Interdisciplinary Handbook
of the Person-Centered Approach

Jeffrey H. D. Cornelius-White
Renate Motschnig-Pitrik
Michael Lux
Editors

Interdisciplinary Handbook of the Person-Centered Approach

Research and Theory

Springer

Editors
Jeffrey H. D. Cornelius-White
Missouri State University
Springfield
MO
USA

Michael Lux
Neurologisches Rehabilitationszentrum
Quellenhof
Bad Wildbad
Germany

Renate Motschnig-Pitrik
University of Vienna
Vienna
Austria

ISBN 978-1-4614-7140-0   ISBN 978-1-4614-7141-7 (eBook)
DOI 10.1007/978-1-4614-7141-7
Springer New York Heidelberg Dordrecht London

Library of Congress Control Number: 2013939050

© Springer Science+Business Media New York 2013
This work is subject to copyright. All rights are reserved by the Publisher, whether the whole or part of the material is concerned, specifically the rights of translation, reprinting, reuse of illustrations, recitation, broadcasting, reproduction on microfilms or in any other physical way, and transmission or information storage and retrieval, electronic adaptation, computer software, or by similar or dissimilar methodology now known or hereafter developed. Exempted from this legal reservation are brief excerpts in connection with reviews or scholarly analysis or material supplied specifically for the purpose of being entered and executed on a computer system, for exclusive use by the purchaser of the work. Duplication of this publication or parts thereof is permitted only under the provisions of the Copyright Law of the Publisher's location, in its current version, and permission for use must always be obtained from Springer. Permissions for use may be obtained through RightsLink at the Copyright Clearance Center. Violations are liable to prosecution under the respective Copyright Law.
The use of general descriptive names, registered names, trademarks, service marks, etc. in this publication does not imply, even in the absence of a specific statement, that such names are exempt from the relevant protective laws and regulations and therefore free for general use.
While the advice and information in this book are believed to be true and accurate at the date of publication, neither the authors nor the editors nor the publisher can accept any legal responsibility for any errors or omissions that may be made. The publisher makes no warranty, express or implied, with respect to the material contained herein.

Printed on acid-free paper

Springer is part of Springer Science+Business Media (www.springer.com)

This book is dedicated to Carl R. Rogers and to people everywhere who reach to understand that which is within and beyond their own world, build bridges with others, and unfold new facts, feelings, ideas, and actions

Preface

Should a humanistic approach pervade science? Will humanists accept science, spirituality, and other assertions from discrepant disciplines? Does the intersection of human values and scientific findings offer unique opportunities to understand and improve the world we live in?

As human beings, we are responsible for unique creations such as the arts or achievements in science and technology—for example, being wirelessly connected with friends and colleagues all over the world. Equally, however, humans are responsible for unbelievable cruelty, destruction, and pain, as in war, nuclear explosions, or through starvation in vast areas of our world. From this we believe that, as the human species, our make-up is highly generic and adaptable, such as to include vast capacities for the constructive, forward moving but equally—and we pause to write this—capacity for the extremely destructive.

Acknowledging this, we are deeply convinced that, to strengthen the constructive potential, we need to contribute to promoting those socio-environmental conditions that research and practice in the person-centered, humanistic orientation has been confirming worldwide, across all continents since more than half a century. Briefly, the conditions of experiencing and mutually communicating empathic understanding, acceptance, and genuineness have countlessly been confirmed across many disciplines to bring to the forefront the inherent, constructive talents in humans. This holds true for individual persons as well as for groups of small and large sizes, covering homogeneity as well as diversity. Hence we feel these socio-environmental conditions are key to the solution of real problems, even of problems and crises of enormous size that seem to require, first of all, (inter)personal immersion, encounter, mutual understanding, and a loosening of rigidly held mental models. This is because problems such as climate change or financial crises or starvation cannot be solved by a single genius or even a single scientific discipline. These problems often are problems of the commons—problems that can only be solved through cooperative effort, often across nations, cultures, and disciplines. Solutions for individuals can actually make the problem harder to solve as they obscure the problem or make it more of a concern for one group than another (see chapter by Fisher in this volume).

Historically, the socio-environmental conditions, which promote the constructive sides of humans and bring along the flourishing of persons and groups, were described and investigated by Carl Rogers and his co-workers about 60 years ago. Rogers formulated a consistent theoretical framework, which embraces his humanistic view of mankind and growth-promoting interpersonal relationships. Over the last years, progress in the human sciences has yielded many significant research findings which are, from our point of view, closely related to key features (such as subception, organismic valuing, self-organization, etc.) of the theoretical framework of Rogers and thus the person-centered approach (PCA). These insights can help to understand the theories of the PCA more fully from a scientific perspective and might even support their social assimilation.

These and similar thoughts come up in our minds when trying to justify our initiative for editing this book. Frankly, to share from the most inner sense of our initiative, we were motivated towards this project by a feeling. It is a feeling born out of our own experience with the PCA and our being in this world that makes us sense that this project is the right thing to do at this time. It requires us to divide our limited time resources between this project and other responsibilities, but, in any case, it feels right to enjoy working on this book. Our huge supply of intrinsic motivation seems to come from each of our own experiencing, our knowledge, as well as from our appreciation of working together on a project we called into life. This is perhaps the more honest explanation why we are editing this book and feel so fortunate that we found Springer Science+Business Media as a renowned publisher as well as top contributors from several disciplines to help us in our bridge-building endeavor.

Not to be misunderstood, when we are saying that reciprocally perceiving person-centered attitudes of empathic understanding, acceptance, and congruence "are key to the solution of real problems" what we absolutely do not intend is to argue that they are all we need. That would be ridiculous. Equally, we do not intend to downplay the invaluable contributions of other disciplines, schools, and theories. What we do, however, endeavor is to build bridges from a person-centered, experiential approach, an approach that equally values the implicit and the explicit processes, to many other disciplines. This is to join forces with them, thereby *never* losing or departing from our deepest human basis—a whole person approach, as originally expressed in the life work of Carl Rogers (1902–1987), or expressed even more broadly, an empathically attuned, self-organizing whole environment approach (Rogers 1983).

More theoretically, the PCA can be seen as providing one meta-model that can help connect many fields of study. It provides a parsimonious explanation and an astonishingly straightforward and elegant theory on how to move forward to address those dimensions of the unique challenges of the present and the future that concern interaction within and between people. It offers constructs that have been supported from many fields of study, but are largely unknown to other fields. To be fully assimilated and understood, however, the constructs of the PCA need to be experienced. This is a limitation of the/any book that readers can overcome only when experiencing a person-centered climate. Nevertheless, this book endeavors to highlight the parsimony, unknown research support, and links within the PCA and from it to various fields of study. While this book focuses on research and theory, the accompanying *Interdisciplinary Applications of the Person-Centered Approach* is devoted to exploring the PCA practice in a multitude of areas including clinical applications, supporting children and families, education, management and leadership, conflict management, and international communication.

The major contribution of this book together with its "sibling book" on applications is to identify and characterize the key bridges—so far only partly recognized—between the PCA and several other disciplines. Crossing these bridges will reveal that scientific disciplines were growing parallel to and decades after the PCA whereby scientific advances occurred with little recognition of the mutuality with and foreshadowing from the PCA. Consequently, the books' main themes and objectives are to:

- Explore the power, depth, and scientific impact of the PCA through its relationship to a broad variety of disciplines.
- Articulate how the theory of PCA is consistent with influential disciplines and in fact has foreshadowed some (e.g., neurosciences, positive psychology, and learner-centered education).
- Propose an integrative framework and conceptual map to depict more of the "geography" surrounding the PCA.
- Respond to international calls for interdisciplinary studies that facilitate dialogue and cooperation with other disciplines to stimulate new ideas and solve twenty-first century problems, such as the tragedies of the commons, globalization woes, and intercultural understanding.
- Introduce people who are less or not familiar with the PCA to reveal it as a meta-approach with widespread scientific support, integrative potential, and influential applications.
- Help those who identify, research, and practice within the PCA—largely psychotherapists, but also educators, consultants, negotiators, coaches, nonviolent facilitators, etc.—to engage with a broader literature, find scientific dialogue with compatible findings from other disciplines, and have increased appreciation for other disciplines.
- Illustrate the importance of the PCA for the research paradigms and competencies to approach and solve the challenges of the world of today and tomorrow.
- Stimulate further research and theory development by identifying open questions.
- Contribute to help us move forward as a human species, regardless of which culture or spiritual tradition we may come from.

Overview and Structure of the Book

This book is set out to be a unique contribution to the literature in so far as it throws fresh light on the *scientific contribution* and foresight of the PCA. It is accompanied by a "sibling book" focusing on the broad, practical *application*, and impact of the PCA. The innovative approach taken in both books is to provide readers with a multidisciplinary and multi-perspective view. Beyond the original psychotherapy theories and applications (client-centered, experiential, emotion-focused, child-centered, motivational interviewing, existential, filial, etc.), influential derived theories and applications have included motivation, mindfulness, interpersonal relationships and group work, cross-cultural communication, parenting, social work and care for people with special needs, learner-centered education, technology-enhanced learning environments, human relations leadership training, life coaching, person-centered medicine, etc.

The book is structured as follows: The first section is an invitation to bridge-building. It introduces the reader to how this book came into being, to the conceptual essence of the PCA, and the broad range of phenomena—research, theory—and disciplines—arts, philosophy, science—in which the PCA interlinks.

Parts 2–8 provide the main part provides transdisciplinary chapters, linking diverse disciplines with the PCA, including neuro- and cognitive science, developmental relating, positive psychology, systems theory, and mindfulness, philosophy, and spirituality. The editors provide concept maps that show how one can understand various chapters' contributions as to "bridge-building" with the PCA.

A reflective and linking section rounds-up the book and points to the "sibling book" that explores PCA applications. It is that "sibling book" that in its very end provides a meta-view on the PCA. It is intended as a generic framework to be specialized for each area at hand such as to reach a broad understanding and be applied or explored through further research or application such as to stimulate further engagement with all the ramifying impacts. This final meta-view chapter was assigned to the second book because it draws upon the research, theories, *as well as* applications substantiated in both "sibling books."

The editors trust you will explore the book in the way that best fits you. Moving through as designed or jumping from topic to topic as your interest or need motivates you! Readers who are new to person-centered thought may want to read the introduction first and thereafter proceed whichever way they prefer.

Reference

Rogers, C. R. (1983). *Freedom to learn for the 80s*. Columbus: Charles Merrill.

Acknowledgments

At this point let us express our deep gratitude to our contributors from all continents and to Springer Science+Business Media for supporting this large-scale project to crystalize and bring together so many important and divergent views and practices. For decades, many scholars have argued for the importance of interdisciplinary collaboration as the primary means to solve difficult social problems and encourage the formation of new paradigms enriched by older traditions. Undoubtedly, without the openness of our contributors to the interdisciplinary adventure, their acceptance of our offerings and constraints, and their empathy towards our shared goals and needs as editors this collaborative work and its thrust would not have been accomplished.

Thanks also go to Mike Bobbitt and Randi Davis, Graduate Assistants in the Department of Counseling, Leadership, and Special Education at Missouri State University, who helped with several miscellaneous tasks, and Dennis Kear, Tami Arthaud, and David Hough, administrators at Missouri State University for support of Jef Cornelius-White's sabbatical, which helped this project come to fruition. Thanks to the Faculty of Computer Science at the University of Vienna, Austria, for their openness to this interdisciplinary project and for providing part of the infrastructure to work on it. Special thanks go to Giorgia Silani, Colin Lago, Will Stillwell, Natalie Rogers, Jenny Bell, Tess Sturrock, and others who provided reviews of various chapters. Thanks to our families for supporting us through so many hours of work!

Renate expresses sincere thanks to Ladislav Nykl for his continuing collaboration and fresh sharing, both critical and appreciative, regarding all the difficult questions that come to the surface when you delve deep into person-centered theories and encounters. Thanks are also due to Sigrid Schmitz who introduced Renate to concept mapping and hinted her to the tool CMapTools from the Institute of Human and Machine Cognition (http://www.cmap.ihmc.us).

Last but not least, we are deeply thankful to Sharon Panulla, Executive Editor at Springer Science+Business Media, for her just perfect and friendly support and encouragement. She contributed significantly to making the genesis of the book an enriching and joyful experience throughout the whole process. Sharon, we appreciate your open-mindedness, prompt, friendly, and helpful responses and your patience with all our questions. For us, you were the best Editor we envisage in this project.

Contents

Part I Introductory Chapters

On the Origins of the Handbook 3
Renate Motschnig-Pitrik, Michael Lux
and Jeffrey H. D. Cornelius-White

The Essence of the Person-Centered Approach................ 9
Michael Lux, Renate Motschnig-Pitrik
and Jeffrey Cornelius-White

Interdisciplinary Research and Theory...................... 23
Jeffrey H. D. Cornelius-White, Renate Motschnig-Pitrik
and Michael Lux

Part II Cognitive and Neuro-Science

An Interactive Cognitive-Emotional Model of the Person-Centered Approach 37
Renate Motschnig-Pitrik and Ladislav Nykl

Carl Rogers Meets the Neurosciences: Insights from Social Neuroscience for Client-Centered Therapy................... 63
Giorgia Silani, Alberto Zucconi and Claus Lamm

The Circle of Contact: A Neuroscience View on the Formation of Relationships.. 79
Michael Lux

Rogers' Generative Framework of Organismic Integrity: Scientific Evidence Challenging Academic, Medical, and Pharmaceutical Forces 95
Carol Wolter-Gustafson

Mindfulness, Authentic Connection, and Making "Right" Decisions: Using Neuroscience to Build a Bridge with the Person-Centered Approach 111
David Ryback

Part III Mindfulness

You Can Inspire Me to Live Further: Explicating Pre-reflexive Bridges to the Other 131
Akira Ikemi

The Awakened Heart: Mindfulness as a Bridge Between the Person-Centered Approach and Eastern Philosophies 141
Karin Bundschuh-Müller

Getting Centered in Presence: Meditation with Gifted Students at Hansenberg Castle............................... 157
Jürgen Flender

Part IV Developmental Relating

On Correspondences Between the Person-Centered Approach and Attachment Theory...................................... 169
Diether Höger

Relational Psychophysiology and Mutual Regulation During Dyadic Therapeutic and Developmental Relating 183
Kymberlee M. O'Brien, Karim Afzal and Edward Tronick

First Relationship, Neuropsychobiology, and the Person-Centred Approach 199
Evleen Mann

Part V Positive Psychology

Person-Centered Theory Encountering Mainstream Psychology: Building Bridges and Looking to the Future.................... 213
Stephen Joseph and David Murphy

Self-Determination Theory, Person-Centered Approaches, and Personal Goals: Exploring the Links 227
Kennon Sheldon

A Strengths-Based Approach Towards Coaching in a Multicultural Environment 245
Llewellyn Ellardus Van Zyl and Marius Wilhelm Stander

Part VI Systems Theory

Person-Centered Approach and Systems Theory 261
Jürgen Kriz

Relationship Worlds and the Plural Self 277
Godfrey Barrett-Lennard

Higher-Order Change Within the Person-Centered Approach 289
Joseph Hulgus

Part VII Game Theory, Research Approaches, and Philosophy

How Can I Trust You? Encounters with Carl Rogers and Game Theory 299
Len Fisher

The Person-Centered Approach in Research 319
David Haselberger and Robert Hutterer

The Learner-Centered Model: Implications for Research Approaches 335
Barbara L. McCombs

A Practice of Social Ethics: Anthropological, Epistemological, and Ethical Foundations of the Person-Centered Approach 353
Peter F. Schmid

Part VIII Spirituality

Christian Spirituality and the Person-Centered Approach 369
Robert Fruehwirth

Formative Empathy as a Mystical Way of Being 381
Francisco Silva Cavalcante Jr and André Feitosa de Sousa

Part IX Concluding Bridge

Reflections and a Preview 387
Renate Motschnig-Pitrik, Jeffrey Cornelius-White and Michael Lux

Editors Biography 391

Index 399

Part I
Introductory Chapters

On the Origins of the Handbook

**Renate Motschnig-Pitrik, Michael Lux
and Jeffrey H. D. Cornelius-White**

The idea for this book was born at the PCE 2010 Conference in Rome. On one nice evening at a small Chinese-Italian restaurant, Michael, after having participated at a fascinating workshop on neuroscience, mentioned to Renate that it would be nice to show to the world in how many areas Carl Rogers' ideas crystallize into beautiful and helpful approaches and furthermore have an increasing, evolving scientific foundation and impact. Renate's response was one of immediate resonance, liking and taking up of the idea. Once expressed, the idea started its own crystallization process and attracted our attention. Renate said: "Sure, we should do something in that direction. I absolutely share your vision. I just participated in a workshop on the person-centered approach (PCA) in academic education and it became very clear to me how much more students gain form a person-centered course than from the more traditional, directive teaching. The PCA is so much closer to situations in real life and so much more alive for both students and instructors/facilitators, irrespective of what type of learner you are or what cultural background you have. You know, I'm so deeply grateful to my mentor Carl Rogers. And I feel our insights must be shared with others, I don't want to keep that for myself."

Michael nodded and continued: "Your early article (Motschnig-Pitrik and Nykl 2003), together with Ladislav (Nykl), on modeling the function of cognition and emotion in the PCA impressed me by your mapping of constructs of the PCA to

---

R. Motschnig-Pitrik (✉)
University of Vienna, Waehringer Strasse 29/6.41, 1090 Vienna, Austria
e-mail: renate.motschnig@univie.ac.at

M. Lux
Neurologisches Rehabilitationszentrum Quellenhof, Kuranlagenallee 2
75323 Bad Wildbad, Germany
e-mail: luxbw@yahoo.de

J. H. D. Cornelius-White
Missouri State University, 901 S. National Avenue, Missouri 65897, USA
e-mail: JCornelius-White@MissouriState.edu

those of neuroscience. I see it as one of the first bridge building endeavors and, as indicated in my book (Lux 2007) would like this direction to be continued." Michael and Renate agreed that it would be nice to collect all the interconnections the PCA has with a multitude of other fields and schools. This might add to the weight and impact of the PCA and help to promote it at universities for still more research that inevitably is necessary for survival and evolution. Renate remembered that recently Jef Cornelius-White had invited her to co-author a paper on "Effectiveness beyond therapy" (Cornelius-White and Motschnig-Pitrik 2010). He had been Chair of the Board of the World Association for Person Centered & Experiential Psychotherapy & Counseling (WAPCEPC) during the completion of a WAPCEPC Taskforce on this theme and had done an extended meta-analysis on learner-centered education (Cornelius-White 2007). Renate: "I suggest we ask Jef what he thinks, I'm convinced that he'll support our project. Perhaps together we could edit a volume on the interconnections of the PCA, something like 'Becoming Interconnected: Perspectives of the Person-Centered Approach'."

Jef listened with excitement and it didn't take us long to get him "on board." And off we took, following the crystallizing idea of building bridges from as well as to the PCA. While the three of us work in quite different areas of engagement in the PCA—Jef at an academic counseling and leadership department, Michael at a neurological rehabilitation center, and Renate at the Faculty of Computer Science, engaged in knowledge engineering and learning technology—what unites us is our felt confirmation that the PCA resonates with the way we want to relate to others, us, and our environment.

It was through extensive mailing across borders and the ocean that we put together a proposal to submit to Springer. This process required us to express our ideas in not too many words, and step-by-step, we consolidated our personal visions to form a growing, shared one. A guiding direction in it was Carl Rogers' reflection when reviewing his life-work. In Gendlin's (1988) words, "Later there was an argument between those who uphold the pure client-centered method and those who expand it. I said we needed both groups. But Carl said, 'I didn't want to find a *client-centered* way. I wanted to find a way to help people'" (p. 128).

Certainly, Rogers and his colleagues helped us to grow in our relationships. This holds true even though we unfortunately did not meet him in person. Based on our experiences in person-centered climates and our knowledge of the PCA, what we do intend is to support people to grow in various relationships, with themselves, their partners, children, students, teams, communities, nations, and the environment. This support or resources for growth can take on various forms and originate from various sources: sharing experience, knowledge, research processes and results, practices, and selves. Therefore, we sought to invite authors from those disciplines and areas of engagement that we felt work toward the same or strongly related "ends" to help us to interconnect the PCA with related "siblings" and thus to produce a conceptual map that is more complete that any map from a separate perspective would be.

The authors whom we decided to invite for a contribution were mainly those whom we knew either through personal contact or through publications.

Thankfully, the vast majority accepted the invitation. So we created a (protected) book homepage with relevant information for contributors as well as the contributors' abstracts for the sake of orientation. For each chapter, one of the co-editors of this book acted as the primary chapter editor to work with the author(s). Almost uniformly, the chapter editor's comments called for a minor or major revision of a chapter. Subsequently, each chapter was read and reviewed by at least two other persons with different nationalities—often but not exclusively the other two co-editors—such as to ensure an international review process of and for high quality. Additionally, from the beginning, we were really keen to propose key issues of the theory of the PCA as a grounded meta-theory for interpersonal growth in a person-centered climate.

But isn't this highlighting of theory and conceptualization contradictory to the priority being "helping people?" We don't think so: Much in the sense of Kurt Lewin's statement: "There is nothing as practical as a good theory," and consistent with our own pleasure in integrating science and experience, thought and feeling, we don't feel any contradiction. On the contrary, forming, confirming, and sharing the forward-directed, lived experience of the PCA provides us with the intrinsic motivation to engage in this book project by (re)searching, practicing, living, and writing within the PCA.

Experientially, the value of integrating thought and feeling became clear for Renate in an encounter group. To make things clearer, let us use a concrete example to explain what we mean by "integrating thought and feeling."

> Unlike several other times before, when facilitators hadn't been "happy" with Renate's "head-focused" responses, one facilitator (Nora Nemeskeri) responded empathically: "Mhm, Renate, this seemed to come from your head, carrying important meaning for you. Now, is there anything else? Anything you feel beneath what you just said? Just take your time …" This felt perfect! I felt respected as a whole human being, inspiring communication between head and organism, arriving at a more complete sense of what I just had expressed. These moments provided me with an intense access to my inner world as it was at that moment without judgment of what was more and what was less valuable. Reflecting back, I gained a deeper, significant rather that just intellectual understanding of my thoughts. I sensed a pervasive "whole-person" understanding of what Rogers (1961/1995) expressed in his paradox, namely, "when I accept myself as I am, then I change" (p. 17).

The encounter experience also opened my door toward truly understanding Rogers' (1983) characteristic of significant learning: "Significant learning combines the logical and the intuitive, the intellect and the feelings, the concept and the experience, the idea and the meaning. When we learn in that way, we are whole…" (p. 20).

So while this book, indeed, is limited by "speaking" through text and figures only, it is centrally aimed at contributing to deep, significant learning in the readers' as well as authors' and editors' experiential fields. It seeks to transcend established disciplinary boundaries to reach out for better informed, more flexible, more self-organizing, and sustainable solutions that our rapidly changing societies and environment require. Just to name a few examples, consider problems like climate change, lacking understanding between peoples, and aging populations.

Elaborating solutions depends, we believe, on creative, open minds, and constructive, collaborative efforts between people and multiple knowledge sources.

Regarding science, as editors of a book that integrates multiple disciplines and hence (re)search approaches and scientific cultures, we take on the attitude that *significant science*, going through early and mature phases, integrates:

- Cognition and feeling and intuition,
- Basic ideas and application-orientation,
- Quantitative and qualitative methods,
- Human and technique/instrument,
- Discipline and art.

In a nutshell, this book aims to explore the contributions the PCA *in interconnection and resonance with other approaches or disciplines* is making to moving forward as a human species.

Following this aim, once we as editors felt satisfied with the coverage of both conceptual and application chapters, we equally realized that the book was getting too big for one physical volume. Fortunately, the flexibility and seamless communicative connection with the publisher helped to turn our dilemma to what we sense benefits all parties. The original book now appears in two physical volumes—the first volume on interdisciplinary *research and theory* and the second on *applications* of the PCA. In this way, you as the reader have the choice to pick one to start with and continue with the other if your interest tells you to proceed. Of course, we hope your time and interest will permit you engage with both books!

If this book contributes to letting you grasp and perceive a more complete, deeper picture of the interconnection of the PCA along with their implication for theory and/or practice, it will have fulfilled its purpose. In our perception, "the facts are friendly" (Rogers 1961, 1995, p. 25) and we trust each reader and contributor to find their own insights and significant revelations.

References

Cornelius-White, J. H. D. (2007). Learner-centered teacher-student relationships are effective: A meta-analysis. *Review of Educational Research, 77*, 113–143.

Cornelius-White, J. H. D., & Motschnig-Pitrik, R. (2010). Effectiveness beyond psychotherapy. The person-centered and experiential paradigm in education, parenting, and management. In M. Cooper, J. Watson, & D. Hölldampf (Eds.), *Person-centered and experiential therapies work. A review of the research on counselling, psychotherapy and related practices* (pp. 45–64). Ross-on-Wye: PCCS-Books.

Gendlin, E.T. (1988). Carl Rogers (1902–1987). American Psychologist, 43(2), 127–128.

Lux, M. (2007). *Der Personzentrierte Ansatz und die Neurowissenschaften. [The person-centered approach and the neurosciences]*. München: Ernst Reinhard Verlag.

Motschnig-Pitrik, R., & Nykl, L. (2003). Towards a cognitive-emotional model of Rogers's person-centered approach. *Journal of Humanistic Psychology, 43*(4), 8–45.

Rogers, C. R. (1961). *On becoming a person: A psychotherapists view of psychotherapy*. London: Constable.

Rogers, C. R. (1983). *Freedom to learn for the 80s*. Columbus: Charles Merrill.
Rogers, C. R. (1995). *On becoming a person*. Boston: Houghton Mifflin. (Original work published 1961).

The Essence of the Person-Centered Approach

Michael Lux, Renate Motschnig-Pitrik and Jeffrey Cornelius-White

1 Introduction

As editors, we feel somehow presumptuous (if not arrogant) wanting to determine—in one single chapter!—what the essence of something so huge like the person-centered approach (PCA) should be. In fact, our true feeling is awe toward the phenomenon of the PCA as a whole and being deeply thankful that our paths took us to encountering it both personally and theoretically. Although none of us was fortunate enough to meet Carl Rogers in person, we had ample opportunities to meet him through his books, videos, and colleagues, and through all the experiential traces somehow embodied in real, genuine, and empathically attuned relationships. Perhaps, if we would just have one sentence to say, we *feel the essence of the PCA in and through the immediate, real, astonishingly fresh, and influential quality of person-to-person encounter*. We appreciate that research in several disciplines like psychology, psychotherapy, learning, systems science, management, philosophy, communication science, etc., constantly confirms the principles of the PCA. At the same time, however, we are also not surprised that the PCA is not a predominant direction in academia. Perhaps, the PCA must be experienced to be fully understood, and this needs time and effort and hence puts a heavy burden on the full and comprehensive recognition of the PCA in all its potentialities.

M. Lux (✉)
Neurologisches Rehabilitationszentrum Quellenhof, Kuranlagenallee 2,
75323 Bad Wildbad, Germany
e-mail: luxbw@yahoo.de

R. Motschnig-Pitrik
University of Vienna, Waehringer Strasse 29/6.41, 1090 Vienna, Austria
e-mail: renate.motschnig@univie.ac.at

J. Cornelius-White
Counseling, Leadership and Special Education, Missouri State University,
901 S. National Avenue, Springfield, MO 65897, USA
e-mail: JCornelius-White@MissouriState.edu

Having said that, we are absolutely aware of the fact that there are as many "essences" of the PCA as there are people. In that way, the approach has a high potential to be meaningful to many persons in their ways and to grow with them, although it will never become an undisputed dogma. Our purpose in this chapter hence is not in any way to prescribe or determine the essence of the PCA. It just plainly is to capture some ground for bridges to be built.

2 Carl Rogers and the Development of the PCA

The PCA was founded by Carl Ransom Rogers (1902–1987), one of the most influential psychologists in history and co-founder of humanistic psychology. According to Rogers (1980), the central hypothesis of the PCA is: "Individuals have in themselves vast resources for self-understanding and for altering their self-concepts, basic attitudes, and self-directed behavior; these resources can be tapped if a definable climate of facilitative psychological attitudes can be provided" (p. 115). The exploration of this climate is one of the most important merits we owe to him. Although he was controversially considered in academic psychology, he was elected president of the American Psychological Association (APA) (1946–1947) and he got several scientific awards, for example the "Distinguished Scientific Contribution Award" (1956 APA) or the "Award for Distinguished Contributions to Applied Psychology as a Professional Practice" (1972 APA). Furthermore, immediately before his dead, he was nominated for the Nobel Peace Prize. He was a gifted writer and reached millions of people by more than 200 professional articles and 16 books. Since the development of the PCA and the life of Rogers are inseparably interlinked, we want to highlight some important aspects of the biography of this great bridge builder between sciences and between humans.

Rogers grew up in a fundamentalist Christian home. He began studying agriculture in Wisconsin and after an influential trip to China at age 20 (Cornelius-White 2012), changed his study to history and then theology at the progressive "Union Theological Seminary" in New York. There he made the acquaintance of liberal theological views, which foreshadowed concepts of humanistic psychology. In this time, he attended lectures of William Heard Kilpatrick who made John Dewey's conception of democratic learning accessible to him. Afterwards, Rogers studied psychology under Edward Thorndike among others at Columbia University. During this time, his acknowledgment of experimental procedures for the acquisition of scientific knowledge was firmly established.

Following studies at university, he began to gather clinical experiences as a child psychologist at the psychoanalytic Child Guidance Institute in New York (1927–1928) and subsequently at the Rochester Society for the Prevention of Cruelty to Children (1928–1940). During this time, he was influenced by Otto Rank's Relational Therapy and the Functional School of Social Work via his colleague Jessie Taft.

Rogers was appointed professor of clinical psychology at Ohio State University (1940–1944). After he developed a program for returning soldiers of World War II (1944–1945), he became professor at the University of Chicago (1945–1957) and at the University of Wisconsin, Madison (1957–1963). During this time, Rogers originated and investigated a new approach to psychotherapy which was called non-directive, client-centered, and later person-centered psychotherapy. He and his research group were pioneers concerning scientific investigation of the exact effects of psychotherapy and of conditions which enable constructive changes in clients. Rogers (1942) was the first psychotherapist who dared to bring transparency in the psychotherapeutic treatment room by publishing a complete treatment of 8 sessions—of course in an anonymous way. Within this approach, several other psychotherapeutic concepts had been developed, for example, Gendlin's Focusing, Greenberg's Process-Experiential Psychotherapy, Prouty's Pre-Therapy, Axline's child-centered play therapy, and Motivational Interviewing by Miller and Rollnick, just to name a few. The work of Rogers and his research group also had profound influence on other psychotherapeutic schools (Goldfried 2007) and became the foundation of the discipline of counseling in the US and UK.

Although Rogers aspired to formulate his theories as hypotheses which can be verified by scientific research, he was aware of the limits of the positivistic, experimental paradigm in psychology, for example, that it does not make enough room for subjective experiences. Later, he (1980) acknowledged that "the old Newtonian conception of science" (p. 237) does not fully fit with his approach and that it is closely related to modern theoretical physics and system theory, for example, the approaches by Fritjof Capra or by Nobel Prize laureate of chemistry Ilya Prigogine.

His openness for scientific discourse becomes apparent in his dialogues with scientists and philosophers like B. F. Skinner, Martin Buber, whom he called one of his favorite thinkers, his friend Michael Polanyi, Gregory Bateson, Rollo May, and theologian Paul Tillich (Kirschenbaum and Henderson 1989a). Additionally, Rogers recognized with some astonishment close connections of his thinking with various philosophical currents. To these belong the philosophy of Søren Kierkegaard, which prompted Rogers (1980) to view his approach as a kind of "homegrown brand of existential philosophy" (p. 39). Later, he noticed conjunctions with Buddhism and with Lao-Tse. For example, he (1980) noted that his own convictions are expressed by the following sayings by Lao-Tse:

> If I keep from meddling with people, they take care of themselves,
> If I keep from commanding people, they behave themselves,
> If I keep from preaching at people, they improve themselves,
> If I keep from imposing at people, they become themselves (p. 42).

Subsequent to his university career, Rogers turned to the potentials of his approach in various social and political domains. In order to emphasize the practical reach of the approach beyond psychotherapy, it was renamed from "client-centered" to "person-centered." At this time, Rogers moved to California where he became a member of the Western Behavioral Sciences Institute (1964) and where he founded in cooperation with others the Center for Studies of the Person in La Jolla (1968). From now on, the approach was utilized in several social fields such as in encounter groups, in organizational consulting, in the development of an experiential education ("significant learning"), in the understanding of marriage and partnership, in a program for medical healthcare professionals, in cross-cultural groups as well as in peace initiatives. Rogers was deeply convinced of the relevance of the PCA for humankind. To propose the way of the future, he states: "Finally, there is agreement that one of the most essential elements of survival is the development of a greater sense of cooperation, of community, of ability to work together for the common good, not simply for personal aggrandizement" (Rogers 1980, p. 332).

During the 1970 and 1980s, Rogers facilitated large groups in many countries, for example, in the Soviet Union before it was falling apart and with conflicting parties in Northern Ireland and South Africa. He also held a group with government officials and policymakers in the "Central American Challenge" in Rust, Austria (1985). Such activities were among the reasons for his nomination for the Nobel Peace Prize. As a result of these various efforts, the PCA was distributed in a wide range of fields all over the world. It is one endeavor of this book to give some insights into the current state of its influence and salience. Before we go into this in more detail, we would like to outline some basic concepts of the PCA.

3 Basic Concepts of the PCA

3.1 The Theory of Personality and its Implications for Mental Health

3.1.1 Actualizing Tendency

Central to the theory of the PCA is the assumption that every being seeks both its maintenance and its enhancement. This motivational tendency to evolve the organism's inherent potentials is called the actualizing tendency. In developing this concept, Rogers was influenced by the neurologist and proponent of Gestalt psychology Kurt Goldstein and by Abraham Maslow, one of the co-founders of humanistic psychology. The actualizing tendency comprises the entire hierarchy of needs by Maslow. Rogers (1980) summarizes its function within the organism as follows:

> We are, in short, dealing with an organism which is always seeking, always initiating, always "up to something." There is one central source of energy in the human organism. It is a trustworthy function of the whole system rather than of some portion of it. It is perhaps most simply conceptualized as a tendency toward fulfillment, toward actualization, involving not only the maintenance but also the enhancement of the organism (p. 123).

On optimal conditions, the actualizing tendency guides the organism toward a constructive development of its inherent potentials. Because humans are social beings, social conditions are essential for the unimpeded unfolding of the actualizing tendency. These conditions are delineated below in more detail. However, the presence of less favorable conditions may bring about an estrangement from the actualizing tendency, which is regarded as the reason for mental disorders and other forms of maladjustment. Such an estrangement is related to a divergence between processes in consciousness and the wisdom of the body, which comes from the actualizing tendency: "While the organism may be constructively motivated certainly the conscious aspects often seem the reverse" (Rogers 1977, p. 243).

3.1.2 Primacy of Experience

The PCA is relatable to the philosophical school of phenomenology and of constructivism. In this sense, the construction of the subjective reality by the individual is essential for his behavior. Thus, proposition I of Rogers' (1951/1995a) originally stated theory of personality is: "Every individual exists in a continually changing world of experience of which he or she is the center" (p. 483). The term "experience" encompasses every psychic process that can be represented in consciousness (e.g., thoughts, feelings, memories, or sensations and the senses). Because subjective reality is crucial for the way the individual orients in the world, empathizing with her/his experiences offers the best opportunity to understand a person.

From the viewpoint of the PCA, two levels of psychic processes can be differentiated. A part of the experiences is symbolized and thus represented in consciousness. The larger part remains beyond conscious awareness. The relationship between conscious and unconscious aspects of totality of experiences is illustrated metaphorically by Rogers (1980) as follows: "It is a tiny peak of awareness, of symbolizing capacity, topping a vast pyramid of nonconscious organismic functioning" (p. 127).

The actualizing tendency is based on non-conscious processes for which reason these are seen in a positive light within the PCA. Mental health is achieved by utilizing these unconscious resources: "When a person is functioning in an integrated, unified, effective manner, she has confidence in the directions she unconsciously chooses, and trusts her experiencing, of which, even she is fortunate, she has only partial glimpses in her awareness" (Rogers 1977, p. 246). These "unconscious choices" signify an organismic wisdom, which transcends the one of the conscious mind alone: "Man is wiser than his intellect" (Rogers 1977, p. 246).

As one potential explanation, Rogers utilizes the concept of "experiencing" developed by his co-worker and the founder of Focusing, Eugene Gendlin, to describe how both levels of psychic processes interact. Following from William James, Gendlin assumes that there is a continuous flow of experiences present in the organism. Within this flow of experiences, there exists an implicit order, the so-called order of carrying forward, which indicates the direction of the actualizing tendency. The implicit order is revealed in a preconceptual felt meaning, which is denoted by Gendlin as the "felt sense." If the felt meaning is exactly symbolized in conscious awareness, a sensible change will occur—the "felt shift" according to

Gendlin. This change is accompanied by cognitive insight, an aha-experience, and feelings of coherence, relief, or bodily relaxation. It expresses that conscious and unconscious processes have become concordant and that the symbolization captures the implicit meaning within the flow of experiences.

Thus, the felt meaning is the point of reference that reveals the accuracy of symbolizations. The term self-exploration describes the search for meaning within the flow of experiences and the attempt to symbolize it as exactly as possible. This is not an easy endeavor as Rogers (1961/1995b) explains in the following statement:

> But in the realm of feelings, we have never learned to attach symbols to experience with any accuracy of meaning. This something which I feel welling up in myself, in the safety of an acceptant relationship—what is it? Is it sadness, is it anger, is it regret, is it sorrow for myself, is it anger at lost opportunities—I stumble around trying out a wide range of symbols, until one "fits," "feels right," seems really to match the organismic experience. In doing this type of thing the client discovers that he has to learn the language of feeling and emotion as if he were an infant learning to speak; often, even worse, he finds he must unlearn a false language before learning the true one. (p. 204)

Self-exploration involves suffering and struggle but within a facilitative relationship, understanding emerges.

3.1.3 The Self as a Process Directing the Symbolization of Experiences

The self or the self-concept is central to intrapersonal and interpersonal processes. It is defined by Rogers (1959) as an "organized, consistent conceptual gestalt composed of perceptions of the characteristics of the 'I' or 'me' and the perceptions of the relationships of the 'I' or 'me' to others and to various aspects of life, together with the values attached to these perceptions. It is a gestalt, which is available to awareness though not necessarily in awareness. It is a fluid and changing gestalt, a process, but at any given moment it is a specific entity which is at least partially definable in operational terms by means of a Q sort or other instrument or measure" (p. 200).

Experiences that are not compatible with the self are subjected to defensiveness; they are denied or perceived in a distorted way in order to stabilize the self. Rogers (1959) explains: "When an experience is dimly perceived (or 'subceived' is perhaps the better term) as being incongruent with the self-structure, the organism appears to react with a distortion of the meaning of the experience, (making it consistent with the self) or with a denial of the existence of the experience, in order to preserve the self-structure from threat" (p. 205).

The flexibility of the self is constrained by experiences during socialization, namely the internalization of conditions of worth. It is assumed that in accordance with the emergence of the self during childhood, a need for positive regard appears. The internalization of conditions of worth occurs if the person does not receive unconditional positive regard but experiences that positive regard is given merely under certain conditions. In that case, the person integrates these conditions within the self and pursues to meet these conditions. In this sense, conditions of worth correspond to socially mediated principles whose compliance should bring along positive regard by other persons. Self-related goals, which stem from the ideal self, "the self-concept which the individual would most like to possess" (Rogers 1959, p. 200), reflect internalized conditions of worth.

3.1.4 Organismic Valuing Process

Person-centered theory posits that the totality of experiences bears a holistic integrative evaluative process and the organismic valuing process (OVP), which expresses the direction of the actualizing tendency. In this way, the OVP has the potential "to enhance the development of the individual himself, of others in his community, and to make for the survival and evolution of his species" (Rogers 1964, p. 165).

Rogers explain the workings of the OVP by using the metaphor of a computer. By calculating all available data from senses, body, memory, and societal requirements, the OVP detects the behavior, which fulfills at best the manifold demands of a given situation. Thereby, the OVP is influenced by previous experiences stored in memory, the uniqueness of the actual situation, and anticipations relating to the future. Rogers was convinced that the totality of experiences is wiser than deliberate reasoning. During his life, he had learned to trust messages from deep within the organism and he had recognized that he can be guided by these: "As I gradually come to trust my total reactions more deeply, I find that I can use them to guide my thinking" (Rogers 1961/1995b, p. 22).

Moreover, under the condition of an undistorted perception of the inner flow of experiences, the OVP makes sure that a positive human nature comes to light: "When man's unique capacity of awareness is thus functioning freely and fully, we find that we have, not an animal whom we must fear, not a beast who must be controlled, but an organism able to achieve, through the remarkable integrative capacity of its central nervous system, a balanced, realistic, self-enhancing, other-enhancing behavior as a resultant of all these elements of awareness" (Rogers 1961/1995b, p. 105).

3.1.5 Incongruence

If important experiences succumb to defensiveness, this is called incongruence—the breeding ground for the emergence of mental disorders and other maladaptive behaviors. Incongruence is associated with an impaired integration of personality. In this regard, the symbolization of experiences, which is determined by the self, is not congruent with the flow of experiences within the organism. Conditions of worth restrict openness to experiences and interfere with the organismic valuing process: "Thus a condition of worth, because it disturbs the valuing process, prevents the individual from functioning freely and with maximum effectiveness"

(Rogers 1959, p. 210). Feelings of tension, anxiety, irritation, or insecurity are subjective markers of incongruence. Within the self, it is revealed as a discrepancy between self and ideal self.

Incongruence comes along with a dissociation of the self-actualizing tendency from the actualizing tendency. It might be, for example, that the self-actualizing tendency makes a person to expose herself to excessive pressure to perform in order to receive other's real or imagined approval. In that case, an organismic need for silence and rest which arises from the actualizing tendency and which is not compatible with a striving after approval is not sufficiently integrated. Rogers (1961/1995b) describes this conflict as follows: "Man's behavior is exquisitely rational, moving with subtle and ordered complexity toward the goals his organism is endeavoring to achieve. The tragedy for most of us is that our defenses keep us from being aware of this rationality, so that consciously we are moving in one direction, while organismically we are moving in another" (p. 194–195).

3.1.6 Congruence

A prerequisite for an optimal utilization of the OVP is the openness of awareness to the totality of experiences. If relevant experiences are symbolized precisely, conscious and unconscious processes are adapted to each other. This condition is called congruence. Within the PCA, congruence is synonymous to mental health and the best possible access to psychic resources. Rogers (1961/1995b) describes this as follows:

> What does this becoming one's self mean? It appears to mean less fear of the organismic, nonreflective reactions which one has, a gradual growth of trust in and even affection for the complex, varied, rich assortment of feelings and tendencies which exist in one at the organic or organismic level. Consciousness, instead of being the watchman over a dangerous and unpredictable lot of impulses, of which few can be permitted to see the light of day, becomes the comfortable inhabitant of a richly varied society of impulses and feelings and thoughts, which prove to be very satisfactorily self-governing when not fearfully or authoritatively guarded. (p. 203)

Openness to experiences means to accept what is present now. This means that there is no avoidance to any experience, whether pleasant or not. This kind of orientation toward reality (Rogers is famous for the phrase "The facts are friendly") allows for change and further development what is called the paradox of change: "The curious paradox is that when I accept myself just as I am, then I can change" (Rogers 1961/1995b, p. 17).

The actualizing tendency guides these changes in direction toward the fully functioning person (FFP)—the ideal case of mental health within the PCA which no one reaches permanently. Rogers had derived the concept of the FFP from observations on developments of persons which benefited from person-centered psychotherapy. According to these observations, the FFP is free of defensiveness. The FFP is not identified with a certain image of one's self and can thus flexibly adapt to the affordances of a given situation: "The self and the personality emerge from experience, rather than experience being translated or twisted to fit a preconceived self-structure. It means that one becomes a participant in and an observer of the ongoing process of organismic experience, rather than being in control of it" (Rogers 1961/1995b, p. 189).

The FFP faces any experience in a mindful and unprejudiced way. Such persons are open to their experiences and perceive sensitively processes within and outside the organism. An FFP lives in the here and now. The application of previous learning experiences does not block one's view on the uniqueness of the current situation. Creativity, a rich emotional life, and trust in the usefulness of intuition in decision-making are additional attributes of the FFP. Due to openness to experiences, an FFP is able to make decisions based on the OVP. Decisions reflect the integration of any information that is available in the central nervous system. Furthermore, Rogers had detected commonalities of value directions in such persons:

> In therapy, such openness to experience leads to emerging value directions which appear to be common across individuals and perhaps even across cultures. Stated in older terms, individuals who are thus in touch with their experiencing come to value such directions as sincerity, independence, self-direction, self-knowledge, social responsivity, social responsibility, and loving interpersonal relationships. (Kirschenbaum and Henderson 1989b, p. 185).

3.2 The Theory of a Growth-Promoting Interpersonal Relationship

3.2.1 Contact

Rogers was the pioneer of research in psychotherapy. He and his co-workers were the first who used recordings of interviews to work out conditions that enable constructive changes during psychotherapy. According to this research, progress of clients in direction of the FFP occurs in a certain interpersonal climate, which is essential for the impact of person-centered psychotherapy. On the therapist's part, this climate is marked by three basic attitudes: empathy, congruence, and unconditional positive regard (see below). Within this kind of relationship, the client experiences security, which facilitates his willingness for self-exploration. In this way, he comes to open up to his experiences and to symbolize these more exactly. The self loses rigidity, whereby the so far repelled experiences can be integrated within the self. Congruence, and thus mental health, increases and the same applies to the consonance of actualizing and self-actualizing tendency. This enables the actualizing tendency to unfold unimpaired. Contact describes a precondition of person-centered relationships (Rogers 1959). It means a mutual influence of the fields of perception of any of the involved persons, a mutual emotional resonance, and minimally connection to consensually validated reality (Prouty et al. 2002).

3.2.2 Non-Directivity

Although each person is an expert for his or her own experiences (e.g., as a psychotherapist, client, teacher, learner) and thus brings in competencies and knowledge the other does not have, contact is realized "at eye level," without rigid hierarchical structures. There is no one who shows the other the way to deal with problems, but instead, there will be established conditions under which this way can be found with a maximum of self-determination. This kind of autonomy supportive, empowering interaction is called non-directivity. In this regard, the actualizing tendency is the base for the trust of person-centered therapists, teachers, counselors, or other facilitators in the potential of clients, learners, consultees, or others for constructive developments. Rogers (1980) expresses the spirit of non-directivity in the following quote: "I go along with Martin Buber and the ancient Oriental sages: 'He who imposes himself has the small, manifest might; he who does not impose himself has the great, secret might' " (p. 45).

3.2.3 Empathy

Empathy is one of the basic attitudes facilitators aspire to put into practice. It is defined by Rogers (1959) as: "The state of empathy, or being empathic, is to perceive the internal frame of reference of another with accuracy, and with the emotional components and meanings which pertain thereto, as if one were the other person, but without ever losing the 'as if' condition. Thus, it means to sense the hurt or the pleasure of another as he senses it, and to perceive the causes thereof as he perceives them, but without ever losing the recognition that it is as if I were hurt or pleased, etc. If this 'as if' quality is lost, then the state is one of identification" (p. 210–211).

Empathy, the attempt to understand the subjective experiences and reality of the other, is based on conscious perspective taking as well as on feeling the inner state of the other with all one's senses. This means that empathy is viewed as a complex phenomenon, which requires cognitive and emotional functions. It implies to resonate emotionally with the other without getting lost in the other's experiences. According to Rogers (1980): "To be with another in this way means that for the time being you lay aside the views and values you hold for yourself in order to enter another's world without prejudice" (p. 143).

Empathy is viewed as an interactional or intersubjective process, a joint search for meaning. By communicating parts from the experiences of the other, the facilitator has understood he helps the other to explore his subjective reality. According to Rogers (1980), empathy "includes communicating your sensings of his/her world as you look with fresh and unfrightened eyes at elements of which the individual is fearful. It means frequently checking with him/her as to the accuracy of your sensings, and being guided by the responses you receive" (p. 142). In this way, empathic understanding stimulates the process of self-exploration by which the felt meaning within the flow of experiences can be symbolized more precisely: "By pointing to the possible meanings in the flow of his/her experiencing you help the person to focus on this useful type of referent, to experience the meanings more fully, and to move forward in the experiencing" (Rogers 1980, p. 142).

3.2.4 Congruence

Another attitude person-centered facilitators hold is congruence. As described above, congruence is synonymous to openness to and acceptance of one's full experiences. The facilitator is attentive to any of his experiences in resonance on the other, and he is able to integrate these experiences for empathic understanding. The relationship between congruence and empathy (and unconditional positive regard) was already mentioned by Rogers (1951/1995a) in a proposition in his originally formulated theory of personality: "XVIII: When the individual perceives and accepts into one consistent and integrated system all his or her sensory and visceral experiences, then he or she is necessarily more understanding of others and is more accepting of others as separate individuals" (p. 520).

Additionally, congruence has an interactive aspect called transparency or realness. This means that the facilitator is not an "empty screen" and does not hide behind a "professional facade." Instead, he encounters the other as the person he is in reality so far as this is appropriate to the current situation: "The more the therapist is him or herself in the relationship, putting up no professional front or personal facade, the greater is the likelihood that the client will change and grow in a constructive manner. It means that the therapist is openly being the feelings and attitudes that are flowing within at the moment" (Rogers 1980, p. 115). A transparent response originates from internal congruence, and a part of that congruence is empathic acceptance. In other words, transparency is not the same thing as impulsivity or selfishness, but an authentic expression of the experience one has while endeavoring to be not only congruent, but also empathic and accepting. This implies that the facilitator communicates without any aspect of falseness but with concordance of verbal and non-verbal communication channels.

3.2.5 Unconditional Positive Regard

The last remaining attitude is acceptance, or unconditional positive regard. It implies that the facilitator is non-judgmental in relation to the experiences of the other. The facilitator unconditionally accepts these experiences and the whole person of the other. This attitude is free of demands on the other but is instead marked by respectfulness for his potential to self-fulfillment and self-determination. This attitude is contrary to the attitude that underlies the internalization of conditions of worth during socialization. Thus, unconditional positive regard conveyed by the way the facilitator is present in the relationship enables experiences which are corrective to those in the past and which offer the opportunity "to be that self which one truly is" (Rogers 1961/1995b, p. 166). The term "acceptance" may be somewhat misleading because it does not fully capture the emotional content of unconditional positive regard. In this regard, by embracing this attitude, the facilitator experiences feelings like compassion, caring, warmth, or non-possessive love (agape in theological terms) toward the other.

3.2.6 Presence: The Ultimate Quality

The basic attitudes of the PCA are closely interwoven and mutually interdependent. We assume that a facilitator's simultaneous holding them, or better "being them," enables her or his "presence" in the relationship. The presence of the facilitator can enable the occurrence of a somewhat altered state of consciousness which Rogers discussed more frequently later in life after he had experienced many intensive phases of therapies or groups and perhaps closely linked with the "magic of encounter," the transforming power of relationships. Rogers (1980) wrote:

> When I am at my best, as a group facilitator or a therapist, I discover another characteristic. I find that when I am closest to my inner, intuitive self, when I am somehow in touch with the unknown in me, when perhaps I am in a slightly altered state of consciousness, then whatever I do seems to be full of healing. Then simply my presence is releasing and helpful. There is nothing I can do to force this experience, but when I can relax and be close to the transcendental core of me, then I may behave in strange and impulsive ways in the relationship, ways which I cannot justify rationally, which have nothing to do with my thought processes. But these strange behaviours turn out to be right, in some odd way. At those moments it seems that my inner spirit has reached out and touched the inner spirit of the other. Our relationship transcends itself, and has become a part of something larger. Profound growth and healing and energy are present. This kind of transcendent phenomenon is certainly experienced at times in groups in which I have worked, changing the lives of some of those involved. (p. 129)

4 Conclusion

The PCA is both a parsimonious explanation of how people grow and change, particularly in a facilitative environment, and an opportunity for complicated connections at biological, psychological, social, cultural, political, and artistic levels in both research and application. The original PCA theories of personality and growth-producing relationships provide a foundation around such concepts as actualization, empathy, congruence, and unconditional positive regard. However, these concepts also have had enormous impact on a variety of applications to shared enterprises and the potential for significantly more influence. Likewise, these concepts foreshadowed findings and theories in other areas not imagined directly during Rogers' lifetime. Furthermore, new findings and theories can help to refine and adjust core person-centered concepts. After the subsequent chapter providing an accessible example of a direct application of the PCA in a dialogue between Rogers and a volunteer experiencing a variety of social, cultural, biological, and psychological stressors, the rest of this book endeavors to outline or draw in detail some of those connections. We hope it stimulates still more bridges to be built in an interdisciplinary fashion around the meta-concept of the PCA.

References

Cornelius-White, J. H. D. (2012). *Carl Rogers: The China diary*. Ross-on-Wye: PCCS Books.

Goldfried, M. R. (2007). What has psychotherapy inherited from Carl Rogers? *Psychotherapy: Theory Research, Practice, Training, 44*, 249–252.

Kirschenbaum, H., & Henderson, V. L. (Eds.). (1989a). *Carl Rogers: Dialogues*. Boston: Houghton Mifflin.

Kirschenbaum, H., & Henderson, V. L. (Eds.). (1989b). *The Carl Rogers reader*. Boston: Houghton Mifflin.

Prouty, G., Van Werde, D., & Pörtner, M. (2002). *Pre-therapy: Reaching contact-impaired clients*. Ross-on Wye: PCCS Books.

Rogers, C. R. (1942). *Counseling and psychotherapy: Newer concepts in practice*. Boston: Houghton Mifflin.

Rogers, C. R. (1959). A theory of therapy, personality, and interpersonal relationships, as developed in the client-centered framework. In S. Koch (Ed.), *Psychology: A study of a science* (Vol. 3, pp. 184–256)., Formulations of the person and the social context New York: McGraw-Hill.

Rogers, C. R. (1964). Toward a modern approach to values: The valuing process in the mature person. *Journal of Abnormal and Social Psychology, 68*, 160–167.

Rogers, C. R. (1977). *Carl Rogers on personal power*. London: Constable.

Rogers, C. R. (1980). *A way of being*. Boston: Houghton Mifflin.

Rogers, C. R. (1995a). *Client-centered therapy*. London: Constable (original work published 1951).

Rogers, C. R. (1995b). *On becoming a person*. Boston: Houghton Mifflin (original work published 1961).

Interdisciplinary Research and Theory

Jeffrey H. D. Cornelius-White, Renate Motschnig-Pitrik and Michael Lux

Carl Rogers' (1959) magnus opus theory statement is not just a theory of therapy, but also of personality, of mental health (the "fully functioning person"), and interpersonal relationships. From an early age onward, Rogers was influenced by science and philosophy alike and foreshadowed and brought to life several of the challenges that the arts and sciences explore today. This section of the interdisciplinary book highlights the bridges that the PCA has and can build with a variety of disciplines.

1 Cognition and Neuroscience

Section 1 elaborates on the bridges between the PCA and cognitive and neuroscience. Starting with extending the cognitive notion of a "chunk" to integrate both cognitive and emotional aspects, Motschnig and Nykl provide innovative

---

J. H. D. Cornelius-White (✉)
Counseling Leadership and Special Ed, Missouri State University,
Springfield 65897 MO, USA
e-mail: JCornelius-White@MissouriState.edu

R. Motschnig-Pitrik
University of Vienna, Waehringerstasse 29/6.41,
1090 Vienna, Austria
e-mail: renate.motschnig@univie.ac.at

M. Lux
Neurologisches Rehabilitationszentrum Quellenhof, Kuranlagenallee 2,
75323 Bad Wildbad, Germany
e-mail: luxbw@yahoo.de

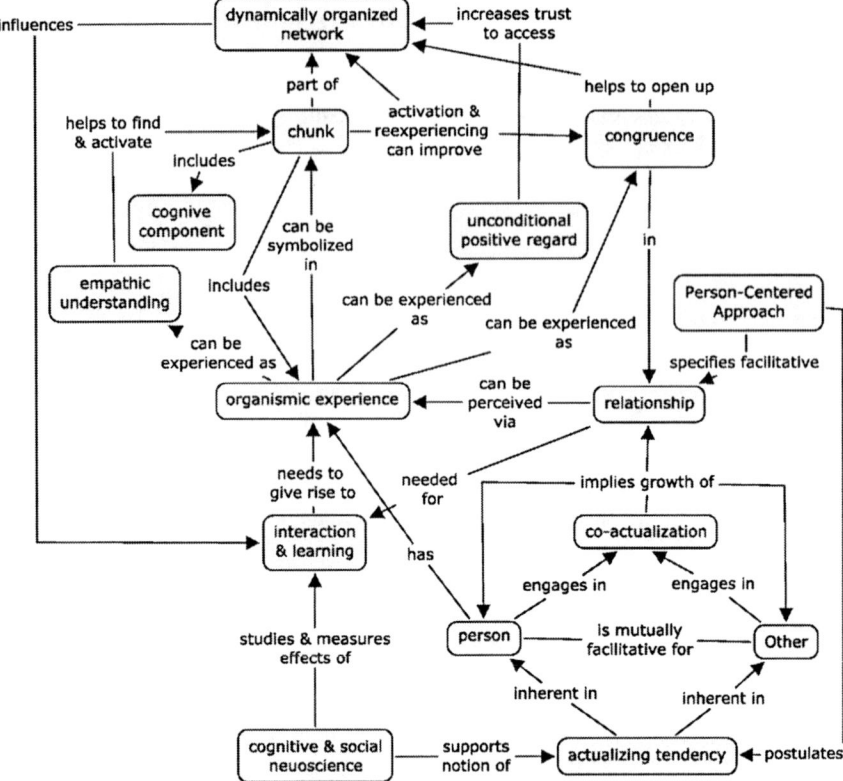

Fig. 1 Concept map illustrating the "bridge" between aspects of the PCA and cognitive science (see Motschnig-Pitrik and Nykl)

connections between learning, mutually facilitative relationships, and cognitive science, especially as concerns organismic experiencing and coactualization. Figure 1 sketches, among others, how a mutually facilitative relationship while forming fosters psychological growth of its partners.

Silani, Zucconi, and Lamm present a view of neuroscience and the PCA centered around research on empathy as depicted in Fig. 2. They link research on social intelligence, emotional regulation, executive functioning, and other aspects with the quality of interpersonal relationships and self-awareness.

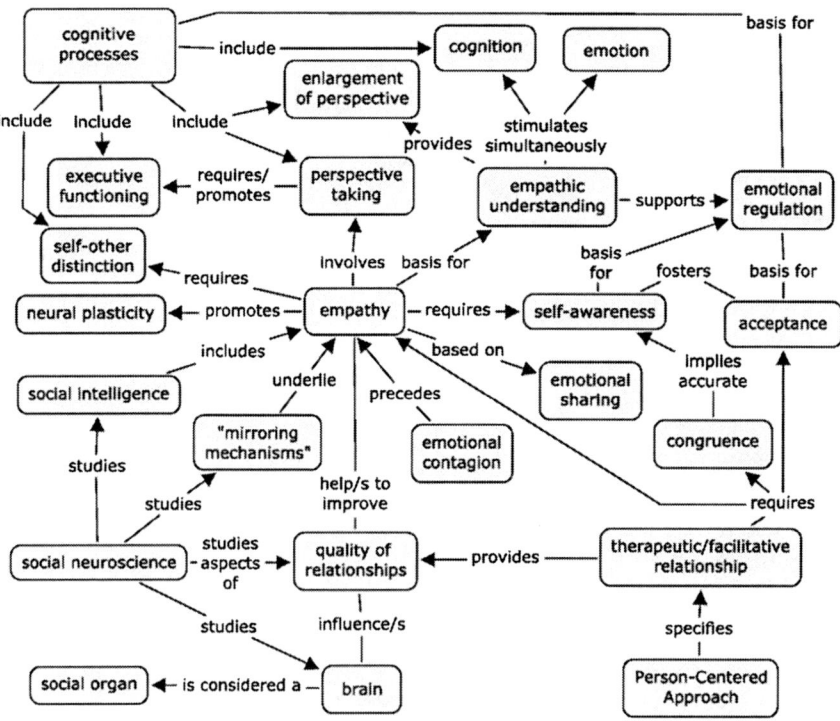

Fig. 2 Concept map showing aspects of the "bridge" between aspects of the PCA and social neuroscience (see Silani, Zucconi, and Lamm)

Lux presents a parsimonious view of how neuropsychological changes in both client and facilitator accompany psychosocial changes in both when fostered by facilitative relationships. This circle of contact shows how the different levels of the human system interrelate as sketched in Fig. 3 and are shown in a detailed figure as part of the chapter.

Wolter-Gustafson adds fresh insight and interconnection from the perspective of neuroscientist Pert regarding communication and cooperation in the human organism. She makes clear how big the gap is in some parts between science and the politics of the pharma industry. Figure 4 exposes key ideas addressed by Wolter-Gustafson. As a result of her investigation and in accord with the view promoted by Seeman, she proposes to consider the PCA as a generative framework for integrity.

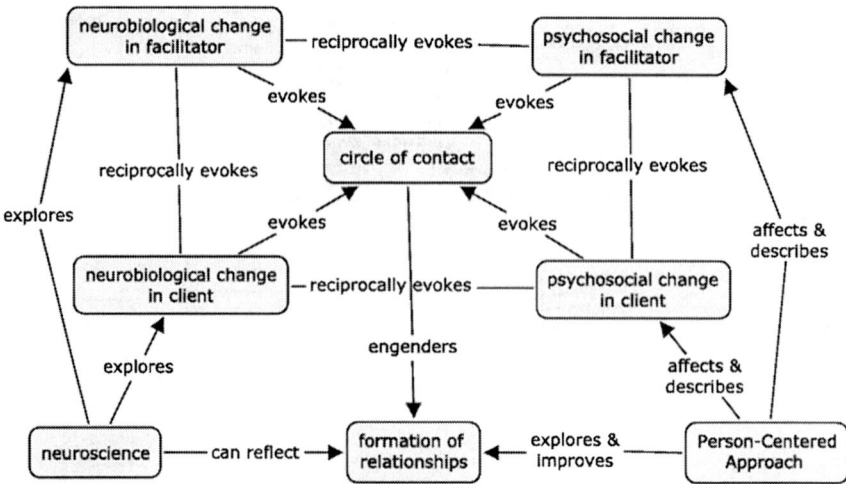

Fig. 3 Concept map illustrating the neuroscience view and the PCA view on the formation of relationship (see Lux)

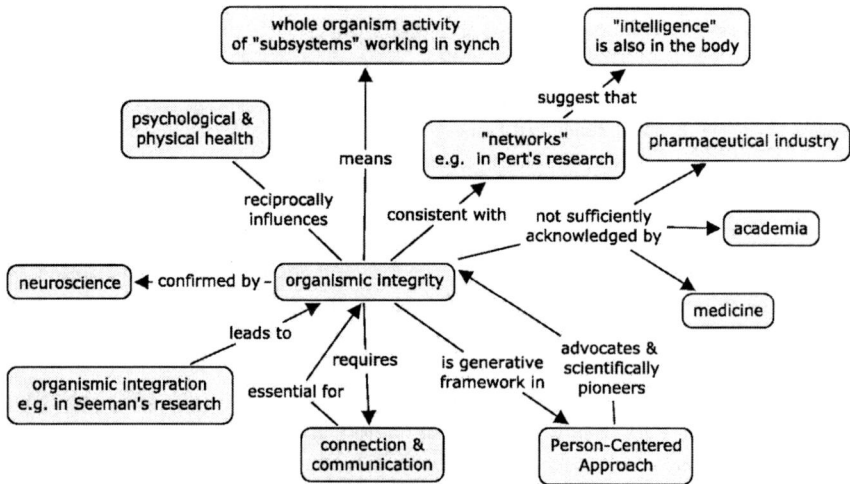

Fig. 4 Concept map on organismic integrity as generative framework and its relationship to neuroscience but ignorance by the pharma industry (see Wolter-Gustafson)

Interdisciplinary Research and Theory

As depicted in Fig. 5, Ryback provides a bridge chapter not only between the PCA and neuroscience but also to the next subsection, as it concerns a neuroscientific perspective on mindfulness. The chapter relies on processes of recursion and reflection with one's thoughts and getting in touch with both one's own and others' feelings and how these processes are manifested in mirror neuron research. Likewise, he links the process of deep authentic presence with the practice of mindfulness and an absence of judgment both intra- and interpersonally.

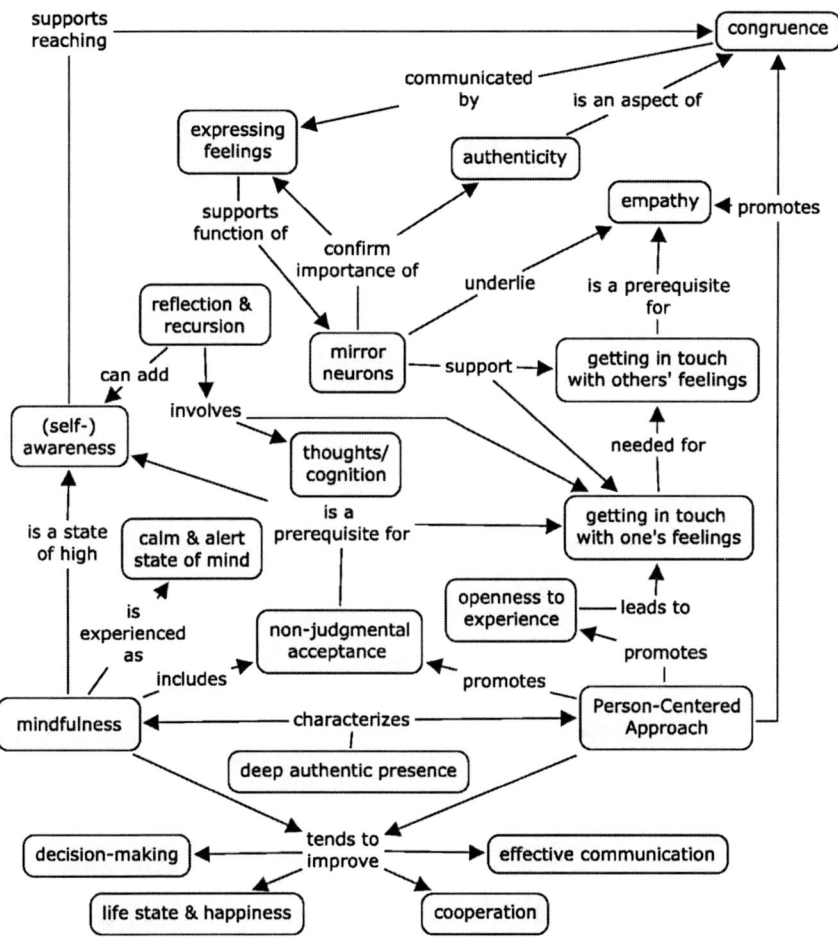

Fig. 5 Concept map depicting aspects of the PCA and their relationships with mindfulness (see Ryback)

2 Mindfulness

Beginning Sect. 2 of Part I concerned with linkages between the person-centered approach and mindfulness, Ikemi provides an elegant, at times poetic, and highly accessible view into the process of living further. As seen in Fig. 6, Ikemi links pre-conceptual understanding and pre-reflective processes to show focusing, mindful presence, and facilitative relationships foster a more alive, richer experience of life.

Additionally, Bundschuh-Müller links the PCA with Eastern philosophies from Buddhism and Taoism. She shows that basic concepts of the PCA can be found in Eastern philosophies and that the PCA builds a bridge between Western and Eastern thinking. She also refers to relationships between the PCA and so-called third wave of behavior therapy. Similarly, Flender provides bridges with mindfulness from the perspective of meditation developed in the Frankfurt School of contemplation using culturally independent practices like preparing, focusing, centering, and opening of consciousness. He also provides how person-centered counseling is integrated with other mindful practices, such as archery and autogenic training to provide a mindfulness approach within school settings.

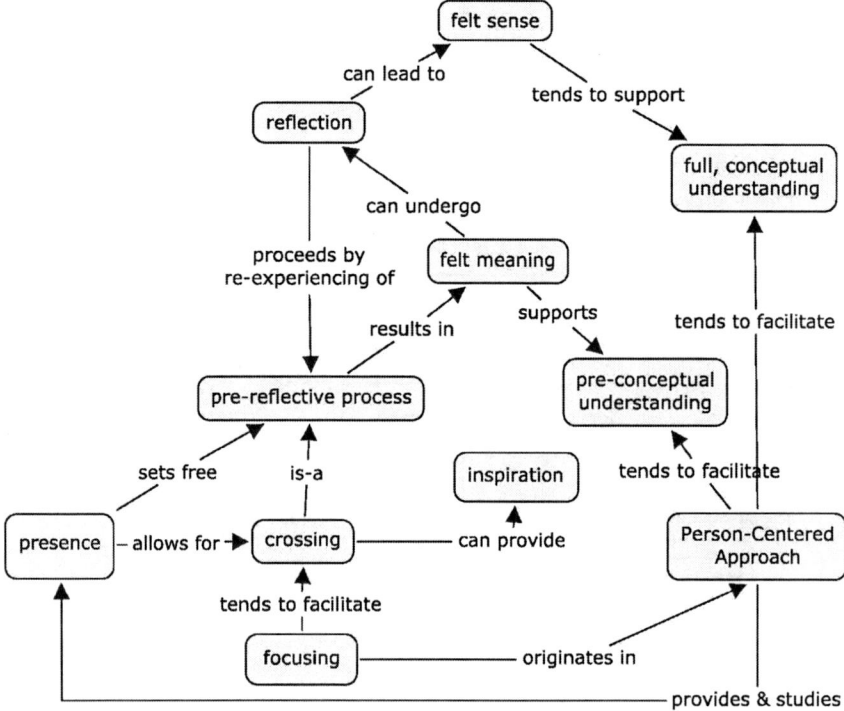

Fig. 6 Concept map showing aspects of the PCA and their relationships to pre-conceptual understanding and focusing (see Ikemi)

3 Developmental Relating

Beginning Sect. 3 of Part I concerned with human development and relating, Höger provides intriguing links to attachment theory. As seen in Fig. 7, both approaches share interest in and similar views on how certain relationship climates foster or inhibit development in fundamental ways. When safe attachments are formed, self-exploration or an exploratory system is activated and the person's development is enhanced.

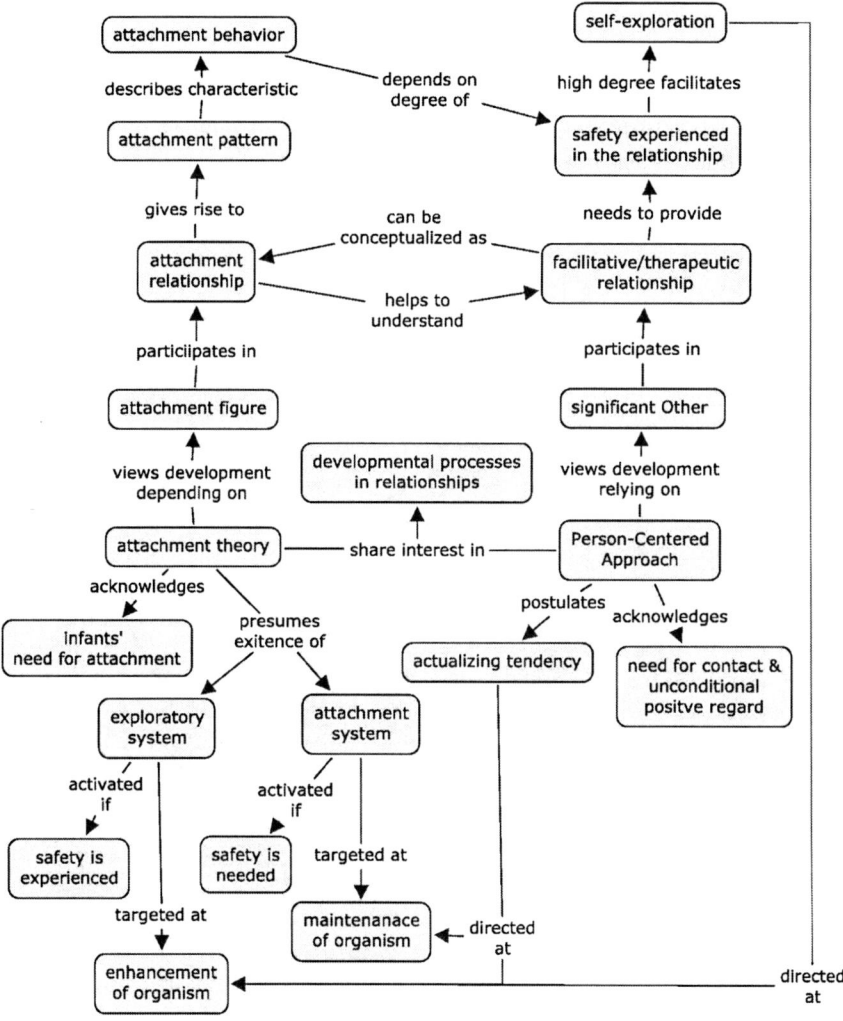

Fig. 7 Concept map matching aspects attachment theory with related notions in the PCA (see Höger)

O'Brien, Afzal, and Tronick show how research on relational psychophysiology involves physiological concordance in mother–infant and therapeutic relationships. They also link nonlinear systems theory to show each person is an agent in mutual growth and development and provide a comprehensive view on these issues. Similarly, Mann describes intensive case study research on mother–infant relationships providing similar links between neurobiology with the person-centered approach.

4 Positive Psychology and Self-Determination Theory

Introducing Sect. 4 of Part I linking positive psychology and self-determination theory with the person-centered approach, Joseph and Murphy show correspondences between self-determination theory, the positive psychology movement, and the PCA and how these intersect in affirming and challenging ways to mainstream psychology and the medical model based on treatment of disorder. They integrate both experiential evidence and phenomenological issues to make their case. Selected aspects are abstracted in Fig. 8.

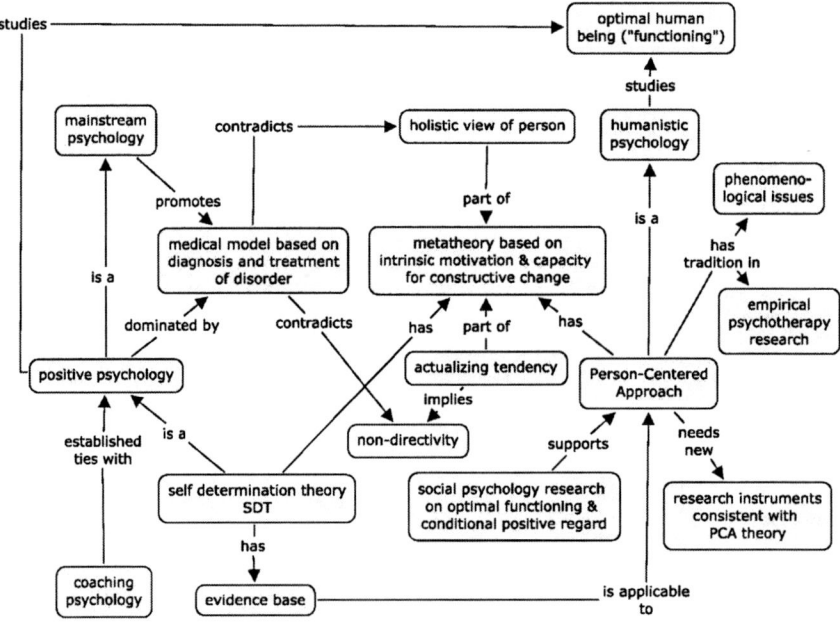

Fig. 8 Concept map illustrating the "bridges" between key issues in positive psychology and the PCA (see Joseph and Murphy)

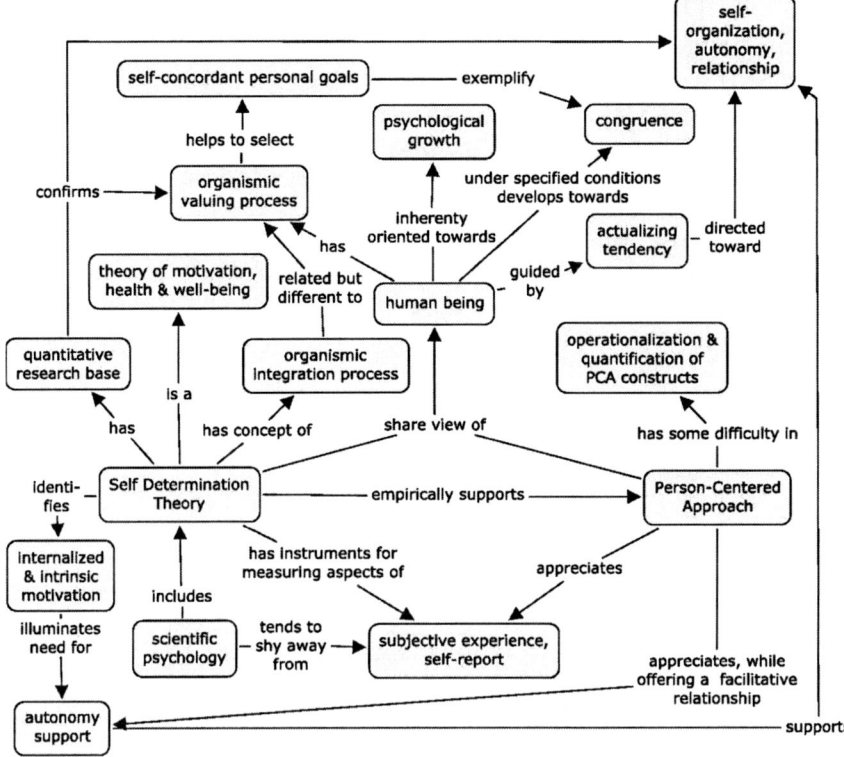

Fig. 9 Concept map depicting "bridges" between constructs of SDT and the PCA (see Sheldon)

In the chapter, "Self-Determination Theory, Person-Centered Approaches and Personal Goals: Exploring the Links" in the section on positive psychology, Sheldon links self-determination theory with the PCA through concepts such as autonomy support and intrinsic motivation of actualization. As seen in Fig. 9, he also shows how both approaches share a very similar view of the human being and evidence bases. Likewise, they both share concern for subjective experience which much scientific psychology shies away from.

Concluding the section, Van Zyl and Stander provide a strengths-based workplace and executive coaching model derived from and relevant for multicultural environments. They provide links to positive psychology and an ecosystemic view of persons.

5 Systems Theory

In the first chapter of the fifth section—Person-Centered Approach and Systems Theory, Kriz describes linkages between interdisciplinary systems theory and the PCA. Figure 10 shows how phase transitions and the actualizing tendency represent parallel descriptions of transformative processes that refute mechanistic metaphors and lead to the extinction of old, inadequate patterns in favor of better adjusted, actualized patterns.

In the chapter, "Relationship Worlds and the Plural Self", Barrett-Lennard continues his lifelong work of researching and describing how persons are relationships, a plurality of selves, and inherently interdependent. Using literature,

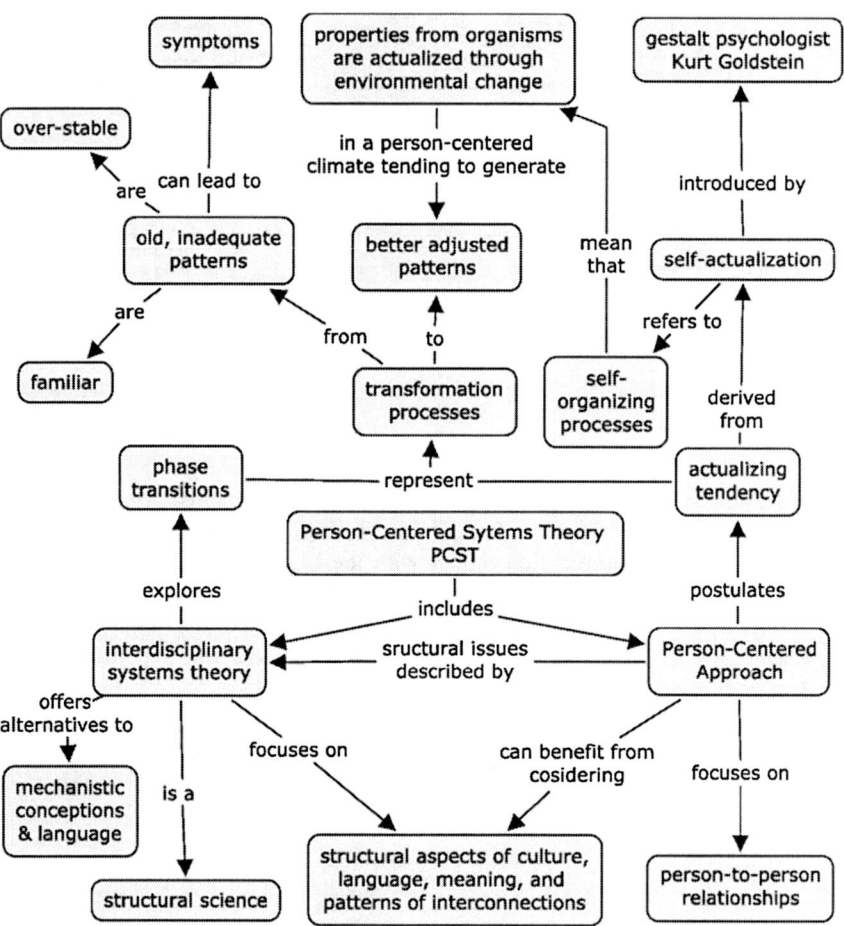

Fig. 10 Concept map showing the "bridges" between constructs of interdisciplinary systems theory and the PCA (see Kriz)

Interdisciplinary Research and Theory

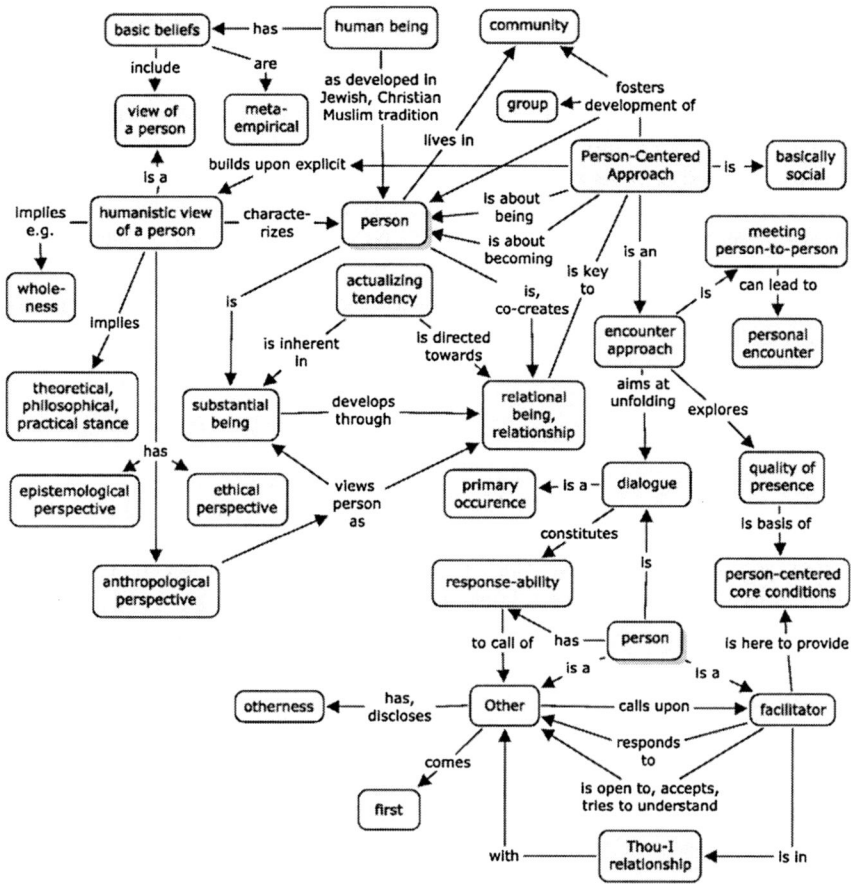

Fig. 11 Concept map summarizing some of the philosophical foundations of the PCA (see Schmid)

psychotherapy dialogs, and research, he shows how both suffering and self-formation are functions of this plurality of self. From another systemic view, Hulgus focuses on how person-centered facilitation shows how emergent qualities of systems can lead to "second-order" solutions that transform persons within psychotherapy, education, and family contexts.

6 Game Theory, Theory of Science, and Philosophy

Len Fisher provides a highly engaging take on how game theory relates to the person-centered approach by showing the limitations of self-interest and how cooperation offers the only solution to certain types of problems. Mutual trust with a credible commitment to maintaining that trust as seen in person-centered acceptance provides an innovative and effective route to seven classes of large social problems that otherwise are insurmountable. Exploring theory of science, Haselberger and Hutterer provide characteristics for research methods that emerge from a person-centered view, especially personal conversation and participatory action research. Exploring roots in philosophy, anthropology, and religion, Schmid provides a well-woven explanation of how the person is substantial and independent yet also relational and interdependent. He links how person-centered relationships and presence foster both aspects in the most ethical sense of what being human means. Figure 11 relates a selection of the concepts that Schmid considers and reveals the complexity inherent in the field of philosophical foundations.

7 Spirituality

Following along religious and ethical lines, Fruehwirth explores how Christian spirituality relates to the person-centered approach through concepts like agenda-free prayer and self-emptying. Such practice of openness and nonpossessive love can lead to possible gains in spiritual and everyday life. Cavalcante and Feitosa de Sousa provide a Brazilian view of presence and formative empathy stemming from the under-explored concept of the formative tendency within the person-centered approach and its inherent mysticism and spirituality.

8 Invitation

The editors invite you to explore, experience, develop, and carry forward the meaning as you read through the contributions!

References

Rogers, Carl. (1959). A theory of therapy, personality and interpersonal relationships as developed in the client-centered framework. In S. Koch (Ed.), *Psychology: A study of a science. Vol. 3: Formulations of the person and the social context.* New York: McGraw Hill.

Part II
Cognitive and Neuro-Science

An Interactive Cognitive-Emotional Model of the Person-Centered Approach

Renate Motschnig-Pitrik and Ladislav Nykl

1 Introduction

The preconditions and the processes of personal growth are precisely described by Carl R. Rogers in several places (Rogers 1951, 1959, 1961, 1980). Although the last decades have witnessed intensive research on process outcome in humanistic psychotherapies (Cain and Seeman 2002; Cain 2010), to the best of the authors' knowledge only few models have been proposed that explain essential aspects of the person-centered approach (PCA) in terms of cognitions, feelings, and interaction in the light of research findings from neuroscience and cognitive psychology. Among these a few are Behr's spiral-model (Behr 2009) of self-exploration, symbolization, and development based on a theory on constructing emotions and accommodating schemas. Already in the previous century, authors like Wayne Anderson, David Wexler, and Fred Zimring (Wexler and Rice 1974) viewed the PCA from a cognitive perspective, focusing on information processing. The model proposed in the current chapter is more encompassing by accounting for cognitive, affective, and experiential aspects of each of the three Rogers variables. A complementary approach to relating the theories of Rogers with cognitive theories of Vygotsky is made by Nykl and documented in (Nykl 2012, 2005; Nykl and Motschnig-Pitrik 2002). Resorting as deeply as to the biological level of neuroscience, Lux (2010) elaborated the neurobiological aspects of congruence, unconditional positive regard and empathy. He proposed a model of reciprocal influence in person-centered relationships calling this phenomenon the "circle of contact" (Lux 2010; see also the chapter by Lux in this volume). Foundations for

---

R. Motschnig-Pitrik (✉)
University of Vienna, Waehringer Strasse 29/6.41, 1090 Vienna, Austria
e-mail: renate.motschnig@univie.ac.at

L. Nykl
Person-Centred Approach, Ledergasse 17/7,
1080 Vienna, Austria
e-mail: nykl@aon.at

this model—amongst a detailed elaboration of PCA-constructs and their neuroscientific counterparts—were laid in his book (Lux 2007). Rogers' 19 propositions of his Theory of Personality and Behavior were related to Damasio's neuroscientific framework in (Motschnig-Pitrik and Lux 2008). Finally, and most central to this chapter, the authors designed the "Abstract Model of Associative Cognition and Emotion" (AMACE) to map constructs of the PCA to those of cognitive neuroscience (Motschnig-Pitrik and Nykl 2003).[1] This chapter revisits the most important features of AMACE in light of new research findings and the growing interest in interpersonal interaction. For the model requirements and the detailed validation of AMACE interested readers are referred to the original article (Motschnig-Pitrik and Nykl 2003).

The motivation for constructing AMACE has been many-fold. First, it shall provide a deeper intellectual understanding of Rogers' approach, based on scientifically accepted lower level phenomena. Based on this, we expect the improved understanding to result in a broader and more profound appreciation of the PCA, fostering relationships to areas such as communication, teamwork, education, systems theory, and management (Cornelius-White and Harbaugh 2010; Kriz 2007, 2008; McCombs 2011; Motschnig-Pitrik 2005; Rogers 1983; Rosenberg 2003; Ryback 1998). Furthermore, the model would provide criteria that allow one to distinguish the PCA from other schools in counseling and psychotherapy.

While it is outside the scope of this paper to compare individual theories of psychotherapy, Nykl (2005) relates aspects of Rogers' theory with psychoanalysis and behaviorism. Rogers' approach is considered unique in so far as all problem solving and change due to re-experiencing and insight are performed by a person within his or her own inner frame of reference. Personal growth is facilitated by perceiving a real, genuine climate of being received, accepted without having to fulfill conditions, and being understood. Since the PCA most intimately respects persons in terms of their immediate experiencing, attitudes, capacities, feelings and values, and—most importantly—their experience, we are convinced of the effectiveness of the PCA to the development of whole persons along with their environment. Confirming evidence of considering the *whole person* comes from the neurosciences, where, for example, Damasio (2012) promotes *the biological value in the whole organism* as our internal navigating device.

In a nutshell, according to Rogers, growth manifests itself in more reliable experiencing in awareness, giving way to more flexible, better adaptable, open and acceptant mind structures, based on the congruence of a person's feelings with his or her cognitions and on an accepting and understanding attitude. Our task therefore will be to find cognitive and affective interpretations of the three variables in order to hypothesize in which ways they influence human mind and experiencing such that personal growth or, in Rogers' words becoming, occurs.

---

[1] The final, definitive version of this paper has been published in JHP, 43/4, 2003 by SAGE Publications, All rights reserved. © SAGE.

An Interactive Cognitive-Emotional Model

Given the immense amount of detail on the lower levels, a key task will be the provision of proper constructs and abstractions. Thus we seek to use abstractions that provide just sufficient information to understand the line of reasoning, no more and no less.

In the next section we describe AMACE based on the requirements that the model accounts for the following:

- The self as a form or configuration that is in constant flux and is potentially available to awareness.
- Mapping of conditions of worth.
- The transition from rigid constructs to more flexible structures.
- The functions of congruence, acceptance, and empathic understanding and their interdependence.
- The function of organismic experience and the interrelation between cognition and emotion.
- The effect of interpersonal relationship on experiencing.

The next section introduces the basic construct of AMACE and relates them to intra- and interpersonal communication. In Sect. 3 we interpret the three Rogers variables in terms of AMACE and Sect. 4 proceeds by discussing implications for interpersonal communication. Section 5 concisely discusses the ways in which the model accounts for the principles and effects of the PCA. The final section summarizes our work and proposes issues for further research.

2 The Abstract Model of Associative Cognition and Emotion

2.1 Model Constructs and Consequent Phenomena

AMACE is intended to serve as a vehicle to explain and to partly visualize essential processes and effects of person-centered communication. As already mentioned the primary task is to find a model that is as simple, as generic, and as reliable as possible, yet sufficiently expressive to meet our goal. While he authors are well aware of advanced cognitive, linguistic, and other models stemming from areas such as cognitive science, artificial intelligence, cognitive psychology,, and linguistics (Anderson 1991; Quillian 1967; Sowa 1984, 2000) an abstract cognitive model that is enhanced by findings on feelings and emotions from the area of cognitive neuroscience (Damasio 2000, 2003, 2012; Squire and Kandel 1999) best fits our purpose. Box 1 summarizes the basic constructs.

Box 1: Basic Constructs
Long-Term Memory. Memories having sufficiently strong encoding that they can be reactivated at long delays are called *long-term memory* (LTM). Activation refers to some transient factor that determines the momentary availability of the memory trace and hence determines access to our memories. Several experiments prove that LTM for semantic or autobiographic knowledge can be seen as an *associative network* of concepts or *chunks* (Anderson 1991; Sowa 1984). For a comparison of various LTM subsystems and Rogers' concept of the self, see Lux (2007).
Working Memory. The term working memory (WM) refers to a limited capacity system that is capable of briefly holding and manipulating information (Baddeley 1986, 1999). Knowledge in WM is the only knowledge that we can currently work with, i.e., think about, compare, match, feel, or restructure.[2] It is essential to appreciate that WM is constrained to hold a limited number[3]– according to (Miller 1956) about seven plus or minus two– of thinkable entities, referred to as *chunks*. Thereby a chunk can be as small as a single proposition, a concept, a structure, and as large as a whole picture. Chunks can either be activated from LTM or equally be constructed from the momentary experience in the "here and now." Chunks in WM do not necessarily have an encoding in LTM.[4]
Spread of Activation. Given a chunk is activated and hence in awareness, how does it influence related chunks to potentially become aware? In AMACE, associations between chunks and their interconnections to mental images of (unconscious) organismic experience play a vital role in the *spread of activation*—some kind of energy flow—that is necessary to activate chunks to be available in WM (Quillian 1967). Spread of activation is comparable to water running through an irrigation system. We assume the following to hold:

- *Activation* spreads in **long-term memory** (LTM) from active chunks to other chunks and this spread takes time.
- The spread-of-activation has *limited capacity*. A source chunk has a certain fixed capacity for emitting activation that can flow to associated

---

[2] In fact, there exist several theories on the concept of short-term- or WM, going back to William James (1890). In AMACE, we just build on some essential features and thus abstract from further details.

[3] As a consequence, highly complex problems can hardly be resolved purely cognitively (Claxton 1998).

[4] Recently (Damasio 2000, p. 200 referring to Baars 1988), the notion of *global working space* has been developed as a way of describing the means by which focused attention and WM cooperate.

chunks (Anderson 1991).[5] This limitation will turn out to be essential in person-centered communication since more distant chunks can be reached only if activation stays focused.
- Associations learned first or repeated more often tend to be stronger encoded and thus faster recalled than associations learned later or repeated less often. Also, various factors (attention, context, mood, etc.) can affect the *amount* of activation that is spread to a knowledge structure (Anderson 1991). Even more importantly, in the context of showing films to subjects, Cahill and McGaugh (1998) have proved that situations that are emotionally more arousing can be accessed more easily and hence receive more activation than emotionally neutral situations. Authors like Piaget (1981) and Nykl (2005) even claim that the *emotional evaluation* of concepts is the primary driving force underlying the spread of activation.
- *Recognition* (e. g., Is Rogers' daughter called Natalie?) is more accurate than *recall* (e.g., What is the first name of Rogers' daughter?) (Sowa 1984). For the sake of recognition, activation can be imagined to spread from the initial as well as the target concept making the corresponding trace easier to find.
- The term *interference* is used to convey the fact that information about a concept or chunk interferes with memory for a particular piece of information. For example, the name of a new colleague may interfere with a similar name of an old friend such that the latter name is overshadowed. In general, interference can cause individuals to fail to remember/process information under some second condition (Anderson 1991)!

Emotional Contagion. *Feelings and moods are contagious*, we transmit and catch them from each other. Referring to John Cacioppo[6] and to Bernieri and Rosenthal (1991), Goleman (1995, p. 132) explains this phenomenon by saying that "we unconsciously imitate the emotions we see displayed by someone else, through an out-of-awareness motor mimicry of their facial expressions gestures, tone of voice, and other nonverbal markers of emotion." We conjecture that emotional contagion and mood-congruent memory (Baddeley 1999), the fact that we remember for example sad experiences when being in a sad mood, are interrelated phenomena having their roots in the body-relatedness of the representation of feelings and emotions.

---

[5] We hypothesize that it equally can flow to other mental images such as those symbolizing emotions and to various processes and dispositions in unconscious areas.
[6] See, for example, Hatfield et al. 1994; Cacioppo and Gardner 1999.

Emotions, Feelings, and Consciousness. Damasio (2000) ascribes fundamental accounts to *emotions*[7] and *feelings*,[8] the body, and subcortical brain systems as sources or preconditions for higher psychological phenomena. Damasio (2000, p. 169) suggests that *core consciousness*[9] occurs when the brain's representation devices generate an imaged, nonverbal account of how the organism's own state is affected by the organism's processing of an object. Note that the term object is used to subsume notions like persons, pictures, situations, physical objects, etc.

While Miller (1956) used the term *chunk* to refer to any thinkable entity, we reintroduce and extend the concept of chunk as a mental image that holds some thinkable entity (such as a concept, a feeling, or a picture) associated with emotional information (Damasio 2000).[10] The weight of the emotional component can vary between approximately zero and values indicating high emotional importance or arousal, in the spirit of Bower's emotional nodes (Bower 1981). There is empirical evidence that the emotional value influences the strength of encoding and activation (Cahill and McGaugh 1998) of the respective chunks. Hence we hypothesize that the degree of flexibility of the emotional values of chunks plays a significant role in the behavior of the individual. While an individual's organismic experience in the current situation leads to a symbolization of cognitions in chunks with a high degree of flexibility, i.e., with rich interconnections to those organismic experiences from which the emotional values are derived, fixed emotional values are characteristic of conditions of worth. The latter typically accompany external evaluations or statements introjected by some significant other or learned purely intellectually. They tend to establish rigid, preconceived patterns or prejudices.

---

[7] An emotion is defined as a "specifically caused transient change of the organism state." (Damasio 2000, p. 282). The brain induces emotions from a remarkably small number of brain sites. Most of them are located below the cerebral cortex and are known as subcortical.

[8] A feeling is defined as "the private, mental experience of an emotion, while the term emotion should be used to designate the collection of responses, many of which are publicly observable." (Damasio 2000, p. 42).

[9] The scope of core consciousness is the here and now. Core consciousness is a simple biological phenomenon; it is stable across the lifetime of the organism; it is not exclusively human.

[10] Damasio 2000, p. 147–148: "The records that we hold of objects and events that we once perceived include the motor adjustments we made to obtain the perception in the first place and also include the emotional reactions we had then. They all are co-registered in memory, albeit in separate systems. [...] p. 161: ...we retrieve not just sensory data but also accompanying motor and emotional data [...] we recall not just sensory characteristics of an actual object but the past reactions of the organism to that object." For the purposes of this article, we emphasize emotional aspects and ignore motor-related ones. However, the function of the body is central in the chapter by Carol Wolter-Gustafson in this volume.

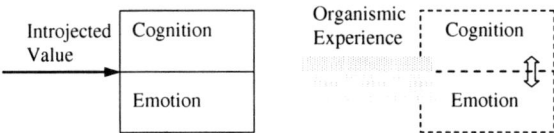

Fig. 1 The abstraction of a chunk and its cognitive and emotional components. Chunks with rigid components (*left*) versus chunks with flexible, richly interconnected components (*right-hand side*)

Figure 1 sketches our abstraction of a chunk, whereby the left-hand side of the figure depicts a rigid chunk that typically appears in rigid constructs. The right-hand side of the figure illustrates a flexible chunk that assimilates its emotional value from organismic experience in the current valuing process. This chunk can be thought to be interconnected with organismic experience and thus is capable of influencing the spread of activation according to the individual's experiencing in the current situation. Note that our notion of interconnected chunks is more abstract but close to Behr's schemas (Behr 2009) and Greenberg and Paivio's (1997) *emotional schemes*. The two notions share the intertwined nature of cognitions and emotions. Our model differs in so far as it is the interpersonal relationship between persons, their attitudes, and the particular situation in the here and now that activates chunks in the first place. In Greenberg and Paivio's framework, it is the emotional schemes for individual emotions that explicitly inform the process of intervention. Complementarily, the function of symbolic representation of experience is convincingly discussed by Watson and Greenberg (1995) and Ikemi (2010). They argue that representing experience in words allows clients to make it perceptible and potentially transformable.

2.2 Intra- and Interpersonal Communication in AMACE

The left-hand side of Fig. 2 sketches the constructs (i.e., structures and processes) we use to model intra- and interpersonal communication. Note that these constructs are more general than Rogers' representation of the total personality (Rogers 1951) sketched on the right-hand side of the figure. This is because we want to track the process of experiencing from its induction to potential awareness about its source and concomitants. The overall structure shows that the construct Person (X) encompasses the totality of a person's organismic experiences at some particular point in time. These arise as subceptions anywhere in the organism (Rogers 1959, p. 199) and are represented in the brain. The precise nature of these processes and their circuitries still constitute a thrilling research question. In Fig. 3, *organismic experience* is denoted by the construct OrgExp that encompasses mental images currently not available to awareness. The interconnections between the LTM, WM, and OrgExp (Organismic Experience) constructs are

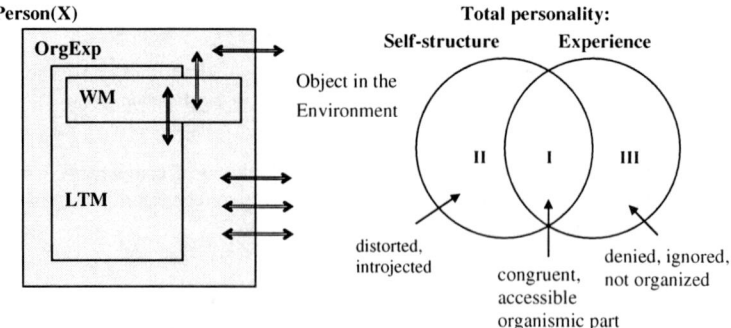

Fig. 2 A sketch of the topology of constructs relevant in intra- and interpersonal communication and their relationship to Rogers' constructs of the Total personality

denoted by drawing the LTM and WM constructs within that of the OrgExp construct. Basically, each chunk of the LTM or WM construct (not shown in Fig. 2 that emphasizes the topology of constructs but depicted in Figs. 3, 4, 5) will have at least some minimal interconnection to the OrgExp construct. Further, the OrgExp construct has, via various messaging systems, modulating influence on higher constructs like LTM and WM. These two constructs have in their common intersection those chunks that have been activated from LTM. For reasons of simplicity, we do not (yet) distinguish further substructures such as various brain systems, the reflexes, the hormonal system, the sympathetic system, etc. Nevertheless, note that the LTM has a configuration or gestalt that takes the form of an associative network of chunks, i.e., mental images that can become aware if activated. This notion is consistent with Rogers' view of the self as an organized, fluent gestalt (Rogers 1959, p. 200).

The bi-directional arrows in Fig. 2 denote communication-links. For example, the bi-directional arrow between WM and LTM means that chunks in WM may be symbolized in chunks of LTM and chunks from LTM can be activated into the WM. Analogously, particular mental images from the OrgExp construct can become conscious and be symbolized as chunks in WM and current experience in the WM can be assimilated in processes and mental images in the OrgExp area. In general, intrapersonal communication is achieved by transmitting information of various intensity and quality along different paths. Thereby information can either be forwarded or inhibited from being spread according to current circumstances signaled in various regions of the organism. Synaptic plasticity and hormonal signaling are just two examples illustrating that changes in response to particular stimuli can cause emotions (Squire and Kandel 1999) and background feelings (Damasio 2000, p. 52). This provides an explanation for the essential influence of experiencing in the current process, leading to effects that cannot be evoked purely cognitively.

Comparing our constructs with Rogers' representation of the self-structure and experience, we observe that Rogers' graphic focuses on illustrating the meaning of the amount of overlap of self-structure and experience. The intersection of Rogers' circles, referred to as zone I in Fig. 2, denotes those experiences where the self is congruent with the organism's experience. In our terminology, zone I corresponds to those chunks in LTM and/or WM that have accurate symbolizations and flexible emotional components (compare right-hand side of Fig. 1) and hence rich interconnections to the OrgExp area that can be thought to encompass Rogers' circle denoting experience. Rigid chunks with valuing conditions (compare left-hand side of Fig. 1) in LTM and/or WM would be placed in Rogers' zone II denoting those parts of the self-structure that lack interconnections to the individual's own organismic experience.[11] Mental images in the OrgExp area with no accessible symbolization in LTM correspond to Rogers' zone III holding denied experiences (being inconsistent with the self-structure) and, more generally, experiences that are ignored or not organized because they have no *perceived* relationship to the self-structure.

3 The Interpretation of Rogers' PCA in Terms of the AMACE Model

The hypothesis underlying our research is that interpreting significant *aspects* of theorizing in the PCA in terms of lower-level phenomena will provide further insight into the way Rogers' approach is effective. Rogers describes the person-centered, growth promoting relationship as requiring three attitudinal conditions, also referred to as the "Rogers variables." Congruence, or synonymously called realness, genuineness or transparency, acceptance or unconditional positive regard toward the other individual, and empathic understanding. Interestingly, more than a decade ago, one of the authors (Nykl 2000, 2005) intuitively assigned the term *dispositions* to refer to Rogers' variables. As will become clear soon, this term matches the "nature" of the person-centered conditions well since they include cognitive as well as organismic components. According to Nykl (2005, 2012), psychological processes in the subceptions (Rogers 1959) include the three dispositions at an unconscious level that influences the self—a view that is taken up in the conceptualization of the orgExp area modeling organismic experience and has interconnections with the chunks of the self structure.

It is these three mutually interdependent conditions or dispositions that we chose to take up and to interpret in cognitive-emotional terms. We are fully aware of the dangers inherent in our enterprise, namely to deprive the approach of its full meaning and make it appear too simplistic. In this context we emphasize that our

---

[11] In fact, two categories of rigid chunks belong to zone II. First, (neutral) learned constructs lacking one's own experience and second, introjections with more or less distorted experience. In our view, based on Damasio (2000), chunks need at least some minimal OrgExp symbolization in order to be able to be symbolized as chunks in WM and LTM.

model is intended to explain *significant aspects* of Rogers' Theory but is *never meant to map all facets* inherent in a real interpersonal relationship! Yet, we also do see the merits of intellectually understanding major aspects of Rogers' theory. In fact, recent research on feelings, motivation, experiencing, and learning points directly to the vital role of person-to person encounters in illuminating, at least partially, the most sophisticated conscious as well as unconscious ways each such encounter influences our self on the basis of our previous self and experience (Barrett-Lennard 2005; Cornelius-White and Harbough 2010; Motschnig-Pitrik and Barrett-Lenard 2010; Nykl 2005).

The three Rogers variables are strongly intertwined (for their characterization see also the chapter on the essence of the PCA in this volume). Nevertheless, we first interpret each variable separately in terms of AMACE components and discuss interdependencies consecutively.

Congruence, Genuineness, Realness, Transparency. The facilitator experiences the feelings that currently exist in him or herself before communicating them to the client, if appropriate. The expression "if appropriate" indicates the necessity of an internal "decision" on which of the inner experiencing to "let through" and which ones to hold back at least temporarily, and rather listen to the client acceptingly and actively. The facilitator may communicate to the client his or her current inner world. Often it will include feelings and meanings that originally the client has initiated and transmitted, thus allowing him or her to re-experience them from a viewpoint enriched by the other person—a viewpoint existing outside of himself or herself. At other times, the facilitator will share parts of his or her inner world and thereby provide a personal reaction or viewpoint, striving for a focused continuation of the client process based on mutual understanding. In both cases, emergent feelings can be experienced and corresponding mental images arise in the brain and can be matched, examined, and acted upon both consciously and unconsciously. Thereby activation, in other words the flow of experiencing is focused on the chunks the client has activated and flows from these chunks to related ones, leading to further focused self-exploration. Once chunks are activated, they can freely be explored and brought into relationship with current or previous experience. In this way, new experiences can be assimilated. Note that mutual sharing of part of one's inner world builds trust and confidentiality and thereby contributes to the client's feeling safe.

To illustrate the importance of a *real* personal relationship targeted at mutual understanding and accompanying the client in her way, we include a snapshot of an interview taken from Bozart et al. (2002). The excerpt shows Carl Rogers talking with Sylvia about her feeling strong within herself to take chances:

Sylvia   Reaching out to people and approaching strangers and uh –
C.R.   Taking all kinds of risks that you hadn't before.
Sylvia   Some. More, which, I mean I, I don't know about all kinds.
C.R.   Yeah.
Sylvia   Quite a few, and it's been exciting and hard.

An Interactive Cognitive-Emotional Model

C.R.   And I guess that leads to a, um, a deeper kind of learning, at any rate a learning that you feel more sure of, I get, I get a sense of assurance in what you're talking about. Assurance in you.
Sylvia   Well, yes. Yes and no. And I, I feel more im-, like I was saying before, I feel more mature and more, and I'm more aware of my immaturity.
C.R.   M-hm.
Sylvia   They're both, uh, a part of each other. ... And uh, does that make—does that, I guess I'm thinking that it just sounds crazy.
C.R.   No, I don't –
Sylvia   To say that I feel more mature because I know I'm how, I know more about how immature I am.
C.R.   Uh-huh. No, that makes a lot of sense to me.

Figure 3 sketches our view of the process by which a person's associative map (the tree-like structure in the LTM area), in particular the fragment available to the WM, gradually changes in response to communicating with the facilitator. The fact that the latter activates and communicates the rightmost chunk from his or her LTM (see the WM context depicted in the middle part of the figure) causes the client in turn to recall a corresponding chunk. By drawing chunks as empty squares we do not make any statement about the relative importance of the cognitive and emotional components of individual chunks. We assume, however, that feelings underlie meanings (Damasio 2000). The thick line in the client's LTM substructure indicates that, under normal conditions, the more strongly associated chunk from the LTM substructure (the one beneath the root) would have interfered with the rightmost chunk and would most probably be activated instead. Generally speaking, Fig. 3 shows the activation of related chunks, i.e., making them available in the WM due to the facilitator's congruent experiencing and expressing his or her perception of the current situation. If the client feels received, this process allows activation to escape from choosing the "usual" pathway. It tends to open up new paths of reaching experience, paths which often are closer to the client's original, undistorted experiencing. This can be seen in analogy to the cognitive notion of overcoming *interference effects*. It is worth mentioning that with genuine reflection, as opposed to cognitive explanation, the process of self-exploration is not interrupted but rather supported to proceed, at its best, guided by the person's own valuing process.

Openness on the side of the therapist fosters openness on the client side. This statement is deduced from the fact that feelings and moods are contagious, as has been argued in Sect. 2. As an attitude, openness tends to be induced from the intuitive, unconscious level, given a safe and accepting atmosphere. In Fig. 3, we use grayscale to illustrate the client's development from being less open (depicted by a darker shade of gray) on the left-hand side of the figure to becoming more open (shown as light gray) on the right-hand side of the figure as a result of communication with a congruent facilitator. Physiological concomitants of openness are opposite to those of fear and appear in all parts of the respective

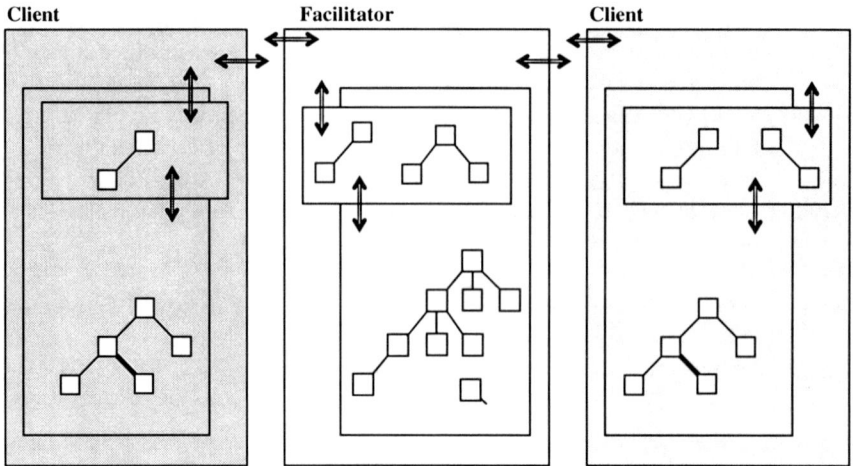

Fig. 3 Mapping of congruence. Chunks from the facilitator's WM help the client to activate related, associated chunks. The client's openness is likely to increase as indicated by the difference in grayscale between the leftmost and the rightmost structure

organism (Damasio 2000, p. 78). The entire organism becomes more open and prepared for reception. This openness improves the flow of experiencing and thus leads to the effect that inhibition, caused by rigid constructs, tends to be overcome more easily.

Although openness, as an attitude manifests itself at the intuitive level (modeled as the OrgExp construct), this level is known to have modulating influence on all other constructs. Hence, intellectual openness, the willingness to be open for receiving and communicating new ideas and experiences, can be traced back to be nourished from lower level structures by the way of influencing the chemical milieu (via chemical messaging) as well as signaling along neural pathways (Damasio 2000; Goleman 1995).

In terms of AMACE, congruence would best be mapped as having a rich repertoire of chunks and other mental images available that truthfully map mental and body states and, furthermore, well developed, rich, and flexible interconnections that encourage communication between all constructs. Thus, being congruent, open, and real manifests itself both at the intuitive and the cognitive levels. Perhaps most importantly, it means a harmonious, uninhibited, truthful interplay fostering communication between these two levels.

From the perspective of neuroscience, Damasio (2003) observes a tightly related phenomenon regarding fluent processes: "The fact that we, sentient and sophisticated creatures, call certain feelings positive and other negative is directly related to the fluidity or strain of the life process" (p. 131). Hence, when associating the psychological notion of congruence with the physiological notion of fluidity of life processes we recognize that they are in tune—both directing us forward. In brief, in accord with Rogers' and Damasio's view, we conjecture the forming, maintaining, and actualizing of fluent communication in terms of complex, flexible mental patterns and messaging to be a lifelong task that rests upon a rich supply of experience.

Viewing openness as linked to acceptance, the perception and at least minimal symbolization of openness by the client support the facilitator's *symbolization* of his or her acceptance. Receiving acceptance in turn helps the client in opening up in communication and allowing him or her to proceed in the exploration of yet deeper levels of self. Naturally, congruence and acceptance can be at odds, needing empathy to mediate in their struggle.

Acceptance, Unconditional Positive Regard. This non-judgemental attitude is essential because evaluation by another tends to move the locus of evaluation outside the individual and thereby distracts the flow of activation and hence the process of self-disclosure. Furthermore, evaluation supplies chunks with rigid emotional values assessed by a significant other rather than incorporating personal values derived from organismic experience. According to Rogers (1961) "Evaluation is always a threat, always creates a need for defensiveness, always means that some portion of experience must be denied to awareness. ...But if judgements based on external standards are not being made then I can be more open to my experience, can recognize my own likings and dislikings... I can begin to recognize the locus of evaluation within myself" (p. 357). In discussing the subtle but sharp difference between acceptance and agreement, Rogers (1961) says: "... to cease evaluating another is not to cease having reactions" (p. 358). Thus, acceptance on the intuitive level must not be confused with agreement with the conversation's subject matter on the cognitive level! To make this distinction particularly clear in AMACE, we model the therapist's reactions as a subdomain of congruence and point to the necessity of gracefully and empathically communicating these two interdependent variables in every instant.

Experiencing and offering acceptance primarily address the realm of feeling and emotion. Thereby the aspects of content and cognition play a subordinate, but nevertheless, at times supportive role. In Fig. 4 the facilitator's attitude of unconditional positive regard is depicted as a waved pattern that is manifest in the OrgExp construct and transmitted to other constructs by means of internal messaging. As with openness, acceptance improves and strengthens the internal flow of experiencing. As a positive feeling it would be aligned with reward which, according to (Damasio 2000, p. 78) "is associated with behaviors such as seeking and approaching. [...] Reward causes organisms to open themselves up and out toward their environment, approaching it, searching it." Acceptance is communicated by various ways of verbal and non-verbal communication such as subtle facial expressions, the tone of the voice, body language, etc., many of which are received by the client at an out-of-awareness level. On the right-hand side of Fig. 4, the waved areas indicate that the client has at least to some degree perceived positive regard. It manifests itself on the intuitive level and spreads to the whole organism.

From the cognitive point of view, acceptance can be interpreted as attentive listening and perceiving of the client's chunks. In Fig. 4, this is illustrated by the

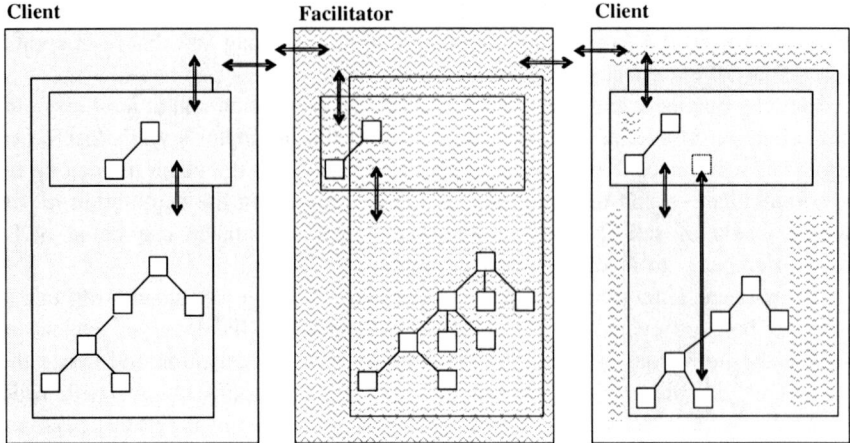

Fig. 4 Sketch illustrating the mapping of acceptance

two-chunk structure the facilitator receives from the current situation, hence primarily the client. The facilitator holds these chunks in an area of the WM that captures current experience and accepts the corresponding feelings and meanings. Thereby the client tends to feel received and can stay within oneself. Activation stays concentrated in those areas that the client activates. In other words, the locus and source of the organismic evaluation process stays within the person, it stays person-centered! In such an internal milieu prepared for flow and devoid of inhibition, activation is more likely to reach even distant chunks on deeper levels that now can be activated and explored in the WM of the client. This is indicated by the long arrow and rightmost chunk in the WM shown on the right hand-side of Fig. 4. Former experience can thus be explored and valued from within and new experience—chunks drifting in from the here and now (not shown in the figure)—can be assimilated.

The recipient perceives that his or her inner world drives the process. This reassures him or her of being a person of worth to the facilitator—usually a person toward whom he or she feels respect. The mutual respect, on the intuitive level strengthened by the phenomenon of emotional contagion, furthermore improves the working alliance between therapist and client which—not surprisingly—has been shown to be an important therapy outcome variable (Cain 2010; Sachse and Elliot 2001). As a further consequence, receiving oneself as someone of worth, the client finds it easier to become aware of feelings and experiences that, in the first place, stem from the current process. This experiencing in awareness has the potential to assimilate chunks that map feelings and hence widens the scope of experience and thereby contributes to congruence, a more informed and reliant intrapersonal communication. The repertoire of chunks is enriched by those that map feelings or bodily sensations and make them available for conscious thought and decision making. As a consequence, the client no longer depends on pure intellect but rather can draw on intellect enriched by intuition. Regarding neurons, we hypothesize that the facilitative atmosphere can cause the strengthening of those terminals and dendrites that support the perception and mediation of acceptance, liking, positive regard, etc. It is these and perhaps other anatomical processes in the brain and body of a person that allow him or her to grow in the direction of greater acceptance of self as well as the environment. Note, in particular, that this adaptation process is out of consciousness and requires, in the first place, experiencing in a favorable atmosphere.

Empathic Understanding. A model of empathic understanding should reflect the facilitator's conscious endeavor to explore the client's inner world in order to support the client in the exploration and potential reorganization of his or her self. Thus, the facilitator temporarily steps into the still unconscious associative maps in the client's LTM area that, according to the facilitator's momentary feeling and understanding, most closely reflect the client's current concerns. The facilitator's sensing of the client's inner world is aided by his or her mirror neuron system—a brain-body circuitry enabling us to perceive (amongst others, aspects of) another persons' emotions as if they were our own ones (Iacoboni et al. 2005; Marci et al. 2007; Rizzolatti and Craighero 2004; Watson 2007).

If the facilitator considers it appropriate, he or she communicates the findings to the client as an expression of a deep sharing. The recipient verifies the message against his or her conception and, in the positive case, feels empathically the correspondence of aspects (mental images) of himself or herself with the facilitator's symbolization . When feeling understood, the client can fully and consciously appreciate the positive regard he or she is receiving and gradually learns the meanings of individual, personal feelings. Thereby new experiences can be assimilated. Occasionally insight—basically a link between organismic experience and cognitions (chunks)—can arise. If, however, the client does not feel understood completely, he or she can report the discrepancies back to the facilitator and the process can be backtracked to proceed in another direction. In case the client (repeatedly) feels totally misunderstood, he or she will withdraw, which means that there is always some risk in communicating empathic understanding. Rogers himself describes the dialogue between a facilitator striving for empathic understanding and a client who compares the reported feelings with his own experiencing and provides feedback on the quality of the match at several places (see e.g., Rogers 1980, chapter on empathy). From this we assume that our LTM is capable of holding concrete symbolizations of feelings—so-called referents (Rogers 1961, 1980; Gendlin 1978)—in response to particular situations that can consciously be checked against perceived symbolizations, as soon as the former are brought into conscious awareness.

The upper part of Fig. 5 illustrates the WM and LTM contents of a facilitator who tries to empathically understand the client. Note that the WM of the facilitator may hold chunks that are not yet in the client's WM (meaning that the client is not yet aware of their contents) but enter it in the next step, possibly along with further related chunks (compare the WM on the top of Fig. 5). The bottom part of Fig. 5 (showing only the WM's) illustrates the continuation of the step-by-step process by which the facilitator accompanies the client in activating chunks and thus

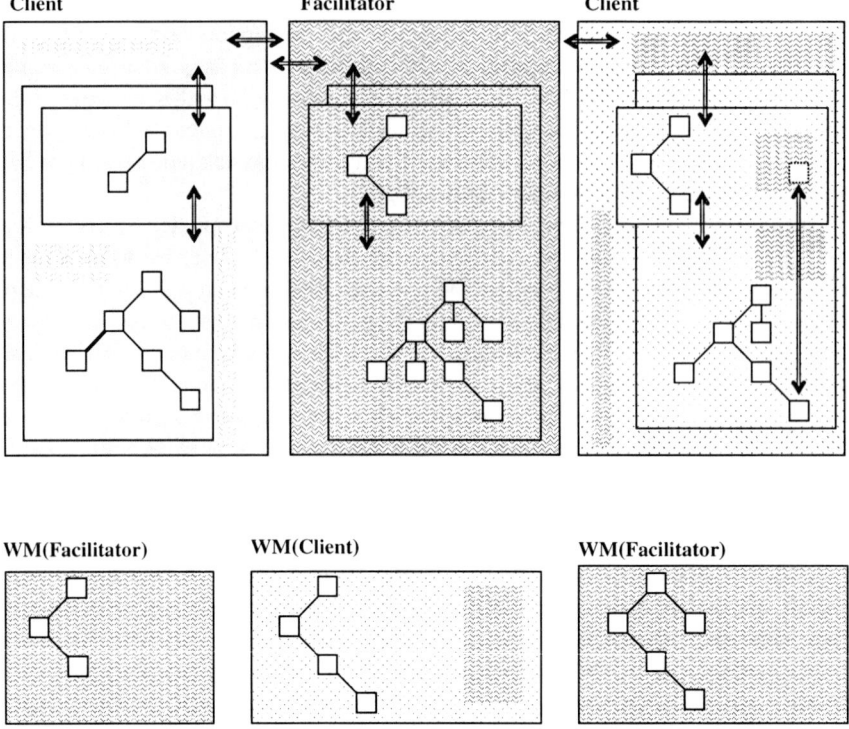

Fig. 5 Cognitive and emotional effects underlying emphatic understanding

making them available in the process. The client thereby experiences the associated feelings in awareness and can explore their old and current meanings. The waved pattern in Fig. 5 illustrates that the client has received the facilitator's acceptance at least to some degree. The feeling of being accepted is intensified by the client's feeling of being empathically understood, as illustrated by the increase of the waved areas in the constructs representing the client. The transition from the light gray area to the dotted area in the client process shall indicate the increase in his or her openness to experience and hence congruence. We emphasize that empathic understanding is a conscious process that is directed toward supporting the other person in experiencing and enhancement of those levels of self (including organismic experience influencing chunks situated at different levels of the associative networks) that so far have been unexplored, denied, or distorted. It depends on an atmosphere where the client feels safe and received, and appears to be strengthened by client resources such as access to his or her inner world combined with skills to verbalize what has been found.

In terms of our model, empathic understanding provides means to override introjected values, causing deep, emotionally initiated interference effects, that stand in the way of accessing relevant chunks or inhibit the assimilation of new experience from the "here and now." Emotionally grounded interferences inhibit the spread of activation to those chunks that hold the client's real, organismic experience. We say that it is denied or in some way distorted. The term "distorted" nicely expresses the fact that other associations are followed due to having higher emotional values instead of the "right" one and thus other chunks are activated in everyday situations. By striving to empathically understand the client, the facilitator cautiously tries to address those chunks from the client's repertoire that he or she feels or believes could contribute to the client's personal growth. Strategically, there seem to be two concrete ways that allow one to resolve interference. Following the first and more powerful way, the facilitator addresses those chunks for the purpose of recognition by the client, which he or she considers relevant. Since recognition needs less activation than recall (compare Sect. 2.2), chunks on levels right beneath the borderline of consciousness can be activated. Whereas the fact that recognition is easier, faster, and more reliable than recall has extensively been proved for cognitive contents, we assume that it equally holds true for the emotional components of chunks. The second way to work around interference is to take up already conscious chunks that are immediately associated with the chunks that hold some key-experience, such that the latter can more easily be recalled.

Complementary to intellectual understanding, matching along chunk networks, the client feels empathically understood. The strength of this feeling will depend partly on the degree of understanding, in more concrete terms on the degree of overlap between the mental images representing the internal state of the client with those mapping the client's perception of the facilitator's understanding of feelings and meanings. A profound overlap would characterize a *meeting at relational depth* (Mearns and Cooper 2005). Complete matching of mental images and neural patterns as if they would touch each other lets activation flow together and causes those intense moments many know as *moments of meeting*. The self is enriched by another, the other momentarily becomes part of self.

As with acceptance, at least some minimal degree of openness and transparency on the side of the client appears to be a precondition for the facilitator's empathic understanding of the client that, in turn, strengthens the client's feeling of being received and motivates further opening. We hypothesize that experiencing empathic understanding strengthens those anatomical connections that enable the matching between organismic experience as represented in mental images (on the OrgExp construct) with corresponding chunks and networks in the WM and LTM constructs. The person experiences his or her feelings in awareness such that his/her disposition over feelings and emotions grows. In other words, fixed chunks gradually give way to loose, fluent structures. Since rigid constructs need no longer be guarded, energy is released and becomes available for the assimilation of experience in flexible chunks and equally for internal valuing processes leading to higher flexibility. The latter leads to a more differentiated perception of the world based on the fact that neither cognitions nor feelings are decisive in their own right. Their interplay, in other words the availability of sensory and visceral experiencing in cognitive tasks, leads to a synergy of all processes and systems. This mutual support and richer interconnection of interacting systems exactly is the reason why stability is not compromised by the higher flexibility of chunks. As a result, improved achievement and optimized behavior ensue.

Summarizing, note that in AMACE all three Rogers variables have organismic or intuitive and cognitive aspects. They support each other in accompanying a person in the direction of increased congruence. Realness enriches the other by having him or her share the facilitator's feelings and meanings with the tendency to trust the client to "decide" (both intellectually and intuitively) what to assimilate or "incorporate" and what to dismiss. Acceptance devoid of conditions encourages internal valuing processes leading to more self-acceptance and less dependence on others while appreciating their caring and collaboration (Cain 2010). Empathic understanding, based on congruence and acceptance, lets individuals feel understood at all levels. It amplifies their own feelings and meanings and makes them available to awareness by linking intuitions and cognitions, thus broadening the field of experience and improving integrated functioning. Some consequences thereof are discussed in the next section.

4 Implications for Interpersonal Communication

While, at any point in time, the number of chunks or units of information we can attend to and process is strictly limited (Miller 1956), our largely unconscious brain-body communication devices support us in interacting widely at conscious and unconscious levels (Damasio 2000; Goleman 1995; Lux 2007; Nykl 2005). Furthermore, advanced measuring techniques reveal more and more about the intricate ways of human preconscious and nonverbal interaction that has a capacity that by far outranges strongly cognitive exchanges (see also chapters by Lux and Ikemi). Consequently, direct human interaction is a particularly powerful way of shaping dispositions. Damasio (2012, p. 63) writes: "I cannot emphasize the word *interaction* enough." In a similar vein and emphasizing interaction with social others Rogers (1951) states in proposition IX: "As a result of the interaction with the environment, and particularly as a result of evaluational interaction with others, the structure of self is formed [..]." Thus let us illustrate the influence of valuing conditions and person-centered dispositions in interaction with the help of a personal example:

Recently, one of Renate's sons said with a sad voice:

S: "I can't find my blue college map with most of the materials for history and some assignments in it."
R: "Hmm, that's unfortunate. Pause. Where was it that you last saw it?"
S: "I had it at school yesterday, but I don't think I left it there, I sense it is somewhere at home."
R (promptly): "I see. The problem is that you leave such a mess in your room that you necessarily lose sight of anything. Frankly, I couldn't find anything in such a mess!"

S (angrily, excitedly, with frustration): "This isn't the reason!! I know you want me to tidy up my room and I'll do so later. But I searched everywhere and just can't find it. ..."
R (softly, looking her son into his eyes): "So you feel like not having the blue college map is quite a loss for you!"
S (sadly yet thoughtfully): "Yes, indeed, mum. (long pause, then clearing up) I'll look out for it in my class and see whether someone put it on the teacher's desk in another class where we had English."
R (confirmingly): "Seems like you know what to do to get it back!"
S: "Yes, and I'll clean up my table tomorrow and if I still don't find the map I'll ask the class-teacher"
R: "Good luck, I'm curious how this will end, make sure you let me know!"

We're including this example since conversation with children can provide such a lot of authentic insight and learning. Let us reflect what had happened. Once I (Renate) brought up the issue with the mess I immediately realized that this was a learned pattern I took over from my parents. Although I had hated it, I curiously enough used it almost automatically! From my son's transparent reaction I knew instantly that, instead of perceiving my child's whole communication, I had diagnosed him with the/my problem, dealt with him like an object, not paying attention to what was going on in him. Fortunately, he didn't turn away completely and I had a chance to 'dis-pose' of my learned construct and rather "re-sort" to my person-centered dispositions to genuinely meeting my son. Feeling understood, he seemed to release all his inner resources to freely explore options for the solution of our problem. Reciprocally, I felt included and part of some larger "project" that was happening between us, perhaps even enjoying a little our cooperation, our joining efforts for meeting a challenge.

The situation can be mapped into AMACE as follows: Strong links such as the bold link between two chunks in the LTM(X) context (in Figs. 3 and 5) might first call the boldly linked chunk into WM and expression, once the source chunk has been activated. In this situation we'd act primarily on fixed, established links (e.g., mess needs cleaning up). However, given strong interconnections between the cognitive structures with their emotional grounding in organismic experience would provide us with connections to deeper levels and richer re-sorting options. For example, chunks residing further down in networks could become activated, informed by activations from organismic valuing *and/or* from recognition of a chunk based on the expression of another person as frequently happens in empathic listening responses. This is illustrated in Figs. 4 and 5 by the long vertical arrow denoting the activation of a low-level chunk into the WM context. Thus, viewing the Rogers' variables as dispositions aiming toward improved communication and flexibility within and between persons leads to exploring the interplay between cognitive and emotion-processing systems (and also between these and motor systems as explored in the chapter by Carol Wolter-Gustafson). Naturally, all these are intricately intertwined as we tried to elucidate throughout and, no doubt, shaped by the *mutual* influence of the *interacting* persons.

While in Sect. 3 we had elaborated the classical "case," namely in which ways a facilitator providing Rogers' core conditions can help another person to reorganize their self structure, this section focused on presenting an instance of *mutually* living the core conditions. It illustrated the potential for mutual unfolding or, in other words, actualization of each person. Elsewhere, one of the authors collaborated in proposing a new construct, termed *co-actualization*, to denote exactly this mutual actualization of partners in a well-functioning, typically but not necessarily longer term relationship (Motschnig-Pitrik and Barrett-Lennard 2010). Besides mutual growth of relationship partners, co-actualization is proposed to result in the forming and growth of the interpersonal relationship as an entity having its own life and influence.

5 Discussion of the Model and the Mapping

This section discusses briefly the ways in which the model accounts for principles and effects of the PCA. A more detailed validation of the model can be found in (Motschnig-Pitrik and Nykl 2003).

The Self Possesses Structure. This claim for structure has been met by foreseeing associative networks of chunks for organizing cognitive as well as emotional knowledge. Furthermore, the abstraction of chunks as network-nodes carrying cognitive as well as emotional components meets the need to combine these two knowledge sources. Rogers' hypothesis regarding a layered structure of self, that typically is explored layer by layer (Rogers 1961), is precisely met and confirmed by a layered traversal or exploration of the network structure such as suggested by the stepwise access to a client's LTM in empathic understanding.

Need for Experiential Learning. In AMACE, experiential learning is taken into account by introducing the construct OrgExp to capture structures and processes relying on organismic experience and by pointing to various "mechanisms" that promote or inhibit communication. Some of these mechanisms are flexible versus rigid emotional components of chunks, changes in the structure of neuronal connections, changes due to synaptic plasticity and the emotionally driven emission of hormones.

Necessity of all Three Rogers' Variables in the PCA. Our mapping confirms this close relationship between the three dispositions in so far as each of them has been shown to contribute individual, yet complementary cognitive as well as organismic effects.

Addressing Areas Denied to Consciousness and Conditions of Worth. In AMACE, for example, empathic understanding has the potential to circumvent interference effects. Furthermore, AMACE acknowledges communication between intuitive (OrgExp) areas of persons and illustrates the changes in these as well as the cognitive areas as caused by psychological contact.

Consistency with Process Outcome Research in Humanistic Psychotherapies. Regarding client processes, AMACE views self-exploration and experiencing as central phenomena following from the therapist's attitudes of congruence, acceptance and empathic understanding. Consequently, their contribution to success appears evident. Equally, the contribution of client's resources, in particular his or her expressiveness, role involvement, and working alliance (Cain 2010) follow directly from AMACE. On the microprocess level, it has been shown that clients profit from deepening proposals, in particular if the therapist has understood the client and anchored his or her response to the client's issues (Sachse and Elliot 2001). This finding appears totally consistent with the way we model self-exploration, namely as stepwise activation of chunks connected to organismic experience and influenced by it.

6 Conclusions and Further Research

This chapter aimed to illuminate significant aspects from Rogers' PCA by (partially) mapping it into an Abstract Model of Associative Cognition and Emotion (AMACE). AMACE employs abstract constructs to overcome the complexity inherent in employing cognitive as well as emotional aspects stemming form disciplines as diverse as humanistic psychology, psychotherapy, communication, cognitive psychology, and cognitive neuroscience. The constructs prove particularly useful in discussing inter- and intrapersonal communication, throwing light onto the influential and potentially reorganizing function of the *interaction* with significant others. Furthermore, the mapping of the PCA into AMACE clarified some of the ways in which the PCA considers an individual's inner frame of reference (Rogers 1951, p. 494) at the organismic as well as cognitive level (Motschnig-Pitrik and Nykl 2001). Given the two levels are well interconnected, other than just linear solution to problems are feasible (compare also the chapter by Hulgus on second-order change). To support phenomena like creative collaborative problem solving and mutual growth, the current version of AMACE emphasized the notion of *interaction* between persons who mutually perceive a person-centered atmosphere. While it was proposed that this would lead to co-actualization of relationship partners (Motschnig-Pitrik and Barrett-Lennard 2010), further research is needed to find out under what conditions relationships tend to retain their co-actualizing capacity over time.

AMACE lets effects of the three Rogers variables (Rogers 1959, 1961; Cain and Seeman 2002) be viewed at a more explicit level, in order to more profoundly and cognitively, imagine and understand them. In our view, the model—today backed with recent research findings as presented in this chapter—contributes to provide further evidence of Rogers' empirical findings and thus would support the PCA to drift into and be acknowledged in all areas involving inter- and intrapersonal communication. By considering experiential learning and concomitant changes in several regions of brain and body, the model, in particular, illustrates the limitations of relying solely on intellect (Goleman 1995; Rogers 1961; Sheldon et al. 2003). Rather, it directly rests upon human dispositions of congruence, acceptance and empathic understanding in any person-to-person encounter and can, *partially*, be accounted for in terms of cognitive neuroscience. The model, however, is abstract and intended to be refined along with the rapid progress being made in cognitive neuroscience (Squire and Kandel 1999; Damasio 2012). In particular, the authors are interested in physiological and biological concomitants of person-centered communication as well as in ways to acquire and deepen person-centered dispositions (Nykl 2005, 2012).

Motschnig-Pitrik has introduced person-centered teaching in her advanced courses on software engineering, project management, and communication. This stream of practice and research is described more fully in the chapter on person-centered learning in Motschnig-Pitrik (2013). The respective experience provided much of the motivation for developing AMACE as a model allowing one to visualize and intellectually capture several effects of the PCA—as something the authors and readers could take and show to students, teachers, management, and significant others. It could help to convince others and make them more aware of the need to connect the intuitive (OrgExp) level with the cognitive one.

Since the PCA plays a significant function in interaction, further research will address the notion of person-centered teams, individual as well as corporate creative problem-solving, flexible or agile approaches to project management, person-centered principles in designing human–computer interaction. Furthermore, we are keen to further explore effects of communicating across cultures in a person-centered way (Lago 2011, Motsching-Pitrik and Nykl 2011).

We trust that this work will contribute to a further assimilation and adoption of Rogers' humane, genuine, and deeply appealing theory and its adaptation to new needs and technologies. To end with Rogers' (1951) words: "If they [these hypotheses] prove to be a stimulation to significant study of the deeper dynamics of human behavior, they will have served their purpose well" (p. 532).

References

Anderson, J. R. (1991). *Cognitive psychology and its applications* (3rd ed.). New York: Freeman.
Baars, B. (1988). *A cognitive theory of consciousness*. New York: Cambridge University Press.
Baddeley, A. D. (1986). *Working memory*. Oxford: Oxford University Press.
Baddeley, A. D. (1999). *Essentials of Human Memory*. East Sussex: Psychology Press Ltd.
Barret-Lennard, G. T. (2005). *Relationship at the centre healing in a troubled World*. Philadelphia: Whurr Publishers.
Behr, M. (2009). Constructing emotions and accommodating schemas: A model of self-exploration, symbolization, and development. *Person-Centered and Experiential Psychotherapies, 8*(1), 44–62.
Bernieri, F. J., & Rosenthal, R. (1991). Interpersonal coordination, behavior matching, and interpersonal synchrony. In R. Feldman & B. Rime (Eds.), *Fundamentals of nonverbal behavior*. Cambridge: Cambridge University Press.
Bozart, J. D., Zimring F. M. & Tausch R. (2002). Client-centered therapy: the evolution of a revolution. In J. Cain & J. Seeman (Eds.), *Humanistic Psychotherapies: Handbook of Research and Practice*. Washington, D.C: American Psychological Association.

Bower, G. H. (1981). Mood and Memory. *American Psychologist, 36*, 129–148.
Cacioppo, J. T., & Gardner, W. L. (1999). Emotion. *Annual Review of Psychology, 50*, 191–214.
Cahill, L., & McGaugh, (1998). Mechanisms of emotional arousal and lasting declarative memory. *Trends in Neuroscience, 21*, 294–299.
Cain, D. J. (2010). *Person-Centered Psychotherapies*. Washington, DC: American Psychological Association.
Cain, J., & Seeman, J. (2002). *Humanistic psychotherapies: Handbook of research and practice*. Washington, D.C.: American Psychological Association.
Claxton, G. (1998). *Hare brain and tortoise mind—why intelligence increases when we think less*. London: Fourth Estate.
Cornelius-White, J. H., & Harbaugh, A. P. (2010). *Learner-centered Instruction: Building relationships for student success*. Thousand Oaks: Sage Publications.
Damasio, A. (2000). *The feeling of what happens—body, emotion and the making of consciousness*. London: Vintage.
Damasio, A. (2003). *Looking for Spinoza: Joy, Sorrow and the Feeling Brain*. Orlando: Harcourt.
Damasio, A. (2012). *The self comes to mind*. London: Vintage.
Gendlin, E. (1978). *Focusing*. New York: Bantam Books.
Greenberg, L. S., & Paivio, S. C. (1997). *Working with emotions in psychotherapy*. New York: The Guilford Press.
Goleman, D. (1995). *Emotional intelligence*. New York: Bantam Books.
Hatfield, E., Cacioppo, J. T., & Rapson, R. L. (1994). *Emotional contagion*. New York: Cambridge University Press.
Iacoboni, M., Molnar-Szakacs, I., Gallese, V., Buccino, G., Mazziotta, J. C., & Rizzolatti, G. (2005). Grasping the intentions of others with one's own mirror neuron system. *PLoS Biology, 3*, 529–535.
Ikemi, A. (2010). Empowering the implicitly functioning relationship. *Person-Centered and Experiential Psychotherapies. 10*(1), 28–42.
James, W. (1890). *The principles of psychology*. New York: Holt, Rinehart and Winston.
Kriz, J. (2007). Actualizing tendency: The link between PCE and interdisciplinary systems theory. *Person-Centered and Experiential Psychotherapies, 6*(1), 30–44.
Kriz, J. (2008). *Self-actualization: person-centred approach and systems theory*. Ross-on-Wye: PCCS-books.
Lago, C. (2011). *The handbook of transcultural conselling and psychotherapy*. UK: McGraw Hill.
Lux, M. (2007). Der Personzentrierte Ansatz und die Neurowissenschaften. [The Peron Centered Approach and Neuroscience, in German] München: Ernst Reinhard.
Lux, M. (2010). The magic of encounter : The person-centered approach and the neurosciences. *Person-Centered and Experiential Psychotherapies, 9*(4), 274–289.
Marci, C. D., Ham, J., Moran, E., & Orr, S. P. (2007). Physiologic correlates of preceived therapist empathy and social-emotional process during psychotherapy. *Journal of Nervous and Mental Disease, 195*, 103–111.
McCombs, B. L. (2011). Learner-centered practices: Providing the context for positive learner development, motivation, and achievement (Chapter 7). In J. Meece & J. Eccles (Eds.), *Handbook of research on schools, schooling, and human development*. Mahwah: Erlbaum.
Mearns, D., & Cooper, M. (2005). *Working at relational depth in counselling and psychotherapy*. London: SAGE.
Miller, B. A. (1956). The magical number seven plus or minus two: some limits on our capacity for processing information. *The Psychological Review, 63*(2), 81–97.
Motschnig-Pitrik, R. (2005). Person-centered e-learning in action: Can technology help to manifest person-centered values in academic environments? *Journal of Humanistic Psychology*, 45 (4), 503–530.
Motschnig-Pitrik, R. (2013). Characteristics and effects of person-centered technology enhanced learning. In J. H. D. Cornelius-White, R. Motschnig-Pitrik & M. Lux (Eds.), *Interdisciplinary applications of the person-centered approach*. New York: Springer.

Motschnig-Pitrik, R. & Barrett-Lennard, G. T. (2010). Co-actualization: A new construct for understanding well-functioning relationships. *Journal of Humanistic Psychology*, 50 (3), 374–398.

Motschnig-Pitrik, R. & Lux, M. (2008). The person centered approach meets neuroscience: Mutual Support for C. R. Rogers's and A. Damasio's Theories. *Journal of Humanistic Psychology*, 48, July, 287–319.

Motschnig-Pitrik, R. & Nykl, L. (2001). The role and modeling of context in a cognitive model of rogers' person-centered approach. In Proceedings of CONTEXT'01, Internat and interdisciplinary conference on the modeling of context, LNAI, *Lecture Notes in Computer Science and AI*. Wien, Heidelberg: Springer.

Motschnig-Pitrik, R., & Nykl, L. (2003). Towards a Cognitive-Emotional Model of Rogers's Person-Centered Approach. *Journal of Humanistic Psychology*, 43 (4), 8–45.

Nykl, L. (2000). Psychologische Kontexte in Rogers' Psychotherapie - das Selbst im Mittelpunkt der Persönlichkeitstheorie. [Psychological Contexts in Rogers'Psychotherapy – the Self in the Center of Personality Theory, in German]. Virya - Zeitschrift für Psychotherapie und Kommunikation. L. Nykl (Ed). 4, 1–108.

Nykl, L. (2005). *Beziehung im Mittelpunkt der Persönlichkeitsentwicklung - C. Rogers im Vergleich mit Behaviorismus, Psychoanalyse und anderen Theorien - Mutter-Kind und andere Beziehungen*. [Relationships in the Center of Personal Development – C. Rogers in Comparison with Behaviorism, Psychoanalysis and Other Theories – Mother-Child and Other Relationships, in German]. Wien: LIT-Verlag.

Nykl, L. (2012). *Carl Ransom Rogers a jeho teorie. Přístup zaměřený na člověka*. [Carl Ransom Rogers and his theories. Person-Centered Approach, in Czech]. Praha: Grada.

Nykl, L. & Motschnig-Pitrik, R. (2002). Uniting Rogers' and Vygotsky's Theories on Personality and Learning. *Proceedings of Carl Rogers Conference* 2002, San Diego, USA. http://textedu.com/f2/download/uniting-rogers-and-vygotsky-s-theories-on-personality-and-learning.pdf (retrieved 2012/02/28).

Piaget, J. (1981). *Über Jean Piaget. Sein Werk aus seiner Sicht*. München: Kindler.

Quillian, M. R. (1967). Word concepts: A theory and simulation of some basic semantic capabilities. *Behavioral Science, 12*, 410–430.

Rizzolatti, G., & Craighero, L. (2004). The mirror neuron system. *Annual Review of Neuroscience, 27*, 169–192.

Rogers, C., R. (1951). *Client-Centered Therapy*. London Constable.

Rogers, C. R. (1959). A theory of therapy, personality, and interpersonal relationships, as developed in the client-centered framework. In S. Koch (Ed.), *Psychology: A Study of a Science*. Vol. 3: Formulations of the person and the social context (pp. 184–256). New York: McGraw-Hill.

Rogers, C. R. (1961). *On becoming a person—a psychotherapists' view of psychotherapy*. London: Constable.

Rogers, C. R. (1980). *A way of being*. Boston: Houghton Mifflin Co.

Rogers, C. R. (1983). *Freedom to Learn for the 80's*. Columbus: Merrill Publishing Company.

Rosenberg, M. B. (2003). *Nonviolent communication: a language of life*. PuddleDancer Press.

Ryback, D. (1998). *Putting emotional intelligence to work*. Boston: Butterworth-Heinemann.

Sachse, R., Elliot, R. (2001). Process-Outcome Research on Humanistic Therapy Variables. In J. Cain & J. Seeman (Eds.), *Humanistic Psychotherapies: Handbook of Research and Practice*. Washington D.C.: American Psychological Association.

Sheldon, K. M., Arndt, J. & Houser-Marko, L. (2003). In search of the organismic valuing process: The human tendency to move towards beneficial goal choices. *Journal of Personality* 71(5), 835–869.

Sowa, J. F. (1984). *Conceptual Structures: Information Processing in Mind and Machine*. Addison Wesley.

Sowa, J. F. (2000). *Knowledge representation*. Pacific Grove: Brooks/Cole.

Squire, L. R., & Kandel, E. R. (1999). *Memory; from mind to molecules*. New York: Scientific American Library.

Watson, J. C., & Greenberg, L. S. (1995). Emotion and cognition in experiential therapy: a dialectical constructivist position. In H. Rosen & K. Kuhelwein (Eds.), *Constructing realities*. New York: Jossey Bass.

Watson, J. C. (2007). Facilitating empathy. *European Psychotherapy, 7*, 61–76.

Wexler, D. A., & Rice, L. N. (1974). *Innovations in client-centered therapy*. New York: Wiley.

Carl Rogers Meets the Neurosciences: Insights from Social Neuroscience for Client-Centered Therapy

Giorgia Silani, Alberto Zucconi and Claus Lamm

1 Introduction

In the last few decades, the number of contributions that neuroscience has offered toward the understanding of the critical role of interpersonal relationships has continually increased. Research on the construction of social and interpersonal realities is no more limited to the instruments of social psychology or psychotherapy: Neuroscience (in particular, the new subdiscipline social neuroscience) has also begun to show that we are constantly engaged in a process of mutual social adjustment of our mental and biological states (Cacioppo 1994; DeVries et al. 2003; Schore 2002a, 2002b, 2005).

By using the currently available neuroscientific techniques, such as functional magnetic resonance imaging (fMRI), electroencephalography (EEG), or transcranial magnetic stimulation (TMS), social neuroscience has provided alternative methods of investigation and scientific validation of significant socio-emotional interactions—such as those that occur in the relationship between the psychotherapist and client. In recent years, this field has produced an increased number of insights into social phenomena from which a new understanding of the human nature and of the enormous power that we use constantly (and often are not even aware of) has emerged. This power is the power of the relationship—how we relate to others, how others relate to us, and how the mutual coconstruction of realities literally changes our brains (Motschnig Pitrik and Lux 2008; Lux 2010;

G. Silani (✉)
International School for Advanced Studies—SISSA, Via Bonomea 265 34136 Trieste, Italy
e-mail: giorgia.silani@sissa.it

A. Zucconi
IACP, Piazza Vittorio Emanuele 99 00185 Roma, Italy
e-mail: azucconi@iacp.it

C. Lamm
University of Vienna, Liebigasse 5, 1010Vienna, Austria
e-mail: claus.lamm@univie.ac.at

Zucconi and Silani 2008; Watson 2011). A new concept has emerged: We now speak of the *social brain*, and we claim that the brain is an organ constructed by social experiences, primarily with caregivers, and that these early experiences will later have an impact on aspects such as parenting, education, psychotherapy, and all interpersonal relationships (Schore 2008, 2009; Cozolino 2010; Decety and Skelly 2011). Therefore, understanding the neurobiological processes behind changes in interpersonal relationships has become of great interest to all psychotherapeutic approaches and in particular to the ones that put the relationship at the center—such as client-centered therapy of Carl Rogers.

2 Client-Centered Therapy

Client-centered therapy is a systemic/holistic approach that focuses on health rather than on disease, on the empowerment of the client rather than on the directivity of the psychotherapist. This approach promotes the development of individuals' and groups' potential through a process that focuses on support and accountability while avoiding the encouragement of passivity and dependence. The central hypothesis of this approach is that humans have innate self-awareness capacities and self-regulatory resources that can be expressed more effectively in relationships characterized by facilitative elements. Carl Rogers postulated—a hypothesis amply confirmed by 70 years of research—that effective psychotherapy is characterized by the quality of the relationship provided by a therapist who sincerely trusts the innate ability of self-awareness and self-regulation of human beings in general and their clients in particular. In this perspective, the effective Rogerian therapist is able to create and manage a setting characterized by acceptance and deep respect, listening, empathic understanding, and genuineness ("congruence," according to Rogers). Based on these premises, the thought of Carl Rogers since the early 1940s had a significant impact in the field of psychotherapy and helping relationships. Rogers formulated hypotheses, to date scientifically verifiable, offering a viable alternative to the prevailing reductionist and negativistic psychology centered on the disease. In fact, a lexicon centered on the dysfunction dominated the language of psychotherapy at his time, and psychotherapeutic theories were theories of psychopathology (Hubble and Miller 2004; Zucconi and Dattola 2007). Even today, such a deficit-oriented view on psychotherapy is dominating outside the person-centered approach (see the discussion by Joseph and Murphy in this book).

And Rogers was right: It is not the therapist who treats the patient, as stated by the paternalistic and mechanistic-reductionist view. Current research shows that the variables ascribable to the clients influence the results of psychotherapy from 40 to 87 %, while the various psychotherapeutic techniques account for only 5 to 15 % of a therapy's success (Miller et al. 1997; Duncan and Miller 2000; Wampold 2001).

According to Rogers, a relationship that facilitates growth is characterized, on the psychotherapist's side, by his real capacity to accept the client, in the sense of a deep respect for the experience of the person, including the absence of any moral judgments. Listening and empathic understanding consists in the ability to understand how the client lives his or her experiences and in being able to effectively communicate that understanding. The authenticity/congruence of the psychotherapist consists in the ability to be in contact and to symbolize his or her own experience without having to resort to defensive distortions and suppressions. A relationship characterized by these elements provides the client with a "safe harbor," a space where he or she can trust, lower his/her defenses, get in touch with uncomfortable and/or unknown aspects of the self, and reach new ways to build realities and to explore new ways of satisfying his/her needs.

Clinical experience and research show that the process of change in psychotherapy is coconstructed: In fact, the three relational qualities of the psychotherapist are able to promote self-awareness, self-understanding, and self-regulation in the client (which translates into more effective connection with himself, the others, and the world) only if accompanied by three additional conditions related to the presence in the client of a minimum capacity of contact with his own experience. These conditions are the motivation to change, which can initially be represented by the painful perception of a lack of consistency, the ability of a psychological contact with the therapist, and the capacity to perceive the relational qualities expressed by the therapist (Rogers 1959, 1961, 1967; Norcross 2011).

The effectiveness of a good relationship between client and professionals is not only evident in the psychotherapeutic setting, but in all helping relationships (Larson 1993; Barrett-Lennard 2005; Anfossi et al. 2008). In the relationship between doctor and patient or between health worker and client, the quality of the relationship is an important variable for the outcome of the treatment, as it affects the levels of compliance, the immune response, user satisfaction, the results of drug treatment, and placebo effects (Krupnick et al. 1996; Zucconi and Howell 2003).

The conditions postulated by Rogers, which he defined as necessary and sufficient, appear effective not only to its paradigm, but in all psychotherapeutic approaches and in any helping relationship. They are the basis of what much later gave rise to the concept of therapeutic alliance, which consists of the relational qualities postulated by Rogers and concepts added later that were already implicit in the formulation of Rogers, as the agreement between therapist and client on the goals of psychotherapy, or the ability of both to repair their working alliance in cases where it is damaged (Horvath and Greenberg 1994; Horvath 2001; Horvath et al. 2011; Norcross 2011).

3 The Client-Centered Therapy from a Neuroscientific Perspective

In recent decades, research in the field of social neuroscience has started to provide insights into the validity of some of the hypotheses proposed by Rogers. As already mentioned, the neurosciences are beginning to find evidence that appears convincing about how the quality of our relationships and social reality influences our brain and our physiology and vice versa (Cacioppo et al. 2002, 2011; Decety 2011).

For example, Cozolino (2010, p. 30) states: "... The warmth, acceptance, and unconditional positive regard demonstrated by Carl Rogers's work embodies the broad interpersonal environment for the initial growth of the brain and continued development later in life." And later, "What might be going on in the brain of a client in client-centered therapy? In the Rogerian interpersonal context, a client would most likely experience the widest range of emotions within the ego scaffolding of an empathetic other. The activation of neural networks of emotion makes feelings and emotional memories available for reorganization. Rogers's non-directive method activates client's executive networks and their self-reflective abilities. Supportive rephrasing and clarification of what clients say may also enhance executive functioning. This simultaneous activation of cognition and emotion, enhanced perspective, and the emotional regulation offered by the relationship may provide an optimal environment for neural change" (Cozolino 2010, pp. 37, 38).

A growing number of authors propose models that associate the development of an optimal human body and also his mental health with an optimal neural integration and growth and, on the other hand, associate psychopathology to a lack of development, integration, and coordination of neural networks. Psychotherapy is seen as a relationship that promotes the creation, reparation, and coordination of the different neural networks involved (Cozolino 2010, Schore 2003a, 2003b).

In other words, the effectiveness of a psychotherapeutic relationship could depend on the ability to promote processes in clients which develop and modify the neuronal structure of the brain and promote integration of the neuronal networks disconnected after trauma and relational deficiencies. The human brain is considered a social organ, and it is assumed that safe and supportive interpersonal relationships provide the ideal climate for the development of social skills and learning and that an empathetic connection with your therapist creates a biochemical environment that promotes optimal neural plasticity (Cozolino 2006, 2010; Elliott and Zucconi 2009; Schore 2003a, 2003b; Watson 2011).

Having discussed the possible contributions that neuroscience can (hopefully) provide to the understanding and validation of the client-centered therapeutic approach, in this paper, we will consider the specific contribution that social neuroscience gave in the understanding of the physiological mechanisms underlying some concepts theorized by Rogers. In particular, empathy and congruence (two fundamental conditions in Rogers' theory) will be described in the following sections using a terminology of cognitive processes (emotional resonance, self–other distinction, emotional regulation) and their neurophysiological substrates, as well as of "bottom-up" (from the periphery to the center) and "top-down" (from the center to the periphery) neuronal mechanisms (see Fig. 1).

 Rogers' concepts	 Cognitive processes	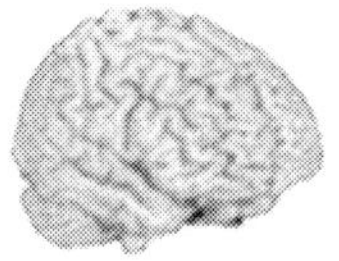 Brain areas
Empathy	Emotional sharing Self-other distinction Perspective taking	AI, TPJ, PFC MPFC, TP, TPJ
Congruence	Self awareness Self-other distinction	MPFC, TP, TPJ TPJ, PFC
Acceptance	Emotion regulation	DLPFC, MPFC, OFC

AI: anterior insula, MCC: mid cingulate cortex, PFC: prefrontal cortex, MPFC: medial prefrontal cortex, TP: temporal poles, TPJ: temporo-parietal junction, DLPFC: dorso-lateral prefrontal cortex, OFC: orbitofrontal cortex

Fig. 1 Comparison between concepts as used by Rogers, cognitive processes associated with these concepts, and putative areas underpinning these processes, as revealed by social neuroscience in the last decade

4 Empathy as Shared Networks Between Self and Other

Among the necessary conditions for a satisfactory and effective therapeutic relationship, empathy (a complex form of emotional resonance with others) has recently received much attention in social neuroscience. According to Rogers (1959, p. 210), the term empathy is defined as "To perceive the internal frame of reference of another with accuracy and with the emotional components and meanings which pertain thereto as if one were the person, but without ever losing the" as if "condition." At a phenomenological level, the concept of "empathy" expresses a sense of sameness, a sharing between one's own feelings and those expressed by another person (Thompson 2001), and at the same time implies a cognitive mechanism that keeps track of the source of the emotional state and thus differentiates the self from the other.

The initial component that precedes empathy is based on the concept of somatic imitation, also known as "emotional contagion," which is the tendency to automatically simulate the expressions, vocalizations, postures, and movements of another person and, consequently, to synchronize emotionally with others (Hatfield et al. 1993). It has been suggested that, initially, unconscious imitation has evolved as a mechanism to promote survival and conservation of the species, allowing the development of communication skills. The pioneering work of Rizzolatti and coworkers (Rizzolatti and Craighero 2004, for review) has revealed some of the putative neurophysiological mechanisms of our ability to resonate with other people's intentions and actions. Through electrophysiological recordings in monkeys, as well as neuroimaging experiments on humans, it has been shown that the mere observation of actions performed by others activates in the person who observes the action the cortical areas involved in the planning and initialization of the same action. This has led to claims that humans and monkey possess a so-called *mirror neuron system* which mainly includes the inferior parietal lobe and the inferior frontal gyrus (pars opercularis) and enables us to mirror the actions of others.

This mirroring mechanism seems to have adaptive value for the survival of individuals. For example, it has been shown that the observation of bodily fear not only produces greater activation in brain areas associated with emotional processes, but also in sectors connected with the representation of action and movement. This mechanism could therefore be interpreted as an automatic response of our brain in the event of perceived danger, allowing an immediate and hard-wired preparation for protective action (de Gelder et al. 2004).

To date, a growing amount of literature suggests that the same neural circuits are also recruited during the direct, first-person experience of an emotion, and its vicarious response to the same emotion resulting from the observation or imagination of others. For example, it has been shown that the anterior insula, a region in charge of the elaboration of bodily changes following the perception of an emotional stimulus (pleasant or unpleasant), is active in response to the presentation of facial expressions of disgust in a similar way as during the firsthand experience of disgust (Wicker et al. 2003). Similarly, the observation and the direct experience of touch are subtended by common neural networks (Keysers et al. 2004).

The perception–action mechanism also seems to underlie our ability to perceive the pain of others. Singer and collaborators investigated the neural responses of participants using functional MRI receiving a painful physical stimulation alternating with trials in which they observed their partner receiving the same type of painful stimulation (Singer et al. 2004). While only the primary experience of pain was associated with activation of the somatosensory cortex that encodes the sensory components of the noxious stimulus, both the firsthand experience and the observation of the partner's pain activated a shared network consisting of the medial cingulate cortex (MCC) and the anterior insula (AI)—which are cortical structures encoding the affective and motivational components of painful experiences. These initial data resulted in the hypothesis of a strong overlap between brain regions that respond to the firsthand experience of pain and the perception of pain in others, a hypothesis that has received today a growing validation as a result of similar findings reported by several research groups (e.g., Morrison et al. 2004; Jackson et al. 2005; Avenanti et al. 2005; see Lamm et al. 2011, for recent meta-analysis). These results suggest that even if we cannot literally feel the pain of others (as neuroimaging studies indicate only a partial overlap of self and others' experience of pain in the anterior insula and MCC), we seem to be equipped with a mechanism enabling us a fast and effortless sharing and understanding of the affective states of others.

5 Perspective Taking and Empathy

In the nineteenth century, the philosopher and Scottish economist Smith (1759) hypothesized that through imagination, we are able to perceive and experience the situation of another as if we were in his or her shoes, becoming somewhat the same person. Through our imaginative capacity, we are able to experience feelings that are similar, though generally weaker than those of the other person. In the same way, as noted above, Rogers (1959) states that empathy "means to sense the hurt or the pleasure of another as he senses it and to perceive the causes thereof as he perceives them, but without ever losing the recognition, that it is as if I were hurt or pleased" (p. 210).

Unlike mimicry and emotional contagion, the ability of perspective taking, which is a fundamental tool for the therapist, emerges later in ontogeny and relies upon higher executive functions (processes which serve for monitoring and controlling thought and actions, including self-regulation, planning, cognitive flexibility, response inhibition, and resistance to interferences) which develop in parallel with the development of the prefrontal cortex that continues to mature from birth to adolescence (Russell 1996; Zelazo 2004).

The ability to adopt the perspective of the other, in other words to overcome our usual egocentrism, allows to adapt our behavior and to create satisfactory interpersonal relationships. In line with this reasoning, social neuroscience has shown that when individuals are invited to adopt the perspective of others, common neural circuits are activated (e.g., Decety and Grèzes 2006). At the same time, however, taking into account the perspective of others involves the activation of specific parts of the frontal cortex that are involved in executive control and the sense of "agency" (which is associated with the sense of being the source of an action or representation; Decety and Jackson 2004). It has been hypothesized that the right inferior parietal cortex, on the border with the posterior temporal cortex (temporoparietal junction, TPJ) (see also following paragraph), may serve to keep the two perspectives of self and other separate, while the frontal lobes help to resist interferences from one's own perspective (Decety and Jackson 2004). Of particular interest are observations in social psychology documenting the difference between imagining others and imagining oneself to be in a certain situation. These studies (Lamm et al. 2007; Jackson et al. 2006a, b) demonstrate that the first case mainly generates empathic concern (defined as a response oriented toward the other, congruent with the difficulties of the person in need), while the second also induces personal distress (which is an aversive self-related response, like being anxious or agitated as a consequence of the other's predicament; see also Decety and Lamm 2009). This observation may help explain why empathic concern and sympathy are such important elements in helping behaviors (notably, empathic concern and sympathy have to be separated conceptually from empathy; see, e.g., Singer and Lamm 2009). If the perception of another person's state of emotional or physical pain arouses personal anguish, the observer would be unable to participate fully in the experience of others, and consequently, this would reduce the likelihood of helping behaviors. Lamm et al. (2007) recently examined the distinction between empathic concern and personal distress. If observing the pain of others from an explicitly self-related (first-person) perspective, this resulted in lower empathic concern responses and higher personal distress, as compared to a third-person perspective in which participants focused on the other person's affective responses rather than on their own. The first-person perspective also evoked a stronger hemodynamic response in brain regions involved in encoding the motivational-affective dimension of pain, such as the insular cortex, and furthermore resulted in increased activation in the amygdala—a subcortical structure critically involved in emotional arousal, including fear-related behaviors (LeDoux 2000).

Overall, these empirical results demonstrate that overlapping ("shared") activations in neural circuits during both direct and vicarious experiences of emotions underlie our ability to empathize with others and that different perspective taking manipulations can trigger and specifically modulate activity in these circuits. However, it is important to note that this overlap is by no means complete. In fact, there are more significant differences in the neural systems involved in direct and vicarious personal experiences than similarities (see next paragraph). This emphasizes the importance of self-awareness and the ability to track who is the "agent" of a state/action. These are key functions for empathy and for appropriate therapeutic responses, as it is important at any point in time during a social interaction not to (con) fuse the emotions originating in the other with those originating in the self.

6 Congruence and Empathy

Empathy is a complex social ability that goes beyond mere emotional contagion, but in addition requires higher order cognitive processes such as the ability to differentiate self-related from other-related representations as well as being aware of your own emotional experience. According to Rogers (1959, p. 206), his definition of congruency includes: "when the self-experiences are accurately symbolized (in awareness), and are included in the self-concept in this accurately symbolized form, that the state is one of congruence of self and experience." A prerequisite for an effective psychotherapeutic relationship is therefore that the two agents can preserve their individuality and each of them are in contact with their inner worlds. As highlighted in the previous paragraph, a complete overlap between self and other in the case of emotion sharing would induce an aversive emotional response or overarousal—which is detrimental to empathy as it will result in self-centered regulatory responses (Batson et al. 1997). When the therapist feels empathy toward the client, he or she must therefore be able to distinguish his or her feelings from the feelings shared with the client.

The sense of "being an agent" is a crucial aspect in representing self- and other-related states. This requires the ability to perceive the self as an independent entity from the outside world (Jeannerod 2003). It allows the existence of a selfless interest in others rather than a selfish desire to escape aversive feelings.

Data from numerous neuroimaging studies as well as studies of neurological patients indicate that the temporoparietal junction (TPJ) plays a crucial role in the distinction between sensory signals arising from the self and signals generated by the social environment (Blakemore and Frith 2003; Jackson and Decety 2004). TPJ is a hetero-modal association cortex that integrates information arising from the lateral and posterior thalamus, as well as portions of the visual, auditory, and somatosensory cortexes. It is reciprocally connected to prefrontal and temporal lobes (Decety and Lamm 2007). Because of these anatomical features, this region is a hinge at the end of multisensory integration of information on bodily sensations and setting up the phenomenological experience of self (Blanke and Arzy 2005). A lesion in this cortical area can produce a variety of disorders associated with body awareness, such as asomatognosia (lack of awareness of the condition of all or parts of your body) or somatoparaphrenia (delusional convictions about their body) (Berlucchi and Aglioti 1997).

The attribution of actions to another agent, which essentially requires the distinction between the behavior of self and others, has also been associated with right TPJ (Farrer et al. 2003; Farrer and Frith 2002; Leube et al. 2003), and this area shows also increased activity in tasks of mutual imitation where it can be difficult to keep track of who is the agent of an action (Chaminade and Decety 2002; Decety et al. 2002). The mental simulation of the behavior of self and other involves a similar mechanism of self–other discrimination. For example, the right TPJ is specifically involved when participants have to imagine how another person would feel in real-life situations that elicit social emotions (Ruby and Decety 2004) or experience painful events, but not when they have to imagine these situations for themselves (Lamm et al. 2007; Jackson et al. 2006a, b). These results stress the similarity between the neural mechanisms underlying proper attribution of actions, emotions, and thoughts to their respective agents when such actions or emotional experiences are experienced in oneself or merely encountered in another individual. Self-awareness is also a necessary condition to make inferences about mental and emotional states of others (Gallup 1982). In two studies involving subjects with alexithymic traits (alexithymia is a subclinical phenomenon marked by difficulties in identifying and describing feelings (Nemiah et al. 1976)), one of the authors recently tested the mechanisms underlying the ability to understand one's own emotions and its relationship to the ability to empathize (Silani et al. 2008; Bird et al. 2010). Notably, she showed that deficits in the understanding of one's own feelings are associated with hypoactivation of AI both when inferring one's own emotional state and when empathizing with another's emotional state, suggesting that a lack of the "embodied simulation" could cause a reduction in empathic behavior. This is in line with Rogers' work: "Proposition XVIII: When the individual perceives and accepts into one consistent and integrated system all his or her sensory and visceral experiences, then he or she is necessarily more understanding of others and is more accepting of others as separate individuals."(Rogers 1951, p. 30). To summarize, self–other distinction and self-awareness play fundamental roles in every social interaction and thus also in empathy. These mechanisms also allow, on a conceptual level, to distinguish emotional contagion from empathy. While the former heavily relies on an automatic link between emotion perception and emotional experiences, resulting in a largely shared emotional experience by means of bottom-up (sensory-driven) processes, a genuine empathic response requires in addition a mechanism that is aware of and keeps track of the source of the emotion felt by the empathizer.

7 Acceptance

The therapist's ability to relate to the client with deep respect—accepting him or her as he or she is—is another of the three relational conditions postulated by Rogers that define the therapist's acceptance as a powerful agent of change. If our own personal experience already tells us that feeling to be accepted and respected is important in a relationship, recent findings in neuroscience provide further evidence of how costly it is for our mind and body to be the object of judgment. For example, recent neuroimaging studies of social rejection have convincingly shown that networks active during the experience of physical pain (AI, MCC) are also involved when experiencing the social pain of being rejected by others (Eisenberger et al. 2003; for review, see Eisenberger 2012). If we then consider that psychotherapy is a learning process, neuroscience could give us further evidence as to how the fear of being judged and excluded from social groups hinders the individual's learning and adaptation process (Elizuya and Rochlofs 2005).

8 Emotion Regulation (Deep Respect and Acceptance)

The ability to regulate one's own emotions has a clear adaptive function in social interactions both for the individual and for our species as a whole. The concept of emotion regulation is defined as the process of initiation, inhibition, retention, and/or modulation of the shape, intensity, and/or duration of an emotion (Eisenberg et al. 2004). It has been shown that people who can regulate their emotions are more likely to have feelings of sympathy and also to implement prosocial behaviors (Eisenberg et al. 1994; Derryberry and Rothbart 1988). In contrast, people whose capacity for modulating their emotions, especially negative emotions, are exposed to greater personal distress as well as aversive emotional reactions such as anxiety when detecting the emotional state of another person (Eisenberg et al. 2001).

"Top-down" cognitive mechanisms seem to be at the base of emotional regulation. A region of the rostral medial prefrontal cortex (mPFC) appears to play an important role in this modulation (Wiech et al. 2005), and different cognitive strategies to regulate emotions have been documented. For example, taking the position of a detached observer when expecting self-related stressful events (such as a painful shock) reduces the subjective experience of anxiety and pain. Recent fMRI studies have identified a limited number of regions in the anterolateral and medial prefrontal cortexes which appear to mediate this function (Kalisch et al. 2005). Another strategy is the emotional re-evaluation ("re-appraisal") of an event that involves a reinterpretation of the significance of a stimulus in order to change the way we react to it. This process is of considerable importance in promoting changes in psychotherapy (Cozolino 2010).

Overall, the ability to regulate our emotions is an important aspect of our ability to interact effectively with other people. The prefrontal cortex is highly differentiated in terms of cellular structures and patterns of interconnectivity with other cortical subsystems. In line with this, neuroimaging studies suggest that these systems interact in specific ways to implement a balanced cooperation between cognition and emotions. However, we have only begun to understand these processes and their complexity. In this regard, we allow us to hypothesize that the therapist's unconditional acceptance of the client's person and his/her experiences may facilitate the client to non-judgmentally perceive and accept these experiences. In this way, person-centered psychotherapy may foster emotion regulation and integrative processes (Cozolino 2010) which are probably of major importance for the Rogerian paradox of change: "when I accept myself just as I am, then I change" (Rogers 1995/1961, p. 17).

9 Conclusions

Models of emotional and social connection have been widely discussed by people working on philosophy of mind and for decades have been the subject of investigation by social psychologists as well as developmental psychologists. More recently, neuroscientific research has begun to unravel the neural systems that support the processes involved in the experience of empathy, including the sharing of emotions, perspective taking, the sense of agency, and emotion regulation.

In a period of exuberant theoretical and clinical developments, the neurosciences offer us new possibilities for the understanding of psychotherapeutic processes and the development of new clinical procedures. What would be the position of Rogers if he were still with us? One of the authors who has had the opportunity of knowing him as a student and then as a colleague for 17 years is convinced that Rogers certainly were interested. Already in 1958, he cited the research of Dittes on the measurement of galvanic skin responses of clients in psychotherapy (Rogers 1958). But in addition to his interest, it is easy to assume that Rogers would have considered it important to be sensitive and alert to any danger of mechanistic reductionism (Zucconi 2008).

He would certainly have had a positive view on the assertion that the neurosciences are entering a season of remarkable development and rich in potential contributions to other fields. However, Rogers would have agreed with those who consider it necessary to develop, in parallel with the neurosciences, modern social epistemologies (Goldman 2008), to update the ethical codes of various professions, and to facilitate a process through which it is possible to reach a thoughtful social construction of a neuroethics that involves clinicians, scientists, philosophers, lawyers, judges, and legislators in the debate (Merkel et al. 2007).

Rogers would have agreed with Cacioppo (2002, p. 21) when he states that "… the mechanisms underlying the mind and behavior will not be fully explainable only by a biological or sociological approach."

Keeping this in mind, it is legitimate to say that social neuroscience will (hopefully) play an important role in shedding light on the complex social, psychological, and neurophysiological mechanisms underlying social interactions in general and psychotherapeutic ones in particular—with the ultimate aim being a far-reaching understanding of the complexity of these phenomena.

References

Anfossi, M., Verlato, L. M., & Zucconi, A. (2008). *Guarire o curare?*. Bari: La Meridiana.
Avenanti, A., Bueti, D., Galati, G., & Aglioti, S. M. (2005). Transcranial magnetic stimulation high lights the sensorimotor side of empathy for pain. *Nature Neuroscience, 8*, 955–960.
Barrett-Lennard, G. T. (2005). *Relationship at the centre: Healing in a troubled world*. London: Whurr/Wiley.
Batson, C. D., Sager, K., Garst, E., Kang, M., Rubchinsky, K., & Dawson, K. (1997). Is empathy induced helping due to self-other merging? *Journal of Personality and Social Psychology, 73*, 495–509.
Berlucchi, G., & Aglioti, S. (1997). The body in the brain: Neural bases of corporeal awareness. *Trends in Neurosciences, 20*, 560–564.
Bird, G., Silani, G., Brindley, R., White, S., Frith, U., & Singer, T. (2010). Empathic brain responses in insula are modulated by levels of alexithymia but not autism. *Brain, 133*(5), 1515–1525.
Blakemore, S.-J., & Frith, C. D. (2003). Self-awareness and action. *Current Opinion in Neurobiology, 13*, 219–224.
Blanke, O., & Arzy, S. (2005). The out-of-body experience: disturbed self-processing at the temporo-parietal junction. *Neuroscientist, 11*, 16–24.
Cacioppo, J. T. (1994). Social neuroscience: Autonomic, neuroendocrine, and immune responses to stress. *Psychophysiology, 31*, 113–128.
Cacioppo, T. J., et al. (Eds.). (2002). *Foundations in social neurosciences*. Cambridge: The MIT Press, Mass.
Cacioppo, J. T., Berntson, G. G., & Decety, J. (2011). Social neuroscience. In A. W. Kruglanski & W. Stroebe (Eds.), *Handbook of the history of social psychology*. New York: Psychology Press.
Chaminade, T., & Decety, J. (2002). Leader or follower? Involvement of the inferior parietal lobule in agency. *NeuroReport, 13*, 1975–1978.

Cozolino, L. (2006). *The Neuroscience of Human Relationship. Attachment and the Developing Social Brain*. NY: Norton & Co.

Cozolino, L. J. (2010). *The neuroscience of psychotherapy. Healing the social brain* (2nd ed.). NY: WW Norton & Co.

de Gelder, B., Snyder, J., Greve, D., Gerard, G., & Hadjikhani, N. (2004). Fear fosters flight: a mechanism for fear contagion when perceiving emotion expressed by a whole body. *Proceedings of the National Academy of Sciences, 101*, 16701–16706.

Decety, J. (2011). *The neuroevolution of empathy* (Vol. 1231 pp. 35–45). NY: Annals of the New York Academy of Sciences.

Decety, J., & Grèzes, J. (2006). The power of simulation: imagining one's own and other's behavior. *Brain Research, 1079*(1), 4–14.

Decety, J., & Jackson, P. L. (2004). The functional architecture of human empathy. *Behavioral and Cognitive Neuroscience Reviews, 3*, 71–100.

Decety, J., & Lamm, C. (2007). The role of the right temporoparietal junction in social interaction: How low-level computational processes contribute to meta-cognition. *The Neuroscientist, 13*, 580–593.

Decety, J., & Lamm, C. (2009). Empathy versus personal distress. In J. Decety & W. Ickes (Eds.), *The social neuroscience of empathy*. Cambridge: MIT Press.

Decety, J., & Skelly, L. (2011). The neural underpinnings of the experience of empathy: Lessons for psychopathy. In K. Ochsner & S. Kosslyn (Eds.), *The oxford handbook of cognitive neuroscience*. New York: Oxford University Press.

Decety, J., Chaminade, T., Grèzes, J., & Meltzoff, A. N. (2002). A PET exploration of the neural mechanisms involved in reciprocal imitation. *Neuroimage, 15*, 265–272.

Derryberry, D., & Rothbart, M. K. (1988). Arousal, affect, and attention as components of temperament. *Journal of Personality and Social Psychology, 55*, 958–966.

DeVries, A. C., Glasper, E. R., & Detillion, C. E. (2003). Social modulation of stress responses. *Physiology and Behavior, 79*, 399–407.

Duncan, B. L., Miller, S. D. (2000). *The heroic client. Doing client-directed, outcome-informed therapy*. San Francisco: Jossey-Bass.

Eisenberg, N., Fabes, R. A., Murphy, B., Karbon, M., Maszk, P., Smith, M., et al. (1994). The relations of emotionality and regulation to dispositional and situational empathy related responding. *Journal of Personality and Social Psychology, 66*, 776–797.

Eisenberg, N., Cumberland, A., Spinrad, T. L., Fabes, R. A., Shepard, S. A., Reiser, M., et al. (2001). The relations of regulation and emotionality to children's externalizing and internalizing problem behavior. *Child Development, 72*, 1112–1134.

Eisenberg, N., Smith, C. L., Sadovsky, A., & Spinrad, T. L. (2004). Effortful control. In: R. F. Baumeister & K. D. Vohs (Eds.) *Handbook of self-regulation* (pp. 259–282). New York: The Guilford Press.

Eisenberger, N. I. (2012). The pain of social disconnection: Examining the shared neural underpinnings of physical and social pain. *Nature Reviews Neuroscience*.

Eisenberger, N. I., Lieberman, M. D., & Williams, K. D. (2003). Does rejection hurt? An fMRI study of social exclusion. *Science, 302*, 290–292.

Elizuya, B., & Rochlofs, K. (2005). Cortisol: Induced impairments of working memory requires acute sympathetic activation behavior. *Neuroscience, 119*, 98–103.

Elliott, R., & Zucconi, A. (2009). Organization and conceptual framework for practice-based research on the effectiveness of psychotherapy and psychotherapy training. In M. Barkham, G. Hardy, & J. Mellor-Clark (Eds.), *A core approach to delivering practice-based evidence in counselling and the psychological therapies*. Chichester: Wiley.

Farrer, C., & Frith, C. D. (2002). Experiencing oneself versus another person as being the cause of an action: the neural correlates of the experience of agency. *Neuroimage, 15*, 596–603.

Farrer, C., Franck, N., Georgieff, N., Frith, C. D., Decety, J., & Jeannerod, M. (2003). Modulating the experience of agency: A positron emission tomography study. *Neuroimage, 18*, 324–333.

Gallup, G. G. (1982). Self-awareness and the emergence of the mind in primates. *American Journal of Primatology, 2*, 237–248.

Goldman, I. A. (2008). *Social epistemology: Theory and applications.* UK: Royal Institute of Philosophy.

Hatfield, E., Cacioppo, J. T., & Rapson, R. L. (1993). Emotional contagion. *Current Directions in Psychological Science, 2*, 96–99.

Horvath, A. O. (2001). The alliance. *Psychotherapy: Theory/Research/Practice/Training, 38*(4), 365–372.

Horvath, A. O., & Greenberg, L. S. (Eds.). (1994). *The working alliance: Theory, research, and practice.* New York: Wiley.

Horvath, A. O., Del Re, A., Flückiger, C., & Symonds, D. (2011). Alliance in individual psychotherapy. In J. C. Norcross (Ed.), *Psychotherapy relationships that work* (2nd ed.). New York: Oxford University Press.

Hubble, A. M., & Miller, D. S. (2004). The client: Psychotherapy missing link for promoting a positive psychology. In P. A. Linley & S. Joseph (Eds.), *Positive psychology in practice.* New York: Wiley.

Jackson, P. L., & Decety, J. (2004). Motor cognition: A new paradigm to study self other interactions. *Current Opinion in Neurobiology, 14*, 259–263.

Jackson, P. L., Meltzoff, A. N., & Decety, J. (2005). How do we perceive the pain of others: a window into the neural processes involved in empathy. *Neuroimage, 24*, 771–779.

Jackson, P. L., Brunet, E., Meltzoff, A. N., & Decety, J. (2006a). Empathy examined through the neural mechanisms involved in imagining how I feel versus how you feel pain. *Neuropsychologia, 44*, 752–761.

Jackson, P. L., Rainville, P., & Decety, J. (2006b). To what extent do we share the pain of others? Insight from the neural bases of pain empathy. *Pain, 125*, 5–9.

Jeannerod, M. (2003). The mechanism of self-recognition in humans. *Behavioral and Brain Research, 142*, 1–15.

Kalisch, R., Wiech, K., Critchley, H. D., Seymour, B., ÒDoherty, J. P., Oakley, D. A., et al. (2005). Anxiety reduction through detachment: subjective, physiological, and neural effects. *Journal of Cognitive Neuroscience, 17*, 874–883.

Keysers, C., Wicker, B., Gazzola, V., Anton, J. L., Fogassi, L., & Gallese, V. (2004). A touching sight: SII/PV activation during the observation and experience of touch. *Neuron, 42*, 335–346.

Krupnick, J. L., et al. (1996). The role of therapeutic alliance in psychotherapy and pharmacotherapy outcome: Findings in the national institute of mental health treatment of depression collaborative research program. *Journal of Consulting and Clinical Psychology, 64*, 532–539.

Lamm, C., Batson, C. D., & Decety, J. (2007). The neural basis of human empathy: Effects of perspective-taking and cognitive appraisal. *Journal of Cognitive Neuroscience, 6*, 1146–1163.

Lamm, C., Decety, J., & Singer, T. (2011). Meta-analytic evidence for common and distinct neural networks associated with directly experienced pain and empathy for pain. *NeuroImage, 54*, 2492–2502.

Larson, D. G. (1993). *The helper's journey: Working with people facing grief, loss, and life-threatening illness.* Champaign: Research Press.

LeDoux, J. E. (2000). Emotion circuits in the brain. *Annual Review of Neuroscience, 23*, 155–184.

Leube, D. T., Knoblich, G., Erb, M., Grodd, W., Bartels, M., & Kircher, T. T. J. (2003). The neural correlates of perceiving one's own movements. *Neuroimage, 20*, 2084–2090.

Lux, M. (2010). The magic of encounter: The person-centered approach and the neurosciences. *Person-Centered and Experiential Psychotherapies, 9*(4), 274–289.

Merkel, R., Boer, G., Fegert, J., Galert, T., Hartmann, D., Nuttin, B., et al. (2007). *Intervening in the brain. Changing psyche and society.* Heidelberg: Springer.

Miller, S. D., Duncan, B. L., & Hubble, M. A. (1997). *Escape from Babel: Toward an unifying language for psychotherapy practice.* New York: Norton.

Morrison, I., Lloyd, D., di Pellegrino, G., & Roberts, N. (2004). Vicarious responses to pain in anterior cingulated cortex is empathy a multisensory issue? *Cognitive, Affective and Behavioral Neuroscience, 4*, 270–278.

Motschning-Pitrik, R., & Lux, M. (2008). The Person-centered approach meets neuroscience: Mutual support for C. R. Rogers's and A. Damasio's Theories. *Journal of Humanistic Psychology, 48*(3), 287–319.
Nemiah, J. C., Freyberg, H., & Sifneos, P. E. (1976). *Modern trends in psychosomatic medicine.* In: O. W. Hill (Ed.), pp. 430–439 London: Butterworths.
Norcross, J. C. (Ed.). (2011). *Psychotherapy relationships that work* (2nd ed.). New York: Oxford University Press.
Rizzolatti, G., & Craighero, L. (2004). The mirror-neuron system. *Annual Review in Neuroscience, 27,* 169–192.
Rogers, C. R. (1951). *Client centered therapy; its current practice, implication and theory.* Boston: Houghton Mifflin.
Rogers, C.R. (1958). The Characteristic of a Helping Relationship. *Personnel and Guidance Journal, 37,* 6–16.
Rogers, C. R. (1959). A theory of therapy, personality, and interpersonal relationships, as developed in the client-centered framework. In: S. Koch (Ed.). *Psychology. A study of a science* (Vol. 3 pp. 184–256): *Formulations of the person and the social context.* New York: Hill.
Rogers, C. R. (1961). *On becoming a person.* Boston: Houghton Mifflin.
Rogers, C. R. (1967). *The therapeutic relationship and its impact: A study of psychotherapy with schizophrenics.* Madison: University of Wisconsin Press.
Ruby, P., & Decety, J. (2004). How would you feel versus how do you think she would feel? A neuroimaging study of perspective taking with social emotions. *Journal of Cognitive Neuroscience, 19,* 988–999.
Russell, J. (1996). *Agency and its role in mental development.* Hove: Psychology Press.
Schore, A. N. (2002a). The right brain as the neurobiologicalsubstratum of Freud's dynamic unconscious. In D. Scharff (Ed.), *The psychoanalytic century: Freud's legacy for the future.* New York: The Other Press.
Schore, A. N. (2002b). Advances in neuropsychoanalysis, attachment theory, and trauma research: Implications for self psychology. *Psychoanalytic Inquiry, 22,* 433–484.
Schore, A. N. (2003a). Affect Regulation and the Repair of the Self. W.W. Norton.
Schore, A. N. (2003b). Affect Dysregulation and Disorders of the Self. W.W. Norton.
Schore, A. N. (2005). Attachment, affect regulation, and the developing right brain: linking developmental neuroscience to pediatrics. *Pediatrics in Review, 26,* 204–212.
Schore, A. N. (2008). Shore Modern attachment theory: the central role of affect regulation in development and treatment. *Clinical Social Work Journal, 36,* 9–20.
Schore, A. N. (2009). Attachment trauma and the developing right brain: Origins of pathological dissociation. in P.F. Dell, & J.A. O'Neil (Eds.), *Dissociation and the dissociative disorders: DSM-V and beyond* (pp. 107–141). New York: Routledge.
Silani, G., Bird, G., Brindley, R., Singer, T., Frith, C. & Frith, U. (2008). Levels of emotional awareness and autism: an fMRI study. *Social Neuroscience 3,* 97–112.
Singer, T., & Lamm, C. (2009). The social neuroscience of empathy. *Annals of the New York Academy of Science, 1156,* 81–96.
Singer, T., Seymour, B., O'Doherty, J., Kaube, H., Dolan, R. J., & Frith, C. D. (2004). Empathy for pain involves the affective but not the sensory components of pain. *Science, 303,* 1157–1161.
Smith, A. (1759). *The theory of moral sentiments.* In: S. M. Soares. MetaLibri, 2005.
Thompson, E. (2001). Empathy and consciousness. *Journal of Consciousness Studies, 8,* 1–32.
Wampold, B. E. (2001). *The great psychotherapy debate: Models, methods, and findings.* NJ: Erlbaum, Mahwah.
Watson, J. C. (2011). The process of growth and transformation: Extending the process model. *Person-Centered and Experiential Psychotherapies, 10*(1), 11–27.
Wicker, B., Keysers, C., Plailly, J., Royet, J. P., Gallese, V., & Rizzolatti, G. (2003). Both of us disgusted in my insula: the common neural basis of seeing and feeling disgust. *Neuron, 40,* 655–664.

Wiech, K., Seymour, B., Kalish, R., Stephan, K. E., Koltzenburg, M., Driver, J., et al. (2005). Modulation of pain processing in hyperalgesia by cognitive demand. *Neuroimage, 27*, 59–69.

Zelazo, P. D. (2004). The development of conscious control in childhood. *Trends in Cognitive Science, 8*, 12–17.

Zucconi, A. (2008). Effective helping relationships: focus on illness or on health and well being? In B. Lewitt (Ed.), *Reflections of human potential: The person centered approach as a positive psychology*. UK: PCC Books.

Zucconi, A. E., & Dattola, G. (2007). La relazione terapeutica nella terapia Centrata sul cliente. In: P. Petrini, & A. Zucconi (Eds.) *La relazione che cura*. Roma: Alpes.

Zucconi, A., & Howell, P. (2003). *Promuovere la salute con un approccio centrato sulla persona*. Bari: La Meridiana. p. 154

Zucconi, A., & Silani, G. (2008). Le conferme delle neuroscienze alle ipotesi della Psicoterapia Centrata sul Cliente di Carl Rogers ed alla teoria dei fattori comuni delle psicoterapie. *Idee in Psicoterapia 1*(3).

The Circle of Contact: A Neuroscience View on the Formation of Relationships

Michael Lux

1 Introduction

Neuroscience has made significant progress in research on neurobiological foundations of human social functioning. In this regard, remarkable parallels between developments in neuroscience and the theories of the person-centered approach (PCA) became apparent. Under the label of a "neuroscientifically based person-centered psychotherapy" Lux (2007, pp. 149–162) proposed how both research areas may be related to each other. The forthcoming chapter deals with a part of this conception, namely that relationships are shaped by the so-called person-centered "core conditions" of empathy, unconditional positive regard, and congruence. The author uses current research findings to provide a compressed overview of the neurobiological processes involved in such relationships.

Neuroscience has made impressive discoveries about the brain's potential to connect humans with each other and to bring them into contact on an emotional level. This is of central importance for person-centered psychotherapy and the PCA. According to Rogers (1995a/1951), "The words—of either client or counselor—are seen as having minimal importance compared with the present emotional relationship which exists between the two" (p. 172). Within the PCA, the presence of such a relationship is seen as an essential prerequisite for a growth-promoting interpersonal climate not only in psychotherapy but also in other contexts such as education, encounter groups, or family and partnership. In the following chapter, neurobiological conceptions are outlined which may play a crucial role in this connection. Although neuroscience has been exploring the social dimensions of the human brain for only a relatively short time, substantial insights have been gained into how person-centered relationships may unfold their potential at a neurobiological level.

M. Lux (✉)
Neurologisches Rehabilitationszentrum Quellenhof, Kuranlagenallee 2,
Bad Wildbad 75323, Germany
e-mail: luxbw@yahoo.de

Our brain is the result of a long process of evolutionary adaptation. It provides us with a great variety of capabilities by which we are prepared to create constructive and mutual supportive relationships. In fact, we humans are very well equipped to build well-functioning relationships and to use these not only for the good of the persons involved but also for others outside of that relationship. Neuroscience has revealed qualities of human nature which are reminiscent of the insights Rogers (1995b/1961) gained from his experiences as a psychotherapist and a psychotherapy researcher. He describes these insights for example, as follows: "One of the most revolutionary concepts to grow out of our clinical experience is the growing recognition that the innermost core of a man's nature, the deepest layers of his personality, the base of his 'animal nature' is positive in nature—is basically socialized, forward-moving, rational and realistic" (p. 91). The prominent neuroscientist Damasio (2003) takes a quite similar view on the social orientation of human nature in stating: "It is reasonable to hypothesize that the tendency to seek social agreement has itself been incorporated in biological mandates, at least in part, due to the evolutionary success of populations whose brains expressed cooperative behaviors to a high degree" (p. 173). Evidence for such a "tendency to seek social agreement" can be seen in studies showing that fair as well as cooperative behavior is accompanied by an activation of the brain's reward centers (Tabibnia and Lieberman 2007). This suggests that such behaviors are intrinsically rewarding and—if I may say so—that they are part of "the innermost core of a man's nature."

It is more than sad that despite our biological equipment, we use our social competencies too often insufficiently. This is not neglected by Rogers: "In my experience, every person has the capacity for evil behavior" [cited in Kirschenbaum and Henderson (1989, p. 254)]. From the viewpoint of the PCA, the psychosocial reason for an estrangement from the fundamental nature of the human condition depends on experiencing the frustration of the need for positive regard, which may range from simple misunderstandings to experiences of violence and abuse. Moreover, though not discussed within the original theory of the PCA, damages or anomalies of certain brain areas are also associated with a reduced capability to utilize social competencies (Damasio 2003; Decety and Moriguchi 2007).

In addition to basic psychological research (see chapter by Sheldon), findings in neuroscience also refer to the enormous importance of social relationships. It was shown, for example, that social exclusion causes in the excluded person an activation of brain regions which are also activated during the perception of one's own pain (Eisenberger et al. 2003). Therefore, it is not too surprising that people strive to avoid social exclusion by adapting to norms and expectations of significant others.

Remarkably, the neuroscientist Hüther (2006) accords with the view of the PCA concerning the developmental impact of social influences: "By starting to suppress everything that has been the most natural and very own part of the self, he [a human being] increasingly becomes a stranger to himself. Because the body and body-related needs stand in the way of the strong need for social belonging and recognition, for identity development and self-unfolding, they will be seen as obstacles which therefore will be suppressed and detached" (p. 88, own translation).

With respect to the horrors people cause each other, the PCA's positive view of human nature may stand out as unrealistic. However, neuroscientific research findings importantly strengthen a vision of humanity which helps us to recognize our inherent potential to create constructive relationships more clearly, to trust them more, and to use them more effectively. Such a vision of humanity can enhance the expectation that other people also possess such potential. Social psychology has sufficiently demonstrated the significance of such expectancies as self-fulfilling prophecies: The image I hold of the other determines how I will behave toward her or him. Trust in a positive human nature characterizes the PCA's vision of humanity. For this reason, at the end of his life, Rogers summarized his experiences with this vision: "If you treat people as if they can be trusted, they are trustworthy" [Rogers, NBC TV, 1983 quoted in O'Leary (2006, p. 232)]—evidence seems to prove him right (see below).

2 A Neuroscience View on Person-Centered Relationships

2.1 The Circle of Contact

If a facilitator successfully offers a person-centered relationship toward another person, then there is an improved probability that positive developmental changes will occur in that person. Rogers (1959) has described such changes in detail. They embrace a greater openness to experiences, improvements concerning creativity, problem-solving skills, social perception and social attentiveness, higher maturity and integration, as well as a decrease in inner tension and anxiety. Evidence indicates that person-centered relationships support transformation in these directions. This chapter will deal with the question of how this happens and which neurobiological processes may be involved therein.

From the viewpoint of the PCA, the formation of a relationship is a reciprocal process which only functions under the condition that the other person perceives at least in part the offer of a person-centered relationship. Neuroscience gives some insights into the great variety of processes which can arise in humans during such interactions. I assume that these processes play a crucial role in the formation of a relationship as an emergent phenomenon during which "I" and "You" become a "We." In this regard I refer to Barrett-Lennard's (2009) view, which sees "the forming of relationship as an emergent process in which a new entity is born, one that is distinct in kind from an individual personality and also has life and influence. Its life is intricately intertwined with those of participant members but is of another order" (p. 82).

Moreover, neuroscience gives not only insight into how the so-called core conditions contribute to the formation of relationships but also on how they are related to each other (see also chapter by Silani, Zucconi and Lamm). In the PCA, it is assumed that they are closely interconnected and that they unfold their constructive impact only under the condition that they are simultaneously present. The relationship between them is characterized by Natiello (2001) with the following words: "They are best viewed as a trinity—inseparable, essential, and mutually interdependent" (p. 6). As far as the current status of research allows, the interconnectedness of the "core conditions" will also be addressed in the course of this chapter.

In the following, the model of the "circle of contact" (see Fig. 1) which was suggested by Lux (2010) to summarize neurobiological processes during psychotherapeutic relationships will be utilized as a frame of reference. The connections mentioned therein will be elucidated by referring to neuroscientific theories and research findings. Furthermore, the model will be generalized from psychotherapy to person-centered relationships in other contexts. Therefore, the terms "therapist" and "client" are replaced by "facilitator" and "other."

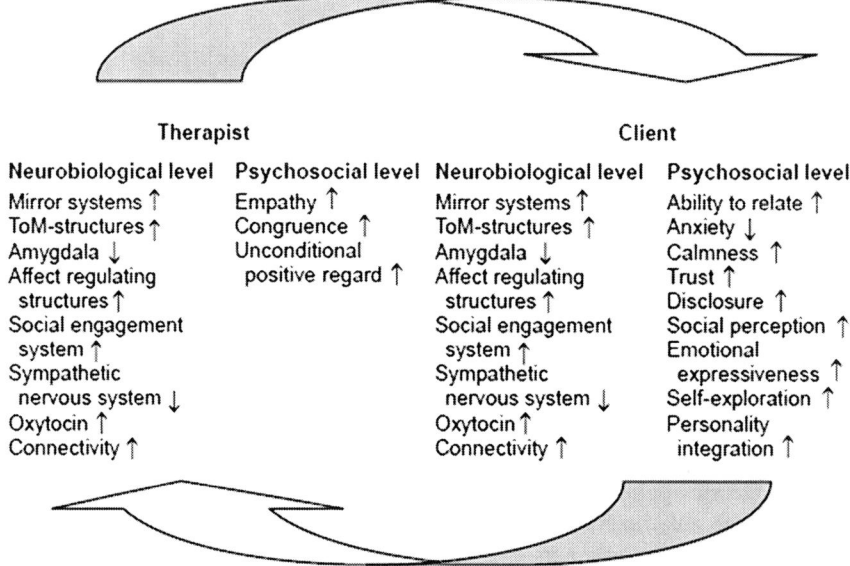

Fig. 1 The circle of contact (*Up arrows* symbolize increase in activation/release, or improvement; *down arrows* stand for alterations in opposite directions.)

2.2 The Impact of a Person-Centered Relationship on the Other

Person-centered facilitators hold the principles of empathy, unconditional positive regard, and congruence toward the other. A growth-promoting interpersonal climate evolves if the other person perceives this. In this way, a relationship evolves which allows for self-exploration and the discovery of new meaning within experiences. Within the PCA, it is assumed that the safety experienced by the other within the relationship is crucial (see chapter by Höger). Rogers (1995a/1951) explains this as follows: "In the emotional warmth of the relationship with the therapist, the client begins to experience a feeling of safety as he finds that whatever attitude he expresses is understood in almost the same way that he perceives it, and is accepted. He then is able to explore, for example, a vague feeling of guiltiness which he has experienced. In this safe relationship he can perceive for the first time the hostile meaning and purpose of certain aspects of his behavior, and he can understand why he has felt guilty about it, and why it has been necessary to deny to awareness the meaning of this behavior" (p. 41).

Research in neuroscience demonstrates that experiencing safety is accompanied by various neurobiological processes, which facilitate interpersonal abilities. From the viewpoint of the polyvagal theory by Porges (2007, 2011; see box (1) the perception of safety influences the autonomic nervous system and causes activation of the social engagement system. In this way, a great variety of processes occur supporting the ability to relate to other persons. On the one hand, emotional expressivity is improved, by which it is easier to express one's emotional state verbally and nonverbally. At the same time, social perception is favorably influenced, for example, by turning one's gaze more toward the other's eye area. In this regard, it can be expected that the improvement of social perception leads to a better recognition of the facilitator's empathy, positive regard, and congruence. This should exert a favorable impact on the psychological contact between the persons which are involved in the developing relationship.

Box 1
The Polyvagal theory
The polyvagal theory, developed by the neurobiologist Porges (2007, 2011), is a theory of the autonomic nervous system. Within this theory, the well-known antagonism between sympathetic and parasympathetic nervous system is replaced by three hierarchically linked systems: the nonmyelinated dorsal vagus, the sympathetic nervous systems, and the myelinated ventral vagus. Like other highly developed beings, humans are equipped with all three systems. Which of these systems is activated depends on a process called neuroception. Neuroception is an evaluation of the safety of a situation and the means to deal with it through unconscious processes.[1] Basically, three results are possible:

---

[1] It can be assumed that neuroception is closely related with the process of subception conceived by Rogers (1959): "Thus it appears that the organism can discriminate a stimulus and its meaning for the organism without utilizing the higher nerve centers involved in awareness. It is this capacity which, in theory, permits the individual to discriminate an experience as threatening, without symbolization in awareness of this threat" (p. 200).

1. The dorsal vagus will be activated if neuroception signals that we are helplessly confronted with a threatening situation with no possibility of escape. By the activation of the dorsal vagus, the organism's energy consumption is minimized, heart rate and breathing frequency decrease, we freeze, become functionally paralyzed, and the experience of pain and other sensations is shut down. These alterations can be seen, for example, as a consequence of trauma or during a severe depression, and are sometimes referred to as dissociation.
2. If neuroception signals that the situation is dangerous but fight or flight are a promising means to deal with it, the sympathetic nervous system is activated. In that case, energy reserves are mobilized and various alterations of the stress reaction occur. An over-active sympathetic nervous system is relevant for anxiety-related problems and for many social and health problems.
3. The third option is that neuroception evaluates a situation as safe. This causes an activation of the ventral vagus, the social engagement system, and a simultaneous deactivation of the sympathetic nervous system. The social engagement system controls facial muscles allowing for an expressive mimic, muscles of the throat, which are involved in the prosody of the voice, eye muscles allowing for establishing eye contact, and muscles of the middle ear supporting the perception of the human voice in background noise. Thus, apart from stress reduction, an activation of the social engagement system can improve emotional expressiveness as well as social perception.

In addition, the activation of the social engagement system is associated with deactivation of the sympathetic nervous system causing a reduction in stress and preventing the impairment of integrative brain regions by an over-activated limbic system. The medial prefrontal cortex is such an integrative brain region that can be impaired by stress. Siegel (2010) explains how it is involved in the attentive registration of experiences and in subsequent integrative processes. Thus, stress reduction supports openness to experiences which characterizes the fully functioning person, the ideal case of mental health, who, according to Rogers (1995b/1961), "makes use of all the information his nervous system can thus supply, using it in awareness, but recognizing that his total organism may be, and often is, wiser than his awareness" (p. 191). In this way, being in tune with the organismic valuing process, fully functioning persons "are surprised at their own intuitive skill in finding behavioral solutions to complex and troubling human relationships. It is only afterward that they realize how surprisingly trustworthy their inner reactions have been in bringing about satisfactory behavior" (p. 191). Neuroscience has elucidated the essential function of nonconscious processes for making appropriate decisions in complex situations. In this field, we owe pioneering work to Antonio

Damasio and his co-workers and their research on the "somatic markers." Somatic markers are emotion-related bodily signals, which reflect an "important reasoning process going on nonconsciously" (Damasio 2010, p. 276). The importance of utilizing body-related signals in decision-making processes is also stressed by Siegel (2010): "Reasoning, once thought to be a 'purely logical' mode of thinking, is in fact dependent on the nonrational processes of our bodies. Such intuition helps us make wise decisions, not just logical ones" (p. 29).

Apart from safety, the offer of a person-centered relationship signals trust toward the other. The fundamental trustworthiness of man is deeply anchored within the PCA. To use Rogers' (1995b/1961) words: "The basic nature of the human being, when functioning freely, is constructive and trustworthy" (p. 194). Person-centered facilitators have a profound belief in the impact of the actualizing tendency and the corresponding competencies for constructive problem solving of each person. Over the last years, the influence of trust on social interactions has been the subject of studies in neuroscience. In these studies, it was shown, for example, that the level of oxytocin is raised in someone who is trusted (Zak et al. 2005; see box 2). Moreover, offering a person-centered relationship can evoke the release of oxytocin in another person by attentive listening (Uvnäs-Moberg 2003) or mutual self-disclosure (Kéri and Kiss 2011) due to the facilitator's transparence. Furthermore, Heinrich and Domes (2008) conclude from their review on studies on oxytocin that it is released by "positive social interactions, such as social support or social proximity" (p. 344). Person-centered relationships can be seen as prototypical examples for such interactions.

Box 2
Oxytocin
In recent years, the neuropeptide oxytocin has been intensively investigated in social neuroscience. It is synthesized in the hypothalamus and acts both in the central nervous system and in the bloodstream. MacDonald and MacDonald (2010), like Uvnäs-Moberg (2003), give an overview of its manifold effects. Oxytocin is linked with attachment processes, and it is released, for example, in situations related to the establishment of social connections. The "trust game" is an example of an experimental design which is utilized in the research of oxytocin. In this game, an investor receives a certain amount of money and passes on as much money as wanted to a trustee. The trustee receives three times this amount and is free to return money in any quantity desired to the investor. Therefore, the amount of money the investor transfers to the trustee is regarded as a signal of trust. Administration of oxytocin causes investors to transfer more money to trustees and thus to show more trust in them (Kosfeld et al. 2005). In addition, Zak et al. (2005) demonstrated that the oxytocin level measured in the trustee's blood plasma correlated positively with the amount of money transferred by the investor. Hence, higher trust in another person increases the oxytocin level of this person. Thereby, it is not the amount of money itself which is related to oxytocin but the amount of money

as a signal of trust. If it is allotted how much money the investor should transfer to the trustee, the oxytocin level will be unrelated to the amount of the transferred money. I would also like to mention that a higher release of oxytocin in the trustee is related to a higher return transfer which seems to confirm an assumption of Rogers: "If you treat people as if they can be trusted, they are trustworthy" [Rogers, NBC TV, 1983 quoted in O'Leary (2006, p. 232)]. Additionally, oxytocin generally enhances generosity both when it is administered by a nose spray (Zak et al. 2007) and by a stimulation of its endogenous release (Barraza and Zak 2009).

Thus, the person-centered offer of a facilitative relationship provides an array of possibilities for stimulating the release of oxytocin in another person. In turn, it has been shown that oxytocin enhances the tendency to trust another (Kosfeld et al. 2005), which can increase the likelihood for self-disclosure. This could be supported by an oxytocin-induced increase in attachment security in insecurely attached persons (Buchheim et al. 2009). Additionally, like an activation of the social engagement system, oxytocin may have favorable effects on social perception by improving eye contact (Guastella et al. 2008). Furthermore, oxytocin has a stress-decreasing effect (Heinrichs et al. 2003) which is probably related to its deactivating impact on the amygdala (Kirsch et al. 2005)—a brain region which is crucial for aversive experiences. As previously stated, stress reduction is advantageous to the process of self-exploration.

In person-centered relationships, the facilitator's empathic understanding fosters self-exploration. During the dialogical process of empathy, the facilitator attentively strives to sense and understand without prejudice the inner world of the other, to communicate this understanding verbally and nonverbally, and to utilize the other's response to achieve a deeper understanding. This allows the other to tune into his experiences in a more mindful way [see the chapters by Bundschuh-Müller and Ryback; Rogers (1995b/1961)]. By communicating the understanding of the other's inner world, the facilitator encourages to explore his or her experiences more deeply. In this process of self-exploration, relationships between different parts of the totality of experiences can be uncovered. The other can clarify how he or she feels toward his or her experiences, how experiences are related to the self-concept or acquired values, or how he or she can utilize "the ongoing psycho-physiological flow within himself" (Rogers 1980, p. 142) as a referent to detect new meaning "and to carry it further to its full and uninhibited experiencing" (Rogers 1980, p. 142).

It can be assumed that self-exploration supports integration within the brain and leads to a strengthening of the neural connectivity between cognitive, emotional, and motivational brain systems. It is important to note that neuroscientists like LeDoux (2002) refer to a reduced neural connectivity between these systems as a fundamental weak point of the human brain and as an important source of threat to mental health. Furthermore, during self-exploration, feelings are perceived with more attention. From the perspective of neuroscience, feelings are important "diagnostic instruments" for the condition of the homeostatic life regulation. In this regard, Damasio (2010) states: "Optimal ranges [of homeostatic life regulation] express themselves in the conscious mind as pleasurable feelings, dangerous ranges, as not-so-pleasant or even painful feelings" (p. 55).

Finally, the facilitator's empathy supports the other's affect regulation (Watson 2007). Empathic understanding helps the other to become aware of and to label emotional experiences. Findings from brain imaging demonstrate that this is accompanied by neural processes which are involved in affect regulation. Lieberman et al. (2007) showed that verbally labeling the emotional quality of an emotion-triggering stimulus activates the right ventrolateral prefrontal cortex which is accompanied by deactivation of the amygdala. Interestingly, self-assessed dispositional mindfulness correlates positively with the aforementioned neural processes associated with affect labeling (Creswell et al. 2007). Thus, it can be assumed that by facilitating mindfulness (see above), person-centered relationships boost the affect-regulating effect of labeling.

2.3 The Impact of a Person-Centered Relationship on the Facilitator

As shown above, offering a person-centered relationship can cause a variety of neurobiological and psychosocial alterations which facilitate the other's willingness to disclose emotional states. Doubtless, if another person discloses experiences, this will affect the facilitator too and will set in motion a wide range of neurobiological processes on this side as well. For one thing, if the emotional state of another person is expressed more transparently, the so-called cognitive empathy of the one who tries to understand this person is improved (Zaki et al. 2008). Cognitive empathy corresponds with conscious perspective taking, that is, to judge another's emotions or cognitions by utilizing observable behavior or context information. Cognitive empathy allows for the conscious recognition of another's emotional state and also for the reasons for that emotional state which is an important aspect of the person-centered conception of empathy [see chapter by Silani, Zucconi and Lamm; Rogers (1959)]. It is scientifically studied under the heading of "Theory of Mind" for which the medial prefrontal cortex, the superior temporal sulcus, and the temporal poles have important functions (Shamay-Tsoory 2009).

Empathy as conceived in the PCA embraces not only cognitive empathy but also emotional empathy, that is, the ability to feel what another person feels. The simulation theory (see Gallese and Goldman 1998) makes an important contribution to the understanding of emotional empathy. Within this theory, it is assumed that the experiences of another person are simulated within the brain of the one who tries to understand him or her. This allows us to experience within ourselves how the other person feels. Gallese (2008) explains this as follows: "The other's emotion is first and foremost constituted and directly understood by means of embodied simulation producing an 'as-if' experience engendered by a shared body state. It is the body state shared by observer and observed that enables direct understanding" (p. 771). Mirror neuron systems in the inferior frontal gyrus as well as the anterior cingulate cortex and the insula are brain regions that are involved in simulation processes which allow for emotional empathy [see chapter by Silani, Zucconi and Lamm; Shamay-Tsoory (2009)]. An enhanced emotional expressivity should ease "embodied" simulation processes and thus emotional empathy. In this regard, Siegel (2010) assumes that simulation processes can induce synchronization of the involved persons at the level of bodily functions. Marci et al. (2007) demonstrated that in psychotherapy such synchronization, which they called physiologic concordance, is closely related to the degree the client perceives the therapist's empathic understanding (see chapter by O'Brien, Afzal and Tronick). Furthermore, this study showed that a higher degree of physiologic concordance is associated with more solidarity and positive regard as measured by trained observers. From the viewpoint of the PCA, this finding supports the interconnectedness of the principles of empathy and unconditional positive regard.

Furthermore, the other's emotional disclosure may lead to an increase in the release of oxytocin in the facilitator. One reason for this is that disclosure of another person may be perceived as a signal of trust which has the potential to evoke the release of oxytocin in the trusted person (Zak et al. 2005). Another reason is that emotional disclosure involves the communication of emotionally moving experiences. It was shown by Barraza and Zak (2009) that watching an emotionally moving video induces the release of oxytocin much more than an emotionally neutral video. Because oxytocin has a reinforcing effect on emotional empathy (Hurlemann et al. 2010), this may also enhance synchronization on a bodily level. Interestingly, in the study by Barraza and Zak (2009), the release of oxytocin correlated negatively with feelings of personal distress (e.g., anxiety, distress, irritation) and positively with feelings of empathic concern (e.g., compassion, warmth, care, or sympathy). In this regard, it should be noted that feelings of empathic concern are present when one holds the principle of unconditional positive regard toward another person (Barrett-Lennard 1998).

In psychotherapy research, a connection was found between the therapist's empathy and feelings like compassion, tenderness, or care toward their clients [Greenberg and Rushansky-Rosenberg quoted after Watson (2007)]. Research in neuroscience confirms such a connection. A study by Lutz et al. (2008) was conducted with persons practicing Buddhist compassion meditation during which feelings of compassion and unconditional love are generated by the meditators. It was shown that during the generation of such feelings, the meditator's limbic systems reacted more strongly to acoustic emotional expressions from other persons compared with a condition without such feelings being present. Isn't it conceivable that such an amplification of neural resonances may be linked to the relationship between bodily synchronization, the therapist's empathy perceived by the client, and aspects of unconditional positive regard found in the study by Marci et al. (2007)?

In person-centered psychotherapy, diminishment of unconditional positive regard can be seen as an "alarm system for the therapeutic relationship" (Eckert 2006, p. 225, own translation) which should be carefully noticed by the therapist. Thus, if deviancies from unconditional positive are recognized, this should be clarified and explored with the help of supervision if necessary. Research in neuroscience refers to the relevance of this "alarm system." In fact, Singer et al. (2006) showed that negative feelings toward a person can diminish emotional empathy toward that person. Thus, once more, a connection between empathy and unconditional positive regard becomes apparent.

In addition to an improvement in emotional empathy, there are other effects which can be expected if oxytocin is released. On the one hand, the facilitator's amygdala should be deactivated (Kirsch et al. 2005). In this way, it is easier for the facilitator to meet the other in a mindful way and to "look with fresh and unfrightened eyes at elements of which the individual is fearful" (Rogers 1980, p. 142). The stress-reducing effect of oxytocin is facilitative to the function of the medial prefrontal cortex which supports the facilitator's congruence and thus her/his awareness of experiences arising in resonance with the client. The PCA and neuroscience agree that these experiences can constitute a bridge into the experiences of the other and that the facilitator's congruence is therefore of great importance for empathic understanding (see chapter by Silani, Zucconi and Lamm). Additionally, oxytocin can help the facilitator to be more trusting (Kosfeld et al. 2005) and to meet the other with transparency and realness. In summary, there are many pathways by which oxytocin can support facilitators in offering a person-centered relationship.

Emotional disclosure can also affect the facilitator's autonomic nervous system. Due to a better understanding of the other, the facilitator may feel safer in the relationship which might then be accompanied by an activation of the social engagement system. As mentioned above, this can have favorable effects on emotional expressivity, social perception, and the sympathetic nervous system—things which support the facilitator to experience and express empathy, unconditional positive regard, and congruence.

3 Concluding Remarks

If someone perceives at least in part the offer of a person-centered relationship from a facilitator, then a variety of neurobiological processes are engaged which can influence emotional expression and other kinds of behavior in the other. This can also affect the facilitator and trigger neurobiological processes which support the ability to create the core conditions of a growth-promoting relationship. This, in turn, creates a reaction in the other by which the circle of contact is completed. It is probable that the aforementioned processes embrace only a part of the mutual resonances which occur during social interactions. With regard to this, I assume that their totality enables the formation of the emergent phenomenon of a relationship—as "a living process at a further level" (Barrett-Lennard 2009, p. 82).

The feedback processes summarized in the circle of contact can be related to concepts about relationships which have been recently developed in the PCA. Here, I would like to address the concepts of "relational depth" and "co-actualization." Relational depth is defined by Mearns and Cooper (2005) as "A state of profound contact and engagement between two people in which each person is fully real with the Other and able to understand and value the Other's experiences at a high level" (p. XII). It describes moments of deep connection, in Buber's terms an "I-thou relationship," during which deception is impossible and a healing power emerges within the client. Mearns and Cooper derived this concept from their experiences as person-centered psychotherapists but acknowledge that this phenomenon occurs in close relationships outside psychotherapy, too. Relational depth expands the classical model of the PCA by emphasizing the client's contribution to the formation of a therapeutic relationship. The client not only perceives the therapist offering a person-centered relationship but is himself pervaded by variations of the "core conditions" in the sense of realness, empathy for the therapist's empathic understanding, and respect for the experiences and the person of the therapist. I assume that in the case of relational depth, the neurobiological processes described in the circle of contact are activated to a high degree which supports the suffusing of the involved persons by empathy, (unconditional) positive regard, and congruence.

The phenomenon of relational depth can be seen as an example of a co-actualizing relationship. The concept of co-actualization was presented by Motschnig-Pitrik and Barrett-Lennard (2010). It describes that in well-functioning relationships, a climate can evolve which supports the unfolding of the actualizing-tendency of every person who is part of the relationship. In addition, co-actualization embraces the unfolding of the relationship itself—"the living process at a further level"—as well as positive influences on the social context of the relationship. Therefore, a person-centered relationship offers the possibility for a growth-promoting climate from which the involved persons, their relationship itself, and higher level social systems may profit. I speculate that the neurobiological processes described in the circle of contact can play—via positive feedback processes—a crucial role in co-actualization. From my viewpoint, such mutually reinforcing effects permit the establishment and further development of relationships like a dyad between therapist and client, an encounter group, a family, a working group, or other social systems.

In principle, it can be empirically investigated whether and how the processes described in the circle of contact are related to relational depth or co-actualization. For example, it can be expected that the "climate of trust which tends to pervade" (Motschnig-Pitrik and Barrett-Lennard 2010, p. 386) co-actualizing relationships is associated with a higher release of oxytocin. The same applies for working at relational depth in psychotherapy. Mearns and Cooper (2005) describe the therapeutic work with a traumatized soldier (Rick) who was mutistic and unable to communicate. From the perspective of the polyvagal theory, we can hypothesize that his autonomic nervous system was dominated by the dorsal vagus (see box 1). I have not the words to express my admiration for the therapist (Dave Mearns) who was able to stand this and to offer 24 sessions of 60 min to a relationship while he was getting almost no reaction from Rick. Then in the 25th session, the following sequence happened: After getting a first small response by the client, the therapist himself felt his own strong emotional involvement in the relationship and began to cry a little. The client noticed this and responded by offering a tissue. Mearns and Cooper (2005) assume that "Dave's crying and Rick handing him a tissue seems to be a real turning point to engage with another" (p. 132). After that episode contact between therapist and client improved more and more which finally allowed for approaching traumatic experiences. There are some questions which concern me: Wouldn't it be conceivable that by being mutually emotionally touched, oxytocin is released in both persons during this episode? Could this perhaps have facilitated Rick to trust Dave, to open up to him, and finally to approach his traumatic experiences?

There are several ways to measure the neurobiological processes which are depicted in the circle of contact. Obviously, the greatest caution is needed lest vulnerable healing processes might be endangered by the context of a scientific study. Yet I would like to suggest some starting points for such an endeavor. Oxytocin is measurable in blood plasma or in urine. However, the short half-life period of measured oxytocin is not easy to handle, and it is not clear how these measures are related to oxytocin in the brain (MacDonald and MacDonald 2010). The situation is further complicated by interindividual differences in baseline plasma levels and contextual influences on the impact of (at least exogenously administered) oxytocin (Bartz et al. 2011). Because of the influence of oxytocin on trusting or generous behaviors, measures of oxytocin-mediated effects are also possible. Operationalizations for this have already been developed in neuroeconomics and thus would be available for evaluation purposes (for an example see box 2). Furthermore, it is possible to measure the activation of the social engagement system by alterations of facial muscles, prosody, exploration of the eye area, or the parasympathetic activation of the heart. In addition, studies on physiologic concordance which have been successfully conducted already (see chapter by O'Brien, Afzal, and Tronick) could show whether bodily synchronization is in fact involved in relational depth or co-actualization.

A problem with such studies would be that neither relational depth nor co-actualization can be reliably produced at the push of a button. Thus, the mentioned relationships will have for the foreseeable future the status of hypothesis. Nevertheless, they are very valuable to me in offering a constant source of inspiration into the mysteries that can happen between humans, the transforming power of relationships, and the magic of encounter.

References

Barraza, J. A. & Zak, P. J. (2009). Empathy toward strangers triggers oxytocin release and subsequent generosity. *Annals of the New York Academy of Science, 1167*, 182–189.
Barrett-Lennard, G. T. (1998). *Carl Rogers' helping system: Journey and substance.* London: Sage.
Barrett-Lennard, G. T. (2009). From personality to relationship: Path of thought and practice. *Person-Centered and Experiential Psychotherapies, 8*, 79–93.
Bartz, J. A., Zaki, J., Bolger, N., & Ochsner, K. N. (2011). Social effects of oxytocin in humans: Context and person matter. *Trends in Cognitive Sciences, 15*, 301–309.
Buchheim, A., Heinrichs, M., George, C., Pokorny, D., Koops, E., Henningsen, P., et al. (2009). Oxytocin enhances the experience of attachment security. *Psychoneuroendocrinology, 34*, 1417–1422.
Creswell, J. D., Way, B. M., Eisenberger, N. I., & Lieberman, M. D. (2007). Neural correlates of dispositional mindfulness during affect labelling. *Psychosomatic Medicine, 69*, 560–565.
Damasio, A. R. (2003). *Looking for Spinoza*. Orlando: Harcourt.
Damasio, A. R. (2010). *Self comes to mind*. New York: Pantheon.
Decety, J., & Moriguchi, Y. (2007). The empathic brain and its dysfunction in psychiatric populations: Implications for intervention across different clinical conditions. *Biopsychosocial Medicine,*. doi:10.1186/1751-0759-1-22.
Eckert, J. (2006). Der therapeutische Prozess in der Praxis. In J. Eckert, E.-M. Biermann-Ratjen, & D. Höger (Eds.), *Gesprächspsychotherapie* (pp. 219–266). Heidelberg: Springer.
Eisenberger, N. I., Liebermann, M. D., & Williams, K. D. (2003). Does rejection hurt? An fMRI study of social exclusion. *Science, 302*, 290–292.
Gallese, V., & Goldman, A. (1998). Mirror neurons and the simulation theory of mind-reading. *Trends in Cognitive Sciences, 12*, 493–501.
Gallese, V. (2008). Empathy, embodied simulation, and the brain: Commentary on Aragno and Zepf/Hartmann. *Journal of the American Psychoanalytic Association, 56*, 769–781.
Guastella, A. J., Mitchell, P. B., & Dadds, M. R. (2008). Oxytocin increases gaze to the eye region of human faces. *Biological Psychology, 63*, 3–5.
Heinrichs, M., Baumgartner, T., Kirschbaum, C., & Ehlert, U. (2003). Social support and oxytocin interact to suppress cortisol and subjective responses to psychosocial stress. *Biological Psychiatry, 54*, 1389–1398.
Heinrichs, M., & Domes, G. (2008). Neuropeptides and social behaviour: Effects of oxytocin and vasopressin in humans. *Progress in Brain Research, 170*, 337–350.
Hurlemann, R., Patin, A., Onur, O. A., Cohen, M. X., Baumgartner, T., Metzler, S., et al. (2010). Oxytocin enhances amygdala-dependent, socially reinforced learning and emotional empathy in humans. *Journal of Neuroscience, 30*, 4999–5007.
Hüther, G. (2006). Wie embodiment neurobiologisch erklärt werden kann. In M. Storch, B. Cantieni, G. Hüther, & W. Tschacher (Eds.), *Embodiment* (pp. 75–97). Bern: Hans Huber.
Kéri, S., & Kiss, I. (2011). Oxytocin response in a trust game and habituation of arousal. *Physiology and Behavior, 102*, 221–224.
Kirsch, P., Esslinger, C., Chen, Q., Mier, D., Lis, S., Siddhanti, S., et al. (2005). Oxytocin modulates neural circuitry for social cognition and fear in humans. *Journal of Neuroscience, 25*, 11489–11493.
Kirschenbaum, H., & Henderson, V. L. (Eds.). (1989). *Carl Rogers: Dialogues.* London: Constable.
Kosfeld, M., Heinrichs, M., Zak, P. J., Fischbacher, U., & Fehr, E. (2005). Oxytocin increases trust in humans. *Nature, 435*, 673–676.
LeDoux, J. (2002). *Synaptic self*. New York: Penguin Putnam.
Lieberman, M. D., Eisenberger, N. I., Crockett, M. J., Tom, S. M., Pfeifer, J. H., & Way, B. M. (2007). Putting feelings into words: Affect labeling disrupts amygdala activation to affective stimuli. *Psychological Science, 18*, 421–428.

Lutz, A., Brefczynski-Lewis, J., Johnstone, T., & Davidson, R. J. (2008). Regulation of the neural circuitry of emotion by compassion meditation: Effects of meditative expertise. *PLoS ONE, 3*(3), e1897. doi:10.1371/journal.pone.0001897.
Lux, M. (2007). *Der Personzentrierte Ansatz und die Neurowissenschaften*. München: Ernst Reinhard Verlag. [The person-centered approach and the neurosciences].
Lux, M. (2010). The magic of encounter: The person-centered approach and the neurosciences. *Person-Centered and Experiential Psychotherapies, 9*, 274–289.
Marci, C. D., Ham, J., Moran, E., & Orr, S. P. (2007). Physiologic correlates of perceived therapist empathy and social-emotional process during psychotherapy. *Journal of Nervous and Mental Disease, 195*, 103–111.
MacDonald, K., & MacDonald, T. M. (2010). The peptide that binds: A systematic review of oxytocin and its prosocial effects in humans. *Harvard Review of Psychiatry, 18*, 1–21.
Mearns, D., & Cooper, M. (2005). *Working at relational depth in counselling and psychotherapy*. London: Sage.
Motschnig-Pitrik, R., & Barrett-Lennard, G. (2010). Co-actualization: A new construct in understanding well-functioning relationships. *Journal of Humanistic Psychology, 50*, 374–398.
Natiello, P. (2001). *The person-centred approach: A passionate presence*. Ross-on-Wye: PCCS Books.
O'Leary, C. O. (2006). Carl Rogers: Lessons for working at relational depth. *Person-Centered and Experiential Psychotherapies, 5*, 229–239.
Porges, S. W. (2007). The polyvagal perspective. *Biological Psychology, 74*, 116–143.
Porges, S. W. (2011). *The polyvagal theory: Neurophysiological foundations of emotions, attachment, communication, and self-regulation*. New York: Norton.
Rogers, C. R. (1959). A theory of therapy, personality, and interpersonal relationships, as developed in the client-centered framework. In S. Koch (Ed.), *Psychology: A study of a science* (Vol. 3, pp. 184–256)., Formulations of the person and the social context New York: McGraw-Hill.
Rogers, C. R. (1995a). *Client-centered therapy*. London: Constable. [Original work published 1951].
Rogers, C. R. (1995b). *On becoming a person*. London: Constable. [Original work published 1961].
Rogers, C. R. (1980). *A way of being*. Boston: Houghton Mifflin.
Shamay-Tsoory, S. G. (2009). Empathic processing: Its cognitive and affective dimensions and neuroanatomical basis. In J. Decety & W. Ickes (Eds.), *The social neuroscience of empathy* (pp. 215–232). Cambridge: MIT Press.
Siegel, D. (2010). *Mindsight*. New York: Bantam.
Singer, T., Seymour, B., O'Doherty, J. P., Klaas, E. S., Dolan, R. J., & Frith, C. D. (2006). Empathic neural responses are modulated by the perceived fairness of others. *Nature, 439*, 466–469.
Tabibnia, G., & Lieberman, M. D. (2007). Fairness and cooperation are rewarding: Evidence from social cognitive neuroscience. *Annals of the New York Academy of Sciences, 1118*, 90–101.
Uvnäs-Moberg, K. (2003). *The oxytocin factor: Trapping the hormones of calm, love, and healing*. Cambridge: Da Capo Press.
Watson, J. C. (2007). Facilitating empathy. *European Psychotherapy, 7*, 61–76.
Zak, P. J., Kurzban, R., & Matzner, W. T. (2005). Oxytocin is associated with human trustworthiness. *Hormones and Behavior, 48*, 522–527.
Zak, P. J., Stanton, A. A., & Ahmadi, S. (2007). Oxytocin increases generosity in humans. *PLoS ONE, 2*(11), e1128. doi:10.1371/journal.pone.0001128.
Zaki, J., Bolger, N., & Ochsner, K. (2008). It takes two: The interpersonal nature of empathic accuracy. *Psychological Science, 19*, 399–404.

Rogers' Generative Framework of Organismic Integrity: Scientific Evidence Challenging Academic, Medical, and Pharmaceutical Forces

Carol Wolter-Gustafson

1 Introduction

I have no doubt Carl Rogers would have been extremely pleased to see this book published. Building connections was his life's work. Like most visionaries, he explored emerging connections flowing from and to his theory and practice.

The concept of the organism is central to understanding Rogers' person-centered theory. Research and theory from person-centered and neuroscience researchers converge describing a singular blueprint of a multi-focal network underlying all organic processes. This powerful paradigm stands in stark contrast to the paradigm that in the USA dominates most medical, psychological, and pharmaceutical practices.

I begin by providing some background to Rogers' contributions, highlighting central theoretical premises of Rogers' and Seeman's work. I then turn to neuroscientific research starting with the works of Candace Pert and Miles Herkenham. Finally, I will position these researchers in the context of current political, ethical, and economic trends. I will suggest that person-centered and neuroscience research that views the organism as a complex whole provides a superior paradigm for fostering the health and well-being of the person and society.

2 Rogers' Contributions

2.1 How Is the Organism Conceptualized? Some Definitions

Rogers (1959) laid out the central framework for his theory of the organism in the most elaborated form in "Psychology: A Study of a Science," edited by Koch.

C. Wolter-Gustafson (✉)
Boston University, 21 Arborway Terrace, Boston, MA 02130, USA
e-mail: carolwg@earthlink.net

The definition of the organism is inextricably tied to the definition of the actualizing tendency. Thus, Rogers (1959) starts with this definition of the actualizing tendency—"the inherent tendency of the organism to develop all its capacities in ways which serve to maintain or enhance the organism" (p. 197).

The organism, that is the human being, is always active and always pointed toward the self-directed tendency of the organism toward healing. Rogers posits that the actualizing tendency is the singular motive in his theory. Central to the thesis of this chapter, he writes that it is, "the organism as a whole, and only the organism as a whole, which exhibits this tendency" (as cited in Koch 1959. p. 196). "In short, organisms are always seeking, always initiating, always 'up to something'" (Rogers 1980, p. 123). It should be noted that Rogers' theory states that the person as organism is implicitly relational and interdependent with the persons and environmental factors with which he or she interacts.

The totality of organismic experience includes an active integration of what we typically call "parts" of ourselves. This *in itself* is radically generative. Given the Western dualistic separation of mind and body, mind being privileged over our lower nature, this in itself provides a substantial and radical contribution to understanding the intricacies of the body–mind connection. Rogers was engaged with nothing less than understanding the whole person.

Next, Rogers' construct is generative and unique in psychology, because it is gender free and as such avoids culturally laden stereotypes about man and woman's "true nature" (Wolter-Gustafson 1999). Another generative aspect of his construct is that it moved away from the theory-centric, intellectualized psychology of Freud and others. Rogers' theory is progressive as he bypasses habituated language that is often dualistic, linear, and encodes gendered binarism (Wolter-Gustafson 2008a, b).

2.2 Empirical Rigor, Epistemological Humility, and Ethical Vision

Three characteristics of Rogers' way of working make his contributions particularly valuable today. They are his empirical rigor, epistemological humility, and enhanced ethical vision.

From his earliest training in scientific agriculture, to being the first researcher to use technology to record clients' therapeutic sessions verbatim, Rogers' empirical drive was apparent. Rogers was certain that breakthroughs in scientific measurement would be capable of discovering more precise mechanisms within the organism. "I would hypothesize that in these moments, had we the measure for it, we would discover improved circulation, improved conductivity of nervous impulses" (Rogers 1961, pp. 147–148). While he received many awards, the one he most valued was The American Psychological Association's Distinguished Scientific Contribution Award presented to him in 1956, its inaugural year. It was created to "express the debt" owed to "the few of us who, in the course of a lifetime...make distinguished contributions to the development of the science of psychology" (as cited in Kirschenbaum 2009, p. 212).

While Rogers was immersed in the empiricism of his time, he valued and espoused alternative epistemological methods. In *Toward a Science of the Person*, Rogers (1964) acknowledged the conventional split between objective and subjective knowledge, and also its inadequacy, "since every instance of knowing involves coming to terms in some way with the subjective and the phenomenological" (p. 110). He valued a third way of knowing, often called intersubjective knowledge. Rogers (1964) believed that this more inclusive method leads to a "newer philosophy of science which will not be fearful of finding room for the person—both the observer and the observed—in his subjective as well as his objective mode" (p. 131). Rogers (1980) writes, "all this goes deeply against the current (and possibly outdated) epistemology of the social sciences, which holds that a 'cause' is followed in a one-way direction by an 'effect'" (p. 122). Once again, Rogers follows the data itself and breaks with the simplistic cause and effect, stimulus–response paradigm prevalent then, and now. He posits multi-focal, organism-wide sources of knowledge.

Rogers was consistently engaged in the context, systems, and cultures in which human beings live. Rather than offering ideological, proscriptive advice, he listened and helped craft temporally and contextually driven solutions. In a privately circulated version of a chapter that was later included in *A Way of Being*, Rogers (1978) noted the loss of political innocence in physics and expressed his concern for the fate of the biological and psychological sciences: "They too may easily become the tools of the massive bureaucratic complex in which movement toward control appears inevitable with no one person responsible for any given step—a hydra-headed creeping monster which would engulf the sort of person I described" (p. 25).

Rogers (1980) accurately predicted that more optimally functioning persons of tomorrow would be opposed by forces working to maintain the *status quo* of national interests, traditions, intellectual hegemony, and the belief that people should be shaped and controlled. Evidence is accumulating that his vision was entirely prescient and all too accurate. In a report, *Prospects and Perils of the New Brain Science*, neuroscientist Rose (2009) echoes Rogers' concerns. In a section called "The Neuroscience of Social Control," Rose (2009) explains that while the title might seem "unduly provocative" (p. 31), he believes it is warranted. Rose is critical of the proliferation of "disturbing classifications" added to the Diagnostic and Statistical Manual. He (2009) challenges the labeling of behaviors previously deemed "eccentric" or resulting from negative social conditions as "diseases, of neurological and perhaps genetic origin, for which psychopharmacological treatment may be appropriate" (p. 31).

2.3 Embodied Organismic Motivation

The organism is embodied. Though redundant, this heading makes explicit our Western linguistically supported, dualistic intellectual habit of seeing motivation as a "psychological" phenomenon. Influenced by Freud, we speak of people being controlled by their Super Ego, self-sabotage, or oppositional defiant disorder. For Rogers (1980), motivation is a "trustworthy function of the whole system, rather than of some portion of it; it is most simply conceptualized as a tendency toward fulfillment, toward actualization, involving not only the maintenance but also the enhancement of the organism" (p. 123).

According to Rogers (1961), a client unable to symbolize part of his or her awareness often feel "stuck." Only after all of his or her "unacceptable" parts have been accepted will the client be able to "experience feelings with 'immediacy and richness'" (Rogers 1961, p. 145). This occurs when that which has been unacceptable is no longer to be "denied, feared, [or] struggled against" (Rogers 1961, p. 146).

Rogers' soma-centric characterization of this stage of movement in clients is noteworthy. He (1961) writes that there are "obvious physical concomitants" (p. 130) and describes "physiological loosening" in which "moistness in the eyes, tears, sobbing, sighs, and muscular relaxation, are frequently evident" (p. 147).

Rogers (1961) writes, "he is making use of his organic equipment to sense, as accurately as possible, the existential situation within and without. He is using all of the data his nervous system can thus supply… he is a fully functioning organism, and because of the awareness of himself which flows freely in and through his experiences, he is a fully functioning person (p. 191)." Explicitly, in client-centered theory, the return to "organic order" is accomplished through organism-wide change.

Of course, finding order amidst the chaos of modern life is a difficult task. In 1956, Jules Seeman wrote, "in our complex culture the chances for intrapsychic disturbance of these laws are manifold, and thus the need for therapy arises. In these terms we may think of therapy as the removal or assimilation of these intrapsychic disturbances and the return to organic order or integration" (as cited in Levant and Shlien 1984, p. 146).

3 Seeman's Contributions

3.1 The Integrated Person and Intellectual Efficiency

Jules Seeman was Carl Rogers' first doctoral fellow at the University of Chicago Counseling Center. As Research Coordinator, Seeman investigated the concept of the fully functioning person and outcomes in psychotherapy. In 1956, he wrote, "the body is governed not by anarchy but by a series of biologically given developmental laws or regularities" (Seeman 1984, p. 146). As Seeman's inquiry evolved, he (1984) saw "organismic integration" as a whole organism activity of various "subsystems" working in a "transactional process that blends...biochemical, physiological, perceptual, cognitive, and interpersonal"[1] in ways that are "congruent, harmonious, and adaptive" (Seeman 1984, p. 146).

This model inspired him to enlist colleagues and students to conduct over 25 experiments exploring the interconnectedness of these subsystems with the person's environment. A number of studies focused on the physiological and perceptual/cognitive systems, utilizing the best technology available to them at the time including galvanic skin response, EEG alpha patterns, skin temperature, heart rate, and biofeedback technology in conjunction with psychological testing metrics (Seeman 1983). Seeman referenced research by Kandel that "describe[s] a regular sequence of biochemically induced neural-circuit impediments that accompany anxiety" (Cain and Seeman 2002, p. 629).

The results of these studies persuaded Seeman (1983) to conclude that a client who has come to appreciate "and trust their basic organismic self" does "not have the need to screen, shut out, or deflect and distort signals in a way that characterizes more vulnerable persons. For the integrated person this ability to receive and process the data of their immediate experience results in the optimal receipt of information" (p. 233).

The key to that trust in psychotherapy is the therapist's capacity to make contact with the client. In relationship, Seeman turned his full focus on contacting the "livingness" of the other. Once an authentic, unconditionally positive, caring connection was established and accurate empathic understanding was given and received, constructive change followed, the vast resources of the client became activated.

Seeman (1983) asserted, "Reality data serve as nutrition, fully as important to the psychological organism as food is to the biological organism" (p. 233). More highly functioning persons "generate more information, and more differentiated information, than their less well-integrated peers" (p. 233). According to Seeman (1983), they also interact more highly with their environment, function with more intellectual efficiency and make excellent use of their resources.

In the late 1990s, Seeman shared his excitement with me over his reading in the field of psychoneuroimmunology. He explained that research on the molecular level is concerned with the mechanism by which cells determine what is "me" and what is "not me." He said, "That sounded familiar to me, I'd heard that language before. Then I realized, why that's the same language we used in describing the self-construct in the process of therapy" (Seeman, personal communication, July, 1995). He explained that the immunologists were using the same language, but on different levels of organismic function. I think he appreciated that neuroscience confirmed a long-held hypothesis that the degree to which a person's self-construct

---

[1] Tracing the development of his own research, Seeman often stated that there was no real difference between Roger's phrase, "organic order" and his own, "organismic integration."

is organized is inextricably linked with a person's physical health: "At the basic organismic level, high-functioning persons are healthier, in terms both of longitudinal health history and daily functioning" (Seeman 1984, p. 151).

3.2 Connection and Communication

For Seeman, these two words hold the key to understanding organismic order and disorder. A consistent pattern emerged from his research; for therapists, making trustworthy connection and communicating with the "livingness" of the client is fundamental. Seeman (2002) saw clearly the "commanding role of communication in maintaining a healthy organism, and the key role of an open, fluid, and unimpeded communication system in maximizing effective human functioning" (p. 628). Conversely, dysfunction results from an organismic breakdown in either connection or communication. This understanding led him to develop his Human Systems Model of Psychotherapy.

Seeman posited that all of the psychopathology in the DSM can be traced to one of two sources, a breakdown of either connection or communication.[2] He explained, "A depressed person shuts down her whole system," is "half dead… out of touch with their digestive system …out of touch with their physiological system. They are not able to relax and put it to rest. They are often unable to sleep. The phobic person shuts out those things of which he is afraid. Does not seek experience. Says no to experience. The dissociative person… is disconnected with her own past" (Seeman, personal communication, 1995). Disorder occurs due to a breakdown of either connection or communication within the various subsystems of the organism.

His research and experience made it clear that the therapist's embodied relationship with the client is healing. What was previously disrupted is reconnected. Taft (1973), an early influence on Seeman, expresses that healing occurs, if at all, in this "one hour of present immediate relationship, however limited, with another human being who has brought himself to the point of asking for help" (p. 11).

Seeman frequently said to me, "Isn't it fortuitous that the things that client centered therapy does best are *exactly* the things that promote health and well-being?" His investigation showed that organismic order and health, as well as disorder and disease, rest on two intricately related constructs embedded in person-centered theory. Health results from an organismic-wide network of fully functioning connection and communication.

---

[2] Jules Seeman sent me a videotape of a talk he gave to graduate students about 20 years into his emeritus status from Vanderbilt University, in the late 1990s. The following quotes came from a recent transcript of that talk.

3.3 Toward Building a Bridge Between the PCA and Neuroscience

The construct of the organism in Rogers' theory provides a solid footing for a valuable bridge between theorists in both the person-centered and neuroscience fields concerned with unveiling the interconnected network of our human patterned complexity.

In the last decade, person-centered writers have been working to build this bridge. While some have drawn on the work of Damasio (Motschnig-Pitrik and Lux 2008), others have emphasized the work on empathy and mirror neurons (Bozarth 2009), and others focus on how neuroscience explains what happens to the brain in therapy, the potential for enhancing the education of therapists, the work of LeDoux, and other significant mutually beneficial points (Watson and Greenberg 2009; Dekeyser et al. 2009).

In his book, *The Neuroscience of Psychotherapy: Healing the Social Brain*, Cozolino (2010) notes that in Rogers' development of psychotherapy, Rogers was always implicitly guided by the principles of neuroscience. Discussing the evidence of the importance of infancy and childhood in shaping our emotional circuitry, Cozolino (2010) writes, "This research establishes attention, care, and nurturance as a way to influence the very structure of our brain" (p. 227). He (2010) notes that psychotherapy later in life becomes an effective biological intervention: "It is odd to think that Carl Rogers may someday find a place next to Crick and Watson in the pantheon of biologists" (p. 227).

4 Pert's Contributions

4.1 Neuronal Communication: Dynamics Govern Connections

Candace Pert began her career researching neurotransmitters and psychoactive drugs as a graduate student at Johns Hopkins University School of Medicine, under Solomon Snyder. She was the first to successfully measure and thus prove the existence of the opiate receptor. Prior to 1987, Pert served as the Director of the Clinical Neuroscience Branch of the National Institute of Mental Health (NIMH) and worked with the top researchers, including Miles Herkenham.[3]

According to Pert (1997), receptors were merely hypothesized to be "living somewhere in the cells of the body" (p. 21). Pert and Herkenham's work shocked

---

[3] Herkenham is now the Chief of the Functional Neuroanatomy Laboratory for NIMH and NIH conducting neuroimmune, neuroendocrinological, and other studies investigating psychosocial stress and environmental enrichment.

neuropharmacologists and other neuroscientists. It reversed researchers' belief that synaptic events occurred in a fixed location and that for receptors and peptides to be communicating across a synapse, they would need to be close together.

Herkenham found that "less than 2 % of neuronal communication actually occurs at the synapse" (Pert 1997, p. 139). Instead, he discovered that what *actually* mattered was the accuracy and specificity of the connections and communication being made.[4]

The receptor was found to be a single molecule composed of smaller units—atoms of carbon, hydrogen, and nitrogen—that come together in a configuration that can be expressed by a chemical formula. These receptor molecules react to various chemical cues by vibrating. Pert (1997) writes, "They wiggle, shimmy, and even hum as they bend and change from one shape to another, often moving back and forth between two or three favored shapes or conformations"(p. 22). More importantly, Pert (1997) explains that "these minute physiological phenomena at the cellular level can translate to large changes in behavior, physical activity, even mood" (p. 24).[5] As experienced client-centered therapists know, this process also occurs in therapy as clients feel increasingly free to wiggle and shimmy (sometimes literally) their way into different shapes or configurations of self-concepts.

According to Pert (1997), receptors work as "sensing molecules...They hover in the membranes of your cells, dancing and vibrating, waiting to pick up messages carried by other vibrating little creatures also made out of amino acids" (p. 23). The right chemical has to swim to the right keyhole: "It's sex on a molecular level" (Pert 1997, p. 23).

Pert's (1997) boldest claim was that opiate receptors, "the first component of the molecules of emotion (p. 21)," are diffused throughout the entire organism, suggesting that intelligence is not solely in our minds. She created the term "mobile brain" as an "apt description of the psychosomatic network where information travels" (p. 188).

According to Pert (1993), "molecules are being released from one place, they're diffusing all over the body, and they're tickling the receptors that are on the surface of every cell in your body" (p. 178). This research establishes that these receptors are distributed throughout the body, located in "far-flung areas" (Pert 1997, p. 139). She calls attention to the "astounding revelation" of endorphins found beyond the brain in the immune and endocrine systems. The phrase she uses is a "psychosomatic communication network" (Pert 1993, p. 178). Like Rogers and Seeman, Pert believes the term "network" most accurately describes organismic functioning.

---

[4] Elaborating the connections between this work and client-centered work on accurate empathic understanding by client-centered scholars (Rogers, Seeman, Brodley, Gendlin, and others) while beyond the scope of this chapter provides an obvious next step.

[5] This echoes Seeman's point that any change within any subsystem can alter the others (Seeman 1983).

4.2 Network in Pert's Research

Pert's most radical finding concerns the multi-focal and non-hierarchal nature of our intelligence. Regarding brain–body function Pert (1997) writes, "A network is different from a hierarchical structure that has a ruling 'station' at the top and a descending series of positions that play increasingly subsidiary roles… you can enter at any nodal point and quickly get to any other point; all locations are equal as far as the potential to 'rule' or direct the flow of information" (p. 186). This perfectly matches Seeman's description (2008) of all entry points being equal in terms of initial access to a person's entire organismic system and also supports Rogers' assertion that the client's direct access to organismic data makes that client the best guide for therapeutic direction.

Pert (1997) demonstrates "the interconnectedness of all systems of the organism" noting that this is a radical departure from the conventional neuroscientist's claims (p. 187). The mind is not separate from the body. "Mind does not dominate body, it *becomes* body—body and mind are one" (Pert 1997, p. 187).

Regarding persons as interdependent, non-hierarchal networks of communication still makes news. In the post-industrial West *being a body*, rather than "having" a body, is indeed a radical departure from the norm.

Starting with Rogers, leading person-centered scholars have already departed. They have embraced new conceptions of science (Bohart 1999; Bozarth 1985; Barrett-Lennard 1998; Coulson 1999; O'Hara and Wood 2004; Kriz 2006; Tudor 2006). Bozarth (1985) examines system theory and quantum physicist Frizof Capra's description of reality, "as an interconnected web of relations that is intrinsically dynamic" and its shared premises (p. 179). Jürgen Kriz (2006) considers it "quite remarkable" that mainstream psychology continues to use "mechanistic models of cause and effect and refers to principles and metaphors which became obscure in the natural sciences in the 20th century" (p. 195). He tells us that a half century of Nobel Prize recipients have demonstrated that humanistic/person-centered principles are more scientifically accurate and effective.

5 Contrasting Paradigms: Health, Disease, Power, and Influence

Client-centered theory and its philosophy appreciate each person as a "dynamic whole." Each person is seen as actively *being* "processes evolving toward complexity, differentiation, and more effective self/world creation" (Raskin et al. 2011, p. 40).This whole person perspective refutes psychology that breaks the person down "in terms of 'parts'—as problematic 'conflicts,' 'self-defeating' behaviors or 'irrational cognitions'" (Raskin et al. 2011, p. 40) and treats those *parts* in isolation. This medical model currently dominates psychology in the USA and elsewhere.

Raskin, Rogers, and Witty counter "Proponents of client-centered therapy see problems, disorders, and diagnoses as constructs that are generated by processes of social and political influence in the domains of psychiatry, pharmaceuticals and third party payers as much as by bona fide science" (Raskin et al. 2011, p. 171). A book review of *Evidence-Based Practices (EBPs) in Mental Health* by K. J. Sher is illustrative. Raskin et al. totally reject Sher's assertion "that therapists should model themselves after '…a thoracic surgeon, a criminal lawyer, an accountant, or even a structural engineer who evaluates how best to fix a home with a broken foundation'" (Raskin et al. 2011, p. 166).

Inevitably, humanistic discussions turn to sociopolitical policies challenging new paradigm values. Rogers consistently outlined the "challenges" and addressed the differences du jour.

Today, the challenges come from two separate, but related and mutually reinforcing forces: First, the epistemological orientation and policies of The American Psychological Association (APA), and second, the Pharmaceutical Corporation's profit-driven policies and marketing effects on neuroscience research.

The first force: Dominant divisions within the APA wield enormous power to define standard psychotherapy practice and to grant recognition of and accreditation to university programs they sanction. Unfortunately, their paradigm of choice remains rooted in the outdated models Kriz describes, instead of one recognizing our scientific uncertainties. Laws governing gravity better match mainstream psychology's views than those governing human suffering.

Bohart (2002) defines empirically supported treatments (EST) as having specific intervention for a specific disorder which is measured by a symptom-based assessment. That core premise of proscribing specific treatments for specific dysfunctions is fallacious, according to Bozarth (2000). Analyzing five decades of data regarding the credibility of diagnosis, and the pattern of psychotherapy outcome research, he found the evidence flawed beyond credulity.

Still in recent decades, the UK, USA, and Sweden all embraced guidelines for EBP. Functionally, only cognitive behavioral therapy (CBT) programs were accredited, and their clinicians licensed. But evidence is mounting that the EST/EBP have not resulted in the promised positive outcomes. According to Miller (2012), Sweden has just reversed its policy. He writes, "The experiment had failed. To be helped, people must have a choice" (para. 10).

Working on behalf of choice, the Humanistic Psychology Division (Division 32) of the APA formally challenged the Board revising the Diagnostic and Statistical Manual of Mental Disorders (DSM-5) in an "Open Letter" also posted online. The Coalition to Reform DSM-5 was created,[6] comprising mental health organizations critical of the proposed revisions. One noteworthy excerpt from that open letter reads,

---

[6] The committee was chaired by Division 32 President David Elkins. Members included Frank Farley, Jon Raskin, Brent Robbins, Donna Rockwell, and Sarah Kamens, who was the letter's primary author.

In light of the growing empirical evidence that neurobiology does not fully account for the emergence of mental distress, as well as new longitudinal studies revealing long-term hazards of standard neurobiological (psychotropic) treatment, we believe that these changes pose substantial risks to patients/clients, practitioners, and the mental health professions in general (Elkins 2012, para 3).

Of particular concern is this conflict of interest: A full 70 % of the DSM-5 Revision Board had research and/or financial ties to pharmaceutical companies.

According to Division 32 President Elkins (2012), the petition was covered by *The New York Times* and over 100 news media. It attracted 13,000 signatures, 45 mental health organizations endorsements (including 13 other APA divisions), and the British Psychological Society of nearly 50,000 members.

The second force: Pharmaceutical companies have been responsible for astonishing breakthroughs in the prevention and treatment of disease. Because of their investments in research and development, drugs like Penicillin, vaccines against Polio and many diseases, other drugs fight AIDS, cancers, and countless other conditions. This, however, does not obviate the need for critical analysis of the power and influence of the pharmaceutical companies, called "Big Pharma"[7] in defining mental health standard of care.

In 1997, lobbying efforts by Big Pharma succeeded when the US Food and Drug Administration (FDA) allowed "direct-to-consumer advertising" (DTCA). Television can and does advertise drugs for every bodily dysfunction conceivable. Central to the medicalization of distress movement is convincing consumers that scientific evidence is sound. Perhaps, this is the point most troubling to me. Antidepressant commercials typically show a simple representation of two points, A and B. The voice-over soothingly reassures the audience something like, "Depression is not your fault. It is due to a chemical imbalance." You take their brand pill and little bubbles float from Point A to Point B. Your chemical imbalance has been fixed. Your bubbles just needed to float a little.

When I first saw that commercial I heard Pert (1997) saying, "less than 2 % of neuronal communication actually occurs at the synapse" (p. 139). She came to understand, "There were numerous alternatives to the synaptic nerve hookups that once seemed indispensable for mind–body communication, and we were beginning to learn what was getting communicated through those connections" (p. 140). Her view of the brain could never be the same again. She was beginning to see the whole organism in its stunning complexity. This is not how Big Pharma wants me to think about how their products work. My view of the pharmaceutical companies could never be the same again.

Increasingly, drug companies use their corporate wealth to lobby policymakers to designate an alarming array of human problems as psychiatric disorders. According to the Center for Responsive Politics, between 1998 and 2005, they spent over $900 million dollars lobbying government agencies. This was more

---

[7] Big Pharma refers to Pharmaceutical Research and Manufacturers of America (PhRMA) and Biotechnology Industry Organization. These are two trade groups representing the top 20 pharmaceutical companies engaged in intensive lobbying of lawmakers and medical groups.

than any other industry in the USA. They have the financial means. In 2002, the top ten drug companies earned more profits than all the rest of the Fortune 500 companies *combined* (emphasis mine) (Angell 2004).

Medicine, psychiatry, and psychology have become reliant on and beholden to the pharmaceutical industry for information on recent scientific breakthroughs, continuing education, research funding, and free "gifts" actually incentives to develop brand loyalty.

These forces combine to create a phenomenon often called, "the medicalization of distress." Pete Sanders writes that, "many decades ago psychology got fatally tangled with the medical model, diagnosis and the medicalization of distress" (personal communication, July, 2008). As Robbins (2012) writes, "pharmaceutical giants have the power and means to invent disorders in order to expand their market share" (p. 32).

One particular revision to the DSM became a lightening rod organizing the previously diffuse electricity surrounding the Boards considerable power. The proposal would designate "sadness" as a psychiatric disorder. The flare of publicity generated great heat and some light. Since no one in life escapes sadness, this one proposal provoked public debate.

An example from Robbins (2012) describes how psychiatrists have shifted their practices. Given the financial constraints of managed care, with less time to spend with patients, receiving less compensation for the patients they see, and with the "escalating costs of medical education and malpractice insurance" (pp. 32, 33). It is easy to understand how mental health professionals could "gravitate to reductive, biological explanations of human suffering that narrow treatment to symptoms checklists and drug prescriptions" (Robbins 2012, p. 32). Robbins (2012) calls these "impoverished practices" that "disproportionately harm the weakest and most vulnerable" (p. 33).

It could be argued that these examples show more author bias than the state of mental health practice. As I reflected on this question, about to submit this manuscript, I read this breaking news from *The New York Times*:

> In the largest settlement involving a pharmaceutical company, the British drugmaker GlaxoSmithKline agreed to plead guilty to criminal charges and pay $3 billion in fines for promoting its best-selling antidepressants for unapproved uses and failing to report safety data about a top diabetes drug, federal prosecutors announced pm Monday. The agreement also includes civil penalties for improper marketing of a half-dozen other drugs (Thomas and Schmidt 2012, para 1).
>
> In the case of the antidepressant Paxil, the prosecutors proved the company used illegal means to market the drug to children, including "helping to publish a medical journal article that misreported data from a clinical trial" (Thomas and Schmidt 2012, para 10). Prosecutors say the $3 billion fine will be of little to no deterrent, since Paxil *alone* brought in $11.6 billion in profit in the past year. "Do no harm" may be the essence of the Hippocratic Oath, but excessive profiteering is the essence of Big Pharma when permitted unrestrained and unregulated powers.

6 Summary

The central themes and theoretical foundation of the person-centered approach advanced by Rogers and colleagues represent an intricate and powerful paradigm for understanding health and wellness. They understood the complexity of the organism's tenacious tendency to maintain and enhance health, wellness, and optimal functioning, as well as the way it becomes disorganized and dysfunctional.

Research by Rogers discovered the precise nutrients required for this organism, called the person, to become fully functioning. Seeman elaborated on the connection between organic order and health. Their findings are corroborated by the emerging neuroscientific research I have discussed. Neuroscience provides the groundbreaking knowledge that previous person-centered researchers could not.

This research, the resurgence of complimentary medical therapies, and mind–body approaches facilitating the "wiggle and hum" of organismic movement confirm the core findings of Rogers et al. and strengthen the place of the person-centered approach beyond the world of psychotherapy and among those advancing mind–body connectedness.

And, although these factors face these friendly facts, we are temporally bound, historically bound, and contextually bound. All these factors challenge our organismic integrity. Seeman (1984) said it well, "In our complex culture the chances for intrapsychic disturbance...are manifold" (p. 146). Inside and outside of therapy, how do we embody our organismic integrity? I believe we must develop our networks. Be in connection and communication. Cultivate our whole body-beingness, our organismic integrity, and what Natiello (2001) calls our "passionate presence."

This emerging paradigm offers us a potent theoretical counterforce to outdated and restrictive mental health policies, one capable of reshaping health policies and services. It remains to be seen whether or not we combine our parallel forces to advocate for more organismically natural and non-toxic ways of healing human dysfunction. Can we reframe public policy to move away from the medicalization of distress and from further dependence on forces driven by corporate profit motives? Can we find creative strategies to push back against the dualistic and entrenched academic, medical, and pharmaceutical forces to better serve science and our interdependent communities?

I am entirely certain Carl Rogers would be highly engaged in finding solutions for these questions. Then, he might ask, "I wonder what we will be able to do together?"

References

Angell, M. (2004). *The truth about drug compainies: How they deceive us and what to do about it*. New York: Random House

Barrett-Lennard, G. T. (1998). *Carl Rogers' helping system: Journey and substance*. London: Sage Publications Ltd.

Bohart, A. C. (1999). *How clients make therapy work: The process of active self-healing.* Washington, DC: American Psychological Association.

Bohart, A. C. (2002). A passionate critique of empirically supported treatments and the provision of an alternative paradigm. In J. C. Watson, R. N. Goldman, & M. Warner (Eds.), *Client-centered and experiential psychotherapy in the twenty-first century: Advances in theory, research and practice.* Ross-on-Wye: PCCS Books.

Bohm, D. (1980). *Wholeness and the implicate order.* London: Rutledge & Kegan Paul.

Bozarth, J. (1985). Quantum theory and the person-centered approach. *Journal of Counseling and Development, 64*(3), 179–182.

Bozarth, J. (2000, August). *The Specificity Myth: The fallacious premise of mental health treatment.* Paper presentation at the American Psychological Association, Washington, DC.

Bozarth, J. D. (2009). Rogerian empathy in an organismic theory: A way of being. In J. Decety & W. Ickes (Eds.), *The social neuroscience of empathy* (pp. 101–112). Cambridge, MA: The MIT Press.

Coulson, A. (1999). Experiences of separateness and unity in person-centered groups. In C. Lago & M. MacMillian (Eds.), *Experiences in relatedness: Groupwork and the person-centered approach* (pp. 167–180). Ross-on-Wye: PCCS Books.

Cozolino, L. (2010). *The neuroscience of psychotherapy: Healing the social brain.* New York: W. W. Norton & Company, Inc.

Dekeyser, M., Elliot, R., & Leijssen, M. (2009). Empathy in psychotherapy: Dialogue and embodied understanding. In J. Decety & W. Ickes (Eds.), *The social neuroscience of empathy* (pp. 113–124). Cambridge, MA: The MIT Press.

Division 32 Committee on DSM-5. (n.d.). *Open letter to the DSM-5 task force (Official Version).* Retrieved June 10, 2012, from http://dsm5-reform.com/the-open-letter-to-dsm-5-task-force/.

Elkins, D. (2012). *Society for humanistic psychology newsletter | April 2012 a President's letter.* Retrieved June 10, 2012, from http://www.apadivisions.org/division-32/publications/newsletters/humanistic/2012/04/presidents-key-achievements.aspx.

Kirschenbaum, H. (2009). *The life and work of Carl Rogers.* Alexandria, VA: American Counseling Association.

Kirschenbaum, H., & Henderson, V. (1989b). *The Carl Rogers reader.* Boston: Houghton Mifflin Company.

Kriz, J. (2006). *Self-actualization.* Norderstedt: BoD.

Miller, S. D. (2012). *Revolution in Swedish mental health practice: The cognitive behavioral therapy monopoly gives way.* Retrieved May 15, 2012, from http://www.scottdmiller.com/?q=node%2F160&goback=.gde_53475_member_125725759.

Motschnig-Pitrik, R., & Lux, M. (2008). The person centered approach meets neuroscience: Mutual support of C.R. Roger's and A. Damasio's theories. *Journal of Humanistic Psychology, 48*(3), 287–319.

Natiello, P. (2001). *The person-centered approach: A passionate presence.* Ross-on-Wye: PCCS Books.

O'Hara, M., & Wood, J. K. (2004). Transforming communities: Person-centered encounters and the creation of the integral, conscious groups. In B. H. Banathy & P. M. Jenlink (Eds.), *Dialogue as a means of collective communication.* New York: Kluwer Academic/Plenum Publishers.

Pert, C. (1993). The chemical communicators. In B. Moyers (Ed.), *Healing and the mind* (pp. 177–193). New York: Doubleday.

Pert, C. (1997). *Molecules of emotion: Why you feel the way you feel.* New York: Scribner.

Raskin, N. J., Rogers, C. R., & Witty, M. C. (2011). Client-centered therapy. In R. J. Corsini & D. Wedding (Eds.), *Current psychotherapies* (pp. 148–200). Belmont, CA: Brooks/Cole Cengage Learning.

Robbins, B. D. (2012). From ice pick lobotomies to antipsychotics as sleep aids for children: A historical perspective. In S. Olfman & B. D. Robbins (Eds.), *Drugging our children: How profiteers are pushing antipsychotics on our youngest, and what we can do to stop it* (pp. 17–33). Santa Barbara, CA: Praeger.

Rogers, C. R. (1959). A theory of therapy, personality, and interpersonal relationships, as developed in the client-centered framework. In S. Koch (Ed.), *Psychology: A study of a science, Vol. 3: Formulations of the person and the social context* (pp. 184–256). New York: McGraw-Hill.

Rogers, C. R. (1961). *On Becoming a Person: A therapist's view of psychotherapy*. Boston: Houghton Mifflin.

Rogers, C. R. (1964). Toward a science of the person. In T. Wann (Ed.), *Behaviorism and phenomenology, contrasting bases for modern psychology* (pp. 109–140). Chicago: University of Chicago Press.

Rogers, C. R. (1978) The emerging person: A new revolution. Unpublished manuscript "for private circulation only". Later published as Rogers (1980). *The world of tomorrow, and the person of tomorrow. A way of being*. Boston: Houghton Mifflin.

Rogers, C. R. (1980). *A way of being*. Boston: Houghton Mifflin.

Rogers, C. R. (1983). *Freedom to learn for the 80's*. Columbus, OH: Charles E Merrill Publishing.

Rose, S. (2009). *Prospects and perils of the new brain sciences: a twenty year timescale*. Retrieved from Resource Document. Royal Society Science Policy Lab. http://www.stevenroseonline.net/SPRR/Welcome_files/Royal%20Society.pdf. Accessed 27 June 2012.

Seeman, J. (1983). *Personality integration: Studies and reflections*. New York: Human Sciences Press.

Seeman, J. (1984). The fully-functioning person. In R. Levant & J. Shlien (Eds.), *Client-centered therapy and the person-centered approach: New directions in theory, research, and practice* (pp. 131–152). New York: Prager.

Seeman, J. (2002). Looking back, looking ahead: A synthesis. In D. Cain & J. Seeman (Eds.), *Humanistic psychotherapies: Handbook of research and practice* (pp. 617–636). Washington, DC: American Psychological Association.

Seeman, J. (2008). *Psychotherapy and the full functioning person*. Bloomington: AuthorHouse.

Taft, J. (1973). *The dynamics of therapy in a controlled relationship*. Gloucester, MA: Peter Smith.

Thomas, K., & Schmidt, M. (2012, July 2). Glaxo agrees to pay $3 billion in fraud settlement. *The New York Times*. Retrieved from http://www.nytimes.com/2012/07/03/business/glaxosmithkline-agrees-to-pay-3-billion-in-fraud-settlement.html?adxnnl=1&emc=eta1&adxnnlx=1341417739-k5/aTLErslxeUFa+cWsr9A.

Tudor, K., & Worrall, M. (2006). *Person-centred therapy: A clinical philosophy*. London: Routledge.

Watson, J. C., & Greenberg, L. S. (2009). Empathic resonance: A neuroscience perspective. In J. Decety & W. Ickes (Eds.), *The social neuroscience of empathy* (pp. 125–138). Cambridge, MA: The MIT Press.

Wolter-Gustafson, C. (1999). Power of the premise: Reconstructing gender and human development with Rogers' theory. In I. Fairhurst (Ed.), *Women Writing in the Person-Centred Approach* (pp. 199–214). Ross-on-Wye: PCCS Books.

Wolter-Gustafson, C. (2008a). Casting a wider empathic net: A case for reconsidering gender, dualistic thinking and person-centered theory and practice. *Person-Centered and Experiential Psychotherapies, 7*(2), 95–109.

Wolter-Gustafson, C. (2008b). Non-dualism and non-directivity: A person-centered concept of health and the fully functioning person. In B. Levitt (Ed.), *Reflections on human potential. Bridging the person-centered approach and positive psychology* (pp. 147–160). Ross-on-Wye: PCCS Books.

Mindfulness, Authentic Connection, and Making "Right" Decisions: Using Neuroscience to Build a Bridge with the Person-Centered Approach

David Ryback

What common basis bridges Carl Rogers' version of empathy and calm mindfulness? If we can consolidate all of the values inherent in both the PCA and mindfulness to be described below, then deep, authentic presence seems to be the common denominator—awareness, both of self and others, and the role of mirror neurons as we influence one another; non-judgmental acceptance; and congruence between mind and body, including the ability to be more fully aware of our thoughts and feelings in the process referred to as meta-cognition, or recursion—thinking about our thoughts. What approach can we consider to better understand the characteristics involved? In this chapter, we look at some of the practical applications—how to approach our social world with authenticity. Looking at a simple model of brain function, we explore bridging the PCA to mindfulness—with the following common elements:

1. becoming more authentic in our communication,
2. taking into consideration others' needs and perspectives,
3. approaching a state of calm mastery with the normal challenges of life, and
4. experiencing the grace of living authentically.

Using mindfulness in person-centered interaction is in part the ability to communicate using the appropriate balance of logic and emotion in making the best decisions while interacting with others. This was one of Carl Rogers' great contributions to our culture.

1 The Musical Mindfulness of Carl Rogers

What Carl Rogers (1951) brought to the table, over half a century ago, was the ability to listen in such a way that the speaker—initially in psychotherapy (1942), but subsequently in classrooms, politics, and organizations (1977)—felt heard in a deep

D. Ryback (✉)
1534 N. Decatur Road, Suite 201, Atlanta GA 30307-1022, USA
e-mail: David@EQassociates.com

and authentic sense. Rogers eventually consolidated his approach to include unconditional positive regard, a type of love and acceptance that required no reciprocation; "congruence," or authenticity, the need to be true to one's inner values and emotionally felt experience, and, of course, empathy (Grobler et al. 2003).

The influence of Carl Rogers greatly surpasses what we commonly acknowledge in the curricula of psychology courses. Arguably, Rogers (1951, 1990) may be one of the most influential individuals to affect how we communicate with one another, spanning the areas of psychotherapy, education (Rogers and Freiberg 1983), as well as commerce (Ryback 1998, 2010, p. 26); and even politics, tackling both civil unrest and international conflict (Rogers and Ryback 1984).

1.1 Carl Rogers on Resolving Conflict by Being Mindful of Others

In any conflict or negotiation, no matter how intense, even between warring factions, Carl Rogers highlighted the importance of understanding the other's perspective as clearly as possible. He then focused on the need to articulate that awareness so the other knew he'd made the effort. It didn't always solve the problem, particularly in the early stages, but it sure beat a more conventional approach of coming in with fists flying, proverbially speaking. And sometimes it worked wonders (Ryback 1999).

No matter how adversarial our opponent might be, Rogers maintained, the more we can immerse ourselves in his or her culture—linguistic framework, way of thinking, preferences—without losing our own style or authenticity, the greater our chances of succeeding in resolving whatever conflict is taking place. Not only will our mindfulness be enhanced—we'll understand much more—but also will our performance. We'll find ourselves much more successful in being heard—in part, because we've taken the effort to respect our opponent's framework of values. If we can approach this adversarial situation with helpful, cooperative mindfulness—using our PCA values rather than with defensive aggression—then the other party will be much more likely to meet us more than halfway, with a minimum of exacerbating conflict (Ryback 2011, pp. 415–416).

1.2 Mindfulness

Mindfulness, as developed by Kabat-Zinn (2005), is a powerful approach to mental and physical healthy lifestyle and can be described as an attitude of open acceptance and witnessing of one's own perceptions and sensibilities—accompanied, according to Lilienfeld and Arkowitz (2008), by a somewhat higher frequency of alpha waves in the brain. It "helps increase our experiences of being in a calm, relaxed and yet alert state of mind that, in most ways, is the opposite of how we feel when anxious or stressed...to be aware of our thoughts without identifying with them or allowing them to 'take over,' which can increase our capacity for introspection" (Ladner 2005, p. 19).

In the last decade or so, there has been increasing interest in understanding how our brains settle into this peaceful mind-set (setting the mind into a settled state). The neuroscience of mindfulness explores the workings of the brain struggling to achieve such a peaceful state (e.g., Burgdorf et al. 2011; Watt 2007; Wright and Panskepp 2011). One of the more spectacular findings is how the brain is reconstructed by intense positive or negative experience (Akirav and Richter-Levin 2002). This concept of brain plasticity—as espoused by Siegel (2005)—reminds us how important it is to be at peace with our everyday experience, in order to keep our brain as healthy as possible and not yield to the temptation of total immersion in electronic communication, where we isolate ourselves from one another and choose the keyboard as our primary means of communication.

1.3 Mindfulness and the PCA in the Age of Electronic Communication

We hear so much about the need for listening skills, particularly from potential employers, relationship experts, educators, and psychotherapists. As we progress in the mechanization of communication, it appears that all this possibility of connecting so well on a person-to-person basis is being displaced by the growing trend to spend more and more time communicating through cell phones, e-mail, Facebook, Twitter, including Skype. It appears that virtual, electronic interaction has taken priority over real, face-to-face sharing.

We've gone through the "Age of Freud, the Existential Self, the Therapeutic Self...the Me Generation, the Culture of Narcissism," writes Siegel (2009), author of *Against the MACHINE*. We're becoming addicted to "electronic" validation, forgetting the joys of authentic, in-person communication. We live narcissistically in our heads more than ever before, he maintains. More and more, especially among the younger generation, we choose to "dial up" our thoughts on blogs rather than interact in two-way conversation. The finding that "nearly 75 % of college students today rate themselves as less empathetic than the average college student did 30 years ago" (Zaki 2011, p. 14) may have something to do with that. To paraphrase John Lennon, bringing this well-versed dictum up-to-date, Life is what happens while you're busy doing other things on the Net.

Virtually (dare I use that word?) every one of us uses the Internet on a daily basis, sometimes many times in a day. To find out what? To see if friends have written us, to get information we need about our lives, to reach out for greater intimacy of varying degrees. At our neighborhood coffeehouse, where books were once read, now we see laptops—people reaching out to millions of potential "friends" across the globe. Some refer to cyberspace as the new home of the mind

(Levine 2011). What was initially a fun way of interacting with others without being in their physical presence has, in too many cases, become an addiction (Linden 2011).

Yet what we're all searching for is that sense of connection that makes life meaningful. Since it's such a challenge to create deep connections with others in our busy lifestyles, especially as electronic invitations to virtual relationships vie for our free time, opportunities for deeply meaningful, personal, face-to-face connections become more elusive. According to neuroscientist John Cacioppo, "Nearly all the initial studies about people who used the Internet for social interaction suggested that they were getting lonelier" (cited by DiSalvo 2010, p. 50).

We use the term "virtual" so freely now that its true meaning seems to evade our understanding. "Virtual," according to Webster's Dictionary (1987), is defined as "being something specified in essence or effect though not in name" (p. 1100, from the old French word, *virtualis*)—in other words, specifying something in terms of effect rather than in terms of fact. So, virtual electronic communication feels like full communication but is not really what it purports to be. We feel as if we're "really" communicating on the Internet but, in fact, that communication is not real since we are not in the physical presence of that person. We can't use our natural senses to connect—no three-dimensional view, no smell, no touch, and usually not in real time. Electronic chats can be delayed—even less than a second long delay has implications for person-to-person contact.

The ubiquity of virtual communication makes actual communication all the more desirable and potentially satisfying. That's why the PCA and mindfulness are becoming more important to those whose reliance on virtual communication has approached becoming an addiction. And gaining a sense of inner calm, one of the aims and benefits of psychotherapy, is increasingly sought after. Mindfulness and the PCA both provide means to actual communication, whether with one's self-in-context (as in meditation and psychotherapy) or with "different" others. A primary principle of the PCA is the yielding of ego to allow for a greater awareness of the other with whom we aspire to connect and whose mind we hope to get into, despite the fact that "our own epistemic baggage encumbers such entry" (Hutson 2012, p. 169).

1.4 Improvising on the Music of PCA

One way to do so is to focus more and more on an empathic approach to the world, allowing our ego to yield to the benefit of the "bigger picture," beginning with those closest to us and ending with all of life, including the welfare of the Earth itself (Neville 2012). Empathy in the PCA can be defined as the delicate, yet powerful, option of allowing mental images and/or emotion sensations of the other's shared or observed experiences to emerge within oneself. I believe there are five stages to this process:

1. Hearing: Listening closely to what is heard, putting what you see/hear into some meaningful context belonging to the other.
2. Inner reflection: Allowing the basic emotion—hurt, anger, sorrow, etc.—to merge with cognitive awareness, yet without judgment, as an in-the-moment experience with the other.
3. Movement: Considering whether this understanding is accurate in terms of the other's experience and, if possible, obtaining feedback from the other as to the accuracy.
4. Framing: Placing this feeling and awareness in the context of the other's in-the-moment experience.
5. Responding: Taking the opportunity (if possible) to check for accuracy of the emotion/awareness once again or, in the alternative, acting in such a manner as to deepen the shared emotion by commitment to connecting with the other by offering support in one form or another, either in words or in actions. (For a viable definition of what is meant by "emotion," please see Eide 2009; Johnson-Laird and Oatley 1992.)

In many ways, empathy at its best can be compared to improvised jazz. "Jazz music," according to Marsalis (2001), "is about communication and connection." Both PCA empathy and jazz have the following:

1. The invitation to improvise—in jazz, among musicians; in conversation, between the two parties. Rogers (1986) puts it this way: "In person-centered therapy, the person is free to choose any direction" (p. 197).
2. Progress of possibilities continues until there is a cohesive theme—in jazz, a shared melody; in conversation, an entrainment of body and mind in both individuals. According to Rogers (1980), "being sensitive, moment to moment, to the changing felt meanings which flow in this other person" (p. 142).
3. An openness leading to togetherness that requires the combination of both skill and creative openness—in jazz, musical technique; in conversation, providing the underlying structure (Barrett-Lennard 1990; Rice and Greenberg 1990).
4. The openness to, and growing respect for, an emerging process of mutual sharing that is new and fulfilling—in jazz, responding to each of the other musician's unique creativity; in conversation, openness to new learning about self and other, daring to transcend the normal bounds of traditional interaction, building on a mutuality of growing shared affect. In Rogers' (1986) words, "a directional tendency inherent in the human organism—a tendency to grow, to develop, to realize its full potential" (p. 197).

Recent research, it turns out, reveals that musical improvisation involves the same part of the brain—the medial prefrontal cortex (MPFC), often referred to as the "self-expression area"—as does talking about oneself (Minkel 2008).

1.5 Nurturing a Happier Brain with Both PCA and Mindfulness

What PCA therapy and Kabat-Zinn's version of mindfulness (2005) both have in common is the aim of achieving a happier, more relaxed state of mind as a by-product of non-judgmental openness. The search for inner and long-lasting happiness, according to Matthieu Ricard (2006), a Buddhist monk and author of *Happiness*, "requires sustained effort in training the mind and developing a set of human qualities, such as inner peace, mindfulness, and altruistic love" (p. 8). This "sustained effort," whether in the form of inner discipline, such as meditation or mindfulness training, or "training" with a therapist, "can alter the structure of the patient's brain," according to Richard Restak (1997), most likely involving "the ability to change the synaptic connections within the brain" (Jenkins 1999). Nowhere is this effect greater—at least in my experience—than when the connection between client-centered therapist and client is deep and fully emotionally engaging (Ryback 2001).

There is a growing literature of research on deep empathy—referred to as linking (Rowan 1986), mutual empathy (Jordan et al. 1991), melding (Sterling and Bugental 1993), authentic knowing (Puhakka 2000) and relational depth, "when each person's words seem to flow from the other's and all self-consciousness is lost" (Mearns and Cooper 2005, p. 11).

Damasio (1994) traces this pathway through the brain and outlines each stage to help us understand and experience it. In the first stage, the therapist identifies the client's emotional affect and chooses some past memory to evoke a similar emotion. The next step involves letting that feeling deepen to form an "acquired dispositional representation" (Damasio 1994, p. 136), allowing the mental image to blend with the physical, emotional reaction. Mind and body are now innervating one another. In the final, third stage, the new and old brains are working in concert as the frontal cortex and limbic system together create the feeling that most resonates with that of the client. This bodily sensation, I deduce, allows the therapist to authentically communicate his/her mutual sharing of a common experience in the moment, expressed by facial expression and other non-verbal aspects along with the reassuring words.

Ultimately, by choosing to engage in such "deep" psychotherapy, or through the discipline of mindfulness, we can take more responsibility for the welfare of our brain. Learning about the neuroscience of deep therapy with Damasio's (1994) description of the steps involved, we can reach for the best function of our most prolific organ that 3-pound marvel of human expression. Becoming mindful about the neuroscience of mindfulness (in the process known as *recursion*, to be discussed later) is devoutly to be desired. When appropriately experienced, both the person-centered approach to communication and mindfulness reduce the need for hiding behind a defensive ego and help us approach a state that can be characterized by humility and grace.

2 The Neuroanatomy of Mindfulness and Recursion

So, let's take a moment for a brief overview of brain function. The new brain, the most recently evolved part, is where thought, planning, and mental control reside. Here is where we choose clear, authentic communication whenever person-centered therapy or negotiation is called for.

As we go through this section, an important thing to keep in mind about the human brain is the distinction between knowing and feeling. The front of the brain, more specifically, the prefrontal cortex, behind the forehead, is the area in which logical thinking arises. This is where decision making of a conscious nature takes place.

Feelings, on the other hand, are much more complex as far as brain anatomy is concerned. Feelings are likely to be generated in the center of the brain, known as the limbic system, including certain small structures of the brain such as the amygdala, which is situated on either side of the brain, close to where our ears are located, and which gives birth to certain intense emotions. Other parts of the emotional brain include the hippocampus (a curved structure along a vertical plane at the center of the brain), which is integral to memory by helping to consolidate it, and the hypothalamus (at the lower end), which is involved with sexual and other basic appetites. It is all much more complex than this simple description, but at least that gives us a starting point.

A new model for the generation of emotion proposes that emotions actually begin "in the midbrain, especially a region known as the periaqueductal gray (PAG), or 'central gray' as it used to be called" (Panksepp and Biven 2012, p. 2). Accordingly, emotional affect begins here and moves through the basal ganglia (or limbic system) and finally to the frontal cortex.

Nor should it be forgotten that within the context of these basic components of the brain is an incredibly complex network, where over a hundred billion neurons connect over a hundred trillion synapses. And, according to a number of researchers, referred to collectively as associationists (e.g., Marcus 1998, 2001), learning takes place when perceptual experience affects existing synchronized neural connections to make them stronger. In his book, *How the Mind Works*, Pinker (1997) refers to the cerebral process as *Connectoplasm*, which takes into consideration how we embed concepts within one another.

2.1 Recursion: Dissecting Our Discussion About That Therapy Session

Consciousness—more specifically, meta-cognition or symbolization, characterized by Nicholas Humphrey as a magic show we stage inside our heads, in his book, *Soul Dust* (2011)—appears to be a uniquely human characteristic, though some (Bering 2010) question whether or not chimpanzees share that attribute with humans. "Theory of mind" refers to the ability to think about what others think and the ability to verbalize such experience in specific, descriptive terms is definitely uniquely human. Also uniquely human is the desire and aspiration to understand the entirety of the universe and our place in it, what Einstein called "comprehensibility." In the book, *The Quantum Universe* (Cox and Forshaw 2012), Einstein maintains that the eternal mystery of the world is its comprehensibility and that the human ability to aspire to comprehend something so much infinitely greater than ourselves is indeed a miracle.

How can the human brain, evolved in a world of finite boundaries, consider the totality of the universe with its own finite boundaries, and, if there are no universal boundaries, how does a material entity, such as the universe, go on forever and ever and ever? In that sense, the meta-cognition process derived in consciousness, including mindfulness, knows no bounds. But the base of all such conscious processes begins with self-awareness or openness to experiences. As Rogers put it: "When I trust a person and try to facilitate his learning, whether in therapy or in education or in encounter group or whatever, I am trying to make it easier for that person *to be open to what's going on within*—the feelings and reaction and so on that he's having...In my mind the person most to be trusted...is the person who is most open to his experiences, both inner and outer" (Cited in Ryback 1989, p. 101, italics added). Being open to "symbolizing" the "infinite" possibilities in the universe begins with the person's self-awareness.

Openness to experiences, or self-awareness, can grow with therapy and is also an inherent component of mindfulness. We can verbalize about our consciousness as well, both in PCA communication (to our therapist) and in mindfulness (to ourselves). Then, after our therapy session, for example, we can verbalize to a close friend, about our experience of that last session. When we share our experiences in the process of therapy with our therapist (let's call this Concept$_1$) and then discuss the therapy in which we talk about it with a close friend over coffee (Concept$_2$), and later wonder, to ourselves, about that discussion about the therapy (Concept$_3$), etc., then we have what Pinker calls "recursion." Webster (1987) defines "recursive" as "capable of being used again, or of being returned to after an interruption" (p. 835).

Pinker's concept of recursion has interesting ramifications for mindfulness, with which we embed our experience of life into our awareness of that experience. Mindfulness is, in essence, our ability to embed certain experiences within an added layer of awareness. It is that added awareness, sometimes referred to as meta-cognition or "open-monitoring meditation" (Reiner 2009), which may give us a sense of control over unpleasant experiences, such as anxiety or anger. It is a unique feature of the human brain to engage in such additional levels of awareness, largely executed in the prefrontal cortex.

I would argue further that recursion is the process in which person-centered therapy takes place (see p. 6). In this case, the therapist embeds the narrative of the client into a framework that allows the emotional and meaningful character of that narrative to unfold fully and then offers that recursion back to the client for consideration. The client's original story is now embedded in the therapist's more nuanced account. The emotion need not be stated overtly; it may be reflected in the therapist's body language, tone of voice, choice of words, etc. But what is going on in the brain as this process unfolds? Let us take a close look at the anatomy of the brains of these two engaging in the process of person-centered therapy.

2.2 Neuroanatomy and Recursion in PCA and Mindfulness

For those who enjoy having a three-dimensional picture of the brain, consider a fist within a boxing glove. The wrist can be seen as the cerebellum and brain stem (responsible for basic functions such as heartbeat, breathing, walking gait), the hand and fingers as the emotional limbic system, and the glove itself as the perceiving, thinking, and motor cerebral cortex. ["Cortex" comes from modern Latin *corticalis*, referring to shell (Webster 1987, p. 219)]. The frontal cortex, or frontal lobes, just behind the forehead, where conscious reasoning and planning take place, makes up about a third of the entire cortex.

On the inside lining of the top of the glove—the medial prefrontal cortex (MPFC)—roughly, lie the anterior cingulate cortex and the orbitofrontal cortex, important in decision making; and, nearby, the insular cortex and the subcortical striatum, concerned with self-relevant information. On either side of the glove is the amygdalae—almond-shaped structures that play a significant role in the processing of emotions.

The discovery of the importance of this small structure residing on both sides of the head—the amygdala—where we process new perceptions that might be frightening, helps us to understand how all new people we meet, including new clients and associates, can be seen as threats. When the threat is great enough (where we to be suddenly and aggressively attacked, whether physically or verbally), we may have "amygdala hijack," when the threatening information goes directly to the amygdalae, short-circuiting the thinking frontal cortex, resulting in a "thoughtless" or irrational impulsive reaction (LeDoux 2004).

Though some find this split-mind characterization too simplistic, it has been widely accepted by a number of others that the right side of our frontal cortex, though only part of our consciousness, is more geared to creativity, spatiality, music, etc., while the left part of the frontal cortex provides the logical function. In his book, *Thinking, Fast and Slow* (2011), Daniel Kahneman describes such complementary functions as System 1—responding automatically and emotionally, acting on the basis of Malcom Gladwell's concept of *Blink* (2005)—and System 2—the slower, conscious "active mind," the thinking "decider" function. In similar fashion, Epstein (1994) divided the brain into an intuitive system—quick, associative, emotional and automatic, and a rational system—slow, deliberate, logical and abstract, much like Kahneman's division.

John Coates, Research Fellow at the University of Cambridge, discovered that when we feel we are winning at some risk (what he terms "the winner effect"), rational System 2 can give way to an erroneous, intuitive System 1 when "our biology can overreact and our risk taking can become pathological"...with increased "confidence and appetite for risk" when a series of successful decisions "morphs into overconfidence" (2012, p. 18). He uses this to explain how biology (System 1, likely a linking between the limbic system and the right brain) can explain what drives bankers (or gamblers) to the brink of disaster.

Again, this is an oversimplification of a very complex dynamic, but gives us an idea as to how the two parts of the frontal cortex—left and right—can interact optimally to provide the right balance of intuition and logic, components of mindfulness. In both the PCA and mindfulness, as we will see, recursion involves the best cooperation between these two parts of the frontal cortex as well as between the entire frontal cortex and the emotional limbic system.

When we experience recursion in mindfulness and also use it in the process of awareness during therapy, both functions of our brain—the logical and the emotional—take part. However, when we totally disengage from either one, then we get into trouble. If we operate from emotion alone, then we have problems with social appropriateness. When we operate from logic without any consideration of emotion, then we have rigidity and lack of empathy.

2.3 Potential Cerebral Dynamics of Making the "Right" Decision

The insular cortex, mentioned above, is the site at which information from both thinking and feeling parts of the brain, including both hemispheres of the cortex, come together in this neural "home" of organismic valuing process (Craig 2009). This flow of information connects with the incoming perceptual data in the moment (visual and auditory, even olfactory and tactile) and then culminates in a sense of the "right" decision in terms of responding to that particular set of circumstances, ranging from anxiety (Paulus and Stein 2006) to empathy (Xue et al. 2010). This is best accomplished when we have a full experience of mindfulness, because then we have the benefit of recursion, an added level of awareness allowing for a clarity and greater accuracy of interpreting these data.

At that moment of decision, when the insular cortex is processing information (Panksepp and Biven 2012, p. 2–5), when our brain is "focused enough to make a split-second decision: when to put a scalpel into a patient, when to execute a stock trade, when to make a putt on the 18th green" (Cloud 2011, p. 52), we tend to absorb as many emotional cues as we can to further our mindful awareness. In a blossoming romance, we might look at our partner's eyes to clarify the authenticity of his/her loving statements. In a tight moment of negotiation, we might look at the facial expression and body language of our adversaries.

The information now travels from the insular cortex to the frontal cortex, and with mindfulness engaged to connect with our emotional sensations, we make our decision (Grosenick et al. 2008). Recursion is the conscious process of considering multiple appropriate responses and, more important, learning from our past mistakes so as not to repeat them. That is what therapy helps us do as well, in a controlled environment, dedicated to that end.

Therapists can even help their clients to master undesirable behaviors by pointing out the importance of the recursive self-awareness aspects of mindfulness. Such awareness can actually help clients take control of their behaviors. A less active prefrontal cortex, according to Davidson et al. (2000), can be associated with difficulty in inhibiting violent behaviors, while a more active one tends to give us more control over unwanted behaviors. The connections between the "mindful" frontal lobes and the emotional limbic system, according to Monaghan and Glickman (1992), provide the lever by which such control can be acquired. So, it is our mindfulness that helps us to master undesirable behaviors stemming from our emotions.

3 Mirror Neurons and Authenticity

Both mindfulness and the PCA involve sensitive awareness of others. Both involve observing others with acute sensitivity as to their needs and intentions, if we elect to be "on the same page."

One of the more useful findings of emerging neuroscience is how strongly we affect one another in our usual, day-to-day interactions with one another. In his research on macaque monkeys by University of Parma neuroscientist Rizzolatti (2006), it was discovered that the mere act of observing a certain action in others triggered the same neurons in the observer that would be required to perform this very action. In other words, to see is almost to do. Observing another's behavior stimulates the same neurons that are activated in doing the exact same action observed. The neurons in the frontal cortex linking observer to observe were called "mirror neurons" by Rizzolatti and his colleagues.

Even more interesting is the research of Marco Iacobini (2009a) in which he was able to cleverly separate perceived motivations on the part of the actors. When the film showed a hand moving toward a teacup in the context of enjoying the drink, there was much more activity in the mirror neurons of the observers than when watching the hand moving toward the same teacup in the context of cleaning up. Apparently, perceived context of particular motivation plays a large role—all this without deliberate reasoning.

Interestingly, these mirror neurons are activated not only by seeing, but also, according to the researchers (Blakemore et al. 2004; Gazzola et al. 2006), by hearing the sounds of certain actions in particular contexts, such as ripping paper to get the food.

If you're thinking "monkey see, monkey do" is more likely to be true of monkeys than of humans, then think again. How does this apply to person-centered therapy? Consider the therapist nodding his or her head while making a salient point, or even wiping away a sympathetic tear.

According to Goleman, "Human mirror neurons are far more flexible and diverse than those in monkeys, reflecting our sophisticated social abilities...The human brain harbors multiple mirror neuron systems, not just for mimicking actions but also for reading intentions, for extracting the social implications from what someone does, and for reading emotions" (2006, p. 63).

In the days of the ancient Greeks, the term *mimesis*, which reflects the modern terms, *mimic* or *imitate* has a lot in common with our understanding of mirror neurons. In Plato's time, according to author Crain (2007), writing in *The New Yorker*, the word mimesis referred to an actor's performance of his role, an audience's identification with a performance, a pupil's recitation of his lesson, and an apprentice's emulation of his master. He goes on to say that Plato himself was concerned that all these situations could involve a kind of trance or emotional enthrallment that came over people in all these situations.

Do these words not describe the best moments in person-centered therapy as well as interpersonal mindfulness? Even Plato could foresee the power of mirror neurons before such an understanding was ever possible. If we allow a mindful attitude to permit the mirror neurons to do their job without defensive barriers, we can have the "emotional enthrallment" of deep connection.

3.1 The Function of Mirror Neurons in PCA and Mindfulness

In my professional reading over the years, I have occasionally come across authors (e.g., Iacoboni 2009b) convinced of the idea that if we imitate others in some physical, behavioral way—walking like them, adopting their expressions, reflecting their postures—then our empathy and interpersonal mindfulness suddenly become superb. We have also had neurolinguistic programming (NLP) around for decades, in which we are told that successful communication involves getting into the rhythm—breathing, speech patterns, sitting posture—of those with whom we are trying to communicate.

Now we have the neuroscientific data to validate such experience. As researcher Marco Iacoboni puts it, "The way we understand the emotions of other people is by simulating in our brain the same activity we have when we experience those emotions" (cited in O'Connor 2004). Or, as primatologist Frans de Waal (2006) at Emory University says, "Try to mimic it a bit, and you will feel internally what other people feel." Both the PCA and mindfulness involve such interpersonal awareness. Now we can understand more clearly what Carnegie (1936) meant when he said that it is easier to act your way into a feeling than to feel your way into action. In other words, actions lead to feelings (see Levenson et al. 1990) (e.g., showing affection leads to feeling it) more than feelings lead to action (e.g., feeling love without action is less likely to lead to demonstrating one's love).

So, to practice the PCA and mindfulness most effectively, we can reflect others' posture and expressions deeply, and authentically "walk in their moccasins," to entrain our brains with theirs, and then experience the highly desired rapport we seek. More than that, the research (Carr et al. 2003) reveals that others, if we do the reflecting well, will also echo our caring emotions in their own minds, "via communication between action representation networks and limbic areas provided by the insula" (p. 5,500), almost visible in their expressions, now feeling cared for where they may have felt neglected or abandoned before.

The emerging data reveal that these "mirror" neurons also act at an unconscious level. This is one of the emotional components of authentic communication—primal awareness, occurring unconsciously in microseconds in both directions. According to Renate Motschnig-Pitrik and Lux (2008), "mirror neurons support us in perceiving and feeling the inner world of persons with whom we are in contact on a conscious as well as subconscious level, to some degree even without conscious effort to do so" (p. 299).

Current research reveals that you can actually "mirror" your own image and be under the influence of your "other" self. Even observing digitally constructed avatars of yourself for 3–5 min "can improve your social skills, calm your anxieties and help you make better…decisions" (Murphy 2011, p. 60). Physical health can be enhanced by your digital doppelgangers as well while observing them on electronic screens during physical exercise. "When the avatars grew slimmer during the exercise portion and plumper during the stationary phase, users performed 10 times as many reps as those whose virtual twins didn't change" (Stanley 2011, p. 40). Exaggerated consequences of exercise to your "mirror" self (exercise leading to slimming; not doing anything leading to getting fat) can influence your decision to work harder—without deliberate reasoning. The dynamics of "mirror" neurons may work just as well with our own images—not to mention with robots "particularly while engaging in meaningful human actions…as long as their behaviors are not too repetitive" (Gazzolla et al. 2007, p. 1,683)—as they do with those of others.

3.2 The Power of the Authentic Moment

As mentioned at the outset, what is common to both the PCA and mindfulness is the capacity for authentic communication—with our emotions open and above board—not lies and deception. The research reveals that mindful awareness involves perceiving involuntary microexpressions of the face, impossible to fake (Gladwell 2005, pp. 209–210). Only by immersing ourselves in our emotions, authentically, and with any associated vulnerability, will this experience of PCA or mindfulness continue. The power of such effective communication comes when we can step back from the ongoing rush of emotional interaction by maintaining an attitude of objective mindfulness, allowing for recursion with an appropriate balance between right and left cerebral hemispheres. Then, we can take stock of our own emotional vantage point in the moment and the direction we decide is important and relevant for effective communication and making the right decision.

3.3 The Dilemma of Appearing *Authentic*

The research on successful psychotherapy tells us that the most effective counseling is done with authenticity (Ryback 2001). By definition, it cannot be faked, so pretending will not work. As Goleman (2006) puts it, "While we can intentionally try to mimic someone in order to foster closeness, such attempts tend to come off as awkward. Synchrony works best when it is spontaneous, not constructed from ulterior motives such as ingratiation or any other conscious intention" (p. 62). Simply trying to *appear* authentic is like the silly book title, *The Five Rigid Steps to Natural Spontaneity*. It is an oxymoron.

So, here's the essence of both the PCA and mindfulness: In order to *appear* authentic, we've got to *be* authentic. We might allow the new brain, our thinking frontal cortex, to imagine ourselves in the situation the other is presenting to us and really *experience*—deeply—what he or she is attempting to convey. We need not hesitate to immerse ourselves in the passion of our innermost feelings. The risk of openness may result in more successful and productive mindful as well as meaningful relationships.

4 Bridging the PCA and Mindfulness

In sum, here are the three common elements that create the bridge between the PCA and mindfulness:

1. **Authenticity**: The capacity to be more self-aware, genuine, congruent, and to reveal our caring for those with whom we're attempting to communicate.
2. **Recursion**: The commitment to become more aware of levels of inner feelings. That's a large component of both person-centered connection and mindfulness, allowing us to become more aware of others' feelings, by simulating them as our own. If we are not mindful of our own feelings, how can we recognize others'? This commonality is straightforward and simple, even though the feelings we communicate are, on the other hand, quite complex.
3. **Mirror neurons**: The ability to communicate those feelings more effectively to others if we can get in touch with our own feelings—of caring, empathy, passion. Research on mirror neurons reveals that people mirror our intentions, but only if we're authentic in our communication—or great actors (Blair 2003; Wicker et al. 2003; Vrij 2008), as the amygdala and insula are particularly sensitive to expressed emotion (van der Gaad et al. 2007, p. 197), and authentic facial expression is quite complex and almost impossible to fake (Ekman 2009; Steimer-Krause et al. 2005, esp. pp. 376–380).

5 ...And So To Bed

As the trite question goes, how do you feel about that? Well, according to the world of neuroscience, that depends on your medial prefrontal cortex (MPFC) as well as your anterior insula because that is where the three elements around authentic connecting meet. "The MPFC," according to Restak (2006), "is responsible both for our concept of how we feel from moment to moment and for our ability to intuit the feelings of other people" (p. 74).

As I finish writing these words, I can only hope that your reading of them finds both acceptance and a sense of integration into your ongoing understanding of how mindfulness and PCA share the three elements. I also hope that my description of the neuroscience of both concepts helps in the understanding of their function and commonality, and that you can more easily comprehend the meaning, influence, contribution, impact, and application of both.

My MPFC and insula must be glowing because I feel connected with you, the reader, and feel gratitude that you've taken the time to hear me out. My right and left hemispheres must be very much in balance, as I feel I've accomplished the intellectual task asked of me, and emotionally satisfied that I've done so in as authentic manner as I could. My hippocampus helps remind me that it's time to quit this activity, and my hypothalamus tells me I'm hungry...and tired. Perhaps I'll have a snack ... and so to bed.

References

Akirav, I., & Richter-Levin, G. (2002). Mechanisms of amaygdala modulation of hippocampal plasticity. *Journal of Neuroscience, 22*, 912–921.
Barrett-Lennard, G. T. (1990). The therapy pathway reformulated. In G. Lietaer, J. Rombauts, & R. van Balen (Eds.), *Client-centered and experiential therapies in the nineties* (pp. 123–153). Leuven: Leuven University Press.
Blair, R. J. (2003). Facial expressions, their communicatory functions and neuro-cognitive substrates. *Philosophical Transactions of the Royal Society, Biological Sciences, 358*(1431), 561–572.
Blakemore, S., Winston, J., & Firth, U. (2004). Social cognitive neuroscience: Where are we heading? *Trends in Cognitive Sciences, 8*(5), 216–222.
Burgdorf, J., Panksepp, J., & Moskal, J. R. (2011). Frequency-modulated 50 kHz ultrasonic vocalizations: A tool for uncovering the molecular substrates of positive affect. *Neuroscience and Biobehavioral Reviews, 35*, 1831–1836.
Carnegie, D. (1936). *How to win friends and influence people*. NY: Simon and Schuster.
Carr, L., Iacoboni, M., Dubeau, M.-C., Mazziotta, J. C., & Lenzi, G. L. (2003). Neural mechanisms of empathy in humans. *Proceedings of the National Academy of Science, 100*, 5497–5502.
Cloud, J. (2011). Thought control. *Time, 178*(19), 52–54.
Coates, J. (2012). Risk factor. *Time, 180*(2), 18.
Cox, B., & Forshaw, J. (2012). *The quantum universe*. Cambridge: Da Capo Press.
Craig, A. D. (2009). How do you feel–now? The anterior insula and human awareness. *Nature Reviews Neuroscience, 10*, 59–70.

Crain, C. (2007). Twilight of the books. *The New Yorker, LXXXIII(41)*, Dec. 24 & 31, 134–139, quotes from 137.
Damasio, A. R. (1994). *Descartes' error*. NY: Grosset/Putnam.
Davidson, R. J., Putnam, K. M., & Larson, C. L. (2000). Dysfunction in the neural circuitry of emotional regulation: A possible prelude to violence. *Science, 289*, 591–594.
de Waal, F. (2006). *Our inner ape*. NY: Riverhead Books.
DiSalvo, D. (2010). Are social networks messing with your head? *Scientific American Mind, 20*(7), 48–55.
Eide, D. (2009). Emotions. In C. Hartel & N. M. Ashkanasy (Eds.), *Emotions in organizational behavior* (pp. 11–44). Mahwah: Erlbaum.
Ekman, P. (2009). *Telling lies*. NY: Norton.
Epstien, S. (1994). Integration of the cognitive and the psychodynamic unconscious. *American Psychologist, 49*, 709–724.
Gazzola, V., Aziz-Zedah, L. S., & Keysers, C. (2006). Empathy and the somatotopic auditory mirror system in humans. *Current Biology, 16*, 1824–1829.
Gazzolla, V., Rizzolatti, G., Wicker, B., & Keysers, C. (2007). The anthropomorphic brain: The mirror neuron system responds to human and robotic actions. *NeuroImage, 35*(4), 1683.
Goleman, D. (2006). Neural WiFi. *Psychotherapy Networker 30*(6).
Gladwell, M. (2005). *Blink*. NY: Little Brown.
Grobler, H., Schenck, R., & Du Toit, D. (2003). *Person-centered communication*. Cape Town: Oxford University Press.
Grosenick, L., Greer, S., & Knutson, B. (2008). Interpretable classifiers for FMRI improve prediction of purchases. *IEEE Transactions of Neural Systems and Rehabilitation Engineering, 16*, 539–548.
Humphrey, N. (2011). *Why everyone (else) is a hypocrite: Evolution and the modular mind*. Princeton: Princeton University Press.
Hutson, M. (2012). *The 7 laws of magical thinking*. NY: Hudson Street Press.
Iacoboni, M. (2009a). *Mirroring people: The new science of how we connect with others*. NY: Farrar, Straus, and Giroux.
Iacoboni, M. (2009b). Imitation, empathy and mirror neurons. *Annual Review of Psychology, 60*, 19.1–19.18.
Jenkins, W. (1999). Quoted in A. Ellin, Can "neurobics" do for the brain what aerobics do for the lungs? *NY Times*, Oct. 3.
Johnson-Laird, P. N., & Oatley, K. (1992). Basic emotions, rationality, and folk theory. *Cognition and Emotion, 6*, 201–223.
Jordan, J. V., Kaplan, A. G., Miller, J. B., Stiver, I. P., & Surrey, J. L. (1991). *Women's growth in connection*. NY: Guilford.
Kabat-Zinn, J. (2005). *Coming to our senses*. NY: Hyperion.
Kahneman, D. (2011). *Thinking, fast and slow*. NY: Farrar, Straus and Giroux.
Ladner, L. (2005, July/August). Bringing mindfulness to your practice. *Psychotherapy Networker*, p. 19.
LeDoux, J. (2004). *Presentation at the meeting of the consortium for research on emotional intelligence in organizations*. Dec: Cambridge, Mass. 4.
Levenson, R. W., Ekman, P., & Friesen, W. V. (1990). Voluntary facial action generates emotion-specific autonomic nervous system activity. *Psychophysiology, 27*(4), 363–384.
Levine, R. (2011). *Free ride: How digital parasites are destroying the culture business, and how the culture business can fight back*. NY: Doubleday.
Lilienfeld, S. O., & Arkowitz, H. (2008). Uncovering "brainscams". *Scientific American Mind, 19*(1), 80–81.
Linden, D. J. (2011). *The compass of pleasure*. NY: Viking Press.
Marcus, G. E. (1998). Rethinking eliminative connectionism. *Cognitive Psychology, 37*, 243–282.
Marcus, G. E. (2001). *The algebraic mind*. Cambridge: MIT Press.
Marsalis, W. (2001). Episode 6: Swing. In Ken Burns (Director) *Jazz*, Florentine Films.

Mearns, D., & Cooper, M. (2005). *Working at relational depth in counseling and psychotherapy*. London: Sage Publications.
Minkel, J. R. (2008). The roots of creativity. *Scientific American Mind, 19*(3), 8.
Monaghan, E., & Glickman, S. (1992). Hormones and aggressive behavior. In J. Becker, M. Breedlove, & D. Crews (Eds.), *Behavioral endocrinology*. Cambridge: MIT Press.
Motschnig-Pitrik, R., & Lux, M. (2008). The person centered approach meets neuroscience. *Journal of Humanistic Psychology, 48*(3), 287–319.
Murphy, S. (2011). Your avatar, your guide. *Scientific American Mind, 22*(1), 58–63.
Neville, B. (2012). *The life of things: Therapy and the soul of the world*. Ross-on-Wye: PCCS Books.
O'Connor, A. (2004). *Brain scans substantiate feel-the-pain sentiments*. Feb: New York Times. 24.
Panksepp, J., & Biven, L. (2012). *The archaeology of mind: Neuroevolutionary origins of human emotions*. NY: Norton.
Paulus, M. P., & Stein, M. B. (2006). An insular view of anxiety. *Biological Psychiatry, 60*(4), 383–387.
Pinker, S. (1997). *How the mind works*. NY: Norton.
Puhakka, K. (2000). An invitation to authentic knowing. In T. Hart, P. L. Nelson, & K. Puhakka (Eds.), *Transpersonal knowing*. Albany: State University of New York Press.
Reiner, P. B. (2009). Meditation on demand. *Scientific American Mind, 20*(6), 65–67.
Restak, R. (1997). Rewiring, *NY Times Book Review, June 22*, pp. 14–15.
Restak, R. (2006). *The naked brain*. NY: Harmony Books.
Ricard, M. (2006). *Happiness*. NY: Little, Brown.
Rice, L. N., & Greenberg, L. S. (1990). Fundamental dimensions in experiential psychotherapy: New directions in research. In G. Lietaer, J. Rombasuts, & R. van Balen (Eds.), *Client-centered and experiential therapies in the nineties* (pp. 397–414). Leuven: Leuven University Press.
Rizzolatti, G. (2006). Quoted in S. Blakelee. Cells that read minds. *New York Times, Jan. 10*, p. C3.
Rogers, C. R. (1942). *Counseling and psychotherapy*. Boston: Houghton Mifflin.
Rogers, C. R. (1951). *Client-centered therapy*. Boston: Houghton Mifflin.
Rogers, C. R. (1977). *Carl Rogers on personal power*. London: Constable.
Rogers, C. R. (1980). *A way of being*. Boston: Houghton Mifflin.
Rogers, C.R. (1986). A client-centered/person-centered approach to therapy. In I. Kutash & A. Wolfe (Eds.), *Psychotherapists' Casebook* (pp. 197–208.) San Francisco: Jossey-Bass.
Rogers, C. R. (1990). Client-centered therapy. In M. Kirschenbaum & V. L. Henderson (Eds.), *Carl Rogers dialogues*. London: Constable.
Rogers, C. R., & Freiberg, H. J. (1983). *Freedom to learn* (3rd ed.). NY: Merrill.
Rogers, C. R., & Ryback, D. (1984). One alternative to nuclear planetary suicide. In R. F. Levant & J. M. Shlien (Eds.), *Client-centered therapy and the person-centered approach*. NY: Praeger.
Rowan, J. (1986). Holistic listening. *Journal of Humanistic Psychology, 26*(1), 83–102.
Ryback, D. (1989). An interview with Carl Rogers. *Person-Centered Review, 4*(1), 99–112.
Ryback, D. (1998). *Putting emotional intelligence to work*. Woburn: Butterworth-Heinemann.
Ryback, D. (1999). *The quiet revolution* (pp. 21–22). January: AHP Perspective.
Ryback, D. (2001). Mutual affect therapy and the emergence of transformational empathy. *Journal of Humanistic Psychology, 41*(3), 75–94.
Ryback, D. (2010). *ConnectAbility*. NY: McGraw-Hill.
Ryback, D. (2011). Humanistic psychology's impact and accomplishments. *Journal of Humanistic Psychology, 51*(4), 413–418.
Siegel, D. (2005, March). The marvel and mystery of the self. Panel discussion at the Psychotherapy Network Symposium, Washington, DC.
Siegel, L. (2009). *Against the MACHINE: How the web is reshaping culture and commerce—and why it matters*. NY: Spiegel and Grau.

Stanley, S. (2011). Dancing with the avatars. *Psychology Today, 44*(5), 40.

Steimer-Krause, E., Krause, R., & Wagner, G. (2005). Interaction regulations used by schizophrenic and psychosomatic patients. In P. Ekman & E. L. Rosenberg (Eds.), *What the face reveals* (pp. 376–380). NY: Oxford University Press.

Sterling, M. M., & Bugental, J. F. T. (1993). The meld experience in psychotherapy supervision. *Journal of Humanistic Psychology, 33*(2), 33–48.

Van der Gaad, C., Minderaa, R. B., & Keysers, C. (2007). Facial expressions: What the mirror neuron system can and cannot tell us. *Social Neuroscience, 2*(3–4), 179–222.

Vrij, A. (2008). *Detecting lies and deceit*. NY: Wiley.

Watt, D. F. (2007). Toward a neuroscience of empathy (with commentaries). *Neuro-Psychoanalysis, 9*, 119–172.

Webster's Dictionary (1987). The New Lexicon Webster's Dictionary of the English Language. NY: Lexicon.

Wicker, B., Keysers, C., Plailly, J., Royet, J.-P., Gallese, V., & Rizzolatti, G. (2003). Both of us disgusted in *my* insula. *Neuron, 40*, 655–664.

Wright, J., & Panksepp, J. (2011). Toward affective circuit-based preclinical models of depression: Sensitizing dorsal PAG arousal leads to sustained suppression of positive affect in rats. *Neuroscience and Biobehavioral Reviews, 35*, 1902–1915.

Xue, G., Lu, Z., Levin, I., & Bechara, A. (2010). The impact of prior risk experience of subsequent risky decision-making: The role of the insula. *NeuroImage, 50*, 709–716.

Zaki, J. (2011). What, me care? *Scientific American Mind, 21*(6), 14–15.

Part III
Mindfulness

You Can Inspire Me to Live Further: Explicating Pre-reflexive Bridges to the Other

Akira Ikemi

1 Presence

Let me start with my favorite story.

One summer day, I was washing my car. I showered the car with the hose from the faucet and I had a sponge in my hand as I was spreading the car wash on the roof of my car. Just as I started to spread the foams on the roof of the car, I felt that someone was watching me.

To be more precise, I felt that my body was being pulled toward the right side, and that someone was watching me from across the street to the right side of me. I did not have to *think* of what I was to do next. My neck and torso "automatically" turned slowly toward the right, in the direction from which my body felt the gaze.

There! A dog! A dog was sitting attentively on the other side of the street, looking at me intensely. The dog was not barking, as it made no sound. Nor did the dog wag its tail. The dog was gazing at me with full attention. I did not *think* of what to do next, "automatically" there was a smile on my face. It felt like there was suddenly a warm glow in my body. I don't know if this is fantasy or reality, but it felt as if the dog had also smiled at me.

The dog was on a leash. The lady who was walking the dog pulled the leash and said, "let's go now, let's go!" The dog got up and took a step and then flipped around and sat again, looking straight at me, again. I did not have to *think* of what to do next. My body already put down the sponge and turned the water faucet off and started to walk across the street to greet the dog. Once I squatted down next to the dog, the dog was all over me, licking my face, brushing its fur all over my body, and showing its tummy to me. The dog was so happy and excited. The lady who was walking the dog said to me: "Sorry to interrupt what you were doing. This dog can identify people who love dogs." I greatly enjoyed the few minutes of our encounter.

A. Ikemi (✉)
Graduate School of Professional Clinical Psychology, Kansai University,
3-3-35 Yamatecho, Suita, Osaka 564-8680, Japan
e-mail: info@akira-ikemi.net

After I parted with the dog and finished washing the car, I sat inside the room with the glow still felt in my body. What was this glow all about? I did not *know*. But much of life is like this anyway. Things happen and change you *before* you know about it. In other words, much happens *pre-reflexively*. Now, I decided to sit down and *reflect* on this experience. As I *re-experienced* the event, several interesting theoretical points came up in me.

First of all, what struck me as I reflected was the power this dog had. The dog did not say anything, not even a bark. The dog's gaze was so powerful that it made me stop whatever I was doing. The dog's gaze literally "took me" across the street. Another way of saying this is that the *presence* of the dog instantly affected me in a very powerful way. As I thought of this, I recalled many situations in which the presence of the other affects me. A smile a certain person has, already puts a smile on my face, before I know why, for example. The presence of the other affects you, before you know about it.

Let us now turn to Carl Rogers, to see what he wrote about presence.

> I find that when I am closest to my inner, intuitive self, when I am somehow in touch with the unknown in me, when perhaps I am in a slightly altered state of consciousness, then whatever I do seems to be full of healing. Then, simply my *presence* is releasing and helpful to the other. There is nothing I can do to force this experience, but when I can relax and be close to the transcendental core of me, then I may behave in strange and impulsive ways in the relationship, ways which I cannot justify rationally, which have nothing to do with my thought processes. But these strange behaviors turn out to be *right* in some odd way: it seems that my inner spirit has reached out and touched the inner spirit of the other. (Rogers 1980, p. 129)

I must beg your pardon, Dr. Carl Rogers, to compare you with a dog. However, there are some parallels here between my experience with this dog and the quote. Yes, it does seem like the dog's inner spirit has reached out and touched my inner spirit. And "simply my (the dog's) presence is releasing and helpful to the other (to me)." Also, the dog must have been behaving in "strange and impulsive ways," to sit down and intently watch a man washing his car, and this must have been interpreted as a particularly impulsive move from the viewpoint of the lady who wanted to continue the walk.

Rogers wrote that he cannot justify rationally these behaviors and that they have nothing to do with his thought processes. As in my example of the dog, my act of crossing the street to greet the dog had nothing to do with my thought process. I did not reason that this course of action was most appropriate. Probably, the dog also had no conceptual reason to be watching a man wash his car.

Rather than rational thought, my *body* turned to the direction from which I felt the gaze. Without any thought process, my body had crossed the street and squatted in front of this dog "automatically," as if were. The body responds to the situation *pre-reflexively*.

Eugene Gendlin (1992) articulated how our bodies interact with the situation before perception. The unity of the world cannot be broken up by percepts, such that there is a perceived dog there and a perceiving subject here, and the percept in between. Our bodies do not have percepts and then think about them, inducing a logically correct next set of actions to be executed by our bodies. Rather, the body already interacts with the situation (environment) before we have percepts and thoughts.

The dog had affected my body before I perceived the dog. My body felt that "someone was watching me," before I found the dog sitting across the street. My body had crossed the street to greet the dog, before I could perceive if the dog was friendly or hostile. The dog was not barking nor wagging its tail. The dog sat very still, just watching me. I had no clue to perceive if the dog was friendly. Yet, my *body* was sure that it was pulled toward the dog in a friendly manner. My body and the dog were already interacting in a pre-reflexive bodily way, before percepts, thoughts, words (barks), or gestures (tail-wagging).

My body responded to the dog before perceiving the attitude of the dog or before making any judgments. We can also say that the dog affected me *pre-reflexively*, before I reflected on whether this dog was friendly or not, or before I could think of how I *should* act toward this dog.

Eugene Gendlin does not write much about presence. In a short lovely passage, however, he describes presence as an essential condition of therapy. Clearly, he does not regard it as a special, "slightly altered state of consciousness" as Rogers did.

> I want to start with the most important thing I have to say: The essence of working with another person is *to be present* as a living being. And that is lucky, because if we had to be smart, or good, or mature, or wise, then we would probably be in trouble. But what matters is not that. What matters is to be a human being with another human being, to recognize the other person as another being in there. Even if it is a cat or a bird... the first thing you have to know is that there is somebody in there... That seems to me to be the most important thing. (Gendlin 1990, p. 205, italics added)

Again, "to be present as a living being" is not something that we should do or some set of logically induced behaviors. It is to be open to the "otherness of the Other" (M. Buber, cited in Gendlin 1973, p. 318), whether the other is a human person, a dog, a cat, or a bird. The *Otherness* of the dog pulled me across the street. The dog was not some machine I could control or manipulate. It would not move, it just continued to gaze at me. It had a will of its own, as a living being, and the lady could not manipulate it to continue the walk. Just as the dog was fully present to me, I was also present to the dog, struck by an overwhelming otherness of the dog.

Just as the dog's presence affected me pre-reflexively, people's presences affect each other, and particularly therapists' presences affects their clients. Rogers' great discovery was that the *relationship* was therapeutic, and that the helping relationship could be characterized by therapists' congruence, unconditional positive regard, and empathy (Rogers 1957), and possibly "one more characteristic" (Rogers 1989, p. 137), which was *presence* in the way that he described it (see quote above).

The whole body of literature in psychotherapy, particularly in client-centered therapy, supports the importance of Rogers' claim. However, there is an interesting subtle discrepancy between these characteristics of the relationship with the discussion above. That is, if the other affects us *pre-reflexively,* and we know what affected us only later upon reflection, how can we know beforehand that these three or four conditions are the essential characteristics of the helping relationship? Gendlin presents this problem eloquently in the passage below.

> ...one wrinkle that I do not remember succeeding in selling him (Carl Rogers) was my argument that the three conditions are sufficient without the proviso that the client has to *perceive* them...I know that perception is not necessary, because my clients are convinced for a year or two that nobody could possibly like them or understand them, and the process works anyway and eventually changes their perception...I know, because I was that kind of client. I always knew that this nice man could not possibly understand my stuff. It took me a long time before I noticed that when I walked into the room, I was already different. The interaction affects you, long before you can think about it. (Gendlin 1990, p. 203)

In the passage above, Gendlin emphasizes that the relationship changes the person before perception. This is entirely in line with his philosophical position as shown above (Gendlin 1992), which is that the body interacts with the situation before perception. I would like to stretch this argument a little further than Gendlin intended. By asserting that the relationship ("interaction" in Gendlin's passage) affects us pre-reflexively, I am emphasizing that we do not know what affected us until we reflect on the relationship, and a possible consequence of such a reflection is that we may discover other characteristics of the relationship that had been affecting us.

In my view (and I believe this view is agreeable with Gendlin's philosophy), the three conditions as presented by Rogers were Rogers' reflective *explications* of the therapeutically effective relationship. Once explicated, these concepts of congruence, unconditional positive regard, and empathy are empowered to serve as helpful guides with which we can think about therapy as well as use them in training therapists to maximize their therapeutic potentials.

However, these explications are not the absolute final say on the therapeutic relationship. The therapeutic relationship is not *defined by* nor *composed of* these three and only three "elements." They can always be exceeded when explicated freshly.

Indeed, each therapy session has a different "flavor," so to speak. The therapist is affected, just as the client is affected by the flavor of the relationship in a particular session. Hence, it is always enriching to *reflect* on a particular session, or on the entire case, and explicate what seems to be working or not working in the relationship. Often, when reflecting on a particular case, therapists find felt senses unique to the client or to the session. For example, a beginning therapist working with a teenager discovered that she felt like she was "turned into a wooden cube by some magical spell the client has" (Ikemi and Kawata 2006). Noticing such a unique way in which the client's presence affect the therapist, and to reflect on it, are helpful to therapists. Now, the therapist is able to detect when the "spell" is coming into the therapy session and the therapist can wonder about the "magic spell" the client is casting on her and others.

In Japan, Professor Yasuyuki Kira (Kyushu University) has published a book (Kira 2010) entitled *Therapist Focusing [in Japanese]* which is an accumulation of his work with his collaborators, including Professors Kenichi Itoh (Gakkushuin University) and myself on the benefits of Therapist Focusing on psychotherapists of various orientations. Since the client affects the therapist pre-reflexively, it is worthwhile to reflect on, or Focus on, the therapy sessions and explicate from the *felt sense* of the therapy sessions. I will elaborate further on this throughout this article.

While congruence, unconditional positive regard, and empathy are valuable general aspects of the therapeutic relationship, the particular ways in which therapists and clients are affected can be explicated freshly, bringing out case-specific understandings. Similarly, in everyday life, the other always affects us before we know it, and reflecting on the ways we are affected brings out fresh new understandings of our interactions with the other.

2 Felt Meaning and Felt Sense

Eugene Gendlin, a close co-researcher of Carl Rogers, is a philosopher, as well as a psychotherapist. His philosophy investigates the nature of how we have experiencing *[Erleben]* (or "consciousness" in Husserl's sense, if you prefer that term). His philosophy deals with the explication of the implicit aspects of experiencing, which is a process central to any thought, philosophy, therapy, art, and almost any human endeavor.

One of the central terms used by Gendlin is *felt meaning*. As a general trend, Gendlin tends to use the term *felt meaning* more often until he developed Focusing, thereafter using the term *felt sense* more frequently. After a close look at these two seemingly interchangeable terms, however, I have come to think of these two terms as pointing to different phenomena. I believe these two terms do not mean the same. Perhaps, the distinction I am making here is roughly in agreement with Gendlin's thinking (personal conversation) but I would like to emphasize this more than he seems to do.

I see felt meaning as functioning *pre-reflexively*. Gendlin writes that "felt meaning functions as an ever-present experienced parallel of all concepts, observations, actions—whatever is meaningful to us" (Gendlin 1962/1997, p. 65.) Felt meaning is "ever-present" whether we reflect on it or not. Every sentence is already imbued with a sense of meaning that is already functioning in our experiencing. Thus, we understand the meaning of the other's speech, without having to think of the definitions of each of the words used in the speech. Gendlin gives this sentence as an example: "Democracy is government by the people" (p. 66). The sentence shows that there is a sense of meaning here, a felt meaning, which is not given by the explication of each of the symbols used in this sentence, such as "government" or "democracy" or "by" or "people."

In exploring about the felt meaning and felt sense, I have referred to a Japanese haiku written in 1686 by the famous haiku poet, *Matsuo Bassho* (Ikemi 2011).

Furuike ya   [Ancient pond(s)]
Kawazu tobikomu   [(A) frog(s) jump(s) in]
Mizu no Oto   [The sound(s) of water]

Translating Japanese to English is difficult, particularly since the Japanese language does not have a singular/plural distinction. Thus, there can be no exact translation of this Japanese poem, since all Indo-European languages require the singular/plural distinction. Although clumsy, the haiku may be translated as the above.

Since the Japanese language does not have a singular/plural distinction, you do not even know if there are one or more of the *furuike* (ancient pond[s]). But to prevent matters from becoming unnecessarily complicated, let us arbitrarily assume that there is only one ancient pond described here. Whether the sound of water is singular or plural would depend on the number of frogs. So, let us make two versions of this haiku; version X assumes that there is one frog in this poem, while version Z assumes that there are more than one frog in this poem.

Version X: Ancient pond/a frog jumps in/the sound of water
Version Z: Ancient pond/frogs jump in/the sounds of water

Then, let me pose a question. How many frogs are there in this haiku? Which of the two versions above (version X or version Z) would you believe to be the vision that the poet had when he wrote this poem?

I have asked this question in many places, not only in Japan, where the haiku originates, but also in Athens, in Rome, and in New York. Most people across the globe, and almost everyone in Japan, see only one frog in this haiku. They believe that version X is what *Bassho* had in mind when he wrote this haiku.

Let me now pose a second question. How did you know that there was only one frog here?

I believe that a *felt meaning* is operating implicitly here. From "ancient pond," a sense of stillness emanates. It is a quiet place. No one has touched this ancient pond for ages. There is a felt meaning of stillness, which is temporality disturbed by a "blop" sound of a frog that jumps into the water. Then stillness prevails again. The felt meaning here says of stillness, so it cannot be a whole group of frogs diving and dancing in the water! The beauty of this haiku is that it sings of silence through the use of words.

We understand that there is only one frog here, from the implicitly functioning felt meaning. It cannot be understood grammatically, because Japanese grammar does not differentiate singular and plural. Moreover, almost anyone who understands Japanese does not have to reflect on this haiku to come to the conclusion that it is one frog. They can instantly "visualize," so to speak, the scene of a single frog jumping into the stillness of an ancient pond. Through this, I am demonstrating that the felt meaning is functioning before we are aware of it, in other words, it functions *pre-reflexively*.

Let me give you an English sentence to show that the felt meaning functions pre-reflexively. A person may say, "My mood started *sinking* after talking to Tom." In this case, we do not have to reflect on the meaning of the verb *to sink*, to understand the complexity of her situation with Tom, and that the speaker is starting to feel depressed or feeling dark or hopeless. All this comes to us pre-reflexively. However, if we were to look up the dictionary for the meaning of the verb *to sink*, we would be puzzled because the verb means immersing in water or some fluid and descending inside the fluid toward the bottom. For someone for whom English is not a native language and who did look up the word *to sink*, the sentence may not be understandable, for moods are not ships and therefore they cannot sink. Felt meaning comes to us pre-reflexively, before reflecting on the explicit meaning of each word, and hence, it enables us to understand the other.

Now, we can choose to *reflect* on how we are experiencing a certain situation, a poem, or the utterance of the other. We will then be intentionally feeling the situation and seeing what might arise. We are then trying to get a *felt sense* of the situation. Gendlin writes about finding the felt sense:

> ...sense how it makes you feel in your body when you think of it [a problem] as a whole just for a moment. Ask "what does this whole problem feel like?" But don't answer in words. Feel the problem *whole*, the sense of *all that* (Gendlin 1981, p. 53).

Now "sensing," "asking," and "feeling" in the quote above are *intentional acts of reflection*. The felt sense comes to form in *reflexive* activity.

We can return to the two versions of the haiku, versions X and Z. If you read them again and *sense* it, *ask* your body what this whole haiku feels like, and *feel* the whole haiku, you will notice that the two versions give rise to different felt senses. For example, from the former, I get a felt sense of "tranquility," "clearness," while from the latter; I get a felt sense of "liveliness," a "jumbled-chaotic-sense." The *felt meaning* which functions *pre-reflexively* can thus be differentiated from the *felt sense*, which comes *reflexively*.

We can thus interact on two levels: the pre-reflexive and the reflexive. We can listen to a piece of music, for example, and be affected by the felt meaning. In this way, the music affects us before we are aware of it, for felt meaning is already functioning implicitly. Before we are aware of it, our legs may be stomping in rhythm with the tune, and our moods can be affected by the key of the melody or by the bits of lyrics reverbing in the background of our consciousness. We can also appreciate the music on the reflexive level by letting a felt sense form from the piece of music. We are then aware of the quality of this music piece and may be wondering about the relevance of this musical quality to our situations.

Interactions with others happen on both the pre-reflexive and reflexive levels.

3 Understanding

In the above, I have already asserted that the presence of the other, their utterances, in fact, the totality of their interactions with us is already affecting us pre-reflexively. There is a pre-reflexive understanding of the other, as the interaction goes on. What is implicit in the other becomes implicit in us.

For example, the fascination of the dog as it watches me wash the car becomes implicit in me, too. So, although I have not reflected on it or thought of the word "fascination," I realize that the fascination is shared between the dog and me.

The stillness that was implicit in Bassho's poem becomes implicit in me as well. Although not perceived as such, an implicit sense of stillness is shared between Bassho and me, as I read his explicit words. In a conversation with the other, the other's excitement about a certain situation stirs in me, and my sense of wonder as I hear the other's story becomes implicit in the other as well. We *cross*, to use Gendlin's terminology.

> Dilthey said that we can understand the authors only if we understand them better than they understood themselves, and this happens only if we carry their experiencing forward with our further understanding, when the author's experiencing is reconstituted by our experiencing—accurately but enriched by ours, as ours is enriched by theirs. Or, as I would say it: these cross so that each becomes implicit in the other. (Gendlin 1997, p. 41)

In therapy, therapists can reflect on the felt meanings they are experiencing. They can get a felt sense of their clients and explicate the meanings implied. Then, although these are explications of the therapists' felt senses, they do, in fact, explicate clients' experiencing, since therapists have already crossed into clients. We see that Carl Rogers was doing this in his interview with Jan, for example. He calls it *presence*, and as such, it is "intuitive." But we can now understand it as his explication of his own felt sense of Jan, which turns out to be an explication of that which is implicit in Jan.

> CARL: Somebody you can relate to. And I guess that—this may seem like a silly idea, but—I wish that one of those friends could be that naughty little girl. I don't know whether that makes any sense to you or not, but if that kind of sprightly, naughty little girl that lives inside could accompany you from the light into the dark—as I say, that may not make any sense to you at all.
> JAN: *(In a puzzled voice)* Can you elaborate on that a little more for me?
> CARL: Simply that maybe one of your best friends is the you that you hide inside, the fearful little girl, the naughtily little girl, the real you that doesn't come out very much in the open.
> JAN: *(Pause)* In fact, over the last 18 months, that naughty little girl has disappeared. (Rogers 1989, p. 148)

Rogers writes about his "intuitive responses" that "they occur infrequently, but they are almost always helpful in advancing therapy." He writes further that: "I know much more than my conscious mind is aware of. I do not form my responses consciously; they simply arise in me, from my non-conscious *sensing of the world of the other*" (Rogers 1989, p. 148, italics added).

Here, we see that Carl Rogers is *crossing into* Jan. He is aware of the felt meanings coming from the other (Jan). It is "non-conscious" in that it is pre-reflexive, to use my terminology, and thus, it is not conceptual thought. I would like to replace Rogers' terminology in this particular instance, from "conscious/non-conscious" to "conceptual/pre-conceptual," because apparently Rogers is conscious, that is, not asleep, at the time he is interacting with Jan, and therefore, he cannot be "non-conscious" in the literal sense of the word. When we thus replace just these particular words, we have Rogers writing: "I do not form my responses *conceptually*, they simply arise in me, from my *pre-conceptual* sensing of the other."

Now we can see that in the interaction preceding the citation above, felt meanings implicit in Jan's statements was carried into Rogers pre-reflectively. Rogers was not explicitly aware of these felt meanings until he started to reflect on some aspects of the felt meaning. With this reflection, Rogers had a felt sense of Jan. Then from the pre-conceptual felt sense, one aspect was explicated, that is, that the "naughty little girl" is needing to "come out in the open." Thus, Jan's naughty little girl came to attention and spoke through Rogers "sensing of the other."

We can now see what Rogers meant by "intuitive." We can see his description of presence in a new light. We can now assure Carl Rogers that it is not the case that he "may behave in strange and impulsive ways" which he "cannot justify rationally" (Rogers 1989, p. 137). We now see Carl Rogers *crossing into* his clients.

Once in a Focusing workshop in Japan, a person who was very new to Focusing came up for a demonstration. After the session, when we shared our experiences of the session with the whole group, she said: "You know, this person (me) is a total stranger! I only met him a couple of hours ago. How can it be that he knows so much about me!"

During the session, I had used one of the standard Focusing responses: "What does this felt sense need?" While I waited for her to answer, I was also asking my felt sense of her the same question. Since she could not come up with an answer, I told her what came to me. As she listened to what I said, her eyes looked startled at first, then tears welled up and laughter came as well. "How did you know that?" she said. "I've closed myself to this, many years ago, but there is that carefree side of me which I valued so much years ago." It was as if I understood the work (the person) better than the authors (the client) did themselves (see Gendlin's articulation of Dilthey's elaboration of understanding quoted above).

This session shows many similarities with Rogers' session with Jan. Jan can live further with the "naughtily little girl" aspect of her, which Carl Rogers explicated. My client can live further with the carefree aspect of her that I explicated. This paper has attempted to show how one can inspire the other to live further. Saying from the felt sense of the other, which has pre-reflexively crossed into each other, can inspire the other to live further.

Acknowledgments I thank Michael Lux for referring me to an article by Nagasawa, M. et al (2009) that shows that a dog's gaze can increase the levels of the neuropeptide oxytocin in its owner. Physiological changes such as these can occur pre-reflexively, and can later be 'explained' by scientific findings.

References

Gendlin, E. (1973). Experiential psychotherapy. In R. Corsini (Ed.), *Current psychotherapies*. Ithasca: FE Peacock.
Gendlin, E. (1981) *Focusing*. New York, Bantam Books.
Gendin, E. (1990). The small steps of the therapy process: How they come and how to help them come. In *Client-centered and experiential psychotherapy in the ninetie*. Leuven: Leuven University Press.

Gendlin, E. (1992). The primacy of the body, not the primacy of perception. *Man and World, 25*, 341–353.

Gendlin, E. (1962/1997). *Experiencing and the creation of meaning*. Evanston: Northwestern University Press. Originally published in 1962 from the Free Press of Glencoe.

Gendlin, E. (1997). How philosophy cannot appeal to experience, and how it can. In D. Levine (Ed.) *Language beyond postmodernism: Saying and thinking in Gendlin's philosophy* (pp. 3–41). Evanston: Northwestern University Press.

Ikemi, A. (2011). Empowering the implicitly functioning relationship. *Person-Centered and Experiential Psychotherapies, 10*(1), 28–42.

Ikemi, A., & Kawata, E. (2006). Aiding the beginning therapist with therapist focusing. *Kobe College Shinri Soudan Kenkyu, 7*, 3–13. (in Japanese).

Kira, Y. (2010). *Therapist Focusing*, Tokyo: Iwasaki Gakujitsu Shuppan (*in Japanese*).

Nagasawa, M., Kikusui, T., Onaka, T., & Ohta, M. (2009). Dog's gaze at its owner increases owner's urinary oxytocin during social interaction. *Hormones and Behavior, 55*, 434–441.

Rogers, C. (1957). The necessary and sufficient conditions of therapeutic personality change. *Journal of Consulting Psychology, 21*(2), 95–103.

Rogers, C. (1980). *A way of being*. Boston: Houghton-Mifflin.

Rogers, C. (1989). A client centered/person-centered approach to therapy. In: H. Kirschenbaum & V. Henderson (Eds.) *The Carl Rogers reader* (pp. 135–152).

The Awakened Heart: Mindfulness as a Bridge Between the Person-Centered Approach and Eastern Philosophiesc

Karin Bundschuh-Müller

1 Introduction

Carl Rogers (1902–1987) initiated person-centered psychotherapy in the 1940s. Many therapists and counselors worldwide consider this approach one of the most important representatives of humanistic psychotherapies. In 1982 and again in 2009, Rogers was rated the most influential psychotherapist (Cook et al. 2009). The basis of the person-centered approach (PCA) is a view of human beings, which emphasizes the capacity for self-development as well as the freedom of decision and self-responsibility, and it puts the relationship between the therapist and the client at the center. It considers certain fundamental attitudes and ways of behaving with which the therapist meets, or rather encounters, the client, to be a healing force, which generates change.

In this chapter, I aim to trace the footprints of Carl Rogers under the perspective of mindfulness in order to find out what the PCA has to offer to the new stream in psychotherapy, counseling, and everyday life which evolved from "the great mindfulness debate," especially held in the field of the behavior therapists. This stream, which is known as the "third wave of behavior therapy," emphasizes Buddhist and Zen meditation practice, acceptance, and mindfulness. Examples of therapeutic approaches from this direction are acceptance and commitment therapy (ACT) (Hayes and Smith 2005), mindfulness-based stress reduction (MBSR) (Kabat-Zinn 2005), dialectical behavior therapy (DBT) (Linehan 1993), and mindfulness-based cognitive therapy (MBCT) (Segal et al. 2002). Some relationships of the PCA with this "third wave" will be addressed later in this chapter.

Various authors (Kuno 2001; Moore 2001, 2003; Schillings 2004) think that Carl Rogers' theory builds a bridge between the Eastern and the Western world. This position is shared from the perspective of Buddhist psychotherapy which

---

K. Bundschuh-Müller (✉)
Focusing Zentrum Frankfurt, Bolongarostrasse 150 H 65929 Frankfurt, Germany
e-mail: bundschuh.mueller@t-online.de
URL: www.focusing-zentrum-frankfurt.de

acknowledges that the PCA offers "some clear ground for fruitful interaction between Buddhist and Western psychological approaches to mind" [Padma (2011) Internet source without page information]. The aim of my chapter is to elucidate some of these bridges.

2 What Does Mindfulness Mean?

It is undisputed that in the Western linguistic, therapeutic, and philosophical spheres the term "mindfulness"—meaning taking care, being careful, paying close attention, being alert—has an important function as well as its own value and tradition. It holds the meaning of awareness, attentiveness, consciousness, regardfulness, sensibility, thoughtfulness, cautiousness, and "watchfulness." It also implies the connotation of accepting what is, just in the here and now. It is obvious that "mindfulness" and "acceptance" in person-centered psychotherapy are of crucial importance. We can even consider them as fundamental.

In a workshop, I asked the participants: "When do you think you are mindful?" One of them answered: "When I am carrying something very precious and fragile, then I am mindful." And this—to me—is really the core of mindfulness in the PCA: encountering somebody very precious and fragile—the client sitting in front of me. In the PCA, the basic principles, which are unconditional positive regard, acceptance, respectful non-judgmental listening, gentle care, and non-intrusiveness, form the basis for constructive change. Person-centered encounter always takes place "in the situation," in the "here and now."

Similar descriptions come from Kabat-Zinn (2003), a microbiologist specialized in integrating the concept of mindfulness in a modern form of stress-coping therapy. He writes that "mindfulness" is connected with special features like mindfulness and consciousness, which can be cultivated and developed by means of meditation. According to him, "mindfulness" means that consciousness is focused on the evolution of experiencing on a moment-to-moment basis. The basis for this is the fact that attention is paid intentionally and without judgment to present moment experiences.

Being mindful reminds us of the inherent actualizing tendency of a person: Mindfulness in its most general sense is about waking up, becoming alert, and being sensitive to our everyday experiences and the direction of personal growth.

3 Carl Rogers: A Mindful Man

> People are just as wonderful as sunsets if I can let them be... When I look at a sunset, I don't find myself saying: Soften the orange a bit on the right hand corner... I don't try to control a sunset, I watch with awe as it unfolds... Carl Rogers.

Carl Rogers was known as an attentive, friendly, unassuming, moderate, and humble man, very authentic, yet radical in his thinking. The way he saw himself was as "walking softly" through life, like Native Americans often "walked softly" through the forest; nobody knew of their whereabouts until they had reached their destination. Carl Rogers, "the quiet revolutionary" (Rogers and Russell 2002) lived in a similar way. Perhaps, it is due to these qualities that he was able to develop a psychotherapy and counseling approach accepted worldwide, describing the fundamental basis of therapeutic change.

Rogers was an example of his own vision of lifelong learning, changing, and growing. When he died the influence of his theory and therapy was widespread and profound. But he worried about the legacy of his theory. He did not want his theory becoming a dogma of truth, but a stimulus for further creative thinking. This was—in his mind—the real goal of a theory. And he did not want to imprison others with his thinking (Demorest 2005). In his view, people should always be open to their own experience and trust in them.

Eastern thinkers "walk softly" as well. They also caused something like a "quiet revolution." They are "warriors" in a special sense. The key to this kind of "warrior ship" is not being afraid of who you are and not being afraid of yourself. We can be heroic and kind at the same time. The essence of being a warrior, or the essence of human bravery, is refusing to give up on anyone or anything. Trungpa (1984) states: "Real fearlessness is the product of tenderness" (p. 47). I believe Rogers embodied this attitude very well.

4 The Core Conditions Under an Eastern Perspective

> I have just three things to teach: simplicity, patience, compassion. These three are your greatest treasures. Lao Tzu.

4.1 Offering Mindful Relationships: Being Genuinely There with an Open Heart

In a lecture, delivered in 1954 on the Nellie Heldt Lecture Fund about "Some Hypotheses Regarding the Facilitation of Personal Growth" Carl Rogers said:

> In my early professional years, I was asking the question: How can I treat, or cure, or change this person? Now I would phrase the question this way: How can I provide a relationship which this person may use for his own personal growth? I recognize that change appears to come about through experience in a relationship. I can state the over-all hypothesis in one sentence: If I can provide a certain type of relationship, the other person will discover within himself the capacity to use that relationship for growth, and change and personal development will occur (p. 1).

We learned that there is a very special way of listening to a person, which fosters personality growth and change. This way of listening has to meet three crucial attitudes, which we call the core conditions: empathy, unconditional positive regard, and genuineness also known as congruence. And even more: They build—if they happen to come into the presence of the living moment of the relationship in the here and now—a special "sacred space" in which healing and growing can take place.

In Rogers' opinion, the most important attitude is "congruence" because without this quality the other two conditions are not trustworthy and reliable: "I have found that the more I can be genuine in the relationship, the more helpful it will be. It is only in this way that the relationship can have reality and reality seems deeply important as a first condition. It is only by providing the genuine reality which is in me, that the other person can seek for the reality which is in him" (Rogers 1954, p. 2).

Congruence means to open to one's experiences: "If a person could be fully open to experience, however, every stimulus—whether originating within the organism or in the environment—would be freely relayed through the nervous system without being distorted by any defensive mechanism" (Rogers 1961/1995, p. 188). Hendricks-Gendlin (2003) suggests the expression "pausing" in order to sense and listen to what is felt right now as a means of authenticity and self-exploration. To pause an ongoing situation, to become aware of one's immediate inner felt sensing creates a space for new possibilities to unfold.

Genuineness and exact sensing what is felt in the present moment meet mindfulness at this point: Solè-Leris (cited by Rose and Wallach 2009, p. 28) defines mindfulness this way: "Mindfulness is the attentive, unbiased looking at all phenomenon, in order to perceive and experience them as they really are, without deforming them emotionally or intellectually" (translated by KBM).

If we follow the perception of Manu Bazzanu, who is an ordained Taoist monk and person-centered counselor, genuineness and congruence find an equivalent in Buddhist terms like "being there with an open heart" or "being there like a host." At the PCE Conference 2008 in Norwich in a workshop, he compared Eastern philosophy and Rogerian theory. In Taoist tradition, a wise individual is called a "true person," a person of integrity, dignity, a person who is whole. If a true person opens up to another person in an encounter, he or she becomes open and vulnerable and he or she has to be aware about the risk of meeting another person on an existential level. Bazzanu also cited Levinas: "We are a host of the other." This hospitality is crucial for the PCA (see chapter by Schmid in this book) as well as for Buddhism. It is due to the awareness: I am a guest in my own dwelling, in the world. I am passing through. And thus I am guest and host at the same time.

On this basis—genuineness, deep openness of the heart, and my own vulnerability—contact, real encounter is possible. When I am meeting the other person with an attitude of not knowing, with openness, wonderment, and curiosity (Buddhists call this attitude a "beginner's mind"), then I am ready to really listen to another person.

Rogers puts this into these words: "I risk myself... I let myself go into the immediacy of the relationship... in these moments there is a timeless living in the experience which is between the client and me. It is at the opposite pole from seeing the client, or myself, as an object" (Rogers 1955, p. 268f). Rogers emphasizes that in these moments helping is mostly a by-product; according to him, what is the most important is that "I want to understand you. What person are you... behind all these masks that you are wearing in real life? Who are you? In this there is the 'desire to meet as a person', not the wish to help" (Rogers and Buber 1994, p. 30). Genuineness and openness causes openness in the other person. Encounter is touching and being touched. This position we share with Buddhist thinking.

4.2 Unconditional Positive Regard: Accepting What Is

What you know is not as important as how you are as a person Carl Rogers.

Rogers characterizes the importance of unconditional positive regard as follows: "I find that the more acceptance and liking I feel toward this individual, the more I will be creating a relationship which he can use. By acceptance I mean a warm regard of him as a person of unconditional self-worth—of value no matter what his condition, his behavior, or his feelings are" (Rogers 1954, p. 3). The concept of unconditional positive regard can also be found in Eastern schools of thought. Shared terms like loving kindness, compassion, tenderness, respect, joy, beauty, patience, gratitude, gracefulness, or unconditional love characterize the bridge between PCA and Eastern thinking.

The fact that the attitude of unconditional positive regard is close to and related to the attitude of mindfulness which Eastern tradition displays is underlined by the estimation of Japanese person-centered psychotherapists of Buddhist orientation. In the Japanese school of person-centered psychotherapy, a special focus is put on the quality of unconditional positive regard. Kuno (2001) recognizes in this quality the core of Buddhism. For him, "unconditional" means that a person is accepted exactly the way he or she is, independent of whether he or she expresses "bad," painful, anxious, or abnormal feelings or a "good," positive, adult, and trusting way of experiencing. To approach another person in an unconditional way of being also means that the therapist himself or herself must learn to accept his or her own negative feelings in the same way as he or she accepts his or her positive feelings.

Buddha's teachings show that everyone can reach this state of mind, if he or she can fully understand the "Four Noble Truths," which are The Truth that there is sadness and distress, the Truth that there is a reason for sadness and distress, the Truth that there is an end to suffering, the Truth that there is a way to end suffering. In order to obtain a better understanding of the third truth, Kuno quotes Brazier's (1995) interpretation of the second Truth which is based on the following logic: If one does not suppress or unnecessarily enhance the emotions which come with suffering, these emotions will gradually disappear without leaving a trace. However, normally we endeavor to escape our suffering, the final result of which is that we aggravate it. Rogers came to realize the same insight which is expressed in the paradox of change: "...the curious paradox is that when I accept myself just as I am, then I change. I believe that I have learned this from my clients as well as within my own experience—that we cannot change, we cannot move away from what we are, until we thoroughly *accept* what we are. Then change seems to come about almost unnoticed" (Rogers 1961/1955, p. 17).

Apart from "unconditionality," Kuno also describes, as a second element, the core variable of "positive regard" from a Buddhist perspective: According to Kuno, Rogers' notion of positive regard corresponds with the teachings of Mahayana Buddhism in the sense that priority should be given to saving others before saving one's own soul. In person-centered therapy, the feelings and the experiencing of the client have priority over the feelings and experiences of the therapist. From the Buddhist perspective, the therapist encounters the client with a behavior that corresponds with the "Four Means of Embracement," which are "to give," "mild words," "philanthropic deeds," and "connection with others" (Kuno 2001).

Also in the Western sphere, some authors point at the parallels between the variable "unconditional positive regard" and Buddhist practice. For example, Moore (2001) emphasizes the deep need for acceptance of the truth and truthfulness of inner experiencing. According to her, this is of existential significance for human growth. Moore describes this attitude of unconditional positive regard as an exceptional letting go, an inner melting, a way of forgetting or losing the self—the aim of Buddhist practice.

Furthermore, unconditional positive regard can be seen as a joy about the truthfulness of the other person. The joy of experiencing beauty only implies seeing the object—a kind of joy which is not possessive or controlling. Joy about beauty is without an agenda. It does not want to possess, to own, to consume, or to control. We are happy observing the object, looking at it. This attitude resonates in Carl Rogers' work and in the work of many others, when they describe the attitude of a person who offers unconditional positive regard to another person. Santorelli (1999, quoted by Iberg 2001, p. 124) adds another specific aspect: "When we stay closely and non-judgmentally with someone exploring pain, we find beauty in the midst of the 'ruins'." It is touching to be present, when a person confronts himself or herself with their problems in a truthful and genuine way. It is truthfulness which "opens the heart" and which evokes feelings of appreciation and respect.

4.3 Empathy: Mindful Listening

> It is as though he listened and such listening as his enfolds us in silence, in which at last we begin to hear what we are meant to be. Lao Tzu (1996).

"It is only as I understand the feelings and thoughts which seem so horrible to you, or so weak, or so sentimental, or so bizarre—it is only as I see them as you see them, and accept them and you, that you can feel really free to explore all the hidden nooks and frightening crannies of your inner and often buried experience. This freedom is an important condition of the relationship" (Rogers 1954, p. 2).

Empathy implies mindfulness, care, and acceptance. In order to be able to enter the world of another person in a healing way, the therapist needs to adopt an attitude of friendly, appreciative, and respectful mindfulness, of "being with" the client: "It means temporarily living in the other's life, moving about in it delicately without making judgments; it means sensing meanings of which he or she is scarcely aware, but not trying to uncover totally unconscious feelings of which the person is totally unaware, since this would be too threatening. It includes communicating your sensing of the person's world as you look with fresh and unfrightened eyes at elements of which he or she is fearful" (Rogers 1980b, p. 142).

Such mindful listening can have a healing power which is very well exemplified by a quote of Hanh (1998): "If the power of mindfulness and of empathic listening is in you, your presence can have a healing and calming effect on other people. You only have to sit there and to listen to the person who trusts you…" (p. 64, translation by Elisabeth Zinschitz). Rud (2003) calls this capacity of empathic listening a contemplative state which leads to transformation. Another important and complimentary aspect of transformation is what happens inside the client. Eugene Gendlin [who was a student and colleague of Carl Rogers at the University of Chicago and influenced him a lot, especially his *concept of experiencing* (1962) and *the way of being with* the client (1984)] explored the question of what clients have to do to improve their own therapy outcome (Klein et al. 1969). He found that it is crucial to develop an attitude of mindful attention toward oneself. When I am able to listen precisely and from moment to moment to myself in a gentle, friendly and curious, nonjudgmental manner, especially to what is bodily felt, change will occur, naturally. As this chapter deals mainly with the impact of Carl Rogers, I will mention the work of Eugene Gendlin only briefly (More about relationships between Gendlin, Focusing and mindfulness can be found in Bundschuh-Müller 2004, 2006, 2007).

4.4 Presence: Wu Wei—A Way of Being With

When nothing is done, nothing is left undone—The way to do is to be—By letting go it all gets done (Lao Tzu 1996).

When he was already at the end of his life, Rogers proposed a hypothesis about a further significant variable which he called "presence." This additional feature is one that exists in the area of mysticism and spirituality (Rogers 1979, 1980b, 1986). He describes in "A Way of Being" (1980b) what happens in a helping relationship, when he is very close to his "inner intuitive self":

> ... When I am somehow in touch with the unknown in me, when I am perhaps in a slightly altered state of consciousness, then whatever I do seems to be full of healing. Then, simply my *presence* is releasing and helpful to the other. There is nothing I can do to force this experience, but when I can relax and be close to the transcendental core of me, ... it seems that my inner spirit has reached out and touched the inner spirit of the other. Our relationship transcends itself and becomes a part of something larger. Profound growth and healing and energy are present (Rogers 1980b, p. 129).

Rogers did not elaborate on an understanding of presence. But today there are several authors who have reflected on this topic. Schmid (2003) assumes that Rogers' "presence" is the existential foundation of the basic attitudes. It comprehensively describes them in an existential way and on a deeper, dialogical–personal level. Thorne (1985), independently, uses the word "tenderness" in this context. Thorne's experience is that tenderness emerges when a relationship is characterized by acceptance, empathy, and congruence and a deep trust in the client's ability to move forward. Thorne describes this as being caught up in a stream of love. Effortless understanding, profound growth, energy, and healing accompany this. This quality can only arise in a climate of faith and a transcending of fear. O'Hara (2000) calls presence "moments of eternity," which for her is a synonym for unconditional love.

Gendlin described this special attitude of "being with" like this: "If there is something bad, sick, or unsound, let it inwardly be and breathe. That is the only way it can evolve and change into the form it needs" (Gendlin 1986, p. 178).

This attitude meets perfectly the principle of Wu Wei which originates from Taoism. Wu Wei means "non-doing" or more precisely not to act against the Tao or the "flow of the universe." "Taoism states that all life forces tend to move toward harmony and balance because it is in their nature to do so. From the Taoist viewpoint, we, as humans, have the choice of consciously aligning ourselves with the way, or remaining in ignorance and resisting the natural order of the Tao. To choose the latter means to remain disconnected from our own personal processes, our own Tao, as well as life's grand flow. Taoist teachings are intended to be utilized as a guide to daily living. Their greatest value lies in their ability to direct us toward our own process of self-exploration, growth, and transformation which connects us deeply to ourselves and to the world around us" (Kardash nd, p. 2). The "going with the flow" of the Wu Wei principle, the "non-doing" can be seen as being/staying with what is just there in the present moment.

Presence is the authentic attitude to be, to fully live in the presence: unconditionally accepting the other, empathically becoming involved in his or her presence, without any prior intention that is with openness and a wonder toward experience and thus meeting the quality of Wu Wei.

To sum up, it seems to me that the core conditions put into practice meditative attitudes (see also the chapter by Flender). In Buddhist terms, these are the qualities of being there with an open heart (genuineness), loving kindness (unconditional positive regard), mindful listening (empathy), and the principle of Wu Wei (which meets the quality of presence).

5 Selected Concepts of the PCA: Reflected by Eastern Wisdom

5.1 Actualizing Tendency

From the viewpoint of the PCA in each person, there is the deep need and desire of "becoming oneself," a longing to become whole, a craving for further development in a direction of growing and becoming what one is meant to be. "It seems to me that at bottom each person is asking, who am I really? How can I get in touch with this real self, underlying all my surface behavior? How can I become myself?" (Rogers 1980a, p. 357) and the reply could be: "At the center of your being you have the answer; you know who you are and you know what you want" (Lao Tzu, internet source). Rogers names this inner quest the "actualization tendency." I dare to assume that the "Tao" is of similar quality: the inner spirit which flows through us, a life force that goes for inner development in a direction of living in harmony, genuineness, and balance. Chuang Tzu refers to this type of being in the world as flowing, or more poetically (and provocatively), as "purposeless wandering." By allowing the Tao to work through us, we render our actions truly spontaneous, natural, and effortless. We thus flow with all experiences and feelings as they come and go (Kardash 1998, 2012 Internet source without page information).

5.2 Openness to Experience

One main basic assumption of PCA is that of the fully functioning person. This (ideal) person is totally free of defense, it is not identified with a special view of itself and flexible to adapt in any situation. "The self and the personality emerge from experience, rather than experience being translated or twisted to fit a preconceived self-structure. It means that one becomes a participant in and an observer of the ongoing process of organismic experience, rather than being in control of it" (Rogers 1961/1995, p. 189). Or, "The good life is a process, not a state of being, it is a direction, not a destination" (Rogers 1961/1995, p. 186). We can understand the attitude of the fully functioning person as mindfulness toward one's own ongoing experiencing in the sense of an attitude of attentive and accepting being with what is going on inside right now without presumption and prejudice. One can also name this "openness to experience." "In general then, it appears to be true that when a client is open to his experience, he comes to find his organism more trustworthy. He feels less fear of the emotional reactions he has. There is a gradual growth of trust, and even affection for the complex, rich, varied assortment of feelings and tendencies, which exist in him at the organismic level. Consciousness, instead of being the watchman over a dangerous and unpredictable lot of impulses, of which few can be permitted to see the light of day, becomes the comfortable inhabitant of a society of impulses and feelings and thoughts, which are discovered to be very satisfactory self-governing when not fully guarded" (Rogers 1961/1995, p. 119).

Gendlin (1962) emphasizes the attitude as one of unconditional positive regard, mindful attention, and curiosity toward oneself and toward what is bodily felt in the present moment. It is a focusing on one's own inner sensing. It carries in it the mood of "beginner's mind" or the position of witness. One uses the core conditions to establish a helpful and friendly relationship toward oneself in order to further personal development.

Quite similarly, Lao Tzu writes that we must be quiet and watchful, learning to listen to both our own inner voices and the voices of our environment in a non-interfering, receptive manner. In this way, we also learn to rely on more than just our intellect and logical mind to gather and assess information. We develop and trust our intuition as our direct connection to the Tao. We heed the intelligence of our whole body, not only our brain. And we learn through our own experience. This means trusting our own bodies, our thoughts and emotions (Kardash 1998, Internet source without page information).

5.3 The Positive View of Human Nature

Within the PCA, a positive view of human nature is held: "One of the most revolutionary concepts to grow out of our clinical experience is the growing recognition that the innermost core of a man's nature, the deepest layers of his personality, the base of his 'animal nature' is positive in nature—is basically socialized, forward-moving, rational and realistic" (Rogers 1961/1995, p. 91).

Eastern philosophies also assume a basic goodness of human nature. Chögyam Trungpa (1984) writes:

> If we are willing to take an unbiased look, we will find out that, in spite of all our problems and confusion, all our emotional and psychological ups and downs, there is something basically good about our existence as human beings. Unless we can discover that ground of goodness in our own lives, we cannot hope to improve the lives of others. Every human being has a basic nature of goodness, which is undiluted and unconfused. That goodness contains tremendous gentleness and appreciation. If they have never developed sympathy or gentleness toward themselves, people cannot experience harmony or peace within themselves, and therefore, what they project to others is also inharmonious and confused. Developing tenderness toward yourself allows you to see both your problems and your potential accurately. That kind of gentleness toward yourself is very necessary. It provides the ground for helping yourself and others. Basic goodness is very closely connected to the idea of bodhicitta in the Buddhist tradition. Bodhi means "awake" or "wakeful" and citta means "heart", so bodhicitta is "awakened heart". Such awakened heart comes from being willing to face your state of mind. That may seem like a great demand, but it is necessary (p. 11).

Both Eastern philosophies and the PCA refer to humans as part of a social system, as having a social responsibility, meant to be part of a relationship from the very beginning. Social responsibility, "social self," being part of something bigger, being a relational person is central to both:

> By listening carefully within, as well as to our surroundings, by remembering that we are part of an interconnected whole, by remaining still until action is called forth, we can perform valuable, necessary, and long-lasting service in the world while cultivating our ability to be at one with the Tao. Such is the power of wu-wei, allowing ourselves to be guided by the Tao (Kardash 1998, para. 11).

One can say the background parallels between the PCA and Eastern approaches involving similar aims, recognition of the essential trustworthiness of human nature, the importance of an internal locus of evaluation, the "process" view of the self, and the therapeutic process which involves a reduction in "incongruence" or "delusion" (Purton 1996).

6 Shambhala: Different Routes—One Destination

In Tibet, there are stories about a legendary kingdom. According to the legends, this was a place of peace and prosperity, governed by wise and compassionate rulers. The citizens were equally kind and learned, so that in general, the kingdom was a model society. This place was called Shambhala. Their people follow the Buddhist path of *loving kindness and concern for all beings*. Among the Tibetan people, there is a popular belief that the kingdom of Shambhala can still be found, hidden in a remote valley somewhere in the Himalayas. Many scholars, however, believe that the stories of Shambhala are pure fiction; it is also possible to see in these legends the expression of the deeply rooted and very real human desire for a good and fulfilling life. Shambhala can be regarded as the ground or root of awakening and sanity that exists as a potential within every human being. Shambhala teachings are found on the premise that there is basic human wisdom that can help to solve the world's problems. This wisdom does not belong to any one culture or religion. Nor does it come either from the East or from the West. Rather it is a tradition of humanistic warriorship that has existed in many cultures and many times throughout history (Trungpa 1984).

Like the hidden land of Shambhala, the PCA and its findings and richness nowadays have moved into the background for many modern psychotherapies. As mentioned before, today many therapists prefer Eastern concepts and techniques and integrate them into their work rather than use "old-fashioned" therapies and concepts of Carl Rogers, Gene Gendlin, and other representatives of humanistic therapies. If I compare these different streams carefully, I don't understand this effort, because there are a lot of similarities between them.

Take, for example, Marsha Linehan, the founder of the DBT, who originally learned a lot from Carl Rogers during her university days. When I attended a retreat with her and Benedictine monk and Zen Master Willigis Jäger about mindfulness and DBT in 2006, she was asked about this noticeable influence of

Rogers, and at this retreat she confirmed Rogers' influence on her. One of the participants, a behavior therapist, asked her about how real change is to come about. He asked: "How can I change, when I accept what is?" Linehan looked at him irritated for a moment, then she smiled and replied: "But acceptance *is* change!"—In other words, she offered to the whole auditorium the Rogerian paradox of change without mentioning him, and perhaps without even realizing it.

Many therapists, especially from the behavioral therapy direction, are just exploring the—for them—radically new findings of the impact of mindfulness and acceptance, without realizing that there is a lot to learn from proven body of experience of the PCA.

Mindfulness meditation is a central element of the "third wave" of behavior therapy (see above). While in these therapies training of mindfulness is generally offered as a pure exercise, in PCA mindfulness is offered in a relationship. In person-centered and experiential therapy we (usually) don't sit on a cushion or bench, we carry mindfulness in the real relationship of the present moment, or in the real relationship with oneself. Here, the dialog is affected and colored by mindfulness; there is a flowing of mindfulness between the two people. In this way, the client is able to learn to be mindful with himself or herself.

But undoubtedly meditation practice is extremely useful (and also Western contemplation practice, see the chapter by Flender in this book). There are an increasing number of person-centered counselors and psychotherapists who practice Buddhist or Zen Meditation. Geller (2003) explains the meaning of mindfulness and meditation:

> Simply being with internal states and accepting what is there—thus enabling the client to be with and accept what is there—is what lies at the heart of working with the core conditions. There is something important in all of this about *being with* in a deeper, more fully "mindful" way that might require a different, perhaps a more precise quality of attention to what is going on- in both self and client- at the level of thoughts, feelings, body language and the felt sense (Cited by Moore 2001). Geller and Greenberg (2002) also offer a very profound and comprehensive research study about the impact of mindfulness practice on person centered and experiential psychotherapists. Additionally, Bazzanu's (Bazzanu 2009) result of a small research project was that "the regular practice of meditation would assist a process of focusing and centering that can make a therapist a better instrument, more finely tune to empathic awareness and congruence, on that can better assist a person in distress, or a person exploring issues in his or her life" (p. 11).

The PCA goes far beyond mindfulness trainings. It aims deeper than pure mindfulness practice. Sometimes very special moments of deep connectedness, like "sacred spaces," arise in the relationship. This is when the quality of presence unfolds. In presence, there is a qualitative jump, which in contrast to meditation practice we cannot make, cannot control with our will. We can direct mindfulness to something, yet presence simply is; it is effortless (yet needs a lot of concentration). It can come when bodily sensation, feeling, and mental activity, such as thinking, are synchronized to a great extent. Rogers (1980b) described an opening in the direction of presence in the sense of this spontaneous state of effortless clarity, precision, lightness, and earthed expansion of perception or consciousness. And so, we are entitled to say: The PCA offers much more than a mere technique!

7 Conclusion

Coming to a conclusion, the quality of being "mindful," being fully and accurately aware of what is going on, both in self and in self-in-relation-to-other is of high value in different schools of thought. Person-centered therapists have known about this for a long time (see "The Essence of the Person-Centered Approach"). I want to state that the PCA is the first and oldest mindfulness-based therapeutic approach of the western hemisphere carrying old and everlasting wisdom from Eastern and Western traditions. Realizing this we are entitled to say: Mindfulness, peacefulness, and "a listening mind" are the crucial characteristics of the PCA. They constitute the spirit of the PCA. They are "the mood" of it.

And I want to bring to mind again the quality of humanistic warriorship. Members of the person-centered community are the keepers of a deep wisdom and competence, which is inherent in the PCA. In the spirit of a warrior, who never gives up, with the sense of bravery and trust, we will wait for a change of the zeitgeist. In the spirit of Lao Tzu, we can say: "I see my path, but I don't know where it leads. Not knowing where I'm going is what inspires me to travel it." And so: We will walk softly and: The path unfolds while walking….

References

Padma (2011). (without date). http://www.dharmanet.org/psychpadma.htm. Accessed 11 Oct 2011.
Bazzanu, M. (2009). Mindful of what? Adlerian year book January 2010. http://www.manubazzano.com/uploads/MINDFUL%20OF%20WHAT%5B1%5D.pdf Accessed 28 Oct 2011.
Brazier, D. (1995). *Zen Therapy*. London: Constable.
Bundschuh-Müller, K. (2004). „Es ist was es ist, sagt die Liebe…. [It is what it is, love says…] In T. Heidenreich & J. Michalak (Eds.), *Achtsamkeit und Akzeptanz in der Psychotherapie* (pp. 405–456). Tübingen: DGVT. (English translation by Elisabeth Zinschitz at http://focusing-zentrum-frankfurt.de).
Bundschuh-Müller, K. (2006). Akzeptieren heißt Verändern. [Acceptance means change.] *Psychotherapie im Dialog, 3*, 258–263.
Bundschuh-Müller, K. (2007). Von Augenblick zu Augenblick—von Angesicht zu Angesicht: Gesprächspsychotherapie als achtsamkeitsbasiertes personzentriertes Verfahren. [From Moment to Moment—from countenance to countenance: Person centered Psychotherapy as mindfulness based method.] *Gesprächspsychotherapie und Personzentrierte Beratung, 2*, 75–83.
Cook, J. M., Biyanova, T., & Coyne, J. C. (2009). Influential psychotherapy figures, authors, and books: An internet survey of over 2,000 psychotherapists. *Psychotherapy: Theory Research, Practice, Training, 46*, 42–52.

Demorest, A. (2005). *Psychology's grand theorists*. New York: Psychology Press.
Geller, S. M. (2003). Becoming whole: A collaboration between experiential psychotherapies and mindfulness meditation. *Person-Centered & Experiential Psychotherapies, 2*(4), 258–273.
Geller, S., & Greenberg, L. (2002). Therapeutic presence: Therapists' experience of presence in the psychotherapy encounter. *Person-Centered & Experiential Psychotherapies, 1*(1 & 2), 71–86.
Gendlin, E. T. (1962). Experiencing and the creation of meaning. A philosophical and psychological approach to the subjective. New York: Free Press of Glencoe.Gendlin, E. T. (1970). Existentialism and experiential psychotherapy, In J. T. Hart & T. M. Tomlinson (Eds.), New directions in client-centered therapy (pp. 70–94). Boston: Houghton Mifflin.
Gendlin, E. T. (1984). The client's client: The edge of awareness. In R. L. Levant & J. M. Shlien (Eds.), *Client-centered therapy and the person-centered approach. New directions in theory, research and practice* (pp. 76–107). New York: Praeger.
Gendlin, E. T. (1986). *Let your body interpret your dreams*. Wilmette: Chiron Publication.
Hanh, T. N. (1998). *Schritte der Achtsamkeit. [Steps of mindfulness.]* Freiburg: Herder.
Hayes, S. C., & Smith, C. (2005). *Get out of your mind & into your life: The new acceptance and commitment therapy*. Oakland: New Harbinger Pubn.
Hendricks, M. (2003). Focusing as a force for peace: The revolutionary pause. *Staying In Focus, 3*(2), 4–7.
Iberg, J. R. (2001). Unconditional positive regard, constituent activities. In J. D. Bozarth & P. Wilkins (Eds.), *Rogers' therapeutic conditions: Evolution, theory and practice (Volume 3: Unconditional positive regard)* (pp. 109–125). Ross-on-Wye: PCCS-Books.
Kabat-Zinn, J. (2003). Mindfulness-based interventions in context: Past, present, and future. *Clinical Psychology: Science and Practice, 10*(2), 144–156.
Kabat-Zinn, J. (2005). *Coming to our senses: Healing ourselves and the world through mindfulness* (p. 606). New York: Hyperion.
Kardash, T. (1998). Taoism: The wu-wei principle, part 4. From http://www.jadedragon.com/archives/june98/tao.html. Accessed 01 July 2012.
Kardash, T. (2012). (without date). Taoism: Ageless wisdom for a modern world. http://www.jadedragon.com/archives/tao_heal/lao_tzu2.html. Accessed 01 July 2012.
Klein, M. H., Mathieu, P. L., Gendlin, E. T., & Kiesler, D.L. (1969). *The experiencing scale. A research and training manual* (Vols. I & II). Madison: University of Wisconsin.
Kuno, T. (2001). An interpretation of unconditional positive regard from the standpoint of Buddhist-based psychology. In J. D. Bozarth & P. Wilkins (Eds.), *Rogers' therapeutic conditions: Evolution, theory and practice (Volume 3: Unconditional positive regard)* (pp. 210–219). Ross-on-Wye: PCCS-Books.
Linehan, M. M. (1993). *Cognitive-behavioral treatment of borderline personality disorder*. New York: Guilford Pubn.
Moore, J. (2001). Acceptance of the truth of the present moment as a trustworthy foundation for unconditional positive regard. In J. D. Bozarth & P. Wilkins (Eds.), *Rogers' therapeutic conditions: Evolution, theory and practice (Volume 3: Unconditional positive regard)* (pp. 198–209). Ross-on-Wye: PCCS-Books.
Moore, J. (2003). *Letting go of what I think I am* (Manuscript of a Talk, given at the PCEPC-Congress 7/2003 in Egmond/Netherlands).
O'Hara, M. (2000). Moments of eternity. *Person, 4*(1), 5–17.
Purton, C. (1996). The deep structure of the core conditions: A Buddhist perspective. In R. Hutterer et al. (Eds.) (1996), *Client-centered and experiential psychotherapy: a paradigm in motion* (pp. 455–467). Frankfurt: Peter Lang. Also available at: http://www.dwelling.me.uk/Deep%20structure.htm.
Rogers, C. R. (1954). Becoming a person. Two Lectures delivered on the Nellie Heldt Lecture Fund. *Oberlin College Nellie Heldt Lecture Series*. Oberlin: Oberlin Printing. Also available at: http://www.centerfortheperson.org/pdf/1954__Becoming_a_Person.pdf Co. 1954.
Rogers, C. R. (1955). Persons or science? *A philosophical question. American Psychologist, 10*(7), 267–278.

Rogers, C. R. (1979). The foundations of the person-centered approach. *Education, 100*, 96–107.
Rogers, C. R. (1980a). What it means to become a person. In A. Arkoff (Ed.), *Psychology and personal growth* (pp. 357–365). Boston: Allyn & Bacon.
Rogers, C. R. (1980b). *A way of being*. Boston: Houghton Mifflin.
Rogers, C. R. (1986). Client-centered therapy. In I. L. Kutash & A. Wolf (Eds.), *Psychotherapist's casebook: Theory and technique in the practice of modern therapies*. San Francisco: Jossey-Bass.
Rogers, C. R. (1995). *On becoming a person. A therapist's view on psychotherapy*. Boston: Houghton Mifflin Company (Original work published in 1961).
Rogers, C. R. & Buber, M. (1994). *Dialog between Martin Buber and Carl Rogers* (K. N. Cissna, R. Anderson, Trans. 1960). Albany: State University of New York Press.
Rogers, C., & Russel, D. (2002). *The quiet revolutionary: An oral history*. Roseville: Penmarin Books.
Rose, N. & Wallach, H. (2009). Die historischen Wurzeln der Achtsamkeitsmeditation—Ein Exkurs in Buddhismus und christliche Mystik. [Historic roots of mindfulness meditation.]. In T. Heidenreich & J. Michalak (Eds.), *Achtsamkeit und Akzeptanz in der Psychotherapie* (pp. 27–48). Tübingen: DGVT.
Rud, C. (2003). Empathy: The adventure of being present. *Person-Centered & Experiential Psychotherapy, 2*(3), 162–171.
Santorelli, S. (1999). *Heal thy self: Lessons on mindfulness in medicine*. New York: Bell Tower.
Schillings, A. (2004). Stillness and awareness from person to person. http://www.focusing.org/spirituality/stillness.htm.
Schmid, P. (2003). "Face to Face" The art of encounter. In B. Thorne & E. Lambers (Eds.), *Person-centered therapy, A European perspective* (pp. 74–85). London: Sage Publications.
Segal, J., Zindel, V., Williams, J., Mark, G., & Teasdale, J. D. (2002). *Mindfulness-based cognitive therapy for depressions*. New York: Guildford Press.
Thorne, B. (1985). *The quality of tenderness*. Norwich: Norwich Centre Publications.
Trungpa, C. (1984). *Shambhala: The sacred path of the warrior*. Boston: Shambhala.
Tzu, L. (1996). *Tao Te Ching: The book of the Way*. London: Kyle Cathie. http://thinkexist.com/quotation/at_the_center_of_your_being_you_have_the_answer/339558.html.

Getting Centered in Presence: Meditation with Gifted Students at Hansenberg Castle

Jürgen Flender

1 Hansenberg Castle

Hansenberg Castle is an upper level secondary school and boarding school established in 2003 by the state of Hess (Germany), focusing on politics/economics, mathematics, and the natural sciences as its main subjects. It is based on a public–private partnership model with strong economical partners, working to provide an environment for motivated, intellectually gifted, and socially competent students. Almost 200 students are prepared to take the A-level in three years. It is Hansenberg's goal to help mold its students into well-rounded individuals who are prepared to assume societal responsibility. Personal growth is challenged and advanced by an attractive program and plenty of opportunities for self-experience within a spirited community. Besides the permanent need for time management, another challenge is the fact that basing one's self-esteem too much on achievement becomes chancy among other high achievers.

As a psychologist, I am involved with the selection of new students, the introduction program, health promotion, and evaluation. Mostly, clinical diagnostics and a repairing psychotherapy are not in demand, but person-centered counseling, for example, to clarify and develop resources, to train assertiveness, or to overcome obstructive perfectionism. In case of diffuse incongruences, Gendlin's focusing (Gendlin 1982) has proved to be an alternative, if not a precondition to rational problem-solving. In addition to counseling, I provide a course in psychology and offer workshops and continuous practice in self- and time management, autogenic training (Wilk 2004), traditional archery (Herrigel 2007), and meditation (Lipsett 1991). As a staff member of the boarding school, I am also responsible for one apartment with eight students. With further activities like staff training and cooperative supervision, I contribute to personnel and organizational

J. Flender (✉)
Internatsschule Schloss Hansenberg, Hansenbergallee 11-13,
65366 Geisenheim-Johannisberg, Germany
e-mail: j.flender@hansenberg.de

development. Within the ambitious Hansenberg community, meditation is a center of reference. I follow a Western philosophical approach that differs from prevalent Buddhist implementations.

2 Meditation and Psychotherapy

In recent years, meditation has been appreciated in psychotherapy as a facilitator of mindfulness and acceptance (Linehan 1996; Heidenreich and Michalak 2004). It is widely accepted that meditation strengthens a healthy awareness of *something* to be experienced in the here and now, for example, sensory stimuli (Kabat-Zinn 2010), inner experiencing (Renn 2011), schemata (Roediger 2011), or helpful imaginations (Wetzel 2011). Although this is doubtlessly useful and matches a widespread form of *object-related* meditation, it misses the crucial point of *silent* meditation (contemplation) as a way leading into *pure* awareness and facilitating free and responsible acting. Rogers showed a strong tendency toward this fundamental awareness when he tried to understand deep experiences of relatedness in terms of Buber's I-thou-philosophy (Buber 1996; Anderson and Cissna 1997). *Presence* for him became a decisive variable of facilitating actualization in helpful relations:

> ... When I am somehow in touch with the unknown in me, when I am perhaps in a slightly altered state of consciousness, then whatever I do seems to be full of healing. Then, simply my presence is releasing and helpful to the other. There is nothing I can do to force this experience, but when I can relax and be close to the transcendental core of me, ... it seems that my inner spirit has reached out and touched the inner spirit of the other. Our relationship transcends itself and becomes a part of something larger. Profound growth and healing and energy are present. (Rogers 1980, p. 129)

Just following the phenomenology of his own experiencing, Rogers crosses conventional borders and enters the sphere of transpersonal psychology (Assagioli 1987) and spirituality (Bundschuh-Müller 2004) without relieving rationality to religious doctrines. This is exactly the core of a modern understanding of meditation: Not limiting actualization to the borders of religious, scientific, or wellness-oriented dogmas, but practicing it as a reasonable form of radical actualization. The main thesis of this article is that a contemporary western understanding of meditation not only is compatible with basic concerns of PCA, but may also lead to an extended understanding of actualization and relatedness.

3 Meditation: A Modern Western Approach

The approach I introduce here is the work of the Frankfurt philosopher Lipsett (1991, 2005), which has been adopted by several teachers of meditation in Europe. Lipsett provides a practical philosophical approach enrooted in occidental tradition, which encourages critical thinking and offers essential meditation exercises without culture-specific decoration.

Lipsett (1991) defines meditation as a process within consciousness ("Meditation is more than sitting up straight."). This process is methodically defined (not just spontaneously occurring), springs from free will (not from drugs, etc.), and takes place under basic conditions (e.g., in a defined setting with specific exercises) with the aim of an extension or deepening of consciousness. As an *exercising practice,* meditation offers a way leading from a self-serving experiencing to an open-minded experiencing of transcendence and true reality. A decisive point can be the experience "to be that self which one truly is" (Rogers 1995, p. 166). Exercising practice trains an "intuition for the here and now" (Lipsett 2012), which on the way back facilitates an *executing practice* with a clear concern for individual as well as for social and political questions. *Contemplation* is a special form of meditation. It means meditating in an unfocused silent mode with the aim of an undisguised experiencing of absolute presence. Contemplation may be seen as a way to promote openness to experiences which is a central attribute of the fully functioning person: "If a person could be fully open to experience, however, every stimulus,—whether originating within the organism or in the environment,—would be freely relayed through the nervous system without being distorted by any defensive mechanism" (Rogers 1995, p. 188). According to Lipsett, the specific process of consciousness is equal in all forms of meditation independent of culture and religion (assumption of convergence).

Based on this definition of meditation, Lipsett systematically searched Zen, Yoga, Taoism, and (because less examined) especially detailed Christian mysticism for universal principles. The four ancient and culturally independent principles he reconstructed are *preparing, focusing, centering,* and *opening of consciousness.* These stages do not describe an empirically founded sequence of practical steps, but the inner logic of the developing process, following Kant's question for the conditions of possibility. According to Lipsett's reconstruction, the immediate precondition for the experience of transcendence and true reality is the *opening of consciousness* as the peak of mystic ways in general.

3.1 Opening of Consciousness

Exercises of this stage train an unfocused mode of consciousness. Even if an awareness of elements remains, attention is no longer bound to specific elements, but directed to "no-thing" (*Nichts, Nicht-Etwas*) or—in equivalent—to "everything" without preference. Culturally specific actualizations of this principle are contemplation (Christian tradition), pure awareness or *shikantaza* (Zen), seizing the tao (Taoism), and pacification of all mental processes, that is, *citta-vrtti-nirodha* (Yoga). An opening of consciousness can occur spontaneously during meditation; most often, a preceding *centering* of consciousness is required. Additionally, it may also occur during person-centered counseling (see below the case example of Toni).

Due to the fact, that this process is actually simple, but not easy to realize, other forms of meditation are useful to fulfill an assisting function. These are assigned by Lipsett to the categories of centering, focusing, and preparing of consciousness.

3.2 Centering of Consciousness

Corresponding exercises direct attention to one single element of consciousness. Meditation on this stage means to reduce awareness to one single element, for example, one word or sentence, one icon, or one overwhelming emotion (Christian tradition). Other traditions reduce attention, for example, to breathing as a whole or make use of koans (Zen), mandalas, or mantras (Yoga). If attention cannot be restricted to one element, a preceding *focusing* of consciousness might be advisable.

3.3 Focusing of Consciousness

Related exercises reduce consciousness to a limited number of changing elements. They bring the volatile mind into a continuous flow. Examples from Christian tradition are singing psalms together, painting icons, or contemplating something, for example, words from the Bible or one's own feelings and wishes. The rich Zen tradition comprises the counting of breath, the reciting of sutras, and attentive walking (kinhin) as well as archery, tea ceremony, ikebana (arranging flowers), and calligraphy. One example from Taoism is T'ai Chi, directing attention toward a prescribed sequence of movements. Yoga also provides a lot of exercises with a focus on the body (asana), breathing (pranayama), gestures (mudra), or conscious action (satyagraha). The focusing principle is central also for autogenic training (Wilk 2004), Gendlin's focusing (Gendlin 1982), and numerous forms of stress relaxation. If a continuous flow of attention is difficult to reach, for example, because of distinct distraction or fundamental doubt, the appropriate principle of meditation might be the *preparing* of consciousness.

3.4 Preparing of Consciousness

On this stage, consciousness is characterized by a discontinuous change of elements. Related exercises prepare the distracted mind for focusing processes. Examples are traditional and contemporary forms of retreat, many of them including a reorganization of the daily routine with opportunities for reading, ethical reflection, helpful discussions, basic counseling, or other activities that facilitate a broad mind for deepening processes.

4 Effects of Meditation

In the long run, exercising practice of meditation aims at a pacification of all mental processes. For an opening of consciousness "motivated non-intentionality" is the appropriate attitude: effects become more probable if they are not intended. At the preparing stages, effects comparable to those of therapeutic processes occur (Lipsett 1991). Especially at the stages of focusing and centering, *physiological* effects similar to effects of autogenic training are possible, for example, perceptions concerning weight, warmth, heartbeat, and breathing. *Emotional* effects are characterized by a typical change between phases of drought and comfort (Teresa von Avila 1979), comprising feelings of aversion, grief, or emptiness during drought and feelings like joy, meaning, and relatedness in phases of comfort. If both extremes are accepted—and ideally reflected in counseling or spiritual mentoring—an enduring imperturbability (*Gelassenheit*) can develop. *Intellectual and spiritual* effects are decidedness, centeredness, a quiet mind, and experiences of relative and absolute transcendence (unio mystica).

5 Meditation Practice at the Frankfurt School of Contemplation

Lipsett's Frankfurt School of Contemplation (FSC) implements the theoretical framework as a contemporary practice that differs in central aspects even from Western adoptions of Eastern traditions (e.g., Enomiya-Lassalle 2005). According to modern epistemology and communication ethics (Apel 1993), truth is not understood as something fixed that can be conveyed, for example, by an outer master; it rather is considered to be a question of finding and following one's inner master within helpful relations—a core condition which FSC shares with PCA. Critical reasoning is considered to be necessary and encouraged to stretch for its own limits. Instead of a master–student model, the FSC favors a mentoring model with a facilitating teacher for a limited time.

Exercising practice within the group takes place in a formally minimized setting. Without a master to be honored or special rituals to be mastered, the individual exercise calls for exclusive attention. Complementary mentoring and intellectual reflection are recommended. Mentoring includes counseling not only of spiritual–intellectual, but also of emotional processes; in certain phases, it can be identical with person-centered counseling. Reflection can be done, for example, in workshops that reframe meditation in mystic, psychological, theological, or philosophical terms. A center of reference is the medieval German mystic Eckehart (1979). The spirit at the FSC is neither a "cold" training of consciousness nor a culture of mindful benevolence, but characterized by an alert struggle for truth, truthfulness, and rightness. These "indispensable" (Apel 1993) principles of communication are the living center of FSC—not shared feelings, experiences, or a common Guru. As Buber puts it: "True community does not come into being because people have feelings for each other (though that is required, too), but rather on two accounts: all of them have to stand in a living, reciprocal relationship to a single living center, and they have to stay in a living, reciprocal relationship to one another" (Buber 1996, p. 94).

6 Using Principles of Meditation to Promote Personal Growth at Hansenberg Castle

A central value of Hansenberg is the close connection between achievement and responsibility. Social and intellectual ability are no end in itself, but ask for actualization in the world. This requires a pronounced awareness for ethical, social, economical, and political questions, appropriate personal values, and distinct self-awareness. Meditation, practiced as a training of consciousness, facilitates relevant actualization processes. It especially trains the "intuition for the moment" (Lipsett 2012), the opening for the crucial questions: What is now? And what is needed now?

6.1 Contemplation Group

Every Wednesday evening, some students and colleagues meet for contemplation in the room of silence. The outer setting comprises exercises in the traditional form of motionless sitting interrupted by attentive walking. Optional elements are a sequence of gestures from monastery tradition and a textual impulse. Interested students get an introduction and advice on the choice of appropriate focusing or centering exercise. Meditation in this minimal form requires nothing but pure awareness. It allows to perceive and to accept what is present now. As a student gratefully put it: "This is the hour where I must not do anything, but just can be."

6.2 Time Management

Usual trainings of time management (e.g., Seiwert 2002) treat time as an objective quantitative variable and provide exercises on how to use hours and minutes effectively. In contrast, Augustinus' time philosophy (Augustinus 1998) demonstrates that there is no other reality than a momentary one: the past consists of memories recalled in this moment, the future is built up from present expectations. We just have this fluent moment (*nunc fluens*)—and we can also become aware of the never-changing (eternal) presence (*nunc stans*). To realize the existence of an unchanging "observing self" (Deikman 1982) beyond all changing, elements and processes can fundamentally convert one's self-concept and contribute to a full actualization of the core variable congruence.

A helpful sensitization for the *nunc fluens* can be supported by exercises from the stage "focusing of consciousness," whereas an experience of the *nunc stans* usually requires continued practice on the stages of centering and opening consciousness. In my trainings of time- and self-management, I use Augustinus' concept in form of an adapted schema to reformulate typical questions of "managing time" in terms of "managing this moment," referring both to *nunc fluens* and *nunc stans*. This may lead to the question of how to become aware of this moment and its potentialities or even to a comprehension of acting as part of a comprehensive actualization. Useful focusing and centering exercises are taken not only from traditional meditation, but also from mental training (Eberspächer 2007), transpersonal psychology (Assagioli 1987), Gendlin's focusing (Gendlin 1982), Gestalt therapy (Stevens 2000), and trainings for acceptance and mindfulness (Heidenreich and Michalak 2004).

6.3 Traditional Archery

Archery provides an athletic form of focusing or even centering of consciousness. We practice it not in the traditional Zen form (Herrigel 2007), but in an adapted form which uses the bow, for example, for a training of volitional skills. Own physical strength is felt and embedded in a sequence of movements, with the central moment of anchoring and releasing. As a powerful form, it allows to detach oneself deliberately from dysfunctional constraints and to liberate energy for volitional aims.

6.4 Autogenic Training

Autogenic training (Wilk 2004) is an approved technique of stress relaxation. By means of evoking sentences, it directs attention to a sequence of bodily areas and perceptions and trains accepting visualization. I introduce autogenic training as an exercise to focus consciousness. Trained participants are invited to centering of consciousness by reducing the sequence to one sentence or visualization. An entire reduction to the basic sentence "I am at peace" actually can serve as an opening of consciousness, if the exercise includes the readiness to abandon even the last preferences of attention.

6.5 Person-Centered Counseling: The Case of Toni

Most Hansenberg students are open-minded about a reflection of their personal growth. Some of them choose counseling for a deeper exploration, often initiated by problems or felt incongruences. Toni was one of them: intellectually gifted, straight, characterful, and willing to explore himself. His achievements in written examinations were brilliant, but he refused to say anything in class, was cautious in social contact, and had a fear of flying. In counseling, he explored the long history of traumatic mobbing experiences in his previous school and revealed a remarkable angst. His actualization process was supported especially by Gendlin's focusing (Gendlin 1982) in combination with techniques of trauma therapy (Reddemann 2003). He created an inner secure place, expanded it to an inner scene play, and for several weeks, he underwent an emotionally intensive process that was driven by its own logic and at the same time fully under Toni's control. Mighty, partly archetypal imaginations occurred that helped Toni to handle his angst and to regulate emotional distance in social contact. Speaking in class became more familiar to Toni and he successfully got through a face-off at his previous school. He passed a flight by airplane and established a local group fighting for human rights.

Nevertheless, after a while, "the system fought back." Psychosomatic pain occurred and clinical treatment was imminent when we met once more for counseling. Toni felt in black despair and found himself caught in fundamental doubt: All imaginations, although he only made selective use of them, had lost their effectiveness, because he recognized them as conceivabilities. Nothing in mind kept him grounded. So I invited him to jump from the observed contents to the "observing self" (Deikman 1982). He jumped—and experienced himself as identical with experiencing. What he verbalized in this moment disclosed a fundamentally changed view on his "problems" within a new experience of reality. He felt an unknown freedom, and we reflected it in the way I introduced in this article. Clinical treatment could be avoided. Toni never shared our meditation group and stayed inclined rather to scientific than to philosophical questions; but an authentic clarity remained perceptible, and he wondered why more and more students and even teachers asked him for advice. Toni was not the first student whose actualization yielded a taste of true being.

7 Concluding Remarks

Meditation means more than sitting up straight or washing dishes in a state of high awareness (Nhat Hanh 2001). In fact, it can be a training of consciousness that enables a comprehensive understanding of actualization that is not limited to individual well-being in satisfactory relations, but implies the potential to reframe relatedness and responsible acting in a verifiable knowledge of oneness. In my opinion, congruence, empathy, and unconditional positive regard are options in the respective moment to be actualized in an absolute presence that is essential for the fully functioning person. Meditation is my way to open myself to this kind of actualization. In Lipsett's theoretical framework and its implementation, I find a reasonable and practicable occidental approach that fits in well with my practice of PCA and convinces me more than Western adaptations of Buddhist traditions

(Enomiya-Lassalle 2005; Nhat Hanh 2001; Wetzel 2011). It offers a chance to overcome common preconceptions and to reconquer the Christian tradition for a coherent Western practice of presence and relatedness.

References

Anderson, R., & Cissna, K. N. (1997). *The Martin Buber-Carl Rogers dialogue: A new transcript with commentary*. New York: State University of New York press.
Apel, K.-O. (1993). *Transformation der Philosophie. Bd. 2: Das Apriori der Kommunikationsgemeinschaft (5. Aufl.)*. [Transformation of philosophy. Vol. 2: The apriority of communication community]. Frankfurt/M: Suhrkamp.
Assagioli, R. (1987). *Die Schulung des Willens: Methoden der Psychotherapie und der Selbsttherapie (4. Aufl.)*. [Training of volition: Methods of psychotherapy and self-therapy]. Paderborn: Junfermann.
Augustinus, A. (1998). *Bekenntnisse*. [Confessions]. Stuttgart: Reclam. (Original work published 397).
Buber, M. (1996). *I and Thou*. New York: Touchstone. (Original work published 1923).
Bundschuh-Müller, K. (2004). "Es ist was es ist sagt die Liebe...": Achtsamkeit und Akzeptanz in der Personzentrierten und Experientiellen Psychotherapie. [Mindfulness and acceptance in Person-Centered and Experiential psychotherapy]. In T. Heidenreich & J. Michalak (Eds.), *Achtsamkeit und Akzeptanz in der Psychotherapie: Ein Handbuch*. (pp. 405–455). Tübingen: dgvt-Verlag.
Deikman, A. J. (1982). *The observing self: Mysticism and psychotherapy*. Boston: Beacon Press.
Eberspächer, H. (2007). Mentales Training: Das Handbuch für Trainer und Sportler (7. Aufl.). [Mental training]. München: Copress.
Eckehart, M. (1979). *Deutsche Predigten und Traktate. Herausgegeben und übersetzt von Josef Quint*. [German sermons and tracts] Zürich: Diogenes.
Enomiya-Lassalle, H.M. (2005). *Zen-Meditation für Christen*. [Zen-meditation for Christians]. Frankfurt/M: S. Fischer. (Original work published 1968).
Gendlin, E.T. (1982). *Focusing: Technik der Selbsthilfe bei der Lösung persönlicher Probleme (6. Aufl.)*. [Focusing: Technique of self-help for solving individual problems] Salzburg: Otto Müller.
Heidenreich, T. & Michalak, J. (Eds.) (2004). *Achtsamkeit und Akzeptanz in der Psychotherapie: Ein Handbuch*. [Acceptance and mindfulness in psychotherapy: A handbook] Tübingen: dgvt-Verlag.
Herrigel, E. (2007). *Zen in der Kunst des Bogenschießens. - Der Zen-Weg (3. Aufl.)*. [Zen in the art of archery. The way of Zen.] Frankfurt/M: S. Fischer.
Kabat-Zinn, J. (2010). *Gesund durch Meditation: Das große Buch der Selbstheilung*. [Healthy by meditation: The comprehensive book of self-healing] Frankfurt: Fischer Taschenbuch Verlag (8. Aufl.).
Linehan, M. (1996). *Dialektisch-behaviorale Therapie der Borderline-Persönlichkeitsstörung*. [Dialectic-behavioral therapy of borderline personality disorder] München: CIP Medien.
Lipsett, P.R. (1991). *Wege zur Transzendenzerfahrung*. [Ways to the experience of transcendence] Münsterschwarzach: Vier-Türme-Verlag.
Lipsett, P.R. (2005). Was ist Kontemplation? Kontemplation und christliche Meditation. [What is contemplation? Contemplation and Christian meditation] *Kontemplation und Mystik*, 6(1), 3–15.
Lipsett, P.R. (2012). Kontemplation–Was ist das? [What is contemplation?] Frankfurter Schule der Kontemplation. http://www.kontemplation-frankfurt.de/sites/kontemplation.html. Accessed 08 June 2012.

Nhat Hanh, T. (2001). *Das Wunder der Achtsamkeit (10. Aufl.).* [The miracle of mindfulness] Berlin: Theseus.
Reddemann, L. (2003). *Imagination als heilsame Kraft: Zur Behandlung von Traumafolgen mit ressourcenorientierten Verfahren (8. Aufl.).* [Imagination as healthful power: Treatment of implications of traumata with resource oriented techniques] Stuttgart: Pfeiffer.
Renn, K. (2011). Focusing: Psychotherapie in innerer Achtsamkeit. [Focusing: Psychotherapy in inner Mindfulness] In L. Reddemann (Ed.), *Kontexte von Achtsamkeit in der Psychotherapie* (pp. 84–100). Stuttgart: Kohlhammer.
Roediger, E. (2011). Achtsamkeit und Schematherapie. [Mindfulness and Schema Therapy] In L. Reddemann (Ed.), *Kontexte von Achtsamkeit in der Psychotherapie* (pp. 67–83). Stuttgart: Kohlhammer.
Rogers, C. R. (1980). *A way of being.* Boston: Houghton Mifflin.
Rogers, C.R. (1995). *On becoming a person.* Boston: Houghton Mifflin. (Original work published 1961).
Seiwert, L. (2002). *Das neue 1 x 1 des Zeitmanagement (27. Aufl.).* [Time-management 101–the new basics] München: Gräfe und Unzer.
Stevens, J.O. (2000). *Die Kunst der Wahrnehmung: Übungen der Gestalttherapie (15. Aufl.).* [The art of perception: Exercises of Gestalt therapy] Gütersloh: Gütersloher Verlagshaus.
von Avila T. (1979). *Die innere Burg.* [Interior castle] Zürich: Diogenes. (Original work published 1577).
Wetzel, S (2011). Aufmerksamkeit, Achtsamkeit und Erwachen–buddhistische Perspektiven. [Attention, mindfulness, and awakening–Buddhist perspectives] In L. Reddemann (Ed.), *Kontexte von Achtsamkeit in der Psychotherapie* (pp. 39–51). Stuttgart: Kohlhammer.
Wilk, D (2004). *Autogenes Training: Ruhe und Gelassenheit lernen (3. Aufl.).* [Autogenic training: Learning rest and calmness] Bern: Huber.

Part IV
Developmental Relating

On Correspondences Between the Person-Centered Approach and Attachment Theory

Diether Höger

1 Introduction

Different theoretical systems can advance when compared with each other. This holds true for the person-centered approach (PCA) and attachment theory (AT). There are similarities between the issues of investigation and the methodological procedures. At first glance, the two approaches follow different research subjects at their outsets: psychotherapy in the case of the PCA and the behavior of infants with respect to their caregivers in AT. The PCA and AT, however, share a central interest in developmental processes in relationships. Also, methodologically, both started by deriving their hypotheses and theories from the results of their field observations.

Prior to having proposed his theoretical concepts, Rogers observed and analyzed the concrete interactions between client and therapist in a large number of psychotherapeutic interviews. By the same token, the starting point for Bowlby and his co-workers was the detailed observation of infants when separated from their caregivers. Both researchers were guided by biological ideas about living organisms and the ways in which they maintained their existence and continued developing in the respective environment. Bowlby drew explicitly from the ethologist Hinde, and Rogers was significantly influenced by the biological studies he conducted at his father's farm.

For further elaborating the correspondences between the PCA and AT, it seems appropriate to first present the basic terms and findings of AT and subsequently relate them to the theoretical concepts of the PCA.

D. Höger (✉)
University of Bielefeld Fakultät für Psychologie und Sportwissenschaft, Bielefeld, Germany
e-mail: diether.hoeger@uni-bielefeld.de

2 Behavioral Systems in Attachment Theory

2.1 Need for Attachment

There is no doubt that the human infant, more than any other creature, depends on the support by caregivers without whom he or she would be desperately lost. Based on this observation, the biologist Portmann (1956) called the human being a physiologically premature delivery. This required that in the course of evolution, he became equipped with the ability to provoke persons whom he met after birth (these are usually but not necessarily his or her parents) to care for him, to look after him, and to support his or her further development. Correspondingly, during evolution, these persons were equipped with affection and abilities to care for the helpless infant, to care for him, and to offer him the feeling of security. The baby's dedicated and effective signaling system prompts them to exhibit this behavior (Dornes 1994).

If this caring and protecting relationship is to fulfill its function, it needs, most of all, continuity. Therefore, the infant or toddler attaches himself to his or her caregiver, in particular the one who has taken over the function of the mother. He shows the need to make sure that she is accessible and undertakes everything to sustain this relationship. In an emergency, he/she discards all other needs in favor of retaining the relationship.

2.2 The Attachment System

Inspired by Hinde (1966), Bowlby developed the idea of a genetically predetermined goal-corrected behavioral system to describe the functioning of the need for attachment. In such a feedback system, the deviations from an organism's given goal are reduced by appropriate activities. According to Bowlby (1969), the variable relevant for the attachment behavioral system is the security experienced by the infant. It is a function of the attachment figure's regard or at least their accessibility. If the experienced security is significantly less than needed, the attachment system will be activated and the individual exhibits attachment behavior. This is the kind of behavior that is apt to re-establish the proximity of the attachment figure and thus provide for the needed degree of security.

Example: An infant wakes up after his afternoon nap and finds himself all alone in the room. The experienced safeness is small and in deficit compared with the needed goal for safety. His attachment system is activated, and he shows attachment behavior, for example he calls "mum" in order to re-establish proximity with her. Should he fail, he chooses some other kind of attachment behavior from his repertoire, for example he starts crying. The mother hears him or her, enters the room, takes the infant up, caresses, and comforts him. This raises the infant's experienced safety, and he calms down. The attachment system becomes

On Correspondences Between the Person-Centered Approach and Attachment Theory 171

deactivated, and other systems can become active. He wants to engage with other things, and with his behavior, he shows that he wants to be put down again.

Attachment behavior can be categorized into various categories:

- *Signaling behavior*. This happens, for instance, if infants look at their mother, smile, wave to her, or call for her. It results in her friendly regard for the infant and establishing contact, smiling back, waving, talking to them, coming closer, etc.
- *Aversive behavior*. This is disturbing primarily for the attachment figure and causing her or him to do something to put an end to it. An example of aversive behavior is crying, shouting, and screaming. To calm the infant, the attachment figure takes her up, cradles her, caresses, and calms her.
- *Active behavior*. This intends something on one's own to establish or maintain closeness, for example to run toward the attachment figure, to follow her, to stretch the arms to her, to clip on her, and to protest in case of separation.

The degree of the security needed can change. In particular, in case of tiredness, misery, distress, or illness, the need for security is significantly higher and hence also the activation of the attachment system. Furthermore, the need for security depends on age, and whereas it stays in place for a person's whole life, it is particularly high in infancy and early childhood. It then declines during puberty and adolescence just to rise again to reach another peak in older age.

During a person's lifetime, the forms of attachment behavior become differentiated. Also, new attachment figures enter the scene, for example partners. There are seven criteria that allow one to recognize an individual's attachment figure. These criteria are as follows:

- *Proximity seeking*: His or her proximity is endeavored.
- *Attachment behavior*: He/she is the preferred addressee of attachment behavior.
- *End of attachment behavior*: His or her positive regard has the highest probability to end the attachment behavior.
- *Separation protest*: Misery and attachment behavior are exhibited as a consequence of an involuntary separation.
- *Reunion is welcome*: The reunion after a longer phase of separation triggers joy and a special welcoming behavior.
- *Secure base*: The proximity of the attachment figure or the sheer knowledge about his or her unhindered accessibility has the meaning of a secure base from which the person can freely move in the world and explore it.
- *Save haven*: The attachment figure provides the locus to which an individual can flee if they feel threatened. If for some reason the attachment figure cannot be reached, the individual feels anxious and uneasy.

Persons with the following features can advance to attachment figures:

- Social partners with the most frequent interactions (in the case of children normally those who are there for them, look after them, and care for them, hence most often their mother and father).
- The person who reacts promptly and responds to attachment behavior (signaling and advances).
- Persons who are kind, accessible, and competent (Bowlby writes: "stronger and wiser").

When there is little choice, the continuity of interaction rather than the quality is decisive. Therefore, even abused children hang on their parents, or adults stay with their violent partner.

2.3 The Exploratory System

Attachment theory presumes the existence of an exploratory behavioral system side by side to the attachment system. This is because people, in particular children, tend to engage in exploratory play as soon as they feel safe and the attachment system is not activated.

The variable responsible for determining whether the exploratory system is active was termed "arousal" by Bischof (1985). It is a function of the confrontation with something new and unfamiliar, be it a foreign person, an unknown environment, or some new object. According to Bischof, the organism's goal is moderate arousal or, in other words, enterprising spirit ("Unternehmungslust"). Too low levels of arousal result in boredom, and the individual seeks new impressions and approaches them—he or she explores. On the other hand, too high levels of arousal cause anxiety such that the individual withdraws and looks out for safety in a trusted environment, optimally in proximity to an attachment figure.

Example: I board a train and see a little girl (approximately 2.5-years old) on the corridor at a distance of about 8 m. She stands besides her mother, smiles, and waves to me. As soon as I wave back friendly, the girl turns around and hides her face in her mother's skirt. In the state of security close to her mother, the "secure base," the girl turned to the stranger with curiosity and greeted him. His waving back causes a frightening overdose of closeness. Hence that girl avoids looking at him and seeks the secure proximity of her mother, the "save haven."

The behavioral systems of attachment and exploration stand in an antagonistic relationship to each other. Depending on the situation, the one or the other comes to the foreground. This relationship stays in place for the whole lifetime of a person. During one's lifetime, the goal prescription "enterprising spirit" develops contrary to the need for security evoked by the attachment system: Whereas the enterprising spirit increases with age, it reaches its peak in puberty and adolescence and then declines with aging (Bischof 1985).

Both systems are of central value to human development: While the attachment system serves to establish and maintain individual's existence, the exploration system assures the enhancement of his or her competences.

2.4 Correspondences with the PCA

Similarities already become apparent in the context of the concept of the behavioral system. Bowlby explicitly contrasts the assumption of a goal-corrected behavioral system with Freud's (1915) drive economy. He argues that Freud did not develop this concept from clinical experience but took over an imagination of that time's zeitgeist. Bowlby himself emphasizes that the initiation and the end of behavior are not caused by excess or exhaustion of drive energy but through larger or smaller deviations from goal states. So, for example, a bird stops building a nest once the nest is done (and not when its "nest-building drive" is exhausted) and resumes immediately after the nest gets damaged.

Rogers did not specifically argue against the energetic drive model. However, for him, emotions were pivotal for regulating behavior. Attachment theory considers exactly these as closely related to behavioral systems.

In Rogers' definition of the actualizing tendency as "…the inherent tendency of the organism to develop all its capacities in ways which serve to maintain or enhance the organism" (Rogers 1959, p. 196), he puts the aspects of an organism's maintenance and the enhancement of its capacities into the center. The behavioral systems attachment and exploration and their mutual relationship—as posited by attachment theory—can be seen as equivalents to Rogers' theorizing. It is noteworthy that maintenance has priority over enhancement. In the case of threat, processes of defense dominate processes of continuing development and hence need unconstrained unconditional positive regard. On its side, the exploration system is always ready to take over control once sufficient security is established.

This can be used to explain therapeutic processes that orient themselves on the PCA: A client seeks therapy because he or she is in the state of distress and misery such that their attachment system is activated. The therapist responds to their attachment behavior, is there for them, is friendly, responsive, caring, and turns out to be stronger and wiser. This makes him or her the client's "secure base" and "safe haven" such that the client's safety rises allowing the exploration system to become active. Consequently, the client can turn to embarrassing issues and in this way enhance their competences for mastering life.

This significantly confirms or supplements Rogers' (1951, p. 51) theory of the function of the therapist: "In the emotional warmth of the relationship with the therapist, the client begins to *experience a feeling of safety* as he finds whatever attitude he expresses is understood in almost the same way that he perceives it, and is accepted. He then is able to explore, for example, a vague feeling of guiltiness which he has experienced. In this safe relationship he can perceive for the first time the hostile meaning and purpose of certain aspects of his behavior, and can understand why he has felt guilty about it, and why it has been necessary to deny to awareness the meaning of his behavior" (italics by the author).

Evidence for these relationships was found in an empirical study involving $N = 54$ clients that had been therapeutically treated according to PCA. Höger and Wissemann (1999) showed the following: Clients who just came from a therapeutic hour experienced more safety and confidence as well as change the better they got along with their therapist.

3 Sensitivity of Attachment Figure and Empathy of Therapist

Hinde (1966) finds it useful to distinguish behavioral features in terms of their "lability" or "stability" with respect to environmental influences. In this sense, the attachment *system* is a stable feature of human behavior as it develops in each human being regardless of any specific environmental factors. Contrarily, the attachment behavior is instable and labile. This is because the way in which a person's attachment behavior manifests itself in concrete situations depends on his or her experiences in their environment, in particular the reactions of their attachment figures.

Ainsworth et al. (1974) described the sensitivity of the primary attachment figure, normally the mother, for infants. They defined it as her "ability to perceive and interpret accurately the signals and communications implicit in her infant's behavior, and given this understanding, to respond to them appropriately and promptly" (p. 127). This definition includes four essential components that the authors describe as follows:

1. Mother's *awareness* of her baby's signals and communications with two aspects: first "accessibility versus ignoring and neglecting" because the mother must be reasonably accessible to the baby's signals before she can be sensitive to them. Second, "thresholds of awareness." The mother with the lowest threshold is alert to the baby's most subtle, minimal, understated cues, whereas the mothers with higher thresholds seem to perceive only the most blatant and obvious communications. Mothers with the highest thresholds seem often oblivious and are, in effect, highly inaccessible.
2. Mother's ability to *interpret accurately* her baby's communications with three main components: her awareness (see above), her freedom of distortion, and her empathy. The precise interpretation of the baby's signals depends on her, taking into account their context, which requires sufficient awareness on her part to be accessible. But when a mother is highly aware and accessible, she may misinterpret communications because her perception is distorted by projection, denial, or other defensive operations. And if she is able to empathise with her baby's feelings and wishes, she can respond with sensitivity.

3. Probably, the most important index of sensitivity is that the mother's responses are *appropriate* to the situation and the baby's communications. In the first year of life, the mother gives the baby what his communications suggest he wants. Toward the end of the first and in the second year of life, it is maximally appropriate to compromise between what the baby wants and what will make him feel most secure, competent, comfortable, etc., in the long run. Finally, an appropriate interaction is resolved, or well rounded and completed. For example, when the baby needs soothing, she soothes him thoroughly, so he is quite recovered and cheerful.
4. *Promptness of response.* An appropriate response that can be perceived by the baby as contingent upon his communication can be linked by him to his own signal. So he can gain some feeling of efficacy and in consequence a "sense of competence" in controlling his social environment.

Viewed from the perspective of actual behavior, these features have nothing in common with those of a therapist. On a superordinate level, however, both situations deal with conditions under which the interacting partners develop in a constructive direction. Furthermore, in both cases, the accurate interpretation means an empathic attunement to the lived experience of the interaction partner, which is free from distortion by incongruences.

Differences, however, provoke further thought. For example, in order to determine the appropriateness of a reaction, Ainsworth et al. focus attention more explicitly on the client's needs and their consideration than is customary in the PCA. If the therapist behaves such that he or she addresses the client's needs and wants and satisfies them, the latter, in Rogers' sense (1959, p. 213), is "more able to perceive the unconditional positive regard for him, and empathic understanding of the therapist." On a hot summer day, a guest is likely to feel better understood if his host not only welcomes him with the words "You sure will be thirsty" but at the same time offers him a drink. Furthermore, it makes sense to take into account how far a therapeutic episode is not just a thematic one but is also resolved, or well rounded and completed with regard to the client's needs.

Particularly, in the beginning of psychotherapy, a client in an emergency situation with his or her attachment system activated will (consciously or not) tend to look for an attachment figure. This means for someone who is responsive to the client's attachment behavior, is competent, and, importantly, through his or her actions provides a "secure base" and a "safe haven." And the therapeutic relationship will be more effective and sustainable if the client is offered all this.

4 Attachment Patterns

Studying infants, Ainsworth et al. (1978) could show that the infants' diverse experiences with their respective attachment figures and their sensitivity had a sustained effect on the infants' behavior in attachment-related situations. The observed differences can be categorized into a limited number of behavioral patterns that the researchers referred to as "secure," "avoidant," and "ambivalent or resistant."

Main (1990) interpreted these attachment patterns as adaptive, conditional strategies of an individual's attachment system. They serve the purpose of responding to the attachment figure's reactions with an own attachment behavior that ensures at least a relative optimum of safety. These strategies manifest themselves in infancy nonverbally. With increasing maturing of the cognitive functions, they are represented mentally in an "internal working model of attachment" (Bowlby 1969). Main et al. (1985, p. 65/66) defined them as "... a set of conscious and/or unconscious rules for the organization of information relevant to attachment and for obtaining or limiting access to that information, that is, to information regarding attachment-related experiences, feelings and ideations."

4.1 The Three Classical Variants of Attachment Patterns

According to Main (1990), there are three basic forms in which attachment figures react to the attachment behavior of individuals in attachment-related situations. The resulting behavioral patterns of infants will be organized schematically rather than categorically:

First, the attachment figure can react to an individual's attachment behavior in a predictable and reliably sensitive form and thus provide him or her with the necessary safety. This results in "primary strategies" corresponding to the attachment pattern "secure." As a consequence, in attachment-related situations, the individual will directly look for (familiar) persons who provide proximity and help and will trust to receive their regard and help. Subsequently, the individual will reorganize himself and be free for exploration and hence expansion of his competences. The corresponding attitude toward life manifests itself in the need and capability to attach themselves closely to a few selected persons and to establish and maintain reliable attachment relationships with them. It also implies the expectation and trust in the feasibility of such relationships as well as in the availability of someone who is going to provide care, empathic understanding, comfort, and support in the case of neediness and misery. Finally, there is also willingness to accept the necessary support.

In contrast, *secondary* strategies develop in the case that direct attachment behavior turns out to be inappropriate since it does not lead to success. These strategies then overlay more or less the primary strategy or even substitute it completely. Two variants can be distinguished: If the attachment figure predictably ignores or rejects an individual's attachment behavior to some degree, he or she depends on other ways to procure their vital safety. This can happen through other behaviors such as receiving positive regard for achievement or self-reliance or needing to cope with the situation on one's own. The consequence is a *secondary deactivating* strategy (according to the "avoiding" attachment pattern). In attachment-related situations, expressions and signals of the attachment system like body contact, crying, or direct seeking of proximity are minimized or completely repressed, whereas independence, self-reliance, and proficiency are emphasized. Experience of distress, misery, or need for help is denied conscious symbolization or is distorted. Need for proximity to other people and related feelings appears threatening and are avoided along with the respective self-experiences.

The second variant of attachment-related reactions of attachment figures is such that—in an unpredictable fashion—at times, they ignore the attachment-related behavior of an individual, and at other times, they accept it, or at yet other times, their own need for attachment lets them seek proximity of the individual who at that moment is not disposed. The results are *secondary hyperactivating* strategies (according to the attachment pattern "ambivalent") with the persistent uncertainty whether the attachment behavior will be satisfied or not. In this case, the attachment system is constantly activated and already small cues trigger the person's attachment behavior, which is particularly intense in truly attachment-related situations. Such situations are characterized by distrust, fear of being abandoned, clinging, and intense claiming of regard and affection. Feelings of worthlessness, furiousness, and frustration are going to break through over and over but must not be expressed due to the impending avoidance by the attachment figure.

4.2 Attachment Patterns and Clients' Ways to Offer Their Relationship

According to attachment theory, one can expect that clients, being in a state of distress and misery when entering psychotherapy, come with an activated attachment system. Furthermore, their way of offering a relationship and hence their behavior with respect to the therapist will correspond to their individual attachment pattern. Individuals with *primary* strategies suffer from psychological problems relatively rarely (Dozier et al. 1999; Strauß 2008) and hence need psychological treatment less frequently. If, nevertheless, they enter psychotherapy, they tend to be trustful and equipped with a rather high ability and readiness for self-exploration such that working with them is likely to be smooth. However, the situation is different with secondary strategies.

In particular, at the very beginning of therapy, clients with deactivating strategies tend to reject therapeutic offerings for help—if they do not reject psychotherapeutic treatment at all and rather want tangible advice and instructions. However, the essence of the person-centered way of offering a relationship is to be regardful, and moreover, it focuses on the client's experiencing. For persons with a deactivating attachment strategy, this offering of intimacy constitutes a threat to their individual equilibrium (Argyle and Dean 1965) against which they need to defend themselves. Hence, they are not able or not willing to talk about their experience. In particular, it will be difficult for them to perceive or express attachment-related needs and feelings. They will tend to minimize or completely deny problems, in particular psychological ones. Therefore, it will be difficult to enter with them into a therapeutic process in the sense of the PCA.

For the therapeutic treatment of such persons and for empathically understanding their situation, the attachment theory reveals that whereas the attachment *behavior* is deactivated in them, their attachment *system* nevertheless is activated (Spangler and Grossmann 1993). Their seemingly dismissing and uncooperative behavior calls for a particularly big portion of the therapist's unconditional positive regard. This is because they are existentially dependent on maintaining their potential relative optimum on safety in a way appropriate for them and thus to maintain their inner equilibrium. Therapeutic progress is possible to such a degree to which the client is free from threat and can—under the safeguard of a therapeutic relationship—find his or her path to a less confining strategy of the shaping of relationships.

The situation is different with *hyperactive* strategies. In this case, clients, to a varying degree, tend to distrust the candor and reliability of the therapeutic offering of the relationship. They often pose excessive demands on the therapists' regard and readiness to help that finally would overstrain them. Moreover, the often ambiguous and embarrassing way in which some of those clients express their need for affection and help such as through rejecting the therapist, insulting or criticizing him/her unfairly is problematic. In such aversive behaviors, the wish to overcome them by finding out that the therapist turns out to be a reliable attachment figure despite all this distrust is truly hard to detect. The therapist's immediate reaction could naturally be embarrassment and defense; hence, the demands on his or her unconditional positive regard are huge. Knowledge about the background and the fact that the aversive behavior is not directed toward him as a person can largely facilitate overcoming such an immediate reaction.

Clients who offer their relationship based on secondary strategies are not only familiar to experienced therapists. They can also be identified by empirical research methods. Factor analysis of questionnaire about the expectations of clients regarding their relationship with the therapist helped to identify three dimensions that summarize the characteristics of these expectations (Höger 1999; Pollak et al. 2008):

1. "Fear of Rejection," defined by items stating a lack of self-confidence and the fear of being rejected.
2. "Readiness for Self-Disclosure" described the ability and readiness of talking about one's inner feelings.
3. "Conscious Need for Care" refers to a person's declared wish for the therapist's attention and care.

Cluster analyses on these dimensions that furthermore proved to be valid for partnerships as well (Höger and Buschkämper 2002; Höger et al. 2007) rendered the identification of five attachment patterns that could be aligned with the strategies described by Main and the secondary strategies figured in two different variants.

1. The primary strategy of a *"securely attached"* individual: Substantial "Readiness for Self-Disclosure" is combined with a "Conscious Need for Care" and little "Fear of Rejection." This configuration indicates openness to communicate about feelings with the anticipation to be accepted.
2. A similar pattern composed of high "Readiness for Self-Disclosure" and low "Fear of Rejection." In contrast to cluster 3, however, no "Conscious Need for Care" is expressed. This attachment pattern was identified by this study for the first time and was referred to as *"partially secure"* because respondents assigned to this cluster are classified as secure by other instruments (see Grau, Clashausen, and Höger 2003; Höger and Buschkämper 2002). However, this pattern cannot be considered a primary strategy, since the expression of some need for care is an essential facet of secure attachment (Main 1990). The lack of any consciously perceived attachment need implies a secondary deactivating strategy.
3. A secondary deactivating attachment strategy *"avoidant-withdrawing"* with very low "Readiness for Self-Disclosure," associated with a low "Conscious Need for Care," "Fear of Rejection" is not perceived.
4. A secondary hyperactivating strategy *"ambivalent-clinging."* Substantial "Fear of Rejection" is associated with a high "Conscious Need for Care." Here, a wish for closeness and attention meets with the fear to be rejected (ambivalent), combined with some "Readiness for Self-Disclosure."
5. Another secondary hyperactivating strategy *"ambivalent withdrawing"* with substantial "Fear of Rejection" and a high "Conscious Need for Care" but communication about feelings is refused (negative values on the "Readiness for Self-Disclosure" scale).

With the help of the Bielefeld Questionnaire for Clients' Expectations (BFKE), Strauss et al. (2006) could show that clients with a "partially secure" attachment profited from psychotherapy relatively most, while clients with the two hyperactivating patterns benefited least. Results from Höger (2004) about clients' satisfaction with their person-centered psychotherapies complement these findings. In contrast to clients with the two hyperactivating patterns, those with partially secure patterns tend to get along with their therapists well. In their therapy hours, they experience safety and confidence paired with change.

5 Concluding Remarks

Consider the following for therapeutic practice: Each person has developed individual strategies for his or her attachment system based on their individual attachment history. We know too little about a client if we classify him or her under an established attachment pattern. The only decisive is the momentary, particular way in which their attachment system reacts to the attachment-related situation "psychotherapy," meaning the concrete form in which deactivating and (hyper) activating strategies display themselves. It is these particular manifestations and the respective experiences toward which our empathic understanding and unconditional positive regard is directed. This is what allows us to provide clients with the safety they need for their free self-exploration and development. The strategies of the attachment systems are not just simple habits but existential needs being essential for sheer survival; hence, they are so significant and decisive.

If the therapeutic relationship shall have the character of a "secure base" and a "safe haven" in order to be constructive, it is suggested to take care that non-directivity of the PCA is not interpreted such a way as to render clients feeling left on their own. At any time, they should be clear that while they need to solve their problems by themselves, the therapist would not leave them alone in doing this, but will carefully accompany them.

In brief, attachment behavior or its avoidance can come up in therapy in versatile, even conflictive forms. Whereas the deeper exploration of particular consequences for therapeutic practice is outside the scope of this article, it can be helpful to understand and to appreciate the respective background as shared in this work.

References

Ainsworth, M. D. S., Bell, S. M., & Stayton, D. J. (1974). Infant-mother attachment and social development: "Socialisation" as a product of reciprocal responsiveness to signals. In M. P. M. Richards (Ed.), *The integration of a child into a social world* (pp. 99–135). London: Cambridge University Press.

Ainsworth, M. D. S., Blehar, M. C., Waters, E., & Wall, S. (1978). *Patterns of attachment: A psychological study of the strange situation*. Hillsdale: Erlbaum.

Argyle, M., & Dean, J. (1965). Eye-contact, distance and affiliation. *Sociometry, 28*, 289–304.

Bischof, N. (1985). *Das Rätsel Ödipus. Die biologischen Wurzeln des Urkonfliktes von Intimität und Autonomie [The riddle Oedipus. The biological roots oft the primal conflict between intimacy and autonomy]*. München: Piper.

Bowlby, J. (1969). *Attachment and loss* (Vol. 1 Attachment). New York: Basic Books.

Dornes, M. (1994). *Der kompetente Säugling. Die präverbale Entwicklung des Menschen*. Frankfurt a.M.: Fischer.

Dozier, M., Stovall, K. C., & Albus, K. E. (1999). Attachment and psychopathology in Adulthood. In: J. Cassidy & P. R. Shaver (Eds.), *Handbook of attachment. Theory, research, and clinical applications* (pp. 497–519).

Freud, S. (1915). *Triebe und Triebschicksale*. In W. X. Ges (pp. 210–232). London: Imago Publishing.

Grau, I., Clashausen, U., & Höger, D. (2003). Der Bindungsfragebogen von Grau und der Bielefelder Fragebogen zu Partnerschaftserwartungen von Höger und Buschkämper im Vergleich [Two German attachment questionnaires compared]. *Psychology Science, 45*, Supplement III, 41–60.

Hinde, R. D. (1966). *A synthesis of ethology and comparative psychology*. New York: McGraw-Hill.

Höger, D. (1999). Der Bielefelder Fragebogen zu Klientenerwartungen (BFKE). Ein Verfahren zur Erfassung von Bindungsstilen bei Psychotherapie-Patienten. [The Bielefeld Partnership-Expectations Questionnaire]. *Psychotherapeut [Psychotherapist], 44*, 159–166.

Höger, D. (2004). Über den Einfluss der Bindungsmuster auf das Erleben des Therapieprozesses. [About the influence of attachment patterns on client's experience of the therapeutic process]. Vortrag vor dem 44. Kongress der Deutschen Gesellschaft für Psychologie in Göttingen. [Paper presented at the 44th Conference of the German Psychological Association].

Höger, D., & Buschkämper, S. (2002). Der Bielefelder Fragebogen zu Partnerschaftserwartungen (BFPE). Ein alternativer Vorschlag zur Operationalisierung von Bindungsmustern mittels Fragebögen [The Bielefeld Partnership-Expectations Questionnaire. An alternative proposal for assessing attachment patterns]. *Zeitschrift für Differentielle und Diagnostische Psychologie [Journal of Individual Differences], 23*, 83–98.

Höger, D., Stöbel-Richter Y., & Brähler, E. (2007). Reanalyse des Bielefelder Fragebogens zu Partnerschaftserwartungen (BFPE) [Re-analysis oft the Bielefeld Partnership-Expectations Questionnaire]. *Psychotherapie, Psychosomatik, Medizinische Psychologie [Psychotherapy, Psychosomatics, Medical Psychology], 58(7)*, 284–294.

Höger, D., & Wissemann, N. (1999). Zur Wirkungsweise des Faktors „Beziehung"in der Gesprächspsychotherapie. Eine empirische Studie [On the Effect of Factor „Relationship"in Client-centered Psychotherapy. Am empirical study]. *Zeitschrift für Klinische Psychologie, Psychiatrie und Psychotherapie [Journal of Clinical Psychology, Psychiatry, and Psychotherapy], 47*, 374–385.

Main, M. (1990). Cross-cultural studies of attachment organization: Recent studies, changing methodologies, and the concept of conditional strategies. *Human Development, 33*, 48–61.

Main, M., Kaplan, N., & Cassidy, J. (1985). Security in infancy, childhood, and adulthood: A move to the level of representation. In I. Bretherton & E. Waters (Eds.), *Growing points of attachment theory and research. Monographs of the Society for Research in Child Development, 50* (1–2, Serial No. 209), 66–106.

Pollak, E., Wiegand-Grefe, S., & Höger, D. (2008). The Bielefeld Attachment Questionnaires—Overview and empirical results of an alternative approach to assess attachment. *Psychotherapy Research, 18*, 179–190.

Portmann, A. (1956). *Zoologie und das neue Bild vom Menschen. Biologische Fragmente zu einer Lehre vom Menschen [Zoology and the new concept of man. Biological fragments for a science of man]*. Reinbek: Rowohlt.

Rogers, C. R. (1951). *Client-centered therapy*. Boston: Houghton Mifflin.

Rogers, C.R. (1959): A theory of therapy, personality, and interpersonal relationships, as developed in the client centered framework. In S. Koch (Ed.), *Psychology: A study of a science* (Vol. 3 pp. 184–256). New York: McGraw Hill.

Spangler, G., & Grossmann, K. E. (1993). Biobehavioral organization in securely and insecurely attached infants. *Child Development, 64*, 1439–1450.

Strauß, B. (Ed.). (2008). *Bindung und Psychopathologie [Attachment and Psychopathology]*. Stuttgart: Klett-Cotta.

Strauss, B., Kirchmann, H., Eckert, J., et al. (2006). Attachment characteristics and treatment outcome following inpatient psychotherapy—Results of a multisite study. *Psychotherapy Research, 16*, 579–594.

Relational Psychophysiology and Mutual Regulation During Dyadic Therapeutic and Developmental Relating

Kymberlee M. O'Brien, Karim Afzal and Edward Tronick

1 Introduction

The purpose of this chapter is to present our work on relational psychophysiology in mother–infant research and offer some ways in which this approach might apply to and inform person-centered psychotherapy research and clinical practice. We first briefly review our theories on infant emotional development that emerged from our empirical research. These theories include the mutual regulation model and our theory on dyadically expanded states of consciousness, which integrates a nonlinear dynamic systems framework into the mutual regulation model. We view the human being as an open, nonlinear dynamic system consisting of many interrelated domains of functioning (physiological, emotional, cognitive/symbolic, and social/behavioral). The core of the chapter presents our latest research, which adds physiological measures and assessment of synchrony across these domains to our mother–infant work. We also review prominent findings in related research on what has also been called physiological "concordance," "mirroring," or "linkage" in dyadic units across the lifespan. Finally, we discuss similarities and possible applications to person-centered psychotherapy research and practice.

K. M. O'Brien (✉)
Child Development Unit, University of Massachusetts Boston, Harvard Medical School, 100 Morrissey Boulevard, Wheatley 3rd Floor, Boston, MA 02125, USA
e-mail: kymberlee.obrien@umb.edu

K. Afzal
Child Development Unit, University of Massachusetts Boston, Fielding Graduate University, 100 Morrissey Boulevard, Wheatley 3rd Floor, Boston, MA 02125, USA
e-mail: karim.afzal@umb.edu

E. Tronick
Child Development Unit, University of Massachusetts Boston, Brigham and Women's Hospital/Harvard Medical School, 100 Morrissey Boulevard, Wheatley 3rd Floor, Boston, MA 02125, USA
e-mail: edward.tronick@umb.edu

2 Relational Psychophysiology

In the spirit of studying physiological and behavioral states as they relate to dyadic relational processes that enhance self-organization and emotion regulation capacities, we believe that psychophysiological variables during relevant social interactions are key to understanding the development of complexity and coherence for each individual, as well the larger social milieu. Psychophysiology is the study of the physical substrates underlying psychological inner states and can be used to assess cognitive, affective, and behavioral processes (Cacioppo et al. 2000). Examples of commonly studied psychophysiological systems are neural activity, electromyography, electrodermal activity, cardiovascular activity, and stress and reproductive hormonal processes. The earliest work investigating behavioral outcomes on physiological linking likely begins with Levenson and Gottman (1983) who examined marital satisfaction as it related to synchrony across multiple autonomic physiological systems and affect. Similar work since then has explored the interrelatedness between social emotions, including empathy and cooperation, as influenced by the ability of adult pairs to be "in sync," once again across multiple physiological systems (e.g., Ekman et al. 2011). We believe that relational psychophysiology has a critical place in the earliest relational sensitivity and in the nascent development of emotion and self-regulation in both infants and their caregivers.

3 The Mutual Regulation Model

For the past three decades, we have studied mutual regulatory processes between mothers and infants during face-to-face (FF) interactions using measures of behavior and affect (see Tronick 2007, for a collection of this work over the past 30 years). We have found that mothers and infants engage in self-directed and other-directed actions during FF interaction in efforts to maintain optimal levels of self- and dyadic arousal and engagement. In the mutual regulation model (Gianino and Tronick 1988; Tronick 1989), infants play a major agenetic role in regulating the interaction. They invite fitted, regulatory scaffolding, with meanings conveyed through eye contact, facial expressions, and emotive expressions such as crying or laughing. They modulate the intensity of interaction and their internal state, again with meanings conveyed through gaze aversion, self-soothing, and expressions of protest. Caregivers vary in the degree to which they apprehend and learn their infant's messages and thus vary in how much they help (or hinder) the infant's regulation. Caregivers smile when infants smile, wait when infants turn away, and soothe infants when they are distressed. In this way, temporal features of the interaction reveal contingencies of signaling, synchrony, and attunement, and both caregivers and infants use nonverbal forms of communication that convey meaning.

Much like the therapeutic interaction, however, the ideal interface is not of absolute synchrony and coordination. Rather, it is "messy." It involves mismatches of affective states, miscoordination of responses, and misapprehensions of relational intentions (Tronick 2007). The actual interaction involves reparation of mismatch and the rejoining of shared relational meaning. In our model, *reparation* is a central mechanism of change and has consequences beyond developing shared meanings. Through reparation, the infant and the caregiver come to implicitly know that the negative experience of mismatch can be transformed into a positive affective match; consequently, the partner can be trusted, and that the infant (and caregiver) is able to act effectively in the world. Out of the reparation of messiness, new implicit ways of being together are co-created and come to be implicitly known (Tronick 2004).

Our research using the FF still-face (FFSF) paradigm (Tronick et al. 1978) has shown the dramatic affect on the infant when the mother's regulatory input is experimentally halted, that is when she offers no feedback to the infant during an interaction. The typical paradigm consists of three relational segments, each lasting 2 to 3 min. In the first episode (mother–infant are face to face), mothers are instructed to play with their infant as they normally do. In the next episode (mother presents still-face), mothers are instructed to face their infant but to no longer respond to their infant in any way. The effect on the infant is dramatic (Adamson and Frick 2003; Weinberg and Tronick 1996). Infants quickly detect the change and use a variety of strategies to re-engage their mothers (smiling, cooing, or fussing). This solicitation cycle may be repeated many times. However, when the attempts to re-engage the mother fail, infants can withdraw, avert their gaze, and lose postural control and begin to self-comfort. Some, but not many, infants cry. In the third episode (reunion), mothers are asked to resume normal interactions with their infants. Mothers often end up having to exert more effort to soothe their infants, and infants display a mix of positive and negative affective states. Over time, with the regulatory engagement of the mother and the fulfillment of infants' intention to elicit interaction once again, and the dyad resumes its typical messy state.

4 Relational Processes

Our work and that of many other developmental and psychological researchers (e.g., Beebe and Lachmann 2002; Fonagy 2002; Tronick 1998) have had a profound impact on the conceptualization of therapeutic processes. It is not an overstatement to say that the early work on mutual regulation was constitutive and foundational to nearly all forms of relational psychotherapies. For example, Safran and Muran's (2000) relational approach to psychotherapy suggests that the type of reparations in relating identified in mother–infant relationships might reflect parallel processes in adult psychotherapy, such that reparations of the patient–therapist relationship facilitate a restructuring of the patient's relational schemas into more healthy relational patterns of expectation. Rogers (1980) was well aware of the importance of supporting the organic process of dyadic relational restructuring within and outside the therapeutic context. He noted, "it seems that the human organism has been moving toward the more complete development of awareness. It is at this level that new forms are invented, perhaps even new directions for the human species. It is here that the reciprocal relationship between cause and effect is most demonstrably evident. It is here that choices are made, spontaneous forms created" (p. 127). Psychophysiological research has established relational linkage as a critical piece for social emotions in particular. Using measures such as cortisol, alpha-amylase, skin conductance, heart rate, and respiration, several social-related emotions such as empathy, loneliness, and disagreement (e.g., Levenson and Gottman 1983) have been associated with concurrent synchrony and time-lagged synchrony (e.g., Butler 2011). Moreover, linkages have been found primarily during reparative processes between social partners, including romantic partners, as well as whole family systems (e.g., Butler 2011; Saxby et al. 2011). Interestingly, this work provides evidence that physiological relatedness is not only present during empathetic or positive affective states, but is a critical underlying process during negative interactions and perhaps negative relationship patterning.

5 Dyadically Expanded States of Consciousness

5.1 Theoretical Framework

We have recently integrated principles of nonlinear dynamic systems theory (Kiel and Elliot 1996; Lewis 2000; Thelen and Smith 1994) into the mutual regulation model and have coined the term "dyadically expanded states of consciousness" to capture our thinking (Tronick 2007). Although we may use the term "consciousness," it is less than ideal because we use it quite differently from neurologists and philosophers and do not believe that all states of consciousness are explicitly realized, but rather much of it is implicit and not in awareness. Nonetheless, we feel that it best captures our belief that the totality of human functioning is involved in the meaning-making processes, from cells to physiological function, from action to awareness. As open dynamic systems, humans move toward more complex and coherent states of self-organization during interaction with their own self and the world of people and things. We refer to this self-organization as a "state of consciousness." This state expresses the entire system of meanings, intentions, and purposes through which one operates and experiences the self in the world. As in all complex systems, there are multilayered, hierarchically organized domains of functioning, and each domain is related to and affects the other. A more coherent state of consciousness occurs when "all" domains are organized into greater (but never complete) harmony with other levels. Coherence is a function of organization, complexity, and flexibility in adapting to different environmental conditions. When one partner in a dyadic process is less coherent, the quality of adaptation and development will necessarily also be less coherent for the other partner. For example, not all caregivers are able to completely and effectively engage with their infant; thus, the infant's ability to engage in social processes, regulate negative emotions and physiological stress, may be compromised. Much prior work has examined the mutual regulation model in healthy populations, as well as dyads where some level of affective or pathophysiology may be present, such as maternal depression and/or maternal anxiety.

An example of work on mutual regulation comes from Feldman et al. (2009) who investigated the effects of maternal depression on infant social engagement, fear regulation, and cortisol reactivity as compared with maternal anxiety disorders and controls. Primarily, the role of maternal sensitivity in moderating the relations between maternal depression and infant outcomes was investigated. The researchers used an extreme-case design; an initial sample of 971 women reported symptoms of anxiety and depression after childbirth, and 215 of those with high and low reports were reevaluated at 6 months. At 9 months, mothers diagnosed with a major depressive disorder (n = 22) and anxiety disorders (n = 19) and matched controls (i.e., no symptoms across the postpartum year; n = 59) were visited at home. Infant social engagement was observed during mother–infant interaction, emotion regulation was micro-coded from a fear paradigm, and mother–infant cortisol values were sampled at baseline, reactivity, and recovery. Mothers' and infants' baseline and reactivity cortisol levels were significantly and positively associated. In addition, the infants of depressed mothers scored the poorest on social engagement and fear regulation at 9 months. Specifically, this group showed the lowest social engagement, less mature regulatory behaviors, greater negative emotionality, and highest cortisol reactivity. The anxious dyads scored less optimally than the controls on maternal sensitivity and infant social engagement. Thus, in this case, the concordant physiology was associated with the dysregulated caregiver and subsequent impaired social, regulatory, and physiological reactivity in the infant.

5.2 Dyadically Expanded States of Consciousness in Psychotherapy

We propose that psychotherapy involves a process of increasing the coherence and complexity of the client's self-organization (state of consciousness). Here, we use coherence to refer to a state in which all domains of functioning resonate with each other and operate harmoniously with each other, like an orchestra playing on point with individual musical streams merging into a sonata that is greater and more beautiful than the sum of its parts.

We suggest that some patients enter therapy because they experience some type of incoherence. They may complain of having a false self, of living a lie, or of not knowing who they are, what they feel, or what they want (e.g., Masterson 1990). They may lack insight or self-awareness (i.e., coherence of identity and meaning with behavior, affect, and physiology). Alternatively, they may lack greater control over their behaviors or emotions (coherence of will and action or feeling). Along these lines, the person-centered approach (PCA) views dysfunction of the self as a failure to be in process; incongruence exists between aspects of the self-concept and daily experience. The person remains stuck in misperceptions or inadequate behavior, while being unable to learn and change (Rogers 1961). From an adult attachment perspective (George et al. 1996), these patients may be identified as dismissive in attachment style and display a poverty of content or report a lack of feeling when discussing attachment issues.

Other patients may present with problems in complexity. Complexity, from a nonlinear dynamic systems perspective, refers to both stability in system organization and flexibility to respond and adapt to changing environmental demands (Siegel 1999). It can be viewed as a chaotic state in which changes emerge out of organizational stability. Low-complexity patients are those who, as the saying goes, find themselves stuck in a hole but keep on digging because they only have a shovel. These patients cannot help but repeatedly make meaning of situations in the same dysfunctional ways or react to situations in the same way (i.e., automatic thoughts, from a cognitive perspective). They may be described as rigid, intolerant, angry, or afraid and are likely to be diagnosed with a personality disorder. Other patients may have disorganized complexity, tending toward randomness. They may become incoherent when anxious, vague, flighty, distracted, and fearful. In the literature on adult attachments, these patients may be categorized as preoccupied and display linguistic and semantic incoherence when discussing anxiety-provoking attachment issues. More seriously, they may present as disorganized, which represents the ultimate level of disruption in self-organization and is often associated with the most severe experiences of trauma or loss.

We believe that therapeutic action lies in dyadically expanding the coherence of patients' self-organization. Any domain of function (physiological processes, behaviors, emotions, conscious awareness, reflective awareness, identity, intentions, and social relationships) can be an effective target for intervention because increasing the coherence in one domain will likely impact the entire system, given the relations of the levels/domains and components of the individual as a system. In this chapter, we highlight the importance of the emotional domain because we believe that it serves as a foundational building block for coherence and is the "product" of domains of function. Thus, it is a critical target for therapeutic intervention and growth. Somewhat like the responsive mother with her child, the therapist must attend to the immediate, moment-to-moment emotional meaning state occurring in the patient, in the therapist, and between patient and therapist. The purpose of this apprehending is to facilitate two overlapping and synergistic processes important in the development of coherence: regulation of affect and awareness of affect. This is not to say that we privilege the emotional domain in therapy, because cognitive therapists have certainly highlighted how alterations in semantic levels of meaning (such as changing cognitive distortions or attributional biases) can have resounding effects on emotions as well. We also acknowledge the interesting work of body psychotherapists (e.g., Ogden et al. 2006), who focus more directly on the nonverbal, sensorimotor domain of function, and believe that this work too can affect self-organization at higher levels.

We also cannot overemphasize the centrality of other people in the development of coherence and complexity. From our clinical experience, one of the greatest sources of malaise in patients is a deep sense of isolation, and many patients report that one of the things that feels best and is most helpful about therapy is the chance to feel heard and understood by another and to have their views on the world validated, their meanings shared. Something magical happens when the patient's most private and shame-inducing vulnerabilities can be shared with the therapist, particularly one who is nonjudgmental, empathic, and accurate in his or her perception (Rogers 1957/1992). The therapist resonates with the patient on an affective, visceral level. Sometimes, on a nonverbal level, vocal rhythms converge (Beebe and Lachmann 2002) and gestures become mirrored (Bernieri and Rosenthal 1991). This alone, however, would be sympathy. The therapist must also accurately convey through language and other forms of communicating meaning that he or she grasps the client's meaning. Empathy requires that the multiple layers of the client's self-organization become resonant with the therapist's and together they co-create a new and greater coherence, a dyadically expanded, harmonically amplified state of consciousness shared between them. This then becomes empathy (Greenberg 1997). We believe that this experience facilitates reconstruction of implicit relational schemas (Tronick 2007) that exist in the body and mind in all organizational levels of the self.

Importantly, these processes are pertinent beyond therapeutic relationships or intimate dyadic interaction, to the development of social emotions and behaviors in the broader societal context. Decades of research have shown that infants' response to the still-face predicts indices of emotional and behavioral health later in development, such as infant attachment classification at 1 year (Braungart-Rieker et al. 2001; Cohn et al. 1991; Kiser et al. 1986) and behavior problems in early childhood (Bates et al. 1985; Moore et al. 2001). We have also documented the impact of maternal illnesses, particularly depression and anxiety, on infant interaction behaviors, leading to more infant hostility, withdrawal, and negative affect that have ramifications on other adult–infant interactions (Tronick 2007) and adult relational style.

Thus, the processes of physiological synchrony can be viewed as having broader social functions, including the enhancement of social cohesion in a cohort. One recent study that reflects this cultural level of meaning making via physiological and affective synchrony comes from Konvalinka et al. (2011). The research team assessed whether heart rate synchrony would occur during a collective ritual: Spanish fire-walking. This study was conducted in a rural Spanish village of 600 inhabitants and occurred during their annual fire-walking ritual. Performed at midnight at the height of the summer solstice, the ritual takes place in an amphitheater, built for this exact purpose. Crowds of up to 3,000 come to watch the spectacle. The researchers chose this particular ritual because it is highly physiologically arousing, but does not involve overt behaviors to be synchronized. Thus the investigators could assess physiological synchrony merely by observing social others' who did not need to synchronized body movements, that is, the spectators who were not walking through the coals.

Specifically, they compared synchronized heart rate reactivity between firewalkers and significant others to unknown spectators. A total of 28 participants walked 7 m over the glowing red coals with surface temperatures of 677 °C. Continuous heart rate data were recorded from three groups of participants: (a) 12 firewalkers, (b) 9 spectators who were either relatives or friends of at least one firewalker, and (c) 17 spectators, not related to any of the locals, who were visiting the village for the ritual. The results demonstrated strong synchronous relationships between the heart rate activity of active firewalkers with their related onlookers, but not with the heart rate of the unrelated spectators. Interestingly, all of the firewalkers' heart rates had a distinctive "signature," with a high peak distributed around the walk itself. This same physiological pattern was found with related spectators, whose heart rates also synchronously peaked for the walk of their relatives and friends. Though the mechanism is unknown, a crucial factor seems to be the nature of the relationship between the walker and the spectator; perhaps something in their mutual knowledge of how emotions are expressed and are not seen by unknown others. This study is one of many that demonstrates that synchrony and relational psychophysiology has a social function in the larger societal context, that is the enhancement of community cohesion and as the authors suggest, "collective effervescence" (Durkheim 1912/1995). Furthermore, shared physiology and subsequent mutual regulation are critical mechanisms underlying social emotions (e.g., empathy, rapport, or cooperation) at group levels (e.g., Maughan and Gleeson 2008; Miles et al. 2009).

6 Physiological Indices and Relational Psychophysiology

The most widely studied psychophysiological signals for social processes are cardiovascular, particularly respiratory sinus arrhythmia (RSA) as an index of parasympathetic tone and emotion regulation (Porges 2003), and salivary cortisol to index social stress reactivity via the hypothalamic-pituitary-adrenal axis system (e.g., Stansbury and Gunnar 1994). Vagal tone or RSA in particular have been well documented as indices of emotion regulation capacities and social competence (Porges 2003). RSA is an indirect measure of parasympathetic influence on heart rate variability (Brownley et al. 2000). The parasympathetic system is generally considered to modulate arousal and activate positive states of rest and digestion. RSA is reflected in heart rate fluctuations that naturally occur with respiration (i.e., increases in heart rate during inspiration and decreases during expiration). RSA can be calculated through spectral analysis of cardiac frequencies and is equivalent to the power density of the high-frequency band typically associated with respiration (Brownley et al. 2000; Task Force of the European Society of Cardiology and The North American Society of Pacing and Electrophysiology 1996). RSA has been shown to be positively related to emotional and behavioral regulation and attentional control (Porges 2003) and is thought to index the "efficiency of central-peripheral neural feedback mechanisms" that control those processes (Thayer and Lane 2000, p. 204). Dysregulated RSA has also been associated with preterm birth status and greater cost to behavioral self-regulation and attentional control (Lester et al. 1996).

In our study on mother and infant behaviors and their own and each other's physiologies, we assessed mother–infant synchrony with RSA because of its widely accepted use as an index of emotion regulation, attention, and social emotions. We also included a measure skin conductance (SC), a measure of sympathetic activity that is much more temporally sensitive.

We found that physiological concordance in fluctuations of sympathetic activity between mothers and infants was related to different social engagement states depending on the contextual demands of the interaction. When mothers are asked to sit still and simply watch their infants without responding, greater SC concordance occurred more when infants spent the most time protesting, fussing, or showing other forms of negative engagement. However, when mothers are asked to resume interaction and make every effort to soothe and attend to their infants, their own parasympathetic systems appear to be come more active in relation to how much their infant fusses and protests during the reunion, as if they are calming themselves in order to calm their infants. Furthermore, greater SC concordance between mothers and infants is no longer related to infant distress, as in the SF context, but instead becomes related to greater synchrony in mother–infant engagement behaviors, our marker of maternal sensitivity (Beeghly and Tronick 2011). The results of our study support the concept that physiology can be used to measure the relational processes that may facilitate the development of emotion regulation capacities and enhance the coherence of what we refer to as dyadically expanded states of consciousness (DiCorcia et al. 2012).

These results pair nicely with the results of Marci et al. (2007). At first, we were disappointed that SC concordance was not related to mother–infant synchrony during the normal FF episode. However, we realized that psychotherapy is also not a normal FF interaction but is more like the reunion (RE) episode, in which one participant (the mother or therapist) is actively focusing on and perhaps even soothing the other (infant or patient). Thus, one might conclude that physiological concordance is most likely to occur when one person is actively attending to another. This conclusion would also be consistent with Marci et al. finding that concordance is related to therapist empathy and positive, affirming behaviors. It is also consistent with the McCraty et al. (2001) proposal that focal unconditional positive regard toward a target person causes entrainment between the target person's cardiac activity and the subject's cortical activity, as measured by electroencephalogram. At the same time, simply interpreting what goes on in mother–infant or therapeutic interactions in a unidirectional fashion is not adequate, because it is not only the mother and the therapist who are responsible for the emergence of synchrony. These processes are bidirectional and require mutual engagement. As the infant is an agent, the patient in therapy must also engage with the therapist in the processes of dissolution and resolution, and ultimately greater coherence and complexity.

7 From the PCA and to the Still-Face Paradigm

The interpersonal dynamics that facilitate relational psychophysiology for the mother and infant and for the therapist and client are couched in Roger's PCA. Rogers is recognized for conducting some of the earliest known experientially based research that examined the "common factors" or "therapeutic factors" in the therapist–client dyad that mediate successful psychotherapy outcomes (Bohart 2005). Specifically, Rogers (1957/1992) found empirical support for the importance that the client be treated with empathy, unconditional positive regard, and genuineness as a unique individual. Psychotherapy research has continued to consistently demonstrate that it is the therapeutic relationship itself and not the therapeutic technique (e.g., manualized treatment plan) that has the most significant and most positive outcome for therapy (Beutler et al. 1986; Hubble et al. 1999; Lambert and Barley 2001). Underscoring these findings, considerable evidence now suggests that the quality of therapeutic alliance and client variables, such as psychological mindedness, account for the bulk of variance in treatment outcome as opposed to therapeutic technique (Messer and Wampold 2002). Additionally, psychotherapy studies examining physiological concordance between the therapist and client have identified its relationship in both client-perceived empathy of the therapist and therapist–client social emotional process during psychotherapy (Marci et al. 2007). Therapeutic alliance and client variables are explicit manifestations of the PCA, including presence/genuineness, empathy, and unconditional positive regard.

The PCA is interpersonal in nature and guides the therapeutic process. Congruence is the therapeutic vehicle for a supportive and collaborative dyadic process that emphasizes a deep appreciation of the client's experiential world, while having the therapist be open to his/her experience. Being congruent also asks that the therapist be genuine about the inner experience that the dyadic interaction evokes (Bugental 1987; Rogers 1957/1992). The concept of empathy, as Rogers described it, echoes the assumption of congruence but also requires more from the therapist. Empathy asks that the therapist understand the client's thinking, feeling, and perception of his/her behavior. The empathic approach includes attending to the client's nonverbal and verbal communication. Rogers explains unconditional positive regard as the basic attitude of distinguishing between the client's dysfunctional behavior and who the client is, in addition to respecting, accepting, and responding to the client "as a full human person" (Holdstock and Rogers 1977, p. 140). The complexity and continuity of verbal and nonverbal cues from the therapist to the client is critical in the patients' perceptions of feeling respected, empathic concern, and genuineness (Tepper and Haase 1978).

PCA is implicit in a mother's interaction toward her infant. It would behoove us to illustrate how Roger's notion of congruence/genuineness, unconditional positive regard, and empathy, provides a theoretical framework for how mother–infant relational psychophysiological dyadic interactions are facilitated. In our research, we see how mothers attempt to maintain their presence during each episode of the FFSF paradigm. For example, during the play episode, the mother will demonstrate unconditional positive regard toward her infant. She will attempt to engage her infant in a play activity, while tolerating her otherwise irritable infant. The still-face episode exacerbates the distress for the infant, while the mother presents a poker face and refrains from interacting with her infant. During the reunion episode, the mother will empathize over her infant's distress, and she will attempt to console her infant. Similar to the therapist–client dyadic interaction from one therapeutic moment to the next, there is a synchronizing or pacing between the mother and infant dyad in each FFSF episode. Moreover, the PCA is similarly "messy" for the therapist or mother to attain or maintain connection, while it may be conceptually straightforward. Congruence, for example, does not always characterize inner harmony for the therapist or mother; the inner sense of physiological harmony comes and goes. Both therapist and mother must initially self-regulate and to strive for congruency with the client and infant, respectively. Active behavioral and physiological subsystems within the dyads are supported through the therapist and mother's efforts at congruence, empathy, and unconditional positive regard. The interpersonal nature of the PCA maintains the momentum of the dyadic relational psychophysiology, which is necessary to engender meaning making for each interacting individual.

Much of the work of therapy is focused on the quality of the relationship or what the analysis sees as transference and counter-transference. Somewhat neglected are the numerous different levels of meaning and how those levels affect both the therapist and the patient. The multilevel nature of communication is spoken to clearly by the data on the synchrony (or not) of skin conductance and heart rate in infants and mothers, the synchrony of heart rate in firewalkers and intimate onlookers, and the heart rate and empathy data of the therapist and the patient. The firewalker findings are particularly telling in relation to multilevel processes involved in working on the relationship because the synchrony was enhanced by the level of relationship between the individuals. While the information that drives the psychophysiological synchrony is still unknown, the linkage only occurred between individuals who are in relationship. Similarly, what happens over time in successful therapy is that the two individuals come to know each other in a multileveled way. New understanding of the processes engaged in authenticity, presence, and positive regard can be illuminated. Unfortunately, these processes—relational psychophysiological processes—may also underlie the failures of therapies when unknown to either patient or therapist, physiological reactivity may belie and betray their lack of presence, authenticity, and positive regard.

8 Person-Centered Therapy Considering Psychophysiology

The nature of relational psychophysiology entails a complex network of interacting behavioral and physiological subsystems. The mechanism of relational psychophysiology for the mother and infant are not unlike what exists for the therapist and client. Rogers referred to this type of mechanistic dyadic process as a stream of becoming in which there is a symbiotic process of conscious and unconscious biopsychological systems that shape the human system. He further explains:

"I am often aware of the fact that I do not know, cognitively, where this immediate relationship is leading. It is as though both I and the client, often fearfully, let ourselves slip into the stream of becoming, a stream or process which carries us along. It is the fact that the therapist has let himself float in this stream of experience of life previously, and found rewarding that makes him each time less fearful of taking the plunge. It is my confidence that makes it easier for the client to embark also, a little bit at a time." (Rogers 1961, pp. 202–203).

In therapist–client and mother–infant relational contexts, the dyads engage in a unique dance of accurate perceptions and misperceptions, which are accompanied with the underlying ebbs and flows of their physiological processes. There is no universal rhythm to learn and prepare for either dyadic dance. Often times, the concordances of the behavioral and physiological systems are messy at best for the mother and infant and for the therapist and client; however, despite such dyadic messiness, these dyads manage to co-create their unique dance steps and routines (Busk et al. 1976; Ham and Tronick 2009; Marci et al. 2007).

A person-centered perspective provides an important theoretical explanation on the mechanism of relational psychophysiology for both mother–infant and therapist–client dyads. Additionally, we can tie this theoretical analysis to the functional purpose of relational psychophysiology for the human meaning-making system, as seen from a dynamic systems position. A dynamic system position explains that dyads endure relationally because of the functional purpose of relational psychophysiology. There is meaning and meaning making that is generated through the relational psychophysiology process. Humans as meaning makers—as open biological systems—have no option but to strive to increase the complexity of their states of interacting behavioral and physiological systems. The whole organism—the totality of human biopsychological processes, including but not limited to what we label mind, brain, and behavior—operates to gain meaningful information about the world in order to act *in* the world and to act *on* the world in alignment with the individual's purposes, intentions, meanings, and sense of the self in the world. Over time, these very processes wind back to create new purposes and intentions and a new sense of self in the world (Tronick 2007).

9 Conclusion

In summary, as research demonstrates, relational psychophysiology may offer insights into the bidirectional, agentic, and "messy" relational processes of dyadic growth. As with interactions between mothers and infants, both are agentic, intentional partners in the interaction. Similarly, patients are not simply passive recipients of the therapist's theories, but the therapeutic exchange is bidirectional, and patients are active and engaged. The processes of empathy, positive regard, and mutual regulation require active engagement in physiology, behavior, and intent in mother–infant and therapist–patient dyads.

References

Adamson, L. B., & Frick, J. E. (2003). The still-face: a history of a shared experimental paradigm. *Infancy, 4*, 451–473.

Bates, J. E., Maslin, C. A., & Frankel, K. (1985). Attachment security, mother-infant interaction, and temperament as predictors of behavior problem ratings at age three years. In I. Bretherton & E. Waters (Eds.), *Growing points in attachment theory and research Monographs of the Society for Research in Child Development* (vol 209, pp. 167–193).

Beebe, B., & Lachmann, F. M. (2002). *Infant research and adult treatment: co-constructing interactions*. Mahwah: Analytic Press.

Beeghly, M., & Tronick, E. (2011). Early resilience in the context of parent-infant relationships: a social developmental perspective. *Infant Mental Health Journal, 41*, 197–201.

Bernieri, F. J., & Rosenthal, R. (1991). Interpersonal coordination: behavior matching and interactional synchrony. In R. S. Feldman & B. Rime (Eds.), *Fundamentals of nonverbal behavior* (pp. 401–432). Cambridge: Cambridge University Press.

Beutler, L. E., Cargo, M., & Arizmendi, T. G. (1986). Research on therapist variables in psychotherapy. In S. L. Garfield & A. E. Bergin (Eds.), *Handbook of psychotherapy and behavior change* (3rd ed., pp. 257–310). New York: Wiley.

Bohart, A. C. (2005). Person-centered psychotherapy and related experiential approaches. In A. S. Gurman & S. B. Messer (Eds.), *Essential psychotherapies: theories and practice* (pp. 107–148). New York: Guilford Press.

Braungart-Rieker, J., Garwood, M. M., Powers, B. P., & Wang, X. (2001). Parental sensitivity, infant affect, and affect regulation: predictors of later attachment. *Child Development, 72*, 252–270.

Brownley, K. A., Hurwitz, B. E., & Schneiderman, N. (2000). Cardiovascular psychophysiology. In J. T. Cacioppo & L. G. Tassinary (Eds.), *Handbook of psychophysiology* (2nd ed., pp. 224–264). Cambridge: Cambridge University Press.

Bugental, J. F. T. (1987). *The art of the psychotherapist*. New York: Norton.

Busk, J., Naftulin, D. H., Donnelly, F. A., & Wolkon, G. H. (1976). Therapist's physiological activation and patient difficulty. *Journal of Nervous and Mental Disorders, 163*, 73–78.

Butler, E. (2011). *Physiological linkage: what it is, when it occurs, and why it matters*. Society for Psychophysiological Research: Poster Presentation.

Cacioppo, J. T., Tassinary, L. G., & Berntson, G. G. (2000). *Handbook of psychophysiology* (2nd ed.). Cambridge: Cambridge University Press.

Cohn, J. F., & Tronick, E. (1988). Mother-infant face-to-face interaction: Influence is bidirectional and unrelated to periodic cycles in either partner's behavior. *Developmental Psychology, 24*, 386–392.

Cohn, J. F., Campbell, S. B., & Ross, S. (1991). Infant response in the still-face paradigm at 6 months predicts avoidant and secure attachment at 12 months. *Development and Psychopathology, 3*, 367–376.

DiCorcia, J.A., Sravish, A.V., & Tronick, E. (2012). *The everyday stress hypothesis: Unfolding resilience from a perspective of everyday stress and coping.* Manuscript submitted for publication.

Durkheim, E. (1995). *The elementary forms of the religious life* (K.E. Fields, Trans). New York: The Free Press (Simon & Shuster). (Original work published 1912).

Ekman, I., Chanel, G., Järvelä, S., Kivikangas, J. M., Salminen, M., & Ravaja, N. (2011). Social interaction in games: Measuring physiological linkage and social presence. Simulation & Gaming, 1–18. doi: 10.1177/1046878111422121.

Feldman, R., Granat, A., Pariente, C., Kanety, H., Kuint, J., & Gilboa-Schechtman, E. (2009). Maternal depression and anxiety across the postpartum year and infant social engagement, fear regulation, and stress reactivity. *J Am Acad Child Adolesc Psychiatry, 48*(9), 919–927.

Fonagy, P. (2002). *Affect regulation, metallization, and the development of the self.* New York: Other Press.

George, C., Kaplan, N., & Main, M. (1996). Adult Attachment Interview (3rd ed.). *Unpublished manuscript*, Berkeley: Department of Psychology, University of California.

Gianino, A., & Tronick, E. (1988). The mutual regulation model: the infant's self and interactive regulation and coping and defense capacities. In T. Field, P. McCabe, & N. Schneiderman (Eds.), *Stress and coping* (pp. 47–68). Mahwah: Erlbaum.

Greenberg, L. S. (1997). *Empathy reconsidered: new directions for psychotherapy.* Washington, DC: American Psychological Association.

Ham, J., & Tronick, E. (2009). Relational psychophysiology: Lessons from mother-infant physiology research on dyadically expanded states of consciousness. *Psychotherapy Research, 19*, 619–632.

Holdstock, T. L., & Rogers, C. R. (1977). Person-centered theory. In R. J. Corsini (Ed.), *Current Personality Theories* (pp. 125–151). Itasca: F.E. Peacock.

Hubble, M. A., Duncan, B. L., & Miller, S. D. (1999). *The heart and soul of change: what works in therapy.* Washington, DC: American Psychology Association.

Kiel, L. D., & Elliott, E. W. (1996). Chaos theory in the social sciences: Foundations and applications University of Michigan Press.

Kiser, L. J., Bates, J. E., Maslin, C. A., & Bayles, K. (1986). Mother-infant play at six months as a predictor of attachment security at 13 months. *Journal of the American Academy of Child Psychiatry, 25*, 68–75.

Konvalinka, I., Xygalatas, D., Bulbulia, J., Schjødt, U., Jegindø, E., Wallot, S., . . . Roepstorff, A. (2011). Synchronized arousal between performers and related spectators in a fire-walking ritual. *Proceedings of the National Academy of Sciences, 108*(20), 8514–8519.

Lambert, M. J., & Barley, D. E. (2001). Research summary on the therapeutic relationship and psychotherapy outcome. *Psychotherapy: Theory, Research, Practice, Training, 38*, 357–361.

Lester, B. M., Buokydis, C. F. Z., & LaGasse, L. (1996). Cardiorespiratory reactivity during the Braselton scale in term and preterm infants. *Journal of Pediatric Psychology, 21*(6), 771–783.

Levenson, R. W., & Gottman, J. M. (1983). Marital interaction: Physiological linkage and affective exchange. *Journal of Personality and Social Psychology, 45*(3), 587–597.

Lewis, M. D. (2000). The promise of dynamic systems approaches for an integrated account of human development. *Child Development, 71*(1), 36–43.

Marci, C. D., Ham, J., Moran, E., & Orr, S. P. (2007). Physiologic correlates of perceived therapist empathy and social-emotional process during psychotherapy. *Journal of Nervous and Mental Disease, 195*(2), 103–111.

Masterson, J. F. (1990). *The search for the real self: unmasking the personality disorders of our age.* New York: Free Press.

Maughan, R. J., & Gleeson, M. (2008). Heart rate and salivary cortisol responses in armchair football supporters. *Medicina Sportiva, 12*, 20–24.

McCraty, R., Atkinson, M., & Tomasino, D. (2001). Science *of the heart: Exploring the role of the heart in human performance* (Publication No. 01-001). Boulder Creek, CA: HeartMath Research Center, Institute of HeartMath.

Messer, S. B., & Wampold, B. E. (2002). Let's face facts: common factors are more important than specific therapy ingredients. *Clinical Psychology: Science and Practice, 9*, 21–25.

Miles, L. K., Nind, L. K., & Macrae, C. N. (2009). The rhythm of rapport: Interpersonal synchrony and social perception. *Journal of Experimental Social Psychology, 45*, 585–589.

Moore, G. A., Cohn, J. F., & Campbell, S. B. (2001). Infant affective responses to mother's still-face at 6 months differentially predict externalizing and internalizing behaviors at 18 months. *Developmental Psychology, 37*, 706–714.

Ogden, P., Minton, K., & Pain, C. (2006). Trauma and the body: a sensorimotor approach to psychotherapy. New York: Norton.

Porges, S. W. (2003). The polyvagal theory: phylogenetic con attributions to social behavior. *Physiology and Behavior, 79*, 503–513.

Rogers, C. R. (1957). The necessary and sufficient conditions of therapeutic personality change. *Journal of Consulting Psychology, 21*(2), 95–103.

Rogers, C. R. (1961). *On becoming a person*. Boston: Houghton Mifflin.

Rogers, C. R. (1980). *A way of being*. Boston: Houghton Mifflin.

Rogers, C. R. (1992). The necessary and sufficient conditions of therapeutic personality change. *Journal of Consulting and Clinical Psychology, 60*, 827–832. (Original work published 1957).

Safran, J. D., & Muran, J. C. (2000). *Negotiating the therapeutic alliance: a relational treatment guide*. New York: Guilford Press.

Saxby, D. E., Margolin, G., Lauren, S. E., & Rodriguez, J. (2011). *Cortisol synchrony during triadic family conflict*. Society for Psychophysiological Research: Poster presentation.

Siegel, D. J. (1999). *The developing mind: toward a neurobiology of interpersonal experience*. New York: Guilford Press.

Stansbury, K., & Gunnar, M. R. (1994). Adrenocortical activity and emotion regulation. *Monographs of the Society for Research in Child Development, 59*, 108–134.

Task Force of the European Society of Cardiology and The North American Society of Pacing and Electrophysiology. (1996). Heart rate variability: standards of measurement, physiological interpretation, and clinical use. *European Heart Journal, 17*, 354–381.

Tepper, D. T., & Haase, R. F. (1978). Verbal and nonverbal communication of facilitative conditions. *Journal of Counseling Psychology, 25*, 35–44.

Thayer, J. F., & Lane, R. D. (2000). A model of neurovisceral integration in emotion regulation and dysregulation. *Journal of Affective Disorders, 61*, 201–216.

Thelen, E., & Smith, L. B. (1994). *A dynamic systems approach to the development of cognition and action*. Cambridge: MIT Press.

Tronick, E. Z. (1989). Emotions and emotional communication in infants. *American Psychologist, 44*, 112–119.

Tronick, E. Z. (1998). Dyadically expanded states of consciousness and the process of therapeutic change. *Infant Mental Health Journal, 19*, 290–299.

Tronick, E. Z. (2004). Why is connection with others so critical? The formation of dyadic states of consciousness and the expansion of individuals' states of consciousness: coherence-governed selection and the co-creation of meaning out of messy meaning making. In J. Nadel & D. Muir (Eds.), *Emotional development: recent research advances* (pp. 293–315). Cambridge: Oxford University Press.

Tronick, E. Z. (2007). *The neurobehavioral and social-emotional development of infants and children*. New York: Norton.

Tronick, E. Z., Als, H., Adamson, L., Wise, S., & Brazelton, T. B. (1978). The infant's response to entrapment between contradictory messages in face-to-face interaction. *Journal of the American Academy of Child and Adolescent Psychiatry, 17*, 1–13.

Weinberg, K. M., & Tronick, E. Z. (1996). Infant affective reactions to the resumption of maternal interaction after the still-face. *Child Development, 67*, 905–914.

First Relationship, Neuropsychobiology, and the Person-Centered Approach

Evleen Mann

Carl Rogers worked for many years with children and often used his experience of mothers, children, and babyhood as anecdotes and supportive evidence for his theories. In his 1959 seminal paper, Rogers (1959) offered no primary research from the mother/baby relationship to support his theories. I attempted to bridge that gap with my Master's thesis, which examined Rogers' (1959) theory of the "Conditions process and outcomes of an improving relationship" (p. 238). This is to me the most apposite theory applicable to a healthy mother/baby relationship, since over time, the mother and baby "improve" their relating and their relationship becomes "growthful" (my neologism).

First, this chapter will explain how I undertook the research, using the qualitative research program ATLAS.ti (1993–2011). Secondly, I will demonstrate how I provided evidence of the presence of Rogers' six conditions of therapeutic process within the first relationship as well as bringing to light serendipitous discoveries arising from the data. Finally, I discuss the implications of this research to therapeutic relating.

1 Research

> First there was the observation of the dynamic event. (Rogers 1959, p. 190)

From 2004–2006, I observed a new baby with his mother in their home, for 1 h per week, until he was 2 years old, an amalgamation of participant/observer and case study research. Although this formed part of my psychoanalytic observational studies diploma, the aim was "to generate thoughts and ideas, not so that it can exemplify theories" (Miller et al. 1989, p. 2). Hence, the written reports of each

E. Mann (✉)
The Dympna Centre, Parkside House, 17 East Parade, Harrogate HG1 5LF, England
e-mail: e.mann@evleenmann.com

observation now provided the material for my new research into Rogers' theory. Rogers (1959) himself valued observation as a tool for creating theory (see the quote above) with the proviso that caution should be exercised in the interpretation of the unfolding events. He noted that "The internal frame of reference is the subjective world of the individual. Only he knows it fully. It can never be known to another except through empathic inference and then can never be perfectly known" (p. 210).

1.1 Method

The written account of the 80 observations, each comprising around 1,200 words, were designated in ATLAS.ti as "primary documents" and the source material for my research. I chose to analyze 14 primary documents, starting when baby was 2 weeks, then roughly 8 weeks apart, and finishing at 2 years. This was to give me an idea of the changes taking place over time. Then, using the grounded theory of (Glaser and Strauss 1967), I went through the material, coding each activity and each experience in order to separate out the elements of mother/baby relating. Using the software program called ATLAS.ti the first set of codes I made were a priori, that is, taken directly from Rogers' theories, for example **contact**, **empathy**, and **unconditional positive regard** (**UPR**). I struggled to identify some of Rogers' concepts: for example, can one observe the **organismic valuing process** (**OVP**) at work? Or indeed someone's **congruence**? ATLAS.ti suggests that we define every code, rather like Rogers attempts to define all terms as thoroughly done in his 1959 paper. These codes and their definitions are easily retrieved in the program for quantifying and qualifying. It soon became clear that the codes would have to be attributed to either mother, baby, father, sibling, or me, the observer, so that I refined my coding into **mother: physical contact**, **baby: physical contact**, and so on. Many other codes emerged during analysis, which are termed *open* or in vivo coding, relating to the minutiae of the relationships, for example **baby: feeding** or **mother: cross**. Also, from the data arose codes without quotations, known as abstract codes, of which **baby** and **mother** are two! This supports Biermann-Ratjen's (1998) contention that we "cannot experience ourselves" but simply our feelings in the moment (p. 108).

For each primary document, I subdivided and broke down sentences and phrases into quotations to which I attached one or more codes. These coded quotations then became the bricks which I assigned to build up new structures, in particular, to examine the constitution of Rogers' six conditions of relating. My personal choice of which codes belonged to which condition was empowered by Rogers' (1959) assertion that "each definition is no more than an abstraction and that same phenomena might be abstracted in a different fashion" (p. 203).

1.2 Examples of Coding

In the following examples, group (a) **premerge codes** show the initial assignment of the individual codes and group (b) **postmerge codes** demonstrate how these individual codes were merged to constitute one or other of Rogers' six conditions of the therapeutic process.

Example 1 A section from an observation of baby at 2-weeks old has the following phrase or "quotation" as ATLAS.ti terms them.

> He latched on very easily and started sucking healthily and making contented sounds.
>
> **Premerge codes** (a) **baby: breastfeeding; baby: congruence positive; baby: vocalisation positive; mother: breastfeeding; mother: physical contact.**
> **Postmerge codes** (b) **Condition 1, Condition 2, Condition 5**
> (Mother's unconditional positive regard is how I defined breastfeeding and feeding in general and see discussion below).

Example 2 Section from an observation at 72 weeks.

> Suddenly he started to rub his face and grumble: 'You are tired' said Mum and plucked him out of the chair. He was happy in her arms and put his face into her neck.
>
> ATLAS.ti enables a Line by Line analysis of quotations, with different colors to differentiate each code hence:
> *Suddenly he started to rub his face and grumble:*
> **Premerge codes** (a) **baby: vulnerable; baby: vocalisation negative; baby: need for positive regard**
> **Postmerge codes** (b) **Condition 2**

You are tired said Mum and plucked him out of the chair.

> **Premerge codes** (a) **mother: vocalising for baby; mother: physical contact; mother: regulates; mother: empathy, baby: physical contact**
> **Postmerge codes** (b) **Condition 1, Condition 4, Condition 5.**

He was happy in her arms and put his face into her neck.

> **Premerge codes** (a) **baby: happy; baby: understood; baby: perception of positive regard; baby: physical contact**
> **Postmerge codes** (b) **Condition 1, Condition 6**

The whole of the section above I also coded with: **baby:dialogue** and **Growthful** interpersonal relationship (IPR). This is because the baby has entered into a dialogue, though wordless, with mother because of a need for positive regard and through communication, baby has had that need contingently met.

Interestingly, except for **mother:congruence**, or **Condition 3**, this small segment contains "proof" that 5 of Rogers' six conditions for therapeutic relating have been met.

1.3 Analysis

ATLAS.ti enables the user to link codes together. For example, baby is crying (coded **baby: crying**), arises from a negative experience which gives rise to negative congruence (**baby: congruence negative**). My proposition that a baby is always congruent and has not yet learnt to hide his feelings because of conditions of worth is supported by Rogers (1961): "he is one unified person all the way through…at the visceral level, the level of his awareness or the level of communication" (p. 339). Tudor (2011) affirms that congruence can be positive or negative: "a person being vulnerable or anxious may also be congruent in terms of being genuine, authentic and accurate about her or his distress or disease" (p. 176). I coded congruent states as **baby: congruence positive** and **baby: congruence negative.** Then, I linked the codes using clauses such as "**is a**" or "**causes**" to join relevant codes to each other. **Baby: anxious** is linked to **baby: congruence negative,** to **baby:cross**, then **baby: vocalisation negative** to **baby: crying** (see Fig. 1). In this way, I was able to build up diagrammatic representations of Roger's theories, in ATLAS.ti terms, "network views" of the concepts I was trying to understand.

1.4 Serendipitous Discoveries from the Data

I noticed that mother always had flowers in the room, crayons for the children to draw with, and tissues to wipe away tears. I coded this aspect of my observation **mother: ambience**. In ATLAS.ti there is a facility to make notes of one's original ideas by writing memos and attaching them to the codes. The memos evoked the parallels between the therapist creating a characteristically peaceful ambience in

Fig. 1 Network view of condition 2: baby's need for positive regard

the consulting room and the mother's efforts at developing an overall atmosphere in the home. Both offer tissues to clean up and could be called "waste disposers"!

Using the network view, I also linked the idea of the umbilical channel pictorially with Mearns and Cooper's (2005) therapeutic concept of relational depth and highlighted the reciprocity contained within the mother/baby and therapist/client relationships. Thus, the program enables verbal and diagrammatic conceptualizations.

1.5 Quantitative Results

The ATLAS.ti program counts how many times a code is used. This can be filtered for each document and compared across baby's developmental age range. For example, over time, we see baby relating more and more to other people (including to me, the observer) and can relate these contacts graphically to other outcomes such as increasing autonomy. The latter too can be simply evidenced by coding for motor developments such as **baby: lying** followed by **baby: crawling** and **baby: walking**.

1.6 Co-occurrence Tool

There is a facility in the program to monitor the frequency with which codes overlap or are associated together. The closer the coefficient is to 1, the more valid is the association. I logged the number of instances of Growthful Interpersonal Relationship versus the presence of Rogers' six conditions. In this mother/baby relationship, the coefficient was over 0.6 for Conditions 1–5 and over 0.55 for Condition 6. This provided supporting quantitative evidence for Rogers's theory of the conditions necessary for the therapeutic process, which are an underlying condition of an "Improving Interpersonal relationship."

2 Discussion of Research and Implications for Practice

Throughout this chapter, I use the gendered pronouns she for "mother" and he for "baby" to clarify who is who, because she carries the baby intrauterinely and in most societies provides his early care.

2.1 First Condition: Mother/Baby Contact

Birth leads to the loss of attachment through the umbilical cord and the protective womb, creating mother's and baby's need to re-establish contact. This physical and psychological closeness acts as a metaphysical channel, through which positive regard, including nutrition, physical support, emotional understanding (empathy), and ensuing regulation, is delivered to the baby, at the beginning of his life and, hopefully, reciprocally, back to the mother during and at the end of her life. Similarly, Mearns and Cooper (2005) describe the therapeutic relationship in-depth: "There is a co-transparency, a co-acceptance, co-understanding, a co-receiving of each other, a flowing backwards and forwards between therapist and client through the channel that connects them" (p. 46). This is affirmed in relational psychophysiology experiments by Ham and Tronick (2009) "the interaction between mothers and infants is bidirectional and infants are active, intentional partners in the interaction. Similarly the therapeutic exchange is bidirectional" (p. 629).

2.1.1 Co-regulation

For the organism to grow fully and to the criterion of the actualizing tendency (Rogers 1959 p. 196), the internal system of the baby has to be able to maintain homeostasis, but be ready to respond to danger/excitement/other stimuli from his internal or external environment. Environmental stress, emotional and physical neglect, and malnourishment and lack of sleep, all cause a rise in cortisol. Gerhardt (2004) writes on "corrosive cortisol" which at high levels destroys cells in the baby's brain and diminishes the growth and the viability of the connections between neurones in vital communication tracts. When mother successfully settles (regulates) her distressed baby, she enables him to be receptive to learning and communication.

So the tighter the connection, and we can assume **attachment** here (Bowlby 1991/1969), the stronger and more open is the channel (the communication) between mother and child. This leads literally to openness in understanding his needs, and a free passage for mother's contingent response to those needs, and for the free return of his response to being responded to.

Astonishingly Rogers, ahead of his time, used this word "regulate" in his 1959 paper, as an outcome of an improving relationship. "Psychotherapy (*or 'mother-baby relationship': my insertion*) is the releasing of an already existing capacity in a potentially competent individual, not the expert manipulation of a more or less passive personality. Philosophically it means that the individual has the capacity to guide, regulate, and control himself, providing that only certain definable conditions exist" (p. 221).

2.2 Second Condition: Baby's Need for Positive Regard

Rogers' second condition for therapeutic process identifies one person as being anxious or vulnerable (p. 213). For a baby, this would include the need for both physical and psychological nourishment and protection, which I reframed as a "need for positive regard" using Rogers' alternative description of this state (p. 208).

2.3 Third Condition: Mother's Congruence

Congruence was the most difficult condition to "evidence" from my observations, as I myself could only empathically infer the mother's internal state of mind as she struggled to respond appropriately to baby's needs. Examples of my codes constituting maternal congruence are **mother: aware**; **mother: attunement**; **mother: relaxed**; **mother: unworried**; **mother: self-regard**.

Lux (2010) defines congruence neuroscientifically, as openness between conscious awareness and inner experiencing "a concordance of processes in explicit and implicit systems" (p. 278). By understanding her own internal frame of reference (Rogers 1959 p. 210), mother metaphorically clears the passage for baby's communications to reach her. Biermann-Ratjen (1998) concurs: It is "important that significant others understand correctly what the child is feeling, and do not react with their own unreflected emotions, if the child is to be able to integrate self-reflective and self-assertive sides into his self-concept and regard itself as a coherent emotional being"(p. 117).

2.4 Fourth Condition: Mother's Empathic Inference

Research by Damasio and Meyer (2008) supports the idea that mother's mirror neurons engender her empathic responding: "mirror neurons induce widespread neural activity based on learned patterns of connectivity; these patterns generate internal stimulation and establish the meaning of actions" (p. 168). Seeing and unconsciously mirroring the child's expressions and body posture enables mother to attune to what the child is feeling, attunement as a resonance with her whole body and vice versa. Similarly, Ham and Tronick (2009) describe the client/therapist thus: "the multiple layers of the patient's self-organization becomes resonant with the therapist's and they co-create a new and greater coherence, a dyadically expanded, harmonically amplified state of consciousness shared between them. This then becomes empathy" (p. 622).

Lux (2010) too examines empathy and its effect on regulation in the therapist/client relationship (p. 182). He suggests that regulation provides emotional security for the adult (akin to physical security for a baby). The recipient (baby/client) of empathic understanding develops trust in the giver (mother/therapist), which generates the hormone oxytocin, giving a sense of security, essential to healthy relating. Paradoxically, oxytocin causes the uterus to contract and expel the baby, but is involved subsequently in breastfeeding and keeping people close. Trust is therefore a mutually affective dynamic which mother and baby co-create. Sullivan, cited in Biermann-Ratjen (1998), calls this "interpersonal security" (p. 112).

Maslow's hierarchy of needs is clear: shelter, food, and drink. Baby cannot state these needs, but mother opens up all her perceptive powers: seeing, sensing, intuition, and experience to empathically infer from the baby's behaviour and type of communications what is required: swaddling, soothing, cleaning, feeding, and rocking to sleep. She also has clues from her own body (her breasts fill up with milk at the baby's cry) which direct her communication. Weighing baby at the clinic gives proof of her success in meeting his physical needs.

2.5 Fifth Condition: Mother's UPR

But initially, it is harder for a mother to be "confident" about communicating the nourishment required for psychological and emotional growth. Often, therapists encourage a client to wait six sessions before giving up on therapy, which parallels the length of time to baby's first reliable smile! It takes time to attune to each other. Schore (2001) laments: "In the U.S. we send mothers back into the work force at 6 weeks, which is the point whereby the face to face joy interactions just begin" (para. 42).

Gerhardt (2004) upholds the indispensability of positive regard to the growth of a baby's brain and body: "looks and smiles actually help the brain to grow" (p. 41). Mother experiencing pleasure triggers baby experiencing pleasure in the form of natural opioids, which nourish the neurones with glucose, helping them to grow and connect. The neurotransmitter dopamine is also released from the brain stem onto the orbito-frontal cortex, energizing it and is also involved in expectation of reward. Schore cited says "positive looks…are the most vital to the growth of the social, emotionally intelligent, brain" (ibid p. 41). Again, Rogers anticipated neuroscientific evidence that UPR promotes growth and is reciprocal. Warner (2005) too values Rogers' ideas around prizing: which is "empathic and genuine" (p. 103). She recognizes their importance in mother/baby attachment and as contributing to the relational depth of all close human connection.

2.6 Sixth Condition: Baby's Perception of UPR and Empathy

Gerhardt (2004) emphasizes the importance of a contingent response (p. 197). This gives the baby the feeling that his needs are being attended to, that his communication is valued, and that he can make himself understood. Ultimately, he becomes confident in his ability to communicate with the wider world. If mother has identified his feelings correctly, this helps the child to reflect on his emotions and understand the meaning they hold in his current situation. Gerhardt asserts that the first relationship informs all other relating. "It is as babies that we first feel and learn what to do with our feelings, when we start to organise our experience in a way that will affect our later behaviour and our thinking capacities" (ibid p. 10).

It seems a mother's role is to help the baby discern his different experiences, separating out the ones which can be named, or mimed, so that she can identify a way of describing them to the child. The child can then use this language (body or verbal) subsequently to return information to the mother and to others about his own state of being. For adults too, naming feelings leads to emotional regulation by deactivating the amygdalae. Lieberman et al. (as cited in Lux 2010) "demonstrated that verbally labelling the emotional quality of an emotional-triggering stimulus activates brain regions, which have the potential to attenuate the activated emotions" (p. 282). Accurate symbolization, Rogers (1959) asserts, is a prerequisite for awareness (p. 198). When mother helps baby name and identify his experiences, he begins to attach outcomes to his emotions.

2.7 Reciprocal Autonomy

Autonomy is an outcome of the actualizing tendency (Rogers 1959, p. 196). From my research, as baby became more autonomous, so did mother. Eventually, baby could feed himself, walk, and talk: his growing independence leaves mother more independent herself to make choices about her life. This might include co-creating another human being with father or going back to work. Rogers (1959) ascribes increasing openness to experience as an important outcome of therapeutic relating, which for baby could be rephrased "flexibility in meeting new environments" (p. 218). Warner (2005) attributes to this facility "much of the adaptive success and dominance of human beings over other species" (p. 100). Conversely, Gerhardt (2004) notes that children who have insecure attachment "lack flexibility because they are essentially defensive" (p. 200).

3 Conclusion

My analysis of this mother/baby relationship supports Rogers' 1959 theory on the six conditions necessary for therapeutic process. Mother/therapist provides an ambient place for meeting, offering contact, a channel, through which empathy and UPR are delivered in response to needs of the baby/client. Often, baby/client does not know the nature of their need, and mother/therapist empathically helps them to uncover and name the need. Recognizing the need provides baby/client with a means to explore meeting that need, either from within his own resources or through other relationships. Additionally, this paradigm fulfills Rogers' "tentative law of interpersonal relationship." "The greater the communicated congruence of experience, awareness and behaviour on the part of one individual, the more the ensuing relationship will involve a tendency towards reciprocal communication with the same qualities" (p. 240). The interchange has reciprocal benefits and, naturally, can convey reciprocal harm. Mother/therapist often takes toxic substances/information away and safely disposes of them. Mother/therapist usually gets help from an experienced other and is supported by other healthy relationships. The ultimate result of the first relationship is to facilitate the baby's experience of how to receive nourishment and give it back to others (to communicate) and subsequently to nourish themselves by becoming independent, resilient, autonomously feeding, and self-regulating. Ultimately, baby/client walks away to lead their own life, confident in meeting their own needs, as does the mother/therapist.

Yet, essential aspects of the first relationship are absent from the typical psychotherapeutic here and now: feeding, physical contact, regulation, and opportunities to play. Yes there are body-related therapies; eating disorder treatment hinges on achieving a healthy weight before psychotherapy is introduced; and sand trays, paints in art, and play therapy reflect an understanding of the importance of creativity in healing. However, these are undervalued compared to language as forms of interpersonal communication. This reflection invites us to explore such maternal additions to traditional therapeutic relating.

References

ATLAS.ti (1993–2011). *Atlasti manual.* Berlin: GMBH.
Biermann-Ratjen, E. M. (1998). On the development of persons in relationships. In B. Thorne & E. Lambers (Eds.), *Person-centred therapy: A European perspective* (pp. 119–130). London: Sage.
Bowlby, J. (1991). *Attachment and loss volume 1 attachment.* London: Penguin (Original work published 1969).
Damasio, A. D., & Meyer, K. (2008). Behind the looking glass. *Nature, 454,* 167–168.
Gerhardt, S. (2004). *Why love matters: How affection shapes a baby's brain.* London: Routledge.
Glaser, B. G., & Strauss, A. L. (1967). *Discovery of grounded theory.* Chicago: Aldine Publishing.

Ham, J., & Tronick, E. (2009). Relational psychophysiology: Lessons from mother–infant physiology research on dyadically expanded states of consciousness. *Psychotherapy Research, 19*, 619–632.

Lux, M. (2010). The magic of encounter. The person-centred approach and the neurosciences. *Person-Centered and Experiential Psychotherapies, 9*(4), 275–289.

Mearns, D., & Cooper, M. (2005). *Working at relational depth*. London: Sage.

Miller, L., Rustin, M., Rustin, M., & Shuttleworth, J. (Eds.). (1989). *Closely observed infants*. London: Duckworth.

Rogers, C. R. (1959). A theory of therapy, personality and interpersonal relationships, as developed in the client centred framework. In S. Koch (Ed.), *Psychology: A study of a science vol 3: Formulations of the person and the social context* (pp. 184–256). New York: McGraw-Hill.

Rogers, C. R. (1961). *On becoming a person*. New York: Houghton Mifflin.

Schore, A. (2001). An interview with Allan Schore-The American Bowlby. http://www.thinkbody.co.uk/papers/interview-with-allan-s.htm, pp. 1–6. Accessed Sep 1, 2012.

Tudor, K. (2011). Rogers' therapeutic conditions: A relational conceptualization. *Person-Centred and Experiential Psychotherapies, 10*, 165–180.

Warner, M. (2005). A person-centred view of human nature, wellness and psychopathology. In S. Joseph & R. Worsley (Eds.), *Psychopathology and the Person-centred Approach* (pp. 91–109). Ross-on-Wye: PCCS books.

Part V
Positive Psychology

Person-Centered Theory Encountering Mainstream Psychology: Building Bridges and Looking to the Future

Stephen Joseph and David Murphy

1 Introduction

Person-centered psychology offers an important theory which has not been as influential within mainstream psychology as it has the potential to be. Over the last decade, however, the world of psychology has been changing in ways that offer new opportunities for person-centered psychologists to influence developments in theory and practice. The task for person-centered psychologists, as we see it, is to now build the bridges to other areas of psychology. In this chapter, we will show that person-centered psychology is situated at the interface of other arenas of psychological research and clinical activity that often go unnoticed by the person-centered community. Many of the core ideas associated with person-centered psychology are topics that are alive and well in contemporary mainstream psychology (see, Joseph and Murphy 2012). There is a renewed interest, for example, in the role of human relationships as a vehicle for therapeutic healing (Duncan et al. 2009; Leahy 2008). One mainstream development, in particular, that person-centered psychologists need to be more aware of is positive psychology—the science of optimal human functioning and well-being. Positive psychology as a new field of psychology began to develop over a decade ago and since then it has gone from strength to strength. The science of positive psychology provides a conduit through which person-centered psychology can engage with mainstream psychology.

The big idea of positive psychology—that we should be interested not only in distress and dysfunction but also in what makes life worth living—has permeated throughout mainstream psychology. It is now commonplace among psychologists

S. Joseph (✉)
School of Sociology and Social Policy, University of Nottingham, Nottingham NG7 2RD, UK
e-mail: Stephen.Joseph@nottingham.ac.uk

D. Murphy
School of Education, University of Nottingham, Nottingham NG8 1BB, UK
e-mail: David.Murphy@nottingham.ac.uk

working in diverse theoretical and applied areas of social, counseling, clinical, health, and occupational psychology to consider optimal functioning and for their research to be published in mainstream journals related to these broader topic areas. As an example, our own work on the topic of posttraumatic growth has been published in the main trauma psychology and clinical psychology journals.

Our aim is to encourage bridge building: first, to advocate a new inclusive approach in which person-centered psychologists engage more fully with mainstream developments such as the research informed by positive psychology; and second, to encourage the person-centered community to disseminate their ideas more widely, and in particular to challenge the dominant medical discourse that now permeates the psychological helping professions. Person-centered psychology is explicitly non-medical in its approach to understanding human distress. It offers a vision for helping in which human relationships are healing in their own right, not only as a precursor to something else. As we will show this vision is founded on an alternative meta-theoretical stance to the medical model and can offer mainstream psychology something new on which to hang the modern approach to positive psychology.

2 Building Bridges

> The aim of positive psychology is to begin to catalyze a change in the focus of psychology from preoccupation only with repairing the worst things in life to also building positive qualities (Seligman and Csikszentmihalyi 2000, p. 5).

Person-centered psychology is often associated with the humanistic school of psychology, but more contemporarily, it can also be aligned with positive psychology because of the shared focus on optimal functioning and well-being, as the above quote illustrates. This is one theoretical issue that has traditionally differentiated person-centered psychology from the mainstream agenda of psychological theory and practice. Person-centered psychology is interested not only in the ways in which people become distressed and dysfunctional but also in their movement toward becoming more fully functioning. The term fully functioning might seem dated, but it essentially captures the characteristics of optimal functioning and well-being, which are now the interest of positive psychologists (Seligman and Csikszentmihalyi 2000). In this sense, person-centered psychology is a positive psychology (see, Joseph and Worsley 2007; Levitt 2008). Shlien, originally writing in 1956, said:

> In the past, mental health has been a 'residual' concept—the absence of disease. We need to do more than describe improvement in terms of say 'anxiety reduction'. We need to say what the person can *do* as health is achieved. As the emphasis on pathology lessons, there have been a few recent efforts toward positive conceptualizations of mental health. Notable among these are Carl Rogers' 'fully Functioning Person', A. Maslow's 'Self-Realizing Persons'... (Schlien 2003, p. 17).

These ideas have been at the core of person-centered psychology for over half a century, but despite this, it never fully entered the mainstream agenda until the advent of the positive psychology movement just over a decade ago. So it is that almost 50 years after the groundbreaking theoretical work of the pioneers of person-centered psychology, it is only now that mainstream practice and policy is changing to accommodate a new agenda of optimal functioning and well-being.

Thus, while we wholeheartedly support the positive psychology movements' vision of an agenda for practice and policy that spans the breadth of human functioning, we are aware that these important new developments have not taken place because of the activities of the person-centered movement. As the changes in mainstream practice and policy toward a positive conceptualization of mental health took hold over the past decade, the person-centered movement was far from the center of influence as economists, social scientists, and psychologists new to these ideas made their voices heard in governments across the Western world. In the midst of these important new developments, there was little active engagement from the person-centered community. Why was this? We wonder whether the person-centered community has to an extent forgotten its roots; person-centered therapists were the original positive psychologists, but having largely adopted the language of distress and dysfunction themselves, the core teachings of person-centered psychology are lost.

The above statement may surprise many person-centered practitioners. But we would argue that the alignment by many person-centered therapists with the medical model delivery of therapeutic services in statutory and managed care services has led person-centered therapists to be caught in the trap of competing with other therapies that are more naturally and congruently aligned with medical model thinking. While there has been much achieved and evidence suggests that person-centered therapy is as effective as cognitive-behavior therapy for the treatment of depression (e.g., King et al. 2000), competition and focus on the reduction in depressive symptoms and other psychiatric disorders are only ever going to lead to the production of medical model therapists. When we start using the language of medicine almost exclusively to evaluate what we do we inevitably lose touch with the core theoretical ideas of the person-centered approach. Here, the quote from Shlien above is never more true as person-centered practitioners become entwined with deficit psychology and attempt to reduce symptoms and find solutions to people's problems in life.

If there is to be competition between therapies, then it must be even-handed. Alongside, the question of how effective is person-centered therapy for depression must sit the mirror question of how effective is cognitive-behavior-therapy for fully functioning behavior. In short, therapies must be evaluated in relation to what it is they propose they do for people. In the past, however, conceptualizing research programs that focus on the development of new aspects of functioning, in ways that are non-specific but directional toward constructive growth, has never been considered within statutory and managed care services. We now need to introduce a language of outcomes that is consistent with person-centered theory. Today, the idea of a more even-handed approach to outcome evaluations is now possible due to the influence over the past decade of positive psychology. Meanwhile, we—the person-centered community—continued to discuss among ourselves how we were marginalized from mainstream practice and policy and how a person-centered approach to living had the potential to transform human lives. Indeed, in the early years of positive psychology, there was little or no acknowledgment of the fact that many of the ambitions of the new positive psychology movement echoed those from humanistic psychology. For some in the positive psychology movement, this was a deliberate strategy of distancing their new movement from what was seen as a previous movement that had failed and lost its way, engaging with spiritual and supernatural practices and abandoning the rigor of science. There is some truth in the positive psychologist's negative portrayal of humanistic psychology but perhaps it was intellectually dishonest to not give more credit to the pioneers of humanistic psychology. As such, the early relationship between positive psychology and humanistic psychology was often contentious (e.g., Taylor 2001). Nonetheless, it was also a politically astute move by the positive psychologists. To be taken seriously by mainstream, funding bodies and scholars required distancing from the embarrassments of humanistic psychology. For younger members of the positive psychology movement, the message that there was little to be learned from humanistic psychology was passed down to them and there was probably a genuine lack of awareness that they were on already well-trodden ground.

Person-centered psychology is not synonymous with humanistic psychology and person-centered practitioners and scholars may be equally embarrassed by their association to the fringe elements of humanistic psychology. As the positive psychology movement has evolved, its leaders now acknowledge that positive psychology builds upon the earlier work of, among others, Rogers and Maslow (Seligman et al. 2005). While this bridge building is heartening to those of us in the person-centered movement, the task remains a long way from completion (Schneider 2011). It is true that Rogers and Maslow had similar visions as the positive psychologists, in terms of wanting to understand the full range of human experience, although their vision was more than simply this. Rogers and Maslow were also trenchant critics of the medical model as applied to psychology, and it was their alternative view of human nature that made their positive psychology also a humanistic psychology. What Rogers and Maslow recognized was that by adopting the medical model, psychology might serve to help people in one sense, but that it also served to alienate and damage people in another. They also recognized that the medical model, as applied to psychological problems, was so pervasive in our way of thinking about psychological issues, and in our culture, that it was hard to see that this was the case. We think this is partly why many person-centered practitioners have become aligned with the medical model without even realizing it. So pervasive is the medical model within the fabric of society that it isn't easy to spot. A consequence of the medicalization of distress (Sanders 2005) is that it has become very difficult to stand outside of the dominant paradigm, perhaps even more so now than when Rogers and Maslow were developing their ideas. Person-centered psychology in theoretical terms remains a truly credible alternative to the medical model paradigm. Practitioners though have to realize this and hold on to their position and speak out against and resist the dominant and oppressive effects of the medical model.

There are some positive psychologists who are similarly critical of the medical model (e.g., Maddux et al. 2004). But positive psychology as a movement largely continues to operate within the medical model (Joseph and Linley 2006a), and thus to implicitly condone the medicalization of human experience. This last statement might also surprise some as the study of positive psychology would seem to be the antithesis of the medical model. However, the medical model nature of much of contemporary positive psychology is disguised by its language of strengths, virtues, and happiness. Because the remit of positive psychology is to supplement traditional psychology, which focuses only on distress and dysfunction, it serves to condone the idea that there is a separation between the negative and the positive aspects of human experience. As such, within the everyday business of positive psychology, the specificity myth continues to rule (Bozarth and Motomasa 2005). The specificity myth is that there are specific treatments for specific conditions which would be the case if one assumes a medicalized view of human experiences. Thus, insofar as new interventions are developed to promote particular positive psychology outcomes, it is true that a medicalized view continues to underpin practice. For example, a client goes to see a coaching psychologist. The problem presented by the client is their lack of self-appreciation. The coach makes a "diagnosis" of low self-worth. The coach suggests a course of gratitude exercises as these are proven to benefit clients with low self-worth. Positive psychology practiced in this way is no different from the medical model paradigm of diagnosing mental illness and treating the disorder and not the person.

The person-centered model offers an alternative meta-theory founded on the assumption that people are intrinsically motivated toward development, growth, and socially constructive behavior, but that the social environment could thwart and usurp this intrinsic motivation leading to distress, suffering, and psychopathology (see, Joseph and Worsley 2005). Thus, therapeutic work is always concerned *simultaneously* with the relief of suffering and the promotion of well-being. The person-centered paradigm demands that there is no division between the negative and the positive aspects of human experience but that these always go hand in glove. Thus, in this sense person-centered psychology is neither a negative psychology, nor a positive psychology, it is both simultaneously.

3 Looking to the Future

3.1 Lessons from Person-Centered Psychology

There is need for person-centered psychologists to communicate their ideas to a more mainstream audience. The field of positive psychology can be a conduit for this communication. For example, there are several ways in which positive psychologists can learn from person-centered psychology. First, it is important to understand that person-centered psychology is not well understood. It is often thought of as dated, lacking in theory, and only about therapeutic relationship. What needs to be communicated is the underpinning meta-theory (Joseph and Linley 2006c; Joseph and Patterson 2008).This, in our view, is the defining feature of person-centered psychology. Positive psychologists may benefit from an understanding of the central theoretical construct of the *actualizing tendency*. Within person-centered psychology, the actualizing tendency is a universal human motivation resulting in growth, development, and autonomy of the individual (Rogers 1963). Rogers argued that it is a tendency toward *fully functioning*. Rogers was clear, however, that fully functioning was an ideal. It is unusual for people to experience such optimal social environments that they might be said to have self-actualized as fully functioning; most people experience to a greater or lesser degree social environments that are less than optimal. Second is the principle of *non-directivity* as the logical response to the actualizing tendency theory. The meta-theoretical position underpins what it means to be person-centered and why person-centered practitioners adopt non-directive approaches. Again, the concept of non-directivity is not well understood outside the immediate community. Grant (1990) distinguished between *principled* non-directivity and *instrumental* non-directivity. Whereas principled non-directivity refers to the therapist's ethical values of non-interference and respect for the self-determination of the other and is itself the goal of the person-centered therapist, instrumental non-directivity refers to a set of behaviors applied by the therapist to achieve a particular goal such as building rapport.

A sophisticated awareness of person-centered psychology is lacking in mainstream psychology which has to a large extent unquestionably adopted the assumptions of medicalization and the need for directivity. Examples of the more outward looking focus and communication advocated here are some work within trauma psychology in which person-centered theoretical ideas have been promoted to a more mainstream audience of clinical psychologists (see, Joseph and Linley 2006b), social workers (see, Murphy et al. 2012), and other work advocating organismic psychology to the positive psychology audience (see, Joseph and Linley 2006c).

3.2 Lessons for Person-Centered Psychology

Despite the developments in the last decade—for example, the philosophical basis of the person-centered approach (Tudor and Worrall 2006), its political impact (Proctor et al. 2006), its conception of psychopathology (Joseph and Worsley 2005), as well as developments in a variety of other areas of theory and practice (Cooper et al. 2007; Kirschenbaum 2007)—these have so far been more inward as opposed to outward looking.

While this is understandable because from the person-centered perspective there is much to be critical of in mainstream psychology, we do not think it is wise for the person-centered community to isolate themselves from what is going on elsewhere. Indeed, as we have already argued, the person-centered community has in the past done just this with the detrimental effects that their influence on developments in contemporary psychology and psychiatry has been marginal. Looking to the future, our focus now should be on how the person-centered community can learn from mainstream developments and be more outward looking.

There are areas of mainstream social psychological research and theory that receive little attention from the person-centered community that do draw on person-centered ideas, or similar ideas. Research shows, for example, that people move toward becoming more fully functioning when exposed to growth promoting climates (e.g., Sheldon et al. 2003), that those who experience greater conditional positive regard are less authentic and exhibit more false self-behavior (e.g., Harter et al. 1996), and that optimal functioning is related to self-concordance in personality (Sheldon 2002; Sheldon and Kasser 2001). There is a wealth of such theory and research evidence from positive psychology and related areas that person-centered psychologists need to be aware of (Joseph and Linley 2006c).

The strongest support, however, comes from an area of research which has developed in parallel to person-centered theory but which offers an almost identical meta-theoretical stance. Self-determination theory (SDT) is a more contemporary organismic theory of human motivation and personality functioning developed over the past 30 years that also emphasizes the central role of the individual's inner resources for personality development and behavioral self-regulation (Deci and Ryan 2000, 2002; Ryan and Deci 2000, 2002). In accord with person-centered theory, SDT views the person as an active growth-oriented organism, attempting to actualize his or her potentialities within the environment he or she functions in. As such, SDT provides a meta-theoretical perspective similar to person-centered personality theory. SDT has three elements:

- The first is that human beings are inherently proactive, that they have the potential to act on and master both the inner forces (viz., their drives and emotions) and the external (i.e., environmental) forces they encounter, rather than being passively controlled by those forces...
- Second, human beings, as self-organizing systems, have an inherent tendency toward growth, development, and integrated functioning...
- The third important philosophical assumption is that, although activity and optimal development are inherent to the human organism, these do not happen automatically. For people to actualize their inherent nature and potential—that is, to be optimally active and to develop effectively—they require nutrients from the social environment. To the extent that they are denied the necessary support and nourishment by chaotic, controlling, or rejecting environments, there will be negative consequences for their activity and development (Deci and Vansteenkiste 2004, pp. 23–24).

Although SDT theorists do not trace the lineage of their work to person-centered psychology, it is clear at the meta-theoretical level that SDT and person-centered theory are synonymous (Patterson and Joseph 2007a). This is an exciting convergence of ideas from these two traditions of psychological thought, and most importantly provides a strong evidence base consistent with person-centered psychology that is otherwise seen by critics as lacking.

As with Rogers's theory, in SDT, the organismic tendency toward actualization is seen as a biological tendency rather than a moral imperative, and as one pole of a *dialectical interface*, the other pole being the social environment which can either be facilitating or inhibiting of the persons' synthesizing tendency. Self-determination theory therefore provides the same meta-theoretical perspective to person-centered personality theory; that is, human beings have an inherent tendency toward growth, development, and integrated functioning but that these do not happen automatically but require nutrients from the social environment (c.f. Deci and Vansteenkiste 2004; Vansteenkiste and Sheldon 2006). Similarities between person-centered theory and self-determination theory have been obscured by the differences in terminology, and separate research trajectories, but on examination, there are such close similarities between these approaches that the extensive research evidence from self-determination theory can be read as providing evidence consistent with person-centered theory (see, Patterson and Joseph 2007a), thus countering criticisms of person-centered theory that it lacks research support. The proponents of SDT also recognize the importance of the meta-theory for mainstream practice and policy when they write:

> Although positive psychology researchers are working to identify factors that enhance individuals' capacities, development, and well-being, only a few…fully embrace and utilize this critical meta-theoretical assumption for grounding their research or building their theoretical perspectives (Deci and Vansteenkiste 2004, p. 24).

3.3 Call for New Research

While it is important that the person-centered community reaches out to include mainstream research that it can learn from and benefit from in promoting itself, it is also important to engage in new research. The person-centered approach has a rich research history dating back to Rogers himself who pioneered psychotherapy research, recording his interviews and publishing the verbatim transcripts for research purposes (Kirschenbaum 2007). Since this, the use of qualitative research protocols using audio and later film recordings has continued and sophisticated methods for analysis have been developed. Perhaps sadly, as a result of the dominance of the medical model paradigm, this attention to the phenomenological was lost within psychotherapy research as for much of the latter half of the twentieth century, many psychotherapy researchers were preoccupied with proving the superiority of their approach over others.

Rogers encouraged empirical research in his early career, and at that time, client-centered therapy was the most "evidence-based" treatment. However, the way that research studies were designed, the purpose and motivations underlying the research questions being posed were also of significance for Rogers. He clearly favored research guided by motivations to uncover the processes of what is observed and not as a rationale for establishing dominance over other approaches (Rogers 1959). But, as Rogers moved away from the competitive world of academia later in his career, and as the trend for cognitive-behavioral approaches to therapy emerged, the person-centered approach became less of a focus for empirical researchers. Rogers himself became increasingly involved in a much wider application of person-centered psychology including working in groups, communities, the administration of organizations, politics, and conflict resolution. Arguably, it is these factors that tilted the rudder, which led to the current marginalization from mainstream clinical psychology practice.

The demand for evidence-based therapies (evidenced in relation to psychiatric diagnostic categories) has disenfranchised those therapies that do not adopt an illness ideology (Bohart et al. 1998). However, while engagement in such research can be incompatible with person-centered principles, it need not be. We call for new research which actively embraces the ethos of person-centered psychology. For example, we see that developing person-centered therapy through randomized controlled trials can be bought closer to the values and principles of person-centered psychology. For instance, when considering the effectiveness of person-centered therapy an alternative model is used as a comparator, both therapeutic approaches might be required to demonstrate their efficacy on their capacity to support and facilitate growth in clients. Turning to the field of psychological trauma, as another example, the field of posttraumatic growth is becoming increasingly recognized as providing a person-centered way of working with traumatized people (Joseph 2004, 2011; Murphy 2009), and the principles of posttraumatic growth are entering the mainstream of practice and research in the field of trauma studies.

Building on the call for new research, there is also a need for routine outcome measurement. The use of outcome measurement has in the past been contentious with the person-centered community—in large part because it has meant introducing ideas grounded in the medical model and incompatible to the growth model—the above developments show that it is possible to use outcome tools consistent with person-centered theory (Patterson and Joseph 2007b). For example, there are already tools within the person-centered literature such as the Unconditional Positive Self-Regard Scale (Patterson and Joseph 2006) that we need to use in preference to, or alongside, measures derived from other mutually incompatible epistemological roots such as the medical model.

The emergence of positive psychology and interest in quantitative research has also led to the development of new psychometric tools consistent with person-centered psychology. For example, work has begun to investigate the study of authenticity as a dimension of personality, with research definitions based in the person-centered conception of authenticity as a tripartite construct, defined by

Barrett-Lennard (1998) as involving consistency between the three levels of (a) a person's primary experience, (b) their symbolized awareness, and (c) their outward behavior and communication (Wood et al. 2008).

Other theory consistent tools, derived from mutually compatible but different epistemological roots also exist, such as the various measures of well-being (Tennant et al. 2007), happiness (Joseph et al. 2004), and growth following adversity (Joseph and Linley 2008). The recently developed Psychological Well-Being-Post-traumatic Changes Questionnaire (Joseph et al. 2012) provides a non-medical model operational definition of functioning that can be used to track adjustment in survivors of traumatic events.

Hence, the development and use of potentiality-based measures and scales can be seen as an epistemology-congruent approach to engaging with the need for research. Person-centered psychologists can conduct research on their own terms by including measurement tools that are consistent with theory (see, e.g., Payne et al. 2007 for an example of small-scale research).

3.4 Person-Centered Coaching

It has been argued that person-centered psychology has for so long been subject to evaluation by the standards of the medical model and so caught up in the language of disorder and deficit that its practitioners have almost forgotten that they were working within a potentiality model. Considering the positive psychology movement, the last decade has seen the rise of coaching and coaching psychology to explicitly address the gap that was left by the absence of the person-centered community in the mainstream discussion of how to go beyond distress and dysfunction (see, Joseph 2006, 2009). However, to the person-centered psychologist, the words counseling and coaching are synonymous—all that is different is what the client brings to a counseling session as opposed to a coaching session. That is to say, the client's expectations of the help sought—whether it is to look back on their life and confront difficulties or to look forward and find new solutions. In either case, the person-centered psychologist remains true to their discipline but the nature of the session and its focus will be different. The person-centered community has not yet understood that it needs to engage with the coaching literature and to articulate how person-centered psychology can be helpful to people seeking to move forward in some way in their lives (see Joseph 2006, 2009 for a full discussion on person-centered coaching).

Thus, in the same way that person-centered therapy has been challenged to show its effectiveness on criteria derived from the dominant medical model, by making the epistemological framework of the person-centered approach clear a new challenge is presented to deficiency-based models to engage with an analysis of their capabilities to promote growth in clients (see, Joseph and Wood 2010).

4 Conclusion

The above discussion is designed to help the person-centered community set a new agenda that propels them to build bridges to other research areas, engage in new research, and influence the issues of what the focus of research should be. Mainstream psychology has changed over the past decade to accommodate many of the ideas from positive psychology about the inclusion of assessment of positive functioning. It is now not unusual for clinical, counseling, health and other applied psychologists, social scientists, economists, and practitioners in counseling, psychotherapy, and social work to be interested in people's strengths, virtues, and how to promote optimal psychological and social flourishing. Meanwhile, the person-centered movement has been fighting a battle elsewhere to ensure its survival as a treatment for psychiatric disorders. As such it had forgotten that it was the original positive psychology, in the sense that it was always ultimately concerned with optimal functioning. But it was a different sort of positive psychology as it challenged the medicalization of human experience with its alternative meta-theory of personal growth. Finally, we think it may be useful for the person-centered community to recognize the overlaps between our own approach and those aspects where a robust evidence base already exists or is emerging and engage more fully with the wider psychological community.

References

Barrett-Lennard, G. T. (1998). *Carl Rogers' helping system: Journey and substance.* London: Sage.
Bohart, A. C., O'Hara, M., & Leitner, L. M. (1998). Empirically violated treatments: disenfranchisement of humanistic and other psychotherapies. *Psychotherapy Research, 8,* 141–157.
Bozarth, J. D., & Motomasa, N. (2005). Searching for the core: The interface of client-centered principles with other therapies. In S. Joseph & R. Worsley (Eds.), *Person-centred psychopathology: A positive psychology of mental health* (pp. 293–309). Ross-on-Wye: PCCS books.
Cooper, M., O'Hara, Schmid, P. F., & Wyatt, G. (2007). *The handbook of person-centred psychotherapy and counselling.* Palgrave: Houndmills.
Deci, E. L., & Ryan, R. M. (2000). The "what" and "why" of goal pursuits: Human needs and the self-determination of behavior. *Psychological Inquiry, 11,* 227–268.
Deci, E. L., & Ryan, R. M. (2002). Self-determination research: Reflections and future directions. In E. L. Deci & R. M. Ryan (Eds.), *Handbook of self-determination research* (pp. 431–441). Rochester, NY: University of Rochester Press.
Deci, E. L., & Vansteenkiste, M. (2004). Self-determination theory and basic need satisfaction: Understanding human development in positive psychology. *Ricerchedi di psicologia: Special Issue in Positive Psychology, 27,* 23–40.
Duncan, B. L., Miller, S. D., Wampold, B. E., & Hubble, M. E. (Eds.). (2009). *The heart and soul of change: Delivering what works in therapy* (2nd ed.). Washington: American Psychological Association.

Grant, B. (1990). Principled and instrumental nondirectiveness in person-centered and client-centered therapy. *Person-Centered Review, 5*, 77–88.

Harter, S., Marold, D. B., Whitesell, N. R., & Cobbs, G. (1996). A model of the effects of parent and peer support on adolescent false self behavior. *Child Development, 67*, 360–374.

Joseph, S. (2004). Client-centered therapy, posttraumatic stress and posttraumatic growth: Theoretical perspectives and practical implications. *Psychology and Psychotherapy: Theory, Research and Practice, 77*, 101–120.

Joseph, S. (2006). Person-centered coaching psychology: a meta-theoretical perspective. *International Coaching Psychology Review, 1*, 47–54.

Joseph, S. (2009). The person-centred approach to coaching. In E. Cox, T. Bachkirova, & D. A. Clutterbuck (Eds.), *The complete handbook of coaching*. London: Sage.

Joseph, S. (2011). *What doesn't kill us: The new psychology of posttraumatic growth.* New York: Basic Books.

Joseph, S., & Linley, P. A. (2006a). Positive psychology versus the medical model. *American Psychologist, 61*, 332–333.

Joseph, S., & Linley, P. A. (2006b). Growth following adversity: Theoretical perspectives and implications for clinical practice. *Clinical Psychology Review, 26*, 1041–1053.

Joseph, S., & Linley, P. A. (2006c). *Positive therapy: a meta-theoretical approach to positive psychological practice.* London: Routledge.

Joseph, S., & Linley, P. A. (2008). Psychological assessment of growth following adversity: A review. In S. Joseph & P. A. Linley (Eds.), *Trauma, recovery, and growth: Positive psychological perspectives on posttraumatic stress* (pp. 21–38). Hoboken, NJ: Wiley.

Joseph, S., Linley, P. A., Harwood, J., Lewis, C. A., & McCollam, P. (2004). Rapid assessment of well-being. *Psychology and Psychotherapy: Theory, Research, and Practice, 77*, 463–478.

Joseph, S., & Murphy, D. (2012). Person-centered approach, positive psychology and relational helping: Building bridges. *Journal of Humanistic Psychology, 53*, 1–26, doi:10:1177/0022167812436426.

Joseph, S., & Patterson, T. G. (2008). The actualising tendency: A meta-theoretical perspective for positive psychology. In B. E. Levitt (Ed.), *Reflections on human potential: Bridging the person-centred approach and positive psychology.* : PCCS Books.

Joseph, S., & Wood, A. (2010). Assessment of positive functioning in clinical psychology: Theoretical and practical issues. *Clinical Psychology Review, 30*, 830–838.

Joseph, S., Wood, A., Maltby, J., Stockton, H., Hunt, N., & Regel, S. (2012). Psychological well-being posttraumatic changes questionnaire: Reliability and validity. *Psychological Trauma: Theory, Research, Policy and Practice.*

Joseph, S., & Worsley, R. (Eds.). (2005). *Person-centred psychopathology: A positive psychology of mental health.* Ross-on-Wye: PCCS books. *4,* 420–428

Joseph, S., & Worsley, R. (2007). Person-centred practice and positive psychology: Crossing the bridges between disciplines. In R. Worsley & S. Joseph (Eds.), *Person-centered practice: Case studies in positive psychology* (pp. 218–223). Ross-on-Wye: PCCS Books.

King, M., Sibbald, B., Ward, E., Bower, P., Lloyd, M., Gabbay, M., et al. (2000). Randomised controlled trail of non-directive counselling cognitive behaviour therapy and usual general practitioner care in the management of depression as well as mixed anxiety and depression in primary care. *British Medical Journal, 321*, 1383–1388.

Kirschenbaum, H. (2007). *The life and work of Carl Rogers.* Ross-on-Wye: PCCS Books.

Leahy, R. L. (2008). The therapeutic relationship in cognitive-behavioural therapy. *Behavioural and Cognitive Psychotherapy, 36*, 769–777.

Levitt, B. E. (Ed.). (2008). *(Ed) Reflections on human potential: Bridging the person-centered approach and positive psychology.* RossonWye: PCCS Books.

Maddux, J. E., Snyder, C. R., & Lopez, S. J. (2004). Toward a positive clinical psychology: Deconstructing the illness ideology and constructing an ideology of human strengths and potential. In P. A. Linley & S. Joseph (Eds.), *Positive psychology in practice* (pp. 320–334). Hoboken, NJ: Wiley.

Murphy, D. (2009). Client-centred therapy for severe childhood abuse: A case study. *Counselling and Psychotherapy Research, 9,* 3–10.

Murphy, D., Duggan, M., & Joseph, S. (2012). Relational approaches to social work. *British Journal of Social Work,* pp. 1–7. Published online at http://bjsw.oxfordjournals.org/. Accessed on 03.05.12, doi:10.1093/bjse/bcs003.

Patterson, T. G., & Joseph, S. (2006). Development of a measure of unconditional positive self-regard. *Psychology and Psychotherapy: Theory, research, and practice, 79,* 557–570.

Patterson, T. G., & Joseph, S. (2007a). Person-centered personality theory: Support from self-determination theory and positive psychology. *Journal of Humanistic Psychology, 47,* 117–139.

Patterson, T., Joseph, S. (2007b). Outcome measurement in person-centred practice. In: Worsley, R., Joseph, S., (Eds). *Person-centred practice: Case studies in positive psychology.* PCCS Books, pp. 200–215.

Payne, A., Liebling-Kalifani, H., & Joseph, S. (2007). Client-centred group therapy for survivors of interpersonal trauma: A pilot investigation. *Counselling and Psychotherapy Research, 7,* 100–105.

Proctor, G., Cooper, M., Sanders, P., & Malcolm, B. (2006). *Politicising the person-centred approach: an agenda for social change.* Ross-on-Wye: PCCS Books.

Rogers, C. R. (1959). A theory of therapy, personality, and interpersonal relationships as developed in the client-centered framework. In S. Koch (Ed.), *Psychology: A study of a Science, Vol. 3: Formulations of the person and the social context* (pp.184-256). New York: McGraw-Hill.

Rogers, C. R. (1963). The actualizing tendency in relation to "motives" and to consciousness. In M. R. Jones (Ed.), *Nebraska symposium on motivation* (Vol. 11, pp. 1–24). Lincoln, NE: University of Nebraska Press.

Ryan, R. M., & Deci, E. L. (2000). Self-determination theory and the facilitation of intrinsic motivation, social development and well-being. *American Psychologist, 55,* 68–78.

Ryan, R. M., & Deci, E. L. (2002). An overview of self-determination theory: An organismic dialectical perspective. In E. L. Deci & R. M. Ryan (Eds.), *Handbook of self-determination research* (pp. 3–33). Rochester, NY: University of Rochester Press.

Sanders, P. (2005). Principled and strategic opposition to the medicalisation of distress and all of its apparatus. In S. Joseph & R. Worsley (Eds.), *Person-centered psychopathology: A positive psychology of mental health.* Ross-on-Wye: PCCS Books.

Schneider, K. (2011). Toward a humanistic positive psychology: Why can't we just get along? *Self and Society, 38,* 18–25.

Seligman, M. E. P., & Csikszentmihalyi, M. (2000). Positive psychology: An introduction. *American Psychologist, 55,* 5–14.

Seligman, M. E. P., Steen, T. A., Park, N., & Peterson, C. (2005). Positive psychology progress. *American Psychologist, 60,* 410–421.

Sheldon, K. M. (2002). The Self-concordance model of healthy goal striving: When personal goals correctly represent the person? In E. L. Deci & R. M. Ryan (Eds.), *Handbook of self-determination research* (pp. 3–33). Rochester, NY: University of Rochester Press.

Sheldon, K. M., Arndt, J., & Houser-Marko, L. (2003). In search of the organismic valuing process: The human tendency to move toward beneficial goal choices. *Journal of Personality, 71,* 835–886.

Sheldon, K. M., & Kasser, T. (2001). Goals, congruence, and positive well-being: New empirical support for humanistic theories. *Journal of Humanistic Psychology, 41,* 30–50.

Shlien, J. M. (2003). A criterion of psychological health. In P. Sanders (Ed.), *To lead an honourable life: Invitations to think about client-centered therapy and the person-centered approach* (pp. 15–18). Ross-on-Wye: PCCS Books.

Taylor, E. (2001). Positive psychology and humanistic psychology: A reply to Seligman. *Journal of Humanistic Psychology, 41,* 13–29.

Tennant, R., Hillier, L., Fishwick, R., Platt, S., Joseph, S., Weich, S., et al. (2007). The Warwick-Edinburgh Mental well being scale (WEMWBS): Development and UK validation. *Health and Quality of Life Outcomes, 5*, 63.

Tudor, K., & Worrall, M. (2006). *Person-centred therapy: A clinical philosophy*. London: Routledge.

Vansteenkiste, M., & Sheldon, K. M. (2006). There's nothing more practical than a good theory: Integrating motivational interviewing and self-determination theory. *British Journal of Clinical Psychology, 45*, 63–82.

Wood, A. M., Linley, P. A., Maltby, J., Baliousis, M., & Joseph, S. (2008). The authentic personality: A theoretical and empirical conceptualization, and the development of the authenticity scale. *Journal of Counseling Psychology, 55*, 385–399.

Self-Determination Theory, Person-Centered Approaches, and Personal Goals: Exploring the Links

Kennon Sheldon

1 Person-Centered Approaches and Scientific Research Psychology

The contributions of Carl Rogers to modern psychotherapy (1961, 1964) can hardly be overestimated. His person-centered approach (PCA) undergirds most therapeutic systems, whether or not this foundation is explicitly acknowledged. The idea that the client's subjective experience must be the starting point for nearly all therapeutic inquiries is now taken as a given, as well as the notion that therapists should be supportive and non-controlling and should try to activate the client's own growth potentials and processes, such that greater congruence and integration are achieved between different aspects of the client's personality. Additionally, no matter what the school or set of techniques used in the therapeutic process, it is generally recognized that the therapeutic alliance between client and provider is vitally important for success (Sheldon et al. 2003b), in part because it facilitates the activation of peoples' own internal resources.

However, the contributions of PCA to empirical research psychology, that is, scientific inquiry into basic psychological processes using experimental methods and quantitative analysis, are much less evident. One problem concerns the difficulty of operationalizing and quantifying important PCA constructs, such as congruence, organismic valuing process (OVP), and actualizing tendency. Such concepts almost necessitate using self-report methodologies, which can provide questionable data when the questions concern "deep" processes inside the personality, processes which are presumably very complex and which also involve self-presentational concerns. Another problem concerns the somewhat rosy or perhaps overly positive view of human nature implied by these terms. Are we really as noble, even as heroic, as such approaches suggest (until we are "messed

K. Sheldon (✉)
Department of Psychological Sciences, University of Missouri, 112 McAlester Hall, Columbia, MO 65203, USA
e-mail: sheldonk@missouri.edu

up by society")? Some are suspicious. A third problem is scientific psychology's reluctance to imbue subjective states of mind with causal properties, a reluctance which began with the rise of operant behaviorism and which continues today in social-cognitive psychology, in the guise of a predominant focus on non-conscious processes and automatic cognitive mechanisms (Bargh and Ferguson 2000). Viewing subjective experience as causal or primary raises very difficult problems and questions concerning the nature of consciousness and its place within the material universe and the question of whether or not people can have some degree of free will in life (versus being merely determined by external or non-conscious forces). As a result of these three problems, many theoreticians as well as empirical researchers shy away from PCA concepts, preferring to identify and study lower level mental mechanisms that impact behavior without the intervention of conscious experience.

In the first part of this chapter, I will discuss the one major exception to this general absence of research into phenomenological processes—namely, self-determination theory (SDT; Deci 1972; Deci and Ryan 1985; Ryan and Deci 2008). SDT is an integrated theory of optimal motivation, health, and well-being, which has been under development for more than four decades. Furthermore, during its development, SDT has relied on the highest quality experimental and quantitative techniques, with findings published in the most rigorous scientific journals. One can make a good case that SDT focuses on exactly the same processes discussed by Carl Rogers and, indeed, that SDT is exactly the kind of research that Rogers would have approved of and supported. Below, I will first provide an overview of the theory, taking a historical perspective. I will then discuss several recent developments within the theory, much of it based on my own work with personal goal-setting. I will show that concepts such as "congruence," " OVP," "actualizing tendency," and "non-directive social influence" are measurable and that they have real impact on peoples' lives, just as Rogers claimed—and that this can be shown by rigorous quantitative data.

2 Self-Determination Theory Provides Empirical Support for Important PCA Concepts

2.1 Reinforcements Can Undermine Intrinsic Motivation

SDT began with the "intrinsic motivation undermining" studies, conducted by Edward Deci in the late 1960s and early 1970s. Deci, trained as an organizational psychologist, set out to test the subversive idea that rewards and incentives can backfire, such that they reduce, rather than boost, people's motivation. This idea runs directly counter to the operant behavioral notion that rewards and external incentives reinforce behavior and bolster motivation (Deci 1972). Deci defined "intrinsic motivation" as the desire to engage in behavior mainly because it is interesting and inherently rewarding to the person. The person acts, not in order to get a subsequent reward, but rather, because the experience of acting is its own reward. Early studies demonstrated that intrinsically motivated behavior is not only more enjoyable, as one might expect, but also that intrinsically motivated behavior is more flexible, persistent, creative, and effective (see Deci and Ryan 1985). When people are intrinsically motivated, they are more likely to enter "flow" states in which they are fully absorbed in the moment (Csikszentmihalyi 1997) and in which all of their capacities are engaged, at the very limits of their abilities; thus, learning and growth tend to occur. Intrinsic motivation can exist for nearly any behavior, including sports, work, parenting, reading, and more. Intrinsic motivation characterizes the play of children, the pleasure of recreation, and the excitement of discovery. Intrinsic motivation is important and should be cherished and nourished wherever it takes hold.

Deci's early experimental studies showed that a formerly enjoyable activity, typically solving interesting puzzles, becomes less enjoyable after participants have been rewarded for doing the activity or for doing it well. As observed through a one-way mirror, participants who received money for each puzzle they solved were less likely to continue doing the behavior during a "free choice" period, compared to participants instructed to do the puzzles for their own sake. These findings have large implications for the fields of education, management, and sports psychology, among other fields, because they suggest that motivators should avoid coaxing behavior by offering external rewards and enticements. Although such enticements may be effective in the short term, they may ultimately undermine motivation or produce lower quality motivation (Kohn 1992).

Later studies showed that many other factors can undermine intrinsic motivation besides rewards, including evaluation, surveillance, competition, deadlines, and ego-involving instructions. An early version of SDT (Deci 1975) argued that these factors share an important commonality; they can all be perceived as controlling and coercive, representing the authority's attempt to "make" the participant do something. Deci proposed that all human beings have a basic psychological need for autonomy, defined as feeling a sense of ownership and engagement in one's behavior. Autonomy need-satisfaction can be thwarted by controlling contextual features, such as proffered rewards, threatened evaluations, and imposed deadlines. When this happens, the experience may be "spoiled" for the person, such that he or she no longer wants to have the experience.

2.2 SDT and the Primacy of Experience

Here, then, is the first tie between SDT and PCA: the notion that experience is primary and the related notion that certain types or qualities of experience are more growth-promoting than others. In SDT, optimal experience is the name of the game, and the theory concerns the deep nature of optimal experiences, and how such experiences can be further promoted. As a second tie with PCA, Deci (1975) also argued that all humans have a basic propensity and potential to become self-organizing and self-regulating, a process which is orchestrated by the subjective sense of self, as it struggles to become more fully conscious and functional both with respect to the external social world and with respect to its own internal processes. The phenomenal self is charged with organizing the person's behavior and personality (Sheldon 2004), organizational processes which unfold naturally when the self is supported, but which can be derailed when the context is too coercive and controlling. These assumptions fit well with PCA's postulate that human beings are imbued with or motivated by an "actualizing tendency" that is a standard feature of basic human nature, but whose unfolding may become suppressed or inactivated.

2.3 SDT and Non-directive Counseling

There is also a third important link between SDT and PCA; according to SDT, the "autonomy supportiveness" (rather than controllingness) of others is the crucial interpersonal factor that impacts growth and thriving (Deci and Ryan 1987). SDT focuses in particular on the dialectical relations between authorities and subordinates (i.e., between parents and children, manager and workers, teacher and students, therapists and clients, and so on). In such "one-up" power relationships, there is a very interesting dependency between the two parties. The authority has some degree of responsibility for the subordinate's behavior, meaning that he/she needs the subordinate to conform. The authority also has the power to coerce or even punish the subordinate, as one possible means of eliciting the desired subordinate behavior. Thus, there is a constant temptation to wield that power, to directly force the desired results. However, according to SDT, yielding to this temptation tends to backfire, because the subordinate may feel resentful and may fail to internalize the forced activity into their sense of self. This means that the subordinate may not do the activity as well or as thoroughly as he/she might and that he/she ceases to do it at all, once the authority (or the controls he/she has implemented) have been removed from the situation.

Consider the resentful student of a highly controlling or overly authoritarian 6th grade math teacher. This teacher is sarcastic; does not trust students to do the right thing on their own; implements strict rules in draconian ways; does not care whether students like the material or accept it; and does not seem to respect students. He assigns boring drills (memorizing multiplication tables) and uses threatened failure to motivate compliance with these drills. Over the course of the academic year, the student loses all interest in mathematics and believes from then on that there is no importance or value in knowing math. Given the twenty-first century goal of producing lifelong learners, able to direct their own further education, this is obviously a very negative outcome.

In contrast, autonomy support involves taking the student's perspective ("I know memorizing multiplication tables may seem difficult or even uninteresting to some of you....."), providing a meaningful rationale for doing it anyway ("but let me show you how many different ways you can use these skills in life, once you master them"), while also providing as much choice as possible in the situation ("so unfortunately, I can't let you just skip this section; but what I can do is let you choose when, how, with whom you do it"). The connections between this vision of the ideal communicative style of an authority, and PCA's vision of the non-directive, supportive therapist, should be obvious. Also, it has been shown that autonomy supportiveness can be taught relatively simply (Reeve et al. 2004).

Notably, autonomy supportiveness is not at all the same thing as permissiveness; supportive authorities can provide lots of structure and can also administer punishments and consequences when the rules they set are not followed (Deci and Ryan 1985). What matters is that they continually acknowledge and support the self of the subordinate, in whatever process or structure they choose and implement. Indeed, Sheldon et al. (2003b) have argued that autonomy support is a *mode* of relating to others, which can be used in the context of *any* type of therapy, from talk to cognitive to interpersonal to psychodynamic therapy, and even to shock therapy. I suggest that autonomy support is precisely the mode of respectful listening and communicating, without forcing any responses, that is advocated by the PCA.

2.4 SDT and Motivational Internalization

Let us talk a bit more about the notion of "internalization," because this idea is of central importance within SDT (Deci and Ryan 1991). SDT now identifies two main forms of autonomous motivation, not just one, namely identified (internalized) motivation and intrinsic motivation. This development of the theory was necessitated by the realization that not all non-intrinsically motivated behavior is undesirable. After all, not everything that we do can be "fun"—there are many behaviors in life (such as paying taxes, changing baby's diaper, taking a required but boring course) which we must do, even if we do not like to do them. Can we stand behind them, "own" them, anyway? The notion of internalization covers this issue, by emphasizing that people's motivation to do "X" can vary on a continuum of internalization, ranging from no motivation at all (helplessness) to motivation that is not at all internalized (external motivation; one does "X" because one feels forced to, or feels one must do it to get a necessary commodity), to partly internalized (introjected motivation; one does "X" because part of the self compels another part of the self, to avoid guilt or contingent self-esteem), to completely internalized (identified motivation; one does "X" because it is important and necessary, even if it is not enjoyable) to automatically internalized (intrinsic motivation is inherently internalized by definition). See Fig. 1 for an illustration of the internalization continuum.

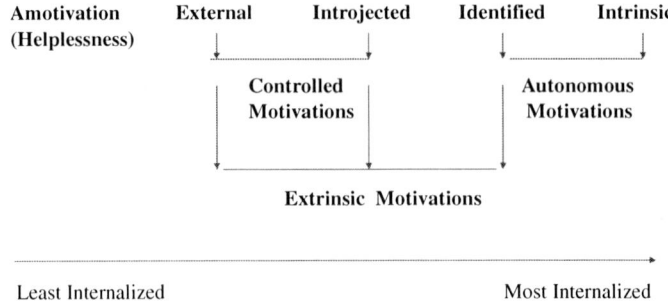

Fig. 1 The internalization continuum: external versus internal "Perceived Locus of Causality"

Notice that these concepts cover all the basics within psychology; external motivation is the province of operant behaviorism, introjected motivation is the province of psychodynamic and ego psychology, identified motivation is the province of existential psychology, and intrinsic motivation is the province of cognitive developmental psychology. As internalization occurs (i.e., as identified and/or intrinsic motivation increases), people develop a more "internal perceived locus of causality" regarding their own behavior, taking greater responsibility as the cause of their own actions, rather than making excuses or engaging in denial (Sheldon and Schachtman 2007).

In this light, the importance of authority autonomy support becomes more apparent; a supportive teacher, boss, or parent can help subordinates to internalize a behavior so that they at least identify with the behavior and agree to its importance, even if the behavior (e.g., memorizing multiplication tables) can never be something they intrinsically enjoy doing. In PCA terms, an autonomy supportive therapist can help ambivalent clients to fully accept the importance of the joint endeavor, defusing resistance, and amplifying engagement in this sometimes-unpleasant process. Similar to central concepts within the motivational interviewing approach (Miller and Rollnick 2002), which Wagner (2013) and Stumm (2013) suggest should be counted among the PCAs, an autonomy supportive coaching style involves avoiding power struggles, rolling with resistance, and slowly enlisting the client's own motivational resources in the process. SDT provides the missing theoretical account of what motivational interviewing is doing and how it works (Vansteenkiste and Sheldon 2006).

2.5 More on SDT and the Actualizing Tendency

Another feature of SDT, relevant to PCA, is its assumption of an "organismic integration process" which occurs naturally, given supportive conditions (Deci and Ryan 1991). In other words, people will automatically tend to internalize their own behaviors over time, integrating them into broader understandings of who they are and what is important. For example, Chandler and Connell (1987) showed that children evidence greater internalization of behaviors such as "cleaning my room," "doing my chores," and "studying for classes" as they move from the preteen to the early teen to the late teen years. I and my colleagues (Sheldon 2009) have shown that this normative process does not end at age 20, for example, in a sample of adults ranging from 18 to 81, Sheldon and Kasser (2001b) showed that chronological age correlated with greater internalization of one's personal goals. Sheldon et al. (2006) showed that middle-aged parents evidence greater internalized goal motivation than did their college-aged children. Sheldon et al. (2005) showed that older people have more internalized motivation than younger people, in performing important social duties such as voting, tax-paying, and tipping service professionals (see Sheldon 2009, for an overview of this research). Note the relevance of SDT's assumption that an organismic integration process unfolds automatically in healthy humans, to PCA's assumption of an inherent actualizing tendency, which tends to move people in growth-promoting directions over the life span. SDT-based research has shown this to be true, using actual longitudinal and temporal data.

2.6 SDT and the Organismic Valuing Process

Another important concept within PCA is that of an " (OVP)," which helps people to know what choices and activities will be growth-promoting and thus how to guide their own development in self-appropriate ways (Rogers 1964). Note that this term sounds similar to SDT's concept of an organismic integration process, which helps people to internalize their own motivations over time. However, there is also a difference, because the OVP is said to be a perceptual faculty that allows people to accurately sense their own internal state as a basis for making growth- and well-being-promoting choices. Obviously, the ability to access an OVP could be a very adaptive faculty for people to have, but is there really such a thing? Maybe not—much social-cognitive research is dedicated to showing how easily people can be fooled, by persuasive messages, non-conscious processes, negative role models, and the like, into making unhealthy or unwise choices or into believing that they caused an outcome that they did not cause (Wegner 2002). Such research typically employs a "self-perception" theory assumption (Bem 1972), in which people have no greater access to their own internal state than anybody else does; lacking such direct access, they must rely on typically inaccurate lay theories of behavior to understand themselves, the same kinds of theories that external observers rely on when making behavior-based judgments about some person. From this perspective, there is no direct pipeline between a conscious self and an underlying personality or a set of personal truths and thus no OVP.

Sheldon et al. (2003a) attempted to empirically demonstrate the existence of an OVP by examining temporal shifts in peoples' endorsements of different kinds of values. For this research, they relied on an important distinction within SDT, between "intrinsic" and "extrinsic" values (Kasser and Ryan 1993; Ryan and Deci 2008). Intrinsic values concern self-expression and self-acceptance, emotional intimacy with others, and helping others and serve a broader community. Extrinsic values concern financial success and material luxuries, status and popularity with others, and physical attractiveness to others. Research (Kasser and Ryan 1993, 1996; Kasser 2002) has shown that endorsing intrinsic values more so than extrinsic values is associated with psychological well-being and other desirable characteristics such as empathy, autonomous orientation, non-contingent self-esteem, and secure attachment. In contrast, when extrinsic values dominate within the person's value system, that person evidences less of a broad range of desirable psychological characteristics and also more stress, anger, and anxiety.

Sheldon et al. (2003a) reasoned that an OVP, if it exists, should move people toward intrinsic (healthy) values and away from extrinsic (problematic) values over time. In other words, when people are asked to reconsider their values, they also move in intrinsic directions, on average. In contrast to this view is the "clueless" human nature described by self-perception theory, according to which shifts in values could just as well move in extrinsic as intrinsic directions, so there should be no net change in any particular direction. In four repeated measures studies, using time spans ranging from only 20 min to more than 6 months, Sheldon et al. (2003a) showed a "biased shift" effect such that value change, when it occurred, tended to move in the intrinsic direction. These researchers argued that an OVP accounts for this biased shift; given a chance to reconsider their choices, people are likely to move toward the more happiness- and growth-promoting choices over time, because of the OVP. Sheldon (2005) found further evidence for such an OVP, showing that college students shifted away from extrinsic values during the four-year course of their college career. Indeed, the tendency of people to shift toward more internalized goals and motives over the life span, discussed above, can be seen as another example of the operation of an OVP. With experience, people learn what goals and values feel best and are most conducive to health and growth. Their OVP becomes honed over time, enabling them to make more accurate choices based on their own distinctive nature and experience.

2.7 SDT, Congruence, and Self-Concordance

Another important concept within PCA is "congruence," defined as a state in which a person's conscious goals, feelings, and self-beliefs are accurate with respect to processes occurring within the deeper personality. My research on the concept of "self-concordance" provides an excellent empirical example of such congruence. When I arrived at Rochester as a post-doc in 1992, to work with Deci and Ryan, I brought an expertise in personal goal assessment—techniques for inviting people to list their own personal goals, as they understand them. Personal goal methodologies are idiographic, because they rely on participants themselves to supply the units of analysis. For example, the "personal striving" assessment procedure (Emmons 1989) invites participants to fill out a blank sheet of paper with a list of 15 or more of the most important things they are trying to accomplish in their daily lives. Example strivings include "do the best I can at everything I undertake," "get regular exercise every day," "control my emotional reactions so I don't go off the deep end," and "stay in touch with those who are important to me."

Although people's self-listed goals can vary in infinitely different ways, it is still possible to compare different people using conventional nomothetic (quantitative) techniques. For example, participants can be asked to rate each goal or striving on a set of dimensions, such that attributes of the entire goal system can be tabulated by summing or averaging across these ratings. In my early work at Rochester, I asked participants to rate their personal strivings (Sheldon and Kasser 1995, 1998) on the four reasons for acting described above: external ("I am pursuing this goal because I have to"), introjected ("I am pursuing this goal because I ought to"), identified ("I am pursuing this goal because I choose to"), and intrinsic ("I am pursuing this goal because I like to"). I then computed an index of "striving self-determination" by summing the identified and intrinsic ratings across the goals and subtracting the external and introjected ratings.

However, in later work, I reasoned that this measure gets at more than the mere self-determination of strivings, that is, more than a mere sense of owning one's behavior in some aspects or area of life. Because the stems of the assessment (i.e., idiographic goals) are self-generated by the participant, they are different from conventional SDT stems, which typically reference motivation in particular life domains (i.e., in school, in relationships, on the sports team). Thus, I argued that the striving self-determination measure actually refers to the extent that the goal-set is "concordant" with the person's deeper personality. Has the person managed to select a set of goals that well represent who he or she is (i.e., his or her growth potentials and health initiatives), or has the person instead become entrapped such that they are pursuing goals that do not fit who they are, that do not emerge from their own internal needs and processes? This can easily happen, as people constantly encounter consumer messages, social norms, and powerful but inconsiderate others who might prompt them to pursue goals that are not good for them or that do not fit them. Indeed, given that people can write down whatever they want on the goal sheet, surprisingly many people report pursuing life goals out of pressure and guilt, goals they do not enjoy and do not believe in. They are stuck with "the wrong goals" for them.

Thus, I now refer to self-determined striving as "self-concordance," conceptualized as an index of the fit or congruence of the goal-set with the deeper personality. Research has shown that self-concordance has many positive correlates, including personality integration, vitality, satisfaction, positive mood, and low stress and anxiety, and furthermore that self-concordance predicts actually trying harder and longer at, and doing better at, one's goals (Sheldon and Kasser 1995, 1998). Sheldon and Elliot (1998) argued that the greater persistence and attainment over time occur because self-concordant goals better represent stable features of personality (long-term interests, enduring values), and thus, they have an enduring source of energy or stable funding within the psychic economy. In contrast, non-concordant goals, which do not represent who the person really is, are more easily swept aside by the vagaries of life or more easily forgotten or abandoned when the going gets tough.

Notice that this line of research relies on self-report to determine whether one part of personality (personal goals) is congruent with another (deeper values and interests). As noted earlier in this chapter, self-reports can be suspect in getting at such issues, because of a participant's lack of self-knowledge or desire to make a good impression. But this observation allows me to highlight a principal advantage of the self-concordance methodology: It does not ask participants to rate their agreement with statements such as "this goal represents who I really am, deep inside" or "this goal channels my growth potentials." Instead, the measure merely asks them to rate a set of reasons for pursuing the goal. Although a person might not know directly that their goals are out of touch with who they really are (because that information may not be consciously accessible or may be too threatening), my assumption has been that people can at least report that they feel some pressure or guilt around the goal or that they feel it is being imposed by others. In this way, researchers may deduce that the goal does not fit or represent who they really are.

What are the data to directly support the notion that self-concordant goals are actually more "congruent" with the person's deeper personality, as I have assumed? Recently, Sheldon and Schuler (2011) integrated concepts from motive disposition theory (McClelland 1985) and SDT to address this question. First, Sheldon and Schuler measured individual differences in participants' need for achievement and their need for affiliation. These two "motive dispositions" are conceived of as learned early in childhood, based on the types of incentives and reinforcements children receive (Schultheiss 2008). Motive dispositions are typically thought of as inaccessible to self-report, being based on non-conscious processes. From a congruence perspective (Rogers 1964), congruent self-listed goals would be goals that well represent, or are consistent with, these deeper features of personality.

This led to the following prediction: When participants are randomly assigned to list a set of achievement goals, they should feel more self-concordant in those goals *if* they are also high in the need for achievement. Similarly, when participants are randomly assigned to list a set of affiliation goals, they should feel more self-concordant in those goals *if* they are also high in the need for affiliation. In their experimental study, Sheldon and Schuler (2011) found exactly these two significant interactions. Consistent with the notion of an OVP that allows people to know their own internal state, achievers assigned achievement goals felt more self-concordant in their goals, and vice versa for affiliation goals. Thus, the self-concordance measure indeed indexes "deep person-goal fit," or in Roger's terms, "congruence" between the conscious goal-setting self and the underlying personality that it represents. Such congruence is a good thing, because it means we can invest our limited supply of volitional energy (Baumeister and Tierney 2011) in ways that are maximally self-sustaining and which maximally contribute to our development and well-being.

3 SDT's Psychological Needs Theory and its Relevance to PCA

Thus far, we have considered how SDT, and goal research based on SDT, can provide empirical support for important PCA constructs such as congruence, organismic valuing, non-directive counseling, and actualizing tendency. Although most research psychology has shied away from these difficult concepts and issues, SDT has approached them directly, with considerable success. In this section, I will describe an important additional feature of SDT which may contribute new understanding to the PCA approach: psychological needs.

Of course, the concept of psychological needs has a long history in psychology, and psychological needs have been conceptualized in a variety of ways. Perhaps, best known is the Maslow's need hierarchy (Maslow 1971), which states that as lower-level needs are met (e.g., for security), higher-level needs emerge (e.g., for belongingness or self-esteem), finally resulting in a person's search for self-actualization. Maslow's theory is a quintessentially humanistic or PCA, demonstrating that psychological need concepts are likely to be commensurate with the Rogerian perspective, even though Rogers himself gave relatively little explicit consideration to the topic of psychological needs.

SDT is ultimately based on a conception of psychological needs which is somewhat different from Maslow's conception. According to SDT, all humans possess three basic psychological needs, defined as qualities of experience that are needed for thriving and growth (Deci and Ryan 2000). Specifically, all humans, regardless of their culture, era, age, or personality type, need to feel autonomous (a sense of volition and ownership regarding one's behavior), competent (a sense of being effective and successful in one's behavior), and related (a sense of psychological closeness with important others). The reasoning is that humans who wanted these experiences would have had an adaptive advantage over humans who did not; psychological needs empower people to do what is adaptive for *them* (rather than being controlled by others who may not have the person's best interests at heart), to do it effectively (rather than ineffectively and inefficiently), and in the process, to form the close social relations which are so essential to healthy human functioning (rather than being isolated or ostracized). Because of this selective advantage, eventually, all humans would have had the three needs (Tooby and Cosmides 1990). These three needs are conceptualized as three separate "nutrients," akin to psychological vitamins (Ryan 1995), each of which are required to produce a fully functioning human being. There is no hierarchical arrangement involving the three needs, just as there is no hierarchical arrangement involving physical vitamins such as vitamins B, C, and D; all of them are necessary.

Much SDT research has focused on showing that these three experiences are essential for well-being and optimal functioning. Sheldon et al. (1996) and Reis et al. (2000) showed that "good days" (i.e., days with the most well-being and happiness) are days in which much autonomy, competence, and relatedness are felt. Sheldon et al. (2001) showed that people's "most satisfying events" are characterized by autonomy, competence, and relatedness, and not by popularity, luxury, meaning, health, pleasure, or security. Filak and Sheldon (2003) showed that the most successful teachers promote all three needs within their students, and Smith (2007) showed that the three needs explain "what's good about good sex." More generally, the importance of autonomy, competence, and relatedness has been supported in multiple domains including medicine, business, sports, and education; within cross-sectional, experimental, and longitudinal study designs; and by assessing satisfaction with a wide variety of life-aspects, including school classes, interpersonal relationships, daily experiences, satisfying activities, and rewarding work activities (Sheldon 2004). It has also been shown in multiple cultures, supporting the hypothesized universality of the needs. For example, Sheldon et al. (2011) showed that autonomy, competence, and relatedness jointly predicted well-being in 4,400 participants, to the same extent in each of 23 different cultural samples.

These findings imply that part of what a good therapist does is helping clients to better meet their needs, helping them to develop a healthy sense of agency and self-ownership, helping them to heal and transform their relationships, and helping them to function more effectively and competently in all spheres of life. As these missing nutrients are added back into the client's life, the client gains the internal resources needed to continue the process of climbing out of the "rut" they have been stuck within. Although Carl Rogers and PCA do not directly address need-satisfaction as a theoretical assumption, there is nothing within Roger's writings that is inconsistent with these ideas, and I suspect that Rogers, were he alive today, would readily concur with the set of needs identified by SDT. Bearing the three needs in mind might help PCA-focused clinicians to better pinpoint what kinds of experiences may be missing within their clients and what kinds of experience to support. To push the vitamin analogy a little further, a good therapist might be, in part, a good "psychological nutritionist," who knows how to diagnose and then correct experiential deficiencies within her clients.

4 Bringing It All Together: An Empirical Example

At this point, the reader may feel bewildered by the large assortment of concepts employed by SDT or at least might be wondering how, or if, they all fit together. In fact, they do all fit together, and I believe that SDT can provide clinicians with an integrated, and empirically well supported, model of the entire process of positive personality change, beginning with the social or clinical context in which a person finds him or herself and ending with either transformation or failed transformation.

To illustrate, let us consider research conducted by Sheldon and Krieger (2004, 2007). Krieger is a clinical law professor who has long spearheaded initiatives toward legal education reform. The need for such reform is shown by research dating all the way back to the 1980s and still being replicated today, clearly showing that law students experience considerable stress and distress during the course of their studies (Benjamin et al. 1986; Shanfield and Benjamin 1985). Although law students start out a little different from students in other professional fields and from the general population (Benjamin et al. 1986; Sheldon and Krieger 2004), soon after law school commences they report large increases in psychiatric symptomology, such as anxiety, depression, hostility, and paranoia. These declines continue into the second and third year of law school and may even persist into their subsequent law careers (Beck et al. 1995; Benjamin et al. 1986).

Many researchers and commentators have proposed that depersonalizing legal education practices may be the common source of some of the problems evidenced by students. Potential aspects of legal education include excessive workloads, deadlines, and competition for academic superiority (Krieger 1998); institutional emphasis on comparative grading, status-seeking placement practices, and other hierarchical markers of worth (Daicoff 1997); excessive faculty emphasis on analysis and linear thinking, causing loss of connection with feelings, personal morals, values, and sense of self (Dammeyer and Nunez 1999); teaching practices which are isolating or intimidating, and content which is excessively abstract or unrelated to the actual practice of law (Glesner 1991); and conceptions of law which suppress moral reasoning and creativity (Hess 2002). Based on such analyses, the recent Carnegie report (Sullivan et al. 2007) and the Best Practices for Legal Education analysis (Stuckey et al. 2007) called for sweeping changes in the way law students are trained, with the latter treatise explicitly raising and addressing the exceptional levels of emotional distress among law students.

When Krieger and I began to collaborate in the early 2000s, he viewed the legal education problems in Maslowian need terms (legal education practices typically activate security needs and thwart the actualizing tendency). I convinced him that SDT provides a more modern and empirically well-supported, humanistic lens through which to view the problems. In our most ambitious study (Sheldon and Krieger 2007), we were able to track students from two different law schools over the entire course of their student careers, examining their changing levels of well-being, need-satisfaction, motivation, and academic performance during that career.

Although both schools admit qualified candidates, with essentially equivalent undergraduate grades and LSAT scores, the schools evidence somewhat different educational and pedagogical philosophies. When hiring faculty, the second school places relatively greater emphasis on law practice/public service experience and demonstrated teaching ability, factors of direct relevance for the professional training of students (Granfield 1992). By contrast, the first school more strongly emphasizes previous and potential scholarly production. The second school also differs from the first school in that it regularly provides teaching skills seminars for its faculty, has many more faculty members devoted to practical skills training, and combines skills and theory instructors into one integrated faculty. All of these factors suggest that there is a stronger person-centered orientation toward student interests and priorities at the second school, which Krieger and I believed might translate empirically into a difference in perceived autonomy support and subsequent outcomes.

And we were right. Figure 2 reproduces the integrative path model that well fit the longitudinal data. Although there was no initial difference between the two schools in how much autonomy support they expected to receive, by the end of the first year, there was a significant difference in actual felt support. This difference then had large downstream effects. Students in the first, more controlling, law school experienced larger reductions in the satisfaction of their psychological needs between the first and third years, which in turn had negative effects on final outcomes, and thus negative effects on student's preparation for their first law job. Specifically, reductions in competence satisfaction predicted poorer academic performance, controlling for initial undergraduate GPA and LSAT score; reductions in autonomy satisfaction predicted less self-determined motivation to go out and work at the first law job; and reductions in all three needs predicted reductions in well-being from the beginning to the end of law school. Interestingly, reductions in competence satisfaction also predicted poorer bar examination performance and passage; students at the first school did worse in the bar examination on average, despite the fact that students from the two schools did not differ in initial undergraduate GPA or LSAT scores. This is a finding that has gotten the attention of the legal education community!

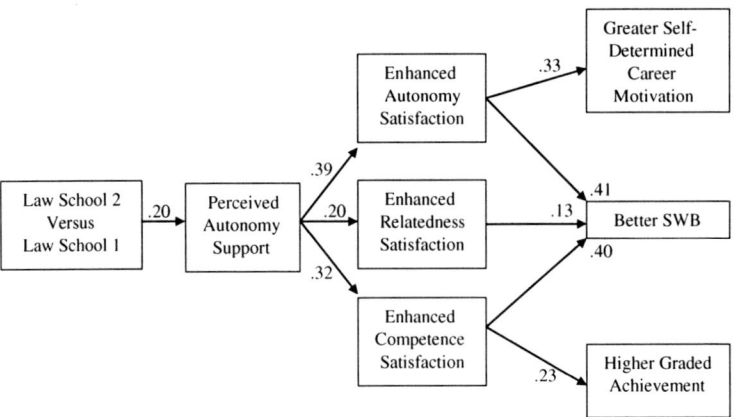

Fig. 2 Parameter estimates for the structural equation model (Sheldon and Krieger 2007) *Note* All downstream variables residualized to remove the effects of race, age, gender, prior job experience, loan balances, and the year 1 versions of the variable (where appropriate)

This empirical example, which I have presented in considerable detail, hopefully shows two things: (1) that all (or at least most) of the major constructs within SDT can be fit within a single temporal process model, leading from social context down to the individual and thenceforth leading to differential individual outcomes over time, and (2) that these concepts and processes may be essentially the same ones that PCA advocates are talking about, in their accounts of how people can be encouraged to change, develop, and thrive. Given the cultural differences between the two law schools described above, a PCA or Rogerian analysis would have easily predicted that the first law school does not serve its students as well as the second law school. The advantage of the SDT approach is that it can provide the quantitative, large-scale data necessary to convince law school administrators that promoting more person-focused legal education might really be a good thing. More generally, I suggest that SDT provides the long missing research framework for the PCA perspective (see Sheldon and Kasser 2001a, for a more general view of how SDT can inform traditional humanistic perspectives on optimal functioning). Using this framework, PCA advocates can test and extend their ideas and perhaps also revise them when necessary.

5 Conclusion

I am not a clinician, and I do not have experience or training in treating people with psychological difficulties. Instead, I am a researcher, interested in theories and the data that support those theories. My goal in this chapter has been to convince person-centered clinicians that research and quantitative data collection are not antithetical to a humanistic or client-focused approach, as is commonly assumed. My firm belief is that if some proposition about people or the world is true, then there must be a way to measure it and prove that it is true. PCA theories and concepts may be harder to measure and test than many other types of theories. Still, it *can* be done, and indeed, it *has* been done, under the auspices of SDT. Readers who want to learn more might start at the SDT website, which can be found at: http://www.selfdeterminationtheory.org/.

References

Bargh, J. A., & Ferguson, M. J. (2000). Beyond behaviorism: On the automaticity of higher mental processes. *Psychological Bulletin, 126*, 925–945.

Baumeister, R. F., & Tierney, J. (2011). *Willpower: Rediscovering the greatest human strength.* New York, US: Penguin Press.

Beck, C. J. A., Sales, B. D., & Benjamin, C. A. H. (1995). Lawyer distress: Alcohol-related problems and other psychological concerns among a sample of practicing lawyers. *Journal of Law and Health, 10*, 1–94.

Bem, D. (1972). Self-perception theory. In L. Berkowitz (Ed.), *Advances in experimental social psychology* (Vol. 6). New York: Academic Press.

Benjamin, G. A. H., Kasznaik, A., Sales, B., & Shanfield, S. B. (1986). The role of legal education in producing psychological distress among law students and lawyers. *American Bar Foundation Research Journal, 11*(2), 225–252.

Chandler, C. L., & Connell, J. P. (1987). Children's intrinsic, extrinsic and internalized motivation: A developmental study of children's reasons for liked and disliked behaviours. *British Journal of Developmental Psychology, 5*(4), 357–365.

Csikszentmihalyi, M. (1997). *Finding flow: The psychology of engagement with everyday life.* New York, USA: Basic Books, Inc.

Daicoff, S. (1997). Lawyer know thyself: A review of empirical research on attorney attributes bearing on professionalism. *American University Law Review, 46*, 1337–1428.

Dammeyer, M. M., & Nunez, N. (1999). Anxiety and depression among law students: Current knowledge and future directions. *Law and Human Behavior, 23*, 55–73.

Deci, E. L. (1972). Intrinsic motivation, extrinsic reinforcement, and inequity. *Journal of Personality and Social Psychology, 22*, 113–120.

Deci, E. L. (1975). *Intrinsic motivation.* New York: Plenum Press.

Deci, E. L., & Ryan, R. M. (1985). *Intrinsic motivation and self-determination in human behavior.* New York: Plenum.

Deci, E. L., & Ryan, R. M. (1987). The support of autonomy and the control of behavior. *Journal of Personality and Social Psychology, 53*, 1024–1037.

Deci, E. L., & Ryan, R. M. (1991). A motivational approach to self: Integration in personality. In R. Dienstbier (Ed.), *Nebraska symposium on motivation* (Vol. 38, pp. 237–288)., Perspectives on motivation Lincoln, NE: University of Nebraska Press.

Deci, E. L., & Ryan, R. M. (2000). The "what" and "why" of goal pursuits: Human needs and the self-determination of behavior. *Psychological Inquiry, 11*, 227–268.

Emmons, R. A. (1989). The personal strivings approach to personality. In L. A. Pervin (Ed.), *Goal concepts in personality and social psychology* (pp. 337–372). Hillsdale, N. J.: Erlbaum.

Filak, V., & Sheldon, K. M. (2003). Student psychological need-satisfaction and college teacher-course evaluations. *Educational Psychology, 23*, 235–247.

Glesner, B. A. (1991). Fear and loathing in the law schools. *Connecticut Law Review, 23*, 627–668.

Granfield, R. (1992). *Making elite lawyers.* New York, London: Routledge.

Hess, G. F. (2002). Heads and hearts: The teaching and learning environment in law school. *Journal of Legal Education, 52*, 75–111.

Kasser, T. (2002). *The high price of materialism.* Cambridge, MA: MIT Press.

Kasser, T., & Ryan, R. M. (1993). A dark side of the American dream: Correlates of financial success as a central life aspiration. *Journal of Personality and Social Psychology, 65*, 410–422.

Kasser, T., & Ryan, R. M. (1996). Further examining the American dream: Well-being correlates of intrinsic and extrinsic goals. *Personality and Social Psychology Bulletin, 22*, 281–288.

Kohn, A. (1992). *Punished by rewards: The trouble with gold stars, incentive plans, A's, praise, and other bribes.* Boston, MA, US: Houghton, Mifflin and Company.

Krieger, L. S. (1998). What we're not telling law students–and lawyers–that they really need to know: Some thoughts-in-acting toward revitalizing the profession from its roots. *Journal of Law and Health, 13*, 1–48.

Maslow, A. (1971). *The farther reaches of human nature.* New York: Viking press.

McClelland, D. C. (1985). *Human motivation.* New York: Cambridge University Press.

Miller, W. R., & Rollnick, S. (2002). *Motivational interviewing: Preparing people for change* (2nd ed.). New York, US: Guilford Press.

Reeve, J., Jang, H., Carrell, D., Soohyun, J., & Barch, J. (2004). Enhancing students' engagement by increasing teachers' autonomy support. *Motivation and Emotion, 28*, 147–169.

Reis, H., Sheldon, K., Gable, S., Roscoe, J., & Ryan, R. (2000). Daily well-being: the role of autonomy, competence and relatedness. *Personality and Social Psychology Bulletin, 26*, 419–435.

Rogers, C. (1961). *On becoming a person: A therapist's view of psychotherapy*. Boston: Houghton Mifflin.

Rogers, C. R. (1964). Toward a modern approach to values: The valuing process in the mature person. *Journal of Abnormal and Social Psychology, 68*, 160–167.

Ryan, R. (1995). Psychological needs and the facilitation of integrative processes. *Journal of Personality, 63*, 397–427.

Ryan, R. M., & Deci, E. L. (2008). Self-determination theory and the role of basic psychological needs in personality and the organization of behavior. In O. John, R. Roberts, & L. A. Pervin (Eds.), *Handbook of personality: Theory and research* (pp. 654–678). New York: Guilford.

Schultheiss, O. C. (2008). Implicit motives. In O. P. John, R. W. Robins, & L. A. Pervin (Eds.), *Handbook of personality psychology: Theory and research* (3rd ed., pp. 603–633). New York, US: Guilford Press.

Shanfield, S. B., & Benjamin, G. A. H. (1985). Psychiatric distress in law students. *Journal of Legal Education, 35*, 65–75.

Sheldon, K. M. (2004). *Optimal human being: An integrated multi-level perspective*. New Jersey: Erlbaum.

Sheldon, K. M. (2005). Positive value change during college: Normative trends and individual differences. *Journal of Research in Personality, 39*, 209–223.

Sheldon, K. M. (2009). Goal-striving across the life-span: Do people learn to select more self-concordant goals as they age? In M. C. Smith & T. G. Reio (Eds.), *The handbook of research on adult development and learning* (pp. 553–569). New York: Routledge.

Sheldon, K. M., & Elliot, A. J. (1998). Not all personal goals are personal: Comparing autonomous and controlled reasons as predictors of effort and attainment. *Personality and Social Psychology Bulletin, 24*, 546–557.

Sheldon, K. M., & Kasser, T. (1995). Coherence and congruence: Two aspects of personality integration. *Journal of Personality and Social Psychology, 68*, 531–543.

Sheldon, K. M., & Kasser, T. (1998). Pursuing personal goals: Skills enable progress, but not all progress is beneficial. *Personality and Social Psychology Bulletin, 24*, 1319–1331.

Sheldon, K. M., & Kasser, T. (2001a). Getting older, getting better? Personal strivings and personality development across the life-course. *Developmental Psychology, 37*, 491–501.

Sheldon, K. M., & Kasser, T. (2001b). Goals, congruence, and positive well- being: New empirical validation for humanistic ideas. *Journal of Humanistic Psychology, 41*, 30–50.

Sheldon, K. M., & Krieger, L. (2004). Does law school undermine law students? Examining changes in goals, values, and well-being. *Behavioral Sciences and the Law, 22*, 261–286.

Sheldon, K. M., & Krieger, L. K. (2007). Understanding the negative effects of legal education on law students: A longitudinal test of self-determination theory. *Personality and Social Psychology Bulletin, 33*, 883–897.

Sheldon, K. M., & Schachtman, T. R. (2007). Obligations, motivational internalization, and excuse-making: Testing and extending the triangle model of responsibility. *Journal of Personality, 75*, 359–382.

Sheldon, K. M., & Schuler, J. (2011). Needing, wanting, and having: Integrating motive disposition theory and self-determination theory. *Journal of Personality and Social Psychology, 101*, 1106–1123.

Sheldon, K. M., Ryan, R. M., & Reis, H. R. (1996). What makes for a good day? Competence and autonomy in the day and in the person. *Personality and Social Psychology Bulletin, 22*, 1270–1279.

Sheldon, K. M., Elliot, A. J., Kim, Y., & Kasser, T. (2001). What's satisfying about satisfying events? Comparing ten candidate psychological needs. *Journal of Personality and Social Psychology, 80*, 325–339.

Sheldon, K. M., Arndt, J., & Houser-Marko, L. (2003a). In search of the organismic valuing process: The human tendency to move towards beneficial goal choices. *Journal of Personality, 71*, 835–869.

Sheldon, K. M., Joiner, T., & Williams, G. (2003b). *Self-determination theory in the clinic: Motivating physical and mental health*. New Haven: Yale University Press.

Sheldon, K. M., Kasser, T., Houser-Marko, L., Jones, T., & Turban, D. (2005). Doing one's duty: Chronological age, felt autonomy, and subjective well-being. *European Journal of Personality, 19*, 97–115.

Sheldon, K. M., Houser-Marko, L., & Kasser, T. (2006). Does autonomy increase with age? Comparing the motivation and well-being of college students and their parents. *Journal of Research in Personality, 40*, 168–178.

Sheldon, K. M., Cheng, C., & Hilpert, J. (2011). Understanding well-being and optimal functioning: Applying the multilevel personality in context (MPIC) model. *Psychological Inquiry, 22*, 1–16.

Smith, C. V. (2007). In pursuit of 'good' sex: Self-determination and the sexual experience. *Journal of Social and Personal Relationships, 24*(1), 69–85.

Stuckey, R., et al. (2007). *Best practices for legal education*. SC, Columbia: Clinical Legal Education Association.

Stumm, G. (2013). Person-centered and experiential psychotherapies: An overview. In: J. H. D. Cornelius-White, R. Motschnig-Pitrik & M. Lux (Eds.), *Interdisciplinary applications of the person-centered approach*. New York: Springer.

Sullivan, W., Colby, A., Wegner, J., Bond, L., & Shulman, L. (2007). *Educating lawyers: Preparation for the profession of law*. San Francisco: Jossey Bass.

Tooby, J., & Cosmides, L. (1990). On the universality of human nature and the uniqueness of the individual: The role of genetics and adaptation. *Journal of Personality, 58*, 17–67.

Vansteenkiste, M., & Sheldon, K. M. (2006). There is nothing so practical as a good theory: Integrating self-determination theory and motivational interviewing theory. *British Journal of Clinical Psychology, 45*, 63–82.

Wagner, C. (2013). Motivational interviewing and client-centered therapy. In: J. H. D. Cornelius-White, R. Motschnig-Pitrik & M. Lux (Eds.), *Interdisciplinary applications of the person-centered approach*. New York: Springer.

Wegner, D. (2002). *The illusion of conscious will*. Cambridge, MA, US: MIT Press.

A Strengths-Based Approach Towards Coaching in a Multicultural Environment

Llewellyn Ellardus Van Zyl and Marius Wilhelm Stander

1 Introduction

Traditionally, helping professions aimed to address psychopathology and deviance. Well-being was defined by the mere absence of distress and pathology, where no emphasis was placed on optimal development (Peterson and Seligman 2004). Focusing on and re-emphasising pathology reinforces low expectations, creates dependency on outside resources and discourages individuals to develop optimally (Seligman 2011). Professionals interested in promoting human potential need to move away from this disease model towards facilitating development through focusing on individual strengths (Park and Peterson 2006) since individuals present with an inherent tendency to develop and grow (Rogers 1961). One approach through which this can be done is coaching (Cilliers 2011).

Coaching refers to a short- to medium-term relationship between an individual and a professional with the purpose of improving an individual's work performance through focusing on changing behaviour and addressing/preventing organisational issues (Feldman and Lankau 2005). Coaching is conceptualised as a practical goal-orientated form of personal and professional development which manifests in various models and approaches (see Biswas-Diener and Dean 2007), yet few are empirically validated (Kauffman 2006; Koortzen and Oosthuizen 2010). Cilliers (2011) argued that these approaches place too much emphasis on 'correcting what is wrong' rather than facilitating optimal development. As a result, the emphasis has moved away from the coachee and has become

L. E. Van Zyl (✉)
Department of Industrial and Organisational Psychology, University of South Africa, Pretoria, South Africa
e-mail: vzylle@unisa.ac.za

M. W. Stander
Department of Industrial Psychology, School for Behavioural Science,
North-West University, Vaal Triangle Campus, Vanderbijlpark, South Africa
e-mail: marius.stander@nwu.ac.za

mechanistic in nature (Biswas-Diener 2010). Consequently, permanent and sustainable change in behaviour may not manifest, which could result in a reoccurrence of the manifested behaviour (Rogers 1951; Seligman 2011).

Rogers (1951) argued that the person (client, student, *coachee*) needs to be at the centre of the developmental process and not the process itself. In order to facilitate change, the facilitator (counsellor, educator, *coach*) should understand the reality of the individual from his/her perspective (Carkhuff 2000; Rogers 1951). Therefore, it is imperative that the coach approaches the process from within the coachee's reality. This is a main theme in positive psychology (Seligman and Csikszentimihalyi 2000). Positive psychology, much like the PCA, assumes that each individual has the capacity for personal growth, to develop strengths, build on positive emotions and develop sustainable resilience which enable individuals. Unlike the PCA, however, positive psychology also considers ways how organisations can flourish (Biswas-Diener 2010; Seligman 2011). Positive psychological coaching refers to the identification, optimisation and application of individual strengths in order to facilitate development of individuals in organisational contexts. Limited research exists on positive psychological coaching within multicultural environments (Cilliers 2011).

Resultantly, the purpose of this chapter is to present a strengths-based coaching model that integrates the psycho-existential, positive psychology, and person-centred approach (PCA) to provide an ecosystemic view of human nature. The approach focuses on enhancing, predicting and utilising individual strengths and its various underlying constructs (e.g. happiness, resilience and meaning in work) in order to enhance individual performance and facilitate well-being. The coach is supposed to concentrate on basic PCA interpersonal attitudes of openness to experience, unconditional positive regard, quality, non-directivity and empathy. A meta-theoretical literature review was used in order to develop a ten-phase strengths-based model for workplace and executive coaching that aims to be applicable within a multicultural environment.

2 A Strengths-Based Coaching Model

One of the basic assumptions of positive psychology, the PCA and psycho-existentialism is that individuals have the capacity to enhance, sustain and actualise their potential (Rogers 1951; Seligman 2011). Individuals' behaviour is the manifested result of this propensity to address this need. Thus, a central tendency of this model is the focus on individual strengths, rather than developmental areas (Smith 2006). Developing strengths buffers against the onset of psychopathology (Smith 2006). Drawing from both the PE and PCA, the model assumes that the development of strengths is based on internal and external forces which address various inherent psychological needs (Seligman 2011). A strength (Peterson and Seligman 2004) is the final outcome of internal struggle with adversity which manifests in (a) experienced meaning and (b) a search for meaning (Sheldon et al.

2011). Fronczak (2006) is of the opinion that integrating signature strengths in coaching interventions may contribute to the quality of happiness and facilitate the pursuit of a meaningful life.

According to So and Kauffman (2010), strengths are psychological traits that render the coachee more capable of identifying, implementing and accomplishing meaningful goals. Linley and Harrington (2006) defined strengths as 'a natural capacity for behaving, thinking, or feeling in a way that allows optimal functioning and performance in the pursuit of valuable outcomes' (p. 88). Gordon and Gucciardi (2011) summarise strengths as something that people are good at and passionate about. Rogers (1978) argued that uncovering, respecting and applying individual strengths manifests in the sustainable change and lasting happiness. The actualising tendency individuals present acts as the foundation through which strengths develop (Rogers 1978).

Linley and Harrington (2006) conceptualised strengths-based coaching as harnessing inner potential to optimise performance and well-being, leading to increased engagement, energy, motivation and hope. Gordon and Gucciardi (2011) described strengths-based coaching as strengths-spotting, learning from successes, proactive, self-directed and collaborative.

The strengths-based coaching model integrates these ideas into a ten (10)-phase model (see Fig. 1). The process is cyclical and rooted in continuous evaluation and feedback. A key part of the model is minimal encouragement, since this act as an indication of complete positive regard. Here, encouragement refers to a process, whereby the coach (a) shows complete acceptance, (b) expresses empathy, (c) shows confidence, (d) focuses on the strengths and resources, (e) effort and improvement of the client and (f) facilitates the implementation of decisions that's made throughout the process. This is essential to facilitate a change in behaviour (Charkhuff 2000; Rogers 1961, 1951). The challenge for the coach will be to facilitate the optimisation of the coachee's resources that will lead to self-directed

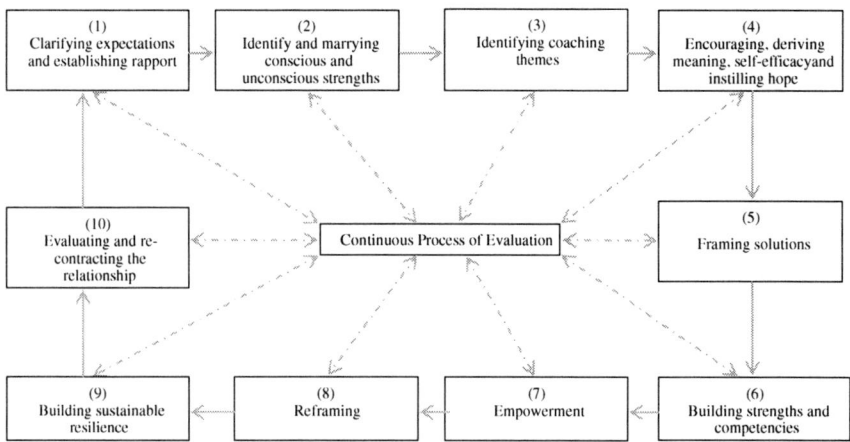

Fig. 1 The strengths-based coaching model

behaviour changes ensuring improved performance for the organisation and wellness for the individual. Strengths must be evoked to overcome obstacles. In the following sections, a brief explanation of each phase will be provided.

2.1 Phase 1: Clarifying Expectations and Establishing Rapport

The purpose of this phase is to clarify the expectations between the various stakeholders in the coaching process and to establish rapport. It is imperative to concentrate development on the needs of the individual within the position (Koortzen and Oosthuizen 2010), as well as within the organisation. Further, this phase aims to understand the utility of the coachee's work-related reality, a concept which is central to the PCA (Rogers 1961). This phase is also central to the tendency of *presence* within the PCA (Rogers 1980). This first phase is divided into four (4) sub-phases:

- Clarifying expectations with Senior Management (either with the Managing Director or with the two levels above coachee).
- Clarifying expectations with the coachee's direct manager.
- Clarifying expectations between the direct manager and the coachee.
- Clarifying expectations with the coachee and establish rapport.

Clarifying expectations and establishing rapport with the coachee is vital to the success of the coaching process (Biswas-Diener 2010). The goal of this phase is to understand the dynamics of the coachee's position and his role within the department/organisation and to develop a foundation from which to approach the process.

In order to establish rapport or 'contact' (Rogers 1961), the coach needs to attend to any physical barriers which might impact or interrupt the process (e.g. switching off the cell phone). The coach should create a calm and trusting environment in order to establish the perception that the coach is providing his undivided attention to the coachee (Carkhuff 2000; Egan 2007; Rogers 1961). This may invoke commitment and involvement from the coachee (Egan 2007; Palmer and McDowall 2010). The coachee is approached in a non-directive manner in order to express trust in his or her constructive tendency and facilitating the establishment of rapport and personal development (Rogers 1951).

Egan (2007) developed a technique which could be used to establish rapport, named SOLER:

S   facing the coachee **Squarely** (sitting in front of him)
O   adopt an **Open,** non-defensive posture
L   **Leaning** forward towards the coachee to show interest
E   Make good **Eye contact**
R   Stay **Relaxed**

Through adopting the SOLER approach, the coachee's perception around the coach's warmth and empathy is established (Egan 2007). Furthermore, the coach should interoperate the interaction from the coachee's reality and therefore present genuine unconditional positive regard, free from judgement. This in turn establishes the perception that the coach is more attentive, empathic and caring. Further, a process of active listening needs to be invoked in order to show that the coach comprehends, retains and responds to what the coachee is presenting (Carkhuff 2000; Rogers 1951). For an outline of this process, see Carkhuff (2000).

In this phase, it is very important to understand the coachee's frame of reference in terms of potential cultural, gender, generations, values, interactional preferences and belief differences (Bennett 1993; Rogers 1961). The coach needs to be sensitive to cultural nuances and needs to interoperate the coachee's messages from his/her perspective (Bennett 1993). Cultural differences must be optimised as a strength within the coaching relationship (Bachkirova 2011). Open, honest communication will be crucial for the success of the coaching process (Rogers 1961). These differences must be discussed and clarified from time to time (van Zyl and Stander 2011).

Furthermore, a psychological contract needs to be established between the coach and the coachee. This process should highlight the expectations of both the coach and the coachee to ensure a clear agreement is derived on both the approach and outcomes of the coaching process (Bachkirova 2011; McGovern et al. 2001). Additionally, during this phase, the process needs to be defined and the coach needs to establish the need to review the process and re-establish expectations on a quarterly basis. A coaching log may be helpful to direct the coaching process towards the stated end results. The coaching log incorporates details of the interaction and acts as a utility for the active listening processes through retaining information for future sessions.

2.2 Phase 2: Identifying and Marrying Conscious and Unconscious Strengths

The purpose of this phase is to uncover the coachee's unconscious strengths and merge it with the coachee's current competencies (Seligman 2011). This phase involves the identification of conscious and unconscious strengths through psychometric measurement and competency-based assessment. Both the psychometric evaluation and the competency-based assessment must be in line with the clarified expectations and measurable end results. The psychometric measures should provide the coach with subjective indicators of the coachee's current mental position (Bachkirova 2011). Psychometric tests can include work preferences, personality and emotional intelligence. Furthermore, the authors suggest a continuous self-report measuring instrument such as the Satisfaction with Life Scale (Diener et al. 1985) to track the developmental process. Additionally, a competency profile needs to be developed (see previous phases), in line with his/her position within the organisation, as well as the identified measurable end results (Bachkirova 2011). A 360° evaluation may be conducted with the competency profile in order to determine the individual's performance based on the developmental competencies. Finally, a strengths-based assessment such as the Values in Action Inventory of Strengths (VIA-IS) (Peterson and Seligman 2004) needs to be conducted in order to provide an indication of the individual's strengths. Some people use interviews or more creative ideas like strengths cards and storytelling to identify strengths. Another technique to identify possible strengths is Appreciative Inquiry (AI) (Sheldon et al. 2011; Whitney and Trosten-Bloom 2003). It is a method of personal and organisational development which emphasises what the individual does well (strengths) rather than focusing on the developmental areas (Whitney and Trosten-Bloom 2003). It is important to note that this is an intervention which is not in line with pure PCA principles of support and empathy, but provides the coach with core information regarding the processing and functioning of the coachee.

2.3 Phase 3: Identifying Coaching Themes

The purpose of this phase is to merge the data obtained from the previous phase and to identify possible developmental themes. The coach shouldn't completely shun the developmental areas (Smith 2006). One has to develop a clear understanding regarding the current challenges in the coachee's life. This is in full accord with a whole person approach focusing on person's experience in the current situation (Rogers 1951). The focus should be on revealing what the coachee believes the problem(s) to be, why it exists, what attributed to the problem, what the consequences are and also what meaning he/she derived from the situation (Bachkirova 2011; Rogers 1951).

The individual's strengths need to be identified and utilised in order to help develop the various competencies (Peterson and Seligman 2004). Strengths develop as a result of a struggle with one's self or a struggle with the external environment (Rogers 1951; 1977). Individuals approach situations within the bounds of their awareness of their strengths (Seligman 2011). One's unique combination of strengths should be utilised in order to develop a strategy to develop competencies (Bachkirova 2011; Seligman 2011). These ideals should then be manifested in a personal development plan (PDP) to facilitate the process (Bachkirova 2011).

2.4 Phase 4: Encouraging, Deriving Meaning, Self-Efficacy and Instilling Hope

The purpose of this phase is to encourage the coachee to utilise his/her strengths and to facilitate the development of meaning, self-actualisation and the inherent potential of the individual. Encouraging a coachee acts as a form of positive reinforcement, whereby the coachee's strengths are emphasised (Lyubomirsky 2011; Smith 2006). Encouragement is a process, whereby the coachee's unconscious resources are developed in order to facilitate the formulation of positive choices (Rogers 1951). Encouragement serves as a vehicle through which the coach 'supports' the current behaviour of the coachee, whereby the coachee internalises it through identifying the behaviour as a strength (Goodyear et al. 2008; Lyubomirsky 2011). In this phase, the coachee experiences self-exploration and reinforcing the presented strengths used in a given situation (Peterson and Seligman 2004). The coach must ensure that the coachee is open to learning from different experiences. Focus should be on the individual's strengths and how these strengths are used to address the developmental areas (Seligman 2011). The coach should reinforce the strengths and probe the coachee on strategies where the coachee can use his/her strengths to address the presented challenges (Sin et al. 2011). As a result, the coachee will discover alternative possibilities to use these strengths through the process of encouragement and probing (Sin et al. 2011). This phase is characterised through the exploration of the self and how it can be used to develop self-identity. This is done so that the coachee can develop his own worldview and to understand where he fits into the larger sub-system (Sheldon et al. 2011).

This self-identity and ideals culminate in the generation of hope (Seligman 2011). According to Peterson and Seligman (2004), hope is the central 'buffering mechanism' which affects the onset of psychopathology. The coach should therefore structure questions in such a manner as to encourage individuals to relive past events where they felt hopeful in order to cultivate optimism (Seligman 2011).

In this phase, both forgiveness and gratitude play an important part. Forgiveness encourages the coachee to release negative energy tied to the past (Smith 2006). Gratitude on the other hand is used to instil lasting happiness within the coachee (Peterson and Seligman 2004). Forgiveness illuminates negative emotions, whereas gratitude strives towards instilling positive emotions about the past and the future (Lyubomirsky 2011).

2.5 Phase 5: Framing Solutions and Action Plans

This phase involves developing or framing solutions to current developmental areas. The coachee needs to be facilitated to develop his own strategies aimed at developmental needs (Smith 2006). This is done through solution-building conversations (Smith 2006), whereby he needs to be made aware of the 'accept, change or leave principle'. According to Justice and Jamieson (2002), there are three high-level responses to most given stressors, namely (a) accepting the status quo or changing the self, (b) changing what one can or (c) leaving the problem situation. Solutions need to be built around these ideals. The coach should try and identify the current working mechanisms in the coachee's life through a process of probing (Smith 2006; Yalom 1980). Through collaboration, the coach and coachee generate solutions to the situation (based on his/her inherent character strengths), whereby the coachee develops and commits to a strategy of change (Smith 2006). One approach would be to identify S.M.A.R.T goals. Doran (1981) explains goals need to be specific, measurable, attainable, realistic and time bound.

Note, in this phase and throughout the whole process, the emphasis on coachee–coach collaboration which can be seen as an expression of mutual positive regard as well as interpersonal transparency of goals and intents (Kirschenbaum and Henderson 1989; Rogers 1951).

2.6 Phase 6: Building Strengths and Competencies

This phase has a strong link to PCA and a multicultural approach in terms of *unconditional positive regard* towards the coachee. The coach engages in a non-judgemental approach towards coachee's experiences, background and preferences. This step is vital for psychological health (Seligman 2011). The coachee needs to identify working mechanisms in himself/herself (Lyubomirsky 2011). These working mechanisms are usually manifested, but repressed strengths (Lyubomirsky 2011; Sheldon et al. 2011). The coach should illuminate these strengths and competencies through a process of self-exploration and encouragement (Sheldon et al. 2011). The coachee must be made aware of the 10, 40, 50 % principle (Lyubomirsky et al. 2005). From this perspective, well-being is determined by a biological set point, the conditions of your current life position (environment) and intentional activities aimed at developing happiness. Each one of these factors declares a fairly large amount of variance in the overall experience of happiness. Research has found that the biological set point declares 50 % of the aforementioned variance, where the current life position declares 10 % and intentional activities 40 % (Lyubomirsky 2011). This means that intentional activities of an individual aimed at increasing well-being has a larger effect than one's current environment on the experience. The coachee should therefore build on his current strengths and apply newly developed strengths in order to identify new ways of utilising them (Peterson and Seligman 2004). This will result in a greater fit between the person and the environment (Lyubomirsky 2011; Seligman 2011). The greater the person–environment fit, the more meaning the individual derives from work (Van Zyl et al. 2010). This results in more engagement and higher levels of performance (Seligman 2011).

2.7 Phase 7: Empowerment

The process of empowerment focuses on activating existing *internal and external resources* of the coachee in such a manner as to promote the coachee's competent functioning through collaboration during the coaching process (Cilliers 2011; Spreitzer 1995). This systemic perspective can be seen as broadening the view of the PCA that emphasises internal resources (Kirschenbaum and Henderson 1989). Psychologically empowering the coachee refers to increasing his intrinsic level of motivational self-efficacy (Spreitzer 1995; Smith 2006). The coach should explore the social origins of the coachee's behaviours and focus on the context in which it resides (Smith 2006). The coachee should be facilitated to try out new ways in which to utilise his/her strengths to attempt a solution to the problem (Peterson and Seligman 2004). The approach depends on both the needs of the coachee and the circumstantial environment in which the coachee resides (Seligman 2011). To be psychologically empowered, the coachee must experience a higher level of meaning, competence and control of his/her environment (Spreitzer 1995).

2.8 Phase 8: Reframing

This phase is characterised by changing current behavioural patterns. The focus is on reframing work and life activities in order for them to become more meaningful. The coach should understand that change is a continuous process and doesn't function in isolation (Rogers 1951). The coachee's strengths are seen as the foundation from which decisions are made (Seligman 2011). These strengths also serve as the catalyst for the need to change (Seligman 2008).

The coachee comes to view mistakes as opportunities to learn and grow which is much in the sense of the primacy of experience as a core idea in the PCA (Rogers 1980; Smith 2006). The emphasis should therefore be on what the coachee does right, rather than focusing on what he/she is doing wrong (LeBon 2001). The primary function of this phase is to facilitate the coachee into understanding and desiring the need for change (Seligman 2011; Smith 2006). This need for change should manifest in a series of small attainable goals, each goal should be slightly more difficult/stretching than the last (Yalom 1980). The coach should encourage the individual through recognising his efforts, improvements and accomplishments even if they aren't fully attained (Smith 2006). These goals should be in line with the goals presented in the previous sections, where the focus should be on the establishment of meaning.

The coachee should change the meaning which he attaches to life circumstances in order to gain clarity (Smith 2006). Through moving away from the negative aspects of the situation, the coachee might be asked what lessons he learned from the situation and how it affected the meaning in his/her life (Seligman 2011).

The coachee should utilise his character strengths in order to reframe the situation and interoperate the events from these strengths (Seligman 2011). Therefore, the life circumstances of the individual have a better chance to change. Smith (2006) conceptualised a theoretical framework for reframing, stating that it comprises eight main steps: (a) recognition, (b) acceptance, (c) understanding, (d) learning there is always choice for how to view adversity, (e) changing the meaning ascribed to an event, (f) deriving lessons from the painful event, (g) redefining ourselves around our strengths and multiple talents and (h) taking constructive action around the new strength-based identities and perseverance. This serves as the foundation for building resilience.

2.9 Phase 9: Building Sustainable Resilience

It is important to understand that building resilience is a multidimensional approach. It is developed through understanding and utilising the internal and external resources available to the coachee. The main goal of this phase is to build a level of resilience which will fortify the internal psychological barriers which buffer against reoccurrences in the future (Steger 2013). The type of approach to instil resilience would be based on the type of complex which is manifested in the coachee's Ego (Jung 1942) or through the coachee's life philosophy as embodied in his/her value system (Rogers 1980).

One possible way of developing resilience is to help the coachee to optimise every incident (successes and mishaps) as a learning opportunity and to identify how he/she can use his/her strengths in a similar situation (Seligman 2011).

2.10 Phase 10: Evaluating and Re-contracting the Relationship

Although evaluation is a continuous process, the final phase is to evaluate the coaching process and to prepare the coachee for terminating the relationship. This phase is also coupled with calculating a Return on Investment for the coaching process (Pedler et al. 2007).

During this phase, both the coachee and the coach should determine whether the initial expectations (as set out in the first phase) were met and whether the coachee has accomplished what he set out to do. The focus should be on determining whether full individuation took place and to which extent the expectations of the direct manager have been met (Van Zyl and Stander 2011). During this phase, a follow-up meeting with the coachee and the direct manager needs to take place in order to determine whether the expectations of the process were met (Pedler et al. 2007). Progress should be measured based on the coachee's expectations and not on what the coach perceived as being right (Rogers 1951).

If the expectations have not been met, or if there is a need for further development, a process of re-contracting could be initiated.

3 Conclusion

This model was developed in an attempt to provide practitioners with a practical model for coaching. The model is rooted in the PCA and drawing from positive psychology and psycho-existentialism. The model is comprised out of ten phases. Each phase is followed by an evaluation process to determine the effectiveness of thereof. This model is presumed to be a unique approach towards coaching in that the coachee is the centre of the process. Development takes place centred on the strengths and competencies of the individuals. The coachee's unique cultural position is optimised as a strength in order to ensure sustainable development. This model is not only practical, but also provides specific criteria against which the success of the coaching intervention can be measured.

As much as being strengths based and coachee centred, this model is context sensitive and systemic since it explicitly deals with the coachee's work situation, managers' expectations and evaluation procedures. The full freedom of a counselling or psychotherapy relationship is streamlined to focus on the work context. While numerous tools and instruments are employed to accelerate the growth process, the basic philosophy highlights personal strengths, the person's potential and tendency to develop his or her potentialities, and the importance of a collaborative climate based on transparency, positive regard and sensitivity to the individual as well as context. Hence, the 'bridge' built through this chapter can be seen to connect core values of the PCA with a special purpose, work-related process for developing persons' work-related strengths.

References

Bachkirova, T. (2011). *Developmental coaching: Working with the self*. Maidenhead: Open University Press/McGraw-Hill Education.

Bennett, M. J. (1993). Towards ethnorelativism: A developmental model of intercultural sensitivity. In R. M. Paige (Ed.), *Education for the intercultural experience* (pp. 21–71). Yarmouth, ME: Intercultural Press.

Biswas-Diener, R. (2010). *Practicing positive psychology coaching: Assessment and strategies for success*. Hoboken, NJ: Wiley.

Biswas-Diener, R., & Dean, B. (2007). *Positive psychology coaching*. Hoboken, NJ: John Wiley.

Carkhuff, R. (2000). *The art of helping in the 21st century*. US: Human Resource Development Press.

Cilliers, F. (2011). Positive psychology leadership coaching experiences in a financial organisation. *SA Journal of Industrial Psychology/SA Tydskrif vir Bedryfsielkunde, 37*(1), 0.

Diener, E., Emmons, R. A., Larsen, R. J., & Griffin, S. (1985). The satisfaction with life scale. *Journal of Personality Assessment, 49*, 71–75.

Doran, G. T. (1981). There's a S.M.A.R.T. way to write management's goals and objectives. *Management Review, 70*(11), 35–36.

Egan, G. (2007). *The skilled helper: A problem-management and opportunity-development approach to helping* (7th ed.). Pacific Grove, CA: Brooks/Cole.

Feldman, D. C., & Lankau, M. (2005). Executive coaching: A review and future research. *Journal of Management, 31*(6), 829–848.

Fronczak, D. B. (2006). Coaching men at midlife. *Dissertations abstracts international: Section B: Sciences and engineering, 66*(10), 5710.

Goodyear, R. K., Murdock, N., Lichtenberg, J. W., McPherson, R., Koetting, K., & Petren, R. (2008). Stability and change in counseling psychologists' identities, roles, functions, and career satisfaction across 15 years. *The Counselling Psychologist, 36*(2), 220–249.

Gordon, S., & Gucciardi, D. F. (2011). A strengths-based approach to coaching mental toughness. *Journal of sport psychology in action, 2*(3), 143–155.

Jung, C. G. (1942). *The structure and dynamics of the psyche. Collected works* (Vol. 8). London: Routledge & Kegan Paul.

Justice, T., & Jamieson, D. (2002). *The facilitator's fieldbook* (2nd ed.). New York: City Press.

Kauffman, C. (2006). Positive psychology. The science at the heart of coaching. In D. Stober & A.M. Grant (Eds.), *Evidence based coaching handbook* (pp. 193–225). New York: Wiley.

Kirschenbaum, H., & Henderson, V. L. (Eds.). (1989). *The Carl Rogers reader*. Boston: Houghton Mifflin.

Koortzen, P., & Oosthuizen, R. (2010). A competence executive coaching model. *SA Journal of Industrial Psychology/SA Tydskrif vir Bedryfsielkunde, 36*(1), 7–22.

LeBon, T. (2001). Wise therapy: Philosophy for counsellors. London: Sage Publishers.

Linley, P. A., & Harrington, S. (2006). Playing to your strengths. *The Psychologist, 19*, 86–89.

Lyubomirsky, S. (2011). *The way to happiness: Action plan for a happy life*. (Katya Benyovitz, Trans.) Or Yehuda, Israel: Kinneret Publishing House.

Lyubomirsky, S., Sheldon, K. M., & Schkade, D. (2005). Pursuing happiness: The architecture of sustainable change. *Review of General Psychology, 9*, 111–131.

McGovern, J., Lindemann, M., Vergara, M., Murphy, S., Barker, L., & Warrenfeltz, R. (2001). Maximizing the impact of executive coaching: Behavioral change, organizational outcomes, and return on investment. *The Manchester Review, 6*(1), 1–9.

Palmer, S., & McDowall, A. (2010). *The coaching relationship: Putting people first*. Hove: Routledge.

Pedler, M., Burgoyne, J., & Boydell, T. (2007). *A manager's guide to self-development* (5th ed.). UK: McGraw-Hill Professionals.

Peterson, C., & Park, N. (2006). Character strengths in organizations. *Journal of Organizational Behavior, 27*, 1–6.

Peterson, C., & Seligman, M. E. P. (2004). *Character strengths and virtues: A handbook and classification*. New York, Oxford, Washington: American Psychological Association.

Rogers, C. R. (1951). *Client-centred therapy*. London, UK: Constable.

Rogers, C. R. (1961). *On becoming a person*. Boston: Houghton Mifflin.

Rogers, C. R. (1977). Carl Rogers on personal power: Inner strength and its revolutionary impact. New York: Delacorte Press.

Rogers, C. R. (1978). *Carl Rogers on personal power*. London: Constable.

Rogers, C. R. (1980). *A way of being*. Boston: Houghton Mifflin.

Seligman, M. E. P. (2008). Positive health. *Applied Psychology: An International Review, 57*, 3–18.

Seligman, M. E. P. (2011). *Flourish: A visionary new understanding of happiness and well-being*. New York: Free Press.

Seligman, M. E. P., & Csikszentimihalyi, M. (2000). Positive psychology: An introduction. *American Psychologist, 55*, 5–14.

Sheldon, K., Kashdan, T. B., & Steger, M. F. (Eds.). (2011). *Designing positive psychology: Taking stock and moving forward*. Oxford: Oxford University Press.

Sin, N. L., Della Porta, M. D., & Lyubomirsky, S. (2011). Tailoring positive psychology interventions to treat depressed individuals. In S. I. Donaldson, M. Csikszentmihalyi, & J. Nakamura (Eds.), *Applied positive psychology: Improving everyday life, health, schools, work, and society* (pp. 79–96). New York: Routledge.

Smith, E. J. (2006). The strength-based counselling model. *The Counseling Psychologist, 34*(2), 13–80.

So, T. T. C., & Kauffman, C. (2010). Positive psychology interventions: An annotated bibliography from the behavioural science literature. Unpublished paper, Institute of Coaching, Harvard University.

Spreitzer, G. (1995). Psychological empowerment in the workplace: Dimensions, measurement and validation. *Academy of Management Journal, 38*, 1442–1456.

Steger, M. F. (2013). Meaning in life. In S. J. Lopez (Ed.), *Handbook of positive psychology* (2nd ed.). Oxford, UK: Oxford University Press.

Van Zyl, L. E. & Stander, M. W. (2011, July). An analytical strength based approach towards coaching. *Research paper presented at the 12th annual Society of Industrial/Organisational Psychologists in conference*, Johannesburg, South Africa.

Van Zyl, L., Deacon, E., & Rothmann, S. (2010). Towards happiness: Work-role fit, meaningfulness and engagement of industrial/organisational psychologists in South Africa. *SA Journal of Industrial Psychology, 36*(1), 1–8. doi:10.4102/sajip.v36i1.890.

Whitney, D., & Trosten-Bloom, A. (2003). *The power of appreciative inquiry*. San Francisco: Berret-Koehler.

Yalom, I. (1980). *Existential psychotherapy*. New York: Basic Books.

Part VI
Systems Theory

Person-Centered Approach and Systems Theory

Jürgen Kriz

1 Systemic Roots in Rogers' Thought

In the eyes of many psychotherapists and counselors, the person-centered approach (PCA) is identified mainly or even only with a practical approach of psychotherapy, originated and developed by Carl Rogers out of carefully observing (including technical recording) and analyzing many sessions of counseling and therapy which he himself and others conducted. One core of this practical part of the PCA is the therapeutic relationship, defined by the so-called *three conditions* that must be present in order for a climate to be growth promoting (Rogers 1959). Undoubtedly, this understanding has not only conquered the field of psychotherapy and counseling but also of family and school conferences or leader training (Gordon 1970, 2001), nonviolent or collaborative communication in mediation and peacebuilding (Rosenberg 2001)—both former students of Rogers—or constructive communication in learning groups (Motschnig-Pitrik and Nykl 2009).

However, observations and other empirical data do not just order themselves but are structured by explicit or tacit ideas, assumptions, or hypotheses of the observer. Accordingly, an explanatory principle in Rogers's thought emerged parallel to the empirically based development of the therapeutic relationship in order to structure and understand the phenomena and data in his practice and research. Rogers has been influenced by Otto Rank, a psychoanalyst, who attended lectures by Alfred Adler, through whom, in 1906, he was given entree into Sigmund Freud's little psychoanalytic circle of Vienna. Rank's thought was nearer to that of Adler than that of Freud. When Rogers (1980, p. 113) stresses that "Alfred Adler later (1933) used Smut's concept of the holistic tendency in support of his view that *there can no longer be any doubt that everything, we call a body shows a striving to become a whole*," this may have been an early influence which shaped

---

J. Kriz (✉)
Department of Psychology, University of Osnabrück, Seminarstrasse 20,
49074 Osnabrück, Germany
e-mail: kriz@uos.de

the way Rogers was looking at the world and empirical facts. A second influence came from Kurt Goldstein, a leading member of the Berlin school of Gestalt psychology, who had to leave Germany due to the Nazi regime and was clinical professor of Psychiatry at Columbia University, 1934–1940. In his book *The Organism* (1939, German edition 1934), Goldstein introduced the term "self-actualization" which became, more generalized as "actualizing tendency," a core principle in Rogers' approach. Forty years later, in a fundamental essay entitled "Foundations of the person-centered approach," Rogers referred to this actualizing tendency as "the foundation block of the person-centered approach" (Rogers 1980, p. 114).

Goldstein coined the term "self-actualization" in order to refer the self-organizing processes of an organism (because "self-organization" was not a common term at that time). In contrast to the classical dichotomy of *imposing* order from outside or *developing* order just from inside, Goldstein stressed the crucial point that self-actualization does not mean that the organism is immune to the events and forces of the external world. Conversely, the structural possibilities of the organism are brought into actualization through environmental changes that act upon it. Therefore, for the organism, the environment is both a source of supplies and disturbances. The expressions of that actualization are the performances of the organism. Through them, the organism can deal with the respective environmental demands and actualize itself (Goldstein 1939, p. 111). And, therefore, the healthy organism is one "in which the tendency towards self-actualization is acting from within, and overcomes the disturbance arising from the clash with the world" (p. 305).

Goldstein's notion of "self-actualization" represents an even more general principle which was important for the classical Gestalt psychology and is important for modern interdisciplinary systems theory: The circular interaction between the macroscopic and the microscopic level of processes and their dynamics—or in terms of Gestalt psychology: between the whole (the Gestalt) and its parts. The paradigmatic example of a "Gestalt" is a melody, because a sequence of tones is perceived (whenever possible) as a melody. This is the bottom-up dynamics of ordering. However, the top-down dynamics is equally important: The elements (tones) do not simply disappear in the Gestalt, as was said in undifferentiated holistic approaches. In contrast, the constituent parts (tones) often obtain a new and specific meaning within these orderings. In a melody, you find the phenomena of the root and the tonic keynote, which gives this tone a particular meaning within the melody that it would not have as an isolated tone, that is, without the top-down influence of the Gestalt.

The dynamic properties of a Gestalt and its dynamic adaptation in the actualization of inherent possibilities to forces from the environment were an important aspect in Gestalt psychology, in Goldstein's organismic theory and in Rogers' thought. In contrast to classical principles, the order of a Gestalt does not need an external "organizer." For example, the environment of an organism does not impose order from outside by way of control nor does it force the individual to behave in a manner that is foreign to his nature. This is a contrary position to the behaviorists' view of treating organisms at that time (and still, to some extent, in contrast to their ideas of learning, training, and controlling). Therefore, Rogers was rather fascinated by the findings of modern systems theory which came up in the 1970s and supported the idea of self-organizing order. When the Nobel Prize in Chemistry 1977 was awarded to Ilya Prigogine for his work on self-organization, Rogers was one of the first psychologists who extensively referred to the correspondence of Prigogine's and his way of looking at the phenomena. In his 1980 book, Rogers wrote:

> Recently, the work of chemist-philosopher Ilya Prigogine ... offers a different perspective, which also throws new light on what I have been discussing. In trying to answer the basic question of how order and complexity emerge from the process of entropy. He has originated an entirely new theoretical system.
> ... Such a system is unstable, has fluctuations or "perturbations," as Prigogine calls them. As these fluctuations increase, they are amplified by the system's many connections, and thus drive the system—whether chemical compound or human individual—into a new, altered state, more ordered and coherent than before...
> The transformation from one state to another is a sudden shift, a nonlinear event, in which many factors act on one another at once. It is especially interesting to me that this phenomenon has already been demonstrated by Don (1977–1978) in his investigation of Gendlin's concept of "experiencing" in psychotherapy (Gendlin 1978). When a hitherto feeling is fully and acceptantly experienced in awareness during the therapeutic relationship, there is not only a definitely felt psychological shift, but also a concomitant physiological change, as a new state of insight is achieved (p. 131).

And he finishes that chapter by stating:

> Thus, from theoretical physics and chemistry comes some confirmation of the validity of experiences that are transcendent, indescribable, unexpected, transformational—the sort of phenomena that I and my colleagues have observed and felt as concomitants of the person-centered approach (1980, p. 132).

Therefore, looking back on Rogers' lifelong work, we can say that the development of the PCA is strongly connected with the view of systems theory—starting from Gestalt psychology (including Goldstein's organism theory) and leading to more recent formulations of systems theory in the field of the natural sciences (including Prigogine's Nobel Prize awarded approach). Although Rogers conducted a lot of empirical research on psychotherapy, he was aware of the limitations of the classical paradigm. The standard approach by which psychologists tend to "make science" on the basis of sophisticated but just linear input–output (or stimulus–response) analysis is ignoring the sudden shifts and nonlinear events of interconnected variables. These, however, are essential for organismic, psychic, and interactive developments. Moreover, while even today many mainstream psychologists ignore both the "ancient" psychological Gestalt theory and the "not psychological" systems theory in the natural science, some leading scientists in the field of modern natural sciences stress the relationship between Gestalt psychology and contemporary interdisciplinary systems theory. One prominent example is Hermann Haken, the physicist and founder of both laser theory and a comprehensive interdisciplinary program of systems theory, called *synergetics* (Haken 1981, 1983).

2 Systems Theory as a Structural Science

However, using Rogers' words, this "*confirmation*" of the actualizing tendency as "*the foundation block of the person-centered approach*" "*from theoretical physics and chemistry*" that he welcomed as an *interdisciplinary* principle helping us to understand, structure, and refer to his personal experiences raised different reactions. Some PCA therapists seem to fear that, if the PCA refers to principles which are also discussed in the natural sciences, we might fall into the pitfalls of present-day technological scientism, reductionism, materialism, and objectivism. Compared to the masses of publications concerning practical aspects of a growth-promoting relationship, there are only a few contributions to deepen our understanding of the actualizing tendency, for example, by Cornelius-White (2006, 2007) or by the concept of co-actualization (Motschnig-Pitrik and Barrett-Lennard 2010).

In any case, according to Grant (2004), stressing that we base our "practice on (implicit) ethical concepts and world-views" (p. 156), we should be aware of the roots of our everyday understanding. Most people believe in the essential difference between repairing a defective engine and working with a patient in a psychotherapeutic manner. But what are the concepts, terms, metaphors, and principles that we have and use as cognitive tools to grasp, explain, and discuss human development, pathogenesis, or psychotherapy?

After 400 years of great success of classical mechanistic science as an essential basis of today's culture, our world is filled with machines, apparatus, tools, and "things" that have changed the face of our planet. Over many generations, our inner images—the metaphors and principles we use in understanding our everyday life—became, of course, more and more related to the outer images of what we perceive and experience: things and mechanical apparatus. No wonder then that it seemed self-evident to use these metaphors and principles to understand and explain other areas of the "world," too—when we are dealing with nonhuman beings, with other humans, and last but not least with ourselves. This tendency seems to be even stronger when we try to give rational or "scientific" explanations. Although science has changed its worldview and its explanatory principles tremendously in the last decades, the informal narratives and metaphors of culture do not adapt as quickly, but instead still convey the "same old stories" of what "science" is. And this still involves the use of a toolbox of mechanistic principles (which are indeed rather adequate in dealing with the restricted apparatus of our technical world).

Therefore, the crucial question is not whether we do or do not use metaphors and principles (also) discussed in the natural sciences. The question is whether we use inadequate (mechanistic) principles or adequate (systemic) ones when referring to life and human creativity instead of machines. Moreover, while examples of self-organization in the natural sciences are connected to *energy*, the examples and phenomena we refer to in this chapter deal with *meaning*. Meaning, however, is not a topic in natural science but only in human and social sciences. As a consequence, by using systems theory to explore and explain phenomena related to meaning, we cannot say that we use tools from "natural sciences." It is most adequate to refer to systems theory as a structural science.

Indeed, my experience is that students on their way to become PCA therapists, often "know" a lot about the relationship, the "three core conditions," or attitudinal qualities. They have read and can repeat a lot of what they *should* do and *want* to do. However, when we listen to the tapes of their first (simulated) steps into "making therapy," we find that what they *really* do is rather different. They are analyzing "the situation" and "the patient," finding out "what is really the case" and giving "advice," they are "applying the core conditions," or "applying encounter groups," and are "using active listening" (techniques)—in other words, they are grasping for information in order to impose "helpful structure" from outside. Although they know that the attitudinal qualities in the PCA are rather different, they feel much more secure and comfortable with a behavior that mirrors (and is influenced by) the principles of our technical understanding of "the world."

Not only the thoughts of patients or of my students but also many PCA texts are full of words, terms, and concepts that refer to those principles, because such an approach to the world has been so successful that it now governs the core ideas of everyday life. For example, references to "blocks," "barriers," and "shields" or the use of phrases such as "he got stuck," "she has no self-control," "I (don't) want to push him," "he does not function well" are much more adequate for dealing with matter and machines than for an encounter with a human being.

As a consequence, in PCA, the ethical position of believing in the essential difference between matter and a person is good but not enough. Without alternatives, we are trapped by the power of our everyday thought in our culture. And by this, we link (implicitly and tacitly) our practice to the metaphors and principles of mechanistic science. The link between PCA and systems theory is meant, therefore, to provide an alternative and not a reduction.

3 Relatedness and Feedback as Basic Concepts of the Systems Approach

A main theme of modern interdisciplinary systems science is to describe and analyze how dynamic order or patterns emerge if input and output are not artificially isolated—as is the case in most classical and technical approaches—but if interconnectedness and feedback are admitted. This core distinction between classical mechanistic and modern systemic approaches is illustrated in Fig. 1a, b.

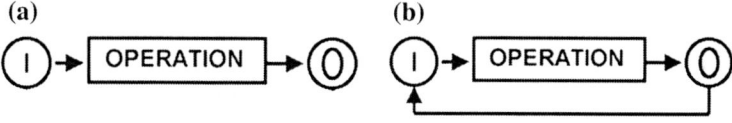

Fig. 1 a Input–output. b Input–output loop

In Fig. 1a, an input "I" is given to the box, which "operates" somehow and gives an output "O." This is not only the classical idea of "making an experiment" but also, accordingly, the underlying perspective of stimulus–response psychology. It is, moreover, often the everyday understanding disseminated in simple textbooks describing social relationships: A wife asks her husband: "what do you mean about X?" And he gives an answer. The question is identified with "I" and the answer with "O," and the interaction takes place because the wife cannot look directly into the "black box" (the man's brain) but has to investigate this box by input–output analysis. Typically, the classical metaphor of experimental input–output analysis applied to human relationship.

However, this description misses the essence of what really takes place when a couple communicates. In contrast to two persons who meet each other for the first time, a couple has a relationship which reflects the common history, some common ideas about the future, and the cognitive processes in the present. Therefore, the man "knows" that certain answers might be interpreted by his wife in a way which he does not want. This belief of course influences the possible answers a great deal. On the other side, "knowing" her husband, and that he "tends" toward "evasive answers," the wife tries to ask in a way that reflects these "tendencies" in order to find out what he really thinks. However, the man has experienced that his wife ....

We could go on telling this story in more and more detail and with more prospective loops which reflect the experiences gained during thousands of previous loops (see Fig. 1b). But even this rough example shows the flaws of a mere input–output analysis in contrast to taking account of the history of feedback loops in which cognitive patterns of beliefs, expectations, interpretations, and so on provide a meaning field that determines the question and answers. Due to interconnections and history, every "stimulus" is also a "response" to what happened before, and every "response" is also a "stimulus" for the further process. Therefore, what happens reflects the pattern of interaction and meaning which emerged in the biography of that couple. This pattern is not imposed from outside (although many influences are important: social and language structure, individual biography, "personality," etc.) but with respect to these influences is self-organized.

Generally, in systems science, interconnectedness and feedback loops are the essence of "emergence" and "phase transitions" (terms we are going to explain later in more detail) of self-organized patterns and order. In chemistry, for example, we find self-organizing patterns of movement of a liquid in a bowl due to chemical reactions or *chemical clocks* where in a test tube, the color might change: red–blue–red–blue–red, etc. In physics, for example, the extremely coherent light wave in a laser can be described by a process of self-organization which synchronizes the emission of light from the individual atoms in such a way that they contribute to a common light wave. Another famous example is the *Bénard Instability*: macroscopic coherent movements (convection "rolls") which typically take on the complicated shape of a honeycomb pattern. In particular, the interdisciplinary systems approach *Synergetics* (Haken 1981, 1983) is presented in more than one hundred volumes with about two thousand contributions, most of them from physics, chemistry, physiology, biology, and other natural sciences.

However, the couple discussed above is an example for such dynamic patterns in social areas, which already combines processes of meaning and behavior (Kriz 2009). Similarly, on the behavioral–interactional level, the rhythmic applause—that is, the spontaneously arising common clapping rhythm, which often emerges from the chaos of applause after a concert—can serve as a last example of emerging patterns here. The individual clapping rhythms, just perceived as "noise" or "thunder," are synchronized in such a way that they contribute to the common rhythm.

4 Emergence and Phase Transition of Patterns

While these phenomena refer to the self-organized *emergence* of order out of chaotic disorder, we often have the case where a state of order or pattern already exists and by passing this gate of disorder a new and different state of dynamic order is established. In the already given quotation of Rogers, he also stressed that this *"transformation from one state to another is a sudden shift."* In interdisciplinary systems theory, this self-organized shift is called *"phase transition."* On the elementary level of perception (including "understanding"), already classical Gestalt psychology referred to such phase transitions of meaning by creating so-called ambiguous figures—such as the Necker cube (Fig. 2a) or Rubinstein's vase–faces (Fig. 2b) or old–young woman (Fig. 2c). Similarly, the famous "aha effect"—that is, that many facts which were interpreted in a particular way for a while can suddenly change "their" meaning, often connected to an unpleasant confusion and then a relaxing "aha!"—is an everyday experience of a phase transition described and investigated by Gestalt psychology a century ago. Moreover, Rogers gives the example of a boy who was an excellent pupil at a small city's school. When he went to a well-known university, however, many students were much better. Therefore, the structure of the self would have needed a phase transition in order to cope with these experiences. But, if this transition is too threatening, the experiences may be denied or given a distorted symbolization—operators of the self to keep the structure stable.

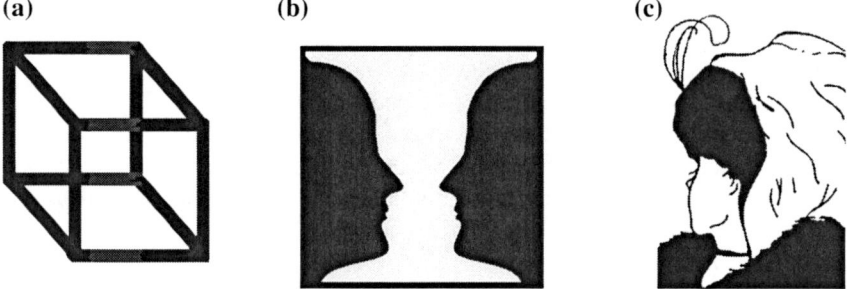

Fig. 2 Phase transitions and ambiguity. **a** Necker-Cube: which side is in front? **b** vase or two faces? **c** old or young woman?

Finally, also the shifting patterns of interaction and interpretations in a "partner crises" can be understood in this way: The benevolent trusting interpretation of actions and comments, mutually understood for a long time, can change into a "climate" of distrust, insinuation, misrepresentations, and allegations which undermines in such a way that this structure dominates and shapes the thinking, perceiving, interpreting, and acting of each partner, forms the patterns of interaction, and contributes in turn to this climate of distrust.

All of these examples have the following in common: The self-organizing process of emergence or phase transition starts due to the fact that the environmental conditions of the systems dynamic have changed. Although the order emerges in a self-organized fashion, it nevertheless represents the environmental conditions of the system in such a way that it represents one (of two or many) possible adaptation to these external conditions. During the self-organized formation of order, the emergence, as well as during the second part of the phase transition (after the order has become unstable), there are different competing possibilities of order. And by means of weak fluctuations, the system "tests" different possibilities. Some of these alternatives of possible order, however, do not represent the overall condition of the system and its surroundings as well as others—as a consequence, they lose the competition and their special contribution to the dynamics becomes weaker and weaker. Other alternatives lose the competition just by chance. Often this can be heard when one is carefully listening to the process when the chaotic clapping changes into a common rhythm: First, some more clear rhythms may be heard. However, some seem to fit better into that what people seem to want unconsciously. When people join into that rhythm, this clapping gets louder and increases the possibility that other people will hear and (mostly unconsciously, too) join into that pattern. This, again, increases the loudness and therefore the chance of being heard and letting others tune into that clapping. Very rapidly, the whole audience will join in clapping that rhythm.

What we find in all examples, too, is the already discussed relationship between bottom-up and top-down influences: The order, pattern, or Gestalt is a phenomenon on a macroscopic level—and is "nothing else" but coordinated dynamics on a microscopic level. Accordingly, the coherent wave of the laser is made up of emitted light (waves) of single atoms; the highly ordered "rolls" of movement in the Bénard Instability are made up of the movements of single molecules; the coherent applause rhythm consists of the hand-clapping of many individuals; the climate of distrust is composed of the interpretations and communications of each partner. These common descriptions of phenomena in totally different realms underline our claim above: These realms and their phenomena are not "reduced to natural science" by referring to these principles in description. Rather, these are descriptions which have their meaning and relevance for understanding dynamics in areas investigated as well in physics, chemistry, etc., as in sociology, psychology, or therapy.

5 Attractors and Over-stability

A last important sub-concept of systems theory should be mentioned here: Although the self-organized order corresponds both to inherent potentials of the system and, equally, to the general conditions of the surroundings, a small change in the environment will normally not change the system's dynamic order which has established itself. Instead, there is always something like an over-stability. This phenomenon can be easily understood in the case of the discussed partner crisis—when, for example, the man has cheated on his wife with a colleague from work. Due to love and trust, earlier hints to the man's unfaithful behavior may have been overseen, ignored, or interpreted in another way by the woman. But suddenly the belief systems change: now she "knows" him and, rethinking some well-known situations, she might ask herself how she could have been so blind to the "facts" since long. The answer is, of course, that there has been an over-stability of trust.[1] However, now a phase transition of the pattern "trustful interpretation" into "distrust" has happened—and, again, we find an over-stability of this new pattern of distrust. It will be rather difficult for the man and may need many "proofs" of faith in order to change this pattern into trust, once more. The same objective situational "facts," which were, in the past, totally OK or even contributions to stabilize the trust, are now "under suspicion" and may even stabilize the distrust.

In systems theory, these dynamically ordered states which are typical for self-organized systems and showing over-stability are called *attractors*. An attractor really "attracts" the possible paths of development of that system to some extent. In the just discussed example, first the forces of trust attract the interpretation of many facts. Disturbing information is leveled out as long as the disturbance is not too big. But when the perturbation becomes too strong, then the system is switching over a phase of instability to a new attractor—in this example: mistrust. The same happens with systems in physics, chemistry, biology, or physiology when they pass from one attractor to another one in a phase transition—and thus necessarily passing a state of instability.

However, interdisciplinary systems theory might be a young branch of science, and even Gestalt psychology started only 100 years ago—but human experience of phase transition is much older. Natural development, particularly of organisms, humans, societies, etc., has to do with transitions between more or less stable states. Therefore, we find very seldom linear development, that is, a steady and continuous movement from one state into another one. Conversely, we find developmental steps in which the system adapts in a nonlinear way and in sudden jumps to the more continuous changing environment. For human beings, this experience is expressed in many cultures by the saying "Die and Become!"—the

---

[1] It should be noticed that such examples and terms like "trust" reduce the complexity and diversity of real life extremely. Of course, the behavior of both the man and the woman has many aspects and reasons.

well-known slogan of transformation coined by the famous German poet Goethe. Structural patterns (of course, only some) have to "die" in order that new patterns can emerge, which are new adaptions to the environmental changes and demands (see Goldstein above). A simple example of this is a functional and useful interactive structure of parents with their 3-year-old son. This would be totally crazy and pathological when it remains the same for 20 years (and the 23-year-old man is treated and let himself be treated as if he would be 3-years old) instead of passing some phase transitions of the structural patterns due to developmental task from the body (e.g., concerning "sexuality"), psyche (e.g., concerning "self-determination"), or culture (e.g., concerning "responsibility"). Already, Goldstein talked about the "reorganization" of old patterns into new and more effective ones with regard to processes of development and healing. Moreover, it should be noted that the idea of growth in PCA and, more general, in humanistic psychology is exactly that "Die and Become" in accordance with the growth of a deciduous tree—letting go all leaves in autumn in order to let new green emerge in spring—and does not mean the "more and more" of growth in economics.

When development, actualization, and psychotherapy are essentially characterized by phase transitions from one state, which is no longer adequate to the environmental demands, to another state, then we can understand why the therapeutic relationship, described by Rogers, is so important. To endure the "death" of familiar patterns and to pass the gate of instability and chaos (at least partly), it is very supportive to have a companion at your side who provides a secure frame and offers a faithful relationship.

6 Person-Centered Systems Theory

Rogers could only make use out of Gestalt psychology and systems theory as far as it was developed until his death. His notion of the actualizing tendency and the necessity of "die and become" in a supporting (therapeutic) relationship without any advice or other interventions that impose order from outside is clearly in accordance with classical approaches of systems theory such as the *Gestalt* approach. Although he noticed the development in modern systems theory during the last few years of his life, he used the principles (outlined in Sects. 3–5) more metaphorically as a confirmation of his thought.

Today, over 25 years after his death, systemic thinking has developed much further because of two influences. One is the extensive development in interdisciplinary systems research, particularly the above-mentioned synergetics. The other, even more important for our field, is the strong dissemination of systemic therapy, which evolved out of family therapy.

In order to unify and more tightly relate Rogers' approach with a more advanced and elaborated use of modern systems theory, the so-called person-centered systems theory (PCST) has been developed (Kriz 1991, 2007, 2008, 2009). Without going into details here, its main advancement is the distinction of different process levels, each characterized by its own dynamics, attractors, forces of stability and instability, and contribution to the overall process of "being in the world" and making meaning. However, due to the central aspect of bottom-up and top-down influences—that is, the circular interaction between the macroscopic and the microscopic level of processes and their dynamics—the process levels are not understood as isolated but interactively interwoven. The main levels in PCST focus on bodily/somatic, psychic, face-to-face, and institutional/cultural processes.

For example, we can describe self-organized order on the interactional level as patterns of communication or interaction. And, in addition, we can describe self-organized order on the cognitive level as cognitive patterns. However, as we have already seen in the above-discussed example of the couple, in most cases, patterns of interaction and cognitive patterns are two aspects of one more complex process in which cognitive and interactive dynamics work together. A simple and often used example is the "nagging wife" and the "withdrawing husband." Let us call the behavior of the female F and of the male M. Then, we can observe the pattern of sequences:

$$\to M \to F \to M \to F \to M \to F \to \ldots$$

and we can understand the feedback loops as shown in Fig. 3 (corresponding to Fig. 1b)

Fig. 3 Dynamic circle of male–female interaction

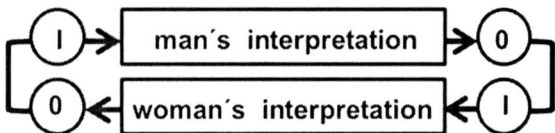

However, in addition to this interactional pattern, we find cognitive patterns. One typical class of such patterning is described as "punctuation" (Watzlawick et al. 1967). In a heterosexual relationship depicted by Fig. 3, the woman interprets the process in one way (Fig. 4a) while, in contrast, the man has another cognitive pattern (Fig. 4b).

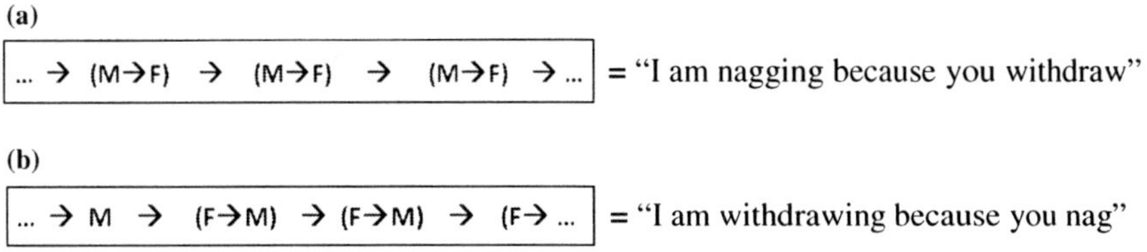

(a)

$\ldots \to (M \to F) \to (M \to F) \to (M \to F) \to \ldots$ = "I am nagging because you withdraw"

(b)

$\ldots \to M \to (F \to M) \to (F \to M) \to (F \to \ldots$ = "I am withdrawing because you nag"

Fig. 4 a Punctuation: woman's perspective. **b** Punctuation: man's perspective

Indeed, therapists who deal with families and couples often observe how reactions to another person's forms of expressing himself have less to do with the communication itself than with some curious rules: offhand one could say that the attempt at communication made by one person—let's call her Sally—as registered and processed by the other person—let's call him Peter—merely acts as a general trigger which causes an "inner film" of expected meaning to start to play. So, Peter does not actually listen any more. In certain situations, if Sally merely opens her mouth, he already knows "what's up." At least, he thinks he knows. But how can he know for sure if he doesn't really listen any more? At any rate, what Peter is reacting to is more his "inner film" than what Sally has said. For therapists, the following brief exchange is therefore typical:

- *Therapist*: What did you perceive?
- *Peter*: The way Sally looked at me I knew what to expect.
- *Therapist*: Did you hear what she said?
- *Peter*: No, sorry. But I already know what she is going to say when she looks at me like that.

When Sally becomes aware that Peter's reactions to much of what she says are always the same because he doesn't listen, she will go to less effort to come up with anything new. This in turn confirms Peter in his belief that he was right in thinking that "Sally always goes on about the same old things." Unfortunately, it is not only Peter who is affected in this manner. We could have observed and related this whole interaction from Sally's point of view. Here, a vicious circle of reduction has been set in motion in which both partners appear to be both active participants and victims of circumstance at the same time. Sadly, this commingling of the roles of perpetrator and victim is typical of many social relationships.

Those interpretation patterns and forms of behavior which (in the sense of the interpretations) are mutually confirmable develop especially well during the common development of a couple or a family. Hence, these persons' degree of freedom can under unfavorable circumstances become increasingly restricted. Finally, this dynamics develops an interaction pattern which an observer experiences and describes as "encrusted, rigid structures." The wife's most likely different utterances and their intentions are all reduced to the category of "nagging," and this is what her husband reacts to. There are simply far too few categories at hand that could be used to understand the partner's behavior.

In order to demonstrate the structural equivalence between the precise notion of an attractor and that what we often observe in the real world of making meaning, Kriz (2009) presented a further example. Let us start with a simple operation according to Fig. 1b: *"Multiply an input number with 0.05, then subtract this result from 2.2, and then multiply this result with the input."* As a consequence, starting with an input "*I*"—which we call "X_{old}"—we can write

$$X_{old} \times (2.2 - 0.05 X_{old}) \rightarrow X_{new}$$

For the first X_{old}, we can begin with a very simple value, for example 10, in order to calculate the right-hand side of the equation—therefore: $10 \times (2.2 - 0.05 \times 10)$, and we get $X_{new} = 17$. In the next step, this value is used again as X_{old} on the right-hand side—therefore: $17 \times (2.2 - 0.05 \times 17)$, which now gives

Person-Centered Approach and Systems Theory 273

22.95. Continuing with this procedure, the process runs after some more steps to the numbers 24, 24, 24....

Amazingly, starting this process from other numbers (out of a rather large basin), it runs into the number 24, too. This is shown in Fig. 5.

Fig. 5 From different starting numbers, the process runs into the attractor 24

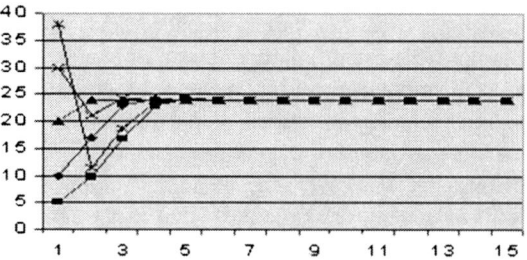

Accordingly, we understand the emergence and function of "meaning attractors" (Kriz 2008), which reduce the interpretative complexity in the "meaning space" into an ordered understanding in strong correspondence with Fig. 5. In the following example, the first six lines of Kevin's behavior which correspond to different complex situations are reduced to the simple, low complex description: "Kevin has a behavior disorder" (Fig. 6).

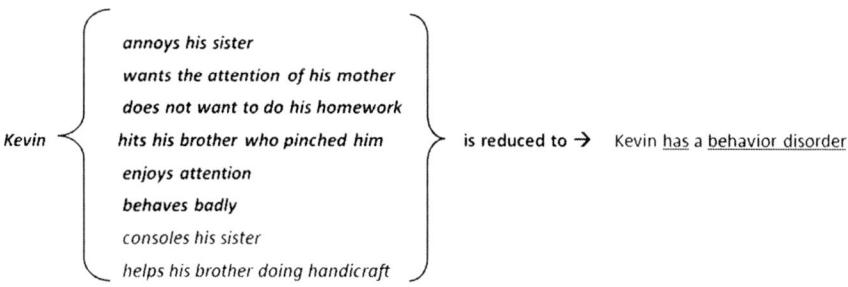

Fig. 6 Reduction in polysemantic complex situations to one interpretation

Even the cognitive processing of the situational behavior, outlined by the last two lines, might be drawn into that "meaning attractor." The reality of counseling shows that this behavior will be ignored, misunderstood, or quickly forgotten. It should be noted that "behavior disorder" is a typical reification which reduces a process to a thing. In addition, the word "has" is rather static and amplifies the encrusted meaning. Therefore, from left to right, we find a pathogenic process of becoming rigid and petrified by reducing a multitude of different dynamic situations with a multitude of meanings and, therefore, a multitude of possible actions into the simple, static, clear but abstract defined, thing-like concept "behavior disorder." No wonder then that also the space of possible action or reaction is rather small. In many approaches, the core of psychotherapy is to go from the right side to the left side, that is, to enrich the abstract and reduced description with more detailed, vivid, sensual, situations which opens not only a multitude of meanings and understandings but, from this, also a many options of action.

Referring to "reification," we make already use of cultural influences on the meaning process in order to understand what is going on in this family. For example, the father's interpretation of Kevin's behavior in a particular situation is as well influenced by his personal biographical experiences as by the self-organizing meaning structures in the family. However, both are influenced by the meaning structure of the culture and, additionally, of subcultures where the family belongs to. Moreover, the meaning influences from culture are not only on the level of content or semantics—that is, the interpretation of the term "disorder"—but also on the level of structure or syntax—that is, the tendency of SAP (*standard average European*—see Whorf 1956) to describe processes as if they were things. Each process level can contribute to stabilize or destabilize meaning processes on the other levels. For example, sorrowful experiences can be stabilized by the interactive patterns of the family and these, again, can be stabilized by narratives in the subculture of the family which, again, might be an expression of historical events (for example, grandfather's fighting in World War 1).

7 Concluding Remarks

From the perspective elaborated in this chapter, it seems that not all process levels and their phenomena are equally elaborated in PCA. On the intraindividual level, pattern formation and its developmental and therapeutic needs with respect to a person-to-person relationship have been extensively presented by Rogers. Additionally, the dynamics of psychic processes with regard to the organism and body, respectively, became a central aspect particularly in Gendlin's *focusing* approach. On the other side, stabilization and destabilization of interindividual patterns and their interwoven dynamics with processes on the psychic level are much better conceived and formulated in systemic therapy and PCST. Moreover, while narratives, interpretative patterns, principles of understanding and explanation play an important role in PCST, because they influence interpersonal and psychic patterns as well as the ability to change these patterns a lot, all these aspects are nearly absent in PCA. The same is true for the influence of language's syntax, such as reification, wrong generalization. Generally speaking, while Rogers stressed the aspects of listening very carefully to the expressed feelings, needs, and contents in the client's verbal expressions, he did not attend to the structural aspects of communication, language, and culture. PCST's concern is to build a bridge between both aspects of a man's life.

References

Cornelius-White, J.H.D. (2006). Environmental responsibility, the formative tendency and wellbeing. *Person-Centered Quarterly*, 11–12.

Cornelius-White, J. H. D. (2007). The actualizing and formative tendencies: Prioritizing the motivational constructs of the person-centered approach. *Person-Centered and Experiential Psychotherapies, 6*(2), 129–140.

Don, N.S. (1977–1978). The transformation of conscious experience and its EEG correlates. *Journal of Altered States of Consciousness*, 147.

Gendlin, E. T. (1978). *Focusing*. New York: Everest House.

Goldstein, K. (1939). *The organism*. New York: American Book.

Gordon, T. (1970). *Parent effectiveness training: The proven program for raising responsible children*. New York: Wyden.

Gordon, T. (2001). *Leader effectiveness training LET: The proven people skills for today's leaders tomorrow*. New York: Perigee Trade.

Grant, B. (2004). The imperative of ethical justification in psychotherapy: The special case of client centered therapy. *Person-Centered and Experiential Psychotherapies, 3*, 152–165.

Haken, H. (1981). *Synergetics: An introduction*. Berlin: Springer.

Haken, H. (1983). *Advanced synergetics: Instability hierarchies*. Berlin: Springer.

Kriz, J. (1991). Mental health: Its conception in systems theory. An outline of the person-centered system approach. In M. J. Pelaez (Ed.), *Comparative sociology of family, health and education* (Vol. XX, pp. 6061–6083). Espania: University of Malaga.

Kriz, J. (2007). Actualizing tendency: The link between PCE and interdisciplinary systems theory. *Person-Centered and Experiential Psychotherapies, 6*(1), 30–44.

Kriz, J. (2008). *Self-actualization: Person-centred approach and systems theory*. Ross-on-Wye: PCCS-books.

Kriz, J., & Molenaar, P. C. M. (2009). Cognitive and interactive patterning: Processes of creating meaning. In J. Valsiner, M. C. D. Lyra, & N. Chaudhary (Eds.), *Dynamic process methodology in the social and developmental sciences* (pp. 619–650). New York: Springer.

Motschnig-Pitrik, R., & Barrett-Lennard, G. (2010). Co-actualization: A new construct for understanding well-functioning relationships. *Journal of Humanistic Psychology, 50*(3), 374–398.

Motschnig-Pitrik, R., & Nykl, L. (2009). *Konstruktive kommunikation*. Stuttgart: Klett-Cotta. [Constructive communication].

Rogers, C. R. (1959). A theory of therapy, personality, and interpersonal relationships, as developed in the client-centered framework. In S. Koch (Ed.), *Psychology: A study of a science: Study 1. Conceptual and systematic: Formulations of the person and the social context* (Vol. 3, pp. 184–256). New York: McGraw-Hill.

Rogers, C. R. (1980). *A way of being*. Boston: Houghton Mifflin.

Rosenberg, M. (2001). *Nonviolent communication: A language of compassion*. Encinitas: Puddledancer Press.

Watzlawick, P., Beavin, J. H., & Jackson, D. D. (1967). *Pragmatics of human communication*. New York: Norton & Company.

Whorf, B. J. (1956). *Language thought and reality: Selected writings*. Carroll): MIT Press.

Relationship Worlds and the Plural Self

Godfrey Barrett-Lennard

1 Introduction

In dialogue, we commonly acknowledge ourselves with use of the first person pronoun 'I': I think, I feel, I believe, I suggest, I want, I hope, etc. Self-reference as 'me' often conveys something about the speaker's receiving or wanting self (e.g. 'he loves me', 'do this for me'). But what is this owned inner being or self we speak of? Is it our whole personality, outlook and style or is it our experiencing self' in an immediate or particular context? Given our hugely complex brains and diverse developmental experience isn't it likely that we would acquire a varied repertoire of ways of being, indeed, that our sense of self would differ in very different contexts?[1] If called on to describe ourselves in distinct and pivotal relationships—with a lover, parent or own child, say—would we come up with same self-picture in each context or find differences reflecting different 'sides' or patterns of self? Person-centred theory as advanced by Rogers has implied that a well- or fully functioning person is essentially free of inner division or conflict and relates from his/her true or genuine self (Rogers 1961, Chap. 8: 'To be that self one truly is'). But what does this mean?

In particular, Rogers stressed the importance of being 'open to experience', of being responsively aware (though not in a self-conscious way) of sensations,

---

[1] This chapter (Relationship Worlds and the Plural Self) is a sibling version of chapter "Interdisciplinary Research and Theory" (The diverse self in and from relationship) of Godfrey Barrett-Lennard's new book on "The relationship paradigm Human being beyond individualism" to be published by Palgrave Macmillan. While both "siblings" share the main theme of self-diversity, this chapter is a shorter and significantly revised version, additionally addressing the "bridge" to the Person-Centred Approach. Thanks to Palgrave Macmillan for granting the permission to include this related version and thus to support another live instance of the concept of plurality.

G. Barrett-Lennard (✉)
Psychology, Murdoch University, Perth, Australia
e-mail: gt_barrett-lennard@iinet.net.au

feelings, images, thoughts and meaning. Being openly in touch in this way can also transform encounter and communication with others. Such holistic process seems counter to notions of constancy or fixity of self. Rogers writes, for example, that clients moving in this direction may find 'that they do not always hold the same feelings towards a given experience or person, that they are not always consistent' (ibid, p. 171). The flowing, becoming process Rogers points to implies self-diversity and I take the further step of linking this diversity to different relationships. Here, I will first present four kinds of evidence of diversity of self, go on to explore the 'yin and yang' of self and relationship, discuss loneliness in connection with the self-relationship nexus and consider the vicissitudes of self in big systems of association.

2 Self-Diversity Revealed in Four Contexts

2.1 Evidence of Self-Diversity from Everyday Experience and Conversation

References to being 'not myself', 'a different person', 'letting myself down', 'in two minds', or to 'having fallen apart', 'turned into jelly', 'pulled myself together', 'slipped back', 'come to my senses', or that 'I don't know what came over me' and other such expressions all reflect an acute awareness of personal complexity and variation. Any genuine expression of being surprised by one's own behaviour or felt reaction suggests that the speaker assumes a familiar self or pattern of being and senses another side of his/her make-up, one that is 'not really like me', 'out of character' or 'not true to who I am'. It may well be, however, that the speaker's surprise and discomfort with this alien or rejected self is a reaction when they are in particular company (for example, a somewhat formal mixed group). In a very different relational context (perhaps with a familiar same sex friend), the same self-behaviour might pass unnoticed or even seem positive.

Great numbers of people participate vicariously in sporting contests, seeming to lose or transcend their everyday selves in the presence of skilled athlete heroes in action with their teams and opponents. In many cases, the pattern change is so marked that it seems clear that a different configuration of self has come into play. So too in some racing carnivals, musical or theatre performances and other situations that arouse and engage people deeply. The evident transitions from one self-mode to another occur spontaneously in response to the contexts in which they occur. On reflection, the person might be quite aware that they 'changed gears' in a way that is natural to them—and which I would say accords with our complex nature as humans. Men and woman can be warriors in armed combat; fierce, dangerous, prepared to overpower or kill a threatening enemy, yet also tender with a loved partner or with their own child. Neither of these almost diametrically opposed patterns need be inauthentic or false in the person's being.

2.2 Evidence of Self-Diversity in Literary Writing

In formally accepting the Nobel Prize for literature, William Faulkner focused on the rendering of personal complexity and conflict as the core element of literary art. Young writers of today, he said, have 'forgotten the problems of the human heart in conflict with itself which alone can make good writing because that is worth writing about, worth the agony and the sweat' (Faulkner 1950). In one later example of such writing—Carey's novel *Oscar and Lucinda* (1988)—the character and core relationships of 'Oscar' come to embodied life with a subtlety and evocative realism that reflect the complexity of human consciousness and the interplay and influence of relationship both within and outside immediate awareness.

In an example of British origin, Arnold Bennett's writing includes his classic 'The old wives' tale' (Bennett 1908). This novel traces the lives, settings and relationships of the two central characters over half a century, from girlhood to death. One striking feature is the interior conversation of the two women. The distinctive plural voices of Constance and Sophie are developed in unusual depth. The interlocking nature of self and qualities of relationship is implied in the extensive self-conversation, withheld and expressed feelings in relationship, and in the different life choices of the sisters.

In Dostoevsky's 'Crime and punishment' (1866), the alienated young man (Raskolnikov) at the centre of this remarkable narrative conceives of and makes himself carry out the murder of an elderly woman pawnbroker, as he sees it, for the sake of his family and to prove to himself that he can stand outside the rules and 'morality' of his world—although afterwards in a developing agony of anxiety and then of inner conflict. The intensity of the book hinges on the sustained and passionate self-talk which, together with interactive communication, exceeds all other text and largely carries the story. Raskolnikov speaks, argues and cries out inwardly, and seeks and hides in strained dialogue with others, in long passages of evocative and mesmerizing writing.

The impact of culture and environment on sense of self, especially with major shifts in life context, is wonderfully illustrated in David Malouf's subtle and powerful novel 'Remembering Babylon' (1993). The central character, Gemmy, worked as a small child in poverty in a sawpit in London and then, with his first sense of belonging, as 'Willet's boy'—in the business of rat catching. At age about 11, he ran through the night from a fire he had started in Willet's abode, climbed into shelter and awoke on a ship at sea, where he entered a further phase of deprivation. Later, at the dawning of his adolescence, he was dropped overboard off the isolated Queensland coast and washed up, alive, on the shore. There he was found by a group of native aborigines who allowed him to follow and attach himself to their band. He became attuned and knowing of their world and grew among them to mid-20s idiosyncratic manhood. Great development in implied selfhood naturally occurred, but without complete severance from his former identity.

Gemmy learned of a coastal settlement of white people near his tribal area, observed them unseen and finally approached a group of children and was then drawn into an affiliation with their family. Although soon accepted into felt relationships with this family and a few others, and on a journey of development from the impoverished 'British' childhood self of his earlier life, Gemmy's aboriginal linkage became disturbing to some other members of the white community. Their threats and abuse divided the community, and Gemmy's fragile membership became unbearable to him, and he disappeared to rejoin the black tribal community. One can speculate that his inner selves never made peace partly because there was no peace between his relationships with the black and white communities in which these selves evolved.

2.3 Evidence of Self-Diversity from Transcripts and Case Studies of Clients in Therapy

In a self at odds with itself differing subself, voices sit in uneasy or opposed relation and the client person may be anxious, depressed and/or stuck in trying to fend off part of his or her own self-being. The illustrations that follow complement those offered in my last book (2005, pp. 8–11). The first to mention is Rogers' (1954) remarkable therapy case study that included a multi-sided focus on the self-concept. For the client, 'Mrs Oak', finding words to express herself was a difficult trial-and-error process, and she struggled to put the pieces of her felt experience and meaning into some sort of coherent whole. She had entered therapy from a context of very disturbed relationships with her husband and daughter, and an implied crisis of meaning in her life. From Rogers' account and interview excerpts, most of her discourse involved difficult self-sharing and searching, with much fluctuation in focus.

Mrs. Oak was a very wounded and vulnerable yet determined person, profoundly lacking confidence at the start in her own voice and capacities and handicapped in connecting felt experience with communicative expression. In effect, the client's overt focus was mainly on relationships within herself, including her gradual discovery that she was and could be a self with agency and ability in relationship. Implicitly, however, she inhabited a very distinctive self with her therapist, she had been almost another person with her daughter and she could not give of herself as a sexual being with her husband. Little or no information is given about relationships with her parents or other family or people in her life. At the time of this study, even though the client's self was closely studied from different vantage points (actual and ideal, as perceived in the past, as seen by the client or by others, etc.), the idea that a person's experience of self naturally differed according to the relational context was not yet in the purview of client-centred thought.

One of the clients Rogers interviewed much later, in the 1970s, was codenamed 'Sylvia'. In the transcript of their published fifth session (Farber et al. 1996, pp. 261–276), Sylvia implies at least four modes of self-being, a firm parent mode with her children, a distinctly different mode in her relationship with Rogers, a third kind with black men—to whom she found herself very strongly attracted—and evidently another mode with her parents. With Rogers, she allowed herself to be dependent (her word), vulnerable and comforted. Her parents' conditional attitudes included clear disapproval of her interest and attraction to black friends (A post-Rogerian understanding of the dynamics of this conflict is briefly discussed in my 2005 book, p. 10.). My own therapy with a former client (Barrett-Lennard 2009) illustrates a more relationship-centred variant of the person-centred approach:

> Sophie (to give her a new name) was at war inside herself and haunted by experiences in relationship, especially in her family. She also felt knotted, stuck and revolted by a bad, almost alien entity inside herself. On the 'outside' she was an attractive and in many ways resourceful young woman. In the self that she mostly spoke to me from she was in an agony of frustration and despair over the dark, sneaky-bad and alien identity she harboured within her outwardly acceptable self. With her parents, especially her father, she held herself stiffly, guarded and with no spontaneity – by implication, in another mode of self-being. She also felt despoiled by her earlier relation with another family member, with its own very disturbing memories. Her way of being with me gradually became more focused and expressive in her path of exploration of self and relationship. Sophie's problems, as she saw them, were stuck within her though rooted in past relationships and with crippling effect on most present associations. She had been largely 'frozen' in the past with men, and felt handicapped in that side of her life.
>
> Sophie's and my relationship, our forming 'we', was born out of where we each came from and it was not an easy birth. Each of us was strongly motivated in distinctive ways and we were able to manage the challenges and come to a productive partnership. Early on, I came to realise that she very easily took my response as 'reading' her from the outside, or explaining her issue, not simply showing I was with her in taking in *her* feeling and meaning. She needed that sense of 'witness' with me, *before she could be sure herself that she was saying what she felt*. One of my own retrospective learnings is that *communicating back and forth is not merely an exchange of messages but always part of the relationship in which they happen. The messages are ripples in the flow or stream of this relationship, and have their meaning within this ongoing flow*. Among other things Sophie was anxious about whether I would take her seriously and 'hang in' there with her for the long haul – and it proved to be a several-year haul! She gradually saw herself in a different light, felt differently in her family relationships, and experimented and spread her wings in more context-sensitive and versatile ways. She did not become less complex but into a different quality of partnership within herself and in her relationships [see Barrett-Lennard (2009) for a fuller picture of Sophie's and my journey through her therapy].

Some other authors in the person-centred orbit have articulated ideas about self-diversity, from observation in their practices (see Vahrenkamp and Behr 2004). One of the first, David Mearns (e.g. 1999), noted that it is not unusual for a client in therapy to identify and even give names to differing inner personalities or subselves. These varied *configurations of self*, he implied, can differ from each other in attitude and ways of coping, and even reflect somewhat differing moralities. The subself systems live together like members of a family, varying in their relation to each other. Gestalt therapist Erving Polster devoted a whole book (1995/2005) to a 'therapeutic exploration of self-diversity'. Polster emphasized that a person is 'host to a population of selves' (p. 41). One of his mentioned clients displayed patterns of self that pivoted on being competent, respected or admired, and determined, patterns that he feared were phony. He is described as feeling worthless inside and negatively stubborn. Through his therapy, the discrepancies greatly diminished though they did not disappear from his thought. Polster evidently considers, as I do, that the forming of multiple patterns of self is a natural part of our complex nature as humans.

2.4 Evidence from Research and Systematic Theory Focusing on Self-Diversity

The directly relevant formal research grows out of my own work and is at a relatively early stage. The roots of this interest are in a paper subtitled *Relations within the self—self within relationship* (Barrett-Lennard 2000/2007). This framed the idea of self-identity forming through varied crucial relationships, each context drawing self-formation in a distinctive direction. The contexts typically would include parent–child relations and any relationships with siblings, with one's own child, with teachers and supervisors or 'bosses', with close friends, with opponents or enemies and in teams or other groups of special importance to the person. How much the resulting 'contextual subselves' varied and how they worked together, for example, as complementary partners or discordant opposites in the person's total make-up, would differ from one person to another.[2]

My method of study centred on development and use of a multi-self-descriptive questionnaire. Earlier client-centred therapy research (Butler and Haigh 1954; Ends and Page 1959) provided a useful pool of self-descriptive items to draw from and adapt. The previous instrument gave what amounted to a generalized picture of self. The new questionnaire, called the contextual selves inventory (CSI), taps into the ways in which self is experienced during engagement in *each one* of a sample of key life relationships. Fifty-eight variously recruited participants answered the CSI in its first 45-item form. Useful data were obtained, but the task proved very demanding for respondents. For the next study, an abbreviated 16-item form was answered by 70 participants in three different workshops (Barrett-Lennard 2008). Participant self-descriptions supported the hypothesis that the way that the self is viewed tends to be highly responsive to context. The data, for

---

[2] At one extreme, a person's subself modes might be so compartmentalized that while manifesting one mode they would disown or be unaware of any other mode. At an opposite well-functioning pole, the person generally would be quite aware of their diversity and each mode of self-being would be a congruent and adaptive expression of self in that context. No mode would simply repeat an exact pattern, but would work as a dynamic resource that continued to evolve through fresh experience and overlap with other permeable modalities. All this could in principle be empirically studied and tested.

example, from all 52 members who provided six self-descriptions yielded statistically marked overall variation in self-descriptions on 14 of the 16 items (ibid). Detailed analyses of answer distributions for the individual items and how the items were inter-correlated and tended to cluster into subgroups or factors (ibid) have contributed to further refinement of the CSI in 24-item form (Barrett-Lennard 2011): Examples of present items are as follows:

> *I take initiative, raise issues, start things.*
> *I look for alibis and excuses for myself if things go wrong.*
> *I forgive easily—don't hold grudges or try to 'get even'.*
> *It is pretty hard to be myself.*
> *I am inwardly on my guard.*
> *I am imaginative and can share my dreams.*
> *I put on a front when I'm uneasy–not showing how I feel.*
> *I tend to follow, letting the other person/people take the lead.*

Respondents rate the CSI items on a scale of 1 (never or not at all like me) to 7 (very or always like me) *in the context of each specified life relationship*. Opposite each self-statement, there are answer spaces arranged in columns on the answer sheets, one column for each relational context. The top of each column shows what that self-context is, for example, with the person's spouse/partner, their mother, father, sister or brother, best friend, boss or teacher and disliked person or enemy. A recently completed (student) research application using the 24-item CSI further confirms promise of the method. Partly to extend the conceptual positioning for related further work, the self-relationship nexus in human life invites further examination, after mention of another source of systematic theory that could lend itself to fresh research.

Close conceptual study of relationship viewed as the primary architect of personal being is at the forefront of Kenneth Gergen's work. Especially, since his 1991 book *The saturated self* came into prominence, this author has been a visible and energetic advocate of relationship-centred thought. The human mind in his understanding develops through and is embedded in relationship. As expressed in his latest book, titled *Relational being* (Gergen 2009), 'our mental vocabulary is essentially a vocabulary of relationship' (ibid. p. 70). The author proposes that 'mental discourse originates in relationship', 'functions in the service of relationship' and amounts to 'action within relationships'—also described as 'co-action' (ibid, pp. 70–76). More broadly, 'rational thought, intentions, experience, memory and creativity are not prior to relational life, but are born within relationships… [they are] embodied actions that are fashioned and sustained within relationship' (ibid, p. 95).

3 The Yin and Yang of Self and Relationship

If personal identity is viewed as only and entirely a relationally derived and socially constituted phenomenon (see discussions by Gergen 1991, 1994, 2009) the whole idea of *a self* as an entity or process in its own right becomes problematic.

However, the same kind of argument could be turned around and applied to the phenomenon of relationship. It might be argued, and indeed has often seemed to be implied, that human association may operate simply in the service of separate autonomous selves. Neither extreme view is credible to me. The concept of a personal self has been pivotal in person-centred theory and research. To jettison, the idea of self would suggest that persons are not distinct—though each one is a whole bounded and individually conscious organism. Granted that this immediate discourse on self and relationship is an enterprise in understanding, not about final truths and reliant on the use of language, there is more to say about the self-relationship connection drawing on the metaphor of yin and yang.

Given that the self or subselves develop and live through relationship, they are an outcome, an outcome rooted in the active potential of the human organism and formed in relationship. The resulting self feeds into the quality of further relationships, which as they develop also act back on the still (and perhaps always) formative self. If one thinks of self and relationship as living systems, this mutuality of influence is just a part of how things work in the real world. No one relationship, nor the whole person, possesses autonomy; each, of their nature, is engaged with other human and non-human systems. This differs from Rogers' thought (e.g. 1963) about well-functioning persons with respect to his stress on the importance of autonomy—which does not work if one thinks systemically. My thought is in accord, however, with having felt agency and responsibility in one's world—as also implied by Rogers.

There can be no self without relationship, understood as the principal vehicle by which self-identity comes into being. Similarly, there can be no relationship without some connection or conjoining of separable entities—as is most evident in the forming of a new relationship. Thus, in their forming, self and relationship are intertwined. They are not the same, not the same order of system, but in general neither can exist without the other. There are exceptions, notably, in the case of an infant in whom a self cannot be said to have formed though the parent–child relationship is one of strong attachment. Also, relationships can be quite asymmetrical, as when one person feels attracted or in some way connected, but without reciprocated feeling by the other or even (as can happen) without the other's awareness of the first person. In this case, the other has subjective presence for the first person, as also is true in vivid memory of an important relationship that the other party has abandoned or where they have died.

A consistent yin and yang of association between self and relationship leaves room for great variation in specific quality. A harshly conditional attitude that a parent or partner might manifest in a relationship then influences the other towards a guarding posture to avoid hurt and, behind this, an inner critic may grow in them that is judgmental of itself. Conditional attitudes can of course be mutual and, in any case, are expressed within a system in which nothing is completely independent in its process or without any returning effect. The phenomenon of loneliness, to turn to next, is complex in its process and of great personal and social importance.

4 Loneliness and the Self

Loneliness has many faces and its varieties may be considered under the three broad headings of self-estrangement, interpersonal loneliness and the loneliness of alienation or non-belonging (Barrett-Lennard 2001, 2005, Chap. 8). Under the first heading, a quality of loneliness can result from subself separation to the point that a part or mode of self is lost from any clear awareness by the most dominant or frequently activated part. This way of being 'out of touch on the inside' seems to sap energy, confidence and vitality, and any sense of being at home with oneself. It may be such a low-grade and chronic detachment within the self and with others that the person is not aware of it except, perhaps, during special moments of self-reflection or exceptional contact with another person.

The literal loss or fracture of a person's sense of self, which may occur when the stresses of their relational and inner world are overwhelming, and the person closes down into a desperate shielding process described as 'acute schizophrenia', is a more extreme form of self and relational disconnection. The not uncommon experience of periodic weird dreams, or other episodes of temporarily slipping out of 'the trance of everyday consciousness', may if we think on it help any of us to feel more fellowship for people who are stuck in their nightmares. A person in such a nightmare may feel an outsider in a slippery, shifting world that eludes them, deeply uncertain of who she/he is, and very afraid of any relationship. All this is to be in a terribly lonely cut-off place.

There is another kind of lack of any distinct sense of self. Some people seem never to have developed much sense of being a known and knowable person. They can appear to live in an almost 'relationless' world, involving superficial or indifferent response from others. Painful attenuation of a personal connection can also develop from the undoing of a foundation of personal life that had been rich with meaning. Ways this can happen include the impact of being transported to a totally different and unfamiliar living environment or handicapped by injury and loss of capacities formerly taken for granted, or caught up in major political and social upheavals in the milieu of 'home'.

Interpersonal loneliness can arise from inexperience and paucity of close relationships as well as from the very disturbing changes already mentioned. As a naturally bonding species, humans have built-in potential for deprivation. The human self is restricted in its development where a person has had no experience in relationships with siblings or other childhood contemporaries; little if any parenting where emotional attachment and example are built-in; and/or an absence of contact with any *un*like others. Such a person is a relative stranger to the process of meeting and engagement. They may live with an unfilled hunger or aching loneliness for closeness of relationship, perhaps for a friend or a lover, for felt companionship or for a child to nurture.

Contexts and kinds of loneliness do not end here. Perhaps because of our tribal origins, it appears to be in our nature to hunger for community, for a sense of belonging within and as part of a larger world than immediate family, friends and close group relations. Without this development and linkage of a communal identity, persons feel no rootedness and sense of inclusion in a world of fellow humans who recognize them and assume mutual belonging. Alienation from the wider world can lead to an exclusive concern with self or to sole reliance on immediate family or other close allies.

Each of these levels and qualities of loneliness is a systemic process with potential to perpetuate itself. However, felt systems can change when qualitatively quite different experiences do happen and register for the person. In view of the nature and origins of loneliness, a crucial new experience would involve other people or, possibly, a striking new engagement with non-human life. Clearly, the new experience would need to be highly relevant in the person's own eyes if it is to meet their lonely thirst for bonding connection and inclusion. Cacioppo and Patrick (2008) have contributed further searching discussion and thought in this area, and my previous book (2005, pp. 108–112) amplifies what is said here. It remains in this chapter to speak briefly about the life and association of the self in big organized modern systems.

5 The Relational Self in Big Systems

Any big system, such as a country, large ethnic or religious community or major organization, embraces a great many more relationships than there are members, since most people would have a range of associative links within the system. For example, in a large nation state, personal selves and face-to-face relationships exist in a vast landscape of human association on many levels. Each person-self defines itself in some degree by its membership in the whole as well as in diverse groups within the whole. The unequal association between a person and their country or nation under its existing leadership may have great significance to them, positive, negative or mixed.

One principle in the study and portrayal of the human associative world is that any relationship is a system associated with other systems on the same level (or of the same generic kind) and is also nested in larger systems of association. Family relationship systems, for example, exist in two-way relation with their ambient community or subculture. Closely linked work teams usually operate in parallel with other teams as well as in interactive relation with the larger organization of which they mutually are part, etc. Thus, person-selves typically live and evolve within a complex environment of relationships, in which systems of relation on a variety of levels carry influence to and from the centre of interpersonal life. Surrounded by this complexity, it is hardly surprising that personal selves are complex and multi-configured.

Zooming out to an even broader view, a nation state that suffers 'civil' war, or war with another state or people, is not only a context for extreme personal suffering and loss of individual life but for destruction, stress-induced breakdown and distortion of relationships. War is itself a way of relating, usually, under the condition of extreme perceived threat or ambition by at least one of the protagonist people systems or their leaders. Some members may develop a rewarded highly combative or warrior subself. Most are greatly disempowered by societal or warring conflict and may develop a quality of victimhood within the self. A change in the balance of alternatives within the self may come from a renewed sense of safety within the larger system and of lived experience in smaller groups.

Even a peacetime pluralistic civil society involves a great ocean of relationships of hugely varied kind and quality. A positive ethos would be one in which the qualitative development and well-being of the human self in relationships and systems at all levels is a generally pervasive value in practice. There are some principles but no blueprint for this movement in this direction, which, necessarily, would be a continuous self-adjusting process (Barrett-Lennard 2012, Chap. 9). Particular contributions by others in the person-centred movement reflect related ideas and a very similar ethic (see Kriz 2008; Neville and Dalmau 2008; contributions in Proctor et al. 2006).

6 Conclusion

This exploration started from the position that self-diversity is a natural expression of our complex make-up and exposure to diverse others. Evidence of the complex multi-configured nature of the human self is all around us in everyday life, in the literature and in therapy discourse. Pertinent systematic research also has begun, but is limited and needed to more fully understand how this natural plurality works. Core propositions are that humans are both creatures of *and* co-creators of relationship and that relationship and self are closely intertwined and interdependent. We crucially overlap each other in features of consciousness though each person lives in a more or less differing orbit of relationships and is distinctive in the totality of his/her conscious being. We tend to experience loneliness through our inner plurality of being, a loss of key relationships or failure of larger systems of belonging. Our big system environments claim coping attention that often leaves us hurrying past one another with little mutual awareness or self-nurturing relation.

References

Barrett-Lennard, G. T. (2000). The warp and weft of therapy: Relations within the self~Self within relationship. Presented at La Trobe University and at the ICCCEP Conference in Chicago. Privately circulated, and later published in French (2007 listing, below).

Barrett-Lennard, G. T. (2001). Levels of loneliness and connection: Crisis and possibility (in English, with summary in German). *PERSON. Zeitschrift für Klientenzentrierte Psychotherapie und personzentrierte Ansätze,* 5(1), 58–64.

Barrett-Lennard, G. T. (2005). *Relationship at the centre: Healing in a troubled world*. London: Whurr/Wiley.
Barrett-Lennard, G. T. (2008). The plural human self under study: Development and early results from the contextual selves inventory. In *Proceedings of the 43rd Annual Conference of the Australian Psychological Society*.
Barrett-Lennard, G. T. (2009). From personality to relationship: Path of thought and practice. *Person-Centred and Experiential Psychotherapies*, 8(2), 79–93.
Barrett-Lennard, G. T. (2011). Contextual selves inventory: Directions and parts A & B. Unpublished research questionnaire available by email from the author.
Barrett-Lennard, G. T. (2012). Relationship as core of the life process. Book manuscript under publisher review.
Bennett, A. (1908). *The old wives' tale*. London: Hodder & Stoughton.
Butler, J. M., & Haigh, G. V. (1954). Changes in the relation between self-concepts and ideal concepts consequent upon client-centered counseling. In C. R. Rogers & R. F. Dymond (Eds.), *Psychotherapy and personality change* (pp. 55–75). Chicago: University of Chicago Press.
Cacioppo, J. T., & Patrick, W. (2008). *Loneliness: Human nature and the need for social connection*. New York: W. W. Norton.
Carey, P. (1988). *Oscar and Lucinda*. St Lucia: University of Queensland Press.
Dostoevsky, F. (1866). *Crime and punishment* (Trans. by Constance Garnett and republished in Cleveland by Fine Editions Press: 1947).
Ends, E. J., & Page, C. W. (1959). Group psychotherapy and concomitant psychological change. *Psychological Monographs*, 73(10, Whole No. 480).
Farber, B. A., Brink, D. C., & Raskin, P. M. (1996). *The psychotherapy of Carl Rogers: Cases and commentary*. New York: Guilford Press.
Faulkner, W. (1950). Untitled *Nobel Prize 'banquet speech'*: http://www.nobelprize.org/nobel_prizes/literature/laureates/1949/faulkner-speech.html.
Gergen, K. J. (1991). *The saturated self: Dilemmas of identity in contemporary life*. New York: Basic Books.
Gergen, K. J. (1994). *Realities and relationships: Soundings in social construction*. Cambridge: Harvard University Press.
Gergen, K. J. (2009). *Relational being: Beyond self and community*. Oxford: Oxford University Press.
Kriz, J. (2008). *Self-actualization: Person-centred approach and systems theory*. Ross-on-Wye, UK: PCCS Books.
Malouf, D. (1993). *Remembering babylon* (p. 1994). London: Chatto & Windus; Vintage.
Mearns, D. (1999). Person-centred therapy with configurations of self. *Counselling*, 125–130.
Neville, B. & Dalmau, T. (2008). *Olympus, Inc.: Intervening for cultural change in organizations*. Greensborough, Victoria: Flat Chat Press (RMIT).
Polster, E. (1995/2005). *A population of selves: A therapeutic exploration of personal diversity*. San Francisco: Jossey-Bass (1995); Gouldsboro: Gestalt Journal Press (2005).
Proctor, G., Cooper, M., Sanders, P., & Malcolm, B. (Eds.). (2006). *Politicizing the person-centred approach: An agenda for social change*. Ross-on-Wye, UK: PCCS Books.
Rogers, C. R. (1954). The case of Mrs. Oak: A research analysis. In C. R. Rogers & R. F. Dymond (Eds.), *Psychotherapy and personality change (259–348)*. Chicago: University of Chicago Press.
Rogers, C. R. (1961). *On becoming a person: A therapist's view of psychotherapy*. Boston:Houghton Mifflin.
Rogers, C. R. (1963). The concept of the fully functioning person. *Psychotherapy: Theory, Research and Practice*, 1, 17–26.
Vahrenkamp, S., & Behr, M. (2004). The dialog with the inner critic: From a pluralistic self to client-centered and experiential work with partial egos. *Person-Centered and Experiential Psychotherapies*, 3(4), 228–244.

Higher-Order Change Within the Person-Centered Approach

Joseph Hulgus

1 Introduction

Whether due to the pressure of modern times or increasing uncertainties in the world, many cultures have drifted into a "results-based" attitude toward others, both individually and collectively. As a psychologist, I see this most prominently in one of the major movements (in the USA, Germany, and the UK, at least) in the field—the "evidence-based treatment" (EBT) movement. However, a similar phenomenon can be seen in U.S. schools and other institutions, often under the banner of increased "accountability" for one group or another. One result of this phenomenon is a business-like focus on "product" versus process, even in things like relationships. Thus, many interpersonal climates are now dominated by social isolation and interpersonal disconnection (Clay 2000; House 2001; Wolf 2006). However, there are exceptions to this relational expectation, some of which may set the stage for fortuitous change and growth to occur.

While PCA was not formally offered as a systems theory, it has many of the characteristics of one (see Kriz elsewhere in this volume). As a path to growth, PCA provides a rich and nurturing context for change in a number of domains (psychotherapy, education, interpersonal relations, etc.). Another thing PCA shares with systems theories is that there is great diversity in views on the ways to promote change, but little agreement on what actually produces change. Fraser and Solovey (2007) have argued that all effective psychotherapeutic approaches share common characteristics of helping people with a particular type of cognitive and perceptual shift that facilitates the resolution of persistent problems. I would argue that this is precisely what PCA has done and does do in a variety of domains and does so in a most humane manner. This chapter will provide some groundwork for this assertion and illustrate how this is so in a variety of domains.

J. Hulgus (✉)
Missouri State University, 901 S. National Avenue, Springfield, MO 65879, USA
e-mail: Josephhulgus@missouristate.edu

2 PCA and Systems Theory

Systems theory is actually a collection of theoretical perspectives that share some common characteristics. Systems theories are holistic in that, as the famous Gestalt saying notes, "the whole is more than the sum of the parts." That is, that a system is not simply a collection of related parts but possessed an "emergent quality" that results from the unique configuration of member elements. Thus, while families, organizations, communities, or nations may have very similar (or even identical) constituents (i.e., members, characteristics, etc.), each is unique in terms of both form and function (von Bertanffy 1962; Miller 1978). So, it is with PCA; every individual (or family, organization, etc.) is unique and can neither be replicated nor be exactly reproduced.

PCA also posits the "actualizing tendency," as described by Rogers (1986) and extensively written about by others (Van Belle 1980; Bozarth and Brodley 1991) which asserts that each of us are biologically and psychologically predisposed to move toward growth and development. As Kriz (2006) points out, this notion was foreshadowed in systemic terms by Kurt Goldstein in 1939 when he coined the term "self-actualization" to refer to the self-organizing tendencies of systems. In a similar fashion (although using decidedly different language), Maturana and Varela (1988) note that systems are marked by "autopoietic processes"—the dynamic and constant interplay between systemic structure and function that works to help systems (a) overcome negentropic (degenerative) forces and (b) aids in maintaining a systemic homeostatic balance (i.e., a dynamic balance between stability and change). Both propositions, the actualizing tendency and autopoiesis, entail systems moving toward ever higher levels of organizational and functional complexity and sophistication. As Rogers (1986) put it, "Practice, theory and research make it clear that the person-centered approach is built on a basic trust in the person... (It) depends on the actualizing tendency present in every living organism's tendency to grow, to develop, to realize its full potential. This way of being trusts the constructive directional flow of the human being toward a more complex and complete development. It is this directional flow that we aim to release" (Rogers 1986, p. 198). Further, both PCA and systems theory acknowledge the importance of self-reference/self-awareness as a basic "systemic" characteristic (of the person or other level of system). Finally, both PCA and systems theory, each in their own way, propose that distress comes from incongruence. Within PCA, this incongruence arises from an individual not being true to who they are (i.e., perceiving/being in line with their self-concept). That is, information from within the individual's perceptual field is denied/distorted/ignored when inconsistent with the person's self-concept. Within systems theory, distress also arises from the failure to utilize discordant (but valuable) "feedback" from the systemic environment (either internal or external). This denial leads to a less-than-optimal adaptation to the environment, which entails making accommodating "adjustments" to maintain the systemic homeostatic balance. If not corrected, this compensation often leads to further compensation and less utilization of pertinent (albeit discrepant) information from the environment. These adaptations are somewhat adequate in re-establishing homeostasis in the short-run, but become more pronounced and less adaptive in the long-run, thus progressively exacerbating systemic distress until either (a) the system enacts a transformative change or (b) a spontaneous discontinuous change occurs.

3 Family Systems Theory

As previously noted, there are a variety of systems theories, including family systems theory. Family systems views arose from a variety of previous traditions including more traditional psychodynamic perspectives, Adlerian conceptualizations, cybernetics, human and biological systems theories, and other types of communications theories. Most relevant to the current discussion is the work of the Mental Research Institute (MRI) of Palo Alto, California. As one of the early sites of research an innovation in family systems work, it became home to many of the leading figures in the development of family therapy, a tradition that is carried on today. While much of the earliest work was led by figures like Don Jackson and Gregory Bateson, a subgroup of psychologists, physicians, and communication theorists provided the theoretical underpinnings of what would become the foundation of all family therapy and systems consultation approaches to emerge from MRI. Summarized in their seminal volume, "Change: Principles of Problem Formation and Problem Resolution," Watzlawick et al. (1974) lay out the guiding threads drawn from philosophy, psychology, mathematics, and logic that would forever shape the Palo Alto group's work. More specifically, they drew on the Theory of Groups and the Theory of Logical Types to craft their theoretical (and later, practical) underpinnings. They tried to contend with the interdependence of persistence and change. Group Theory, primarily drawn from mathematical logic, deals with (among other things) relationships between elements and the whole of which they are a part. It concerns change within a system that stays relatively invariant as a whole.

The Theory of Logical Types is a philosophical perspective, which fundamentally postulates that systemic change cannot be instigated from the same level as the system in question, but must be influenced by the systemic level at the next higher level of abstraction or above. That is, it is not possible to change the system (group) from within the system (group). While this has some logical appeal, when applied to living systems, it runs counter to everyday experience. That is, we note changes all around us (and in us) all the time. However, from the perspective of the Theory of Logical Types, what's happening is that we are simply not making distinctions between levels of groups. That is, you can have change within a group, but for the group to fundamentally change its nature, you would need a "change of change" (i.e., meta-change), instigated from (at least) the next higher logical level of abstraction. To illustrate, Watzlawick et al. (1974) note a common example often offered by Gregory Bateson. Bateson noted that motion is an excellent example of change. Thus, you can move or not, either being a change from the previous state (i.e., motion or rest). However, the notion of acceleration implies a change of motion (i.e., a meta-change). Thus, at one level you can move or not, but once moving you can go faster or slower. A related example is to consider an automobile with a manual transmission. If you put the vehicle in first gear and depress the accelerator, you will move forward. However, the "range of allowable behavior" of the gear you are in will limit your speed. Thus, you will only go so fast and no faster. To go faster than first gear allows, you need to shift gears into a higher gear, which will allow a new range of behavior for the vehicle.

To help characterize this process, Watzlawick et al. (1974) proposed what they called "first-order" and "second-order" changes. First-order change, in behavioral terms, is a simple change of behavior that solves some problem. It could be anything from moving left instead of right to overcome an obstacle to talking in shorter sentences instead of longer ones to help promote understanding in communication. It is a simple change of behavior, but not a change in ways of behaving. This type of change is the most common form we encounter in human behavior, given that most problems encountered can be overcome with a simple change of behavior. However, sometimes we become stuck attempting to apply solutions to a problem from within the same solution set and become stuck.

4 Problem Formulation and Resolution

Fraser and Solovey (2007), working from this general conceptual model, provide further explication of how problems arise. They note that problems can actually come from four sources: (a) attempting to solve a problem when one does not actually exist; (b) under-responding to a problem that requires a solution; (c) over-responding to a problem that requires a solution; or (d) responding to a problem at the wrong level (i.e., applying a first-order solution when a second-order solution is needed). Thus, a problem of type (a) might be when a parent attempts to "motivate" a child toward a behavioral change for which they are not developmentally ready. Problems of type (b) would be things like a parent not responding immediately, clearly or assertively when told by a child about being abused by someone. Problems of type (c) can be seen in situations such as adults responding to children's sexual exploration as if it is sexual abuse. Finally, a problem of type (d) might be avoiding things (i.e., objects, places, circumstances) that produce a phobic response, thus reinforcing the phobic response. In each case, the solution to the problem often times requires a somewhat surprising, even paradoxical solution to resolve the "stuckness."

As noted previously, most problems are usually and easily resolved by a simple first-order solution. When they are not, however, there is the possibility of creating "stuckness" through the application of repeated first-order solutions. As others have noted (Watzlawick et al. 1967, 1974), this cycle of first-order change attempts (a) often results in considerable frustration for those involved, (b) fails to solve the original problem, and (c) generates a new problem (i.e., the successive application of first-order solutions when a second-order solution is needed). This situation has variously been called the "game without end" (Watzlawick et al. 1967) or "the same damn thing over and over again" (Fraser and Solovey 2007, p. 51). Fundamentally, it is when the original problem fades into the background and the new problem is the attempted solution.

To break out of this repetitive problem, a second-order shift is required (i.e., a solution from outside the current solution set). Such shifts, however, are met with hesitance or clear resistance, due to their very nature. As Watzlawick et al. (1974) noted, "the occurrence of second-order change is ordinarily viewed as something uncontrollable, even incomprehensible, a quantum jump, a sudden illumination which unpredictably comes at the end of long, often frustrating mental and emotional labor, sometimes in a dream, sometimes as an act of grace in the theological sense" (p. 23). Thus, it reflects that transformative moment when an unexpected solution or perspective on a problem situation shifts (or begins to shift), allowing for some transformation of the previously experienced "stuckness."

Fraser and Solovey (2007) have gone so far as to propose that this transformative shift is what underlies many psychological interventions. Examples from psychotherapy include such things as follows: working with a phobic person to decrease their reactivity to a feared object through progressively approaching it; helping a client openly express thoughts and feelings that are highly intropunitive and are constantly reverberating internally; and helping a couple discuss a feared topic openly and thoroughly. Examples from other domains are also illustrative:

- When a parent refocuses away from trying to force a particular "attitude" in their child toward focusing on the particular behavior they want to see.
- The Zen practice of focusing on the fundamentals of archery (i.e., breathing properly, drawing the bow, correct body posture), rather than hitting the target.

5 The Alliance and Influence

Research on psychotherapy notes the importance of the alliance, which incorporates the core conditions (empathy, genuineness, unconditional positive regard), as well as cognitive and mutual goal-related aspects (Horvath and Luborsky 1993; Summers and Barber 2003). Generally, however, it is often used interchangeably with "relationship." Psychotherapy research has long sought to separate out relational aspects from intervention aspects. However, efforts to do so have generally not been successful. In fact, research (Luborsky et al. 1975; Lambert 1992; Wampold 2001) has suggested that interventions, regardless of theoretical bent, tend to have similar degrees of influence on therapeutic outcomes, and less of an influence than relational variables.

If it is not meaningful to separate intervention from relationship, then in significant ways, relationship *is* the intervention, a view consistent with PCA. This notion gains support from a somewhat unexpected source—interpersonal communications theory. Watzlawick et al. (1967), in addressing the relationship between communication, behavior, and intervention, note that

1. you cannot not behave (i.e., behavior has no opposite)
2. since communication is behavioral, then one cannot not communicate
3. all communication has some value/meaning
4. within interpersonal contexts, since we cannot not behave and communicate, then we cannot not influence each other in some way
5. thus, we cannot not influence each other (regardless of whether it is our intent to do so or not).

Thus, all relationships are "influential," regardless of intent. This is also a long-standing notion within PCA. The question still remains, however: *How* are they influential? That is, how are relationships transformational? Borrowing from a long, earlier tradition of thought (Watzlawick et al. 1967, 1974; Fraser and Solovey 2007), I offer that it is the nature of the relationship that promotes change. While many others have offered this same observation, here I emphasize the nature of the underlying structure as the contextual phenomenon that promotes transformation. Specifically, within a relationship in which one member is PCA informed, the juxtaposition of the core conditions embodied within this perspective provides a perspective-shifting opportunity for the other member of the relationship who does not normally operate from within a PCA framework. That is, (sadly) the world at large generally does not relationally operate from a base of empathy, genuineness, and unconditional positive regard. Thus, when an individual encounters "stuckness" from repeated application of first-order changes when a second-order change is needed, they often spark greater levels of pessimism, engendering feels something like, "it must be your own damn fault," in line with Seligman's (1990) attributional style characteristics pertinent to an actor's level of pessimism. With heightened levels of pessimism, failure is attributed to an actor's constitutional characteristics, while success is attributed to outside forces (Seligman 1990). In response, they attempt to apply another solution (from within the same solution set), which compounds the problem, and inadvertently reinforces the notion that they are the source of their own problem. Encountering another with a PCA orientation, however, shifts the relational field, presenting the opportunity for a perceptual shift and the possibility for second-order change. Thus, when the person experiencing the "vicious cycle" of first-order change (Fraser and Solovey 2007, p. 23) encounters true empathy, genuineness, and positive regard instead of blaming, distain, and/or indifference, the contextual influences change and offer the opportunity of a shift in perspective. For instance, such encounters may offer the opportunity for the individual experiencing the problem to simply gain a degree of acceptance of the problem (and, by extension, of themselves). Or, it may offer the opportunity for either reframing the problem or even normalizing it. Each of these possibilities reflect possible second-order shifts on the part of the person experiencing the problem that may offer a way out of the cycle of failed first-order solutions. While this may sound like it occurs more in encounters like psychotherapy, it is equally applicable to things like education. Consider how students frequently get "stuck" in trying to understand a new concept and then experience that "aha" moment when facilitated by a teacher who understands and empathizes with the struggle that learning can be.

From one perspective, the notion offered here, that PCA promotes a discontinuous shift into a second-order change partly through contrast with a harsh and unsupportive world, is dismaying. Thus, the question may be asked whether PCA would continue to have the same influence it has if the world were better at enacting the core conditions, regardless of endeavor? My contention is that it would, simply because it is not just the external environment with which PCA is contrasted but also the internal, often intropunitive environment that often arises with "problem stuckness." Further, I would contend that it is precisely these types of second-order shifts that promote self-actualization in general.

References

Bozarth, J. D., & Brodley, B. T. (1991). Actualisation: A functional concept in client-centered therapy. In A. Jones & R. Crandall (Eds.), Handbook of self-actualization. [Special Issue] (Vol. 6, pp. 45–60). Journal of Social Behavior and Personality.

Clay, R. A. (2000). Linking up online: Is the internet enhancing interpersonal connections or leading to greater social isolation? *APA Monit, 31*(4), 20.

Fraser, J. S., & Solovey, A. D. (2007). *Second-order change in psychotherapy.* Washington, D.C.: American Psychological Association.

Horvath, A. O., & Luborsky, L. (1993). The role of the therapeutic alliance in psychotherapy. *Journal of Consulting and Clinical Psychology, 61*(4), 561–573.

House, J. S. (2001). Social isolation kills, but how and why? *Psychosomatic Medicine (American Psychosomatic Society), 63*(2), 273–274.

Kriz, J. (2006). *Self-Actualization.* Norderstedt, Germany: BoD.

Lambert, M. J. (1992). Implications of outcome research for psychotherapy integration. In J. C. Norcross & M. R. Goldfried (Eds.), *Handbook of psychotherapy integration.* New York: Basic Books.

Luborsky, L., Singer, B., & Luboraky, L. (1975). Comparative studies of psychotherapies: Is it true that "everyone has won and all must have prizes"? *Archives of General Psychiatry, 32*, 995–1008.

Maturana, H., & Varela, F. (1988). *The tree of knowledge.* Boston: Shambhala.

Miller, J. G. (1978). *Living systems.* New York: McGraw-Hill.

Rogers, C. R. (1986). Client-centered approach to therapy. In I. L. Kutash & A. Wolf (Eds.), *Psychotherapist's casebook: Theory and technique in practice.* San Francisco: Jossey Bass.

Seligman, M. E. P. (1990). *Learned optimism.* New York: Knopf.

Summers, R. F., & Barber, J. P. (2003). Therapeutic alliance as a measurable psychotherapy skill. *Academic Psychiatry, 27,* 160–165.

Van Belle, H. A. (1980). *Basic intent and therapeutic intent of Carl R. Rogers.* Toronto Canada: Wedge.

von Bertanffy, K. L. (1962). *Modern theories of development.* New York: Harper.

Wampold, B. E. (2001). *The great psychotherapy debate: Models, methods, and findings.* Mahwah, NJ: Erlbaum.

Watzlawick, P., Beavin, J. H., & Jackson, D. D. (1967). *Pragmatics of human communication: A study of interactional patterns, pathologies and paradoxes.* New York: W.W. Norton.

Watzlawick, P., Weakland, J., & Fisch, R. (1974). *Change: Principles of problem formation and problem resolution.* New York: W.W. Norton & Co.

Wolf, E. (2006). Social connections in decline. Universe. Retrieved February 5, 2012, from nn.byu.edu/story.cfm/61082.

Part VII
Game Theory, Research Approaches, and Philosophy

How Can I Trust You? Encounters with Carl Rogers and Game Theory

Len Fisher

1 Introduction

In Smith's novel *Daughters of Darkness* (1996), her ruthless character Ash is asked "You always look after Number One, don't you?" "Doesn't everybody?" he replies with surprise.

Although Ash doesn't know it, he is following in a long philosophical tradition that began with Socrates two and a half thousand years ago. Socrates took it as an axiom that "everyone seeks what is most serviceable to oneself or what is in one's own self-interest".[1] Prominent followers in that tradition have included Niccolò Machiavelli (1532), who argued that a wise ruler ought never to keep faith when by doing so it would be against his interests, and the philosopher Thomas Hobbes (1651), who saw rational self-interest as the cardinal human motive.

Nearly four centuries later, the pursuit of rational self-interest remains a fundamental cornerstone of many Western societies. It forms the foundation of classical free market economics, for example, in which economists view us as members of the disinterestedly rational species *Homo economicus*, making informed decisions based solely on the best outcomes for ourselves (Anon 2005). Some philosophers have even attempted to justify it on moral grounds. Ayn Rand (1964), for example, sees rational self-interest as the "proper moral purpose of a person's life".

Psychologists and sociologists are well aware that this simple picture fails to acknowledge the complexity of our motivations and under-emphasises the role of such factors as public spiritedness, empathy, commitment and justice (Miller

---

[1] Socrates' basic axiom appears in several different guises in the Socratic dialogues reported by Plato. This particularly clear paraphrase is that which is used on the Lander University philosophy course website (http://philosophy.lander.edu/ethics/socrates.html) under the heading "Socratic Paradox".

L. Fisher (✉)
School of Physics, Tyndall Avenue, Bristol BS8 1TL, UK
e-mail: len.fisher@bristol.ac.uk

1999). There is no doubt, though, that the philosophy of looking after Number One runs deeply through Western culture.

The personal and social consequences of looking after Number One are the subject of *game theory*, which looks at our social interactions as games that we play[2] for the highest personal rewards with the lowest possible risk. Game theory was developed in the 1940s, first by the brilliant Princeton mathematician John von Neumann (von Neumann and Morgenstern 1944), thought by some people to have been the model for the remote and impersonal Dr. Strangelove, and later by the mathematical genius John Nash (1951), known to many as the schizophrenic anti-hero of the film "A Beautiful Mind".

These mathematical antecedents are no accident, because game theory is concerned with calculating the odds of success or failure for the various social strategies that we might adopt. Until John Nash came along, however, no one had any idea that game theory would expose a social paradox that has been staring us in the face since the dawn of human society—a paradox which means that the use of "rational self-interest" as a guide to social interactions can often land us in situations where self-interest is the last thing that is being served.

The paradox concerns situations where cooperation would serve everybody's interests, but where the logic of self-interest dictates that an individual can do even better by putting his or her own interests above those of the group and breaking the cooperation (in game theory parlance, *defecting*). What is sauce for the goose is sauce for the gander, however, and when all of the individuals in the group use the same ironclad logic, cooperation collapses and everyone ends up worse off than if they had maintained the cooperation in the first place.

This vicious logical paradox can affect us in many real-life situations, from divorce to war, from the breakdown of individual relationships to global problems such as pollution, resource depletion and climate change; so many, in fact, that it has been proposed as the basic problem of society, since our efforts to live together in a cooperative and harmonious way are so often undermined by it.

But is it a necessary paradox? Or does it arise because we live in an increasingly depersonalised society, where it has become essential to look after Number One, or risk going under? Is there some way that we can change our approach to social interactions and so avoid the paradox?

It has turned out that the key to resolving the problems exposed by game theory is the evocation and development of *trust* (Fisher 2008). Game theorists have so far tackled this question by developing strategies based on the logic of self-interest. Enter Carl Rogers. Rogers' pioneering work on the spontaneous evolution of trust and acceptance in encounter groups (Rogers 1970) and on the evocation of trust through unconditional positive regard in the person-centred approach (Rogers 1942, 1951; Wilkins 2010), offers possibilities for a very different approach.

---

[2] Note that these are *not* the psychological games that Eric Berne refers to in *Games People Play* (1964). Berne does not refer to mathematical game theory in his book, even though it was written 20 years after formal game theory had been established.

My aim in this chapter is to help open a dialogue between psychologists and psychotherapists on the one hand (focussing particularly on the person-centred approach) and game theorists on the other hand[3] to investigate further development of trust and cooperation in human relationships, and how it can help to resolve the paradoxes exposed by game theory. These two groups approach the problem from very different viewpoints, using different axioms and modes of thinking. I believe that it is vitally important for each to understand the other, and to be informed by the other, if we are to make real progress.

My approach is frankly speculative and designed to stimulate discussion rather than offer dogmatic solutions to problems that have been with us since the dawn of civilisation. If I succeed in getting experts from either side of the fence to think about the possibility of a two-pronged attack on these problems, or at least the possibility that there is more than one way of looking at them, then I will have done my job.

2 The Prisoner's Dilemma

I begin by looking at the problem of cooperation from the game theorist's point of view. That point of view is encapsulated in the now-famous parable of *The Prisoner's Dilemma*, which the Princeton mathematician Albert Tucker invented when he was asked to explain game theory to a group of psychologists at Stanford University. As recounted later by his colleague Kuhn (1994):

> Tucker was on leave at Stanford in the Spring of 1950 and, because of the shortage of offices, he was housed in the Psychology Department. One day a psychologist knocked on his door and asked what he was doing. Tucker replied: "I'm working on game theory", and the psychologist asked if he would give a seminar on his work. For that seminar, Al Tucker invented the Prisoner's Dilemma (p. 161).

The story has since appeared in various incarnations. In one of them, two thieves (let's call them Bernard and Frank, after two of the conspirators in the Watergate scandal) have been caught by the police, but the prosecutor has only enough evidence to put them behind bars for 2 years on a charge of carrying a concealed weapon, rather than the maximum penalty of 10 years that they would get for burglary. So long as they both plead "not guilty", they will both get only 2 years, but the prosecutor has a persuasive argument to get them to change their pleas.

---

[3] I am not a practitioner in either field, but a scientist who has written and lectured extensively on game theory in everyday life in an effort to make its socially important discoveries more widely known (see, for example, my *Rock, Paper, Scissors: Game Theory in Everyday Life* (Fisher 2008)). My appreciation of the person-centred approach has come principally from my wife Wendella, a counsellor who uses and has great experience with the person-centred approach, and with whom I have attended a number of encounter groups.

He first approaches Bernard in his cell and points out that if Frank pleads guilty but Bernard doesn't, Frank will receive a reduced sentence of 4 years for pleading guilty, but Bernard will get the maximum 10 years. So, Bernard's best bet, if he believes that Frank will plead guilty, is to plead guilty as well, so as to receive 4 years rather than ten. "Furthermore" says the prosecutor "I can offer you a deal that if you plead guilty and Frank doesn't, you can go free for turning state's evidence!"

No matter what Frank does, it seems that Bernard will always do better for himself by pleading guilty. The logic seems irrefutable—and it is. The trouble is that the prosecutor has made the same offer to Frank, who has come to the same conclusion. So, they both plead guilty—and they both end up in jail for 4 years, rather than the 2 years that they would have received if they had both kept their mouths shut.[4]

Tucker's story of the Prisoner's Dilemma goes straight to the heart of the paradoxes that can arise when we use rational self-interest as our guide to action. It has struck resonances with many people, and literally thousands of articles and dozens of books have been devoted to examining the consequences of its insidious logic and to proposing solutions to the paradox. Not all of these books and articles have been by game theorists. As the journalist William Poundstone recounts in his 1993 book *Prisoner's Dilemma*, philosophers, religious leaders, politicians, psychologists, sociologists, and the inevitable collection of cranks have all had their say.

3 Trust

One of the major conclusions from all serious contributors to the debate is that the key to a solution lies in *trust*. If each of the prisoners in Tucker's story had been able to trust the other not to give them away, their problem would have been solved. But how can such trust be achieved?

Promises are clearly insufficient, as the *dramatis personae* in Puccini's opera *Tosca* discover to their cost.[5] The heroine (Tosca) is faced with an unenviable choice. Her lover (Cavaradossi) has been condemned to death by the corrupt police chief Scarpia. Tosca is left alone with Scarpia, who thinks that he is on to a good thing when he offers to have the firing squad use blank bullets if Tosca will let him have his wicked way with her. Tosca agrees—but is her commitment credible?

Scarpia thinks it is, because he has Tosca on her own in a room from which there seems to be no escape. But Tosca has spied a knife on the table and has

---

[4] If you think that this little story has uncomfortable parallels with the U.S. practice of plea bargaining, you are dead right. This is why plea bargaining has been made illegal in many countries.

[5] This example is due to Bill Poundstone (1993).

worked out that she can win both ways by agreeing to Scarpia's proposal, but actually stabbing him when he comes close.

Unfortunately for Tosca, Scarpia's commitment wasn't credible either! It was no more than an empty verbal contract and (as Hollywood producer Sam Goldwyn is supposed to have said), verbal contracts aren't worth the paper they are written on. In fact, Scarpia has worked out that *he* can win both ways by having his way with Tosca, but not really telling the firing squad to use blank bullets. The upshot is operatic mayhem. Cavaradossi dies, Scarpia dies, and when Tosca finds out what has happened, she flings herself off a castle parapet and she dies too. Everyone is a loser, as is often the way with opera.

Everyone is a loser in real life as well when promises can't be trusted, whether the promise has come from a partner, a politician or a passerby. But how are we to achieve such trust?

The game theorist's answer lies in *credible commitment* to the promise that has been given. Such commitment can be evoked by using the logic of self-interest if (a) the person offering the commitment puts themselves in a position where it is obvious to the other party or parties that the commitment is irreversible, or (b) it can be seen by the other party or parties that it would be too costly for the person offering the commitment to change their mind later.

How might do such strategies work in practice? Below I offer a series of examples. They show that the logic of self-interest can quite often produce practical strategies for demonstrating credible commitment, but that all too often there is a loophole which allows one or other party to cheat on the cooperation for personal advantage and without having to pay too heavy a penalty.

3.1 Deliberately Cutting Off Your Escape Routes

There are three broad ways to do this, each scarier than the last.

3.1.1 Use a Mandated Negotiating Agent

With a legally binding contract, that agent is the law. But there are many "contracts" that we enter into which are not legal contracts, but which are contracts nonetheless. When my brother and I divided up the household jobs between us, our verbal agreement was a contract, and it was enforced because we had a mandated negotiating agent—our father!

If the two prisoners in Tucker's story had each had friends on the outside who could be relied upon to punish the other for giving him away, these would also be acting as "mandated negotiating agents" and would have saved the day.

The loophole with contracts is that they can often be renegotiated (witness what happens when countries or business firms declare bankruptcy) and can in any case be difficult and costly to enforce.

3.1.2 Cut Off Communication

We've all done it. We do it whenever we post a letter, press the "send" button for an e-mail, turn off our mobile phones, or even when we have written our wills. Once we've done it, that's it. We've made a commitment, and that commitment is credible because there is no going back. But we can apologize for the e-mail, change our wills up to the moment that we die and say that we "forgot" to turn our phone on. There's usually a way out.

3.1.3 Burn Your Bridges

Cutting off communication is one way to "burn your bridges", but there are many others. A striking example is that of the Spaniard Hernando Cortés, who led an expeditionary force to invade Mexico in 1519. Cortés scuttled his ships in full view of the on-looking Aztecs, thus making it impossible for his force to retreat, and demonstrating to the Aztecs his commitment to remain.

Two friends of mine found another way to burn their bridges when they decided to do a parachute jump. Both of them got an attack of nerves, with each saying to the other "if you go first, I'll follow you". Neither would really trust the other to follow until they hit on the idea of offering credible commitment by each taking a grip on the other's wrist, so that when one jumped, the other was forced to follow.

Of all the logical strategies for credible commitment, burning your bridges is the one with the most force.

3.2 Making It Too Costly for You to Change Your Mind Later

There are many possible strategies. Here are four major ones:

3.2.1 Put Yourself in a Position Where Your Reputation Will Be Damaged if You do not Deliver

This can be a powerful strategy in personal relationships, because letting down others in the group can do you future damage when they then fail to trust or accept you. It seems to be much less powerful in politics, where promises made in order to gain power are frequently broken later.

A particularly important, and much studied, possibility is to use *repeated interactions*. If you know that you are going to have to cooperate with someone again in the future, you are much less likely to cheat on a promise or renege on a bargain. But people still do.

3.2.2 Move in Steps

Breaking a promise or threat into a series of steps means that, when you get towards the end, most of the promise or threat will have been fulfilled, as happens when homeowners or developers pay builders at the end of each completed phase of a project. But there is a trap here. If you *know* that it is the last step, you may be tempted to renege. A developer, with the project completed, may refuse the last payment, leaving the builder out of pocket, or with the stress and cost of taking the developer to court. A tenant may skip without paying the last month's rent, as has happened to me as a landlord more than once. The message is clear; make the steps (or at least, the last few steps) as small as possible so as to minimise the risk of loss. In the last month of a lease, for example, make the payments weekly rather than monthly, or ask for payment in advance.

3.2.3 Enter Into a Contract

Some contracts are binding, as Faust discovered when he entered into a contract with the devil. But most contracts are not so binding and can be subject to renegotiation. To make them stick, it often needs something extra, such as a penalty clause. The person or body who enforces the clause must also have a good reason to stick to their responsibility. Penalty clauses are of little use if a local planning officer can be bribed into passing a shoddy piece of building work, for example, even though that work does not meet the standards of the contract.

3.2.4 Use Brinkmanship

"I'll shoot" screams a man standing at the counter of a bank "unless you pass over that bag full of money!" How realistic is his threat? It doesn't really matter, because the outcome will be so drastic if he carries it out. That's the essence of brinkmanship, a term coined by U.S. Presidential candidate Adlai Stevenson at the height of the cold war in 1956. Stevenson used it to criticise Secretary of State John Foster Dulles for "bringing us to the edge of the nuclear abyss". It demonstrates credible commitment by making the cost of escape too high, although it is certainly the least likely of the lot to lead to genuine cooperation!

4 Enter Carl Rogers

Logic is not the only way to generate credible commitment. Close involvement within a group can do just as good a job, even between strangers, as Carl Rogers discovered when he studied the behaviour and evolution of encounter groups in the

1960s. Here are some of his observations that I believe are relevant to our discussion here (from Rogers 1970; pages 18, 14, 16, 40, 28 and 50, respectively):

> ... the soil out of which this demand [for encounter groups] grows has two elements. The first is the dehumanization of our culture ...
> A climate of mutual trust develops [in encounter groups] out of [the] mutual freedom to express real feelings, positive and negative.
> ... one of the most common developments is that a sense of trust slowly begins to build ...
> One member ... speaks of the "commitment to relationship which often developed on the part of two individuals ..."
> One of the most fascinating aspects of any intensive group experience is ... the manner in which a number of the group members show a natural and spontaneous capacity for dealing in a helpful, facilitating and therapeutic fashion with the pain and suffering of others
> ... the group seems like an organism, having a sense of its own direction even though it could not define that direction intellectually.

In other words, many people feel alienated and isolated in our wider culture and compelled in self-defence to adopt the dehumanizing "rational self-interest" approach to handling their interactions with most other people—an approach that can lead to the serious problems exposed by game theory. When people are given an opportunity to get together in an initially unstructured group, however, their human qualities come to the fore, trust and mutual support emerge, and the group eventually takes on a dynamic of its own.

This is obviously a very broad generalisation (albeit one that is supported by research), and I put it forward here as a catalyst for discussion rather than as a dogmatic assertion. It shows, at least, that there are at least two possible routes to credible commitment—via strategies based on the logic of self-interest, or through spontaneous group dynamics. In the latter case, I would suggest that the potential for the development of the mutual trust necessary to overcome the paradoxes of game theory depends very much on the size of the group, as illustrated schematically in Fig. 1:

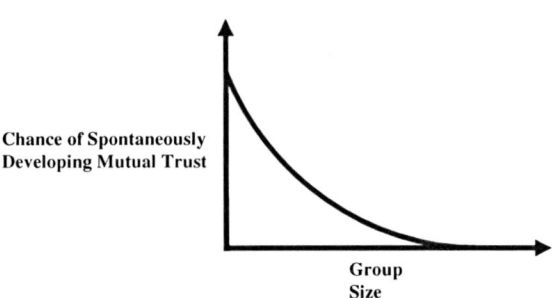

Fig. 1 Potential for mutual trust development sufficient to overcome the paradoxes of game theory as a function of group size

The question is: "Could either of these routes to credible commitment (used separately or in tandem) help us in practice to avoid or escape from situations such as that exemplified by the Prisoner's Dilemma?"

5 The Seven Deadly Dilemmas

Game theorists have identified seven basic situations [which I call *The Seven Deadly Dilemmas* (Fisher 2008)],[6] where the use of rational self-interest takes us to a less-than-ideal place. In addition to The Prisoner's Dilemma, there are

- *The Tragedy of the Commons*, where individuals who share a common resource are each tempted to take more than their fair share. When they all follow this strategy, however, the resource becomes overused and can even disappear, as witness the collapse of many fisheries.
- *The Free Rider* problem (a variant of the Tragedy of the Commons), which arises when some people in a community take advantage of a group resource without paying for it.
- *Chicken* (also known as *Brinksmanship*), where each side tries to push the other as close to the edge as they can, with each hoping that the other will back down first. It can arise in situations ranging from someone trying to push into a line of traffic to confrontations between nations that could lead to war, and which sometimes do.
- *The Volunteer's Dilemma*, in which someone must make a sacrifice on behalf of the group, but if no one does, everyone loses out. Each person is hoping that someone else will be the one to make the sacrifice, which could be as trivial as making the effort to put the garbage out, or as dramatic as one person sacrificing his or her life to save others.
- *The Battle of the Sexes*, where two people have different preferences, such as a husband who wants to go to a ball game while his wife would prefer to go to a movie. The catch is that each would rather share the other's company than pursue their own preference alone. But how can they make the decision?
- *Stag Hunt*, a situation where cooperation between members of a group gives them a good chance of success in a risky, high-return venture, but where an individual can win a guaranteed, but lower, reward by breaking the cooperation and "going it alone".

Here, I examine each of these dilemmas in turn and ask whether logic-based and/or person-centred routes to credible commitment could help to resolve the dilemma.

5.1 The Prisoner's Dilemma Revisited

The prisoners in Tucker's story may have been able to escape their dilemma if each of them had had friends on the outside, willing and able to punish the other

---

[6] Formal logical analysis requires a concept known as the *Nash equilibrium*, which is not difficult to master, but which I have avoided using in the context of this chapter. A description of the seven deadly dilemmas in terms of the Nash equilibrium may be found in my book *Rock, Paper, Scissors* (Fisher 2008).

for giving their friend away. If each prisoner regarded the threat as credible, then rational self-interest would dictate that each should keep his mouth firmly shut. As with so many instances of rational self-interest, however, there could be a loophole. The ratting prisoner's friends might protect him, for example, or the authorities might provide protection, or even a new identity.

Practical experience has also shown that criminals are unlikely to rat on each other if they are members of the same criminal gang. This could be due to the development of trust within the group, the fear of loss of reputation within the group, the anticipation of repeated interactions, or a combination of all of these.

But this story is not just about criminals and criminal gangs. The same principles apply to *any* situation where one individual might be tempted to cheat on cooperation with another for personal gain, whether it be within a marriage, a community or a business arrangement.

5.1.1 Credible Commitment and the Prisoner's Dilemma

"Credible commitment" via a marriage settlement, a contract or fear of loss of reputation provides one possibility for evoking trust, although experience has shown that these logic-based mechanisms are not always reliable. Mutual membership of a group where trust has evolved spontaneously provides a more reliable mechanism—witness the degree of support that members of small communities often offer each other, not to mention church groups or organisations such as the Masons (which provided great support to my mother after my father died).

There is also another possibility—mutual respect based on Rogers' principle of unconditional positive regard, where the reward works both ways. "I have found it highly rewarding", Rogers wrote in his 1961 essay *This Is Me* "when I can accept another person". The person who has received the unconditional acceptance is unlikely to cheat on the person who has offered it, if for no other reason than the risk that the source of acceptance might be cut off. The person who has offered the unconditional acceptance is also unlikely to cheat, not just because of the reward that Rogers wrote about, but simply because he or she *has* offered unconditional acceptance.

Unfortunately, these considerations carry less weight with my next Dilemma—The Tragedy of the Commons, which game theorists have proved may be formally viewed as a set of Prisoner's Dilemmas played out by all of the different pairs of individuals within a group.

5.2 The Tragedy of the Commons

This scenario was brought to public attention by the Californian ecologist and game theorist Garrett Hardin in a 1968 essay with the above title, although philosophers have been worrying about it since the time of Aristotle. Hardin illustrated it with the parable of a group of herders each grazing their own animals on common land, with one herder thinking about adding an extra animal to his herd. An extra animal will yield a tidy profit, and the overall grazing capacity of the land will only be slightly diminished, so it seems perfectly logical for the herder to add an extra animal. The tragedy comes when all the other herders think the same way. They all add extra animals, the land becomes overgrazed and soon there is no pasture left.

The intractable paradox exemplified by the tragedy of the commons underlies family disagreements about inheritance, divorce settlements where the lawyers end up with the bulk of the proceeds, and choices about who should take responsibility for aged parents. On a wider scale, it is responsible for resource depletion, global warming and a host of other global problems (up to and including war).

At its heart lies an insidious logic. When just two people are involved, a gain for one is going to be an obvious loss for the other, and a balance may be struck. When many people are involved, however, the gain for an individual is palpably obvious, but the loss is spread across the group and can be so diluted as to become almost invisible.

We even see it with teaspoons. When a group of Australian medical epidemiologists started wondering about the way in which teaspoons were disappearing from the communal area of their office, they had a lot of fun at first dreaming up unlikely explanations. One was that the spoons had escaped to a planet entirely populated by spoon life-forms, there to live an idyllic existence where they were not being dunked head-down in cups of hot tea or coffee. Another was *resistentialism*—the belief that inanimate objects have a natural antipathy towards humans and are forever trying to frustrate us, in this case by hiding when they are most wanted, in the manner of single socks in a washing machine.

The true explanation, of course, was that they were faced with a domestic version of the Tragedy of the Commons. "Teaspoon users", they said "(consciously or otherwise) make decisions that their own utility [i.e. the benefit to themselves] is improved by removing a teaspoon for personal use, whereas everyone else's utility is reduced by only a fraction per head (after all, there are plenty more spoons…). As more and more teaspoon users make the same decision, the teaspoon commons is eventually destroyed".

It sounds funny when applied to teaspoons, but if you replace the word "teaspoon" by "land", "oil", "fish", "forest", or the name of any other common resource, you will soon see that some very serious global problems have their origins in this vicious circle of logic, which can make its unwelcome presence felt whenever profit goes to an individual person or group of people, but costs are shared by the community as a whole.

5.2.1 Credible Commitment and the Tragedy of the Commons

The Tragedy of the Commons is one of the most serious problems facing us in the world today. The failure of international agreements on fishing quotas, rainforest preservation, global pollution and the like shows how difficult it can be to produce credible commitment by supposedly rational means.

There is no easy solution (in some cases, there may be no solution at all) in terms of the "rational" strategies for producing credible commitment as suggested by game theory. One possibility, however, that has been discussed in many contexts is that of "modularization" of the problem—in other words, breaking the system up into smaller, more self-sufficient units that are less dependent on each other. This has been suggested in the context of the international banking system (May et al. 2008), ecosystems (Allesina and Tang 2012), and social-ecological systems (Ostrom 2009). The key point is that the groups which make the decisions must be small enough to be able to perceive the costs to themselves of various strategies, rather than looking at the benefits and assigning to costs to some nebulous larger group—small communities where the members know and trust each other, villages rather than towns, local communities rather than central bureaucracies. It should work in theory, and Carl Rogers' experience with groups suggests one of the reasons why it can work in practice [as it has been shown to do in many individual instances (Fisher 2008)]. Whether it can be made to work in face of the relentless trend towards social aggregation, and agglomeration is another matter.

5.3 Free Rider

The free rider problem applies to any situation where a resource that has to be paid for cannot easily be restricted to those who have paid for it. The problem can become especially acute when it comes to the care and use of communal resources. The Greek philosopher Aristotle was one of the first to point out its existence when he observed that "That which is common to the greatest number has the least care bestowed upon it".

The Chinese authoress Aiping Mu provides a poignant modern example in her book "Vermilion Gate", which tells the story of her growing up during the cultural revolution:

> During the "storm of communization", peasants put much less energy into working for the collective economy than for themselves, because the rewards were the same no matter how much or how little they worked, and no one could be bothered to take care of the collective property. The most painful experience was eating at the mass canteens, which were supposed to liberate women from daily cooking and hence to increase their productivity and increase the quality of life. The outcome was just the reverse.
>
> Misled by the propaganda, peasants assumed that a life of abundance had begun, and they could eat their fill ... ... the peasants lost nearly everything, even their cooking utensils and food reserves ... ... When the famine ended ... one estimate put the number of deaths in rural China at 23 million (as cited in Fisher 2008, pp. 67–68).

5.3.1 Credible Commitment and the Free Rider

"Free riding" encompasses such actions as littering, fare-dodging, tax-dodging and illegal dumping on both small and large scales. As with the Tragedy of the Commons, it is difficult to deal with because the benefit goes to an individual, but the community shares the costs.

In this case, however, some of the logic-based strategies suggested by game theorists could work. For example, the threat of social disapproval for littering is so strong in Scandinavian countries that there is scarcely a problem, while the threat of punishment in Singapore brings a different sort of severe cost. "Free riding" is also much less prevalent in smaller communities, because repeated interactions with others bring an unacceptably high social cost.

Perhaps the Rogers approach could also help here in the form of a lesson: if each of us first learns to take responsibility for ourselves, and cherish ourselves as individuals, then we are more likely to take communal responsibilities and cherish others.

5.4 Chicken

"Chicken" is not just a game for teenagers. It is all around us, even at the very highest levels, as the philosopher Bertrand Russell pointed out during the Cold War between the U.S.S.R and the United States in the 1950s (Russell 1959):

> Since the nuclear stalemate became apparent, the Governments of East and West have adopted the policy which Mr. Dulles calls "brinkmanship". This is a policy adapted from a sport which, I am told, is practised by some youthful degenerates. This sport is called "Chicken!". ... ... As played by irresponsible boys, this game is considered decadent and immoral, though only the lives of the players are risked. But when the game is played by eminent statesmen, who risk not only their own lives but those of many hundreds of millions of human beings, it is thought on both sides that the statesmen on one side are displaying a high degree of wisdom and courage, and only the statesmen on the other side are reprehensible. This, of course, is absurd. Both are to blame for playing such an incredibly dangerous game. ... (p. 30)

We are constantly playing games of chicken in our everyday lives, whether we are walking towards someone on a narrow sidewalk, hoping that someone else in a group will offer to buy the next round of drinks, or waiting for someone else to tell the boss that he's got things wrong. Whoever makes the first move loses out, while the others gain, but if no one makes a move to resolve the situation, everyone loses out.

5.4.1 Credible Commitment and Chicken

How can we resolve such situations? "Credible commitment" to your threat is hardly an answer (especially if it involves commitment to nuclear warfare!), but there is a different approach—to coordinate your actions.

If both parties simultaneously move slightly aside when walking towards each other, for example, then perhaps neither of them need step down into the gutter. If people agree to talk to the boss as a group, no individual will be singled out. In 1961, for example, towards the end of the Cold War, Kruschev and Kennedy defused the Cuban missile crisis by agreeing to make simultaneous moves—Kruschev to remove the missiles, Kennedy simultaneously lifting the blockade (Fisher 2008).

Simultaneous moves need negotiation, which takes us straight back to trust and credible commitment—each side must trust the other to be committed to fulfilling their side of the bargain, and the commitment must be credible. Strategies based on the logic of self-interest to demonstrate credible commitment to the promise can and do work. But how much easier if the trust is already there through prior small-group interactions!

5.5 The Volunteer's Dilemma

The now-extinct Yagan Indians of Tierro del Fuego had a wonderful word for a situation that we have all experienced. The word was *mamihlapinatapai* and it means "looking at each other hoping that the other will offer to do something that both parties desire to have done but are unwilling to do themselves". It was described in the 1993 Guinness Book of Records as "the most succinct word in any language".

The Yagan Indians did not become extinct through *mamihlapinatapai*, but it certainly encapsulates what we now know as The Volunteer's Dilemma, where someone has to make a sacrifice on behalf of the group, but if no one does, then the whole group will suffer.

Being the volunteer, though, can require a courage amounting to heroism. When a grenade was lobbed into the middle of a platoon led by Sergeant Laszlo Rabel of the U.S. infantry, the platoon members would have died or been seriously injured if they had all stood back hoping that someone else would act. Sergeant Rabel did act, falling on the grenade and sacrificing his own life to save those of his companions.

It is not diminishing Sergeant Rabel's heroism to say that The Volunteer's Dilemma is not usually that extreme. It can amount to no more than offering to put the trash out. But how can we make the decision?

5.5.1 Credible Commitment and the Volunteer's Dilemma

The best answer is for people to *want* to take action on behalf of the group, even though it involves some sacrifice (small or large) to themselves. Offering unconditional positive regard may be seen as such a sacrifice, at least in the short term. So might taking action to relieve others of the responsibility. In both cases, the conditions that have repeatedly appeared in the discussion of other dilemmas come into play—in particular, the spontaneous evolution of trust within small groups.

5.6 The Battle of the Sexes

At last, a problem for which game theory has a solution! It is a problem that confronted me and my English wife when we agreed to divide our time between Australia (where I was born) and England. The problem was that I would like to spend more time in Australia, she would like to spend more time in England, but both of us would rather be together than apart.

The answer was discovered by the Israeli-American game theorist Robert Aumann, who shared the 2005 Nobel Memorial Prize in Economics "for having enhanced our understanding of conflict and cooperation through game-theory analysis". Aumann's answer was for both people to agree to some random way of determining their strategy, such as tossing a coin or drawing a card. In our case, it was the toss of a coin, with the prearrangement that if it came up "heads" she was to stay longer in England before coming out to Australia to join me, with the reverse arrangement if it came up "tails".

We were both better off with this arrangement. Aumann called it a "correlated equilibrium", because it binds the choices of the two parties together in a very neat way. It may seem trivial when a coin toss decides the issue, but Aumann has proved mathematically that it is the most efficient strategy. It can even help to resolve some games of "chicken" where the participants seem to be locked into a mutually destructive collision course, with neither prepared to give way.

5.6.1 Credible Commitment and the Battle of the Sexes

The only problem is credible commitment to abide by the result of the coin toss. Mutual trust is essential. Answers on a postcard, please (they can be copied from any of the discussions above).

5.7 Stag Hunt

The name of this dilemma comes from a story told by the French philosopher Jean-Jacques Rousseau (1754) about a group of villagers hunting a deer:

> If a deer was to be taken, every one saw that, in order to succeed, he must abide faithfully by his post: but if a hare happened to come within the reach of any one of them, it is not to be doubted that he pursued it without scruple, and, having seized his prey, cared very little, if by so doing he caused his companions to miss theirs (para. 9).

Rousseau saw the story as a metaphor for the eternal tension between social cooperation and individual freedom. In his words, when referring to the "social contract" between the individual and the state: "True freedom consists in giving up some of our freedoms so that we may have freedom".

Stag Hunt represents the fragile circumstances in which so many of the world's people now live, especially when it comes to the preservation of individual liberties, freedom of expression, and even the freedom to hold private conversations. When I visited Tibet recently, for example, I found that it was impossible to talk freely with individual Tibetans about the problems in their country because they were frightened that their conversations, or even the fact that they had had a conversation with a Westerner, would be reported by one of their neighbours to the authorities. The Stag was the freedom to talk. The Hare was the more certain reward of spying and reporting secretly on your neighbour. Divide-and-rule works. It is not an easy thing to change, even with the tools of game theory.

5.7.1 Credible Commitment and Stag Hunt

I do not pretend to have an answer, even a theoretical one. If I had, I would be out there, shouting it from the rooftops. To solve such problems requires credible commitment and trust on a massive scale. Perhaps, sadly, the human race is simply not ready for it.

6 Fairness and Empathy

Game theory provides an accurate description of what happens *if* we rely on the logic of self-interest to guide our actions and out interactions. Our very human feelings for fairness and empathy, however, can turn this logic on its head.

One example, which surprised game theorists and psychologists alike when it was first observed, occurs in the "ultimatum game". This game has been played primarily in psychological laboratories (usually with students as subjects) although it has many uncomfortable parallels in real life.

In the game, an experimenter gives an amount of money or other goods to someone, who is then required to offer a proportion to a second person. The second person can then either accept or reject the offer. If they accept it, the money or goods are shared accordingly. If they reject it, neither of them gets anything. That's it. There is no further bargaining; it's a one-off.

What should the "proposer" do? His or her obvious and logical course is to offer as little as possible, because the receiver has to accept it or get nothing. This sort of "take it or leave it" negotiating tactic has been widely used by the powerful to take advantage of the weak and helpless. It is a weapon for those in positions of power.

When researchers handed that power to volunteers in the "ultimatum game", though, they received a surprise. They found that most "proposers" did not try to keep as much as possible for themselves, but offered around half of the total, even when real money was involved. Even more surprisingly, when "receivers" were offered less than 30 %, they often exerted their own power by rejecting the offer, even though this meant that they lost out along with the proposer. "Receivers" seemed very willing to cut off their noses to spite the other person's face—not only in affluent America, but also in countries such as Indonesia, where the sum to be divided was a hundred dollars, and where offers of thirty dollars or less were frequently rejected, even though this was equivalent to 2-week wages (Cameron 1995)!

Our inbuilt senses of empathy, and the altruism to which it can lead, can also help. These senses can be swamped by the perceived need for self-preservation in today's often anonymous and depersonalised society, but they are always there, even in toddlers and chimpanzees (Warneken et al. 2007). There is some evidence that altruistic behaviour provides us with a physiological reward (in the form of the release of brain chemicals that give us the "warm glow" (Moll et al. 2006; Tankersley et al. 2007; Harbaugh et al. 2007)).[7] It would be absurd reductionism to say that brain chemistry and physiology alone account for our feelings, but they obviously play a substantial part. Whatever the origin of these feelings, though, it is clear from our earlier discussion that they offer the most substantial hope of overcoming the serious social dilemmas exposed by game theory—so long as we can learn to use them to create and maintain an atmosphere of mutual trust.

Such an atmosphere arises in encounter groups, where sharing works on two levels. One has its basis in game theory. If I share a personal secret with you, this makes it safer for you to share a secret with me, because you know that, if I betray your secret, you are in a position to betray mine.

The other level is psychological and lies in the fact that sharing creates an empathic bond. There is also a run-on, positive feedback effect that can run through the group, with one bit of sharing triggering memories for others and enabling them to share similar experiences. As those who have felt it know, the empathic bonds that are thus created can be extraordinarily powerful. As Professor Renate Motschnig pointed out in her review of an earlier version of this chapter, the next step is to understand further what "'causes the magic', how it could be transferred to the 'real world' and how aspects of it, combined with other PCA characteristics, could address the dilemmas".

7 Conclusions

The game theorist's approach to credible commitment lies in logic-based strategies where the person offering the commitment demonstrates publicly and conclusively to the other parties that he or she would lose out if they went back on their word. An approach based on Rogers' research and ideas offers a different route—the

---

[7] This "reward" motive provides an interesting link between psychology and game theory, as I discuss in detail in *Rock, Paper, Scissors* (2008).

development of genuine trust through personal interactions based on unconditional positive regard, or in group situations where trust can develop spontaneously.

Both of these approaches have their place when it comes to resolving the problems posed by The Seven Deadly Dilemmas. They can work more effectively (especially those based on Rogers' research and ideas) in societies that contain many small groups, rather than consisting of a large and relatively homogeneous mass. The important thing in either case, though, is that we should be aware of these dilemmas, and of the serious social threats that they pose. Only then can we make genuine progress towards their solution.

References

Allesina, S., & Tang, S. (2012). Stability criteria for complex ecosystems. arXiv:1105.2071v1.
Anon, J. (2005). Homo economicus? Sound economics may lie at the heart of humanity's evolutionary success. *The Economist* (April 7th). (http://www.economist.com/node/3839749).
Berne, E. (1964). *Games people play*. New York: Ballantine Books.
Cameron, L. (1995). Raising the stakes in the ultimatum game: Experimental evidence from Indonesia. Working paper #345, industrial relations section, Princeton University. In R. Slonim & A. Roth (1998) Learning in high stakes ultimatum games: An experiment in the Slovak Republic. *Econometrica, 66*, 569–596.
Fisher, L. R. (2008). *Rock, paper, scissors: game theory in everyday life*. New York: Basic Books.
Harbaugh, W., Mayr, U., & Burghart, D. (2007). Neural responses to taxation and voluntary giving reveal motives for charitable donations. *Science, 316*, 1622–1625.
Hobbes, T. (Thomas Hobbes of Malmesbury). (1651). *Leviathan, or the matter, forme, and power of a common-wealth ecclesiasticall and civill*. London: Andrew Crooke, at the Green Dragon in St Paul's Church-yard. http://socserv.mcmaster.ca/econ/ugcm/3ll3/hobbes/Leviathan.pdf.
Kuhn, H., et al. (1994). The work of John Nash in game theory *nobel seminar* (December 8). http://www.nobelprize.org/nobel_prizes/economics/laureates/1994/nash-lecture.html.
Machiavelli, N. (1532). *The prince* (W. K. Marriott, Trans.). Chapter XVIII. (http://ebooks.adelaide.edu.au/m/machiavelli/niccolo/m149p/chapter18.html). The actual quote is "a wise lord cannot, nor ought he to, keep faith when such observance may be turned against him.".
May, R., Levin, S., & Sugihara, G. (2008). Ecology for bankers. *Nature, 451*, 893–895.
Miller, D. T. (1999). The norm of self-interest. *American Psychologist, 54*, 1053–1060.
Moll, J., Krueger, F., Zahn, R., Pardini, M., de Oliveira-Souza, R., Grafman, J. (2006). Human fronto–mesolimbic networks guide decisions about charitable donation. *Proceedings of the National Academy of Sciences of the U.S.* (Vol. 103, pp. 15623–15628).
Nash, J. (1951). *Non-cooperative games. Annals of Mathematics* (Vol. 54, pp. 286–294). This is surely one of the shortest papers ever to have won its author a Nobel Prize (the 1994 Nobel Memorial Prize in Economics).
Ostrom, E. (2009). A general framework for analyzing sustainability of social-ecological systems. *Science, 325*, 419–422.
Poundstone, W. (1993). *Prisoner's dilemma*. New York: Anchor.
Rand, A. (1964). *The virtue of selfishness*. New York: Signet. See also Rand, A. (1992). *Atlas Shrugged* (35th anniversary edition). New York: Dutton.
Rogers, C. (1942). *Counseling and psychotherapy*. New York: Houghton Mifflin.
Rogers, C. (1951). *Client-centered therapy*. London: Constable.
Rogers, C. (1961). This is me. In *On becoming a person* (p. 20). London: Constable.

Rogers, C. (1970). *Encounter groups*. London: Penguin.
Rousseau, J. (1754). *A discourse on a subject proposed by the Academy of Dijon: What is the origin of inequality among men, and is it authorised by natural law?* (G. D. H. Cole, Trans.). Rendered into HTML and text by Jon Roland of the constitution society. (http://www.constitution.org/jjr/ineq.txt).
Russell, B. (1959). *Common sense and nuclear warfare*. London: Simon and Schuster.
Smith, L. (1996). *Daughters of darkness*. New York: Simon and Schuster (This is the second novel in her *Nightworld* series).
Tankersley, D., Stowe, C., & Huettel, S. (2007). Altruism is associated with an increased neural response to agency. *Nature Neuroscience, 10*, 150–151.
von Neumann, J., & Morgenstern, O. (1944). *Theory of games and economic behaviour*. Princeton: Princeton University Press.
Warneken, F., Hare, B., Melis, A., Hanus, D., & Tomasello, M. (2007). Spontaneous Altruism by Chimpanzees and young children. *PLoS Biology, 5*, e184.
Wilkins, P. (2010). Unconditional positive regard reconsidered. *British Journal of Guidance and Counselling, 28*, 23–36.

The Person-Centered Approach in Research

David Haselberger and Robert Hutterer

1 Introduction

For Carl Rogers, research enables the researcher to clarify personal thought or experience: "It seems to me that in the best of science, the primary purpose is to provide a more satisfactory and dependable hypothesis, belief, faith, for the investigator himself" (Rogers 1961/1995, p. 219). It is a way to gain insight into phenomena we perceive as relevant to ourselves. In his article "Toward a More Human Science of the Person," published in 1985, Rogers outlines several models of science that differ from reductionist scientific viewpoints. More and more, a person-centered approach to research appears to be required. Various researchers such as Wolter-Gustafson (1990), Ulph (1998), or Wilkins and Mitchell-Williams (2002) express an experienced need for person-centered attitudes in search for a scientific perspective that allows for holistic involvement of the researcher and that is in tune with a desire to be "respectful to the data" (Wilkins 2010, p. 219). If researchers live authentically in their research endeavor, try to empathically grasp patterns in their research field not illuminated or appreciated before, and encounter their environment with an attitude of unconditional positive regard, this can hardly be cast in a concrete method, but rather appears to be a personal approach to scientific research. Wilkins and Mitchell-Williams (2002) argue that the effectiveness of a person-centered approach to research depends on the communication of the necessary and sufficient conditions (Rogers 1957). While not explicitly elaborated here, this aspect is interwoven in our considerations.

D. Haselberger (✉)
Postgraduate Center, University of Vienna, Spitalgasse 2, Hof 1 1090 Vienna, Austria
e-mail: david.haselberger@univie.ac.at

R. Hutterer
University of Vienna, Department of Educational Science, Sensengasse 3a 1090 Vienna, Austria
e-mail: Robert.hutterer@univie.ac.at

In this chapter, we are interested in whether characteristics of researching can be discerned that are closely related to attitudes and ideas that form core concepts of the person-centered approach. By means of a review of selected articles written by researchers reflecting on research in the context of the person-centered approach, we try to characterize key aspects of a person-centered approach to research. We found it valuable to summarize and organize commonalities in approaching research by person-centered researchers to reflect upon our own ways of researching. The characteristics we gathered can be seen as a collection of expressions of experiences open for supplement and rearrangement. They are primarily intended to support questions such as "What does research mean to me?" "What is my personal way of researching?" "How do I want to encounter my field of research?"

In the first part, we list and discuss six principles fostering ways of researching closely related to essential concepts in the person-centered approach that could be deduced from a literature review of selected articles. In the second part, examples of contemporary research methods in tune with person-centered principles in the fields of social sciences and educational technology are portrayed. We first depict personal conversation as research instrument enabling insight into personal life experiences as elaborated by Inghard Langer (2000). Then, action research is presented as a set of tools to evaluate and change educational settings as applied in courses at the University of Vienna by Motschnig-Pitrik (2006). In the conclusion, the main characteristics of a person-centered approach to research are summarized and an outlook on research processes sustained by person-centered values is given.

2 Characteristics of a Person-Centered Approach to Research

Many researchers who explore the person-centered approach in fields such as psychotherapy, education, or organizational development have implicitly or explicitly written about their way of researching. In order to find out what is essential to person-centered approaches to research, we reviewed the literature, especially the following:

- "Persons or Science? A Philosophical Question" by Rogers (1955) and (1961/1995), a pivotal contribution to a person-centered perspective on research,
- "Researching in a Person-centered Way" by Wilkins (2010), an exploration of connections between person-centered attitudes and ways of researching, and
- "Authentic Science" by Hutterer (1990), an elaboration of implications of person-centered values and attitudes on science.

We summarize and organize vital statements on research and the person-centered approach that may support the reflection on personal ways of researching. Findings comprise key assumptions on relations between primary concepts in the person-centered approach and how research is put to action. They were arranged in seemingly separate subsections to provide for structure and clarity. In a more encompassing view, they appear highly interdependent and interwoven. Yet, the structure of the characteristics is rather a proposition to be experimented with in personal reflection and dialog.

2.1 Persons as Originators of Research

"Science exists only in people. Each scientific project has its creative inception, its process, and its tentative conclusion, in a person or persons" (Rogers 1961/1995, p. 216). This is an inherent characteristic of authentic scientific research. "Accordingly, to be engaged in authentic science means that investigators are involved as subjective human beings, committed to their values and intrinsically motivated to investigate a specific area of interest" (Hutterer 1990, p. 60). Authentic research is first of all about authentic persons, it is about what understanding of science is authentic for a person in contact to research.

Organismic experiencing such as intuition, feelings, and intellect is equally momentous in the creative process of scientific exploration. "Authentic research is based on increased self-awareness and acceptance of all facets of the researchers' unique experience: motivational, sensory, emotional, and cognitive" (Hutterer 1990, p. 70). Researchers follow a personal vision encountering the phenomena that are most intriguing for them. "Authentic science ... seeks to discover a hidden reality and unrealized potentials in human nature by virtue of a personal vision. Scientists' involvement in this endeavor implies commitment, self-discovery and self-transcendence in order to arrive at a new intellectual identity in accordance with new perspectives of reality" (Hutterer 1990, p. 71). Kriz (2000) shares his impressions on the reflection of the personal disposition to science. In his view, one's decision to be either a biochemist or a molecular biologist is not solely based on rational quantitative analyses of the question, what scientific paradigm could help solve problems most effectively, but rather on personal preferences, competencies, interests, life experience.

For McLeod (2001), the plausibility and trustworthiness of the researcher are the key factors constituting validity of scientific results. "If a piece of research is carried out with integrity, then there is almost certainly something of value in it, there is some truth in it" (McLeod 2001, p. 188). Being conscious of personal values and understanding their influence on perception, being aware of personal bias, is for Maslow (1954) the only way to provide for trustworthy, valid scientific research. "Granted that the ideal of science is to reduce to a minimum these human determinants of theory, this will never be achieved by denying their influence, but only by knowing them well" (Maslow 1954, p. 7). Polanyi states that personal and passionate involvement of the researcher makes research "objective in the sense of establishing contact with a hidden reality" (Polanyi 1962, p. vii).

The use of research outcomes and results is dependent on their relevance for persons involved in the research endeavor. "What I will do with the knowledge gained through scientific method—whether I will use it to understand, enhance, enrich, or use it to control, manipulate and destroy—is a matter of subjective choice dependent upon the values which have personal meaning for me (Rogers 1961/1995, p. 223)."

2.1.1 Individuality as Resource

Individuals can draw from their personal experience to shape creative research questions they perceive as significant for themselves and their environment. "Every researcher/scientist is an individual with a special learning and growth process. Living in a particular cultural setting, during a particular historical period, the scientist's values, convictions, and aims are part of his or her individuality. Additionally, the cultivation of certain ways of perceiving, along with the researcher's theoretical orientation, makes him or her a distinct individual. ... Authentic scientists are committed to this individuality. They acknowledge the problems they study as a discovery in its own right that is personally relevant to them. In developing a personal vision they seek to fulfill what is appropriate to their deeper selves" (Hutterer 1990, p. 73). The consideration of individuality is vital in modern standpoint theory (Harding 2004; Hartsock 1983; Smith 1974). Jürgen Kriz, who experienced postwar confusion as son of a mother that had to care for three children alone, later in his life explored systems theory in psychotherapy. He (2008) states that part of his life was always characterized by a "deep fascination for 'chaos'" (p. 21).

2.1.2 Research Is an Endeavor in Networks with Others

Not only does research commence in a creative effort of an individual or group of people, but it involves subjects with their interests and interpretations as respected partners in the research process (Hutterer 1990, p. 60/61). Kriz (1999) explains that since Popper, Kuhn, and Feyera bend the truth step-by-step had to give way to intersubjective acceptance in the context of given valid paradigms or disciplinary matrices. Rogers states: "It is important that scientists agree upon certain ways as good means to prevent self-deception" (Rogers, 1961/1995, p. 220). For Rogers, trustworthiness of a theory does not derive from applied methods, but from the open communication among (co-)researchers sharing their experiences and perspectives (Hutterer 1990, p. 65). Transparent discussion of methodological and methodic premises may increase validity (Kriz 2000). Reflection of personal values, being open to new findings, sentiments, experiences, and rather unconditional respect for others' views and attitudes, discovering parallels, and distinguishing differences in perception and understanding, can be seen as basic to the movement of scientific dialog. To engage in scientific exchange, it is necessary to be familiar with terminologies, values, and basic beliefs in the respective scientific communities. "No theory can be adequately understood without some knowledge of the cultural and personal soil, from which it springs" (Rogers 1959, p. 185).

Living and experiencing person-centered dispositions can be seen as contributing to the trustworthiness of person-centered research for they establish a highly threat-free environment and may minimize distortion of co-researchers' perceptions (Mearns and McLeod 1984, p. 385).

Authentic involvement with (co-)researchers can facilitate reflection on personal bias (Reason and Heron 1986). If research participants are seen as co-researchers supporting discovery and construction of meaning and "value is placed on the wealth of experience and views of all concerned and products of the research are co-constructed and co-owned, the experience of co-researchers is of empowerment" (Wilkins 2010, p. 221). Collaborative power can be perceived as enhancing personal power by co-researchers (Natiello 1990, p. 272). Because of this, Wilkins and Mitchell-Williams (2002) argue that collaborative research methodologies are closest to person-centered dispositions and values. "Also collaborative effort (because it involves the statement of personal views which are then refined in the light of the views of others) results in the co-construction of meaning. Because it evolves from a consensus, this increases the trustworthiness of findings" (Wilkins 2010, p. 222).

2.2 Primacy of Experience

"Science, as well as therapy, as well as all other aspects of living, is rooted in and based upon the immediate, subjective experience of a person. It springs from the inner, total, organismic experiencing which is only partially and imperfectly communicable. It is one phase of subjective living" (Rogers 1961/1995, p. 222). In his research, Carl Rogers was attentive to his experiences in practice. In his view, science is based on the recognition of a dimly sensed gestalt—a hidden reality. "This gestalt or pattern appears to give meaning to disconnected phenomena. The more that this total apprehension of a pattern is free from cultural values and is free from past scientific values, the more adequate it is likely to be" (Rogers 1968). Creating theories can be described as a process of symbolizing experiences, so that previously isolated phenomena appear related and show an inner order. Thus, theorizing adds (inter)subjective meaning, integration and order to otherwise disparate facts (Hutterer 1990, p. 65).

A person-centered approach to research is an approximation to an inclusive, authentic science. "In this context, 'inclusion' means a science which is attentive to a broad range of realities: cognitive processes, as well as personal and emotional meanings; and the phenomenological world, as well as outward appearances, behavior and reactions. It means a science … which goes beyond the narrow concepts of traditional scientific approaches" (Hutterer 1990, p. 60). Experience is related to the perception of prevailing circumstances. In a person-centered approach to research, attention is given to personal, subjective experiences, the context of the research, and the frames of reference of involved co-researchers. "Some very fruitful discoveries have grown out of the persistent disbelief, by a scientist, in his own findings or other. In the last analysis he may place more trust in his total organismic reactions than in the methods of science. There is no doubt that this can result in serious error as well as in scientific discoveries, but it indicates again the leading place of the subjective in the use of science" (Rogers 1961/1995, p. 219).

Hutterer (1990) highlights that "passion (orig.: Passion, ed.) and involvement are necessary to realize hidden and deeper structures of reality" (p. 70).

2.3 Acknowledgment of Early Phases of Research

From a person-centered perspective, research starts already before the formulation and testing of hypotheses. The researcher "senses the field in which he is interested, he lives it. He does more than 'think' about it—he lets his organism take over and react to it, both on a knowing and on an unknowing level. … Out of this complete subjective immersion comes a creative forming, a sense of direction, a vague formulation of relationships hitherto unrecognized. Whittled down, sharpened, formulated in clearer terms, this creative forming becomes a hypothesis—a statement of a tentative, personal, subjective faith" (Rogers 1961/1995, p. 216/217).

Research starting as personal endeavor is guided by an intuitive vision and is based on aims and values that are meaningful to the researcher (Rogers 1961/1995).

In the first phases of a scientific endeavor, a researcher may ask himself[1]: "Can I approach my field of interest with a well-informed, but open mind?" "What is my heart truly burning for?" "Can I immerse myself in all the observations I have collected, live with them until patterns begin to emerge, themes and concepts begin to be evident?"

Empathy can help to identify or clarify relevant research questions. Deep understanding of people's needs, even on a level maybe just dimly aware, can bring forth significant research endeavors (Rogers 1985). Langer et al. (1981), for example, developed a concept of understandable expression in texts on the basis of empathic indwelling in the joys and frustrations of people trying to comprehend the contents of books.

2.4 Extensional Relationship to Reality

A person engaged in scientific exploration lives in relationship to himself or herself, his or her field of interest, and (co-)researchers. The quality of these

---

[1] These questions are primarily adapted from Rogers (1985), except for "What is my heart truly burning for?" which was adapted from a question Jürgen Kriz asked doctorate students in a course on scientific methods at the University of Vienna in the summer term 2012.

relationships has tremendous impact on conduct, trustworthiness, and validity, lastly the whole process of research. Being acceptant of all sorts of findings, intuitive directions, contradictory information and associated feelings, open to holistic organismic experience, the scientist lives extensional in the relationship to his or her field. "It is when people approach phenomena with an openness to their experience … that they are most likely to discover significant meaning" (Wilkins 2010, p. 220). Additionally to an extensional relationship to the field, constructive, empathic, caring inner communication of different aspects of self involved in the research endeavor may lead to deeper, clearer understanding of the investigated events (Rogers 1961/1995). Empathy enables deep sensing of diverse mental models of aspects to explore (Senge 2006, p. 401). Active, empathic listening can be considered a core skill of scientific interviewers (Wilkins 2010, p. 218).

Extensional differentiation and assessment of various approaches to view the research field helps finding suitable models of aspects of reality the researcher wants to explore. Each model is a representation of a perspective on the field of interest and therefore, even if it is contradictory to other models, associated with a part of the researched reality. When evaluating various ways of getting in contact with significant aspects of the research field, it may be valuable to reflect upon the particular ways chosen, the motives behind these choices, the bumps encountered and promising tracks to clarify the personal research process, and to make this process comprehensible for others. Concerning results and findings of scientific investigations, Rogers framed his personal maxim that the facts are always friendly (Rogers 1961/1995, p. 25).

2.5 Methodological Openness

"The methodology chosen must be appropriate to the question being asked. This is very important, because, if taken seriously, it will prevent new rigidities from developing" (Rogers 1985). To "check with reality" and to avoid self-deception, Rogers utilized empirical experimental research.

According to Hutterer (1990) "The application of methods and methodological rules to the conduct of authentic research is important, but only in an auxiliary way" (p. 61). Scientific methods are employed to prevent self-deception and to create a basis for reciprocal understanding of findings and conclusions with colleagues. Scientific methods standardize and simplify scientific discourse among participants of scientific communities (Kriz 1999).

Hutterer (1990) and Kriz (2000) argue that combining a plurality of perspectives and forms of discovery enables the exploration of a vast number of puzzling questions and makes research a comprehensible personal and social process. Applying a variety of methods, naturalistic and experimental, and cooperating with other scientists could offer deeper insights through the tension between different, maybe contradictory, perspectives on the researched phenomena (Hutterer 1990, p. 68).

2.6 Research Is Process

> It is my opinion that the type of understanding which we call science can begin anywhere, at any level of sophistication.... A closely related belief is that there is a natural history of science—that science, in any given field, goes through a patterned course of growth and development. ... Science is a developing mode of inquiry, or it is of no particular importance (Rogers 1959, p. 189).

If science is perceived as existent in persons and in the relationships between persons' process characteristics of scientific research become evident. In this sense, an objective body of knowledge equally understood by everyone is not plausible. "There are only tentative beliefs, existing subjectively, in a number of different persons. If these beliefs are not tentative, then what exists is dogma, not science" (Rogers 1961/1995, p. 219). Theories, in that sense, are not rock-solid concepts of truth, but rather changing, provisional attempts to design and refine maps of some aspect of perceived reality. They become "a stimulus to further creative thinking" (Rogers 1959, p. 191), a "springboard for further investigation" (Rogers 1961/1995, p. 218).

3 Examples of Research in Tune with the Person-Centered Approach

The person-centered approach evolved closely connected to scientific research. Rogers states:

> ...client-centered therapy has always existed in the context of a university setting. This means a continual process of sifting and winnowing of the truth form the staff, in a situation of fundamental personal security. It means being exposed to the friendly criticism of colleagues,... This has helped greatly to keep the client-centered orientation an open and self-critical, rather than a dogmatic, point of view (Rogers 1961/1995, p. 246/247).

Person-centered ways of researching emphasize collaboration, holism, openness to the total experience of all concerned and they are permissive and elective (Wilkins 2010, p. 236). Subsequently, two examples of researching attuned to a person-centered approach to research are portrayed.

3.1 The Personal Conversation as Way of Researching

Langer (1985) elaborated the personal conversation as research instrument. Personal conversations are opportunities to gather, process, and give insight into life experiments people engage in every day. Generated knowledge can be offered to concerned people. Though, personal conversations differ from interviews. Personal conversation is a reciprocal human encounter, a deep sharing between people to a common issue. Bias through the researcher is minimized if personal conversation works out. Through a nonjudgemental attitude of the researcher, the partner is enabled to freely express his/her individuality, which can be completely different from the researchers'. Though there appear to be overlaps with dialog by Bohm and Nichol (1996), the research method of personal conversations differs slightly as it is a primary concern of the researcher to provide for a maximum of free development of the conversation partner, whereas in dialog personal articulation is equally valuable. Due to new impressions and insights gathered in conversation, the research process needs to be flexible and can hardly be planned in advance. The researcher describes his/her learning process in relation to the research topic and the conversations and structures his/her reflection.

3.1.1 Preparation

In advance to the conversation, the researcher may talk to somebody about his/her personal concern, how the research topic relates to his/her life and focal points of the topic.

3.1.2 The Conversation

- Clarity and contact

At the beginning of the conversation, personal exchange that is not related with the research topic may help to decrease feelings of strangeness in the situation.

- Understanding resonance

Central to understanding conversation in the context of research is that people are understood in their inner world, their very own values, attitudes, feelings, and thoughts, to establish an empathic relationship in which the essence of their experiencing and behavior may be grasped.

- Questions

After the free disclosure of the conversation partner, the researcher may pose questions that go beyond direct understanding which are relevant for the research as well.

- First record of the conversation

Both research partners may accentuate at the end of the conversation what were main results and what was specifically relevant or touching.

- Fade away of conversation

It is important to stay in contact with the conversation partner, as conversations about personal topics can bring about new memories, experiences, points of view that clarify and get communicable in the following days, such that follow-up contact may be worthwhile.

3.1.3 Evaluation of Conversations

- Every conversation is a single case study

As a lot of information can be gathered by one conversation, every conversation may be evaluated separately at first.

- Condensed report

Keywords of essential contents of the conversation and literal statements related to the keywords can be arranged to accentuate the substance of the conversation in a comprehensive form. The conversation partner may be asked whether he/she finds himself/herself in the summary of a conversation.

- Informing the conversation partner of the results

In the process of communicative validation, both conversation partners can check whether the publication accommodates the need for personal security.

- The overall result

In the condensed report of the first conversation, the researcher can consider whether essential contents concerning the research topic were touched upon. The condensed reports of the following conversations can be summarized paying attention to what main issues are explored and how often certain keywords are stated.

A detailed description of this way of researching can be found in Langer (2000). Projects working with this research method are listed at: http://www.inghardlanger.de/PDF/Dipl-dr.pdf

3.2 Action Research to Improve Person-Centered Technology Enhanced Learning

Action research is an aggregate of research methods from social sciences to facilitate social change (Wilkins 2010, p. 234). Many contemporaneous action research approaches can be traced back to research methods of Kurt (Baskerville 1999). In action research, aims of researchers and co-researchers are considered. "Any meaningful investigation must consider the frame of reference and underlying social values of the subjects" (Baskerville 1999, p. 4). Ideally, the researcher is actively involved, generated knowledge can be directly applied, and the research process integrates theory and practice.

In participatory action research, researchers and co-researchers synergistically work together to produce knowledge and action directly applicable in the community (Wilkins 2010, p. 235). Responsibility for the research process is shared among all involved in the research endeavor. Co-researchers collaboratively shape ideas that influence their future action. In the following, one research cycle of participatory action research is illustrated by tracking its five phases aiming to improve educational settings in a course in "Project Management Soft Skills" at the University of Vienna (Motschnig-Pitrik 2006).

3.2.1 Participatory Action Research in a Course on "Soft Skills" at the University

- Investigating

The development of soft skills besides intellectual knowledge is highly appreciated in industry and educational contexts. Thus, it is an aim of the course on "Project Management Soft Skills" at the Faculty of Computer Science at the University of Vienna that students have the opportunity to learn as whole persons, on an intellectual, a skill, and a personal level.

A key question was how development at the skills and personal levels can be achieved and evaluated (Motschnig-Pitrik 2006).

- Action Planning

"The course is aimed at addressing students at all three levels of competence or learning: knowledge, skills, and attitudes with a clear emphasis on experientially developing soft skills such as active listening, effective communication and negotiation, moderation, team competencies, etc." (Motschnig-Pitrik 2006, p. 2). The course design integrates face-to-face meetings and eLearning. Through the synergy of present meetings and web-supported learning, students can benefit from the advantages this blend offers.

- Action Taking

Students can find material concerning the course for self-appropriated learning online. In the beginning of the course, requirements and learning methods in the course are discussed. Further, students assign themselves to teams. Ten moderated face-to-face workshops enable the exploration of individual interests in the framework of "soft skills project management" in a highly interactive work environment. After each workshop, students submit an online reflection that provides manifold perspectives on the workshop for the participants. At the end of the course, students evaluate themselves online. They conduct peer-reviews of the topics elaborated by other student teams, and they fill out a questionnaire to evaluate the course (Motschnig-Pitrik 2006, p. 3).

- Evaluation

In the evaluation stage, questionnaires were statistically assessed. Results were complemented by analyses of feedback and self-evaluations students wrote during the course.

- Specifying learning

If the first face-to-face meetings are facilitated in a person-centered way, participants seem to grow together as a group and perceive a constructive working climate (Motschnig-Pitrik 2006, p. 5).

An essential feature of the course are the units that are facilitated by student teams. "... The degree of self-initiated, experiential learning—from successful elements as much as from mistakes—is astonishing....

This course structure appears to be more stable in terms of providing learning to all participants than pure encounter groups, perhaps due to the loose but transparent course structure and the responsible activities in small teams. However, I'd be eager to compare long term effects of this setting when compared with person-centered encounter groups."[2]

Further readings concerning action research in the area of educational technology at the University of Vienna can be found in Motschnig-Pitrik (2004, 2006), Motschnig-Pitrik et al. (2007), Motschnig-Pitrik and Mallich (2004).

4 Conclusion and Outlook

In this article, we discerned characteristics of researching that are related to primary concepts in the person-centered approach. We portrayed research as a phenomenon that commences in and builds on personal experiences, involves other persons, and has meaning for persons. The research examples presented show that various methodological approaches can be attuned to person-centered principles, if the researchers live in an authentic, extensional relationship with their field of interest, reflect their personal process, their individuality, their motives in the research endeavor, consider their own vulnerabilities and biases in contact with their research field, are open for different, maybe even contradictory, viewpoints, try to co-construct the research process with co-researchers. We presented personal conversation as a way to mutually collect experiences and thus open them up for others involved (Langer 2000). Further, we depicted (participatory) action research

---

[2] Personal contribution by Renate Motschnig in an online conversation with the first author in 2012.

as opportunity to design and realize courses at universities with adjustments to students' and facilitators' needs, interests, and ideas (Motschnig-Pitrik 2006).

The fruitfulness of a person-centered approach to human science is not a self-propelling and self-explaining process. The power of mainstream research is inevitably influential and cannot be ignored, nor the temporary fashions and passing fads. To stay discerning of the literature and self-critical are ongoing challenges. An informed stance is necessary for not stepping into the common trap to criticize perspectives even the mainstream has already overcome.

There are still many open questions. In his last article on human science 1985, Rogers was aware of new movements in the field of research that fully blossom today. The first is the qualitative research movement with its many differentiations and types of inquiry. It opens a rich discussion about producing knowledge, about its validity and limitations. Today in many fields of human research and social science, there is a growing susceptibility toward methodological pluralism, which includes quantitative, as well as qualitative and mixed method research (Creswell 2009; Denzin and Lincoln 2011). There is no need to fight against old-fashioned positivism and to pronounce exclusively phenomenology or old-fashioned hermeneutics. There are fresh ways to look at and use these cognitive resources in several types of qualitative and mixed methods research. But it is a big challenge to show the fruitfulness of these transformed approaches in actual research projects. A second movement that gains influence and power of discernment over the last decades is the critical realist perspective in philosophy of social science according to Bhaskar (1998, 2008), Collier (1994) and others.

Today, it is fashionable to see the person-centered approach in line with a constructivist position, which seems to fit perfectly to social practices like counseling and psychotherapy. There are different traditions of constructivist ideas, but many seem to play down a causal dynamic in the social world. Additionally in the course of a relativizing postmodern discussion, there are interpretations of constructivism that come close to irrealism. A critical realist perspective is compatible with a mild constructivist position: The objects of social research are socially produced and concept dependent in themselves while we cannot avoid socially defining them and approaching them in a theory-dependent way in the course of inquiry. But unlike postmodern and constructivist perspectives, it holds a strong ontological realism: There is an ontological objective existence of reality, independent of our beliefs and our knowledge about it. To follow a methodological pluralism is not just a compromise or the result of human imperfection but a logical necessity to understand the complexity of social practices. It seems a promising perspective to make experiential learning in counseling, psychotherapy, and education more transparent and to come to a depth understanding of the predictable and the indeterminate personalized dimensions of social relationships as well. Rogers (1985) was close to this realistic perspective when he stated about experiential learning: "We can communicate about it, or we can create conditions that facilitates it, but it cannot be communicated directly" (p. 8).

Reflection of the personal approach to researching may help to find out about rudiments of the personal understanding of research and what it means to oneself.

As research takes place in contact with others, it appears to be necessary to reflect upon the influences of culture and social circumstances as well as the traditions and values of the scientific communities it relates to and stems from. If research is perceived as an ongoing process of development, differentiation, and refinement, a key concern may be to engage in research that can be brought in connection to further research.

References

Baskerville, R. L. (1999). Investigating information systems with action research. *Communications of the Association for Information Systems, 2*(19), 1–32.
Bhaskar, R. (2008). *A realist theory of science.* Oxon: Routledge.
Bhaskar, R. (1998). *The possibility of naturalisms. A philosophical critique of the contemporary human sciences.* Oxon: Routledge.
Bohm, D., & Nichol, L. (1996). *On dialogue.*, Routledge Classics Series London: Routledge.
Collier, A. (1994). *Critical realism. An introduction to Roy Bhaskar's philosophy.* London: Verso.
Creswell, J. W. (2009). *Research design. Qualitative, quantitative and mixed methods approaches.* Thousand Oaks: Sage Publications.
Denzin, N. S., & Lincoln, Y. S. (2011). *The Sage handbook of qualitative research.* Thousand Oaks: Sage.
Harding, S. (2004). A socially relevant philosophy of science? Resources from standpoint theory's controversiality. *Hypatia, 19*(1), 25–47.
Hartsock, N. (1983). *Money, sex and power.* Boston: Northeastern University Press.
Hutterer, R. (1990). Authentic science: Some implications of Carl Rogers's reflections on science. *Person-Centered Review, 5*(1), 57–76.
Kriz, J. (1999). Von der "science-fiction" zur "science": Methodologische und methodische Bemerkungen zur Frage der "Wissenschaftlichkeit von Psychotherapie-verfahren". [*From "science-fiction" to "science": methodological and methodic notes on the question of "scientificalness of psychotherapy-methods".*] *Report Psychologie, 24,* 21–30.
Kriz, J. (2000). Perspektiven zur "Wissenschaftlichkeit" von Psychotherapie. [*Perspectives on "scientificalness" of psychotherapy.*] In M. Hermer, (Eds.), *Psychotherapeutische Perspektiven am Beginn des 21 Jahrhunderts* (pp. 43-66). Tübingen: DGVT-Verlag.
Kriz, J. (2008). *Self-actualization. Person-centred approach and systems theory.* Ross-on-Wye: PCCS-Books.
Langer, I. (1985). Das persönliche Gespräch als Weg in der psychologischen Forschung. [*The personal conversation as way in psychological research.*] *Zeitschrift für personenzentrierte Psychologie und Psychotherapie, 4,* 447–457.
Langer, I. (2000). *Das persönliche Gespräch als Weg in der psychologischen Forschung.* [*The personal conversation as way in psychological research.*] Köln: GwG-Verlag.
Langer, I., Schultz von Thun, F., & Tausch, R. (1981). *Sich verständlich ausdrücken.* [*Expressing oneself understandably.*] München: Reinhardt.
Maslow, A. H. (1954). *Motivation and personality.* New York: Harper & Row.
McLeod, J. (2001). *Qualitative research in counselling and psychotherapy.* London: Sage.
Mearns, D., & McLeod, J. (1984). A person-centered approach to research. In R. F. Levant & J. M. Shlien (Eds.), *Client-centered therapy and the person-centered approach: New directions in theory, research and practice* (pp. 370–389). New York: Praeger.
Motschnig-Pitrik, R. (2004). Blended Learning in einer großen Informatik-Lehrveranstaltung: Personenzentriert oder Handlungsorientiert? [*Blended learning in a large computer science*

course: person-centered or activity-oriented?] In *Handlungsorientiertes Lernen und eLearning: Grundlagen und Praxisbeispiele* (pp. 219–246). Wien: R. Oldenbourg Wissenschaftsverlag.

Motschnig-Pitrik, R., & Mallich, K. (2004). Effects of person-centered attitudes on professional and social competence in a blended learning paradigm. *Educational Technology and Society,* 7(4), 176–192.

Motschnig-Pitrik, R. (2006). Participatory action research in a blended learning course on project management soft skills. In *36th ASEE/IEEE Frontiers in Education Conference* (pp. 1–6). Presented at the 36th ASEE/IEEE Frontiers in Education Conference, San Diego.

Motschnig-Pitrik, R., Kabicher, S., Figl, K., & Santos, A. M. (2007). Person-centered, technology enhanced learning in action: Action research in a course on organizational development. In *37th ASEE/IEEE Frontiers in Education Conference* (pp. 6–11). Presented at the 37th ASEE/IEEE Frontiers in Education Conference, Milwaukee.

Natiello, P. (1990). The person-centered approach, collaborative power, and cultural transformation. *Person-Centered Review,* 5(3), 268–286.

Polanyi, M. (1962). *Personal knowledge: Towards a post-critical philosophy.* Chicago: University of Chicago Press.

Reason, P., & Heron, J. (1986). Research with people: The paradigm of co-operative experiential inquiry. *Person-Centered Review,* 1(4), 456–476.

Rogers, C. R. (1955). Persons or science? A philosophical question. *American Psychologist,* 10(7), 267–278.

Rogers, C. R. (1957). The necessary and sufficient conditions of therapeutic personality change. *Journal of Consulting Psychology,* 21(2), 95–103.

Rogers, C. (1959). A theory of therapy, personality, and interpersonal relationships, as developed in the client-centered framework. In S. Koch (Ed.), *Psychology, a study of a science* (Vol. 3, pp. 184–256)., Formulations of the Person and the Social Context New York: McGraw-Hill.

Rogers, C. R. (1995). *On becoming a person.* New York: Houghton Mifflin Company. Original work published 1961.

Rogers, C. R. (1968). Some thoughts regarding the current presuppositions of the behavioral sciences. In W. Coulson & C. R. Rogers (Eds.), *Man and the science of man* (pp. 55–72). Columbus: Charles E. Merrill.

Rogers, C. R. (1985). Toward a more human science of the person. *Journal of Humanistic Psychology,* 25(4), 7–24.

Senge, P. M. (2006). *The fifth discipline: The art and practice of the learning organization.* New York: Double Day.

Smith, D. (1974). Women's perspective as a radical critique of sociology. *Sociological Inquiry,* 44, 1–13.

Ulph, M. (1998). *Stolen lives: The effects of the development of self of men who have experienced sexual abuse in childhood.* Unpublished master's dissertation, University of East Anglia.

Wilkins, P. (2010). Researching in a person-centered way. In M. Cooper, J. C. Watson, & D. Hölldampf (Eds.), *Person-centered and experiential therapies work: A review of the research on counseling, psychotherapy and related practices* (pp. 215–239). Ross-on-Wye: PCCS Books.

Wilkins, P., & Mitchell-Williams, Z. (2002). The theory and experience of person-centered research. In J. C. Watson, R. N. Goldman, & M. S. Warner (Eds.), *Client-centered and experiential psychotherapy in the 21st century: Advances in theory, research and practice* (pp. 291–302). Ross-on-Wye: PCCS Books.

Wolter-Gustafson, C. (1990). How person-centered theory informed my qualitative research on women's lived experience of wholeness. *Person-Centered Review,* 5(2), 221–232.

The Learner-Centered Model: Implications for Research Approaches

Barbara L. McCombs

> *We're at a crossroads, of sorts, and here's why: Talking around notions of collaborative cultures is easy, in the same way people banter about collaborative innovation. Small wonder there's such a buzz about it. But fostering cultures that spawn collaborative behaviors is hard work. I wonder: do we have the resolve to take it on?*
> **Collaborative Culture: Insights from Peter Senge on the Foundations of Organizational Learning** January 11, 2011.

1 Introduction

As researchers tackle the challenges of twenty-first century, transformational learning models that offer personalized and individualized instruction tailored to unique student qualities, interests, and learning preferences, research methodologies have changed. These research methodologies are capitalizing on the core person-centered principles of the whole person, including acknowledging the power of learner voice and the changing role of all learners in the learning process. This chapter explores these significant and emerging trends and offers readers the opportunity to reflect on what these trends mean for future research, practice, and policy.

1.1 The Power of Research on Learner Voice and Changing Roles in Learning

One of the most important assumptions in person- and learner-centered theories is that individual learners of any age or position in the learning relationship (teacher, student, peer, parent, administrator, etc.) all have a unique view of what supports or hinders their learning and motivation to learn in various contexts. This means without giving the learner a voice and allowing them to work together collaboratively on various research projects centered on understanding and developing both

B. L. McCombs (✉)
Center for Human Motivation, Learning and Development (HMLD),
Applied Research & Technology Institute (ARTI),
University of Denver, Denver, CO, Colorado
e-mail: bmccombs@du.edu

lifelong learning dispositions and necessary skills and competencies in core content areas, learners will not "own" or invest in the research and may sabotage the quality of research data (cf. McCombs 2012, in press). Research has shown that inviting students as young as 6- to 7-years old and in first or second grade to "be a scientist" and find clues as to how they can be more engaged in learning necessary learning processes, skills, and content pays off in the quality of data collected. That is, the data are more reliable and valid and in the collaboration, students also acquire critical-thinking and decision-making skills needed to apply the scientific method.

Expert teacher-as-facilitator and learning guide skills are called into play as well as support from the research community in various person-centered approaches to applying the scientific method in real-world learning contexts. As Carl Rogers recognized decades ago,

> Science has its inception in a participating person who is pursuing aims, values, purposes which have personal and subjective meaning for him.... he immerses himself in the relevant experience.... He senses the field in which he is interested, he lives it. Out of this complete subjective immersion comes a creative forming, a sense of direction, a vague formulation of relationships hitherto unrecognized.... It is indeed the matrix of immediate personal, subjective experience that all science, and each individual scientific research has its origin (Rogers 1964: On Becoming a Person, p. 217).

We need an approach to transformation in our research paradigms and methodologies that reflects that all learners are as naturally self-regulated and self-motivated agents of our own learning. We need to rethink whether we want to do things *to* and/or we want to do things *with* the natural learners (all of us) that we are for a lifetime. We need to move away from our fears about giving students and teachers choices and agency as argued by Walls and Little (2005) and Zimmerman and Schunk (2001), for without choice self-regulation and responsibility cannot be developed in learners of any age or stage of development.

Researchers in England and other European and Australian cultures are discovering the importance of giving students leadership roles in framing quality research and being part of a collaborative research team whose aim is to provide the most engaging and personalized education possible given the current context of testing and accountability prevalent round the world. For example, British researcher (Fielding and Bragg 2003) describes some of the theoretical underpinnings of radical approaches to student voice that are part of what he sees as our transformative future. The notion of voice is explored within the framework of current research on constructivism and research approaches that show the power of student voice in producing quality research outcomes. Fielding examines a number of practical issues that need to be addressed and critiques theories that are in two major categories. He states (p. 295),

> The first, *Deconstructing the presumptions of the present*, explores the largely ignored problematic of much student voice work. (1) 'Problems of speaking *about* others', (2) 'Problems of speaking *for* others', and problems of (3) 'Getting heard' reveal a range of issues that need to be better understood and acknowledged. The second, *On the necessity of dialogue*, attempts a resolution, exploring the possibility of (4) 'Speaking about/for others in supportive ways' before offering the preferred (5) 'Dialogic alternative: speaking

with rather than for' and further developing that line of enquiry through (6) 'Students as co/researchers'. Finally, (7) 'Recalcitrant realities, new opportunities' offers some ambivalent, but still hopeful thoughts about current realities and future possibilities.

Similarly, Mitra (2004) has studied whether increasing student voice in schools can lead to gains in youth development. She sees this trend in student decision-making roles as a potential strategy in this twenty-first century for improving not only the success of school reform efforts but also for demonstrating research consistency around the growth of agency, belonging, and competence that has led to new multivariate models that focus heavily on data from students as the source of their own feelings and experiences. These research data demonstrate how giving students voice in the context of supporting positive adult/student relationships can fundamentally influence youth development outcomes that emerge.

A working paper by Clark (2007) explores the methodology and initial issues raised in seeking to involve young children in the design process. It reports a study concerned with how young children can play an active role in the designing and developing of children's spaces. The focus is on children under 6-years old in early childhood provision. Clark describes over 10 years of research with children as young as 3- and 4-years old who were given voice to share their views and experiences of their early childhood center experiences in Britain. Children and the adults supporting them were given central roles in the design of their learning experiences. The researcher was able to take pictures, tape record, and take notes describing the expertise these young children could demonstrate. Clark points out that this is part of an international impetus from the United Nations Convention on the Rights of the Child (UNCRC) ratified in 1991 and a later report in 2006 that supports a view of children as "acute observer of their environment." This has led to new policy initiatives in the UK that place a duty on local authorities to take account of the views of young children in designing their early childhood experiences. It has also led to a recognition of the value of research that focuses on what these views add to the quality of their learning and educational outcomes. In turn, that has led to researchers being committed to an active role for children and young people in the research itself.

1.2 Emerging Research Approaches and Methodologies

In exploring what research means to all fields of science, Adams et al. (2009) make the point that what is considered research has many meanings depending on who is asking the question and what topic they are analyzing. What those doing research of all kinds, from the most simple to the most complex, do agree upon is that research is a deep inquiry into a problem to be solved or the discovery of new facts. Current research models require a diligent and studious search for relevant prior research information. They require knowing what questions to ask and what information to collect to answer those questions. New research models often lead to the revision of current theories in light of new information or ways of thinking about and interpreting existing evidence. As an academic approach using the basic research steps known as the scientific method, new *collaborative action research* enhances our understanding of what is already known, extends our knowledge of our world in areas where very little is known, or basically help us better understand real issues confronting us in the worlds in which we live.

Adams et al. (2009, p. 20) explain the three main types of research most often used: (1) descriptive research aimed at describing phenomena and useful for setting a baseline or starting place (exploratory study) for a research project; (2) explanatory research aimed at deeply describing why behavior is the way it is, leading to advancing knowledge about structures, processes, or the nature of events that can lead to the building, testing, or revising of a theory; and (3) prediction research goes beyond explaining behavior to predicting future behavior due to changes in any of the explanatory variables that are relevant to a particular phenomenon or issue in question, often leading to changes that improve current outcomes. Descriptive Research is a phase early in the collaborative research project involving the students as well as adults in the system where, for example, in our research, we carefully listened to young children and older students while constructing our self-assessments tools and found ways to word items that were clear and easily understood by children at different ages and developmental stages (cf. McCombs and Miller 2007, 2008). That led us to write articles, book chapters, and presentations for colleagues in the field to critique and provide suggestions for further testing our learner-centered model (LCM) and identifying the key variables at each developmental stage. From there, our research efforts turned to various prediction models that have been tested, retested, and refined over the last 15 years and continuing into the present (see McCombs 2013, in press and other chapter in this volume).

The scientific method is understood as a process that is aligned with common problem-solving and critical-thinking models. The two major categories of the scientific method are applied in the areas of (a) theoretical and thinking concepts and (b) measurement and statistical concepts. As discussed by McCombs (2013, in press), most researchers are trained in the ways scientists think. That means they first learn how to formalize their thinking in terms of science so as to produce knowledge not previously known and, in some cases, to verify what others have already found in some contexts but not others. Second, research training helps individuals understand that there is a language of science that also extends to terms and concepts used to better understand the truth of scientific inquiries. They describe careful and accurate ways to classify facts, discover scientific laws, and ensure findings are clear and capable of representing the best methodologies of data collection.

Even today, there is not universal agreement of what defines the scientific method, but the following are the commonly accepted steps used in the social sciences: (1) recognize the problem, (2) define the problem, (3) develop the hypotheses, (4) develop the research design, (5) define the research methods and measures, (6) collect the data, (7) analyze the data, and (8) draw conclusions and document results. Research designs follow logically from identified research question(s) and the information learned from an extensive literature review. The key features of research designs is that they will generally be in the categories of descriptive, explanation, or prediction research, depending on the state of the field and what is known about the issue or problem. In addition, Robson (2002) suggests that everything starts with the research questions in terms of what assumptions are made and the designs for the research that is selected—a view pioneered by Rogers (1964). The field is acknowledging that research designs are increasingly moving toward a mixed method approach because human phenomena require a degree of complexity in designs in order to fully understand particular issues or research questions.

The following are what many be considered to be the types of design issues that researchers at all levels of expertise should constantly be aware (cf. McCombs 2013, in press): (1) *Pragmatism*, (2) *Qualitative Research Designs*, (3) *Quantitative Research Designs*, and (4) *Mixed Methods Research Designs*. These designs offer researchers the flexibility to combine methods associated with qualitative and quantitative research designs to more completely understand individual and social phenomena of interest. A research design comes with its own set of assumptions philosophically, scientifically, and from a methodological perspective. Sweeney (2010, downloaded from www.pegasus.com on 12/3/10) puts her finger on the problem when she states, "The problem, arises when we use analyses 'mindlessly,' assuming that the world stands still as we study it. That puzzling situations will stand still while we bring them into their component pieces, and that the relationship between the pieces aren't important."

As seen in Fig. 1, the learner-centered model is built on scientifically validated learner-centered principles that cover four domains or sets of factors that impact learning. They provided a holistic look at what it means to be a learner. They apply to all of us. Together, the domains provided a framework and a new paradigm that helps us put the educational system back into balance. The challenge then became how to figure out how the learner-centered principles could translate into practice. This involved putting them into a theoretical framework. It also involved identifying the personal characteristics and practice characteristics that research has demonstrated is most related to important learner outcomes.

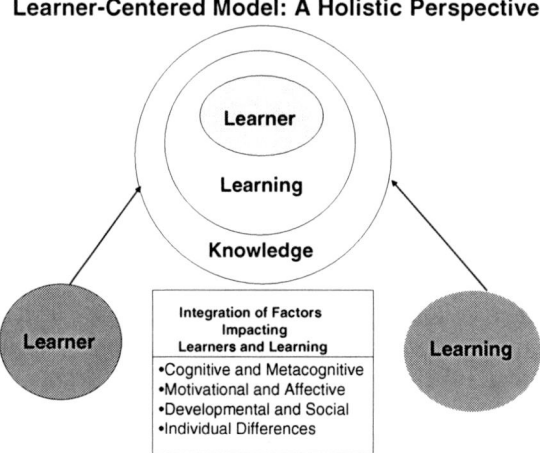

Fig. 1 Learner-centered model: a holistic perspective

The understanding researchers bring to the classes of variables that can be measured in a research study include those defined by Graziano and Raulin (2010, p. 56). These include the following: *Behavioral Variables* or any observable responses of an organism; *Stimulus Variables* or environmental factors that have actual or potential effects on an organism's response; *Organismic Variables* or characteristics of an organism that can be used to classify the organism for research purposes; *Independent Variables* that are actively manipulated by the researcher to see what its impact will be on other variables; *Dependent Variables* or variables that are hypothesized to be effected by the independent variable manipulation; *Extraneous Variables* or any variable, other than the independent variable, that might affect the dependent variable in a research study; and a *Constant Variable* or any event that is prevented from varying. In our own work (see Fig. 2), we have validated the following general model of significant variables for middle school and high school students and teachers, which is generally also supported at the college level (McCombs and Miller 2007, 2008).

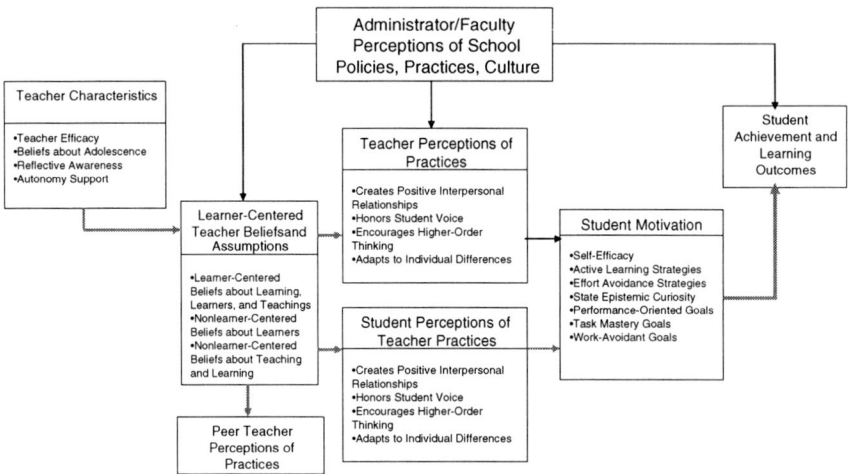

Fig. 2 A learner-centered model of relations between teacher beliefs, teacher practices, and student outcomes

As can be seen in this figure, *Behavioral Variables* include teacher and researcher observations of student behavior while learning and student self-reports of their perceptions of classroom practices and their learning strategies and motivation while learning in a particular classroom with a particular teacher and content area. *Stimulus Variables* are the content, teacher relational and teaching processes, and other classroom variables as uniquely perceived by the students per our LCM. *Organismic Variables* collected in our research collaboratively by students and adults include gender, ethnicity, age, grade level, and socioeconomic status. *Dependent Variables* are also collaboratively selected but generally include engagement and a variety of learning outcomes from student self-assessments of their own performance and progress, teacher performance evaluations, and state-mandated tests or other objective measures of learning outcomes relevant to a particular school system and context. *Extraneous Variables* are context specific and may include peer teacher observations or self-assessments, administrator evaluations, and parent self-assessments per our LCM and its assessment tools. Finally, the constant is any variance due to teacher or student fluctuations in behavior or other school-related practices and policies that influence student perceptions at a particular point in time. These are all part of the various statistical models we have used to refine the models shown in Figs. 1 and 2.

2 New Directions Emerging in Learning for a Lifetime

Work on emotional intelligence begun in the early 1990s is described. The report research over more than a decade confirms that humans have an emotional as well as an intellectual (or analytical) brain, both of which are in constant communication and involved in learning, motivation, leadership, and well-being (Goleman 1995). This research acknowledges that there is more to human effectiveness than SAT scores, IQ scores, and employment tests focusing on cognitive ability. Research evidence exists on the inseparability of intellect and emotion in learning (e.g., Breckler 2010; Elias et al. 1997; Lazarus 2000, 2003; Lee 2011; Pekrun et al. 2010; Radel et al. 2010) and the importance of emotional intelligence to human functioning and health (e.g., Kristjansson 2010; Lazarus 2003; Seligman and Csikszentmihalyi 2000).

2.1 Implications for Teachers as Learners

Studies clearly show the measurable impact great teachers have on students' acquisition of social and emotional skills. One example is the Students First organization that has been supporting student voice and advocating for students to speak out for and against what practices best serve them in their schools. On February 21, 2012, they announced the results of their six-word essay contest on what it means to "be a great teacher." At http://studentsfirst.org/last-chance-to-vote, you can judge for yourself how inspiring the stories are about the hard-working teachers who middle- and high school students found had changed their lives. Here is one example from that site:

> My 6th grade teacher, Mr. Brown, provided a classroom environment where I felt at ease expressing myself. After our weekly science class, I would go home and make a project that pertained to the lesson. The next day, Mr. Brown would encourage me to present my latest project to the class. I realize now that this probably took up precious classroom time, but Mr. Brown always made me feel that what I had to share was important. I was a shy little girl who had found an interest in science and he recognized it. In fact, he promoted it! Years later, I became the lead electrician in the installation of the dual Harpoon system on the battleship U.S.S. Missouri. Thank you, Mr. Brown. Jackie K. of Texas.

As a further recent example, the Talent Development community at http://www.hci.org/lib/leveraging-technology-onboard-and-engage-gen-y had a webcast on February 22, 2012, to discuss what it takes to retain the current millennial generation embarking on their career paths. The increased expectations these youth have of work and their low sense of company loyalty are leading to premature and expensive turnover. Research is reported that shows collaborative and personalized policies and cultures both attract and retain Millennials. This technology-oriented expects access to information at the "moment of need" and in personalized formats that prepare them to immediately contribute to the organization. Millennials also expect to use social media and work with peers in team problem-solving approach. It is easy to see that these are the approaches of learner-centered models and another indicator of their current and ongoing effectiveness in teaching not only emotional intelligence but other critical intellectual and relational skills needed for innovative contributions to the workforce. As Williams (2012) explains, she is working on a new US Department of Education project that will focus on fostering innovation by online learning communities of educators who are new to those who are already involved in networking and collaboration with colleagues about these best practices. More information about this project can be found at http://connectededucators.org/.

2.2 The Value of Collaborative Research Approaches

Simple rules can often be the best approach to data management and decisions about data reduction according to Gilbos and Schmeidler (2011). These collaborative researchers from the University of Tel-Aviv and Ohio State University have determined an *axiomatic* approach to problems of prediction, classification, and statistical learning. Their methodology uses inductive conclusions derived from existing databases that apply consistency rules and similarity-weighted aggregation to estimate a similarity function from the data. This rule-based reasoning can be incorporated into case-based predictions that follow research-validated principles and practices in any given human system.

Crump (2011) describes the IT issues involved when organizations are faced with the challenges of storage with big data infrastructures available in the research web 2.0 fields. This includes large data sets needed to validate in various contexts and cultures the learning and change models emerging in the field of educational psychology nationally and internationally. Crump's solution is scalable as virtual environments become more demanding from a performance perspective and as these environments become increasingly dense. As a Senior Analyst for Storage Switzerland, LLC, Crump advocates user-developed storage systems that are reliable, simple, affordable, and can be ideally served by what he calls "scale-out storage." Problems are caused when the storage system reaches maximum capacity and needs to be upgraded in way that do not create multirole silos of data. One solution has been offered by Isolin Systems (a Seattle, WA-based company specializing in large data storage solutions) in a single system that can handle all data in a single pool that can incrementally scale capacity and storage. Workloads that can run on a single system and that makes big storage reliable, reduces costs, and simplifies the complexity of research data storage, analyses, and ongoing validation studies.

3 Implications for Research, Practice, and Policy

Rebecca A. Clay, a writer who works in Washington DC and who is also an experienced researcher for the American Psychological Association (APA), shows the current shifting views about what constitutes quality research in the social sciences (Clay, 2010). She argues:

- In spite of a decade of arguments in favor of randomized clinical trials (RCTs) as providing the highest level of scientific proof, many critics are arguing that researchers will get better results if they also embrace other methodologies.
- Other methodologies that are seen as providing good sources of evidence include epidemiological studies, single-case experiments, the use of historical controls, or other sources of clinical evidence of effectiveness for particular interventions.
- The strengths of RCTs are that they provide an estimate of the effect that is unbiased and consistent, providing the gold standard of perfection when it is possible to randomly assign participants to treatment groups.
- Major weaknesses of the RCT approach is that they do not provide researchers with the critical information that is needed about individuals, such as which participants are going to benefit from the treatment and which are not—unless a very large sample is used.
- Supplementing the RCT design with other more qualitative, individually focused methods that allow an in-depth look at how behavior changes over time is particularly recommended in those studies where there is a concern that the method used may influence the results obtained.

3.1 Policy Changes Needed

Policies are increasingly acknowledging the relational aspects of learning and the value of each person in the system. Policies in applied educational psychology and its vast research capacity must acknowledge the knowledge base on effective communication and organizational development in outlining guidelines for dealing with diversity and inclusion in research. Research must be supported by all people in and around the educational system and all those interested in quality research projects should be educated to follow their burning questions to find answers needed to transform learning for the betterment of all learners. Policies must also value human models of functioning and give priority to those variables validated by experience, intuition, and scientific research—looking for a convergence of "truth" from all sources.

The role of funding agencies in shaping the future of research in all fields is a topic explored recently by Fox (2012 February 8) in The Washington Post section on leadership. The director of the National Science Foundation (NSF), Subra Suresh, an engineer and scientist formerly dean of the School of Engineering at the Massachusetts Institute of Technology, describes his role as "the science of leading scientists." With responsibilities for funding over 250,000 US individuals and 2,000 institutions, Suresh reports that a big challenge is to keep the agency and its staff of 1,400 in-house employees curious about understanding nature through science and passionate about education.

To lead in this service-oriented agency, a leader and his or her staff must keep both the agency and staff on the cutting edge with opportunities to engage with exciting and leading scientific discoveries. With an annual budget of 7 billion dollars, the biggest challenge Suresh admits is the increased number of proposals and severe workloads for staff in dealing with the number of outstanding proposals that are beyond the number that can be funded. Collaborative leadership strategies are being set up and multiple conversations with the use of hardware and software solutions to support two-way communication forums and all-hands town hall meetings. Allowing the best ideas to "bubble up" and vetted with the larger research community is fundamental to the NSF mission of leading basic and applied research.

3.2 Producing Credible Research: Implementation and Evaluation Considerations

If we sincerely want to produce credible research on learner-centered principles and practices that is valued and acted upon by all levels of people involved with our educational and learning systems, this research needs to be based on both knowledge-centered principles and a combination of community- and learner-centered principles as well. Developing new implementation and evaluation strategies that include innovative assessment methods can lead to an understanding of what makes particular learning communities viable and how best to support learning in both online and offline learning communities. Assessment measures can be designed to provide data about the balance between individualized and group learning processes, instructional strategies and activity structures, and outcomes within different types of learning communities (Duffy and Kirkley 2004; Hannum and McCombs 2008; Horwitz and McEwan 2011; McCombs 2001, 2007, 2009; McCombs 2013, in press; McCombs and Vakili 2005; Wheatley 2011; Wheatley and Frieze 2011).

As discussed in more detail by McCombs (2013, in press), there are a host of other issues that will expand into the twenty-first century concern about the growth of technology-based learning environments. In such environments, the PCA researchers in collaboration with practitioners and policymakers can play a central role in defining research implementation and evaluation data requirements. Some of the most significant include the following:

- Acknowledging the complexity of human behavior and the need for integrative theories and research that contextualize teaching and learning in schools as living systems that are themselves complex, dynamic, and built on both individual and relational principles.
- Looking at humans and their behavior holistically and focusing not only on cognitive and intellectual processes, but also on social and emotional processes that differentially influence learning, motivation, and development.
- Situating the study of teaching and learning in diverse school contexts and in particular content domains with a mix of quantitative and qualitative methodologies.
- Seeing teachers as learners whose own professional development must mirror the best of what we know about learning, motivation, and development.
- Rethinking critical assumptions about human abilities and talents, reciprocity in teacher and learner roles, and the function and purpose of schooling such that we can better prepare students for productive contributions to a global world and lifelong learning with emerging technologies.
- Acknowledging the central role of learners' thinking and perceptions of their experiences in learning and motivation, for all learners in the system including teachers, administrators, parents, and students.
- Basing our educational and learning systems on a new set of assumptions that are based on natural learning principles that are in keeping with twenty-first century learning and teaching principles and technologies that work from the inside out and not the outside in, thereby acknowledging unique learner attributes and lifelong learning goals.
- Adopting a new way of thinking and a new set of assumptions that can propel us to a radically different educational paradigm that aligns what we know about learners and learning with what the world is already doing.

Implementing these suggestions helps us see global connections and that we can learn from each other in ways that are more meaningful and relevant than current schooling practices. When dealing with a rapidly changing landscape that is likely to accelerate in the days and years to come, the educational system must be viewed as organic and living in service to the natural learning of people—students, teachers, administrators, and parents alike. It must be grounded on a core belief in the inherent tendency of all people to learn for a lifetime and must start with a value all can embrace: *schooling and education are the fundamental means to develop each learner's unique potential to contribute to a global world in a way that is meaningful and relevant to him or her.* Any other basic value will have the consequences of not transforming our current educational and research paradigms is appoint, recently acknowledged by many current researchers such as Ackerman (2010), APA Work Group of the Board of Educational Affairs (1997), Blaxter et al. (2006), Caine and Caine (2011), Ceci and Papierno (2005), Deakin-Crick et al. (2007), Deci and Ryan (1991), Dede (2009), Fullan (2010), Gilburg (2010), Greene and Azevedo (2010), Jukes et al. (2011), Lambert and McCombs (1998), Levine (2007), McCombs (2004), McNabb et al. (2001), Patall et al. (2010), Penuel and Riel (2007), Pink (2009), Polsky (2011), Ryan and Deci (2000), Sabelli and Dede (2001), Stewart (2007), Suarez-Orozco and Sattin (2007), and Surdam (2011).

It is time to rethink where we start with a natural learning and person-centered {education} model of the learner. It is also time to acknowledge the validity of learner and/or student perceptions of their learning experiences as a foundational variable that can most accurately predict learning outcomes we value.

4 Future Directions

4.1 The Bottom Line for Collaborative Research

To get the highest quality results that are free from internal and external threats to validity, it is always better to use many different methods relevant to the research.

Similarly, Blythe and Machold (2011) report the following: Since the Sarbanes–Oxley Act and other more recent regulatory actions have been implemented, organizations are increasingly seeking a sound risk control culture. Many are looking to governance, risk management, and compliance (GRC) frameworks and processes to effect improvement. Though an official, standard definition does not exist, GRC is established to ensure that an organization acts ethically and effectively in accordance with its risk appetite, internal policies, and external regulations through the alignment of strategy, processes, technology, and people.

The GRC framework described by Blythe and Machold (2011) is one wherein:

- Governance ensures that information reaching the executive team is sufficiently complete, accurate, and timely to enable appropriate management decision making and that controls are in place to confirm executive strategies and directions are carried out ethically and effectively.

The Learner-Centered Model

- Risk management identifies, analyzes, and addresses risks that can adversely affect the organization's strategic plan and ability to operate. Identified risks can be managed by mitigation, avoidance, acceptance, or risk-sharing methods.
- Compliance addresses the consistency in which the organization adheres to applicable regulations, laws, policies, contracts, values, and strategies. Many well-intentioned GRC programs tend to be centered on strategy, process, and technology. In many cases, however, these efforts tend to either neglect or underemphasize the human dimension, that is, the personal characteristics, competencies, and actions that make GRC successful. The all-too-frequent result is that the "rubber never meets the road," and the real work of risk dialogue and critical risk/reward decision making never actually takes place.

The best GRC strategy, process, and technology will most often fail if the organization's people are not fully committed at a personal level. Perhaps, the most fundamental and frequently asked question in GRC practice is how to influence people throughout the organization (from the boardroom to the mail room) toward becoming fully invested in establishing and maintaining a true culture of ethical governance, risk management, and compliance. In addressing this question, we will look to two generally accepted and proven models of leadership development and behavior management. The US Army's "Be, Know, Do" model serves as an overall organizing construct for evaluating the GRC process, and the "Pinpoint, Record, and Reward" formula is presented as a device to influence the right GRC management behaviors. The "Be, Know, Do" model of leadership development is particularly useful when applied to and tailored for today's GRC environment, which often struggles to attain full engagement from the organization's people. The model is simple and practical and can help a board, executive management team, managers, and supervisors influence a healthy and thriving GRC culture:

- **Be**: What are the character attributes and personal values that lead to an effective GRC culture?
- **Know**: What do all people throughout the organization need to know in order to develop and maintain an effective GRC culture?
- **Do**: What are the highest impact actions that will overtly demonstrate a strong and significant governance, risk, and compliance culture?

Behavior management specialists have a simple formula to influence behavior in desired directions, that is, "Pinpoint, Record, and Reward."

- **Pinpoint**: The organization must concretely define (or pinpoint) the exact set of behaviors desired. If people are not clear about what is expected, the desired behavior is unlikely.
- **Record**: If desired behaviors cannot be counted or timed, they cannot be adequately monitored and controlled. Behaviors that are monitored tend to improve. So, people throughout the organization must know that management is monitoring desired GRC behaviors or else adherence to those behaviors will erode.

- **Reward**: There must be a consequence that makes compliance matter. Preferably, the consequence will be in the form of meaningful rewards, for example, anything meaningful from recognition to financial incentives. But, a negative reinforcement will also put "teeth" into the GRC program, as needed.

With these new trends in leadership, the next section suggests research directions now needed in our field and in our data reduction models that can produce the transformation in our research methodologies in keeping with those needed when studying the effectiveness of person- and learner-centered programs.

4.2 Research Directions Needed

Both basic and applied research directions are needed as described below.

Basic Research Directions—In making the knowledge base from educational psychology more visible and accessible to educators and policymakers, some basic research directions are needed. Findings from laboratory studies versus the real-world contexts of applied research define main differences between these research categories. From the preceding chapters in this volume and my own perspective, a number of suggestions can be made for basic research, including the following:

- Research that can further refine and elucidate alternative conceptions of ability and intelligence and broaden our understanding of the interplay between cognitive, affective, neurobiological, and social factors that influence the development of competencies.
- Research on voluntary study groups, effective uses of problem-based learning, intersections of cooperative learning and curriculum, strategies for professional development and follow-up support for cooperative learning, and how well cooperative learning works for gifted students or other students at the margins.
- Research on adult literacy, along with more research on how teaching word recognition also affects normal and gifted readers (not just struggling readers) and how to develop teachers to deliver motivational reading and writing programs.
- Research on the cultural aspects of learning and contrasts between activity theory and contextualism as alternative views for understanding the sociocultural context of the teaching and learning process.
- Research that explores relations between self-regulation and volition, the development of self-regulation in children, self-regulation and the curriculum, and self-regulation across the life span.

Applied Research Directions—Ongoing collaborative research is needed on the real-world contexts of learning environments and the complex interactions between personal, organizational, and community levels of learning in schools as living systems. This includes special attention to applied research in the following areas:

- Research on school-based methodologies for studying the complex interrelationships between and among individual, organizational, and community levels of learning and functioning that can provide solid and credible evidence to support conclusions about causal connections between variables.
- Research on sharing the data reduction and other technology strides being made with quality research projects with others in the spirit of open source twenty-first century emerging technologies and data management platforms that can be shared in new web 2.0 and higher cloud technologies to enhance understanding of what we know.
- Research on the types of partnerships needed to disseminate results that are available more generally to the public, other researchers, practitioners, and policymakers so that awareness of the new thinking and approaches to implementing and sharing research data and findings can be made more cost-effective and efficient.

5 Conclusion

One major conclusion is that researchers interested in exploring person- and learner-centered transformational educational models have a responsibility to educate other professionals surrounding the enterprise of education and schooling—running the gamete from the researchers and educators to the policymakers, parents, and the public in our country and abroad. We have a unique opportunity to join forces with media partners, diverse groups of research collaborators from the ground up and top down. Not only do we need to help others understand new conceptions of learning, motivation, and development, but we also need to help them understand that learning and change are flip sides of the same social-psychological process—the process of changing one's mind. Processes and contexts that support learning are also those that support change. Based on the contributions in this book and in the field generally, this is also a challenge to help change the future preparation of researchers, practitioners, and policymakers.

A second conclusion is that we as a group of concerned researchers who understand the value of person- and learner-centered principles and practices must use our collective wisdom and data to work with media and policy groups to provide them with appropriate research briefs and other short stories that capture the attention of journalists, funding sources, and policymakers. These partnerships and collaborations offer an innovative way of solving the persistent educational problems facing all learners here and around the globe. We have the data and now is the time to creatively share it in ways our partners help create—in true communities of learners and practice.

References

Ackerman, G. L. (2010). Bridging 21st century gaps: An essay review of Mehlenbacher's technology and instruction. *Education review, 14(3)*. Retrieved Mar 4, 2011, from http://www.edrev.info/essays/v14n3.pdf.

Adams, J., Khan, H. T. A., Raeside, R., & White, D. (2009). *Research methods for graduate business and social science students*. New Delhi and Thousand Oaks: Response Books and Sage Publications (4th printing).

APA Work Group of the Board of Educational Affairs. (1997). *Learner-centered psychological principles: A framework for school reform and redesign*. Washington, DC: American Psychological Association.

Blaxter, L., Hughes, C., & Tight, M. (2006). *How to research* (3rd ed., pp. 122–126, 245, 246). New York: Open University Press (Read selected parts as needed of pages).

Blythe, B. T., & Machold, R. J. (2011). *The human side of GRC: The essence of governance, risk and compliance*. Atlanta: Crisis Management International. Downloaded on Dec 14, 2011, from http://tnwinc.com/files/Human_Side_of_GRC.pdf?webSyncID=26ed75de-ef90-4d81-87c9-edf91530a808&sessionGUID=f1484057-8d66-4fa8-b33b-e85a24d4b0ae&spUserID=NDk1MDMzOTc4MAS2&spMailingID=2457015&spJobID=35388742&spReportId=MzUzODg3NDIS1).

Breckler, S. J. (2010). The myopic vision of technology leaders. *Monitor on Psychology, 41(8)*, 23.

Caine, R. N., & Caine, G. (2011). *Natural learning for a connected world: Education, technology, and the human brain*. New York: Teachers College Press.

Ceci, S. J., & Papierno, P. B. (2005). The rhetoric and reality of gap closing: When the "have-nots" gain but the "haves" gain even more. *American Psychologist, 60(2)*, 149–160.

Clark, Alison. (2007). *Early childhood spaces: involving young children and practitioners in the design process*. The Hague: Bernard van Leer Foundation.

Crump, G. (2011). Solving corporate IT storage challenges with big data infrastructures. Downloaded on Dec 13, 2011, from bc_newsletters@response,webbuyersguide.com.

Deakin-Crick, R., McCombs, B., Haddon, A., Broadfoot, P., & Tew, M. (2007). The ecology of learning: Factors contributing to learner-centred classroom cultures. *Research Papers in Education, 22(3)*, 267–307.

Deci, E. L., & Ryan, R. M. (1991). A motivational approach to self: Integration in personality. In R. Dienstbier (Ed.), *Nebraska symposium on motivation Vol. 38. Perspectives on motivation*. Lincoln, NE: University of Nebraska Press.

Dede, C. (2009). Technologies that facilitate generating knowledge and possibly wisdom. *Educational Researcher, 38(4)*, 260–263.

Duffy, T. M., & Kirkley, J. R. (2004). *Learner-centered theory and practice in distance education*. Mahweh, NJ: Lawrence Erlbaum.

Elias, M. J., Zims, J. E., Weissberg, R. P., Frey, K. DS., Greenberg, M. T., Haynes, N. M., Kessler, R., Schwab-Stone, M. E., & Shriver, T. P. (1997). *Promoting social and emotional learning: Guidelines for educators*. Alexandria, VA: Association for Supervision and Curriculum Development.

Fielding, M., & Bragg, S. (2003). *Students as researchers: Making a difference. Consulting pupils about teaching and learning*. Cambridge, UK: Pearson Publishing.

Fullan, M. (2010). The big ides beyond whole system reform. *Education Canada*. Retrieved Mar 15, 2011 from http://www.michaelfullan.ca/Articles_10/BigIdeas-CEA.pdf.

Gilbos, R., & Schmeidler, D, (2011). *Case-based predictions*. In World scientific series in economic theory. London: Imperial College Press.

Gilburg, D. (2010). *Leader as convener not problem solver*. Waltham, MA: Pegasus Communications.

Graziano, A. M., & Raulin, M. L. (2010). *Research methods: A process of inquiry* (7th ed.). Boston, MA: Allyn & Bacon.

Greene, J. A., & Azevedo, R. (2010). The measurement of learners' self-regulated cognitive and metacognitive processes while using computer-based learning environments. *Educational Psychologist, 45*(4), 203–209.
Goleman, D. (1995). *Emotional intelligence*. New York: Bantam Books.
Hannum, W. H., & McCombs, B. L. (2008). Enhancing distance learning for today's youth with learner-centered principles. *Educational Technology, 48*(3), 11–21.
Horwitz, J., & McEwan, P. J. (2011). *Brookings small reforms report a useful contribution, Says independent review: Report highlights successful education reform efforts largely missed by media and policymakers*. Boulder, CO: National Education Policy Center (NEPC). Available at http://tinyurl.com/6wv43v5
Jukes, I., McCain, T., & Crockett, L. (2011). Education and the role of the future educator in the future. *Kappan, 92*(4), 15–21.
Kristjansson, K. (2010). Positive psychology, happiness, and virtue: The troublesome conceptual issues. *Review of General Psychology, 14*(4), 296–310.
Lambert, N., & McCombs, B. L. (Eds.). (1998). *How students learn: Reforming schools through learner-centered education*. Washington, DC: APA Books.
Lazarus, R. S. (2000). Toward better research on stress and coping. *American Psychologist, 55*(6), 665–673.
Lazarus, R. S. (2003). Does the positive psychology movement have legs? *Psychological Inquiry, 14*, 93–109.
Lee, C. D. (2011). Soaring above the clouds, delving the ocean's depths: Understanding the ecologies of human learning and the challenge for education science. *Educational Researcher, 39*(9), 643–655.
Levine, M. (2007). The essential cognitive backpack. *Educational Leadership, 64*(7), 16–22.
McCombs, B. L. (2001). Self-regulated learning and academic achievement: A phenomenological view. In B. J. Zimmerman & D. H. Schunk (Eds.), *Self-Regulated learning and academic achievement: Theory, research, and practice* (2nd ed., pp. 67–123). Mahwah, NJ: Lawrence Erlbaum Associates, Publishers.
McCombs, B. L. (2004). The learner-centered psychological principles: A framework for balancing a focus on academic achievement with a focus on social and emotional learning needs. In J. E. Zins, R. P. Weissberg, M. C. Wang, & H. J. Walberg (Eds.), *Building academic success on social and emotional learning: What does the research say?* (pp. 23–39). New York: Teachers College Press.
McCombs, B. L. (2007). Balancing accountability demands with research-validated, learner-centered teaching and learning practices. In C. E. Sleeter (Ed.), *Educating for democracy and equity in an era of accountability* (pp. 41–60). New York: Teachers College Press.
McCombs, B. L. (2009). Commentary: What can we learn from a synthesis of research on teaching, learning, and motivation? In K. R. Wentzel & A. Wigfield (Eds.), *Handbook of motivation at school* (pp. 655–670). New York: Routledge.
McCombs, B. L., & Miller, L. (2007). *Learner-centered classroom practices and assessments: Maximizing student motivation, learning, and achievement*. Thousand Oaks, CA: Corwin Press.
McCombs, B. L., & Miller, L. (2008). *The school leader's guide to learner-centered education: From complexity to simplicity*. Thousand Oaks, CA: Corwin Press.
McCombs, B. L. (2012). Educational Psychology and Educational Transformation, In W. M. Reynolds and G. E. Miller (Eds.), Comprehensive Handbook of Psychology, Vol. 7 *Educational Psychology* (2nd edn.). New York: John Wiley & Sons pp. 952–1025.
McCombs, B. L. (2013, in press). Using a 360 degree assessment model to support learning to learn. In Deakin-Crick, R., Stringher, C., & Small, T., Learning to learn for all: theory, practice and international research: *A multidisciplinary and lifelong perspective*. London: Routledge.
McCombs, B., & Vakili, D. (2005). A learner-centered framework for e-learning. *Teachers College Record, 107*(8), 1582–1609.

McNabb, M. L., McCombs, B. K. (2001). *Designs for e-learning: A vision and emerging framework.* Paper prepared for the PT3 Vision Quest on Assessment in e-Learning Cultures. Available at www.pt3.org.

Mitra, D. L. (2004). The significance of students: Can increasing "student voice" in schools lead to gains in student development. *Teachers College Record, 106*(4), 651–688.

Patall, E., Cooper, H., & Wynn, S. P. (2010). The effectiveness and relative importance of choice in the classroom. *Journal of Educational Psychology, 102*(4), 896–915.

Penuel, W. R., & Riel, M. (2007). The 'new' science of networks and the challenge of school change. *Phi Delta Kappan, 88*(8), 611–615.

Pekrun, R., Goetz, T., Daniels, L. M., Stupinsky., & Perry, R. P. (2010). Boredom in achievement settings: Exploring control-value antecedents and performance outcomes of a neglected emotion. *Journal of Educational Psychology, 102*(3), 531–549.

Pink, D. H. (2009). *Drive: The surprising truth about what motivates us.* New York: Riverhead Books.

Polsky, L. (2011). *The 8 greatest lessons 2011 taught us about change leadership.* Posted DEC 05, 2011, 12:00:00 AM EST, from http://www.humanresourcesiq.com/talent-management/columns/the-7-greatest-lessons-2011-taught-us-about-change/.

Radel, R., Sarrazin, P., Legrain, P., & Wild, T. C. (2010). Social contagion of motivation between teacher and student: Analyzing underlying processes. *Journal of Educational Psychology, 102*(3), 577–587.

Robson, C. (2002). *Real world research* (2nd ed.). Malden, MA: Blackwell Publishing.

Rogers, C. R. (1964). Toward a modern approach to values: The valuing process in the mature person. *Journal of Abnormal and Social Psychology, 68,* 160–167.

Ryan, R. M., & Deci, E. L. (2000). Self-determination theory and the facilitation of intrinsic motivation, social development, and well-being. *American Psychologist, 55*(1), 68–78.

Sabelli, N., & Dede, C. (2001). *Integrating educational research and practice: reconceptualizing the goals and process of research to improve educational practice.* unpublished. http://www.virtual.gmu.edu/integrating.html and http://h2oproject.law.harvard.edu/educational_funding.pdf.

Sabelli, N., & Dede, C. (2012). *Integrating educational research and practice: Reconceptualizing the goals and process of research to improve educational practice.* (in press) http://www.virtual.gmu.edu/integrating.html and http://h2oproject.law.harvard.edu/educational_funding.pdf

Seligman, M. E. P., & Csikszentmihalyi. M. (2000). Positive psychology: An introduction. *American Psychologist, 55*(1), 5–14.

Stewart, V. (2007). Citizens of the world. *Educational Leadership, 64*(7), 9–14.

Suarez-Orozco, M. M., & Sattin, C. (2007). Wanted: Global citizens. *Educational Leadership, 64*(7), 58–62.

Surdam, G. (2011). *Bright start family literacy—success stories.* Email sent to team on December 19, 2011.

Sweeney, L. B. (2010). Systems thinking: A means to understanding our complex world. *Pegasus Communications.* Downloaded on Dec 3, 2010, from www.pegasus.com.

Walls, T. A., & Little, T. D. (2005). Relations among personal agency, motivation, and school adjustment in early adolescence. *Journal of Educational Psychology, 97*(1), 23–31.

Williams, C. (2011). New department of education initiative: Online communities for education professionals. Downloaded on February 18, 2012 from http://www.linkedin.com/groupItem?view=&srchtype=discussedNews&gid=2811&item=80066691&type=member&trk=eml-anet_dig-b_pd-ttl-cn&ut=2ZKSzPqf3e9B81.

Zimmerman, B. J., & Schunk, D. H. (Eds.). (2001). *Self-regulated learning and academic achievement: Theoretical perspectives* (2nd ed.). Mahwah, NJ: Lawrence Erlbaum Associates.

A Practice of Social Ethics: Anthropological, Epistemological, and Ethical Foundations of the Person-Centered Approach

Peter F. Schmid

The person-centered approach (PCA) is fundamentally based on a philosophy of *dialogue*. It is dialogue where the human being, both unique and interrelated from the very beginning, fully becomes what occidental philosophy calls a *person*.

This does not mean that it has its grounds in metaphysical, ontological ideas. On the contrary, both its roots and its foundation lie in *ethics*, the philosophy of how to lead one's life. Therefore, to speak about dialogue does not mean to merely speak about mutual exchange and the issue of equality; it denotes a practice of responsibility, based on the response—ability of human beings. It is a practical philosophy of the person, even more accurate: a *practice of social ethics*. Thus, the PCA is a consequence of an ethical stance.

If psychotherapy and related professions in particular and facilitative relationships in general are understood in a personal way, they are an ethical enterprise. By doing psychotherapy (or counseling, helping, facilitating, teaching, upbringing, engaging in social or pastoral work, etc.)[1] and by reflecting this theoretically, a decision is made to respond to the need, to the life of another person, and to share his or her joys and sorrows. It derives from being addressed by the Other, from being touched, from being asked, from being called, and from being

---

[1] The philosophical underpinnings described in this chapter apply to all kinds of person-centered work. For reasons of readability, I use the terms facilitative or helping relationship, facilitator or helper, and client or helpee. All these relationships have in common that they imply an imbalance of power: One is the "helper" and the other one(s) is (are) the "helpee(s)." They are called *person (or client-)-centered relationships* and are a special case of *personal relationships*, that is, person-to-person relationships. Relationships are called "personal," when the individuals involved are regarded as persons in the meaning described below, regardless whether the relationship implies a "hierarchy" (like in counseling) or not (like partners, friends, colleagues, peers, etc.).

P. F. Schmid (✉)
Sigmund Freud University, Vienna, Koflergasse 4 1120 Vienna, Austria
e-mail: pfs@pfs-online.at

appealed to. This means that the need of the Other is there first and that all these ways of relating are responding, answering to a demand. Thus, they take their origin at the Other. They see him or her as a call. In particular, starting from a phenomenological consideration, as Carl Rogers did (and not out of morals), they must be regarded as ethical phenomena. In these interpersonal encounter relationships, addressed, and asked to respond, the therapist (counselor, helper, facilitator, teacher, parent, social or pastoral worker, etc.) assumes a deep responsibility toward the client (helpee, group or community member, student, child, etc.), an obligation in which their fellow humans expect him or her to render the service we owe to each other and thus to fulfill our duty (Schmid 2002a, p. 66).

This chapter explores the underpinnings of person-centered philosophy as the practice of personalization, being, and becoming a person by briefly examining the core terms of its theory and practice and their grounding in philosophy. It has a look at the implications for human living-together in general and therapeutic and related fields of social work in particular.[2]

1 The Image of the Human Being: A Basis for Thinking and Acting

It is important to be aware that every human being has an idea about what it means to be human. All our living and thinking is grounded in basic beliefs, in a more or less consistent image of the human being as part of our worldview. Basic beliefs about the nature of humans (such as the question whether humans are good, evil, or both or whether they are free or determined) cannot be verified or falsified, and they are meta-empirical. Therefore, it does not make sense to argue about different images of the human being or to try to convince each other (It rather makes sense to pay attention to those areas of our worldview that experience difficulties in understanding when we try to explain them to others and therefore need to be critically further developed).

Each human being bases their acting and thinking—consciously or not, reflected or not, scientifically (i.e., systematically) investigated or not—on assumptions of what and how people are. We all have an image of ourselves and the human being in general that constitutes our anthropology, our understanding of us as humans. We all have conceptions: Why we act and think in a specific way and not in another one (theory of motivation), how we develop and grow (theory of personality including a developmental theory), how we relate to others (theory of relationship), how and why processes occur that make us suffer or unhappy (theory

---

[2] This chapter builds on an invited lecture, given at the 5th World Congress for Psychotherapy in Beijing, 2008, a keynote lecture at the 3rd Conference of The British Association for the PCA, in Cirencester, UK, 2007, and a paper, given at the World PCE Conference, Norwich, UK, 2007. See Schmid 2007b, 2008b, c, 2012a, b, c for more details.

of "disorders," e.g., psychopathology), and how we can help each other or, generally, influence each other (theory of change including a theory of therapy, education, pedagogy, social and pastoral work, etc.).

This is the reason why there are different theories and practices of helping relationships. Schools of therapy, pedagogy, etc., are different because the underlying image of the human being is different. Therefore, it is important to consider one's image of the human being as the foundation for one's acting and thinking, for example, in order to hold consistency in one's mind and to offer consistency in helping relationships.

The so-called humanistic and existential orientations in psychotherapy are the only ones which have so far explicitly taken the image of the human being as a starting point for practice and theory building. The anthropological, epistemological, and ethical convictions of the humanistic image of the human being were summarized in the form of theses by James Bugental (1964), in what is called the "Magna Charta" of humanistic psychology. Among them are the statements that the human being supersedes the sum of their parts (a holistic perspective including "body," "soul," and "mind"), which they live consciously, have the free will to decide, and live toward aims. An important conclusion of such assumptions is that a science adequate for the human being, namely a *human* science as opposed to *natural* science (hence named "humanistic"), is still to be developed.

Humanistic psychotherapy and related work as the practice resulting from this image of the human being mark a profound revolution in psychology and psychotherapy, a true change of paradigms, not yet fully sounded out. The philosophy, theory, and practice that radically adhere to this image of the human being are that of the PCA.

2 Central Philosophical Terms in the PCA

2.1 Person: The Human Being as a Relational–Substantial Being

The name of the approach does not come by coincidence. The PCA is founded out of the conviction that the image of the human being most adequate to our experience we have been developing so far in the history of humankind is to regard him and her as a person. This term denotes the essential conclusion of the process of reflection about ourselves in the European tradition during more than two and a half millennia from the Judeo-Christian and Greek tradition via the Muslims and the Enlightenment until today (Schmid 1991, 1998a).

To be a person means that the human being is intrinsically and dialectically both substantial and relational: being from oneself and thus autonomous and being from relationship and thus interdependent with others. Human beings have an innate capacity, need, and tendency to develop on their own *and* in relationships.

Both autonomy and interrelatedness constitute the one human nature. According to Rogers (1958), the human is motivated by the actualizing tendency (see below) as the inner force and resource to lead one's own life out of one's own capabilities which only can be tapped, if the individual is facilitated by a special kind of relationship, that is, an encounter relationship (see below).

Thus, the two essential dimensions of person-centered anthropology, of being a person, are *interconnectedness and independence*. To be a person depicts an understanding of the human being as a *relational–substantial being*, interdependent, *and* autonomous, characterized by solidarity *and* self-responsibility. (Schmid 1991, 1994, 1996, 1998a, b, 2012c).

In particular, a deeper realization of the relational dimension of personhood within the paradigm has been achieved during the process of reflection by Rogers and other scholars. This has been termed (with slightly different accents) *relationship therapy* (Rogers 1942), *interpersonal* (Rogers 1962b), *person to person* (Rogers and Stevens 1967), *encounter approach* (Schmid 1994), *dialogical approach* (Schmid 1996, 2006a), or *meeting at relational depth* (Mearns and Cooper 2005). Such an image of the human being with its profoundness and radicalism and the dialectical balance of substantiality and relationality can only be found in a genuine PCA and is the foundation of the identity of this approach and the state of the art of a genuinely PCA in theory and practice today.

2.2 Encounter: The Relationship Person to Person

If a person enters a relationship with another human being as a person, this is termed an encounter relationship. "Encounter" derives from the Latin word "contra" ("against"). To encounter means to be open to be surprised, "to be touched by the essence of the opposite" (Guardini 1955). The term "encounter" denotes a relationship where the other person is not regarded as an alter ego, but met as truly being an *Other*. I cannot simply conclude from me and my experience to the self and experience of the other person. The attitude rather is to open up and genuinely accept and empathically try to comprehend what the partner in the relationship is going to disclose. This marks a far-reaching epistemological paradigm change, based on phenomenology and constructivism. It means that I no longer draw conclusions from the way in which I experience the other person or understand their experiences, thus putting them into my categories, but instead open up to what the Other is going to disclose and wants to be understood.

Therefore, the PCA no longer follows an epistemology of "egology"—a very meaningful term by Emmanuel Levinas (1957, p. 189)—taking as its starting point the self, or that which is already known. Instead of trying to understand itself by itself, it acts upon an epistemology of transcendence, of *alterity*, and of dialogue (see below), where the movement goes from the Other to me. The respective epistemology can correctly be named a *Thou-I-relationship*, because it has its origin in the opening up of the "Thou." The Thou precedes the I—a basic stance for the way of understanding in a person-centered approach, possible only in the authentic attitude of presence (see below; Schmid 1994, 1996, 1998c, 2012c).

Such a way of understanding and relating to each other enables the *interpersonal, co-creative process* of personalization (see below), of becoming a person, making therapy and related fields an issue based on a fundamental We (see below). So the PCA has developed a bi- or multi-polar psychological model.

While many other orientations "use" the relationship as a means, "in order to," as a precondition for the task to perform, the work to do as such, the unique stance of the PCA is that the relationship itself is the help. Psychotherapy (education, teaching, group work, etc.) is the art of encounter, dialogue from the very beginning (Schmid 2006a; Schmid and Mearns 2006).

As persons we are not only in relationship, we are relationship (Schmid 2002b, 2004). This becomes clearer, if we have a look at the dialectical nature of the actualizing process.

2.3 Personalization: The Dialectical Nature of the Actualizing Process

In-depth investigations (see Schmid 2008a) into the origins of the idea of the actualizing tendency (Rogers 1963) brought to the fore that the idea of an actualizing tendency with its roots and surprising parallels in the classical doctrine of energeia and dynamics or act and potential by Aristotle and Thomas Aquinas is in itself a dialectic principle. According to them, the potential can never become reality without an efficient cause (causa efficiens); it needs something or somebody from the outside to become what it can become—in personal terminology: it needs an other, another thing, or person.

For the understanding of personality development, this means that life is the actualization, the realization of the given possibilities, the potency, which needs an "influence" from outside, that is, by somebody else and by another human being. This is the foundation for the essential importance of relationship also from a substantial viewpoint. Although the actualizing tendency is a tendency inherent to the individual, the presence of the other is needed to make it work. The relational and the substantial are not independent dimensions but two sides of the same coin. With the very idea of actualization, "the Other" is inevitably connected. With this, the PCA has indeed moved on from the "self-centered period" of the so-called humanistic movement with its numerous self-terms, like self-development, self-determination, and self-realization. We cannot even think of a person without thinking of their relationships.

Therefore, the actualizing tendency must be seen as a dialectical axiom. It must also be regarded as a relationship-oriented and therefore a social construct and ultimately at the human being with their specific *human* quality as a *personalizing tendency* or *personalizing process*, characterized by freedom and creativity (Schmid 1994, 2008a).

So the PCA finds itself in a tradition that appreciates the possible in the same way as the real and therefore does not reduce the person to what can be found obviously and superficially. Instead of trying to understand itself by itself, it follows an epistemology of dialogue.

2.4 The Fundamental We: The Importance of the Group and of Society

Rogers (1962) was convinced that "the interpersonal relationship" is "the core of guidance." This "encounter person to person" as the core of an *intersubjective, co-creative process* springs from a fundamental We (Schmid 2003); its nature is to co-respond to the situation the client finds himself or herself in. This also means that helper and helpee are co-responding to the relationship they find themselves in the very moment of their being-together. They are co-creating the relationship out of mutual encounter.

The client's contribution to this fundamentally dialogical process is to actualize their potential and thus "make therapy work," that is, to actively make use of their inherent capacity to be fostered by the acknowledgment and empathy of the facilitator (see Bohart and Tallman 1999 for psychotherapy) by "informing" the helper and by actively bringing the helper in form to relate to and understand the client in order to better understand himself or herself (Schmid 2003).

The contribution on the helper's part is to be present (see below). This means to respond to the call of another person; client and helper co-respond to the demand of life and to the relational situation they are in.

Such a stance of interconnectedness includes the importance of *transcending the pair* in helping relationships. Levinas and other philosophers of dialogue remind us that we do not live in a world of two and that the pair is not the ultimate form of living-together. One more consequence of the meaning of being-oneself when being in relationship is that there is not only the Other; there is also the Other of the Other. In short, we live in a world of smaller and larger *groups*.

The PCA is not about two in a relatively secluded space. It rather is *social* psychology by its very nature always having in mind "the Third" (Levinas 1974)—a term that serves as a metaphor for the Other of the Other. We live in groups our whole lifelong. The very focus of the approach is on the community beyond the relative seclusion of the pair, which makes the group the primary reality and locus of facilitating. The group, as already emphasized by Rogers (1970), is the interface of the individual and the society where the person experiences themselves in their substantial and relational dimensions. Thus, it can be shown that the PCA is essentially a group approach (see Schmid 1994, 1996; Schmid and O'Hara 2012) and psychotherapy and related fields are essentially social therapy in the meaning of a therapy for and by society—with all political consequences (see below). One outcome was that from Rogers onwards, the approach dealt with larger communities and engaged in peace work (Rogers 1980; Schmid 1996).

2.5 Presence: The Elementary Facilitative Attitude

Building on these assumptions, the question arises what can be done to do justice to the others and ourselves as persons and how can attitudes be fostered that facilitate an encounter relationship, in other words: What is the adequate posture and approach?

It obviously is not an attitude of diagnosing and assessing but of being open to the Other, that is, to expose oneself to the Other in the "here and now," in a word: to be present. This is an understanding of "here and now" that matches the kairotic quality of presence in the philosophy of kairology and the philosophy of the right acting in the right moment (Kierkegaard 1855)—named after Kairos, the Greek God for the quality of time (Schmid 1994, 2002b, 2003, 2006a).

Presence—literally the underlying Latin word "prae-esse" means "to be fully there"—is the existential foundation and deeper meaning of the well known, yet all too often superficially misunderstood core conditions of authenticity (congruence, genuineness), acknowledgment (unconditional positive regard, praise, acceptance), and comprehension (empathy). These basic attitudes, carefully elaborated by Rogers (1957) with profound parallels in encounter philosophy (e.g., Buber 1961), are seen as three dimensions of one fundamental attitude toward life: presence—*the* core condition of encounter and of "being-with and being-counter" (Schmid and Mearns 1996).

The facilitator's task is to realize these continuously and in any given situation—thus responding to the challenge of the relationship in its concrete context. This provides a climate of safety, trust, and respect for the client enabling him or her to more and more face and develop themselves.

2.6 Dialogue: The Realization of Responsibility in Solidarity

"Dialogue" is a term with specific notions in the history of philosophy. A brief look into the evolving notion of dialogue in anthropology can help to understand its profound meaning for facilitative relationships. (For more details, Schmid 2006a, 2012b).

$Διά$ (dia) means between or through. Literally, "dialogue" means "between" or "through words." One might translate it with "conversation," but also with "flowing of (or: through) meaning." According to this, usually dialogue is understood as human conversation face-to-face, as mutual exchange, characterized by symmetry and equality: a meeting of the one with the other.

Martin Buber and his understanding of dialogue can be seen as the underlying idea of most humanistic orientations. For him, the significance of dialogue is not in the one and not in the other partner and not in both together but in their exchange. Thus, dialogue is what *follows* from interpersonality. "The sphere of the interpersonal is the opposite-to-each-other; its unfolding is what we call dialogue" (Buber 1961, pp. 275–276). True dialogue is not transmission of information; it is participation in the being of the Other. The respective attitude toward the Other is referred to as "I-Thou-relationship."

But this view was also disapproved of and developed further. *Emmanuel Levinas* emphasized that dialogue is not to merely understand each other, expressing mutual empathy. He criticized that Buber got caught in circularity—in the enclosed circle of the I–Thou. According to Levinas, dialogue rather is a step beyond the thinking of the one and the other. Dialogue is not the experience of a meeting of persons talking with each other. Dialogue is not a consequence of meeting each other: Dialogue is of original "im–media–cy," is not mediated (Levinas 1989, p. 72, 74).

Buber emphasized that dialogue is not a consequence of an experience. On the contrary, *dialogue is an original, primary occurrence,* as Levinas (1989 p. 74) puts it, it is the interpersonal relationship, "the original sociality," that occurs in dialogue. So far, both are in line. But in Levinas' view, dialogue is not about symmetry, as stressed by Buber, but dissymmetry in the relationship. "It is precisely because the Thou is *absolutely* different from the I that there is—from the one to the other—dialogue" (Levinas 1989, p. 76). So it is the other way round: It is dialogue now that constitutes interpersonality.

The fundamental We is not a symmetric We. It is asymmetric by nature. When we speak of a Thou-I-relationship, the Other comes first: The Other calls me, the face of the Other addresses me, it is a provocation, it "demands." Therefore, dialogue constitutes responsibility, solidarity, and a commitment. The Thou calls the I into service. "The Other *orders* me to serve him," Levinas (1986, p. 74) says. Hence, diacony ($\delta\iota\alpha\kappa\text{o}\nu\iota\alpha$, service) is not a result of dialogue, and it is the fundamental essence of the human relationship (Levinas 1989; Schmid 1994, pp. 147–148).

Solidarity now is not a second-order category deriving from experience, but a basic human condition. Such thinking is the turn from monologue to dialogue, from *thinking about* the other to *addressing* the concrete fellow person. It is the willingness and readiness to simply say: "Here I am" (Levinas 1986). It means to be *for* the Other, not simply being *with* him.

Such dissymmetrical relationship is the origin of ethics. *The I is constituted by his or her responsibility* to the call of the Other. Nobody can be replaced in facing this unconditional demand.

This radically turns the usual order between self-consciousness and dialogue around: Encounter in dialogue is the precondition for self-consciousness and self-confidence. Dialogue is the non-indifference of the I toward the Thou or to formulate it positively, attention, care, unconditional positive regard. In other words, dialogue is an expression of love. Levinas prefers to think of philosophy as the "wisdom of love" rather than the "love of wisdom" (the literal Greek meaning of the word "philosophy").

To sum it up, dialogue is neither the consequence of an insight nor an action to be taken. Dialogue is a primary fact of and in the human condition, an original occurrence. And so it follows: The human person *is* dialogue, from the very beginning (Schmid 1998a, 2006a). To be in the world is to be in dialogue.

This is more than a nicely put statement, because it puts our understanding of our being in the world and with each other on new ground: Being in the world is being in dialogue. From a dialogical point of view, persons are not only seen as being in relationships; as persons, they are relationship. (Schmid 2004; Schmid and Mearns 2006). Persons are dialogue.

3 Personal Social Ethics: Dialogue as the Realization of the Fundamental We in the Encounter Person to Person

Accordingly, psychotherapy and related work means to enter dialogue.

This is why Levinas' understanding can be seen as an explication of the stance of the PCA: The client comes first: Facilitation, help, and therapy are for the client, and the helper is "their deacon" and is at their service (Schmid 2003, pp. 112–114).

Levinas (1957, 1986) criticizes the so-called humanistic approaches as not humane enough—still putting the ego in the center and taking it as standard and rule for everything. This central position of the ego needs to be replaced by the unconditional demand of the Other. In my eyes, there is some truth in the reproach that many forms of humanistic therapy including some strands in the PCA are only or mainly concerned with the therapists' tasks and therefore are forms of "egology." If the therapist is only concerned with what to do, how to behave, and how to realize the conditions, if client-centered therapy mainly consists of investigating the side of the therapist, we might really find ourselves again in the trap of being concerned with ourselves, with therapist-centeredness, and with egology—whereas client-centered means that the client comes first and the relationship is for the client.

Taking the aforementioned notion of dialogue serious, then dialogue is not the consequence or the aim of person-centered work. Rather *to help means to enter dialogue*. It is of interest to note that "enter" has the same root as "inter"—"between," the Greek "$\delta\iota\alpha$"—and derives from the Latin "intrare" which means "go into." Help means to enter—to go into—to enter a room that is already there.

So, a closer look at Rogers' understanding of "therapy as encounter" reveals dialogue as primary occurrence and the facilitating relationship intrinsically as dialogue, as entering the "challenge of the Other" (Schmid 2006a). Thus, dialogue is in the very beginning of such a relationship.

Dialogue is definitely not "a means in order to ...," something the helper has to achieve or perform, nor is it a precondition, let alone a technique. Dialogue is also not an expression of equality, mutuality, and reciprocity, as we are used to think. It does not signify moments of intensive exchange in the facilitative relationship. It is not a goal for it and not an outcome of it.

Dialogue is "more." The persons engaged in a facilitative relationship *are* dialogue. This completely turns around our traditional thinking of helping relationships. We must not come into dialogue in the meaning of achieving it, or making it happen; we must come into dialogue in the meaning of coming to what is already there, *we enter dialogue!* Dialogue takes place before the first word is spoken, and the first glimpses are exchanged. We need to *realize* that there is dialogue regardless whether we are aware of it or not. "In the beginning" (Schmid 1998a), *there is dialogue*, primary, fundamental, basic, deeply rooted, and thus seminal.

The helping relationship is the unfolding of this dialogue. Therefore, dialogue is not a consequence, but a fundament of community. It is about realizing the preceding common We—in all its dissymmetry. *Dialogue is realizing the healing and challenging quality of the essential human We.* The *restoration of this underlying We is the therapeutic or facilitative in these relationships*. This is done by presence as the realization of the core conditions. Hence, presence is not a precondition for dialogue; rather it is dialogue that comes to the fore in presence. Presence is an expression of the fundamental "Here I am." *To say* "Here I am" (in the full meaning of being-with and being-counter) *is all what we have to do.*

To encounter a person is to realize to be in dialogue. It is only in dialogue that persons really are addressed as persons. Therefore, by definition, a PCA is an approach that unveils the dialogical quality already there. We just have to realize it. Person-centered work is the realization of the fundamental We.

It is not to *make* something happen with or in the client, not to teach the client to do something or behave in a specific way, and not to achieve something, but to be present in the full meaning of the word, to let happen, what is there, even before we realize it. Dialogue in helping relationships is not *bringing* the client or oneself into dialogue; it is rather unearthing and unfolding the interpersonal quality of what at a first glance might seem one-sided begging for advice, helplessly being at the mercy of somebody, stuck development, intellectual stuttering, refusal of growth, provocation, testing the helper, and so on.

Dialogue is not a means or an instrument to communicate; *it is rather the* "way of being with"—*and ethically seen*—*the* "way of being for" *another person, a fundamental existential stance.* Dialogue is taking serious to be responsible (response–able) and to owe a response to a demand, a cry for solidarity. Dialogue is an irreversible principle and condition of being human. Humans substantially rely on dialogue, better: They *are* dialogue. It follows: *The facilitative relationship substantially relies on dialogue, better: It is dialogue.* This denotes the foundation of the person-centered approach.

4 A Political Conclusion

Helping is not a method of repairing problems or fostering personal happiness. That is psychotechnique. On the contrary, from the outlined image of the human being follows, that is, fundamentally an *ethical* and a *political* task.

I am convinced that a dialogical understanding of helping will, in the long run, prevail in all orientations of helping and facilitating. Although at the moment problem-centered and solution-focused orientations along with a passion for the invention of sophisticated techniques seem to prevail, humanity will finally win.

This image of the human being and the ensuing understanding of psychotherapy are also a *political statement*. To be a person-centered facilitator is not only a personal, but a political challenge. It means to be existentially challenged as a person, as a role model, and, where applicable, as a professional to foster empowerment. In questioning established paradigms and patterns, any genuinely PCA defies current trends toward problem- and solution-centeredness. It resists the temptations of expertise and the seductions and damnations of self-selected experts. Placing itself at the edge of human knowledge and at the frontier of the human's search for self-understanding, it is an ongoing provocation to established science and the customary politics and policies of the helping professions, in a word: to the habitual conventions of society. Holding a clear stance with its image of the human being and its values, it takes the risk of developing a truly human science, research, and practice. (Schmid 2007, 2012a).

References

Bohart, A. C., & Tallman, K. (Eds.). (1999). *How clients make therapy work*. Washington: APA.
Buber, M. (1961). *Das Problem des Menschen*. [*The problem of being human.*] Heidelberg: Lambert Schneider.
Bugental, J. F. T. (1964). The third force in psychology. *Journal of Humanistic Psychology, 4*(1), 19–26.
Guardini, R. (1955). Die Begegnung: Ein Beitrag zur Struktur des Daseins. [Encounter: On the structure of presence.] *Hochland 47*(3), 224–234.
Kierkegaard, S. (1855). *Øieblikket*. [*The moment.*] Copenhagen.
Levinas, E. (1957). Die Philosophie und die Idee des Unendlichen. [The philosophy and idea of the infinite.] In: E. Levinas, *Die Spur des Anderen*. [*The trace of the Other.*] (pp. 185–208). Freiburg: Alber 1983; orig. 1957.
Levinas, E. (1974). *Autrement qu'être ou au delà de l'essence*. [*Different than being or beyond essence.*] Den Haag: Nijhoff.
Levinas, E. (1986). *Ethik und Unendliches*. [Ethics and the infinite.] Graz: Böhlau.
Levinas, E. (1989). Dialog. [Dialogue.] In F. Böckle et al.(Eds.), *Christlicher Glaube in moderner Gesellschaft* [*Christian faith in modern society*], (vol.1, pp. 61–85). Freiburg i.Br.: Herder.
Mearns, D., & Cooper, M. (2005). *Working at relational depth in counselling and psychotherapy*. London: Sage.
Rogers, C. R. (1942). *Counseling and psychotherapy: newer concepts in practice*. Boston: Houghton Mifflin.

Rogers, C. R. (1957). The necessary and sufficient conditions of therapeutic personality change. *Journal of Consulting Psychology, 21*(2), 95–103.
Rogers, C. R. (1958). The characteristics of a helping relationship. *Personnel and Guidance Journal, 37*(1), 6–16.
Rogers, C. R. (1962). The interpersonal relationship: the core of guidance. *Harvard Educational Review, 4*(32), 416–429.
Rogers, C.R. (1963). The actualizing tendency in relation to 'motives' and to consciousness. In: M.R. Jones, (Ed.), *Nebraska Symposium on Motivation*. Lincoln: University of Nebraska Press, pp. 1–24.
Rogers, C. R. (1970). *On encounter groups*. New York: Harper and Row.
Rogers, C. R., & Stevens, B. (1967). *Person to person. The problem of being human*. Walnut Creek: Real People Press.
Rogers, C. R. (1980). *A way of being*. New York: Houghton Mifflin.
Schmid, P.F. (1991). Souveränität und Engagement: Zu einem personzentrierten Verständnis von "Person" [Souvereignty and engagement: On a person-centered understanding of person]. In Rogers, C.R. & Schmid, P.F. (1991). *Person–zentriert [Person–centered]* (8th edn. 2011; pp. 15–164). Mainz: Grünewald.
Schmid, P.F. (1994). *Personzentrierte Gruppenpsychotherapie [Person-centered group psychotherapy], vol.I: Solidarität und Autonomie [Solidarity and autonomy]*. Cologne: EHP.
Schmid, P.F. (1996). *Personzentrierte Gruppenpsychotherapie in der Praxis [Person-centered group psychotherapy in practice], vol. II: Die Kunst der Begegnung [The art of encounter]*. Paderborn: Junfermann.
Schmid, P.F. (1998a). *Im Anfang ist Gemeinschaft: Personzentrierte Gruppenarbeit [In the beginning there is community: Person-centered group work]*, (vol.III). Stuttgart: Kohlhammer.
Schmid, P. F. (1998b). 'On becoming a person-centered therapy': A person-centred understanding of the person. In B. Thorne & E. Lambers (Eds.), *Person-centred therapy: A European perspective* (pp. 38–52). London: Sage.
Schmid, P. F. (1998c). 'Face to face': The art of encounter. In B. Thorne & E. Lambers (Eds.), *Person-centred therapy: A European perspective* (pp. 74–90). London: Sage.
Schmid, P. F. (2002a). Knowledge or acknowledgement? Psychotherapy as 'the art of not-knowing'—Prospects on further developments of a radical paradigm. *Person-Centered and Experiential Psychotherapies, 1*(1&2), 56–70.
Schmid, P. F. (2002b). Presence: im-media-te co-experiencing and co-responding. In G. Wyatt & P. Sanders (Eds.), *Contact and perception* (pp. 128–203). Ross-on-Wye: PCCS Books.
Schmid, P. F. (2003). The characteristics of a person-centered approach to therapy and counselling: criteria for identity and coherence. *Person-Centered and Experiential Psychotherapies, 2*, 104–120.
Schmid, P. F. (2004). Back to the client: A phenomenological approach to the process of understanding and diagnosis. *Person-Centered and Experiential Psychotherapies, 3*, 36–51.
Schmid, P. F. (2006). The challenge of the other: Towards dialogical person-centered psychotherapy and counselling. *Person-Centered and Experiential Psychotherapies, 5*, 241–254.
Schmid, P.F. (2007). Psychotherapy is political or it is not psychotherapy: The actualizing tendency as personalizing tendency. Keynote lecture, 3rd BAPCA Conference: Cirencester.
Schmid, P. F. (2008a). A personalizing tendency: philosophical perspectives on the actualizing tendency axiom and its dialogical and therapeutic consequences. In B. Levitt (Ed.), *Reflections on human potential* (pp. 84–101). Ross-on-Wye: PCCS Books.
Schmid, P. F. (2008b). Active responsiveness. Person-Centered Psychotherapy—a dialogical approach. Invited lecture, World Conference for Psychotherapy, Beijing.
Schmid, P. F. (2008c). *How person-centred is dialogical? Therapy as encounter—an evolutionary improvement? an arbitrary deviation? a new paradigm?* Paper, World PCE Conference Norwich.

Schmid, P. F. (2012a). Psychotherapy is political or it is not psychotherapy: The person-centered approach as an essentially political venture. *Person-Centered and Experiential Psychotherapies, 11*, 95–108.

Schmid, P.F. (2012b). Dialogue as the foundation of person-centred therapy. In R. Knox, D. Murphy, S. Wiggins, M. Cooper (Eds.), *Relational depth: New perspectives and developments*. Houndmills: Palgrave Macmillan. In print.

Schmid, P.F. (2012c).The anthropological, relational and ethical foundations of person-centred therapy. M. Cooper, M. O'Hara, P.F. Schmid, A. Bohart (Eds.) *The handbook of person-centred psychotherapy and counselling*. In print. Houndmills: Palgrave Macmillan.

Schmid, P. F., & Mearns, D. (2006). Being-with and being-counter: Person-centered psychotherapy as an in-depth co-creative process of personalization. *Person-Centered and Experiential Psychotherapies, 5*, 174–190.

Schmid, P.F. & O'Hara, M. (2012). Working with groups. In M. Cooper, M. O'Hara, P.F. Schmid, A. Bohart (Eds.) *The handbook of person-centred psychotherapy and counselling*. In print. Houndmills: Palgrave Macmillan.

Part VIII
Spirituality

Christian Spirituality and the Person-Centered Approach

Robert Fruehwirth

1 From Secular Counseling to Religious Experience: Kenosis in Christian Contemplation and Person-Centered Therapy

1.1 Introduction: Facilitating a Mutual Openness

For decades, there has been debate about the relationship between the person-centered psychotherapy and spiritual experience and practice. This debate has been wide-ranging, encompassing therapist and client experience in therapy sessions, as well as arguments about statements made by Carl Rogers late in his life, indicating his sense of transcendental or mystical dimensions in therapy and group facilitation (Rogers 1980, p. 129). What drives this debate is not conceptual curiosity, but the awareness that something other than a normal functioning of self, something more like a loss of self, or a mediation of something Other through the self, appears to occur in therapist and client experience, appears to be beneficial to both parties, and occurs with enough regularity to create a public discussion about what is happening (Leonardi 2010). This is especially so among therapists who already engage in spiritual practice and who note a similarity, approaching an identity in this kind of therapeutic experience and what they otherwise experience spiritually (Thorne 1998, 2002).

In this paper, I step aside from the debate regarding Rogers' controversial later statements about spirituality and mystical experience. I also resist arguing for a correct symbolization of the kinds of therapeutic experiences described above—whether this is, for instance, an experience of love in the context of a theistic God (Mearns and Thorne 2000, pp. 60–66) or Aloneness and a Buddhist Nothing (Thorne 2002, pp. 50–51), or relational depth (Mearns 2010; Mearns and Cooper

---

R. Fruehwirth (✉)
The Norwich Centre for Personal and Professional Development, 7 Earlham Road,
Norwich, Norfolk NR2 3RA, UK
e-mail: rgfruehwirth@gmail.com

2005). Instead, my intention, more modestly, is to demonstrate a deep resonance between the uncontested heart of person-centered therapy—the offering of the core conditions of empathy, congruence, and unconditional positive regard as already defined in the introduction to this volume—and the heart of the Christian spiritual tradition, as realized particularly in the experience of contemplation, or wordless prayer.

To have said this much is already to have entered highly questionable terrain, as difficult for the person-centered community as for those invested in Christianity. On the person-centered side, there can be significant anti-religious and anti-Christian bias, which sees nothing helpful in Christianity, which has been experienced as authoritarian, dogmatic, and judgemental—and thus inimical to person centeredness. Famously, Carl Rogers himself renounced Christianity in his journey to developing what is now the person-centered approach (Thorne 2003a). And on the Christian side, there may not be a recognition of contemplation or wordless prayer as representing anything like the heart of the Christian spiritual tradition, which can seem to be more about preaching, morality, or activism. From the outset, both parties may be uneasy or unclear about what I am proposing.

My tactic for navigating these difficulties is first to demonstrate how wordless contemplation can be considered as the heart of the Christian spiritual tradition and then to open a conversation between this experience and that of the therapist offering the core conditions. To do this, I draw on the writings of Cambridge theologian Sarah Coakley to explore the meaning of an ancient Greek term, kenosis, meaning self-emptying, arguing for its centrality to the Christian tradition and its realization in contemplation. What we are after, in the experience of contemplation, rooted in kenosis is not Christian metaphysics or doctrine, but a spiritual experience of self-emptying openness that is felt to be a participation in what Christians understand as "God's way of being in the world," as enacted by Jesus of Nazareth. That Coakley is widely regarded as one of the most eminent theologians of our time, philosophically rigorous and deeply concerned with women's and men's flourishing, lends weight to this interpretation of the Christian spiritual tradition and its likelihood of engaging with therapeutic theory, and concerns for human well-being.

My argument is that once Christianity can be seen as having something like an experiential self-emptying that is also self-actualizing at its core, then it becomes possible to see that something similar, or deeply resonant, is occurring at the experiential heart of the two traditions. This "something similar" seems to be a different type or way of being a self, even though this is happening in very different contexts and with very different conceptualizations—the Christian participating in Jesus' self-emptying way of enacting God's presence in the world, and the therapist in offering a therapeutic context for a client. My aim is not to collapse either tradition into the other nor to subordinate one to the other, but in the kind of "multi-directional partiality" dear to person-centered facilitation (O'Leary 2012, pp. 17–18), to hold the heart of each tradition open to the other, so that each can sense something of itself in the other, as well as to note distinctive differences. There is much that is challenging in such a sustained holding open of the two traditions to each other, but much also to be gained. In a concluding postscript, I bring these possible gains into focus by sharing the personal significance of the conversation for myself as someone shaped by two decades living in an Anglican monastery devoted especially to the contemplative traditions, yet now living in a different way of life, married and "in the world," and working in a secular context as a person-centered therapist.

1.2 Kenosis and Christian Contemplation

1.2.1 The Original Use and Meaning of Kenosis

Sarah Coakley's offering of a description for Christian contemplation occurs at the end of an extensive reflection on the theological and spiritual history of the Greek term kenosis (Coakley 2002, pp. 3–39). This term, normally translated into English as "emptying," has historically been highly contested and problematic, yet occurs only once in the whole of the Christian Scriptures, in an early letter of St. Paul of Tarsus to the Christian community in Phillipi. According to a majority of commentators, the passage in which it occurs appears to be drawn from an already existing Christian hymn (Coakley 2002, p. 6) and thus comes from an ancient, primitive strata of Christian prayer and liturgical experience. In the hymn, Christians are urged to have the "same mind" among themselves as Jesus of Nazareth, who, though in the form of God, did not exploit this equality with God to dominate human beings, but emptied himself in his human life, in chosen humility and vulnerability, to the point of undergoing death as a scorned criminal:

> Let the same mind be in you that was in Christ Jesus,
> who, though he was in the form of God,
> did not regard equality with God
> as something to be exploited,
> but emptied himself,
> taking the form of a slave,
> being born in human likeness.
> And being found in human form,
> he humbled himself
> and became obedient to the point of death—
> even death on a cross (NRSV Translation, Philippians 2: 5–8).

As Coakley details in her essay, this single, seemingly poetic use of the reflexive, verbal form of kenosis has generated an extensive debate over nearly 2000 years, with shifting interpretations and concerns related to the theological assumptions and questions of particular cultures. What does it mean that Jesus emptied himself? That he was in the form of God? That he did not exploit or grasp at this? Is it, for instance, a matter of Jesus, understood as already divine, emptying himself of divine powers such as impassibility in allowing himself to be born as a vulnerable human being? Or is it Jesus, in his humanity, emptying himself by refusing false forms of worldly power and not seeking to be godlike among human beings in the socially expected way? The debates are complicated, and in her essay, Coakley defines six different possible interpretations of what Jesus' kenosis can mean, seeming to locate her own position in one more likely to be meaningful to non-Christians: that Jesus, as a human being, emptied himself, not of preexisting divine powers but of certain types of worldly, human powers counter to God's way of relating (Coakley 2002, pp. 33–38). In this interpretation, Jesus, historically, appears as a non-grasping, non-exploitive, vulnerable human being who enacted God's empathic closeness to humanity, who intervenes in human life primarily through the context of accepting relationships, and who suffered violence and public execution as a result. Moreover, it must be kept in mind that Jesus' self-emptying, however, it is understood, is intended as a model for Christians in their spiritual practice: that they should have the "same mind" in their relationships vis-a-vis God, worldly powers, and each other. This is the overarching rhetorical and pastoral aim of the passage. Kenosis appears to be at the center of what Jesus did, who he was, how he enacted what he understood as God's way of being in the world, and how Christians and the Christian community are likewise invited to be.

1.2.2 Contemplation as a Christian Realization of Kenosis

Inviting others into kenotic self-emptying vulnerability and humility is not, however, unproblematic. The main drive of Coakley's essay is in fact to meet concerns, largely from feminist writers, about the historical misuse of this invitation to self-emptying by already empowered men to further oppress and diminish the socially and personally less powerful, usually women. For these writers critical of kenosis, it is at best a gendered, compensatory spiritual need for already empowered men, but inappropriate for women who need to travel in the opposite direction of self-empowerment (Coakley 2002, p. 32).

Such concerns—the unavoidable centrality of kenosis in Christian belief and practice, evidence of historical misuse and abuse, and a need to support both women and men's spiritual flourishing—lead Coakley to look for a way of enacting kenosis that honors her understanding of the term as describing Jesus and yet, when practiced spiritually, can lead to self-actualization. Is there, in short, a kind of self-emptying—a letting go, as the current author might say, of an agenda for one's own self-development—that is also self-empowering? Is there a humility and a vulnerability that paradoxically makes one not less but more secure, not less but more creative and more capable, both in oneself and in the social and political sphere?

Coakley's response to such questioning is to locate Christian self-emptying primarily in relationship not to other human beings but with God, and this self-emptying humility and vulnerability in relationship to God as being realized with special power and clarity, in the diverse traditions of Christian contemplation, or silent prayer. Coakley (2002) says: "I know of no better way to express it [a way of kenosis that meets the above concerns] than by reflection on the practice of prayer, and especially wordless prayer, or 'contemplation'" (p. 33).

Helpfully, Coakley (2002) notes that in asserting this she is making an extension from theological reflection into spiritual practice:

> This is to take a few leaps beyond the notion of kenosis as a speculative christological theory about the incarnate life of Jesus...The 'spiritual' extension of Christic kenosis, then...involves an ascetical commitment of some subtlety, a regular and willed practice of ceding and responding to the divine. The rhythm of this askesis [ceding and responding to God] is already inscribed ritually and symbolically in the sacraments of baptism and eucharist; but in prayer (especially the defenceless prayer of silent waiting on God) it is 'internalized' over time in a peculiarly demanding and transformative fashion...What I have elsewhere called the 'paradox of power and vulnerability' is I believe uniquely focused on this act of silent waiting on the divine in prayer. This is because we can only be properly 'empowered' here if we cease to set the agenda, if we 'make space' for God to be God (pp. 33–34).

While there is not space here to trace out all of Coakley's concerns around contemplation, it is interesting to note how she describes it: as "waiting" and "making space" for God in contemplative prayer, as involving not only a lack of agenda, but also a "narrative 'gap,' the hiatus of expectant waiting" (Coakley 2002, p. 39). Contemplation involves the self in a practice of setting aside its own agenda, stepping out of its immersion in its self-developing narrative, and in this hiatus of self, opening in vulnerability to a divine Other—or, alternately, resting without narrative or agenda in the enclosure of that Other. In the words of one Christian mystic, John of the Cross from sixteenth-century Spain, our normal agenda-driven and narrativized life becomes like a house that is "all still," and from which our soul, our awareness, slips in darkness, unseen, to meet with God (St. John of the Cross, The Dark Night, Book 1, Transl. Kavanaugh and Rodriguez 1979). Or, in the words of another Christian mystic and theologian, Julian of Norwich, from fourteenth-century England, the contemplative, having abandoned their own agenda and entered a hiatus of expectant waiting, can do nothing except as they are moved by the divine Other. The contemplative's actualization is experienced not in self-motivation, but in being moved by the divine Other:

> And thus the soul by prayer comes to agree with God. When our gracious Lord by His particular grace shows Himself to our soul, we have what we desire, and then we do not see for that time what more we should pray for, but all our purpose with all our might is fixed wholly upon the contemplation of Him. This is an exalted incomprehensible prayer, as I see it, for the whole cause for which we pray, is to be one-ed to the vision and the contemplation of Him to whom we pray, marvelously rejoicing with reverent fear and such great sweetness and delight in Him that for the time being we can pray absolutely nothing except as He moves us (Julian of Norwich, Revelations of Divine Love, Ch. 43, Transl. Swanson 1988, p. 98, emphasis mine).

Such descriptions sound wholly unproblematic, but Coakley is also aware of concerns for the psychological health of the person embarking on this way of prayer, in which the self-protective security of an agenda and narrative are left behind. It can be internally painful, bewildering, and disruptive, allowing "a too sudden uprush of material from the unconscious" (Coakley 2002, p. 35). Thus, contemplative silence, involving an attitude of expectant waiting, and a kind of bracketed openness to a non-objectified Other, can leave one also uniquely open to the hitherto ignored urgency of one's own experiencing, past and present.

This can be destabilizing, but Coakley's thesis rests on the idea and experience that contemplation is in general empowering, actualizing, even transformative, because the contemplative, in that vulnerable openness to both self and God, is understood as receiving something positive from God through the experience. Coakley (2002) adds:

> If, then, these traditions of Christian 'contemplation' are to be trusted, this rather special form of 'vulnerability' is not an invitation to be battered, nor is its silence a silencing (if anything, it builds one in the courage to give prophetic voice.)…this special self-emptying is not a negation of self, but the place of the self's transformation and expansion into God (p. 35–36).

Such contemplative self-emptying is thus both vulnerable and secure. It is a practiced humility that allows for greater personal power. It is a silence that may build a greater public voice.

1.3 A Counseling Model of Kenosis

1.3.1 The Core Conditions and Kenosis in Jesus of Nazareth's Way of Being

Coakley's articulation of contemplation as empowering kenosis is groundbreaking, but might there also be a way of relating with another human being that also realizes kenosis in a similarly positive way, supporting the flourishing of those who practice it and those who come into contact with it?

Is there in short a "counseling model of kenosis," a chosen way of being for the therapist that has enough similarity to the contemplative kenosis already described to be recognizable to Christians as such, yet which happens in a counseling room, in relationship to another person, in a context that is self-defined as secular? If there is, and if such counseling kenosis is not an idiosyncratic occurrence, but is present in the basic intent of offering the core conditions of the person-centered approach, then we will have achieved something significant: the heart of the Christian tradition, as realized in contemplation, and the heart of the person-centered approach will appear as open to each other, not extrinsically or analogically, but at the basic level of their identities and experiential realizations. From this point, we could have Christian contemplatives gazing into the heart of the person-centered core conditions and recognizing something of what they already understand as God's way of being and relating in the world. Likewise, we could have person-centered therapists seeing into the heart of the Christian traditions and finding there the distinctive marks of the person-centered approach.

Obvious parallels are easy to draw. Just as Jesus, though "in the form of God," did not count this as something to be exploited to gain status, power, or personal security over humanity, so the person-centered therapist, although having undergone extensive training and having perhaps decades of experience, does not exploit this in relationship to the client to assume a status in any way superior to the client, as an expert in a place of invulnerable power. Rather, the person-centered therapist actively works to renounce such power and by a deliberate, practiced, sensitive waiting on the client's self-articulation and self-adjudication, invites the client to take up the role of the expert in the middle of their own lives. Moreover, just as this renunciation of a superior and invulnerable status allowed Jesus, as understood in the Christian tradition, to come alongside humanity to experience the full vulnerability of being human, so the person-centered therapist, in the renunciation of an expert status or intent, finds a capacity to offer themselves as what might be called "a field of empathic sensitivity" for the client. This allows them to pick up the experience of the client and to experience it as if it were their own, without being lost within it.

Complementing this empathic sensitivity is unconditional positive regard, an acceptance of what the client brings and how the client uses the therapeutic space, suspending judgment of the client or on behalf of the client, or an agenda for the therapeutic process. This too is a dimension of therapist self-emptying, and it touches on one of the experienced paradoxes at the heart of the person-centered approach, that when warm, positive regard for the client is offered unconditioned by therapist concerns for any particular therapy outcomes, the offering seems to become more therapeutic. As Rogers (1951) questioned:

> But is the therapist willing to give the client full freedom as to outcomes? Is he genuinely wiling for the client to organize and direct his life?...To me it appears that only as the therapist is completely willing that any outcome, any direction, may be chosen—only then does he realize the vital strength of the capacity and potentiality for the individual for constructive action. It is as he is willing for death to be the choice, that life is chosen; for neuroticism to be the choice, that a healthy normality is chosen. The more completely he acts upon this central hypothesis, the more convincing is the evidence that the hypothesis is correct (pp. 48–49).

In the person-centered therapist's offering of the core conditions, the Christian is thus confronted with someone who, like Jesus in his self-emptying relationship with humanity, attempts to renounce anything that elevates himself above the client, in order to empathically experience the client's reality, and to combine this with a cherishing regard of the client regardless of what they bring, or how they choose to present themselves or engage in the therapeutic process.

Furthermore, just as Jesus did not lose touch with his identity while vulnerable to humanity, but articulated himself over against social expectations, so the person-centered therapist remains, ideally rooted in a congruent awareness of their own experiencing. Thus, while experiencing the client, the therapist can choose to articulate themselves to the client, sometimes cutting across the client's expectations of them, and becoming visible as a distinct and different human being (Barrett-Lennard 1998, p. 110; Wyatt 2001).

1.3.2 The Core Conditions and Kenosis in Contemplation

Such loose analogies seem obvious and fitting. But more strictly: can the therapist, in practicing these core conditions, be said to be engaged in some kind of kenosis, some kind of self-emptying that resonates with the Christian meaning of the term? Here is where Coakley's description of self-emptying in contemplative silence, in the Christian attempt to have the same mind as Jesus, or to be in the world in the same manner as a Christian believes God was in the world, seems particularly helpful.

As we have seen, Coakley describes contemplative prayer as an expectant waiting, a narrative gap, and a lack of agenda. These are phrases which suggest a situation in which a self while consciously opening itself to experience, is not, for a time, seeking to further the narrative of its own self-development, to determine the direction of its movement, to further itself at all. It is instead holding itself opening in a gap in its own narrative and agenda to the influence of an other. In Coakley's case, this other that is expectantly awaited on is God, and this occurs largely in silence when the self has stopped even trying to move itself forward in words, that is, in symbolization, but has become "all still" and also supple to movements God is believed to make in the self.

My argument is that this experience of a Christian way of being a self in silent contemplation vis-a-vis God is very close to the therapist's way of being a self vis-a-vis the client. The person-centered therapist is not seeking to further her personal narrative in that hour with the client, or achieve her agenda, but waits expectantly on the client to make an impact on the field of the therapist's experiencing. The sense is that this, combined with an adequate energy of therapist self-acceptance in which the client is included, and an adequate level of self-awareness and honest communication when needful, provides a context in which a client can feel themselves understood and genuinely accepted, in other words, received. The person-centered therapist, classically, does not have to seek to do anything more than this, recognizing though that developing a capacity to do this demands a particularly open and accepting relationship with oneself and is in that way the work of a lifetime.

In conclusion, then Christian contemplation is a human, self-emptying reflection of Jesus' self-emptying, which in Christian belief is seen to be revelatory of God's self-emptying way of relating with humanity. I have argued above that both loosely, in a kind of analogy with Christian belief about what Jesus did, and more strictly in terms of a similarity with the Christian experience of contemplative silence, the person-centered therapist is engaged in what Christians think of as self-emptying kenosis. Or, to put it differently, that the Christian belief about God's way of being in the world, as enacted by Jesus of Nazareth, along with the experience of contemplative prayer, have a kind of deep, structural resonance to therapist experience in offering the core conditions of the person-centered approach. In this sense, both traditions can be seen as open to each other at a relatively deep level of their own experiencing and practice.

The question we are left with is what might be gained by such mutual openness?

1.4 A Concluding Reflection on Possible Gains Both Therapeutic and Spiritual

Having lived for nearly twenty years in a Christian monastery devoted to contemplative spirituality, and now living in a different way—married, in the secular world, and working as a person-centered therapist—it is natural for me to stand between the two traditions of person-centered therapy and Christian contemplation, in which I am still involved. Facilitating a mutual openness between the two traditions arises as a natural need within myself and in conversation with persons in the different communities that I regularly cross into, the secular and therapeutic on one side and religious and contemplative on the other.

The basis of my belief in the fundamental fit between the two traditions and experiences is not, however, my current experience, but my past: while still living as a monk, and as the leader of a small monastic community, I experimented with person-centered ways of relating, facilitating, and responding to pastoral crises. Before having received formal training in person-centered therapy, I was discovering by trial and error in my monastic community a different way of being with others that I now recognize as person centered, but which I felt then was a natural emergence and expression of my daily practice of self-emptying contemplation. At that time, I was attempting to relate to others with the same kind of "self-emptied self" I had already nurtured and experienced in wordless contemplation, and it had effects that seemed both "miraculous and predictable," to quote Brian Thorne's description of Rogers' sense of person-centered process (Thorne 2003a, p. 35).

Presently, standing between the two traditions of contemplative and person-centered therapist experience, in the mutual openness created by reflection on the term kenosis, I can report simply and non-polemically the gains that occur for me in this kind of sustained, existential openness, a place of meeting which is my personal home and for which this essay has argued.

On the one hand, as a person practicing a Christian spirituality, and thus seeking to have in myself "the same mind" as Jesus in his non-grasping, non-exploitive vulnerability, I have some experience of this as a narrative gap and loss of agenda in my contemplative silence where I wait on the Other whom both Jesus and I call "God." This spiritual experience of kenosis in contemplation seems fairly clearly connected with my sense of Christian faith. However, life, and the Christian life, includes much more than expectant waiting. It's not all narrative gap, or a quiet emptiness in the solitary self. Jesus himself displayed a profound quality and breadth of human interaction—a presence, a sensitivity, and a caring acceptance of other human beings that, in shorthand, could be called love, and which is a kind of active realization of kenosis.

Thus, as a Christian, what I gain from openness to the person-centered tradition is precisely a schooling in love that is enacted not in contemplative silence but in spontaneous interactions with other human beings, a capacity and skill that is developed through professional training, personal self-exploration, and in mindful practice within the central relationships of my life. To say this is to follow on much of what Brian Thorne has said and written about his discovery of the person-centered tradition as being just such a school of love (Thorne 2003b, pp. 16–21). However, I would like to emphasize that as a Christian, I find in the person-centered tradition the heart of the Christian response and experience of God being realized, without any religious language whatsoever, and being accomplished moreover with great rigor, consistency, and skill. People are in fact successfully trained in this approach! Here is a practical way of learning how to love, a way of learning how to participate in what I believe in as God's way of being in the world.

On the other hand, as a person-centered therapist, what do I gain from being open to the Christian spiritual tradition through the experience of contemplation? This is more difficult to spell out, but if we are willing to see self-emptying kenosis as the heart of Jesus' reality, and thus the heart of the Christian spiritual tradition, and if we are willing, equally, to see kenosis as describing something of what occurs in the person-centered offering of the core conditions, then we very quickly gain a sense of the possible therapeutic meaningfulness of 2000 years of religious and spiritual culture for the therapeutic venture. There exist at hand 2000 years of images, narratives, conceptual languages, philosophical discussions, and liturgical rites, a great deal of which is tied back to the experience of kenosis, and which thus has resonance with what is being offered in the therapy session.

On a personal level, participating in a religious and spiritual culture—looking on icons, sharing in liturgies, meditating on sacred narratives—has the effect of creating a kind of outside resonance for my work as a therapist which does not at all contain or guide the therapist offering, but reflects it back and feeds it from within. More generally, I'd also like to suggest that Christianity's twenty centuries of experiential learning and philosophical and theological explorations of what it is to be a self, to be in relationship, to empty and die to oneself, might be a profound dialogical resource for conceptualizing therapist process in the person-centered tradition. In Christianity, there is a deep and complex tradition of experiential self-reflection and articulation to be accessed and possibly learned from for the sake of increased sensitivity and articulation of therapist process.

Thus, as a concluding example: within Christian spirituality, there is already a highly developed conceptual language for differentiating types of experience in contemplation. Sometimes the self-emptying of contemplation seems more like an active task, almost like a skill that can be acquired, while at other times it is experienced as a passively received gift that is surprising, intensely deep, and which happens almost in spite of oneself—in the terminology, it is "infused"

(Garrigou-Lagrange 1999, Part III, Chs. 31–33). Such distinctions could be helpful in distinguishing and discerning the value of different kinds of self-emptying experiences that therapists have in attempting to offer the core conditions. Some therapists report that beyond the normal, workaday offering of the core conditions, something much more radical can happen, not the normal activity of a practiced self-emptying, but the self suddenly being emptied out without any effort of its own and being swept along in a way of being that feels dimensionally new yet not discontinuous with the previous offering of the core conditions (Rogers 1980 pp. 129–130; Moore 2001; Thorne 2002, pp. 75–85). These two types of therapist experience, in their relationship with each other, have a marked similarity to what the Christian tradition in the West has generally described as the difference between the acquired (active, workaday) form of self-emptying contemplation and its infused (passive, unexpected, and intense) realization.

This is simply one possible avenue for deeper conversation between the two traditions, traditions which, it is hoped, are now more open to each other and can sense what can be gained from this openness—even if this is, in the beginning, only a further articulation of difference. This is a conversation the current author is bound to have and which he hopes can be helpful to others.

References

Barrett Lennard, G. (1998). *Carl Rogers' helping system: Journey and substance.* London: Sage.
Coakley, S. (2002). *Powers and submissions: Spirituality, philosophy, and gender.* Oxford: Blackwells.
Garrigou-Lagrange, R. (1999). *The three ages of the interior life* (New ed.). Charlotte: Tan Publishers.
Kavanaugh, K., & Rodriguez, O. (1979). *The collected works of John of the Cross.* Washington: ICS Publications.
Leonardi, J. (Ed.). (2010). *The human being fully alive: Writings in celebration of Brian Thorne.* Ross-on-Wye: PCCS Books.
Mearns, D. (2010). On faith and nihilism: A considerable relationship. In J. Leonardi (Ed.), *The human being fully alive: Writings in celebration of Brian Thorne.* Ross-on-Wye: PCCS Books.
Mearns, D., & Cooper, M. (2005). *Working at relational depth in counselling and psychotherapy.* London: Sage.
Mearns, D., & Thorne, B. (2000). *Person-centred therapy today: New frontiers in theory and practice.* London: Sage.
Moore, J. (2001). Acceptance of the truth of the present moment as a trustworthy foundation for unconditional positive regard. In J. Bozarth & P. Wilkins (Eds.), *Unconditional positive regard.* Ross-on-Wye: PCCS.
O'Leary, C. J. (2012). *The practice of person-centred couple and family therapy.* Basingstoke: Palgrave Macmillan.
Rogers, C. R. (1951). *Client-centered therapy.* London: Constable.
Rogers, C. R. (1980). *A way of being.* New York: Houghton Mifflin.
Swanson, J., & Trans, J. (1988). *A lesson of love: The revelations of Julian of Norwich.* New York: Walker.

Thorne, B. (1998). *Person-centred counselling and Christian spirituality: The secular and the holy*. London: Whurr.
Thorne, B. (2002). *The mystical power of person-centred therapy: Hope beyond despair*. London: Whurr.
Thorne, B. (2003a). *Carl Rogers* (2nd ed.). London: Sage.
Thorne, B. (2003b). *Infinitely beloved*. London: Darton, Longman, and Todd.
Wyatt, G. (2001). The multifaceted nature of congruence within the therapy relationship. In G. Wyatt (Ed.), *Congruence*. Ross-on-Wye: PCCS.

Formative Empathy as a Mystical Way of Being

Francisco Silva Cavalcante Jr and André Feitosa de Sousa

According to Brazilian theologian Faustino Teixeira (2004), "the mystic is someone familiar with their interior vision, who goes beyond ordinary consciousness, living the radical nature of the presence of something totally new and free; living an experience that touches the profound and hidden dimensions of reality" (our emphasis and translation). In its Greek root, the verb myein from which mysticism derives means "to close ones eyes and lips" (Teixeira 2004, p. 27).

It is in these moments of presence that the mystic is surprised by the repercussions in their practice, as affirmed by Carl Rogers (2000) later in his life:

> As I recently said, I find that when I am the closest to my inner, intuitive self—when perhaps I am somehow in touch with the unknown in me—when perhaps I am in a slightly altered sate of consciousness in the relationship, then whatever I do seems to be full of healing. Then simply my presence is releasing and helpful. At those moments, it seems that my inner spirit has reached out and touched the inner spirit of the other. Our relationship transcends itself, and has become part of something larger. Profound growth and healing and energy are present. (p. 36)

The state of presence allows us to penetrate the concept of formative empathy, which has been the objective of our studies and practice in psychotherapy and education (e.g., www.casa.ufc.br) in Brazil. Formative empathy is founded on the formative tendency of the PCA (Cavalcante and Sousa 2009; Rogers 1980). Rogers asserted the formative tendency "exhibits itself as the individual moves from...knowing and sensing bellowing the level of consciousness, to a conscious awareness of the organism and the external world, to a transcendent awareness of the harmony and unity of the cosmic system, including humankind" (Rogers 1980, p. 133). Our formative empathy concept was also influenced by the important

F. S. Cavalcante Jr (✉)
Instituto de Educação Física e Esportes—IEFES, Universidade Federal do Ceará (UFC),
Av. Mister Hull, s/n—bloco 320—sala 8, Campus do Pici, Fortaleza, CE 60455-760, Brazil
e-mail: fscavalcantejunior@gmail.com

A. F. de Sousa
Faculdade Fanor/De Vry Brasil, Av. Santos Dumont, Dunas, Fortaleza, CE 7800, Brazil
e-mail: andre_feitosa@msn.com

contribution of the Brazilian psychologist Maria Constança Villas-Bôas Bowen and her spiritual conception of the PCA. We give her the credit for the development of mysticism in our approach. Her life path led her to migrate toward "therapeutic responses to issues of the soul," as affirmed by Maureen O'Hara (personal communication quoted in Cavalcante (2008), p. 131):

> Maria was greatly loved by many people who worked with her. It was a great loss to all of us that she died so early. By the end of her life, her interests were moving from therapeutic concerns to concerns for the soul. I am sure that if she had remained with us she would have become a leader in the evolution of the spiritual dialogue within PCA. She was making the link between the world of psychology and the world of the great mystics. She, (like me) believed Carl was a mystic and that he had access to levels of truth that only mystics have. I think Maria could also be thought as a mystic and when she died her husband Jack reported that he felt that she had prepared herself for death so completely that she had become an enlightened being.

According to Maria Bowen, Carl Rogers developed a psyche that was spiritual in nature. Even though this spiritual nature only was visible on rare occasions as Rogers reported from his clinical sessions, we can identify in the case of his work with Jan, an important example of formative empathy:

> I have begun to value highly these rare intuitive responses—this is the first that I have on tape—that are almost always useful for the progress of the therapy. At these times, perhaps I am in an altered state of consciousness, inhabiting the client's world and completely in tune with that world. My unconscious takes control. I know more than my conscious mind can perceive. My responses are not formed consciously; the replies are simply born in me, from my unconscious feeling about the world of the other. (Rogers 1987, p. 82, our translation)

To become *one* with the client is the highest expression of formative empathy in the PCA. Bowen (1987) reflects that at moments of unity, "it seems to me that he [Rogers] goes into an altered state of consciousness, in which the duality between him and the other person disappears. He becomes one with the client" (p. 112). These are the moments when psychotherapists find themselves in tune with the client's world, and the unity of the encounter allows responses to emerge without the predominance of reason. For Bowen (cited in Cavalcante 2009) on the level of empathy of unity, "Therapist and client *share the same world at the same time*" (p. 26, author's emphasis) and come to share a reality which transcends the dualism of "I" and "You."

According to her, what made Rogers a brilliant psychotherapist was not his capacity to reflect on what his clients said, but "Carl's ability to enter the client's world" and remain there during the dialogue relationship with the client, in a profound unity with him/her (Bowen 1987, p. 112).

Bowen (1991) concluded that the greater the degree of empathy, the more the therapist is able to enter into the client's world, so that he/she needs to communicate less information to the therapist, who in turn can respond quickly and sensitively to the experiences the client is sharing.

For Bowen, the empathy of unity "is felt by the **PRESENCE** of the other" (cited Cavalcante 2009, p. 59, emphasis of the author), a quality of presence that emerges from silence and a type of relationship where one is not merely entering the reality of the other as *if it* were your own. Formative empathy is transcendent or cosmic in nature.

For Alfred Adler (cited in May 2001), empathy is "a cosmic feeling and a reflection of the linking of the whole cosmos living in each of us. It is an inevitable characteristic of being a human being" (p. 63). According to Maria Bowen, formative empathy occurs when "the Spirit moves us" to say something. Mysticism speaks when we close our eyes and our lips (Teixeira 2004) and open to the formative nature of the universe that lives in us to make itself present in the relationship of unity.

In his latter writings, Rogers emphasized that these moments are rarely seen in human relationships; however, being rare does not mean that they cannot be developed. Rogers' wisdom was still developing when, in his seventies, this dimension of empathy became more textured, especially in his work with encounter groups and the large, influential groups that were part of his life from 1974 until his death in 1987.

Rogers (1980) came to believe that he and other practitioners of the PCA "have underestimated the importance of this mystical, spiritual dimension" (p. 130). Conceptions of the mystical dimension of the PCA had previously been presented and defended by other scholars of this approach (e.g., O'Hara 1995; Thorne 2002; Ellingham 2006).

The efforts of our team in Brazil (Cavalcante et al. 2008) have consisted of the inclusion of the formative mystical dimension that "transforms" the work of the experiential humanistic psychologist regarding organisms filled with mysticism and its continuous theoretical updating. The importance of mysticism as conceived by Rogers (1980) fortunately allows us to "create new and more spiritual directions in human evolution" (p. 134) with a PCA that remains in the vanguard of the twenty-first century, a revolutionary paradigm that continues to surprise us the more we dedicate ourselves to its development and application in the Brazilian context.

References

Bowen, M. C. V. (1987). Espiritualidade e abordagem centrada na pessoa: interconexão no universo e na psicoterapia. In: Em A. M. dos Santos, C. Rogers, M. C. V. Bowen (Eds.), *Quando fala o coração: a essência da psicoterapia centrada na pessoa* (pp. 86–122). Porto Alegre: Artes Médicas.

Bowen, M. (1991). *Intuition and the person-centered approach*. Trabalho apresentado na 2nd ICCCEP, Stirling, Inglaterra.

Cavalcante, F. S. (2008). Trilhas de vida e espiritualidade em Maria Bowen: "Interconexão no universo e na psicoterapia". Em F. Cavalcante, Jr. E. Olinda (Eds.), *Artes do existir: trajetórias de vida e formação* (Coleção Diálogos Intempestivos, vol. 51, pp. 126–139). Fortaleza: Edições UFC.

Cavalcante Jr., F. S., Sousa, A. F., Correira, L. F. B., Branco, P. C. C., Vasconcelos, T. P. (2008). Vidas que se encontram e que trans-formam psicoterapeutas: Contribuições à aprendizagem experiencial no referencial da psicologia clínica humanista. Em E. C. Souza & M. C. Passeggi (Orgs.), *Pesquisa (auto)biográfica: cotidiano, imaginário e memória* (pp. 127–245). São Paulo: Paulus/Natal: EDUFRN.

Cavalcante Jr., F. S. (2009). A empatia formativa é! Em F. S. Cavalcante Jr. & A. F. de Sousa (Orgs.), *Humanismo de funcionamento pleno: Tendência formativa na Abordagem Centrada na Pessoa (ACP)* (pp. 59–63). Campinas, SP: Alínea.

Cavalcante Jr., F. S. & Sousa, A. F. (2009). (Orgs.), *Humanismo de funcionamento pleno: Tendência formativa na Abordagem Centrada na Pessoa (ACP)*. Campinas, SP: Alínea.

Ellingham, I. (2006). Towards a Rogerian theory of mysticism. Em J. Moore & C. Purton, *Spirituality and counselling: experiential and theoretical perspectives* (pp. 81–98). Ross-on-Wye: PCCS Books.

May, R. (2001). *A arte do aconselhamento psicológico*. 13. ed. Petrópolis, RJ: Vozes.

O'Hara, M. (1995). Carl Rogers: scientist and mystic. *Journal of Humanistic Psychology, 35*(4), 40–53.

Rogers, C. (1980). *A way of being*. Boston: Houghton Mifflin.

Rogers, C. R. (1987). Abordagem centrada no cliente ou abordagem centrada na pessoa. In A. M. dos Santos, C. Rogers, & M. C. V. Bowen (Eds.), *Quando fala o coração: a essência da psicoterapia centrada na pessoa* (pp. 67–85). Porto Alegre: Artes Médicas.

Rogers, C. (2000). Interview with Carl Rogers on the use of the self in therapy. In: Em M. Baldwin (Ed.), *The use of self in therapy* (pp. 29–38). (2a. ed.). New York: The Haworth Press.

Teixeira, F. (2004). O desafio da mística comparada. In: F. Teixeira (Org.), *No limiar do mistério: mística e religião*. São Paulo: Paulinas.

Thorne, B. (2002). *The mystical power of person-centred therapy: hope beyond despair*. London: Whurr.

Part IX
Concluding Bridge

Reflections and a Preview

Renate Motschnig-Pitrik, Jeffrey Cornelius-White
and Michael Lux

The chapters in the *Interdisciplinary Handbook of the Person-Centered Approach: Research and Theory* have provided an expansive "arch" reaching from quite firm ground in the realms of cognition, neuroscience, and psychological and educational theories to the softer ground of multicultural coaching, philosophy, spirituality, and mysticism. As co-editors of this discipline-transcending enterprise, we have been aware of the conceptual "bridges" leading to and from the person-centered approach (PCA). In fact, "bridges" may be more appropriate than "arch" since bridges can be traversed and traveled. In any case, we still are astonished, even awed, at the richness of the landscape resulting from seeing the bridges side by side, packed into chapters of the *Handbook*.

Despite the visible diversity of landscapes, all the bridges share one particular, unique quality: Each of them either builds upon or connects to the heritage of Carl Rogers. Indeed, the authors are willing and often happy to state this connection openly and candidly! But fortunately, they don't stop there! They are not constrained to seeing the PCA as their dogma—something that dictates the truth and is followed blindly as a legacy, gradually destined to become outdated. The authors all grant life and development to the PCA. Some of them accomplish this by bringing inherent concepts closer to the surface through crystallizing and explicating them, such as with the notion of motivation, self–other distinction, "mirroring mechanisms," and co-actualization. Others contribute to the development of

---

R. Motschnig-Pitrik (✉)
University of Vienna, Waehringer Strasse 29/6.41, 1090 Vienna, Austria
e-mail: renate.motschnig@univie.ac.at

J. Cornelius-White
Missouri State University, Springfield, USA

J. Cornelius-White
University of Missouri, Columbia, USA

M. Lux
Neurological Rehabilitation Center Quellenhof, Bad Wildbad, Germany

the PCA by confronting its theories with current experience and knowledge. This "knowledge" includes new scientific findings such as those in the neurosciences, in biology, and in constructivist education just to name a few. Thus, emerging from their unique qualities, the bridging chapters appear to accomplish more than pure interconnection: They show that the PCA as alive and expanding, forming, and provoking dialogue and pioneering and nurturing new ground, much in the spirit of the formative tendency directed toward moving forward.

But the studies of theories and research directions would not be complete without considering the applications of the PCA. Thus, with undivided attention and interest, we as co-editors set forth to also collect application of the PCA that would come with "bridge-building" characteristics.

Naturally, collecting bridging chapters focusing on PCA applications revealed a landscape similar to the one resulting from the conceptual bridging chapters. Thus, in many ways, the theories and applications appear like siblings. They tend to follow their lives and expressions in different countries, even at different continents. As an example, take person-centered systems theory (see chapter by Kriz in this volume). Though developed in Germany, the "application" of the PCA to families, groups, and communities has been found around all over the world since before Kriz began writing. At other times, such as in education or coaching, the evolution of theory and practice often co-occurs and even is co-located. In this particular field, it becomes also evident that new technologies are integrated as allies for increased collaboration and transparency rather than being viewed as threatening dangers or being ignored to maintain purity and tradition.

In brief, once we felt satisfied with the coverage of both conceptual and application chapters, and happy to provide a conceptual map for the whole landscape, we equally realized that the book is getting out of bounds for one physical volume. Fortunately, the flexibility and seamless communicative connection to the publisher helped to turn our dilemma to what we sense benefits all parties. The original book now appears in two physical volumes—one on interdisciplinary research and theory and the other on applications of the PCA. For you as the reader, each book is more handy and easier to take with you, easier to hold and read. Also, it is up to you to choose one to start with and get the other only if your interest tells you to proceed. To facilitate your decision whether to read the "sibling book" on applications of the PCA, let us end this volume with a brief preview of the applications book.

The *Interdisciplinary Applications of the Person-Centered Approach* starts off with a short chapter that guides the reader through the sections of the book. Next comes an experiential example most central to the roots of the person-centered approach: A comprehensive transcript from a demonstration interview of Carl Rogers and Dadisi, an African-American volunteer. This interview is available as a video from the Center of Studies of the Person, La Jolla, USA, but had not been previously published in written form. Subsequently, the application chapters follow.

The application chapters are organized into five sections starting with *clinical applications* discussing person-centered and experiential psychotherapies, person-centered medicine and care for special needs persons, continuing with *education with and without technology integrations*, followed by developmental relating with *children and in families*, proceeding to the realm of *organizations, business, and leadership* and following on with *conflict management and international, constructive communication*. The *book on applications* is concluded by a chapter co-authored by the co-editors that provides a *meta-view* on the PCA as an "Overarching Paradigm," drawing on both the theoretical and the application chapters in each of the books.

Figure 1 comes from the final meta-view chapter of the applications book in order to visualize the two focal emphases in the two "sibling books." While the research and theory *Interdisciplinary Handbook* focuses on the upper half of the figure, the *book on interdisciplinary applications* addresses the lower part.

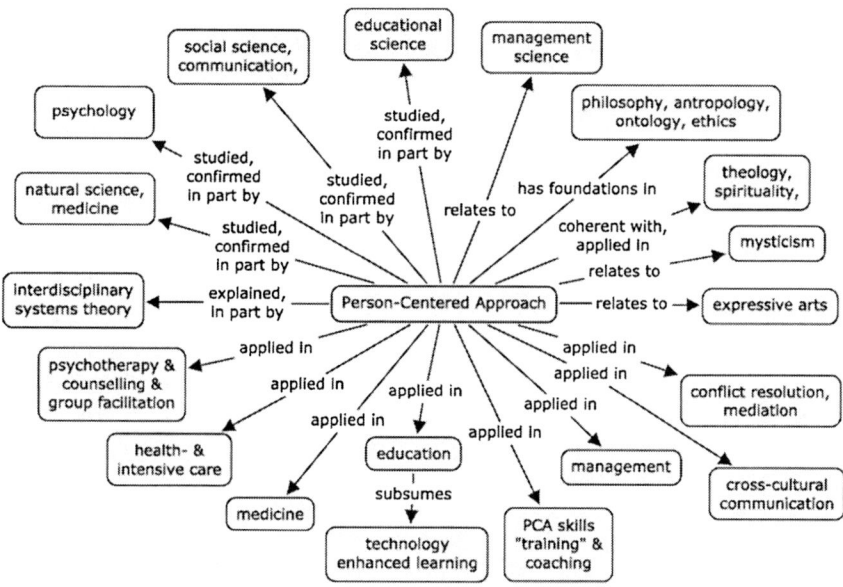

Fig. 1 The spectrum of scientific fields and application areas interrelated with the *Person-Centered Approach*

As editors, we leave you here, wishing you intriguing insight and revelation from whichever way you decide to use either one or both of the interdisciplinary books.

Editors Biography

Jeffrey H. D. Cornelius-White Psy.D., LPC is Professor of Counseling at Missouri State University and doctoral faculty at the University of Missouri-Columbia. He is former editor of *The Person-Centered Journal* and former chair of the World Association for Person-Centered and Experiential Psychotherapy and Counseling. He has published more than 75 works, including *Learner-Centered Instruction* (Sage, 2010 with Adam Harbaugh), *Facilitating Young People's Development* (PCCS, 2008 with Michael Behr), and *Carl Rogers: The China Diary* (PCCS, 2012). Jef studied at the Chicago Counseling Center and the Pre-Therapy Institute and is a graduate of Argosy University-Chicago. He enjoys cycling, volleyball, his friends, and family.

Michael Lux born in Stuttgart, Germany, has Master degrees in Psychology and Gerontology. He is a certified person-centered psychotherapist and works as a psychotherapist and neuropsychologist in the Neurological Rehabilitation Center Quellenhof in Bad Wildbad, Germany. Over the past few years, he has been intensively engaged with linkages between the person-centered approach (PCA) and neuroscience. As a result, he developed the model of a neuroscientifically based person-centered psychotherapy, which he described in a book and in scientific articles. Furthermore, he gives lectures and workshops on the neuroscientific bases of the PCA at conferences and training institutes.

Renate Motschnig-Pitrik born in Ostrava, Czech Republic, is a professor of computer science and head of the Computer Science Didactics and Learning Research Center at the University of Vienna, Austria. Renate held positions at the RWTH Aachen in Germany, the University of Toronto, Canada, and teaches and cooperates with the Masaryk University in Brno, Czech Republic. She participated in encounter groups and several events based on the person-centered approach. She is deeply interested in the multiple ways in which mutual understanding and whole-person learning happen. She is an author/co-author of more than 130 scientific articles, one book, and is determined to foster a style in education that is based on person-centered attitudes, our co-actualizing potential, and thoughtful support by Web-based technology. She appreciates synergies between presence and distance, and a multitude of (scientific) disciplines and cultures.

Additional Contributors

Karim Afzal MA, Doctoral Student, received his bachelor's degree in Psychology from Wheaton College (Massachusetts) and his master's degree in Psychology from Adelphi University. He is pursuing his Ph.D. in Clinical Psychology in Fielding Graduate University's doctoral program. His research experience is diverse and includes working in a radiology laboratory at Beth-Israel Deaconess Medical Center/Harvard Medical School where he earned co-authorships on studies focusing on developing image-guided, minimally invasive therapies for malignant cancerous diseases. In Dr. Ed Tronick's laboratory, he is participating in a research project on examining maternal-infant dyads in a naturalistic home setting, and his dissertation is investigating infant social referencing and memory of mother-stranger interactions. Clinically, he has a strong existential and humanistic orientation, and his extensive psychotherapy experience includes working with developmental disability populations at FEGS and YAI, in addition to psychiatric populations in New York University/Bellevue Hospital and Albert Einstein School of Medicine/Jacobi Medical Center.

Godfrey (Goff) Barrett-Lennard studied with Carl Rogers at the University of Chicago, graduating with a Ph.D. from there. He is honorary Doctor of the University at Murdoch and Fellow of American Psychological Association and its Australian equivalent. Search and research into relationship in therapy and life systems is his primary focus. Goff's career in Australia and North America has balanced scholarly contributions, teaching, and practice. His later writings include three books completed in "retirement" plus journal articles, chapters, and research questionnaires. A new book, pending publication, reflects his original blend of forward-reaching experiential and systemic thought on human nature and relations.

Karin Bundschuh-Müller is a licensed psychologist and psychotherapist based in Frankfurt am Main, Germany. She was born in 1949 and was trained in Client-Centered Psychotherapy (GwG), Hypnotherapy (M.E.G.), Behavior Therapy (DGVT), and Focusing (especially with Eugene Gendlin in Chicago). She is Leader of the "Focusing Zentrum Frankfurt," a Trainer and Certifying Coordinator with the Focusing Institute of New York, and a Trainer of Person-centered Counseling with the GwG (the German Person-Centered Association). The main topics of her research and work include psychotherapy, training, teaching, coaching, and supervision.

Francisco Silva Cavalcante Junior is associate professor of educational psychology at the Federal University of Ceará (Brazil) where he coordinates the Laboratory for Studies of the Possibilities of Being (LEPSER) and the Augusto Boal Circle of Artful Studies (CABEARTES). Building person-centered communities of learning in Higher Education has been his focus of work and research since 2009. With André Feitosa de Sousa they are the book editors of *Humanismo de Funcionamento Pleno: A tendência formativa na Abordagem Centrada na Pessoa* [Fully functioning humanism: the formative tendency in the Person-Centered Approach].

André Feitosa de Sousa is a person-centered psychotherapist and assistant professor of humanistic psychology at Faculdades Fanor-DeVry (Brazil). He coordinates person-centered training courses for socioeconomic vulnerable groups in Brazil and has authored several book chapters in Portuguese about the PCA. With Francisco Silva Cavalcante Junior, he is the book editor of *Humanismo de Funcionamento Pleno: A tendência formativa na Abordagem Centrada na Pessoa* [Fully functioning humanism: the formative tendency in the Person-Centered Approach].

Len Fisher Ph.D. (Physics of Surfaces), M.Sc. (Radiation Chemistry), was born in Australia and followed a research career in experimental physics, food science, and biophysics with several Universities and Research entities, especially in the UK and Australia. For the past decade, he has worked as a writer and broadcaster, aiming to open up the closed world of science by showing how scientists think about the problems of everyday life. Most recently, he has focused on the problems of living in a complex world with a trilogy—*Rock, Paper, Scissors: Game Theory in Everyday Life* (2008), *The Perfect Swarm: The Science of Complexity in Everyday Life* (2009), and *Crashes, Crises and Calamities: How We Can Use Science to Read the Early-Warning Signs* (2011). These deal respectively with the problem of cooperation, strategies for handling life's complex situations, and ways in which we can foresee and handle upcoming sudden changes in our personal lives and our societies.

Dr. Jürgen Flender is a person-centered counselor (GwG) and psychologist at Hansenberg Castle, a German boarding school for gifted students (www.hansenberg.de). After having obtained degrees in Music and Theology (University of Siegen) and a Ph.D. in Psychology (University of Heidelberg), he finished a 10-year-training with Dr. Peter Lipsett as a Contemplation Teacher at the Frankfurt School of Contemplation (www.kontemplation-frankfurt.de). Continuous practice and critical reflection of meditation since 1995 have led to a contemporary western conception that is very compatible with PCA. Jürgen Flender is married and the father of three children.

Robert Fruehwirth was a member of an Anglican monastic community devoted to the contemplative Christian tradition for 20 years. He is currently married and living in Norwich England, where he works as a person-centered counselor, Anglican priest, and serves as chairperson of the Friends of Julian of Norwich. His previous publications include *Words for Silence: A Year of Contemplative Meditations*, published in the US and the UK in 2008.

David Haselberger after finishing teacher training in Psychology, Philosophy, and Computer Science at the University of Vienna, David started to work as a high school teacher and to participate in research projects concerning soft skills and interpersonal communication. He considers his work at school and doctoral work at the University of Vienna to be propelled by a deep curiosity in human relationships and distinct ways of growth.

Diether Höger born 1936, studied from 1957–1962 and received his doctorate at the University of Freiburg i.Br., Germany. He served as assistant professor at the Child Guidance Clinic (Institut für ärztlich-pädagogische Jugendhilfe) at the

University of Marburg-Lahn. From 1964 to 1969 he was assistant professor and from 1969 to 1971 associate professor at the Department of Psychology at the University of Freiburg i.Br., where he received his habilitation, post doctoral qualification, in 1968. In 1971, Dr. Höger was called for a full professorship at the University of Pedagogy ("Pädagogische Hochschule") Westfalen-Lippe, Division Bielefeld. As of 1980, he served as a full professor at the School of Psychology and Sports Science ("Fakultät für Psychologie und Sportwissenschaft") at the University of Bielefeld until his retirement as a Professor Emeritus in 2001.

Joseph Hulgus Ph.D. is a family psychologist and Associate Professor at Missouri State University. He has been active in the field of systems therapy for over 30 years, and has published on a variety of related topics. Dr. Hulgus' current interests include multi-level systems therapy and addressing mental health as a public health issue.

Robert Hutterer was Professor at the Department of Education and Human Development at the University of Vienna. He taught education, person-centered counseling, and humanistic psychology. He did some pioneering work in developing person-centered training programs in Austria and was founding member of various associations facilitating the person-centered approach in psychotherapy and education. As psychotherapist, trainer and teacher he was working on a realistic perspective of person-centered counseling and psychotherapy as complex human practices modeled by an efficacious setup of real mechanism, processes, and structures. Robert passed away during the copyediting of this book.

Akira Ikemi Ph.D. is a professor at the Graduate School of Professional Clinical Psychology at Kansai University, Japan. Having studied with Professor Eugene Gendlin at the University of Chicago graduate school, he has since authored many books and journal articles on Focusing in Japanese and English. One of the founders and past-presidents of the Japan Focusing Association, he is currently board member of the Focusing Institute and the World Association of Person-Centered and Experiential Psychotherapy and Counseling.

Stephen Joseph Ph.D, AfBPsS, is Professor of Psychology, Health and Social Care in the School of Sociology and Social Policy at the University of Nottingham. Stephen is a British Psychological Society (BPS) Chartered Psychologist and on the BPS Register of Psychologists Specializing in Psychotherapy. Stephen's research interests are in the applications of social psychology specializing in person-centered psychology, the psychology of well-being, traumatic stress and posttraumatic growth. He is the author of *What Doesn't Kill Us: The New Psychology of Posttraumatic Growth* (Basic books, 2011).

Jürgen Kriz is professor emeritus of psychotherapy and clinical psychology at the University of Osnabrück and guest-professor at several universities in Europe and the USA. He is the author of a 2008 book *Self-Actualization: Person-Centered Approach and Systems Theory*. He is a practicing psychotherapist, supervisor, and for many years the chairman of the scientific council of the Person-centred Society in Germany (GwG). Among other honors, Kriz received the "Grand Viktor Frankl Award of the City of Vienna" for his life work concerning humanistic psychotherapy.

Claus Lamm holds a professorship for Biological Psychology and heads the Social, Cognitive, and Affective Neuroscience Unit at the University of Vienna. His current research focus is the neural, psychological, and biological mechanisms of empathy and other social emotions, and how these emotions are linked to prosocial and antisocial behavior.

Barbara McCombs Ph.D. is a Senior Research Scientist and Director of the Center for Human Motivation, Learning, and Development (HMLD) with the Applied Research and Technology Institute (ARTI), University of Denver, Denver, CO, USA (email: bmccombs@du.edu). She is the author of several works on the learner-centered model including *A School Leader's Guide to Creating Learner-Centered Education: From Complexity to Simplicity* (2008). She has served in leadership capacities within the American Psychological Association and the American Educational Research Association, such as being the primary author of the Learner-Centered Psychological Principles (LCPs): Guidelines for School Redesign and Reform. Much research has utilized several forms of the Assessment of Learner-Centered Practices (ALCP) she developed. McCombs' research encourages new leadership models for redesigning schooling and learning.

Dr. Evleen Mann MBBS, PGDip in Psychoanalytic Observational Studies, MSc in Person-Centred Psychotherapy and Counselling is a Member of UKAHPP and UKCP. After working for 20 years as a general practitioner, Evleen recognized that much physical and mental distress was created by psychological and social problems, which are not amenable to medication. Turning to psychiatry, Evleen worked for 6 years with people suffering from eating disorders, then several years in gender dysphoria. She continued her NHS work in substance misuse, specifically with the pregnancy and parenting team, alongside retraining in person-centered psychotherapy. She works in Harrogate and London.

David Murphy Ph.D., AfBPsS, is a British Psychological Society (BPS) Chartered Psychologist and on the BPS Register of Psychologists Specializing in Psychotherapy. He is also registered with the Health Professions Council as a counseling psychologist. He is in practice in the Centre for Trauma, Resilience and Growth as a person-centered psychotherapist. He is program leader for the Master of Arts degree in Trauma Studies: A Person-Centered Approach at the University of Nottingham. David's research interests are in person-centered psychology, mutuality, the therapeutic relationship, interpersonal relations, and trauma.

Dr. Ladislav Nykl Ph.D. was born in Bohemia, Czech Republic. In his thirties, he moved to Vienna, where he studied economics and worked as a software analyst. His interest in psychology emanated from his participation in encounter groups. He holds doctorates in psychology from the Charles' University in Prague/CZ and the University of Vienna/Austria. During the last 30 years, he has been intensively engaged in counseling and psychotherapy, leading training programs in Bohemia, writing seven books, and facilitating courses in the PCA at the Masaryk University in Brno, Czech Republic. Currently, he runs a private practice, facilitates encounter groups, lectures at the University of Vienna, and acts as an active consultant in a project of the European Union on promoting constructive international communication.

Kymberlee O'Brien M.Ed, Ph.D. is a Postdoctoral Fellow at the Horizon Center for Excellence at University of Massachusetts, Boston, and Harvard Medical School, Children's Hospital Boston. She was awarded the American Psychological Association Dissertation Research Award on her dissertation titled, "Moral Certainty Under Stress: Psychological and Physiological influences on Socio-Moral Assessments." She was also awarded the Brandeis University Provost Award for outstanding research. In 2011–2012, she was named a Harvard University Sackler Scholar in Psychobiology. She developed and implemented the first graduate student Psychophysiology Journal Club and received the Brandeis University Prize Instructorship to teach an advanced seminar on Social Psychophysiology. She also served as a Chair for the American psychological Science RISE-UP program to enhance minority inclusion in higher education. Currently, she is focusing her research on the effects of stress on infants and their mothers and their relation to health disparities in community samples.

David Ryback received his Ph.D. from the University of Hawaii and then traveled through Europe and Asia for a couple of years to further his education in human nature. He returned to Georgia to direct a conference on humanistic education to which he invited Carl Rogers as keynote speaker, and then a working friendship ensued, resulting in a co-authored paper, "One alternative to nuclear planetary suicide." After years as associate editor of the *Journal of Humanistic Psychology*, David settled into consulting with business and government organizations on applying the principles that Rogers engendered to make bottom-line success more easily attainable. He is the author of *Putting Emotional Intelligence to Work* (Butterworth-Heinemann) and *ConnectAbility: 8 Keys to Building Strong Partnerships with Your Colleagues* (McGraw-Hill) and is book review editor for *The American Journal of Family Therapy*. With fiction writing as his hobby, David is under contract with Tiger Iron Press to publish his first novel, *Beethoven in Love,* due out in 2013.

Peter F. Schmid [Univ.Doz. HSProf. Mag. Dr.] is Chair of the Department for Person-Centered Psychotherapy at the *Sigmund Freud University, Vienna*, Austria, part time faculty member at *Saybrook University, San Francisco*, USA, person-centered psychotherapist, supervisor, and coach in private practice, and founder of the *Institute for Person-Centered Studies (IPS of APG)* in Vienna. He co-operated with Carl Rogers in the 1980s and was a founder of person-centered training in Austria and a co-founder of the *World Association for Person-Centered and Experiential Psychotherapy and Counseling (WAPCEPC)* and the *Network of European Associations for Person-Centred and Experiential Psychotherapy and Counselling (PCE Europe)*. For 40 years in Austria as well as internationally, Peter Schmid engaged in both, genuine and innovative development of Carl Rogers' work. He is the author and/or co-editor of 19 books and more than 300 academic publications about the foundations of the PCA and anthropological, epistemological, and ethical issues of person-centered psychotherapy and counseling. Likewise, he is co-founder and a previous co-editor of two major international academic person-centered journals: the German language journal *PERSON* and the English language journal *Person-Centered and Experiential Psychotherapies*. His websites include www.pfs-online.at and www.pca-online.net

. **Ken Sheldon** is a Professor in the Department of Psychological Sciences at the University of Missouri. He received his Ph.D. from UC Davis and completed postdoctoral work at the University of Rochester. Professor Sheldon's research interests center on the intersection of Self-determination theory and Goal theory, with particular emphasis on what types of goals and motives promote optimal personality development and psychological well-being. He is the author of *Optimal human being: An integrated multilevel perspective* (2004), co-author of *Self-determination theory in the clinic: Promoting physical and mental health* (2003) and co-editor of *Designing positive psychology: Taking stock and moving forward* (2011).

Giorgia Silani is senior researcher and head of the Collective Emotions and Social Cognitive Neuroscience Lab at the International School for Advanced Studies (SISSA-ISAS), Trieste, Italy. As a neuroscientist and trained psychotherapist, her research interest covers the field of social neuroscience, in particular empathy, morality and the intersection between psychotherapy and neuroscience.

Marius Stander is a professor and management consultant specializing in the assessment and optimization of talented people and teams. He has been lecturing postgraduate students in Industrial Psychology at the North–West University, University of Namibia as well as UJ (previously RAU). He studied at the North–West University and holds an MCom (cum laude) and Ph.D. in Industrial Psychology. He is a registered Industrial Psychologist and Supervising Psychologist (HPCSA), as well as a Master HR Practitioner and Mentor with the SABPP. He has acted as study leader for more than 40 Master's students and as supervising psychologist for more than 50 Intern-Psychologists. He has published and delivered various International and National research papers in journals and at conferences.

Ed Tronick Ph.D. a developmental neuroscientist and clinical psychologist, is a world class researcher and teacher recognized internationally for his work on the neurobehavioral and social emotional development of infants and young children, parenting in the U.S. and other cultures, and infant-parent mental health. Dr. Tronick is a University Distinguished Professor of Psychology at the University of Massachusetts, Boston, Director of the UMB Child Development Unit, a Research Associate in Newborn Medicine at the Brigham and Women's Hospital, and a Lecturer in Pediatrics, Harvard Medical School. He is also on the faculty of the Maternal and Child Health at the Harvard School of Public Health and Human Development at the Harvard School of Education. He is a member of the Boston Psychoanalytic Society and Institute. Over the course of his career, Dr. Tronick has co-authored and authored more than 300 scientific papers and chapters and 3 books, as well as numerous videos on infant development.

Llewellyn van Zyl is a registered psychologist (Industrial) with the Health Professions Council of South Africa. He holds a Doctorate, Masters (cum laude), Honours (cum laude), and Bachelor's (cum laude) degree in Industrial Psychology from the North–West University. Llewellyn is an active researcher with accepted publications in peer-reviewed journals, chapters in international peer-reviewed books and presentations at national and international conferences. He is currently involved with the University of South Africa (Unisa) as a Senior Lecturer in Industrial Psychology. Furthermore, he is involved with the *South African Journal of Industrial Psychology* as a section editor. Llewellyn has a passion for strengths-based people development, coaching, happiness, and consumer behavior.

Carol Wolter-Gustafson received her Ed.D. from Boston University's Department of Humanistic and Behavioral Studies. As a graduate student she met Carl Rogers at a nine-day residential workshop in New York. Subsequently, she has facilitated groups and lectured in the United States, Europe, and Japan, and is committed to learning in large groups, exploring themes of gender, personal power, community power, and cross-cultural communication. As an adjunct professor at Lesley University's Graduate School of Education, Carol taught philosophical, psychological, and counseling courses for 25 years and was a Visiting Professor at the Universidad Iberoamericana (Mexico). Her personal and professional life has centered on cultivating a pathway out of the "us-versus-them" thinking and rhetoric that fuels subtle and outright violence locally and globally and moving through the so-called body-mind split. She maintains a client-centered psychotherapy practice in Boston.

Alberto Zucconi is the president of the Person-Centred Approach Institute (IACP), a non-profit international organization, co-founded with Carl Rogers and Charles Devonshire. It is dedicated to research in human behavior, the promotion of health, and the training of professionals. He has been working internationally for 35 years as a trainer, lecturer, and consultant for public and private organizations and is currently teaching at the postgraduate level at the University of Siena, School of Medicine (Italy).

Index

A
Ability to relate, 83
Abstract model of associative cognition and emotion (AMACE), 38–40, 43, 45, 46, 48, 49, 53, 55–57
Acceptance, 39, 45, 48–54, 56, 57, 64, 66, 72, 73, 141, 142, 145–148, 152, 158, 163
Accepting atmosphere, 47
Action research, 320, 328–330, 338
Activation, 40–42, 46, 47, 49, 51–53, 55, 57
Active behavior, 171, 193
Active listening, 249
Actualization, 158, 159, 162–164, 220
Actualizing process, 357
Actualizing tendency, 12, 13, 15–18, 96, 142, 149, 227, 228, 230, 232, 237, 262, 264, 270, 290, 356, 357
Affect regulation, 87
Agenda-free prayer, 373, 376
Alexithymia, 71
Altruism, 315
Ambivalent, 179, 232
Ambivalent-clinging, 179
Ambivalent-withdrawing, 179
Amygdala, 70, 86, 87, 89
Anterior insula, 68, 69
Anthropology, 354, 356, 359
Anxiety, 81, 84, 88, 89
Archery, 157, 160, 163
Asomatognosia, 71
Assessment of positive functioning
Attachment, 204, 206, 207
Attachment behavior, 170, 171, 174–177, 180
Attachment figure, 170, 171, 175–177
Attachment patterns, 175–178
Attachment system, 170, 172, 174, 175, 177–180

Attachment theory, 170, 172, 173, 178
Attractor, 269, 272, 273
Authenticity, 112, 120, 121, 124, 221
Authentic research, 321, 325
Autogenic training, 157, 160, 161, 163
Autonomous, 355, 356
Autonomy, 203, 207, 284
Autonomy support, 230–232, 240
Autonomy supportiveness, 230, 231
Autopoiesis, 290
Aversive behavior, 171, 178
Avoidance, 16, 180
Avoidant-withdrawing, 179
Avoiding, 64, 232, 292
Awareness, 158–160, 162, 164, 186, 188
Axiomatic approach, 342

B
Balance, 148, 149
Behavioral-systems, 170, 172, 173
Big Pharma, 105
Bodily synchronization, 89
Body, 80, 85, 88, 150, 152, 160
Brain, 63, 64, 66, 68, 70, 79, 80, 84, 86–88, 91
Brazilian, 381–383
Breathing, 160, 161
Brinksmanship, 307
Buddhism, 144–146
Burn your bridges, 304

C
Calmness
Candace Pert, 95, 101
Caregiver, 184, 185, 187

Carl Rogers, 3, 4, 9, 10, 95, 98, 101, 107, 111, 112, 132, 134, 135, 138, 139, 141–143, 146, 147, 151, 169, 173, 175, 300, 305, 310
Case study, 280
Centering, 159–163
Cerebral dynamics, 120
Change, 289–295
Changing your mind, 304
Chicken, 307, 311, 313
Chunk, 40–49, 51–57
Cingulate cortex, 68
Circle of contact, 81, 82, 89, 90
Client-centered therapy, 64–66
Closeness, 124, 171, 179, 204, 237, 285, 372
Coaching, 217, 222
Co-actualization, 56, 90, 91
Co-construction, 63
Co-creative, 357
Cognition, 37, 38, 42, 52–54, 66, 73
Cognitive behavioral therapy, 104
Cognitive empathy, 87
Cognitive flexibility, 69
Cognitive psychology, 39, 57
Collaboration, 252, 253
Collaborative action research, 338
Collaborative research approaches, 342
Comfort, 161
Communicate, 19, 46, 47, 51, 86, 111, 112, 116, 124, 207, 331
Communication, 99–102, 105–107
Communication ethics, 161
Communication skills, 68
Community, 354, 358, 362
Competency-based assessment, 249
Conditions of worth, 39, 42, 56
Congruence
Congruent, 41, 43, 44, 47
Connection, 95, 96, 99–102, 105, 107
Connectivity, 86
Conscious need for care, 178, 179
Consciousness, 41, 42, 51, 53, 56, 116–119, 142, 148, 149, 153, 159–164, 186, 187, 381, 382
Constructs, 246
Contact, 200, 203, 204, 208, 248
Contemplation, 158, 159, 161, 162, 369–374, 376–379
Context, 278–280, 282, 283, 286
Conversation, 278, 279
Cooperative behaviors, 80
Core conditions, 79, 82, 89, 90, 143, 144, 148, 293–295, 370, 374–379
Counseling, 157, 159–161, 163, 164
Credible commitment, 303–315
Crossing, 132, 138, 139
Crossing into, 138, 139
Culture, 264, 265, 269, 270, 273
Cut off communication, 304

D

Deactivating, 86, 177, 179, 207
Death, 270
Defenses, 65
Denied, 43, 49, 52, 56
Descriptive research, 338
Development, 27, 28
Developmental areas, 246, 250, 251
Dialectical interface, 220
Dialogic communication, 337
Dialogue, 353, 356–362
Die and Become!, 269, 270
Disclosure, 88, 89
Disgust, 68
Disposition, 40, 45, 53–58
Distorted, 43, 45, 52
Distress, 88
Drug, 101, 105, 106
Dualism, 382
Dyadically expanded states of consciousness, 183, 186, 187
Dynamics, 262, 268, 271, 272, 274

E

Eastern philosophy, 144, 150
Ecosystemic, 246
Efficacy, 221
Electronic communication, 113, 114
Electrophysiological recordings, 68
Emergence, 266–268, 273
Emotion, 37, 39–41, 43, 44, 51, 53, 66, 68, 70, 72, 73, 87, 88, 145, 146, 149, 150
Emotional contagion, 41, 51
Emotional empathy, 87–89
Emotional expressiveness, 83, 84, 88, 89
Emotional regulation, 66
Emotional resonance, 66, 67
Emotional schemes, 43
Emotional sharing, 72
Emotional stimulus, 68
Empathic understanding, 39, 45, 51–54, 56, 57
Empathize, 70–72
Empathy, 18–20, 79, 82, 83, 86–89, 133–135, 144, 146–148, 164, 184, 189, 191–193, 200, 205–207, 299, 314, 315, 370, 381–383
Empathy of therapist, 174
Empirical rigor, 96

Empirical support for person-centered approach, 228, 237
Empowerment, 253
Emptying, 371, 372
Encounter, 354, 356–362
Encounter group, 300, 305, 315, 383
Energy, 264
Epistemological humility, 96
Epistemology, 222, 356, 358
Escape routes, 303
Ethical vision, 96
Ethics, 353, 360, 361
Eugene Gendlin, 4, 132, 133, 135
Evidence-based treatment, 221, 289
Executive coaching, 246
Existential, 355, 359, 362, 363
Expectations, 247–249, 254, 255
Experience, 9–11, 13–20, 64, 65, 68–73, 143–150, 152, 185, 186, 188, 189, 192, 277, 278, 280, 285–287, 319–323, 325, 326, 328, 330, 381, 382
Experiencing, 135, 137, 138, 142, 145–147, 149, 158, 159, 164
Explanatory research, 338
Explication, 134, 135, 138
Exploration, 10, 19, 51, 91, 163, 172, 251, 287, 320, 325, 329
Exploration of self, 177, 180
Exploratory system, 28, 172
Extensionality, 324, 325, 330
Extensional relationship, 324, 325, 330
Eye area, 83, 91
Eye contact, 84, 86

F
Face-to-face still-face, 185
Facilitator, 46–53, 55, 81–83, 85–89
Fairness, 314
Family systems theory, 291
Fear, 187
Fear of rejection, 178, 179
Feeling, 37–39, 41, 44–49, 51–54, 87–89, 145–147, 149, 150, 152, 188, 192, 193
Felt meaning, 135–139
Felt sense, 134, 136, 139
First-order change, 292, 294
Flow, 229
Fluent processes, 48
Focusing, 134, 135, 139, 157, 159–164
Formative empathy, 381–383
Formative tendency, 381
Forming of relationship, 81
Framing, 115

Free Rider, 307, 310, 311
Frontal cortex, 115–119, 121, 124, 125
Full functioning
Fully functioning person, 84
Fundamental We, 357, 358, 360–362

G
Galvanic skin responses, 73
Game theory, 31, 300, 301, 306, 310, 313–315
Gaze, 83
Generative, 96
Genuineness, 45, 46, 64
Gestalt, 262, 263, 267–270
Gestalt psychology, 262, 263, 267, 269, 270
Gestures, 160, 162
Goal setting, 228, 236
Group, 354, 357, 358
Group theory, 291
Growth, 214, 215, 219–222

H
Happiness, 217, 222
Harmon, 148–150
Health, 95, 100, 101, 103–107
Hearing, 115, 121
Helping relationship, 64, 65
Hemodynamic response, 70
Hermann Haken, 263
Holistic, 261, 262
Homeostatic life regulation, 87
Human computer interaction, 58
Human development, 173
Human functioning, 100, 237
Humanism, 383
Humanistic, 355, 357, 360, 361
Human organism, 96, 100
Human potential, 245
Hyperactivating, 177, 179

I
Image of the human being, 354–356, 363
Imagination, 69
Imitation, 67, 71
Imperturbability, 161
Inclusive approach
Incoherence, 188
Independence, 356
Individuality, 322, 327, 330
Infant, 183–185, 187, 191–194
Infant observation
Inherent nature, 219

Inherent potential, 81
Inherently proactive, 219
Inner reflection, 115
Instrumental non-directivity, 218
Integration, 15, 17, 71, 81, 86, 96, 125, 227, 232, 233
Intellectual efficiency, 98, 99
Interaction, 38, 54, 57, 58
Interconnectedness, 88, 356, 358
Inter-connections, 4, 6
Interconnectivity, 73
Interdependent, 96, 103, 107, 355
Interdependent partners
Interdisciplinarity, 6
Interdisciplinary, 262–265, 269
Interdisciplinary research, 387, 389
Interdisciplinary theory, 387, 389
Internalization continuum, 231, 232
Interpersonal, 354, 356, 358, 360, 362
Interpersonal communication, 39, 43, 54, 294
Interpersonal growth, 5
Interpersonal relationship, 17
Intrapersonal communication, 44, 51, 57
Intrinsic motivation, 217, 228, 229, 232
Introjected value, 43, 52
Intropunitive, 293, 295
Intuition, 159, 162, 321, 381, 382
I-thou relationship, 90

J
John Bowlby, 169, 170, 172, 173
Jon Kabat-Zinn, 112, 116

K
Kenosis, 369–374, 376–378
Kurt Goldstein, 262
Kurt Lewin, 5

L
Language, 266, 274
Learner-centered model, 338–340
Learner-centered principles, 339, 344, 349
Learner-centered, 335, 338–340, 344, 348, 349
Learning for a lifetime, 341
Learner voice, 335
Limbic system, 116, 117, 119–121
Listening, 85, 142, 144, 146–148, 153
Literary writing, 279
Locus of causality, 232
Logical types, 291
Loneliness, 278, 285–287

Long-term memory, 40, 44
Love, 145, 148, 369, 378
Loving kindness, 145, 148, 151

M
Mainstream psychology, 103, 104, 213, 214, 219, 223
Meaning, 262, 264, 266, 267, 271, 273
Measure, 221, 222
Medial prefrontal cortex (MPFC), 84, 87, 89, 115, 119, 125
Medical model, 214–217, 222
Medicalization, 105–107
Medicalization of distress, 105
Meditation, 141, 142, 152, 158, 161, 162, 164
Meditation exercises, 158
Meta-analysis, 68
Meta-theoretical, 214, 218–220
Meta-theory, 389
Methodological openness, 325
Methodology, 169, 325
Mind-body, 105, 107
Mindfulness, 26, 27, 111–113, 116, 117, 119, 121, 122, 124, 142, 144, 152, 153, 158
Mirror neurons, 121–124
Mirror neuron system, 68
Mirror system, 88
Mixed methods research designs, 339
Moments of eternity, 148
Moments of meeting, 53
Mother/baby relationship, 199, 208
Motivational internalization, 231
Move in steps, 305
Movement, 115
Multicultural environment, 246
Multi-self, 282
Mutual, 284, 286, 287
Mutual openness, 369, 377
Mutual regulation model, 183, 184, 187
Mutual resonance, 90
Mysticism, 381–383

N
Narrative, 373, 374, 376–378
Need, 229, 230, 236–240
Network, 95, 100–103, 107, 322
Neural network, 66, 68
Neural process, 117, 120
Neuro-anatomy, 117, 119
Neurobiological processes, 79, 81–83, 87, 89, 91
Neuroception, 83, 84

Neuro-economics
Neuro-ethics, 74
Neuroimaging, 68, 71–73
Neuronal communication, 101, 102, 105
Neuronal mechanisms, 66
Neuronal structure, 66
Neurophysiological substrates, 66
Neuroscience, 23–26, 37–39, 48, 57, 63, 65–67, 69, 72, 74, 79, 81, 84, 85, 89, 95, 97, 99, 101, 104, 107, 113, 121, 125
Neurospsychobiology
Non-directive counseling, 230, 237
Nondirectivity, 218
Non-doing, 148
Non-judgmental, 19, 73, 116, 142, 146
Nonjudgmental acceptance, 111

O

Observation, 68, 69
Observer, 88
Observing, 162, 164
Opening, 159, 162, 163
Openness, 144, 145, 148, 149
Optimal functioning, 97, 107, 237
Optimal motivation, 228
Orbitofrontal cortex, 119
Order, 261, 262, 265–273
Organismic, 96, 98–100, 103, 107, 218–220
Organismic experience, 39, 40, 42–45, 49, 52, 53, 56, 57, 321, 323
Organismic integration process, 233
Organismic motivation, 98
Organismic theory, 262
Organismic valuing, 227, 233, 237
Organismic valuing process (OVP), 15, 200, 227, 228, 233, 234, 236
Organization, 286
Originators of research, 321
Otherness, 133
Other-related states, 71
Over-arousal, 70
Over-stability, 269
Oxytocin, 85, 86, 88, 89, 91, 206

P

Pain, 80, 84, 87
Paradox, 300–302, 306, 309
Partially-secure, 179
Participatory action research, 329, 330
PCA workshops, 3
Peacefulness, 153
Perception, 207

Person, 353–358, 360–363
Personal conversation, 320, 326, 327
Personal goals, 233, 234
Personal growth, 37–39, 53
Personality, 38, 43
Personality integration, 81
Personalization, 354, 357
Personalizing tendency, 358
Person-centered, 95, 101, 103, 107
Person-centered approach (PCA), 9, 10, 12, 13, 16, 20, 21, 116, 141, 157, 159, 161, 163, 188, 192, 193, 227, 301, 387, 388
Person-centered community, 214–216, 219–221, 223
Person-centered psychology, 213–218, 221, 222
Person-centered psychotherapy, 79, 89
Person-centered relationship, 79, 81, 82, 85–87, 89, 90
Person-centered research, 320, 323
Person-centred coaching
Person-centred systems theory, 270
Perspective taking, 69, 70, 73, 87
Peter Lipsett, 158, 159, 161, 164
Pharmaceutical industry, 105, 106
Phase-transition, 266–270
Phenomenology, 331, 356
Philosophy, 23, 31, 353–355, 359, 361
Physiologic concordance, 88, 91
Physiological indices, 190
Pinpoint, 347
Pluralistic, 287
Plurality, 325
Plurality of self, 287
Political, 359, 363
Polyvagal theory, 83, 91
Positive psychology, 213, 215–217, 221–223, 246
Positive view of human nature, 150
Postmerge codes, 201
Power, 103–106, 147, 151
Power of the relationship, 63
Pragmatism, 339
Prediction research, 338, 339
Prefrontal cortex, 69, 73, 84, 87, 89
Premerge codes, 201
Preparing, 159–161
Pre-reflexive, 132, 133, 135–137, 139
Presence, 20, 111, 114, 132–134, 137–139, 144, 147, 148, 152, 158, 159, 164, 165, 192, 193, 357, 359, 362, 381, 382
Primacy, 323
Primacy of experience, 229
Primary strategies, 176, 177

Principled non-directivity, 218
Prisoner's Dilemma, 301, 302, 306–308
Problem formulation and resolution, 292
Process, 321–323, 325–332
Prosocial behavior, 72
Proximity, 85, 170–172, 177
Proximity seeking, 171
Psycho-existential, 246, 255
Psychological needs theory, 237
Psychology, 28–30
Psychometric measurement, 249
Psychometric tool, 221
Psychoneuroimmunology, 99
Psychopathology, 64, 66
Psycho-physiological flow, 86
Psychophysiology, 184, 190, 192, 194, 195
Psychosomatic, 164
Psychotherapy, 64–66, 72, 73, 158
Psychotherapy outcome research, 98

Q
Qualitative research designs, 339

R
Rapport, 247, 248
Readiness for self-disclosure, 178, 179
Realness, 45, 46, 54
Re-appraisal, 73
Reasoning, 161
Recall, 41, 42, 47, 53
Reciprocity, 203
Recognition, 41, 53, 55
Record, 337, 347
Recursion, 111, 116–120, 124
Re-experience, 132
Reflect, 132, 134–139
Reflexive mode of consciousness, 138
Reframing, 294
Regulation, 204, 206, 207
Reinforcement, 228, 236
Rejection, 72, 178, 179
Relational, 355–358
Relational deficiencies, 66
Relational depth, 90, 91
Relational processes, 184, 185, 191, 195
Relational psychophysiology, 184, 190, 192, 194, 195
Relational qualities, 65
Relationship, 132–135, 278–287
Reparation, 185
Research process, 320, 322, 325, 327, 329, 330
Resilience, 246, 254
Respect, 64, 65, 72, 81, 90
Responding, 115, 119, 120
Response, 266
Responsibility354, 356, 359, 360
Reunion, 185, 191, 193
Reward, 347, 348
Rogers' six conditions, 199–201, 203

S
Safe haven, 173, 175, 180
Safety, 83, 85
Safety in the therapeutic relationship, 180
Science, 319–321, 323, 324, 326, 328, 329, 331
Scientific method, 336, 338
Scientific research psychology
Secondary strategies, 176–179
Second-order change, 292–295
Secure base, 171, 173, 180
Securely attached, 179
Security, 170–173
Self, 5, 39, 40, 44, 45, 49, 51–53
Self-actualization, 237, 262, 290, 295
Self awareness, 64, 65, 70–72
Self-concept, 14, 70, 162, 205, 290
Self-concordance, 234–236
Self-determination theory (SDT), 219, 220, 228
Self-diversity, 278–280, 282, 287
Self exploration, 83, 86, 87, 144, 148
Self-identity, 282, 284
Self-organizing systems, 219
Self-other distinction, 72
Self-perception, 233, 234
Self-structure, 43–45
Self-unfolding, 80
Sensing, 137–139
Sensitivity of attachment figures, 174
Sensitization, 163
Separation, 96, 171, 285
Shambhala, 151
Shift, 289, 292–295
Signaling behavior, 171
Significant learning, 5
Silence, 374, 376–378
Silent, 158, 159
Simulation, 87, 88
Social brain, 64
Social competencies, 80
Social engagement, 83, 84, 86
Social ethics, 353, 361
Social exclusion, 80
Social interaction, 72, 74
Social neuroscience, 63, 65, 67, 69, 74
Social perception, 81, 83, 84, 89

Society, 358, 359, 363
SOLER, 248, 249
Solidarity, 88, 356, 359, 360, 362
Somatic markers, 85
Somatoparaphrenia, 71
Somatosensory cortex, 68, 71
Spirituality, 32, 33, 369, 377, 378, 382, 383
Stag Hunt, 307, 313, 314
Still-face paradigm, 192
Stimulus, 265, 266
Strengths based coaching, 246–248
Strengths, 246–255
Stress, 84, 85, 89
Structural equation model, 240
Structural science, 264, 625
Subjective, 321–324, 326
Substantial being, 356
Superior temporal sulcus, 87
Symbolization, 37, 42, 45, 48, 51, 52
Sympathetic nervous system, 83, 84, 89
System, 268, 269, 281, 284, 286, 287
Systematic theory, 282, 283
Systemic, 253, 255, 286, 290, 291
Systemic PCA, 289, 290
Systems parenting
Systems theory, 28, 30, 32, 263–265, 267, 269, 270, 289–291
Systems therapy, 291

T
Taoism, 148
Temporal poles, 87
Temporo parietal junction, 69, 71
Tenderness, 143, 145, 148, 150
The Battle of the Sexes, 307, 313
The emotional re-evaluation, 73
The exploratory system, 172
The integrated person, 98, 99
The Seven Deadly Dilemmas, 307, 316
The Volunteer's Dilemma, 307, 312
Theory of mind, 87
Therapeutic relationship, 180, 218
Therapist, 82, 83, 88–91
Third wave of behavior therapy, 141
Thought, 145, 147, 153

Thou-I-relationship, 356, 360
Time-management, 157, 162
Tragedy of the Commons, 307–309
Transcendence, 356
Transformation, 147, 148
Trauma, 214, 218, 221
Traumatic experience, 91
Trust, 81, 85, 86, 89, 91, 143, 148, 150, 153, 269, 300–304, 306, 308, 310, 312–316
Trustworthiness, 85

U
Unconditional positive regard, 15, 17, 19, 20, 37, 45, 49, 79, 89, 142, 145, 146, 148–150, 164, 192, 193, 300, 308
Unconditional positive self-regard scale, 221
Unconditional regard, 200
Unconscious level, 45, 47
Understanding, 135, 137–139, 158, 164, 321, 322, 324, 325, 327, 331

V
Variables, 338–341, 344, 349
Virtual, 113, 114, 123

W
Way of being, 145, 147, 285, 362, 370, 372, 374–377, 379
Well-being, 95, 214, 215, 217, 222, 228, 234, 237, 238, 240, 287
Well-functioning relationships, 80
Working alliance, 65
Working memory, 40, 44, 47, 55
World Association for Person-Centered and Experiential Psychotherapy and Counseling (WAPCEPC), 4
Wu Wei, 147, 148

Y
Yin and yang of self, 278, 283

CPSIA information can be obtained at www.ICGtesting.com
Printed in the USA
LVOW071439130613

338472LV00001B/1/P